MEDIA USA

PROCESS AND EFFECT

ARTHUR ASA BERGER

San Francisco State University

Longman

New York & London

MEDIA USA: Process and Effect

Longman Inc., 95 Church Street, White Plains, N. Y. 10601

Associated Companies:
Longman Group Ltd., London
Longman Cheshire Pty., Melbourne
Longman Paul Pty., Auckland
Copp Clark Pitman, Toronto
Pitman Publishing Inc., New York

LONGMAN SERIES IN PUBLIC COMMUNICATION
Series editor: Ray Eldon Hiebert

Executive editor: Gordon T. R. Anderson
Production editor: Elsa van Bergen
Text design: Laura Ierardi
Cover design: Jacqueline T. Ghosin
Production supervisor: Judith Stern

Library of Congress Cataloging-in-Publication Data

Media USA.

(Longman series in public communication)
Includes index.
1. Mass media — United States.   I. Berger, Arthur Asa,
1933–   . II. Series.
P92.U5M45 1988   001.51'0973   87-3143
ISBN 0-8013-0063-0 (pbk.)

Compositor: Best-set Typesetter Limited
Printer: Malloy Lithographing, Inc.

88 89 90 91 92 93 9 8 7 6 5 4 3 2 1

CONTENTS

BOOKS   95

RADIO   135

ALTERNATIVE TABLE OF CONTENTS
Organized by Theme

ACKNOWLEDGMENTS

I would like to express my appreciation to all the people who have helped me with this book. Let me start with my editor, Gordon T. R. Anderson, who suggested I do the book. I appreciate his confidence in my judgment and his resoluteness in facing the tidal wave of letters I sent his way. I also appreciate Elsa van Bergen's invaluable assistance in producing the book. Then, there are a number of people who evaluated what turned out to be my first approximation of the book (the articles it would contain) and offered numerous suggestions. I have followed many of these suggestions and benefited a great deal from them. I am particularly grateful to Ray Hiebert who looked over my preliminary version of the book and suggested that my publisher give me the green light.

Many people were kind enough to write articles specially for this book and I owe them all a debt of gratitude: Rick Boyer, Benjamin W. Cate, Dan Coffey, Edwin E. Ewry, John Fell, Lynne Schafer Gross, Lynn Hershman, R. Dean Mills, George E. Steiner, Anthony Tiano, and Herbert Zettl. Jim Lull and Marsha Kinder were kind enough to revise previously written essays especially for the book.

I also appreciate the following individuals (and sources) who provided me with photographs and other graphics materials: Edwin E. Ewry (and S&O Consultants, who were kind enough to do the wonderful cover, also), CBS, KNBR, Lynn Hershman (for stills from her video LORNA), The San Francisco State University Audio-Visual/ITV Center (and, in particular, Frank Moakley and Hal Layer), Scott Meredith, *The San Francisco Examiner*, Mike Noll, and the Rykmuseum Kroller-Muller (for permission to use the Mondrian painting).

I also am grateful for the assistance of a legion of permissions editors all over the country, who have been extremely patient and cooperative. My colleagues in the Broadcast Communication Arts Department were supportive, my wife Phyllis was patient, and my dog, Patches, was always willing to take walks with me while I thought about which articles I should use and what I should say about them in my introductions.

Editing this book has been an exciting and challenging task. I hope my readers will find the result — *Media USA* — worth my time in doing it and their time in reading it.

INTRODUCTION

This book is about the mass media and how they affect and reflect various aspects of American society...but the book is about more than that. For while the articles deal with newspapers, books, radio, television, film, and new technologies, among other things, in the final analysis this book is about how people arrive at definitions of themselves, at what is sometimes called "an identity." And, by implication, it is about how you, the reader, arrived at your identity. My assumption is that the mass media play an important role in our lives as socializing agents, and are not just trivial entertainments that we use to kill time or provide kicks or whatever.

Reading this book will be, among other things, an adventure in self-discovery ...and there should be a number of times when you experience what might be called a "shock of recognition," when you find out that the media — the shows you watch, the films you see, the songs you listen to — are the source of an idea you hold or some notion about life that seems to have always been part of you. Where did you get your ideas about what you might accomplish in the future? Where do you get your notions about how to relate to members of the opposite sex, about what political party to identify with, about what is moral and immoral?

It would be oversimplifying things to say that all of our (or your) ideas come directly from the mass media. We know that parents, peers, professors, preachers, politicians, and all kinds of other people play an important role in our lives. But consider, for a moment, how much time we spend involved with the media. We know that the average person in American watches something like 3½ hours of television per day. We also listen to the radio for a couple of hours each day, read newspapers and magazines, listen to records, and see films (increasingly on VCRs).

Our media diet is, then, enormous. And if you believe, as I do, that "we are what we eat" as far as the media are concerned and that the media are powerful socializing and acculturating (culture reinforcing) institutions, it is only logical, then, that we examine them carefully and look at them in terms of the impact they have had (or may be having, if you are skeptical) on our lives and on our society.

A number of the articles in this book are "theoretical" and are written at a somewhat general level. One essay, for instance, deals with the question of media and effects and the many different positions that scholars have taken on this topic. I might point out that there is a good deal of disagreement among scholars about the impact of the media as well as about almost every other aspect of the communications field. The summer 1983 issue of *The Journal of Communication*, one of the most important scholarly journals in the area, was devoted to what was called "Ferment In The Field." It was full of articles by prominent scholars who disagreed with one another about almost every area of communications.

In addition to the theoretical essays in this book, there are some essays that are thematic, and cover a variety of media. One essay deals with stereotypes in the media and another considers the way women are now portrayed in *Playboy* magazine.

Other articles are more interpretative and offer analyses and explanations of the meaning *of films*, such as *Star Wars*, or television commercials or radio programs. Some of these essays are based on empirical research, while others are based on the application of various critical (that is, interpretative) techniques.

Among these are certain essays included because they will provide methods you can use to make your own analyses of films or television shows or rock videos. Thus, for example, I have several essays on the use of formulas — conventional ways of structuring stories. One of these essays deals with "The Lone Ranger" and the other deals with situation comedies and action-adventure programs.

Once you understand how formulas work, and the impact that formulas have on how programs are written and produced (and, perhaps on our psyches), you will be able to apply this concept to films, television programs, popular romances, and other works that strike your attention.

To make things as simple as possible, I have designed the book so it covers, first, specific media and then, media in general and theories about the media and their impact upon society. That is, in the first part of the book I have sections that cover the print media — newspapers, books, magazines — and electronic media — radio, television, film, and recording. Then, I have sections dealing with issues about the media, their effects on people, advertising (and packaging), public relations, business and regulatory aspects of the media, and new technologies.

In addition, I have supplied an Alternative Table of Contents, which uses a topical format and enables readers to investigate subjects that are dealt with throughout the book.

One of the topics considered in this book deals with the broad area of politics and economics and the media. Related to this is the matter of what is called "cultural imperialism" (also known as Coca-colonization) and the impact that American mass media have on other cultures — especially Third World ones, which import a great deal of media from America.

Another topic involves the way women, blacks, and other groups are portrayed in the media. Consider, for example, the amount of anger generated when *The Color Purple* was released...or when National Public Television aired a documentary on AIDS in the spring of 1986. Topics such as stereotypes and "images" of women, blacks, gays, athletes, or whomever seem abstract and remote until a film or television program is produced that offends some group; especially if it is one to which you belong.

Other topics involve such matters as the impact of the media on our values, lifestyles, social and political institutions, and psyches. Terms such as "mass media" or "mass communications" seem terribly remote and abstract, somehow. You watch television and listen to the radio and go to the movies, but your use of media probably seems to you to be personal and maybe even insignificant. What do your tastes have to do with the mass media and what do they have to do with your life?

Don't be misled by terms. This book is about *Playboy* and how it gives males an identity, about politics in the comics, about bestsellers, about how Germans interpret "Dallas," about *King Kong*, about the Fairness Doctrine, about situation comedies, about media concentration, about compact disks and MTV, about television aesthetics, about advertising, about *Star Wars* and *Star Trek*, about stereotypes, about pornography and censorship, about satellites and new technology and media ethics...about all kinds of things that, I would argue, have had a significant effect upon society and, indirectly, upon you, your values, your taste, and your relations with other people. You may not have recognized this before, but I believe this book will help you make the connections.

You will find that the introductions I have written for the essays in this book are somewhat unusual. The introductions are most always micro-essays on the topic of the article under consideration, and they do not always deal with the specific content of a given article.

I use these introductions to "import" relevant ideas, to provide you with quotations worth thinking about, and to raise issues and questions you might find worth thinking about.

I hope you will find this innovation useful and that these introductions will enhance your understanding of the articles that follow them. I didn't want simply to summarize what was in the articles but to bring in new ideas and to enrich your understanding of the topic being dealt with.

To some essays I have added illustrative material.

Many of the articles you read tend to be critical of the media. This, itself, is a topic worth considering, for the fact is that the general public in America *loves* the media. Why else would people watch television so much? Or listen to the radio so much? Or buy so many records? Or rent so many movies for their VCRs?

One reason for the critical tone you find is that many of the researchers believe the media are not functioning in a responsible manner and are not worthy of the "trust" we put in them. Thus the tone of much scholarly work on the media is critical or even alarmist. What we must consider is whether these scholars and researchers are correct in their assertions. Are their criticisms of the media heroic attempts to save us from some kind of mass-mediated moronization (and manipulation and many other things, equally destructive) or are they based on something else? Television has been described as a cultural "wasteland." Is it? And if so, why? Whose responsibility is it to do something about this situation?

I hope that you will find this book provides you with ways of better understanding the media and the role they have played in your life. It offers a number of ideas to consider and ways of thinking about the media that should help you in this effort. Those critics who believe that the mass media have, in the main, a destructive effect on people and on society (in America and all over the world) may be wrong. You can think about their ideas and their arguments, and come to your own conclusions. But what if they are right?

NEWSPAPERS

Newspapers are part of our everyday experience, and when people are deprived of their papers (even for a day, when a delivery person forgets to leave one) they experience a considerable amount of anxiety and anger. Statistics suggest that something like 60 percent of Americans get most of their news via television, but the news we get on television lacks the detail and depth of newspaper articles.

The term "newspaper" is really inadequate now, for newspapers carry much more than news — especially political and economic news, as we have traditionally understood the term. Newspapers are changing to meet the competition provided by television. They have become, in recent years, much "softer" and full of entertainment material, much to the chagrin of press critics. As newspapers have evolved, there is a question about whether they are losing their main reason for existence — to help people keep up-to-date with important political, economic, and social events and understand their significance.

This kind of news is considered "hard" news — it deals with important and complicated issues and is often difficult to understand and not particularly pleasant. That is because this kind of news involves not only important events (what is happening) in our political life but also what these events "mean" and what impact they might have on society. Sometimes it is difficult to find out what is happening — as the situation involving selling arms to Iran shows.

Marshall McLuhan once suggested that all news is "bad." Good news, he said, is advertising. Thus, the idea that newspapers (and news programs) should focus on "happy" news or "good" news is really quite silly.

The other kind of news, "soft" news, is used to describe much of the other material we find in newspapers — sports news, entertainment news, movie reviews, gossip columns, and that kind of thing. Many newspapers now have entire sections devoted to this soft news — style sections, sports sections, food sections, and business sections, to name some of the more common ones.

It is difficult, at times, to make rigid distinctions between hard and soft news. At either end of the spectrum — news about politics and about sports, for example, it is easy. But there are areas, such as reports about health or business matters, in which the hard/soft distinction seems to break down. There is also the matter of analysis and opinion. Many articles are analytic (and often labeled as such) and deal with *interpretations* of news events rather than the events themselves. We see this in editorials and columns, where writers offer their opinions.

There is a good deal of controversy among journalists about what news is and about whether one ever gets news without some kind of interpretation. The term "interpretive reporting" is now used, though some people consider this a contradiction in terms. There is always some principle of selection involved in covering an event, and even if all reporters want to do is tell the "who, what, where, when, why and how" of things, they must select from the information at their disposal and this selection means, ultimately, some kind of interpretation is happening.

Newspapers are also businesses; we must not forget that fact. There is a kind of schizoid split that editors face, for editors have a responsibility to readers but also to boards of directors, who are interested in profits. Many of the changes that have occurred in newspapers are the result of marketing decisions. Market researchers conduct elaborate surveys to find out what readers want and then, too often some would say, editors change newspapers around to suit the alleged interests of their readers.

The question is this — should editors give readers what readers *want* or what readers *need*? There is often quite a difference. From the marketing perspective, newspapers are "products" to be sold; from the editorial perspective, newspapers have an obligation to their readers and to society at large and popular taste should not be the deciding factor. Editors have had to find a way to appeal to the general public and, at the same time, produce papers that carry out the traditional mission of newspapers, which is to find out what is going on and report it.

In America, there are a few newspapers that have the most prestige and that play a major role in shaping public opinion. The most important of these would be the *New York Times*, the *Washington Post*, the *Los Angeles Times*, the *Wall Street Journal*, the *Christian Science Monitor*, and perhaps a couple of other papers. Our newspapers range from newspapers of record, such as the *New York Times*, to television-influenced papers such as *USA Today*, which has been described as "McPaper," suggesting that it is like fast-food, and not particularly nourishing or valuable. Whatever its value, *USA Today* has forced many newspapers to change their look, use more color and use more soft news. Indications are now, however, that things are changing and the pendulum is beginning to move in the other direction, back toward hard news.

PRIVACY VS. THE PRESS*

John Hulteng

The essay that follows deals with an important issue: where do you draw the line "between the public's need to know and the individual's right to privacy?" The branch of philosophy that deals with such questions is known as normative ethics; it considers what is right or obligatory. There are two schools of thought in this area — the consequentialists (who stress the consequences of actions) and the non-consequentialists (who focus upon the intentions of "actors" and matters such as obligation, duties, and rights). The latter school is concerned with the act itself or the agent of the act and not with the consequences of the act.

Among the consequentialists we find:

1. *Utilitarians* who focus upon "the greatest good for the greatest number." How this is done is often problematical, however.
2. *Hedonists* who argue that pleasure is the goal of life and direct their actions toward maximizing their pleasure.
3. *Egoists* who argue that the individual self is what is all-important and are concerned with the consequences of acts only as they relate to themselves and their well being.

Among the non-consequentialists we find:

4. *Kantians* who believe in "the categorical imperative." Only acts that can be universalized are ethical.
5. *Aristotelians* who argue that "moral virtue is an appropriate location between two extremes." They search for a "golden mean."
6. The *Judeo-Christians* who believe that people are ends in themselves and should not be used as means toward some other end. This is sometimes expressed as "do unto others as you would have others do unto you."
7. The *situationalists* who argue that ethical decisions always must be determined relative to a given situation.
8. *"Emotionalists"* who stress conscience and feelings as the primary determinants of ethical actions.

When people argue about what is right or wrong, more often than not one of the above notions is the basis for their position (whether they recognize this or not). And, as we can imagine, there is a good deal of controversy about which basis is correct. In thinking about media and ethics, it is useful to consider the

---

* From *Stanford* Magazine, Fall, 1985. Reprinted with permission of *Stanford* Magazine.

material discussed in this micro-essay on normative ethics. If you are interested in this subject you should consult a good ethics textbook as well as one of the numerous books on media ethics.

A news photographer's lens catches the anguished, unbelieving faces of five small children seated in a police car, watching as firemen carry the body of their mother from her burning home. The picture appears on page one the next morning. A wire service files from Hollywood a lengthy story on the arrest of the son of a famous actress, now past her peak but still remembered throughout the world. The son has been charged with making pornographic movies involving pre-teenage boys, and the story includes references to reporters' vain efforts to get comments from the actress. A TV camera crew in a southern town gets a tip that a man is going to set himself on fire in a local park. The reporter and cameraman go to the park, and the man waits until their camera is set up and ready to roll before dousing himself with gasoline and igniting his clothes. For a long half minute the journalists record the scene until one finally rushes forward to put out the flames — but not before the deranged victim has been badly burned. Later the graphic film is aired on the local channel and the networks.

These actual instances from the news media illustrate several of the ways in which the rights and sensitivities of individuals are violated by journalists hot on the trail of a story. They also suggest why the public's opinion of the ethics of the news media has been at historic low levels in recent years.

Virtually every working day, journalists face occupational challenges like the several cited above. Much of the time their responses to these challenges are well-considered and defensible; but sometimes they reflect a cynicism, an arrogance, or a callousness that violates ethical standards and erodes the public's confidence in the media.

Was there news value in the picture of the five children that warranted its use? Or should it have been filed unpublished, on the ground that it represented only a morbid exploitation of a moment of shattering grief?

Would the story about the Hollywood star's son have merited a place on the national wire service if it had involved an unknown with no newsworthy family connections? Is it justifiable to build up a story at the expense of an innocent third party?

How should the TV crew have dealt with the man who wanted to burn himself? Did they incite his act by setting up their equipment to film his immolation? Should they instead have tried to deter him? Should they have left the matter to police and stayed away from the scene? After the fact, should they have put the grisly footage of the burning on the air?

Such questions are often posed by critics of the news media. But they are also raised within the journalistic family, whose members must struggle to resolve conflicting pressures and make the painful choices that sometimes are forced on them in the dual roles of messengers and gatekeepers.

The primary objective of the media and those who work with them is to bring readers, listeners, and viewers as honest, accurate, and complete an account of the day's events as is possible. We who are consumers of the media's end products have a very real need to know about the events of the day — in order to function within society, to be informed enough to monitor the actions of our representatives at various levels of government, to be warned of dangerous trends or incipient demagogues, to be made aware of opportunities. The need to be informed is so great that the Constitution provides the press with a First Amendment standing that is unique among business enterprises.

But as with most grants of power, there is an accompanying responsibility, not constitutionally mandated but nonetheless well understood: that the power of the press must be used responsibly and compassionately.

GROPING FOR COMPROMISE

The newspaper and TV accounts of the news obviously can't be literally complete and wholly accurate. The media reports emphasize some details and leave out others; only a tiny fraction of events and issues find their way into the limited packages of newsprint and air time with which the daily media must work.

Moreover, it is inevitable that almost any news story will in some way cause embarrassment, injury, or worse to some individuals who are principals or walk-ons in the episode being reported. If the news event is important enough to the public interest, the damage to individual rights may have to be accepted, written off as the price to be paid for informing the people.

In the process, though, journalists must somehow find a viable compromise between the duty to get the news and their ethical responsibility to respect individual rights and sensitivities. And they must find that compromise under pressure of tight publication or broadcast deadlines.

How carefully is the balance struck between the public's need to know and the individual's right to privacy? What guidelines do journalists follow? How much do craft conditions and conventions influence their decisions? Are ethical lapses more frequent and more consequential now than in the past, or less so?

The answer to the first of these questions — how fairly is the balance struck — may seem obvious. There are telling examples in every day's news diet: a cluster of microphones and cameras being thrust into the face of some harried, hurrying suspect or celebrity; tasteless questions being shouted by a pressing pack of correspondents at a bereaved relative ("How do you feel about the babysitter who let your child fall to her death?" or

"What did you think when the police told you that your son was the North End rapist?").

There was the running story of a dying child who got her last wish — a trip to Hawaii — and then was dogged every step every day by reporters and photographers who milked the saga for every possible sob, every pathetic image. Or the case of the British photographers who focused their long-distance lenses on a private Caribbean beach so that they could bring the world pictures of the pregnant Princess Diana in a bikini.

A dispassionate analyst of journalistic history would probably conclude that there are no more such excesses today than in earlier eras of journalism; very likely there are far fewer. But those abuses that do persist may be more damaging and more intrusive now, thanks to the ubiquitous TV and the wire service distribution networks. And the public may be more sensitized to media lapses today than it used to be.

Whatever the reasons, opinion polls have rarely shown the news media in lower repute with the public — right down at the bottom of the scale, barely above politicians. It is fair to ask why this should be, why journalism in the 1980s should display *any* excesses redolent of an earlier day.

PRESSURES FROM WITHIN

Some explanations are to be found in the nature of journalism itself. News is gathered, processed, edited, and distributed in a hurry; the deadlines are inexorable and there is precious little leeway within which to check facts or weigh values. Many of the lapses that give offense can be traced to this fact of life in the news business.

But there is another internal factor that is more significant and less excusable. Competition, despite the trend to one-newspaper towns, *is* still a force. The old *Front Page* rivalry among reporters representing many newspapers in a single community may be a thing of the past, but cross-media competition among print, radio, and TV is still lively.

Within television the scramble among the networks drives the camera crews and producers. And at the local level there are typically two, three, four, or more television outlets all competing for Nielsen ratings and advertisers' dollars. These competitive forces account for the thicket of cameras and microphones at a news scene, and for such unseemly episodes as the flood-lit coverage of the funerals of the Atlanta child victims of a serial murderer.

Another form of competition also affects the way news is covered: the internal pressures within a newspaper organization or a network news staff. It was this kind of internal competition that led to a major journalistic scandal when a young reporter for the highly respected *Washington Post*, eager to hype her story so that it would earn a front-page byline and advance her career, invented an eight-year-old heroin addict whose misadventures made such gripping reading that the reporter's account won a Pulitzer Prize and the admiration of her colleagues. When the truth finally came out, the prize had to be returned, and the reporter resigned in disgrace. Had she not felt pressured to produce, she might not have been tempted to cut corners.

Sometimes the pressure within is blatant. A Detroit news editor several years ago circulated to his staff a memo setting out policy for the selection of front-page stories for the paper. It read, in part:

> I want at least one, preferably two or three, stories on [page] 1-A that will jolt, shock, or at least wake up our readers. Go through the last few weeks of the early edition and you'll see what I want: "Nun charged with killing her baby," "Prison horrors revealed," "They chummed together — and died together." Sure, we've got to cover hard news — but you've got the whole rest of the paper for all but the hardest news. Look for sex, comedy, and tragedy. These are the things readers will talk about the next day — and that's what I want.

It should be noted that this editor's attitude is far from typical; on most newspapers much more conservative policies are in effect.

The reporters, camera crews, and editors who work for TV are under internal pressures peculiar to their medium. For TV, action is an essential news ingredient; stories of movement, violence, and drama can almost always beat out "talking-head" interviews for the precious few minutes of air-time. Frequently the events that can be illustrated with lively or bloody action footage are selected from the broad array of available news stories even though they may distort the reality of that day's news.

To provide the indispensable action factor, complex economic or political issues are reduced to a few frames showing an aggrieved farmer or a fleeting view of an empty storefront. Never mind that such shorthand treatment grossly oversimplifies a complicated issue and blurs public understanding.

BLOOD IN THE WATER

A different internal craft convention or occupational pressure is responsible for another category of press sins — the sometimes relentless pursuit and misrepresentation of well-known public figures on the seeming assumption that such persons have no privacy rights or else have forfeited them by going into public life. The case of the actress's son cited earlier falls into this category, as does the harassment of Princess Diana in her bikini, Bert Lance, and Geraldine Ferraro.

There is, of course, nothing new about journalistic hot pursuit. And in some situations it is triumphantly justified. In an earlier era the newspapers' dogged exposés of New York's Boss Tweed (aided by the deadly cartoons of Thomas Nast) helped eradicate a civic cancer. And if the news media had not kept an unwavering spotlight focused on Richard Nixon and friends throughout the long Watergate ordeal, the worst governmental scandal in American political history might have been glossed over.

But in the post-Watergate era the exploits of the *Washington Post*'s Robert Woodward and Carl Bernstein so captured the imagination of their colleagues that investigative journalism became the vogue in just about every newsroom in the country. Fired by visions of uncovering another Watergate, reporters followed every tip, pored over every municipal record, suspected every public official. Sometimes they hit pay dirt and the polity benefited. In many other instances, however, their efforts began to take on the dimensions of a witch hunt.

Some editors, taken aback by the development, saw the overzealous investigators as consumed by a "wolf pack syndrome." Ben J. Wattenberg, press critic and observer, said such reporters "have the bias of the piranha fish — they will go after anything that bleeds." San Francisco columnist Herb Caen complained about "vendetta journalism" in which some public figure is singled out for daily sniping until the cumulative damage finally brings him down. Even Howard Simons, then managing editor of the *Washington Post*, was dismayed by the eagerness of some elements of the press to "rush in to get a bite of that bleeding body in the water."

Less sanguinary practices also stemmed from the Watergate period. Anyone in public life became fair game for constant and critical scrutiny, and any well-known figure might be dragged into the news though only peripherally involved, or even when there was no legitimate news link at all, as in the following opening paragraph of a newspaper story: "The son of President Reagan's tax attorney has been described in a psychiatric evaluation as schizophrenic and an isolated, chronic bed-wetter who is incompetent to stand trial for the rape and murder of his mother."

BLATANT INTRUSION

Television frequently offends in unnecessary and egregious fashion, as when a CBS crew was sent to follow a Marine officer to the home of a soldier killed in Beirut so that their camera could film the faces of the family members as they were given the first word of their loss. The film was shown on several stations, but the anchor person on at least one of them followed it immediately with an apology. NBC got similar footage but anchor Tom Brokaw and his colleagues decided it was blatant intrusion and refused to show it.

It was on TV that vendetta journalism found unusual expression when such programs as "60 Minutes" and "20/20" developed the ambush interview technique. This involved setting up unsuspecting individuals for an on-the-air surprise confrontation, during which the target could almost invariably be counted on to stumble, blurt out incriminating admissions, or simply flee the scene, leaving the audience with an impression of guilt, whether or not such an impression could be supported by evidence admissible in a court of law.

WHAT ROLE TO PLAY

Let's turn, finally, to yet another form of invasion of privacy: the roles journalists sometimes play to gain access to news that would otherwise be barred to them. In one instance, a TV reporter donned a white medical jacket and borrowed a stethoscope so that she could get into a hospital wing where an artificial-heart patient was being treated. Her story went on the evening news with details that partially contradicted information given out by hospital spokesmen.

Was the reporter behaving responsibly? Did the fact that her story contradicted the official version justify the deception? Most editors would probably agree that it did not.

The issue of deception by reporters is not clear-cut, though, as illustrated when the *Chicago Sun-Times* published a series of articles exposing corruption among municipal and state agencies charged with making sure that places of business were safe and sanitary.

The material for the exposé came from an unusual sting enterprise. The newspaper had financed two of its staff members to open a neighborhood bar. The two represented themselves as entrepreneurs, got a license, found a location, and opened their doors. They did not, of course, let it be known that they were actually reporters. The bar's sly name: The Mirage.

During the weeks that they were in business the proprietors of The Mirage amassed evidence about the shady ways of state and city inspectors who would, in exchange for a modest bribe, give their OK to substandard fixtures and equipment. Hidden cameras and microphones recorded the transactions, all of which were promptly reported to the Illinois Department of Law Enforcement, which had been aware of the operation from the beginning.

Was the Mirage caper a brilliant stroke of investigative journalism, or was it entrapment? Under what circumstances can reporters traffic in deception in order to get a story?

The Mirage series was nominated for a Pulitzer Prize, but the Pulitzer board's discussion was long and heated. In the end the board members passed it over because they could not agree on the ethical questions inherent in the situation. Editor Benjamin C. Bradlee of the *Washington Post*, a member of the Pulitzer board that year, reportedly asked his colleagues: "How can a newspaper fight for honesty and integrity when they themselves are less than honest in getting a story?"

The guideline most widely accepted seems to be that if the news situation is sufficiently important to the public, and if the masquerading reporter does not claim false credentials (posing as a doctor or a policeman) deception is sometimes permissible.

BLURRED ROAD MAPS

The vagueness and elasticity of this statement of principle is typical of the codes and policies drawn up to give ethical guidance to journalists.

There are many codes. Most major newspaper and electronic news organizations have one. National organizations such as the American Society of Newspaper Editors and the Society of Professional Journalists have overall codes of general application. So do organizations of radio and TV journalists.

Yet their chief utility seems to be to adorn office walls and sustain the already converted. They lack effective enforcement powers. They are generalized, and it is typically left to the individual journalist to figure out how to apply the lofty principles to actual cases.

But the codes and policies do at least reflect concern on the part of media managers, who have in recent years become much more sensitized to the need for improved journalistic practice. To address that need, editors and broadcasters have experimented with various approaches beyond drafting codes.

One approach has been to set up press councils, appeal bodies made up chiefly of nonjournalists and charged with receiving and investigating complaints from readers and viewers. Several regional and local councils are still in business, but the National News Council folded last year after an eleven-year run because major newspapers refused to finance or cooperate with its investigations.

Another approach has been to designate ombudsmen, an idea imported from the Scandinavian countries, where such officials are appointed to act as the public's representatives, sorting out grievances and redressing wrongs. In the American press version, the ombudsman is a staff member of the news organization, given autonomy to ride herd on mistakes and excesses and report regularly to the public. But only about three dozen papers out of the 1,700 dailies in the U.S. have experimented with this approach, and some of them have discontinued the office after giving it a try.

The truth is that media people are very thin-skinned about criticism, even though they regularly rake over almost every other institution in society. They are always suspicious of any form of critical overview, fearing it might be a precursor to governmental intervention and the eventual death of press freedom. But however thin their skins, the press and TV managers should do more than they have been doing to assure quality control. There are measures that could be taken without jeopardizing the independence and integrity of the media.

For one thing, the National News Council should be revived. It may not have been a complete success, but it did provide a forum to which victims who felt that they had been mangled by media machines could turn for a hearing. In its new incarnation the council ought to be fully independent, endowed by foundation grants so that its directors would no longer have to go around, begging bowls in hand, seeking funds from the very publications and networks the council was intended to monitor.

As a routine adjunct to its investigative and judicial activities, a newly independent council should be enabled to present a monthly report to the public, on the Public Broadcasting Service if not on the commercial TV networks. Such a report would briefly detail cases, outlining the arguments that had been weighed and the judgments reached. This open accounting would at one stroke enhance the public's understanding and lend more force to the council's admonitions.

Secondly, the media managers ought to make wider use of the institution of the ombudsman, providing that office with enough autonomy so that its potentialities as a bridge to the public can be realized.

Finally, standards and priorities ought to be more constructively defined — particularly in the case of TV — in order to reduce the incidence of abuses caused by internal or craft pressures.

Unless steps like these are undertaken voluntarily by editors, publishers, and broadcasters, it is conceivable that public confidence in the various branches of the media might become so eroded that the way would be opened for those various interests (Jesse Helms isn't the only one) that are watchfully waiting for a chance to weaken the First Amendment buckler that has protected the press so well from assaults in the past.

A CAVEAT — AND A HOPE

In fairness, I should acknowledge that this article has been, of necessity, a condensed chamber of horrors. Most of the distasteful instances that have been described are exceptions, not the norm. Yet the very fact that there are this many exceptions suggests that the need for improvement is real and that the owners and operators of the media should take seriously their responsibility to act.

I do want to add a final, hopeful note. Whatever the media managers may do or not do to foster and institutionalize incentives to quality, there is one additional factor that represents perhaps the most consistent force for improvement in press practices: the consciences and idealism of the individual men and women who work in the business and make the daily, front-line decisions on ethical questions. And — fortunately for us — that is a solid factor to lean on.

The people in the news business are often perceived by the public as an arrogant lot, more liberal than the majority of the population, hungry for power, uncaring about the rights and sensitivities of individuals they write or broadcast about, interested only in sensationalism, headlines, and exposure on the national TV networks.

I admit that there are some journalists who do fall into one or even all of these perceptual categories. But there are many who fall into none of them. My forty-five years in and observing journalism leave me with the belief that a clear majority of journalists do respond to what might be called a central ethic of journalism: informing the people as accurately and as completely as possible. They look on their work as a form of public service. Sure, they like to earn bylines or they covet an anchor slot. But they are also aware that the vast media machines they operate can wreak dreadful injury on the men and women who are swept into the news stream, and they try very earnestly to minimize the injury. Their efforts and their influence are significant; they are, after all, the first gatekeepers.

2   THE NEWS MEDIA AS A CURRICULUM*

MICHAEL J. ROBINSON

News, like everything else, doesn't just appear out of the blue sky, from nowhere. News is the product of some organization devoted to obtaining it, interpreting it, and disseminating it via the various media.

This essay deals with two questions about news: what is news and what role do news organizations play in gathering it for use by the media? But the essay does more than that, for it enables us to see how news can be used as an effective topic for teaching. Hence the title — the news media as a curriculum.

What Robinson likes about the news is that it enables him (or any teacher) to deal with a number of important topics or considerations: facts, citizenship values, analytical skills, and philosophical values. Let us examine each of these topics in more detail.

Teaching the news requires students to learn a good deal of factual information about our political system, and to keep up-to-date with current events. Robinson cites some statistics that reveal that many American students know very little about the American political system or what is going on in society. Since news (at least hard news) tends to be about political matters, teaching the news forces

---

* Michael Jay Robinson, "The News Media as Curriculum," reprinted with permission of the Poynter Center, Indiana University, © 1979.

students to learn some factual information about our political system and how it is evolving.

Teaching news also develops analytical skills, since students are constantly forced to reconcile differing descriptions of "fact," different opinions about what should be done to solve problems, and deal with important issues. Here, values come into play and students have to consider what role they think government should play in dealing with problems (and what problems government should deal with).

The second part of the essay deals with news organizations and forces students to think about how organizations function and the role they play in the scheme of things. This process leads students to see the difference between individual and corporate morality and, one would hope, think about how ethics applies to corporations and other such entities.

Ultimately, studying news "liberally" educates students, gives them greater understanding of themselves and people in general, and generates a greater tolerance for human error as well as a more profound understanding of human fallibility and limitations.

This essay was written by Robinson to suggest how the news might be taught and why it is a valuable teaching device. For students, this represents an unusual opportunity to see how teachers think and why they design courses the way they do.

Generally, I hate vogue. I own neither a Bee Gees album nor a pair of Frye boots. But some vogue I do like; some I even practice. My favorite academic trend right now is teaching "the news" and teaching about the "news media."

Teaching news and about news is a vogue that merits more than promotion — it merits what social scientists would call institutionalization. I find no happier recent development in teaching political science than that which brings the news and the news media into the classroom — both as a resource in and a focus for teaching.

WHAT IS TO BE TAUGHT?

One might say that in political science, and generally in the liberal arts, there are *four major goals* — types of lessons — to be achieved in the classroom. An instructor can, really should, attempt to teach (1) *facts;* (2) *citizenship;* (3) *analytical skills,* and (4) *philosophical values.* These are the basics of education.

Obviously, any curriculum that provides lessons in two or three of these basic areas is worthwhile. But teaching "news" and "news organization" provides, happily, for instruction in all four categories — without stretching our definition of a news curriculum very much. Still, in order to get the most out of teaching from and about news — in order to achieve all four major goals — instructors must keep in mind that there really are two separate topics to be addressed here — *news* and *news organization*.

Taken separately, each of these two topics — news and news organization — provides its own lessons and "advantages" among the four major categories of instruction. Each topic should, in fact, be considered as distinct, when the curriculum begins. But as the curriculum develops the two subjects can be and should be melded together. *When melded, the study of news and the study of news organization provides a grand and unique set of philosophical lessons — a set of lessons as important and understandable as any offered within political science or social science generally.*

"NEWS" IN TEACHING: LESSONS IN CONTENT

The obvious questions are how and why does a dual curriculum in news and news organization do so much? The answers to those questions range from the obvious to the subtle, but in every instance the academic advantages are there.

Most obvious, perhaps, is the fact that by simply teaching news content *per se* — either print or electronic — one provides a considerable amount of basic, factual information.

Fact: By bringing news into the classroom, and into the curriculum, a political scientist promotes most directly the acquisition of political facts. And as instructors, we need all the help we can get teaching political facts. Most recent research among our student-aged population reveals just how badly political facts are being communicated in contemporary educational environments.

National survey data from 1976 compiled by the National Assessment of Education Progress (NAEP) demonstrate that among other horrors:

- 47 percent of our high school seniors believed that Presidents can appoint people to Congress;
- 47 percent of our high school seniors did *not* know that each state has two senators;
- 54 percent of our high school seniors did *not* know Congress has the right to increase our income taxes by a factor of two;
- 28 percent of our high school seniors did *not* know that starting a new party, other than the Democratic or Republican party, is legal;
- 46 percent of our high school seniors believed that Congress can declare Presidential troop commitments "unconstitutional."[1]

This advertisement was part of a campaign by the *San Francisco Examiner* satirizing local television news broadcasters.

Our young citizenry is, quite apparently, in trouble when it comes to basics.* But by compelling students to read a newspaper or watch television news, we, as faculty, force students to learn these rudimentary political facts — and, obviously, many more.

Logic and intuition both support this not-too-surprising notion that newspapers teach *political* facts. Newspapers and news programs, after all, have their biases. We make much of the alleged partisan biases all the time. But one bias that we tend to ignore completely — because it is so total — is that news, TV or print, is *political* news. (It needn't be that way and, in fact, it has not always been that way, even in the U.S.) But besides this "political" bias, newspapers practice a second — but from our perspective, fortunate — bias. American newspapers cover politics *factually*. That is, the newspaper story about politics is built around who, what, when, where. And, while it is demonstrably true that almost every American daily newspaper contains as much grocery advertising as political fact, newspapers do, to a considerable degree, stress their political information, placing it up front on page one.

Students even come to us in the classroom assuming that "news" is factual, political news. So, assigning the newspaper is tantamount to assigning a political factbook, day-by-day. This simple truth about American news is as obvious as it is important to teachers of political science trying to cover basics.

One might begin a course on and of the media by stressing the factual advantages in reading the newspaper — any newspaper.† One might even suggest to his or her students that by reading the local newspaper day-to-day they, by the term's end, will have more political facts at their disposal than the overwhelming majority of the American adult population, including, most likely, their own parents. (This particular "truth" about adult ignorance should, at first, impress students, but by the end of the semester a good instructor will have used this "truth" to unnerve them.)

It is not, however, my own simple intuition and logic that allow me to argue the premise that the news teaches facts. Empirical research dealing with mass media generally finds that the one — and often the only — consistent impact of "news exposure" upon children, adolescents, or adults is increased factual information.[2] Media, apparently, do not convince nearly as well as they inform.[3] Newspapers, and even television, may not persuade but they do "teach," at least according to the majority of the scholarly research dealing with this particular topic.[4]

It comes down to news as fact. Think of television's own Sgt. Joe Friday — who, like a good journalist, always started out asking for "just the facts,

<hr>

* Quite remarkably, seniors did best on questions about "rights under arrest" and the criminal justice system generally — a fact NAEP attributes to "Crime-Time" television; something we might legitimately term the "Kojak effect."
† Journalists and instructors usually develop an acute snobbishness about good newspapers. But virtually no American daily is so poor that it doesn't "teach" students that states have two senators, that states have varying numbers of representatives, that Congress can change law, and that third parties are legal — facts that NAEP demonstrates students do not now know.

ma'am, just the facts." All serious news media — and even most of the frivolous news media — start out with the facts.

Citizenship Values: The twin biases in newspapers toward "facts" and "politics" are important, if not surprising. And those two biases imply clearly that news itself reflects and must reflect basic cultural values — which are, to be honest, cultural biases. But these biases are so deeply engrained we essentially disregard them, just as we disregard the bias toward facts on page one.

Newspapers and news programs are products of — and promoters of — basic cultural values, especially the values of our social, economic, and political elites. Therefore, when followed closely, newspapers achieve a second, beneficial effect in students. They teach *good citizenship*, as defined by our American political culture, and as interpreted by American communication elites.

By this I mean that newspapers and the electronic media urge readers to learn and to practice the political values of "the system." After all, we know that no daily newspaper advocates — on its editorial page or anywhere else — that readers should *not* vote, should *not* practice community spirit, should *not* "get involved," should *not* learn more about government. Newspapers advocate precisely the opposite in every instance. Virtually all daily newspapers and all licensed broadcasters counsel their readers and their audience to obey the law, to do their share, and to be active in their community.

In essence, then, one advantage of using news as a pedagogical tool is that news and newspapers represent cultural propaganda that encourages good citizenship.

In one sense, newspapers trumpet this propaganda to such an extent that they, themselves, fall victim to it. For example, "Republican" newspapers inevitably urge that, regardless of one's choice among candidates, a citizen should vote — although most of us take it for granted that when Republican newspapers get apathetic people to vote that usually helps the Democrats and hurts the Republicans. But the vote is another form of apple pie, so newspapers — Republican or not — are in favor of voting, no matter whom it helps.

Each of us has been taught some citizenship by the media and the more news we consume the more likely we are to reflect the "good citizenship" we are given by the news media. One might object to this use of newspapers and news programs as a channel for inculcating elite values into our citizenry — especially our young citizenry. But, if the system is "legitimate," if it is "worth saving," one can, without much gagging or embarrassment, accept this very mild form of propaganda. The values expressed, almost unthinkingly by the news media, are so culturally based, so widely shared, so consensual that it would be difficult to object to their transmission. How *does* one, after all, object to news that tries to "indoctrinate" our young into being better citizens, or becoming voters, or getting more knowledgeable?

Analytical Skills: As I have already attempted to make clear, newspapers contain more than citizenship values. Alongside the pieces that promote citizenship and community values are pieces that provide hard news. The hard news permits students to place the society's values beside the society's "facts." Hard news provides "data" necessary for comparing the society to its own culturally defined standards.

In that comparison lies another general lesson that newspapers can teach. By placing the student in an intellectual tension in which facts and values do not always mesh, news pushes students into an analytical exercise. Newspapers require reconciliation between hard news and soft, between news and opinion, and between opinions themselves.

If we return to the issue of "voters" and "voting," we can see how this might work. Any serious student who reads an editorial claiming that public opinion will not stand for another Congressional delay in tax reform will obviously find that assertion suspect if our student has just seen the poll on page one which shows that the public does not even know that Congress makes tax law. Inconsistencies like this demand some sort of reconciliation. And political analysis is a first derivative of this reconciliation.

More than a traditional text, the newspaper and the news program provide information that works to support several discrepant approaches and several less-than-consistent theories. Newspapers were the original college "reader" in this respect — a "reader" being simply a compilation of pieces requiring some considerable degree of intellectual synthesis.* News is, in essence, a perfectly good way to teach analytical skill — by forcing the student to swim, or drown, in this sea of discrepant information and opinion.

In sum, "The News," in and of itself, does much that most teachers of political science and other social sciences should want done with their students. The news provides students with facts and data; the news inculcates civic values into its youth; the news presents fact and opinion that require readers to think about what is happening, or should be happening, in politics. And, finally, most of our news does all this without selling a wholly partisan — or even observably partisan — line. (Almost none of the empirical research demonstrates any major partisan impact from print or electronic news, if partisan impact is defined as advantage for the Democrats or the Republicans.[5])

So, from the perspective of fact, value, citizenship, and analysis, news-

---

* Interestingly enough, although newspapers would seem to demand more analytical competence than news programs — because of their size and format — *news programs may actually prove better at teaching analytical or synthetic skills.* Acting within the constraints of the Fairness Doctrine — the rule that compels licensees to present "both sides" of controversial issues — networks and stations present conflicting opinion and discrepant fact in almost every news item which takes longer than thirty seconds. Watching both sides simultaneously requires analytical thinking in the mind of any but the most casual viewer. Despite this strange advantage of the electronic media, all news sources will trigger some intellectual dissonance in audiences, and thereby elicit some need to put things together.

papers and news programs make a singularly good "text" for American political science.

"NEWS ORGANIZATIONS" IN TEACHING: LESSONS IN FACT AND ANALYSIS

Despite the advantages in teaching "news," any faculty member who only teaches "the news," as content, misses a great opportunity. Studying the news *process* and the news *organization* is, in my opinion, just as beneficial for students as reading or watching content.

As in studying content, studying the process teaches lessons that are both factual and analytical. Studying news process and news organization does not, obviously, have as large and as immediate a payoff in facts as studying the content directly. But by focusing on large news organizations — especially network news — one first magnifies student interest in learning political facts, facts both about news makers and about news-making.

Students often come to these types of courses regarding Walter Cronkite, John Chancellor, and Barbara Walters, among others, as distant, influential relatives, relatives about whom students wish to know practically everything there is to know. Even drugstore book racks have paperbacks about prominent TV personalities. News organizations are, in this respect, almost "bait" for students, specifically those students who need or like some form of packaging to make facts more palatable. Media classes — especially television classes — draw students heavily, from all departments and from all majors (an important consideration these days) and teach them facts about the news business. Admittedly, at this starkest level, teaching news organization and process teaches facts about current events because students enjoy following the news as their TV heroes and favorite anchor people report it. Thankfully, however, teaching news organization and news process does much more than attract large numbers of registrants who are really looking for facts and anecdotes about television personalities.

From the educator's perspective, beyond the advantage of sugar-coating current events and attracting students to one's department, the greatest academic advantages in teaching about news organizations inheres in teaching about "organizations" themselves.

Organization is one of the most important variables in politics, or political science for that matter. Organizational analysis is a critical skill. Yet, undergraduate students rarely appreciate or understand organization as a political dimension — except in the most pejorative terms. But, by mastering the how, what, and why of organization, students learn some of the most important lessons political science has to teach. Indeed, studying organization, even *without* considering news organizations as a special case, gives added meaning to modern politics, to modern sociology, and, quite literally, to our "corporate state." But by focusing specifically on the case of news organization — TV or print — one has three special advantages in teaching.

First, and of practical importance, there is a considerable amount of literature about "news as organization" — most of it readily available in paperback. One can use the popular trade books like Dan Rather's *The Camera Never Blinks*, Daniel Schorr's *Clearing the Air*, Timothy Crouse's *The Boys on the Bus*, Bob Woodward and Carl Bernstein's *All the President's Men*, or Gay Talese's *The Kingdom and the Power*.

One can also use what might best be called intermediate level books, works such as Robert MacNeil's *The People Machine*, Lou Cannon's *Reporting*, or Fred W. Friendly's *Due to Circumstances Beyond Our Control* — all of which successfully fill the gap between journalism and social science.

One can also use the growing number of professional analyses of news organizations — the two best, perhaps, being Leon V. Sigal's *Reporters and Officials* and Edward Jay Epstein's classic, *News From Nowhere*. (Epstein's book, to my mind the best of the lot, is his doctoral dissertation, written at Harvard for James Q. Wilson, possibly the most distinguished authority in political science studying political organization *per se*.) Regardless of the level of literature one chooses — or even the specific book — there is a large and worthwhile bibliography to draw from to teach organization by teaching news organization.

Second, because the *product* which any news organization provides is continuous, public, and cheap, students can test their notions and theories about organizational behavior by analyzing the product itself — the news. News organizations are, in this respect, unique in their unintended capacity to provide material for students and scholars to assess. This availability of news makes any lesson or any idea about organization more meaningful and vivid for students. In a word, it makes analysis simple.

If, for example, one believes that news on television is more a function of what is filmable than what is significant (and who doesn't believe that?), students can "test" that hypothesis, which is based in organization theory, simply and directly, by merely going home and watching TV. Students can watch and count the number of airplane landings, arrival ceremonies, or limousine departures on the network programs just to get a sense of the "tyranny of film," which does, in fact, dictate a good deal of news policy in television.

Obviously, the study of news organization and news process at this level does more than teach students "about" news; it also demands *analytical thinking* of a fairly high order — forcing students first to draw hypotheses from their reading and, second, to test those hypotheses by assessing the "content." By forcing students to analyze news organizations by analyzing their product, one goes beyond teaching analytical thinking. One teaches, in elementary form, the scientific method. What, after all, is the scientific method other than developing hypotheses, selecting indicators, collecting evidence, and evaluating results?

The third advantage in studying news organizations, as distinguished from general organizations, is that students will be forced to consider the idea that *news organizations are not inherently "good" organizations — and that other forms of organization are not inherently "evil."* When approaching the study of organizations, students often expect to discover that Exxon, as an example, behaves selfishly. Exxon does so, students surmise, to sustain itself and to please its stockholders. Students, in other words, tend to presuppose corporate "immorality," when contemplating most large organizations — especially "Big Business" organizations.

But students are less likely to see network news (with Walter Cronkite) or major newspapers (with Woodward-Bernstein) as modern organizations in this same vein. News, to students, is both personal and moral. (Personal often implies moral to most of us.) But by studying news process and news organization, students will discover that the news media have bureaucrats, subscribers, public relations people, shareholders, and budgets — all of which must be accommodated — very much in the manner that Exxon must accommodate its bureaucrats, subscribers, PR people, shareholders, and budgets.

In terms of "social values" students should see that large corporations — whether selling oil or selling news — have at least as much in common as they have in opposition. The major lesson here may well be corporate, organizational *amorality*, as opposed to the so-called corporate immorality.

Whatever the exact lesson in values, it is almost inevitable that teaching news process and news organization will make students understand that organizational behavior is different from individual behavior. CBS is more like Exxon than either organization would like to admit. And both Richard Salant, the President of CBS News, and Walter Cronkite recognize that CBS as an organization compels them to do much of what they do, greatly influencing the way they do it. Clifford C. Garvin, Exxon's Chairman of the Board, contends with and obeys most of the same organizational imperatives as the people at CBS.

Perhaps the ultimate lesson here is that news is more like "product" than it is like "goodness," despite the motivations and sincerities of individual journalists, producers, cameramen. A corporation by any other name....

TEACHING NEWS AND NEWS PROCESS TOGETHER: THE ESSENCE OF A LIBERAL EDUCATION

So far I have dealt with the unique lessons one learns in studying "the news" and studying "the news media." For the most part those lessons have been factual or analytical — only rarely normative.[*] However, I contend

---

[*] In the vernacular of modern day social science, "normative" is defined as that which pertains to values and value judgments — good and evil.

that when we use both together — when we combine what we know about news and about news-making — we teach one final lesson to students, and just possibly the most important lesson of all.

This lesson is normative and philosophical, and it might best be termed the Lesson of a Liberal Education. The lesson holds that what we know and what we can know is limited. Therefore, what we believe in, and what we do, should be limited as well.

This lesson starts with what we have learned about news and about the news process — and what we have already taught our students about both. I believe that students, having learned what news production and news organization really are, having learned the inherent *limitations* of our information and even our information-gathering apparatus, will better understand intellectual "relativism," or what I call "academic liberalism."

Students who learn that news is neither pure nor comprehensive, neither absolute nor necessarily important (and these lessons are all but inevitable), will recognize that the foundations upon which their opinions are built are inherently weak. Not evil, merely weak.

I argue that this is true for all of us, not just students — that all of us have foundations, in fact, with serious weaknesses. But, if you, as reader, consider your own foundation sound, and regard only the other person as having limited rationality, consider this case of news-based opinion — and consider what it means for your own sense of relativism and values.

First, ask yourself, who is, at this moment, Africa's most despotic black leader?

I suspect that you have already selected President Idi Amin, pariah of Uganda, beast of Kampala. Why do you believe so? For those very few who have been to Kampala, the answer may well be "experience." For me, and for the rest of us, the answer, of course, is the media.

The media have created a vivid and heinous picture of President Amin in our heads — complete with uniform and cap. After all, we have been to Entebbe; we have been to Kampala — via the media. We know about Amin.

So given his media "image," Amin is not by any stretch an unreasonable selection as "Africa's worst" or even the "world's worst" leader. But Amin is the wrong selection. (At least I think he might be.) Read the following sentences from a recent news dispatch:

The worst African oppressors are often the blacks.

A blood-curdling example is Francisco Macie, the president-for-life of Equatorial Guinea.

During the nine years of his terrorist reign, Macie has slain an esti-mated 50,000 persons. And, 150,000 have fled the country.

Two years ago, for example, Macie celebrated Christmas with his national militia in Fernando Po soccer stadium. As a recording of "Those Were the Days, My Friend" blared over the stadium's loudspeakers, Macie's troops shot and hanged 150 of the regime's opponents. The year before, a similar grisly mass execution was publicly performed on Christmas Eve.

Dissent in Equatorial Guinea means certain death. A foreign minister, Dr. Atansio Ndongo, died when Macie ordered him thrown from the third floor window of the presidential palace.

With megalomaniacal fervor, Macie has ordered a new law passed which requires that he be praised in the Catholic Mass. He has proclaimed a "hymn of the republic" which reads: "God has created Equatorial Guinea through the will of Papa Macie. Without him Equatorial Guinea would not exist. Forward with Macie. Nothing without Macie. Everything with Macie."

Commented Herbert Spiro, the last American ambassador to Equatorial Guinea: "Compared to Macie, Idi Amin...is a great statesman."

This passage appeared in *The Washington Post* on March 29, 1978. None other than Jack Anderson wrote it from accounts he had been given from his own sources in Africa. And, even though this information (like almost *all* information) came to me through the mass media (suggesting that some part of the media knows "everything"), and even though Jack Anderson too could be in error, the point I want to make should come through rather clearly. Even if we have read everything there is to read — *we do not really know who is the world's worst leader, or even Africa's worst leader. We can only know what the media are capable of telling us, or are inclined to regard as newsworthy, or are permitted to cover.* In Amin's case the media might just possibly have told us "wrong." Compared to Papa Macie, Amin may be just another awful despot. If Anderson is correct in his story, Amin can be viewed as the victim of a press vendetta, which is, for better or worse, what Amin maintains. Perhaps the most reasonable interpretation of this case of Amin *vs.* Macie is that among those currently receiving greatest media attention, Idi Amin ranks as the world's worst political leader.

In any event, Amin's case serves a point: *Our information and, hence, our reason are suspect.* Walter Lippmann recognized this when he argued that news puts pictures in our heads; that news is ephemeral; that news is relative; that news is never complete. I say that to know what Lippmann knew is to develop a sense of intellectual modesty and, therefore, a sense of relativism and a sense of tolerance.

I think that to understand that news is what the news media are prepared to discover; to realize that news is so heavily culturally defined; to learn that news is not only limited by quick judgments but also by budgetary

---

* "Permission" is especially important outside the United States. The reason, for example, that the press tended to dwell on atrocities committed by South Vietnamese soldiers during the War in Vietnam was not that the press was pro-North. The major reason was that North Vietnamese soldiers permitted virtually no press coverage of their atrocious conduct.

constraints is to recognize the limitations of our own intellectual resources, our own faculties, and even our own rationality.

To know what news is, therefore, is to learn a sense of liberalism — not left-of-center liberalism, not New Deal liberalism, but liberalism defined as an academic and an intellectual philosophy.

Liberalism is, in this sense, an acceptance of one's own, and society's own, limitations. Liberalism is a recognition of other people's rights, other people's facts, other people's values — because we can never know truth, either through our own senses or our own media.

For students to recognize that the limitations of their reason are vast and inevitable is to understand and to accept academic liberalism. This is, perhaps, the most important lesson that any political scientist, social scientist, or humanist can teach. Teaching the news, teaching the news process, is nothing short of a great assignment.

STRATEGIES IN TEACHING THE NEWS

Fortunately all the advantages which accrue in teaching news and news-making are relatively simple to attain. News is, in fact, one of the few things that can be as effectively taught using either traditional pedagogy or "classrooms without walls."

I have three specific suggestions that might help in constructing a "news curriculum." These suggestions run the gamut from the traditional through the progressive, and were chosen to show how wide-ranging the alternatives can be. Obviously, of course, my list is not close to being an exhaustive one.

Quizzes: I have found that nothing works better in teaching news content than simply telling students, at the outset of the course, that some modest percentage of their grade — I usually allocate 10 percent — will be based upon what old-fashioned teachers might call current events quizzes.

I recommend giving six quizzes, or somewhere near that number, and permitting students to miss one quiz, or to drop their lowest score. With quizzes teachers can give instructions to follow a particular newspaper, network, or whatever. But the point with quizzes is not so much to teach differences in media, or the process of news, but instead to teach the rudimentary facts of the day — something the usual political science curriculum often does not attempt to do.

One nice advantage to quizzes is that they allow the teacher, by his or her instructions, to guide students to precisely the type of news or news sources the teacher wishes to stress. The quizzes, and the instruction concerning them, serve as an "invisible hand," moving students toward the precise information the teacher wants to convey. Another advantage in short-answer quizzes is that students actually come to appreciate them — because quizzes force students to do something they actually believe in — reading the newspaper.

Ride-along: One other approach, one that takes students away from the traditional classroom, is the "ride-along" technique. I have used this strategy when teaching criminology courses — in that case negotiating an arrangement with the local police so that students literally rode with the officers in their cruisers, for periods of up to four hours. This same strategy should work just as well with local journalists.

The class should be small and each student must be prepared and briefed about his or her assignment. But the essential plan involves merely arranging to have a student stay with one reporter (or camera crew) for one full workday, or for one complete story. By negotiating with all types of news sources, the instructor can almost be certain that students will learn something about journalism, and about the inherent differences and similarities among media, as each student discusses his or her own experiences with a particular medium.

Grading a ride-along program is simple. Students should file two stories shortly after their trip. The first should be a straight news piece about what he or she covered during that day. The second story should assess the experience itself. Each student would attempt to answer one major question. What did the ride-along tell me about news, journalists, and journalism?

Reality Testing: The most unusual suggestion I have to offer is also the most difficult to orchestrate. It involves, first, selecting an event with which students are intimately familiar, or, better, an event with which they could be made intimately familiar before some future point.

The best strategy would be to select a *planned* event that would take place in the not-too-distant future, and, of course, in the local area. On campus this would probably entail an event dealing with student politics or student life. And, of course, the larger the event — in scope or in meaning — the better. (The current mood on campus will probably make big political events hard to find.) The most important thing, however, is that students will have been there when the event took place — and to have been there in large enough numbers to have a sense of what really went on.

The next step involves collecting all the media coverage of the event that is available from virtually every source. Clearly, it is essential to choose an event big enough to attract the local media.

The last phase is, of course, to place the separate and collected "realities" of the event alongside each other — the reality of having been there, the reality of print, the reality of television, etc.

I am not the inventor of this strategy for studying news and news process. Kurt and Gladys Lang used it in 1951 to study the separate realities of "Douglas MacArthur Day" in Chicago, as depicted "on television" and "in life."[6]

Regrettably, few social scientists have used the technique for teaching or research since the 1950s. But I regard this strategy as splendid. It is doubtful that students in your school will witness an event as big as "MacArthur Day" during any given term. But the technique should apply to mini-events too, especially if students have been given an opportunity to understand what Lang and Lang were up to before going into the field. The point of the exercise is a direct understanding of what news is — what it focuses on, or ignores, how it chooses to cover events, or not cover events. Nothing, in my opinion, teaches the limitations and strengths of news better than comparison between what one really knows about, and what one then reads about or watches.

"Reality testing" is a tricky and a risky technique. It takes events, literally, out of the hands of the instructor. But this approach carries with it an advantage that almost no other approach can offer. It places media coverage up against a known quantity. In that there is much to learn and to see.

CONCLUSIONS

For those who might have missed it, the point here has been that a news curriculum not only teaches political facts; it also teaches analytical skills, citizenship, and academic liberalism. By building a curriculum that blends the study of news and the study of news process, an instructor can teach almost everything, from constitutional law to scientific method. And the methods for teaching a news curriculum are every bit as varied as the lessons that are offered.

Besides all that, teaching news is enjoyable — the news process is enjoyable. It is almost embarrassing to teach the news because it *is* so enjoyable. One gets to feel that he or she has clearly invented a curriculum to excuse the two full hours of reading required each day to get through a first-rate newspaper from cover to cover. But don't be embarrassed in establishing a "Citizenship and News" curriculum. This essay has been a set of honest justifications, and not just rationalizations for teaching news. I can't even imagine a more useful curriculum in political science, or social science, generally, than a curriculum of news. And, for me, that's the way it is.

NOTES

1. *Education for Citizenship: A Bicentennial Survey* (Denver: National Assessment of Educational Progress, 1976), pp. 26–27.
2. For a classic treatment of what the news does teach, see Steven H. Chaffee, L. Scott Ward, and Leonard Tipton, "Mass Communication and Political Socialization," *Journalism Quarterly*, Vol. 47, 1970, 647–659, 666.
3. *Ibid*; see also Steven H. Chaffee, Marilyn Jackson-Beeck, Jean Durall and Donna Wilson, "Mass Communication in Political Socialization," in *Handbook of*

Political Socialization: Theory and Research, ed. Stanley Allen Renshon (New York: The Free Press, 1977), pp. 223–58; Charles Atkin and Walter Gant, "The Role of Television News in the Political Socialization of Children," paper presented to Political Communication Division of the International Communication Association, Chicago, 1975.

4. Michael J. Robinson, "Mass Media Television and Political Perception Among Non Adults." Unpublished manuscript.

5. For recent data that show that the news does not influence voting directly, see Thomas Patterson and Robert McClure *The Unseeing Eye: The Myth of Television Power in National Elections* (New York: Putnam, 1976). For a contrasting view see John Robinson, "Perceived Media Bias and the 1968 Election," *Journalism Quarterly*, Vol. 49, 1972, 239–246.

6. Kurt and Gladys Lang, *Politics and Television* (Chicago: Quadrangle, 1968), chapter 2.

3 POLITICS IN THE COMICS*
Arthur Asa Berger

We have had comics in America for about a hundred years; the comics are part of our growing up experiences and thus seem both natural and, somehow, innocent. This may be, I would suggest, because we start reading them when we are very young and tend to associate childhood with innocence. The very term "comics," which is actually misleading, suggests humor, lack of seriousness, and perhaps even triviality. I have said the term comics is misleading because many of the comics, especially the classic American comic strips of the forties through the seventies, were serious action-adventure strips and were not funny at all.

This essay deals with social and political themes reflected in such comics as *The Yellow Kid* (our first comic strip), *Little Orphan Annie, Superman, Krazy Kat, Dick Tracy, Pogo,* and *Doonesbury*. We can, I suggest, read comic strips on two levels. On one level they are action-adventure stories or gag strips that we enjoy and find entertaining. This is the way we usually read the comics. But for those who investigate the way these strips reflect interesting things about our society and culture, we read the strips differently.

At this level, we look at the strips for stereotypes they may contain, for the way women are presented (and the roles they are given), for allusions to social and political matters, and for the way they reflect fundamental values and beliefs. That is, we can examine the comics as "historical documents" that reflect many different things about our society. Many of the early comics, for example, are

* Arthur Asa Berger, "Politics in the Comics," reprinted with permission from *Crimmer's*, 1976.

racist, anti-semitic, anti-ethnic, and full of sexism and other things that would be impossible now.

Because the comics are a relatively "naive" kind of art, and because there was a lot of racism and anti-semitism and bigotry in our earlier days, we find the early comics full of these things. The comics we will be examining are much more sanitized and self-conscious, but they still tell us a good deal about our beliefs and values. You will find discussions of our anti-authoritarian beliefs, of our morbid preoccupation with crime, of curious parallels between Superman's origin tale and the experiences of our Puritan forefathers and a number of other topics of a similar nature.

I would hope that you might use this chapter as a kind of model for your own research into the comics. I would also suggest you would find it fascinating to look at some of the comics from our earlier days, to get a reading on our values and beliefs and see what your parents read in the papers when they were growing up. You might find it very revealing.

The comic strip is one of those art forms whose very all-pervasiveness and ubiquity blind us to its significance. Certain people, I would call them elitists, suggest that comics and all forms of popular culture are subliterary, mass-produced artifacts that cater to the "lowest common denominator" and that they are of no significance, except as indicators of the power of the mass media to dominate a culture — in the service of bourgeois capitalism, invariably.

I would counter this by suggesting that all forms of expression are connected with ideologies, and the popular culture (and, indeed, elite culture) of nonbourgeois societies is far from innocent and devoid of particular points of view (a charitable term). If the comics and all forms of popular culture do express this so-called "lowest common denominator," that is perfectly fine, because we need to know more about the ideas of the common man — *his* point of view, his notions about the good life and the good society.

The comics can be characterized as having the following attributes: continuing characters, speech in balloons, and a left to right sequence of boxes and balloons. Some comics have continued stories while others, humorous "gag strips," have a new and complete episode each day. Sometimes comic books — actually magazines of comics — carry adventures of various characters and appear regularly, though this innovation is a mere forty years old.

IMPORTANT THEMES IN AMERICAN COMICS

It is difficult to characterize, with any degree of accuracy, American comic strips and comic books. After all, we are dealing with an art form that started in the 1890s and which has flourished since that time. Some of the classic strips are now forty years old and still appearing, and the number of comic books (conventional and underground) is staggering. There is a veritable pantheon of comic characters — heroes, villains, clowns, fools, people, animals, humans, inhumans, robots, machines, spooks, and androids — and with every week that passes, new creations (especially villains to fight with the heroes) find their way into the American "collective imagination."

Nevertheless, American heroes and superheroes do arise out of the American experience and must have meaning to children socialized in America. So despite the diversity of characters in comicdom, there are some things they tend to have in common. In my book, *The Comic-Stripped American*, I detected several themes which are of interest to us here: first, the notion that Americans are "spiritual orphans"; and second, a fundamental anti-authoritarianism, balanced in part by some characters who had great reverence for authority.

I discerned these themes after I had written on more than a dozen important American comics and looked back over my "findings" to see what patterns and configurations emerged. What I will be discussing, then, could be described as the theory of politics of the common man as found in comics. In some cases, such as *Pogo*, there is direct and outspoken (and even courageous) comment on specific political figures and events in American politics, but in most cases, we will be dealing with innate social and political philosophy.

It is these attitudes and values which give shape to American political life, which "condition" our political behavior, and if the comics do not as a rule focus upon specific issues in American politics, this does not mean that they lack a political dimension.

SPIRITUAL ORPHANS IN THE NEW WORLD PARADISE

By spiritual orphans I mean the notion, found in many American comics, that we have either been "abandoned" or that we lack, or have escaped from, history and the past; that we have cut ourselves off from our "motherland" and "fatherland." Loneliness is the price to be paid for freedom to create the future. Americans are cultural or spiritual orphans, free to create ourselves without the burden of a past or of institutions — but the cost is great.

Our very first comic strip, *The Yellow Kid*, reflects a strong sense of abandonment. The strip takes place in a mythical "Hogan's Alley," where a multitude of abandoned kids play. They are children but are not childish;

many wear big derbies, some smoke cigars and cigarettes, others have beards, many are grotesque. They fill the frame (*The Yellow Kid* generally was not sequential but was instead a tableau) and reflect, in a subtle manner, the feeling Americans had at the time that they were to be overwhelmed by the spawn of Europe.

Outcault's style might be described as extremely "busy." Sometimes he had fifty or so characters in a tableau, as well as numerous animals, signs, posters, and speeches made by some characters. The *ambiance* was chaotic and bodies were inserted everywhere (sometimes hanging out on a line, like stockings which had just been washed). There was no place for "nature's nobleman," the American of the forest in this world; instead, it was peopled by tough little immigrant kids, Negroes with kinky hair, mangy animals, and despondent adults.

While most of the episodes in *The Yellow Kid* had a political dimension, in certain cases there was direct political commentary. The line between the political cartoon and the comic strip with political relevance becomes very blurred at times.

In one episode, done by Outcault's successor, George Luks, we see President-elect McKinley visiting Hogan's Alley. He stands in the foreground, majestic, holding two little babies in one hand and the Yellow Kid with his other hand. The walls are covered with bits of advice for "the major," written in dialect and, as was typical of the strip, misspelled. Another episode was devoted to the gold versus silver question which was important in the McKinley-Bryan election of 1896. In this cartoon, the Yellow Kid's robe contains the following statement, "fer O'Brien. At least I am inter politics."

Though *The Yellow Kid* is generally considered a humorous strip, beneath the absurdity and nihilism is a strong element of despair at the degradation of millions of Americans during the waning years of the nineteenth century. And yet there is also a certain kind of heroism in these kids, who are full of spirit and energy — and even social awareness — despite the awesome forces they must contend with. They have been abandoned, left to play in the alley, and must contend with a dehumanizing society, and yet they manage to maintain a sense of perspective and humor.

Many other characters in American comics are abandoned — or even orphans, both real and spiritual. Little Orphan Annie, Superman, Batman, Spider-Man...they are all orphans and their histories reflect with surprising accuracy important constellations of values in America.

LITTLE ORPHAN ANNIE

In Harold Gray's *Little Orphan Annie*, the distinction between the political cartoon and the comic strip disappears, for the strip is one long political diatribe in support of conservative values and politics. It is a legacy of the

Coolidge era and was introduced (in 1924) when "The business of America is business" was the prevailing social philosophy. Gray sees the good society as a result of free competition by individuals in a laissez-faire ambiance, though Annie cannot explain how the selfishness of each (in a so-called free enterprise economy) leads to the welfare of all.

America is not what it should be — a paradise — and it is Annie's function to rail against the society in which she finds herself and to suggest that all is not lost, that there is a way for America to redeem herself. America has lost its way and the urban, complicated, cosmopolitan, bureaucratic, socialistic society in which she finds herself is a monstrosity that must be destroyed. America can be redeemed by liberating a dynamic force — the benevolent capitalist, the morally superior businessman. Freed from a destructive governmental bureaucracy, he can recreate the old, virtuous, simple America. Into the natural paradise of America the serpent of European ideas had glided, and when this snake is destroyed, we can return to the "good old days."

Given this ethos, it is only logical that the hero of this strip should be a titanic individual, one "Daddy Warbucks" (the name is most revealing) whose intrigues involve nothing less than the survival of the free world. Calling him "Daddy" humanizes him. Look, Gray is telling us, billionaires aren't that much different from anyone else, though there may also be an element of paternalism in the term. His real first name is Oliver.

And true to the dictates of the Gospel of Wealth, he is a servant of man and aware of the awesome responsibilities his great wealth imposes upon him. The strip has an aura of mystery and fantasy about it which suggests that Warbucks is the product of some kind of "higher law" which creates dynamic and heroic individuals like him. He always has special positions, secret missions, and we are to infer from his adventures that as a private individual he is able to avoid all the bureaucratic redtape which immobilizes our governmental officials. Daddy Warbucks engages in "direct action."

We are shown that history is a record of great men who transcend their societies and spend their time, in the case of the American experience, fighting foreign conspiracies. The strip reflects a diffuse paranoia to be found in many paramilitary groups; a sense that the enemy is everywhere, that the government is full of traitors, and that only a few people can be trusted.

In American society, which is egalitarian in terms of our value system, we have an economic but not a social or hereditary aristocracy (though we may be moving in this direction). Given this situation it can be seen what the basic function of Daddy Warbucks is — *mystification*. His role is to act as an apologist for capitalism, to suggest that those on the top are there on the basis of special capacities and virtues. And furthermore, that the only way to have a good society is to liberate these men so they can function efficiently. Yet the very ethos of the strip, which is full of desperate and pathetic "little people" contradicts this notion.

Indeed, *Little Orphan Annie* reflects the failure of what is probably the most important organizing myth in American culture, the myth of success and the self-made man, the so-called American Dream. Annie's tragedy is that she refuses to recognize the truth of this failure; her blank eyes cannot or will not acknowledge it.

Little Orphan Annie is really a prolonged morality play, a sustained jeremiad, exhorting Americans to return to "innocence" and implying that our salvation lies in a repudiation of Europe and history and institutions. Her confidence reflects another myth — that of the "chosen few" (in this case corporate capitalists) who will redeem American society. Annie's cause is hopeless, though, for she does not acknowledge the Great Crash, which destroyed America's faith in moral superiority of the businessman.

SUPERMAN AND THE PURITANS

Although there are other orphans and abandoned souls in the comics, I would like to conclude my discussion of this theme with a look at one of the greatest heroes of comicdom, *Superman*. Since Superman first appeared in 1938, he has changed in terms of his looks, his attitudes towards women and sex, the kinds of adventures he has had, and even his powers. But his significance as an American hero has not, and it is to this subject I would like to turn my attention.

The origin tale of *Superman*, the first two pages of the strip, is a remarkable reflection of the American ethos in an incredibly condensed but comprehensive form. *Superman is a paradigmatic hero whose experience recapitulates, so to speak, the American experience to an "extraordinary" degree.* The accompanying table illustrates the parallels. He leaves a doomed planet, Krypton, just as the Puritans left a corrupt and destructive society, Europe. He becomes a real orphan. "Poor thing...It's been abandoned," says the woman who found him. The Americans become spiritual orphans who abandon their fatherland and the past. He had a "perilous" journey in an experimental spacecraft; and so did the Puritans and founding fathers, in their small ships. He comes to a new land where his powers are enormous. The same applies to the Puritans, who were free to set up a Holy Commonwealth, a totalitarian theocracy, in which their powers were absolute.

Superman had a strong sense of mission. As the origin tale says: "Clark decided he must turn his titanic strength into channels that would benefit mankind. And so was created — Superman, champion of the oppressed, the physical marvel who had sworn to devote his existence to those in need."

The Puritans, likewise, had a strong sense of mission and believed that they would establish a perfect society which would lead to the eventual regeneration of mankind. Both had a single-mindedness that was quite remarkable, and both had a fear of the old world. Superman was weakened by exposure to fragments of his planet of origin, Krypton, and the Puritans feared (like countless generations of Americans after them) that exposure to old-world practices and ideas was morally corrupting and destructive.

Both Superman and the Puritans can be characterized as being psychologically complex (the Puritans with their belief in predestination and Superman with a dissociated personality). And both reflected the primacy of the super-ego. The Puritans had an obsession with evil, and Superman can be seen as a manifestation of this phenomenon. He is a supreme super-ego

SUPERMAN AND THE AMERICAN EXPERIENCE

The American Experience	Superman
Leaves a corrupt land — Europe: Destructive Godless, not "pure."	Leaves a doomed planet, Krypton.
Becomes a spiritual orphan: Abandons fatherland, the past.	Becomes a real orphan: "Poor thing, It's been abandoned."
Perilous journey on small ships.	Perilous journey on experimental rocket.
Comes to new land — America.	Comes to new land — Earth (by chance USA).
Great Power Here: sets up city on a Hill; theocracy semi-totalitarian.	Great Power: Superhuman strength while on earth (can use strong-arm methods).
Sense of Mission: regenerate man.	Sense of Mission: use powers to help man.
Single-Mindedness: everything subjugated to mission.	Single-Mindedness: no sex, only work (until later on).
Fear of Corruption by Old World: European institutions, the past.	Weakened by exposure to Old Planet: Kryptonite (the past).
Psychological Complexity: Predestination and Willpower Effort-Optimism.	Psychological Complexity: Dissociated self; Clark Kent/ Superman.
Super-Ego Society: Guilt, God punishes the evil.	Super-Ego Figure: no escape (even has X-ray vision).
Middle-Class Values: effort-optimism, strive and thrive.	Middle-Class Figure: Delayed Gratification Pattern, Forgo Fleeting Pleasures.
Inhuman Society crumbles: prosperity impossible strain.	Superhuman figure humanized: less square women.
Great Impact on American Culture: ideal of achievement, etc. values institutionalized.	Great impact on Popular Culture: caped crusaders model for others.
Conservative Elements: self-reliant Individual saves self; willpower (Psychology) basic.	Conservative Elements: strong father saves, focus on superstructure not base?

figure with super powers to punish wrongdoers. He was even given X-ray vision to seek out evil people no matter where they might be hiding. With Superman there is no escape.

The comparison can be extended further. Superman is an essentially middle-class figure who forgoes fleeting pleasures, as Nietzsche said supermen should, and attains "happiness and dominance through the exercise of creative power." This is quite close to the middle-class pattern of *deferred gratification*, and Superman is notorious (in his earliest supermanifestations) for avoiding sexual relations. Likewise the Puritans, with their effort-optimism, strive-and-thrive philosophy, championed middle-class values.

Superman, however, eventually became humanized and more complicated, and the Puritan experiment eventually crumbled, in part because it was based on an inhuman ideal and asked men to be what they were not — namely supermen. Also, increased prosperity seemed to weaken its grip on people. But Puritanism had an enormous impact upon the American psyche, and to a great degree, even to this day, its influence can be found in the basic American personality structure and in our values and beliefs. *Superman* also was formative: the first caped crusader was the model for later ones, though there have been great modifications in the kinds of heroes to be found in the comics.

Ultimately *Superman* is a conservative figure, for he focuses his attention upon problems of the superstructure, and not, to adopt Marxist terms, the base. He works like a demon, but he is always occupied with criminals and malfunctions at the most superficial level of society. He lacks political awareness and, at times, even verges on a kind of watered-down fascism, glorying in violence and direct solutions via a super bash in the teeth. He reflects the basically conservative views of the American public. We have, traditionally, posited the self-reliant individual as the means for achieving the good society; success is a function of willpower in a "just" society, in which people are not enslaved by traditions and institutions (such as royalty or the church).

The irony in America is that instead of a nation of individual supermen, we find a country full of seemingly powerless weaklings, full of fantasies of potency, while the state has become a superstate, with prodigious powers and, so it seems at times, a will of its own. The recent cataclysmic events in America surrounding the Watergate hearings have had a traumatic effect on the American political consciousness; the presidency has been demythologized and few Americans can maintain the fiction that the president is a combination of Superman and Jesus Christ Superstar, though once upon a time we tended to believe this.

ATTITUDES TOWARD AUTHORITY: NON-CONFORMISTS, GUNG-HO TYPES, AND OTHERS

Generally speaking, as a consequence of our egalitarian ethos, most Americans can be characterized as "anti-authoritarian," and I have explored this theme in some detail in the first chapter of my book, on *Li'l Abner*. In a comparative study of similar (in time of appearance and kind of hero) American and Italian comic strips, I discerned an important difference between American and Italian comics in terms of the way authority is treated. The Italian comics reflected a conservative approach towards experience and saw authority as valid and rebellion against it as futile. The American comics, on the other hand, had an "irreverential" approach towards authority, were much more "antisocial," and saw rebellious activity as having a strong possibility of being successful.

The dominant thrust in American comics is an anti-authoritarian or nonconformist one, though there are some strips, such as *Dick Tracy* and possibly *Batman*, which might be classified as authoritarian or, to use the vernacular, "gung ho." Probably it is best, and certainly it is safest, to see cultures as containing within them contradictions and engaging, in various ways, in dialogues about important issues. Certainly we find both positions or both points of view about authority in the comics.

Krazy Kat, George Herriman's brilliant strip (which is generally considered to be our greatest strip and the one which elevates the lowly comic strip into "art") is a case in point. The strip involves three characters: Ignatz Mouse, a malevolent, willful, egotistical, brick-throwing creature, who is always testing authority and generally paying the consequences for his antisocial behavior; Offissa B. Pup, a police figure, and the keeper of the jail where Ignatz spends much of his time; and Krazy Kat, a silly cat who loves Ignatz Mouse and interprets the bricks he uses to "crease" her noodle with as signs of love. Pup loves Krazy who loves Ignatz who loves to throw bricks, and for thirty years Ignatz threw bricks and Offissa Pup vainly tried to protect Krazy, whose passion grew greater with every knock on the head.

There are two important themes in this strip: the valuing of illusion (the brick as love) over reality and the attitude towards authority, which might best be characterized as one involving rebelliousness (on Ignatz's part) and an unwillingness to submit to authority. These two themes inform the strip, giving it an aura of poignancy.

Curiously enough, there is reason to believe that Herriman, the author of this strip, was a Negro who masqueraded as a white man. Thus the themes of illusion and rebelliousness stem from Herriman's personal situation and the difficulties he faced as a black man posing as a white. *Krazy Kat* can be characterized as an anti-authoritarian strip, for though Ignatz submits to superior power (in the form of Offissa Pup), he never admits the legitimacy of Pup's authority, and we always know that right after he gets out of jail he will heave another brick.

DICK TRACY'S PREOCCUPATION WITH EVIL

There is an officer, however, who represents a different attitude towards authority, an attitude which might be described as reverential or perhaps obsessional. *Dick Tracy* is about as far removed from the fantasy and mirthfulness of *Krazy Kat* as you can get. The *ambiance* of *Dick Tracy* is morbidity. A Calvinistic passion for scourging evil from the land pervades it. Chester Gould, who does the strip, has created a veritable bestiary of criminal monsters, grotesques, and freaks who succumb, inevitably, to Tracy.

He is activated by an overwhelming sense of purpose and seems to be a reflection of a super-ego of almost pathological proportions. The strip, drawn in strong blacks and whites, is permeated by a preoccupation with evil that is terrifying. He is a reflection of American evangelical Protestantism and stems from a long line of conscience-ridden Protestants who peopled the country, working strenuously to vanquish evil — in thought and deed. Tracy can be seen as a symbol of this tradition, which recoiled in horror at the evil in the world and threw up bloody avengers to root out the evil monsters who were trying to intrude into the American paradise.

Gould's use of grotesques is very significant. These figures are physically and morally ugly, and this facilitates a guilt-free aggression on the part of the readers. But are not grotesques creations of a grotesque society? Gould does not seem to consider this matter; he is too busy sending Tracy out in the relentless pursuit of criminals, a servant of a stern God striving to rid America of evil in the neverending quest for the sublimity of a community of saints. Alas, he never quite succeeds. Dick Tracy is probably an extreme instance, though the avenger is a common figure in American comics — but in comic books rather than comic strips, which are carried in newspapers and read by children as well as adults.

Batman is a good example of a comic-book hero motivated by vengeance. Like Superman, he too is an orphan and he too is engaged in a holy war against evil. As he says in his origin tale, "I swear by the spirits of my parents to avenge their deaths by spending the rest of my life warring on all criminals." I see Batman as a reflection of the pietist-perfectionist strain in American culture. This belief imposes upon each individual the responsibility to confront evil and try to root it out whenever possible. It has been described as: "the belief that every individual is himself responsible for deciding the rightness or wrongness of every issue (large or small) in terms of a higher moral law...and having made his decision, he must commit himself to act upon it at once, taking every opportunity and utilizing every possible method to implement his decision...."

This is what creates the "crusader" and also leads to a widespread sense of guilt, since we cannot live up to such impossible ideals. In such a situation it is comforting to have a heroic fantasy figure who "redeems" us by his magnificent actions.

POGO AND McCARTHYISM

Unfortunately, this pietistic thrust frequently turns sour — in the case of McCarthyism, for example. Yet here too, in the face of this aberration, the comic had a role to play and the courageous satires of Walt Kelly in *Pogo* are thought to have had some role in helping to stem the hysteria that McCarthyism produced in America. Kelly attacked McCarthy in many episodes, portraying him as a lynx named Simple J. Malarkey, who becomes involved in all manner of nasty things. In one tale he leads an "anti-bird" campaign designed to protect the swamp, where Pogo and his friends live, from "unwelcome immigrants." This adventure had episodes involving book burning and attempts to "smear" innocent animals by tarring and feathering them — making them, in effect, birds.

But McCarthy wasn't the only politician Kelly satirized in his caricatures and fables. He drew Spiro Agnew as a creature that resembled a hyena, wore a military uniform like that of the Greek colonels, and talked an absurd gobbledygook.

In *Pogo* we find satirical and frequently nasty portrayals of other figures such as Richard Nixon, Lyndon Johnson, Bobby Kennedy, and Nikita Khrushchev. Kelly turns some of his characters into animals (George Wallace becomes a cock, Khrushchev a pig, Johnson a longhorn steer) and others into toys (Bobby Kennedy is shown as a wind-up toy man).

The Okefenokee Swamp is portrayed as a primitive paradise that is under attack from all kinds of evil characters — religious fakes, confidence men, political cranks, and fools, just to name a few. And it is Kelly's mission to present the American public with cautionary tales that have, frequently, very direct implications for American political life.

Kelly denies that he has a political stance or is trying to make a statement of any kind. All he wants to do, he claims, is "have fun and make money at the same time," but such denials are typical of humorists. By claiming they are not serious, they defend themselves from being attacked or sued by their "victims." In America it is also necessary to "take a joke," and dignifying an insult is a dangerous ploy.

I ought to mention a few other comics, if only in passing, before I conclude this discussion of authority and rebellion in the American comics. For a long time *Li'l Abner* was one of the most inventive and remarkable comic strips in America. It satirized and ridiculed, with brilliance and inventiveness, a large number of absurdities in American society — the predatory businessman, the stupid politician, gangsters, show business types, and so forth.

Al Capp, who wrote and drew the strip, was at the height of his powers one of America's most gifted satirists and social critics. Unfortunately, during the last ten years or so, his strip has lost its character. Capp has moved from a liberal to a conservative, and perhaps even reactionary, political stance.

The place Capp vacated as a liberal critic of American mores and politics has been taken by Gary Trudeau, whose *Doonesbury* is one of the most interesting new strips. The characters in *Doonesbury* are skeptical and iconoclastic, and Trudeau has been one of the most savage critics of Nixon. The strip is probably the closest thing in the American newspapers to the American underground comics, which attack American social, political, and sexual values and behavior with considerably severity and occasional wit. Interestingly enough, there was one series of episodes in *Doonesbury* in which one of the characters was banished to the garage by his father, who wanted to make money by renting out his son's room. Even in the 1970s we find American children being "abandoned" or rejected; it is not much of a move from the garage to the alley, which would complete the circle and bring us back to *The Yellow Kid.*

The popularity of *Doonesbury* leads me to believe that Americans are now reading newspaper comics selectively, for the same newspaper might carry both *Little Orphan Annie* and *Doonesbury,* which represent considerably different belief structures. What is happening in the newspapers is that the long serial adventure strips are losing their popularity and the "gag" strips are taking over. Thus *Orphan Annie* is an anachronism in philosophy and form.

There are, of course, many other strips which bear mentioning: *Mutt and Jeff, The Katzenjammer Kids, Popeye, The Wizard of Id,* and so forth. Fortunately, scholars in many different disciplines have "discovered" the comics in the last decade and serious attention is now being paid to them — not only in America but in many other countries.

CONCLUSIONS

While I was in the middle of writing this essay a cartoon by Feiffer appeared (Sunday *Observer*, May 19, 1974) that is most relevant. One of his characters is delivering a monologue, which goes as follows:

Someday...
There'll be a world without authority
Without bureaucracy
Without rules
Where there'll be freedom
and sharing
and love.
And still I won't fit in.

This cartoon deals with the two themes I've been discussing — the abandoned child/spiritual orphan and the rebel — and suggests their logical outcome, namely alienation.

For spiritual orphans have broken their ties with their fatherland, and those who will tolerate no authority can have few ties with their fellow man, and can never "fit in." Thus the anti-authoritarian spiritual orphan pays an enormous price for his co-called freedom; he is doomed to a kind of loneliness and solitude. Feiffer's character wants, it seems, to "fit in" more than anything else. That is, he wants to be able to think of himself as a social person, as a member of something bigger than himself. Man is, after all, a social animal, and Americans, having rejected history and sacrificed the past to the future, often find themselves in a bind. When there is no authority, no bureaucracy, and no rules, is there a society? Is there anything to "fit in" to? And is there, we might ask, freedom? Is a collection of alienated anarchists what the utopian dream of America is all about?

I think not, though if you push the themes of the spiritual orphan (voluntarily so) and anti-authoritarianism to their "logical conclusion" you do end up there. There is another side to this, which I have not dealt with, though my suggestion that cultures all engage in dialogues with themselves would indicate it. And as the great organizing myth of the self-made, self-created man disintegrates and reveals itself to be sterile, the communitarian myth, the myth of man as a social being, as a member of the family of man, grows stronger. The hunger of America for communes, for utopian societies, for voluntary associations is part of that side of the American personality, and it too is a part of the comics, though I have not time for it here.

The matter of the relation that should exist between the individual and society is a central question in politics. This question is dealt with explicitly and implicitly in the comics, in America and elsewhere. For the most part, Americans have thought they were being anti-authoritarian when they were only being antisocial. But things are changing! In America we have comics dealing with social problems, with ecology, with sexual politics, with almost any subject you might name.

As I write this a thousand new comic heroes are being born, to wage war upon a thousand fiends, and contribute to the education — political and otherwise — of all who follow their exploits. And who knows — somewhere, in some distant planet in some obscure universe of the American imagination, a new hero is speeding towards us, with new powers and a new social message. Will we listen?

4   HOW U.S. NEWSPAPER CONTENT IS CHANGING*

LEO BOGART

The American newspaper is undergoing fundamental changes and this article, based on a survey of more than 1300 newspapers, shows what is happening and offers some reasons for why these changes have occurred. One trend is to a different size page, one that is a standard thirteen inches wide with six columns, which makes it easier to place advertisements in them.

Along with this change in size came redesigned mastheads, changes in typography, and an increased use of photographs. Many of the changes are related to the computerization of newspapers. By installing computerized systems, newspapers can be made-up electronically, which represents considerable financial savings and an increase in flexibility and composition speed.

More newspapers are using color now, Bogart reports, and many of them have become sectionalized. Some 38 percent of our daily newspapers have added life-style sections and beefed up their sports and business coverage.

One interesting finding of the survey is that readers say they want a substantial amount of national and international news, yet newspapers are increasing the amount of local news in their papers, at the expense of national and international news. They are doing this because newspaper editors feel they cannot compete with the television networks in these areas.

There is reason to believe that the sectionalization of newspapers makes them more accessible and more predicatable, and this predictability creates emotional ties to the newspapers in the readers. They know they can count on finding certain features in the paper in certain places and this, research suggests, is emotionally reassuring.

What newspapers can do, better than any other medium, it seems, is provide special features that deal with the interests and needs of their readers. They have to do this, yet not become too specialized and lose their mass audience. In recent years, there have been three trends, Bogart concludes: first, the ratio of features (or soft news) to hard news has increased; second, the ratio of local news to national and international news has increased; and third, the amount of staff-written specialized or feature material has increased and the number of columns has decreased. What Bogart's survey indicates is that over the years there have been a number of small decisions that editors have been making that don't seem significant until added up, and you find that major changes have taken place.

* From the *Journal of Communication*, 1985: 35 (2): 82–90. © 1985 Reprinted by permission. *Author's Note:* The 1983 survey was directed by Charles Lehman with the assistance of John Kelley. Their contribution is gratefully acknowledged.

The American press has changed rapidly under the pressures of urban depopulation and transformation, the explosion of broadcast news, and technological improvements in newspaper production methods. The extent and character of the changes have been tracked in a series of four surveys of daily newspaper managements conducted since 1967 by the Newspaper Advertising Bureau. In several significant respects, the editorial changes run counter to the opinions expressed by newspaper readers in surveys conducted during the same period (See Reference 1).

In the fourth of these studies, conducted in the spring of 1983, mail questionnaires were returned by 1,310 U.S. daily newspapers, which represent 77 percent of the total number and about 90 percent of the full circulation. The returns have been weighted statistically for papers of different size to make the results projectable to the entire American daily press. The questionnaire asked newspapers about recent editorial and format changes and also about the standing features and columns that they carry on a regular basis (at least once a week or more often) to deal with specialized interests.

Two out of three papers report that in those four years they made "substantial changes" of some specific kind in editorial content, and 71 percent report "substantial changes" in graphics or layout. As Table 1 shows, the changes have come most often in larger papers, but even among the smallest papers (under 10,000 circulation) a majority has made such changes.

The most common changes in graphics relate to formatting. On July 1, 1984, American newspapers moved to a standard six-column, 13-inch-wide page designed to facilitate the placement of advertising. (Tabloid papers adopted a compatible format.) The trend toward six columns and narrower page widths was already apparent in our 1979 survey, and the changes have accelerated since then, with 43 percent of the papers in 1983 reporting modifications in column widths, 25 percent in the number of columns, and

Table I	PERCENT OF NEWSPAPERS MAKING "SUBSTANTIAL CHANGES," 1979–1983	
	In editorial content (%)	*In graphics or layout (%)*
All papers	64	71
Circulation		
100,000 plus	82	83
50–100,000	73	77
25–50,000	75	76
10–25,000	61	74
Under 10,000	55	63

GREAT MOMENTS IN HISTORY / *1968 -- Soviet Union seizes Czechoslovakia*

Russian Blitz Crushes Czechs -- LBJ Warning

Mostly Fair

Mostly fair through tomorrow night. Increasing coastal cloudiness tonight and increasing high cloudiness Friday. Slightly warmer most areas afternoons. Low tonight in the 50s. High tomorrow 68 to 78
Full Report on Page 35

San Francisco Examiner

9 STAR FINAL LATEST SPORTS

104th Year   No. 45   ☆☆☆☆   SU 1-2424   WEDNESDAY, AUGUST 21, 1968   64 PAGES   DAILY 10c

Soviet armored vehicles rumble past Central Committee Building in Prague as citizens maintain a sullen silence

Women observers watch invading horde in streets of Prague

Contempt of Court

Companion of Newton Jailed

By SAM BLUMENFELD and RUSS GREENLEE

Huey P. Newton's mystery companion on the night of the police shoot-out took the witness stand today—and was promptly jailed for contempt of court when he refused to answer the prosecutor's questions.

He gave his name as Gene Allen McKinney when called to defense attorney Charles Garry. Asked if he'd been a passenger in a car with Newton at 7th and Willow Streets at 5 a.m. on Oct. 28, the witness answered calmly:

"Yes I was."

Asked what he was wearing, he said he couldn't recall.

To further questions by Garry and assistant district attorney Lowell Jensen, the witness refused to testify on grounds that he might incriminate himself.

REFUSED TWICE

Superior Court Judge Monroe Friedman directed McKinney to answer a few questions related to the testimony about being in the Black Panther leader's car. But he twice refused.

"Take to miss jail," he told a bailiff.

Although the presence of another man in the car is the subject of considerable testimony, it was the first mention of the phantom witness by name.

ANSWER REFUSED

McKinney, accompanied by attorney Harold Perry, wore a dark turtleneck sweater and colorful green trousers. After the first two questions, Garry asked if

—Turn to Page 6, Col. 1

Dynamite Rescue of 9 Guards

COLUMBUS, Ohio—(UPI)—An assault force of police and National Guard troops blasted their way through a hole they blasted in the wall of an Ohio State penitentiary cellblock today and at less than 30 rebelling convicts had been holding prison guards hostage by 200 rebelling convicts for 29 hours.

When the cellblock wall was blown out by demolition experts, the assault force of 200 stormed the prison through heavy machine gun emplacements rifles and teargas.

Five convicts were shot to death. A sixth had his throat slashed by fellow prisoners.

Lt. Sam George was the only casualty among the hostages. He suffered a cut over the right eye.

Shortly before the charges were exploded, Warden M. J. Koloski gave the convicts an ultimatum — "come out immediately or we are coming in."

Koloski said One Gus James Rhodes gave the order to storm the cellblock in how the hostages are and the whereabouts.

The nine guards screamed from cellblock windows for freedom to be released.

The rebel prisoners had threatened to kill the hostages.

Lt. George told authorities over a telephone before the

—Turn to Page 5, Col. 4

Ted Tells 4 Steps To Peace

WORCESTER (Mass.)—AP—Sen Edward Kennedy (Dem-Mass.) called today for an unconditional end to the bombing of North Vietnam.

Speaking politically for the first time since the assassination of his brother, Sen Robert Kennedy, Edward outlined a four-point program to end the war in Vietnam.

The other three points outlined in Kennedy's prepared speech were:

* Negotiate with Hanoi and the military withdrawal from South Vietnam of all foreign forces, both allied and North Vietnamese.

* Accompany the withdrawal with "whatever help we can give to the South Vietnamese in the building of a viable political, economic, and legal structure that will not promptly collapse upon their departure."

Kennedy said he was rejecting suggestions that he retire from public life, saying . . . "There is no safety in hiding. Not for me, not for any of us here today, and not for our children, who will inherit the world we make for them."

Kennedy said he would not propose halting the bombing

—Turn to Page 1, Col. 4

Eyewitness

Long Night in Prague Described

By DENIS BLEWETT
London Express

PRAGUE—The dramatic announcement of the Russian invasion of Czechoslovakia was made over Prague Radio at 2 o'clock this morning, and within minutes planes began to zoom over the capital.

From my balcony window I watched aircraft swooping across the city. Some were piston-engined planes with navigation lights glowing. Others were jets making screaming dives bombing down runs.

The radio announcement appealed for calm and urged the Czechs not to resist the Russians. Neither the Czech Army nor the people's militia had been called out, it said.

In the streets outside my hotel, as police cars raced past with sirens wailing and lights flashing, the low late night strollers showed little shock at the news. There was fear on their faces, and an atmosphere of panic quickly began to spread around the city. Inside the hotel student arguments began to break out. A receptionist shrieked:

"The facts, what can they hope to win?"

Soon after the first broadcast ended, Radio Prague began another announcement. It began "Here is a special

—Turn to Page 11A, Col. 6

Paralyzed, Silent Susan May Testify

By WILLIAM O'BRIEN
Examiner News Staff

SAN JOSE—On the first anniversary of her brutal rape and near-fatal shooting, the possibility was raised today that Susan Bartleman, 18, would be carried into the trial of her accused attackers in a prosecution witness.

The girl is paralyzed and can communicate only with one-finger sign language and with her eyes.

But in Ukiah, her home, one of her doctors said she's "making a very good progress. She should be going some any day now. She's so happy she can almost succeed."

Dist. Atty. Arthur Broaddus of Mendocino County, the prosecutor, said the final decision as to her appearance would have to come from the doctors. His office hinted for among 70 potential prosecution witnesses.

"I certainly would like to call her," Broaddus added.

Observers at Mendocino County Hospital, where the girl was in a coma for six months, said she is mentally "very sharp" and using her

LBJ Calls On Russ— Withdraw

WASHINGTON—(UPI)—President Johnson today called on the Soviet Union and its communist allies to withdraw their troops from Czechoslovakia. He said "It is never too late for reason to prevail."

Johnson said:

"It is a sad commentary on the Communist mind that a sign of liberty in Czechoslovakia is deemed a fundamental threat to the security of the Soviet system.

"The excuses offered by the Soviet Union are patently contrived. The Czechoslovakian government did not request its allies to interfere in its internal affairs. No external aggression threatened Czechoslovakia," Johnson said.

The President said the action by the Warsaw Pact allies was a "flat violation" of the United Nations charter and as a result the U.N. government was urgently calling other nations to consider what steps should be taken in the United Nations.

The UN Security Council was summoned into emergency session at 7:30 p.m. (PDT) today.

Johnson and UN Ambassador George Ball had been instructed to join with other nations in the Security Council "to insist upon the clearer rights of Czechoslovakia and its people."

Other U.S. officials, sur-

—Turn to Page 16, Col. 1

Russ Seize Czech Chiefs

PRAGUE—(UPI)— Invading troops from the Soviet Union and four allied nations overthrew Czechoslovakia's liberal government today by arresting its leaders and overwhelming a handful of freedom fighters.

Defiant Czechs abandoned any major attempt to resist the takeover by force of arms. An official Czech statement demanded the invaders get out at once.

Sporadic street fighting ebbed as the National Assembly raised the threat of a general strike against the occupation forces which seized Alexander Dubcek, First Secretary of the Communist Party, President Ludvik Svoboda and their aides.

The Czechoslovak news agency CTK said late tonight Dubcek and other reform leaders had been "taken to an unknown place" by occupation troops. CTK said Central Party's Central Committee had been "kidnaped."

CASUALTIES

At least seven persons were reported killed and 57 wounded in fighting in Prague, bystanders and Soviet soldiers fired into Soviet tanks, cannon and machine guns. Russians shots blew the head off one Czech youth in Prague.

The National Assembly, protesting the "most concentrated invasion" by the Soviet Union, Poland, Bulgaria, East Germany and Hungary, demanded the release of Dubcek, Premier Oldrich

—Turn to Page 11A, Col. 1

Gunfire All Around —Shirley

Shirley Temple Black, trapped in Prague by the Soviet invasion, reported "machine gun fire all around us" today.

She was all fine in the hotel, in good shape. Our rights in good and we're sticking together"

She was interrupted by a commotion, clearly heard over a telephone line to San Francisco.

NOISE OUTSIDE

There's a big noise outside" she said "I'm at a padded phone booth and can't tell what it is."

Shirley reported.

"The first I heard was machine gun fire near the hotel. I couldn't believe it. I was sort of in a deep sleep, and I thought it was practicing at first.

"But then my door was rapped on; an associate knocked and said the city was controlled by Soviet soldiers.

Shirley was eaten and composed despite the drama and potential peril of the story.

She and her husband, Charles A.

—Turn to Page 11A, Col. 3

The Czech Crisis at a Glance

By The Associated Press

Prague — Slight significance is a crucial in the Czechoslovakian capital after the Soviet Union and four Warsaw Pact allies invade the sleeping nation.

Johnson denounces the Soviet move and calls on emergency meeting of the National Security Council.

New York — At the request of leading Western powers, the UN Security Council opens an emergency session.

Moscow — Radio Moscow tells the Soviet people that their armed forces have moved into Czechoslovakia to save that country from the enemies of communism.

Washington — President

Belgrade — President Tito deplores the Soviet invasion and calls a session of the Communist Party's central committee's presidium.

London — British Prime Minister Harold Wilson calls a cabinet meeting and Parliament is summoned into session tomorrow.

Bucharest — The Romanian Communist Central Committee is called into special session to deal with the situation.

Rape of The Czechs

See Editorial Page 38

IN THIS EDITION

There was a note of hope in 1968 when talks began in Paris designed to bring an end to the war in Vietnam. But in Europe, a nation lost its hope as hordes of Soviet and Warsaw Pact troops invaded Czechoslovakia to crush the liberal regime of Alexander Dubcek and bring a new reign of repression.

MIDDAY EDITION ★R

San Francisco Examiner

25¢ WEDNESDAY, APRIL 1, 1987 ★ MIDDAY EDITION

Concern over communications secrecy; third embassy Marine arrested

Spy scandal may hinder Shultz's Soviet trip

By Stewart M. Powell
EXAMINER WASHINGTON BUREAU

WASHINGTON — Breaches in security by Marines protecting the U.S. Embassy in Moscow are threatening to complicate secret communications by Secretary of State Shultz during his upcoming mission to the Soviet capital, officials said Tuesday.

U.S. diplomats in Moscow are concerned that embassy codes and communications equipment have been compromised by penetration of the embassy by Soviet agents with the alleged assistance of U.S. Marine guards.

Officials preparing for Shultz's visit April 13 worry that he will be forced to rely on the limited communications aboard his U.S. Air Force plane rather than embassy channels, an administration source said.

Diplomatic communications in Moscow, including reporting from sophisticated eavesdropping operations, have been effectively brought to a standstill until new codes and procedures can be adopted to thwart Soviet monitoring, the source said.

Sensitive messages are being hand carried to Frankfurt, West Germany, by U.S. diplomatic couriers, a cumbersome procedure that slows two-way communication with Washington as preparations are laid for Shultz's trip to Moscow.

A State Department spokesman said: "Every effort is under way to provide adequate security for the trip. We will do whatever needs to be done."

The investigation into the sex-for-secrets scandal inside the U.S. Embassy in Moscow widened Tuesday with the arrest of a third Marine enlisted man, who was charged with lying about relationships he had had with

— See MARINE, back page

Robert Stufflebeam
Deputy commander of embassy detachment held as 'possible suspect'

Big banks hike prime to 7.75%

Surprise announcement by 3 N.Y. institutions

EXAMINER NEWS SERVICES

NEW YORK — Three of the nation's largest banks took the business world by surprise by announcing increases in their prime lending rate to 7.75 percent from 7.5 percent.

Citibank, the nation's largest commercial bank, said late Tuesday afternoon that it had increased the prime rate, which had been 7.5 percent since Aug. 26.

It was followed soon after by Chase Manhattan, the nation's third-largest bank.

On Wednesday, Manufacturers Hanover, ranked fourth in deposits, announced it too was raising its prime rate to 7.75.

All three banks are based in New York.

The new rates, effective immediately, came just after the close of the stock market. However, they were in time to send the Treasury bond market into a tailspin and the dollar higher.

Financial analysts said other banks were likely to follow the example.

Major banks generally follow

— See PRIME, A-6

A victorious William Stern brushes away tears as he, wife Elizabeth and attorney Gary Skoloff talk to reporters Tuesday in Hackensack, N.J. A judge awarded custody of Baby M, right, to her father and she was officially named Melissa. The baby's natural mother, Mary Beth Whitehead, left, surrendered her rights in a surrogate motherhood deal with the Sterns

AP photos

Total victory for Baby M's natural father

Judge denies surrogate mother custody or even visiting rights

By Michael J. Kelly
and Betsy August
SPECIAL TO THE EXAMINER

HACKENSACK, N.J. — In a decision with major implications for surrogate motherhood, a judge ruled Tuesday that the surrogate-mother contract in the celebrated "Baby M" case is valid, and he awarded sole custody of the child to the father, William Stern.

The ruling by Superior Court Judge Harvey R. Sorkow terminates all parental rights of natural mother Mary Beth Whitehead to the blue-eyed baby girl she gave birth to a year ago last Friday.

Baby M was adopted immediately by Stern's wife, Elizabeth, at the suggestion of the judge, who conducted the adoption in his private chambers. He also directed that the child's birth certificate be changed to read Melissa Stern, the name given to her by her father — rather than Sara Whitehead, the name chosen by her natural mother.

Judge Sorkow's sweeping 121-page decision, which went beyond the recommendations of Baby M's court-appointed attorney, stunned the Sterns and their lawyers, but also drew immediate criticism.

"This case furrows new legal

— See BABY M, A-7

The Baby M verdict

☐ How will baby Melissa be affected? Page A-6
☐ Rejoice and despair greet judge's ruling Page A-6
☐ Decision seen as key win for surrogates Page A-6
☐ Whitehead's sister: 'She took it well' Page A-6

U.S. adviser is killed in El Salvador

EXAMINER NEWS SERVICES

EL PARAISO, El Salvador — Troops rushed north and garrisons throughout El Salvador were on alert Wednesday after guerrillas killed at least 43 soldiers, including a U.S. adviser, in one of the boldest attacks of this 7-year-old civil war.

The army was investigating how several hundred Farabundo Marti National Liberation Front fighters managed to mass without being detected for the assault on El Paraiso military base in northern Chalatenango province, before dawn Tuesday, an army spokesman said.

That was when guerrillas raided the base, killing the first U.S. military adviser to die during battle in the civil war.

El Salvador's military commander said the American, identified as Staff Sgt. Gregory A. Fronius, 27, of Greensburg, Pa., had been killed by mortar fire near a command post.

The military said 35 soldiers had been wounded by leftist rebels who assaulted the base behind a barrage of cannon, mortar and grenade fire. Base commander Col. Gilberto Rubio, who was slightly wounded, said the number of attackers had not been determined.

Officials said seven guerrillas had died in the attack on the 4th Infantry Brigade garrison. Some, carrying explosives, penetrated the camp.

El Paraiso is nearly 40 miles north of San Salvador, capital of this Central American country.

— See ADVISER, back page

Scott Rice
'The teaching of writing is too stifled'

It was a dark and stormy bag of mail

By John Flinn
OF THE EXAMINER STAFF

SAN JOSE — Every day, the mailman brings another stack of post cards full of shattered syntax, Osterized metaphors and truly frightful puns to English Professor Scott Rice's cramped office at San Jose State University.

They arrive from virtually every state in the United States, from Finland, Japan, India, Saudi Arabia, the Netherlands, Great Britain and Taiwan. A gentleman in Southern California has mailed in enough to form a stack 3 feet high.

It is only two weeks until April 15, a day synonymous with bad fiction. That is the deadline for entries to the fifth annual Bulwer-Lytton Fiction Contest, which seeks to discover the nadir in deliciously awful writing.

Among this year's contend-

— See BULWER, back page

Chile church must fight for freedom, Pope says

By Don Lattin
EXAMINER RELIGION WRITER

SANTIAGO, Chile — Pope John Paul II said that in its defense of human rights, the Roman Catholic Church in Chile should follow the example of the Philippine church, which was vital in the ouster of President Ferdinand Marcos last year.

Even before his Alitalia Boeing 747 landed in South America Tuesday, the pope was questioning the legitimacy of the right-wing dictatorship of President Augusto Pinochet.

During the trip from the Vatican to his first stop, in Montevideo, Uruguay, the pope was asked whether he thought it would be possible for the Chilean church to engage in the same type of activism that the church in the Philippines had carried out to defend human rights and freedom.

"I think it is not only possible but necessary," the pope said, "because this is part of the pastoral mission of the church. The rights of man, justice, are among the contents of our mission."

The church in Chile, the second stop on the pope's two-week Latin American tour, has been in the

— See RIGHTS, back page

Reagan addresses AIDS issue twice in one day — a record

☐ Experts warns against illegal 'remedy' for AIDS Page B-1

By Julie Johnson
BALTIMORE SUN

WASHINGTON — After nearly seven years of silence on a disease the administration expects to kill 179,000 people by 1991, President Reagan twice in one day discussed AIDS.

Tuesday morning, Reagan announced that U.S. and French scientists would split the patent rights over AIDS screening tests.

Hours later, Reagan responded to questions about acquired immune deficiency syndrome at a White House dinner in honor of French Prime Minister Jacques Chirac, who participated in the patent-sharing announcement.

"We want an all-out campaign," Reagan said. "This is one of the greatest health threats the world has ever known."

Asked whether he favored sex education in public schools and discussions of AIDS, Reagan said, "Yes, I think so, as long as they teach that one of the answers to it (AIDS) is abstinence."

He said students should not be taught "how to do it, but that you don't do it."

These were the first public comments Reagan has made concern-

— See AIDS, back page

INSIDE

A legend dies

John Swanson, a fixture in San Francisco sports circles, is dead.
Page F-1

Strike move

As San Francisco shipyards enter the third day of a pipe fitters' strike, the San Francisco Central Labor Council may extend its official sanction, a move that could bring 15 other unions into the dispute.
Page B-1

Changing the books

PG&E says a change in the bookkeeping for its Diablo Canyon nuclear plant will cut its 1987 profits sharply.
Page C-1

Star sheets

Dave and Maddie are hardly the first co-stars of a contemporary series to crawl under the covers together. But never has it been done with such hype or such style.
Page E-9

Bridge ... E-6 Movies ... E-6
Business ... C-1 Rob Morse ... D-1
Classified ... B-10 Obituaries ... B-9
Comics ... E-10 Stocks ... C-6
Editorials ... A-10 Sports ... F-1
Horoscope ... E-2 Style ... E-1
Ann Landers ... E-2 Television ... E-8
Metro ... B-1 Weather ... B-2

122nd Year, No. 252

House defies Reagan veto of highway bill

FROM EXAMINER STAFF AND WIRE REPORTS

WASHINGTON — Favoring local political interests over national partisan concerns, more than half the House Republicans joined their Democratic colleagues Tuesday in voting to override President Reagan's veto of the $88 billion highway bill.

The 350-73 House tally easily exceeded the two-thirds majority required to revive the legislation in that body.

But Reagan was said to be within a few votes of blocking a similar action in the Senate, where he has made a strong personal appeal for help in quashing a bill he calls too costly and demonstrating presidential strength.

Robert Byrd, D-W.Va., the Senate majority leader, attempted to bring the veto up for a quick vote after the House action Tuesday, hoping to move before the administration could pick up the additional support it needs. He was thwarted, however, by a GOP stall. The vote was put off until Wednesday.

At least 60 senators must also vote to override Reagan's veto in order to resuscitate the highway bill, which would free already-collected gasoline-tax money to finance hundreds of highway, bridge and mass transit projects in time for this construction season.

Working against Reagan in the Senate is the strong support of Western Republicans for an

— See HIGHWAY, A-7

38 percent in page size. It is noteworthy that in those four years, 36 percent of papers redesigned the masthead, 35 percent used more photography, 30 percent changed typefaces, and 23 percent went to a modular layout.* The proportions are even higher among the larger papers. All this, coming on top of similar dramatic reports of change between 1977 and 1979, indicates that the American press has a very different look than it did just a half dozen years ago.

A typical weekday paper has an average of eighteen news and editorial pages. A majority of publishers have maintained the size of the editorial package, even in the face of a shift of advertising out of the run of the press and into preprinted inserts.† Naturally, the greater the circulation of the paper, the greater the number of news pages. The very largest and the very smallest papers most often increased their total editorial content between 1979 and 1983 (see Table 2). In the middle-size range, similar proportions increased and decreased their editorial content.

The number of physically separate sections carried on the average weekday ranges from two for the smallest circulation papers to five for the bigger ones, with an average of three.

For a typical paper, photos and illustrations make up between 10 and 20 percent of the newshole. For 13 percent of the papers, pictures represent less than 10 percent of the editorial content. For 24 percent of the papers, they represent 20 percent or more.

Even before the launching of *USA Today* in 1982, color in editorial matter had been increasingly visible in the American press. Only 17 percent of all papers report that they do not use editorial color at all, and 28 percent are using full color (rather than one or two spot colors plus black) in their weekday editions.

One important development of recent years has been the introduction of geographically zoned editions that include editorial matter as well as advertising. The introduction of zoned editions was in large part a response by metropolitan papers to growing suburban competition and by dailies generally to the rise of free-distributed weekly "shoppers" in the 1970s. Eighteen percent of all daily newspapers, with 43 percent of the circulation, now offer some kind of zoned editorial coverage. Between 1979 and 1983, fourteen percent of all newspapers added editorial zones. (The proportion was 43 percent among the larger papers.)

Another striking change has been sectionalization. In the previous four

---

* The use of modular layouts will be spurred as newspapers move to adopt computerized page makeup systems to replace pasteup, which had only recently in turn replaced the metal makeup procedures that had been in use for a century.

† A separate analysis of 164 papers with circulations over 100,000, representing 56 percent of total circulation, shows that total weekday pages (including advertising preprints) increased by 33 percent between 1977 and 1983, while news and editorial pages increased by 34 percent. Total Sunday pages grew 50 percent and Sunday editorial pages by 40 percent. Although many papers reduced page width during these years, this only slightly offsets the very substantial expansion in the bulk of both news and advertising.

Table 2
PERCENT OF NEWSPAPERS SHOWING INCREASES AND DECREASES IN
AVERAGE NUMBER OF WEEKDAY NEWS AND EDITORIAL PAGES, 1981–1983

	Average no. of pages (n)	More than in 1981 (%)	Less than in 1981 (%)
All papers	18	52	34
Circulation			
100,000 plus	30	59	28
50–100,000	26	44	39
25–50,000	21	41	43
10–25,000	17	49	39
Under 10,000	14	59	27

years, 25 percent of papers added "life-style" sections, and this proportion goes up to 38 percent among papers of over 100,000 circulation.

There have been substantial increases of news coverage in two areas: sports and business. Less than one percent of the papers reported any substantial decrease in coverage for either subject, while two out of five built up each of these important areas. The figures are even higher among the bigger papers that account for a substantial part of circulation. Although readership studies show that sports and business news attract many women readers, both have traditionally been thought of as subjects of special interest to men. There has been no commensurate increase of editorial emphasis in the areas generally considered of primary interest to women.

Op-ed pages are another phenomenon that has been increasingly evident as editors in single-ownership towns seek to avoid charges of media monopoly by presenting an assortment of viewpoints besides their own editorial opinions. In 1979, about one-third of the papers were running op-ed pages at least once a week; about one in five ran them every day. By 1983, over half of all papers, with three-fourths of the circulation, offered op-ed pages, and almost all of those offered them every weekday. Two out of three Sunday papers were also carrying an op-ed page. These pages have become a preferred site for institutional advertising. Only 30 percent of newspapers now report that they would not position corporate ads on the op-ed page if requested. Twenty-seven percent say their decision would depend on the individual ad, and 43 percent take them all as a matter of course.

Readers like some kinds of subjects more than others, but they expect the paper to give them both facts and fun and to encompass both the trivial and the earthshaking. Our national surveys of the public's interest in specific items (1972) or reported readership of those items (1982) consistently show that every subject has a constituency among readers, although no reader is uniformly responsive to every subject.

The same surveys show that readers come to the newspaper mainly for the news rather than for the entertainment content. Faced with a forced choice, 49 percent (in 1982) would opt for a paper that is mainly news and 20 percent for one that is mostly features.

On balance, readers are more interested in news of what is going on in the larger world and in the nation than they are in what is going on in their own local areas, though they want to know about both. These conclusions are derived not just by asking people directly in general terms what they are interested in, but also by measuring their responses to hundreds of thousands of individual articles and news items. International news items score 29 percent higher than the typical local story; national news scores 11 percent higher (see Reference 1, pp. 202–246; Reference 2).

However, among the one-third of all newspapers that made substantial changes in the ratio of hard news to features in the period 1979–1983, the ratio runs two to one for more features and less news. This is especially true among smaller papers of under 25,000 circulation.

Almost half of the papers report substantial changes in the ratio of national and international news to local and state news, just within those four years. Nearly five times as many increased local coverage at the expense of international coverage as did the reverse. This is true of papers of every size. Many editors may have been going this route in the belief that people want "chicken dinner news" from their newspapers at a time when television is bringing them battle scenes live from the Middle East and Central America. Some may have become discouraged at the thought of competing with the TV networks in the arena of authoritative reporting on national and world affairs.

Seventy percent of all papers run a daily main news section and a daily sports section, but only 25 percent have a labeled business section (see Table 3). Among papers of 100,000 circulation and over, which represent 55 percent of total circulation, practically every one has a main news and a sports section every day, and over half run a business section. Over the course of a week, these proportions are even higher. (Two out of three food sections now run on Wednesdays.)

Sectionalization makes the newspaper more accessible to readers by making its content more predictable, by packaging content in a convenient and manageable form. Among the expectations with which readers come to their papers is that they will find a certain element in a certain place, whether that element is a comic strip or a political columnist. It is that predictability that develops readers' emotional ties to the features, that brings readers back to the paper day after day, that makes the paper's content seem familiar and comfortable amidst the endless turmoil and daily turnover in the subject matter of the (predominantly unpleasant) hard news.

In our four surveys of content, we have taken an inventory of the standing features or columns that appear either on a daily or less frequent basis. With a few changes made based on our experience, we have tracked about seventy different subjects since 1967 and in Sunday newspapers since 1979.

Table 3   PERCENT OF NEWSPAPERS CARRYING IDENTIFIABLE SECTIONS, 1979–1983

	Every day	At least once a week	
	All papers (%)	All papers (%)	100,000 plus (%)
Sports	70	74	96
Main news	70	71	95
Entertainment	28	54	68
Food	3	53	85
Lifestyle/Women	39	52	72
TV/Radio	30	49	38
Second news	41	45	77
Business/Finance	25	43	72
Fashion	4	13	38
Home	2	13	20
Food/Home	3	9	9
Farm	1	7	3
Travel	1	5	9
Science	1	4	13

Regular standing coverage has diminished on almost every single subject of special interest. The trends are documented in Table 4. All the numbers are much higher if circulation is taken into account, as it is in the two right columns, which show the weekday and Sunday figures for 1983.

Newspapers representing substantial chunks of the total circulation continue to provide, week in and week out, columns and features that speak to an enormous assortment of segmented concerns on a scale beyond the capacity of other mass media. For example, less than half of all newspapers offer a movie timetable or movie reviews on a regular basis, but those papers represent seven out of ten copies sold. Less than one-third of the papers regularly review records and tapes, and only one in four regularly reviews books. Only 11 percent have a weekday travel feature. (Travel, movies, books, records, and performing arts are of special interest to young people, whom newspapers have been seeking to attract.)

What was once called "society news," the minutiae of community life, used to carry its own special heading. While 93 percent of all papers covered it on a regular basis in 1967, that proportion is now down to 80 percent. Only half carry regularly scheduled reviews of television programs at least once a week.

Seven percent of the papers have started a feature for personal computer buffs, but only 9 percent now carry a science or technology column or feature on a regular basis.

There are fewer papers with action lines and career columns. Although

Table 4   PERCENT OF NEWSPAPERS CARRYING FEATURES AT LEAST ONCE A WEEK, 1967–1983

	% of newspapers				% of total circulation	
					Weekday	Sunday/weekend 1983
	1967 (%)	1974 (%)	1979 (%)	1983 (%)	(%)	(%)
Business, financial	77	78	66	67	87	90
Farm and ranch	53	43	40	34	22	14
Real estate	—	—	—	16	21	57
Security, commodity tables	67	66	56	48	74	74
Automotive	18	18	18	13	25	24
Boating	25	16	—	—	—	—
Outdoors, camping, hunting	64	60	47	44	59	68
Sports	95	99	—	—	—	—
Sports (spectator)	—	—	92	88	91	93
Sports (participant)	—	—	86	78	79	76
Beauty	45	36	36	23	36	25
Fashion, women	57	47	41	26	46	30
Fashion, men	18	20	26	16	31	16
Fashion, teenage	25	28	27	16	29	10
Sewing patterns	62	57	50	44	57	51
Etiquette	31	22	13	12	21	22
"People"	—	—	—	50	70	77
Personal advice	76	82	74	71	81	80
Society, social news	93	95	85	80	69	79
Religion	—	—	58	48	30	40
Home building, repair	47	37	29	22	25	46
Home furnishings, decorating	39	35	28	18	26	37
Household hints	—	—	—	43	44	47
Radio	32	22	—	—	—	—
Radio log	43	29	22	16	38	48
Television	73	80	—	—	—	—
TV reviews	—	—	61	51	73	76
TV log	91	91	85	87	92	96
Gardening	53	47	43	37	39	55
Pets	18	21	14	14	15	34
Photography	17	13	9	6	9	26
Stamps, coins	—	—	8	6	8	43
Computers (personal)	—	—	—	7	16	10
Environment, ecology	—	—	16	9	11	9

Health and medical	68	71	66	63	74	61
Science, technology	34	24	14	9	21	20
Weather	94	98	—	—	—	—
Weather map	—	—	63	65	87	93
Books	49	38	33	25	28	81
Motion pictures	61	60	—	—	—	—
Movie reviews	—	—	46	46	72	69
Movie timetable	—	—	50	48	67	68
Theater	56	56	54	41	64	73
Travel and resort	23	22	19	11	11	81
Music, records, tapes	—	—	37	31	44	61
Child care	36	22	17	11	16	11
College	30	33	16	10	8	9
School news	73	66	61	52	36	25
Youth, teenage	61	45	24	24	22	29
Best food buys	—	—	50	50	68	11
Diet, nutrition	—	—	—	44	60	29
Recipes	81	78	78	74	85	40
Restaurants	—	—	—	28	48	38
Wine	—	—	15	14	36	23
Advice on personal finance	—	—	42	38	62	54
Career advice	—	—	15	11	23	26
Consumers (action line)	—	—	28	21	37	35
Retirement, Social Security	—	—	33	23	28	29
Astrology, horoscope	—	75	78	84	92	92
Bridge	60	62	57	55	78	75
Games and puzzles	—	81	75	78	84	89

the population is aging, fewer papers are now offering a regular feature dealing with retirement and social security matters.

The trend holds for papers of every size in every part of the country. (There is one notable exception: newspapers have been increasing their coverage on a regular basis in one field — astrology.)

On many of these subjects, features tend to come predominantly from syndicated sources, as Table 5 shows. Thus, the reduction in regular coverage may represent an attempt by editors to increase the amount of staff-written content. It may also be that, as part of the "sectional revolution," papers have been covering subjects of special interest on an individual assignment basis and varying the content from one week to the next, rather than trying to hold to identifiable, labeled features on a week in, week out basis.

Table 5   SOURCE OF NEWSPAPERS' MOST WIDELY CARRIED STANDING FEATURES, 1982

	Syndicated (%)	Locally produced (%)	Both (%)
Astrology	98	2	—
Bridge	96	2	2
Personal advice	92	6	2
Games and puzzles	90	6	4
Health and medical	82	6	12
Weather map	77	16	7
TV log	76	22	2
TV reviews	67	18	5
"People"	49	35	16
Best food buys	29	48	23
Business, finance	24	41	35
Recipes	21	46	33
Op-ed	11	35	54
Sports (spectator)	3	49	48
Sports (participant)	2	61	37
Social news	2	91	7
School news	—	97	3

Whatever its causes, this trend runs in the face of an increasing segmentation of people's interests in a complex, mobile society. This is what has fueled the growth of specialty magazines, of selective programming on cable and radio. Newspapers' mass character derives from the fact that they deal not only with common interests, but with innumerable idiosyncrasies. Readership surveys may show that relatively few people share any one particular interest, but they are not likely to show how intensely they feel about it.

Overall, the mix of newspaper subject matter has not changed very much. A sampling of articles in our 1971, 1977, and 1982 surveys did not show dramatic shifts in the proportions dealing with such subjects as crime, public health, taxes, or Hollywood. But even though newspapers may be running as much space in general on fashion or travel as they ever did, they are less likely to be running it in a format that readers can expect, look forward to, and find easily. For stereo buffs or stamp collectors, there is quite a difference between occasionally coming across an article dealing with their peculiar predilections and knowing that there will always be a goody waiting in a regular place.

The substantial changes in both the appearance and content of the

American press we have documented are stimulated by new technology, a growing sensitivity to reader interests, and the acute competitive marketing pressures that newspapers face as a business. But three trends can be identified that run counter to the conclusions of research on reader interests: (a) increasing the ratio of features to hard news content, (b) reducing the relative balance of national and world news to local news, and (c) reducing the number of regular standing columns and features dealing with specialized interests. These trends were not set in motion by any conscious policy decisions. They arise from a multitude of small day-by-day decisions that editors make as a matter of course. But over time, these little decisions add up to significant changes in newspaper content.

REFERENCES

1. Bogart, Leo. *Press and Public: Who Reads What, When, Where, and Why in American Newspapers.* Hillsdale, N.J.: Lawrence Erlbaum, 1981.
2. Bogart, Leo. "The Public's Use and Perception of Newspapers." *Public Opinion Quarterly* 48(4), Winter 1984–1985, 709–719.

I·MAG

The Journal of the Magazine Industry   Spring 1989

MAKING MEGABUCKS AS A
SECRET AGENT BY **B 2689**

MAGAZINES

If you look in a dictionary, you will find that the first definition of the term magazine means "storehouse." In the military, magazines are places in boats or forts where munitions are stored. This notion of being a "storehouse" applies, also, to what we know as magazines when we think of the media — a periodical containing articles on a variety of topics.

At one time, in the 1950s, there were a number of very important weekly magazines — *Collier's, Life, Look,* and *The Saturday Evening Post* — which might be described as "general interest" publications that had circulations in the millions. These magazines could not compete with television, however, and went out of business. It was thought by some at that time that both magazines and radio would also die out, but that hasn't been the case. Instead, magazines have redefined themselves and have become more focused and specialized in many instances.

It is generally held that the first magazine was *The Review*, which started in England in 1704 and was published by Daniel Defoe, author of *Robinson Crusoe*. (See the introduction to the section on Books for a discussion of Daniel Defoe and his archetypical hero, Robinson Crusoe.) Four decades later, the first regularly published magazines appeared in America, *The American Magazine*, published by Andrew Bradford, and *The General Magazine*, published by Benjamin Franklin. Neither lasted more than a few issues or so, but it did not take very long for magazines to take root in America and by the mid-nineteenth century, the industry was prospering. Several magazines that started in this period — *Harper's* and the *Atlantic Monthly* — are still being published, though neither has the prominence it once did.

Magazines were the first national medium and as such they played an important role in our political life. As a result of improvements in printing technology, it became possible to publish large numbers of magazines quickly and cheaply and there were thousands of magazines flourishing in America in the late 1800s. The *Ladies' Home Journal* was founded in this period (1881) and *The Saturday Evening Post*, which was published weekly until 1965. In the 1920s some of the magazines that we are familiar with got started: *Reader's Digest* (1922), *Time* (1923) and *The New Yorker* (1925).

Television forced magazines to redefine themselves and find new audiences. Magazines, like television, deliver audiences to advertisers. It is the size of the audience and its demographic features that determine the rates magazines can charge advertisers. Thus a magazine that appeals to affluent people, all things being equal, can charge more than one appealing to people with moderate incomes. Advertising is generally sold on the basis of "cost per thousand" (CPM) of readers or viewers, but demographic factors also play an important role. An advertiser who reaches millions of readers and viewers who aren't interested in his or her product or don't have much discretionary income to purchase it, is not spending his or her money wisely. So "cost per thousand" isn't the only consideration.

Since magazines tend to be rather specialized, advertisers can target their audiences rather precisely, which is one reason the industry is doing so well. It has found a way to compete with television by offering services that television cannot provide. One of these services, curiously enough, is to tell people what is on television. *TV Guide* has the largest circulation of any magazine in America. The next largest magazine, in terms of circulation, is *Reader's Digest*, a journal full of condensed reprints (and some original articles) that appeals to "middle-America."

There are approximately 10,000 magazines published in America, of which about 4,000 are monthlies. Something like a third of all magazines are published in New York, which is also the center of book publishing. There are a large number of trade magazines, which provide information to people in various industries. These trade magazines cover everything from toys to food processing, from advertising to running supermarkets.

Magazines have been used by sociologists and other researchers to gain information about American character and values. Magazines are a good source for research because they have been around so long. It is possible, for example, to make content analyses of the values found in magazine articles that cover fifty or more years of our history. By doing these longitudinal studies, we can get an idea of how our values and beliefs have been evolving. And magazines are relatively easy to study, since you don't have to worry about moving images and that kind of thing.

The articles that follow in this section deal with such topics as values in *Ms.* magazine, the remarkable world of trade magazines, and the cultural significance of *Playboy* magazine. Our magazines, you will see, tell us a great deal about a variety of topics — including ourselves.

5 · A PERSONAL VIEW OF A THIN SLICE OF HISTORY*

BENJAMIN W. CATE

All too often, when we read an article in a news magazine, we forget that it was written by someone with feelings and emotions. For a long time, articles in *Time* and *Newsweek* just appeared — the product of some mysterious group editing process. In recent years, they have started putting attributions in *Time*, at the end of articles. Even so, we don't usually feel the presence of the writer (or writers). After all, isn't journalism "just the facts, please?"

When people function as reporters, they do suppress (to the extent that this is possible) their immediate feelings and emotions and they take on the persona of the no-nonsense fact finder and reporter of what happened...or what is happening. But if you scratch beneath the surface, you find that reporters also have intense personal reactions to the events they witness and the people they meet. Journalists learn to keep these feelings hidden and we tend to assume that these feelings are irrelevant. Maybe that's why we often see reporters as cynical, unfeeling people. We confuse their professional personas with their real selves.

In this remarkable article, Ben Cate, who worked for *Time* for more than twenty-six years (and was bureau chief in Houston, Bonn, Chicago, and Los Angeles) offers a personal view of news journalism. And, in a revealing series of vignettes, he shares with us his reactions to the events he covered and the people he met. Let me offer an example:

> Staten Island 1960. Many of the dead were still in their seats. The Constellation has been chopped in half by the DC-8 and had fallen from the sky. The jet age was here. The smell of death on that cold, raw winter day permeated the air. There were shoes and shredded Christmas packages in puddles of water on the ground. The taxi fare back to Manhattan was $18. After writing all night for *Time*, I finally got home to my dank Greenwich Village apartment and threw up. I had been at *Time* all of six months.

This essay is a micro-autobiography and will give you a good idea of the kind of experiences Cate had in his exciting and remarkable career. And when Cate says "personal," in his title, he means it...he talks about everything from covering the lunar landing to spending time with "long-legged blondes." The essay is full of emotion and passion — something, curiously, we don't expect to find in our

---

journalists, though this idea is quite absurd. Journalists, Cate shows, may learn to hide their feelings but they can never learn to stop having them.

Journalists view the world through different glasses. While they are usually not active participants in the events they witness, they are none the less instant historians. They must balance accurate reporting with sound judgement meeting daily deadlines as the clock races forward minute by minute. Their egos not surprisingly are enormous, and little wonder. Stanley Walker, the longtime city editor of the old *New York Herald Tribune*, once described a good newsman (there were few newswomen then) as someone who "knows everything. He is aware not only of what goes on in the world today, but his brain is a repository of the accumulated wisdom of the ages. He is not only handsome, but he has the physical strength which enables him to perform great feats of energy. He can go nights on end without sleep. He dresses well and talks with charm. Men admire him; women adore him; tycoons and statesmen are willing to share their secrets with him. He hates lies and meanness and sham, but keeps his temper. He is loyal to his paper and to what he looks upon as his profession: whether it is a profession, or merely a craft, he resents attempts to debase it."

Perhaps a bit flowery but certainly very accurate. Journalists rub shoulders with the great and the near-great and the not-so-near great. They witness the beautiful and the horrible, the truth and the lie, the noble and the ignoble. Is it any wonder that they often view the world with cynicism?

Yet it is a badge of the profession that the events swirling about them do not affect them, for they are there to record and observe, not to participate.

But there are events in a journalist's life that never see printer's ink, nor are they ever flashed on the television screen. There are feelings and emotions that are hidden from view. There are thoughts and opinions seldom expressed. This is the stuff for diaries or writers of fiction. Still, all these things happen but journalists seldom record them because they're not really part of instant history — just reporting it. And yet they are in a very personal way part of the history they are reporting.

With that in mind, I decided to look back over the thirty years I have been a journalist and describe the world I have seen through a series of vignettes, some light, some serious. The purpose is to capture in a microcosm some of the drama and pathos, both big and small, of the thin slice of history I was experiencing in a personal way. It is something journalists normally never delve into.

And with some reason. They're observers, reporters supposedly immune to events swirling around them. Editors don't care nor do they want to hear about "your" feelings. Nor does the public care or need to hear about "your" feelings. After all, you are just a byline or a face on television or a voice on the radio. And yet, we correspondents and reporters are real people with feelings.

The events we witness, experience, and write about are buried in our memories. Sometimes they are good memories. Sometimes they leave scars. Sometimes they hurt for the folly or the horror of it all, for we all too often witness the stupidity of man to his fellow man. So it shouldn't be surprising that we are cynics who could easily live by Mike Hammer's code, "Live fast, die young and have a good looking corpse"! Only other journalists will understand what that means.

Florida, 1955. His name was Ogden Sharpnack and he was the night city editor of *The St. Petersburg Times.* He didn't like Yalies. When I turned in my first obit, all three paragraphs of it, he snarled that I didn't know how to write, tossed the copy into the waste basket, and ordered me to do it again. It was a sobering experience and taught me a great deal about the unabashed power editors wield. Sharp, as he was known, was a member of the old school — he didn't like educated people.

Washington 1956. The Army was a dreadful experience. But being single, with no children I could claim and not being in graduate school, I got the call. Most of my classmates took the easy way out — they got married, too early, or ducked out in graduate school. What a bore the Army was. Two years wasted writing inane press releases for dumb colonels.

But there were moments. Catching training hops to Florida to spend a few hours with a long-legged blonde. Then racing back to police the barracks. Two years and one day — Uncle Sam still owes me one day.

Staten Island 1960. Many of the dead were still in their seats. The Constellation had been chopped in half by the DC-8 and had fallen from the sky. The jet age was here. The smell of death on that cold, raw winter morning permeated the air. There were shoes and shredded Christmas packages in puddles of water on the ground. The taxi fare back to Manhattan was $18. After writing all night for *Time,* I finally got home to my dank Greenwich Village apartment and threw up. I had been at *Time* all of six months.

Paris, 1962. Her name was Robin Webb. She was a pert Australian blonde who worked for *Newsweek* in the Paris Bureau. I fell in love, desperately. We became engaged, my first and last experience with that vestige of older times. It means nothing, I was to learn.

Detroit, 1962. Robin Webb ran off with Phillip Graham, the publisher of *Newsweek* and husband of Katharine Graham who owned The Washington Post Company. He did it with limos, roses, and promises of heaven on Bali, all on his expense account. It ended tragically enough a few months later when Phil Graham shot himself in the head.

I wrote Robin later about how sorry I was. She wrote back and said she was sorry too...but it had a hollow ring. She was sorry because she had lost the limos, the roses, and the trips to Bali...and the job at *Newsweek.*

Detroit, 1962. Many thought the end of the world was at hand. I knew it was and my hands became cold and clammy. John Kennedy had ordered the blockade of Cuba and both the U.S. and the Soviet Union were rattling their missiles. Henry Luce's cocktail party at the annual automobile show bombed as people retreated to their homes to ponder armageddon. The vast emptiness of cavernous Cobo Hall was a Daliesque scene — gorgeous models, glistening new cars, but no people.

"Let's have a drink," I said to the blonde model standing near an ugly new Buick, "because there's nothing else to do." "Yes there is," she said. And she was right. The world didn't end that night but if it had, it would have been a helluva way to go.

I don't know what Henry Luce did but I know I had a better time than he did. He was probably busy on the phone all night trying to avoid nuclear war. He was that kind of man.

Detroit, 1963. The affair with the blonde model lasted more than a year. On the way to lunch one day I stopped by the AP wire machine in the office. The President had been shot. No one ate lunch that day. The nation wept for days if not years. I wept too as I watched the sickness of the moment again and again on television. I wept knowing but not knowing what it all meant…it was an evil omen as it turned out. The killing of public figures had begun. It would lead us all to the Gulf of Tonkin and eleven years of Vietnam. Where had all the flowers gone? But I was too involved in the space program to really notice until later.

Houston, 1967. His name was Joe Shea and he was boss of NASA's Apollo program — the lunar landing mission. We had just returned from Cape Canaveral. He was to be on the cover of *Time*. "I'll see you tomorrow, Joe," I said as we shook hands. Little did we know that as we parted, Grissom, White, and Chaffee were being burned alive, trapped inside their burning spacecraft perched atop a Saturn rocket. And it was just a simulation — a high tech term for a dry-run! So much for dry-runs.

That night I didn't go to bed. I wrote about what it was that made these men (and today it would be these men and women) do these things. The conquest of space symbolized one of man's oldest and basic drives: the quest for knowledge, the lure of a new frontier, the challenge of the impossible, and the aphrodisiac of fame.

Joe Shea never made the cover of *Time*. He was fired. Somebody's head had to roll. It was his. He was a big, burly guy who loved martinis. When we finally had dinner a few weeks later, Joe Shea was a broken man, his world shattered by an accident that should never have happened. He was bitter. He heaped much of the blame on North American Aviation, the prime Apollo contractor (the aerospace part of Rockwell International today).

He took me into his bedroom and swore me to secrecy. He opened his dresser drawer and underneath his socks he pulled out a blue baseball hat with white lettering over the bill which read N$SA. North American had a big party after they got the multi-billion dollar Apollo contract, Joe explained, and these were the hats they passed around.

"That tells it all," said Joe. Indeed it did. That was 20 years ago and it seems as if nothing has changed.

Paris, 1968. There were only five guests in the posh George V hotel. Every night the helmeted riot police fought the students and anyone else up and down the streets of the Left Bank. The boom of concussion grenades, the baton charges, the raw smell of tear gas filled the air. The days of rage had begun.

In his Elysée Palace bunker Charles de Gaulle tried to figure out what was happening, what was happening to "his" France as if he were some kind of latter day Louis XIV. Why were they so angry, he wondered aloud to aides who mumbled, "Mais, mon général..."

And then he had had enough. He made a deal and the tanks suddenly appeared in the quiet woods outside the city. On a brilliant day late in May, a million people took to the Champs Elysée chanting "Vive de Gaulle." The guttural sound of diesel engines throbbing disturbed the birds in the woods. But the students heard it also. It reminded me of Napoleon and his whiff of grape shot.

De Gaulle had made a deal, a cynical deal. He had agreed to free hundreds of imprisoned military officers who had opposed him in return for the support of a general whom he hated but who controlled two armored divisions. "Free these men or lose your kingdom," was just about the way Général Jacques Massau put it.

The students got the message and so did de Gaulle. The rioting stopped and the tanks went back to their garrisons. The next spring the people voted. De Gaulle lost, rejected once again. But the great man never bowed his head. He left as abruptly as he had come — in the dark of the night.

Madrid, 1969. The moon was huge and full. The giant 60-foot dish antenna was pointed at it. NASA staffers at the tracking station sat around on wooden chairs outside on this mild summer night. Up there near the moon a crab-like vehicle was making its slow descent to the lunar surface. As Neil Armstrong ticked off the descent — 100 feet, 90 feet, 50 feet, 20 feet — everyone stood staring at the moon as if hoping that by some miracle we would actually see the Eagle landing. Our eyes strained moonwards. Then came Armstrong's terse voice: "The Eagle has landed." It sounded like he'd just landed a piper cub somewhere. Everyone cheered and hugged one another pointing stupidly at the moon as if we could see Armstrong's lunar lander. Joe Shea would have loved it. It was to have been his moment in the sun — his moment in history, the man who put America on the moon *first.* But Joe Shea wasn't there or anywhere. But he really was there but nobody knew it. And it won't show up in the history books.

Warsaw, 1970. In the gray of a winter day, the only audible sound was the hiss of two gas-burning seven-pronged candelabras. There for thirty seconds knelt Willy Brandt, the Chancellor of Germany, before the great slab of granite which serves as a memorial to the Jews who died in the Warsaw Ghetto uprising of April 1943.

It was an extraordinary moment. A German leader kneeling at a memorial to millions of Jews who had perished during the Holocaust.

Some thought it was a grandstand play. But they didn't know Willy Brandt. The night before he had slept fitfully, if at all. He sipped brandy after brandy as he pondered what symbolic gesture he could make at the wreath laying the next day. Aides wrung their hands with worry, bereft of ideas. Brandt wanted to show the Polish people and the world that the Germans were repentant. At the same time he wanted to remind his people, as he frequently liked to stress, that "no man can run away from the history of his people."

It was not until he faced the slab that Willy Brandt knew what he had to do. It was only then he knew he must fall to his knees in silent prayer.

The hiss of the gas-burning candelabras was joined by the gasp of the crowd as it watched this man of peace kneel before the slab.

Now this was a man. It was a true moment of greatness for here was this man making peace for his people so long despised for the evils their countrymen had wrought to mankind. If there is a God, he was there in Warsaw on that gray, grim day.

New York, 1974. Some said the media hounded him out of office but that was not the case. Richard Nixon had done it all himself and all the press did was expose his lies. And now there was talk that Ted Kennedy might be running for office in 1976. It seemed only natural to take another closer look at the bizarre events of Chappaquidick on the night in July 1969 that Kennedy's Oldsmobile went over the bridge killing a young woman campaign worker at almost the same time Neil Armstrong was landing gently on the lunar surface.

I headed a small task force, six in number, with the mission of finding out what really happened that night on earth. Our investigation lasted only six weeks, halted abruptly when Kennedy took himself out of the 1976 presidential race. Our reason for the investigation — who wanted two years of Chappaquidick? — had ceased. We were later criticized for not going ahead though at the time I concurred with the decision.

While we never solved the riddle of Chappaquidick we were certain of one thing — people had lied. The fix was in. Another cover-up had been perpetrated. Some day the truth will out and it will be a far different story than has been told to date.

Elk City, Okla. 1975. The small four-seater plane bumped to a halt on the uneven surface of Elk City's weed-covered airstrip. Out hopped a short, gray-haired man, garment bag slung over his shoulder. It was a big day for Elk City. No presidential candidate had visited Elk City since William Jennings Bryan had stopped there seventy years before. But who was this presidential candidate? It was Jimmy Who? then.

There were 300 people at the Ramada Inn. And they listened as Jimmy Carter promised to bring decency back to government and never tell a lie. Never tell a lie? Jimmy shook hands with everyone in the room, grinning widely all the time. No one took him very seriously. It was all slightly quixotic.

Later in a car, the smile vanished. The warm blue eyes turned cold. The act was over. And it was an act as I observed this man who professed that he would never tell a lie, take off his jacket and roll up his sleeves, all of it carefully calculated to impress his audience. It did. But it didn't impress me.

In 1976, I voted for Gerald Ford, the first and last Republican presidential candidate I have voted for up to now. And I voted for Ford because I knew that Jimmy Carter, for all of his intellectual brilliance and knowledge, was a fraud. He was a man who had calculated every move, every statement, every gesture with one goal in mind — to become President of the United States. The fact that he might have to govern if elected had apparently never crossed his mind.

We journalists should have known better when he published his so-called autobiography "Why Not the Best?" Somehow many of us missed the gross arrogance of it all. I had missed it too, for a while, caught up in the excitement and frenzy of this "new face" challenging the aging denizens of the New Deal — Fair Deal — Great Society Democratic Party.

There were two things that convinced me that Jimmy Carter was not what he said he was, a man who would never tell a lie (which in hindsight is a preposterous statement for anyone running for the Presidency to make). During that swing through Oklahoma in the fall of 1975 when he was still Jimmy Who?, Carter would carefully doff his jacket at every meeting and meticulously roll up his shirt sleeves — but only three turns so that his shirt sleeves were rolled up between his wrist and his elbow, no further. It was always the same — a calculated piece of body language to make him appear to be "one of the boys," which he distinctly was not.

His first words proved that. "I'm Jimmy Carter. I'm running for President of the United States (the usual applause). I'm a nuclear physicist...." And then about three more minutes about Jimmy Carter ending up with "I'll never tell a lie." Perhaps he didn't tell a lie, but he told an untruth as it turned out. He was *not* a nuclear physicist (which implied a Ph.D. and all that) but a nuclear engineer — a vast and significant difference. The little "white lie" caught up with him quickly enough and he hurriedly amended his opening line.

The media, in its great wisdom, forgave him this "minor" indiscretion. And then it was forgotten. Why, I don't know. Perhaps because he ended up running against the man who pardoned Richard Nixon. But Ford did what he had to do to save the country two more years of anguish.

Ford, for all his shortcomings, was not a fraud. The decision to vote *for* Ford was easy.

Chicago, 1975. Mayor Richard Daley. Hizzoner, as he was known. The audience was in his office. His massive desk faced no fewer than fifty chairs lined up in precise rows — fifty chairs equaled fifty aldermen who rubber stamped Dick Daley's dictums. There were only four of us and we were dwarfed by forty-six empty chairs as the great man strode into his office and plunked himself into his massive green chair. Power. Yes, power radiated from this ruddy-faced Irishman. Chicago's de Gaulle with a midwestern accent or maybe the Pope as politician. When you're in the presence of power you know it. This man had power.

Storm Lake, Iowa, 1978. They're crazy in Iowa, sort of. Every summer some 5,000 bicycle nuts (I hear it's up to 8,000 now) trundle out their $600, 10-speed machines and for seven days peddle like mad across the state from the banks of the Missouri on the west to the banks of Mississippi on the east. It's become an annual ritual known as RAGBRAI — The Register's (as in Des Moines) Annual Great Bicycle Ride Across Iowa — a quintessential Heartland happening.

They sleep out-of-doors in tents and drink gallons of Gatorade and orange juice and ice tea as they peddle up and down for 450 miles across the gorgeous rolling hills of Iowa. The corn in midsummer is a deep, rich green canopy stretching from highway shoulder to highway shoulder, 10-feet tall. As far as the eye can see, there's nothing but corn — the world's greatest breadbasket right here in our Heartland. Food to feed the world. The corn-fed Iowa girls with their smooth, tanned legs serve only to distract from the cornucopia of plenty that extends from horizon to horizon.

Fifteen years ago no one in his or her right mind would have thought of biking across Iowa in the searing August heat. But that was fifteen years ago. Times have changed. Last summer (1986) former Arizona Governor Bruce Babbitt and his leggy wife did it. Democrat Babbitt is running for President.

Teheran, 1978. At best, Teheran is a dreadful city — a giant paved parking lot smothered in smog. The parking lot slopes down from the mountains so the rain water is always flooding the hovels where the city's millions of poor try to live. So being in Teheran during a revolution had more than just a few drawbacks. Six people in a 600-room hotel is, well, bizarre. (The foreign press corps, more comfortable with their own herd, stayed elsewhere.)

But what was happening and did happen in Teheran and continues to happen there is not unlike what happened in France in 1789 and the years after. It was and is a revolution of the have nots against the haves. They came out of their filthy, water-soaked slums and slaughtered their royalty. Forget all that business about religion. This was and is a revolution over bread, butter, and roofs. But we don't understand that because we're mesmerized by a shrunken Muslim priest.

Curfews are never pleasant but they usually don't last long. Except in Teheran where the curfew became a way of life. In by eight, was the word. Long nights on the hotel balcony, the city blacked out, listening to the chatter of machine gun fire and the occasional thump of a mortar. You knew it was just a question of time before they got him — the Shah. All his fancy British-made tanks and American-built F-4s and Bell helicopters couldn't keep him in power.

The foreign community knew it too. So they drank themselves silly at all-night parties in the private suites of the now-empty hotels. And around 3 AM, someone would slip an X-rated video cassette into the VCR and everyone howled with joy. It must have been like that in Rome under Nero.

Paris, 1978. And in a farmhouse outside the city, a funny, shrunken old man sitting on a Persian rug was directing the show back in Teheran. The show by the have nots, that is. Ayatollah Khomeini never looks a visitor in the eye. Indeed, one feels that he is barely aware that anyone else is around.

He talks in a whisper, without gestures or emotion. Expressionless. And the talk sounds like so much medieval mumbo-jumbo. The man is stubborn to the point of being mulish. No power here, for sure. But power in what he stands for — the have nots against the haves. And the have nots, because they are so many, will always win. And win they did. Just like in 1789 in France and 1918 in Russia and 1949 in China and 1959 in Cuba and 1979 in Nicaragua and...where will the next one be?

Edwards Air Force Base, CA, 1981. At 55,000 feet, it was a mere speck in the sky picking up the sun's early morning rays. Nothing more than a gleam. In three minutes the Shuttle was kicking up a rooster tail of sand on the dry lake bed having done in 180 seconds what would take an average jetliner 45 minutes to do. A new age in space travel had arrived.

Los Angeles, 1986. There would be a price, of course. Joe Shea could tell you about that. There had to be a catastrophic accident. What experimental program, aeronautic or otherwise, didn't have one or more. But success breeds complacency and arrogance. NASA and America became complacent and arrogant.

So when the Challenger blew, I was not surprised. I was sad and horrified as I watched the replays of those fireworks in the sky. I wept by myself for a few minutes. And then it was over because I knew it had to happen — and it will again, alas. And that's not a cynic speaking. It's just reality. Man will always be playing with the outer edge of whatever envelope he's testing — it makes no difference whether he's racing cars, climbing the north face of K-2 or reaching for Mars — the outer edge of the envelope is the unknown and it is fraught with danger. It always will be.

I thought of this as I stood in the chilly desert morning awaiting the arrival of the toothpick-like Voyager about to end its round-the-world non-stop flight. It was a couple of days before Christmas 1986. What the hell was I doing there anyway? And what were all these thousands of other people doing there as dawn broke over Rogers Dry Lake? They were witnessing history.

And then I realized this is what I have been doing over the course of my career. Witnessing history. Which isn't a bad way to make a living. You'll never be rich. But you'll also never be dull. You'll learn that it's difficult to tolerate fools and with a bit of luck you may help make a difference somewhere. But you'll probably never know it.

6   THE MAGAZINE INDUSTRY: DEVELOPING THE SPECIAL INTEREST AUDIENCE*

BENJAMIN M. COMPAINE

Magazines have a long history in America. Magazines have been with us since their first appearance in 1704. A glance at the magazine rack at a good bookstore shows that there are hundreds of consumer magazines (magazines directed to the general public as contrasted with trade magazines, which are directed to specialized groups of people). But even within the general public, magazines have become specialized.

This is because television is now the dominant mass medium in America. To survive, then, magazine publishers have focused on serving the needs of specialized audiences. "This change does not mean," writes Benjamin Compaine, "as has been reported, that the mass circulation, general interest magazine is dead. It does mean that an increasing proportion of magazines published...will be accounted for by special interest or limited audience publications."

Consider, as a case in point, the development of computer magazines — at one time a very "hot" form of magazine publishing. As home computers started becoming popular, the purchasers of these computers needed information about different software programs that were available and about new developments.

Magazines were developed for computers in general and for particular computers: Apple computers (in particular, the Apple II series), IBM personal computers (and IBM compatible computers and IBM clones), the Macintosh, *ad infinitum*. The market expanded rapidly, a number of publishing companies launched new computer magazines, and then there was a fallout, leaving (still) a large number of computer magazines around. And with the development of desktop publishing, new magazines have appeared trying to capture that market.

This case history shows that the magazine is a very flexible kind of publication and that as soon as publishers perceive that there is a good-sized market for a magazine, they are quick to respond. There are some remarkable failures in magazine publishing, let me add. Time, Inc. has launched several magazines in recent years, in a rather big way, with disastrous results — losses of tens of millions of dollars.

The variety of magazines is good a reflection of the incredible variety of interests Americans have. There are people who are passionate about everything

* From the *Journal of Communication*, 1980; 30(2): 98–103. © 1980 *Journal of Communication*. Reprinted by permission.

from birdwatching to hang gliding, from writing software to growing orchids. And for every group, no matter how arcane its interests, there are magazines.

The threshold of the 1980s finds the magazine industry having substantially completed a fundamental change. As a modern publishing form, the magazine is barely a hundred years old. For much of their lives, magazines served as the primary mass medium in American society. Now that other media, principally television, have usurped that purpose, magazine publishers are justifying their existence by serving either portions of the entire literate audience, or small groups of readers with intense interest in particular subjects. This change does not mean, as has been reported, that the mass circulation, general interest magazine is dead. It does mean that an increasing proportion of magazines published — and probably of total magazine circulation — will be accounted for by special interest or limited audience publications.

Magazines evolved because of two unique characteristics that differentiated them from newspapers. First, since they did not have to carry up-to-the-minute news, they could rely on more leisurely delivery systems than newspapers, especially to spread-out rural areas. More importantly, in an age before television and radio, they were able to offer advertisers national coverage. As Americans spent increasing amounts of money on raising their material standard of living, magazines benefited from the expanding market for the goods and services advertisers offered.

Throughout the twentieth century, the magazine responded to the dynamics of several factors (Servan-Schreiber, 1978):

Job specialization. A more complete society creates a need for specialized subgroups of managers, engineers, researchers, and financiers. To meet the needs of these subgroups, many of which do not understand the language of the other, there are special publications tailored to them — the business and professional press.

The assertion of new freedoms and tastes. American society is becoming more permissive, resulting in magazines that have responded to different groups asserting their potential as a new market. This includes the "new" women's magazines like *Ms.*, the city magazines like *Philadelphia*, or the sex magazines, from *Playboy* to the more explicit *Penthouse*. Youth is served as *Rolling Stone* moves beyond rock music to youth culture, while blacks are finding a continually widening range of magazines directed at them.

Spread of education. In the past two decades, higher education has become mass education in the U.S. Half of all high school graduates now go on to college. In the past ten years more than 12 million individuals have received a bachelor's degree (millions more attended college but did not receive a diploma) and the number receiving degrees in the next ten years will be even greater. The result has been the creation of a vast college-educated, literate audience with a multiplicity of personal and intellectual interests.

A consumer haven. With a market as vast and wealthy as that of the U.S., almost any well-presented idea can create a highly lucrative, if limited, submarket for itself.

Increased opportunities to pursue interests. In addition to increased leisure time, Americans have the discretionary income to embrace a wide variety of pursuits, from bowling to camping, furniture building to wine-making. People with similar interests join together, identifying with each other.

The magazine has always faced competition in taking advantage of these changes. In the early years of the century, newspapers and to a lesser extent books were the primary competition. Soon movies became an important form of entertainment. In the twenties, radio swept the nation, unmatched in speed of penetration until television came along beginning in the late 1940s. And inexpensive paperback books, getting under way just before World War II, have become a major form of mass media in the past two decades.

Just as book publishers have learned that a successful movie spurs rather than harms book sales, so magazine publishers have learned to take advantage of television. Popularity of televised spectator sports has stimulated sales of sports magazines, and fast-breaking news on TV has created opportunities for deeper analysis and perspective in the news weeklies (since 1946 the combined circulation of the news weeklies has about quadrupled).

But perhaps the most significant reason for the magazine's survival has been its ability to adapt to a changing role in society. It is no longer needed as a national advertising tool for mass-oriented products; television can simultaneously supply far-flung regions with the same advertisement. Nor is it needed for purely entertainment purposes, as television and the movies satisfy those needs. Whereas most magazines used to be published for a mass readership, today even most of the so-called mass consumer magazines have narrowed their audiences down to smaller proportions.

This trend of specialization applies not only to consumer interests, but also to the diverse information needs of business and the professions, as evidenced by a steadily increasing number of trade magazines with both paid and controlled (sent free to an eligible population) circulations. As with consumer magazines, business magazines serve the need of advertisers who wish to reach a well-defined audience for their product or service.

One indication of this specialization is that the number of magazines has been growing, even though total magazine circulation is fairly level. In 1950 there were 6960 periodicals in the *Ayer Directory of Publications*. By 1978 the number had increased by almost 38 percent, although with deaths and births the actual number of different titles is no doubt much greater. Most of these have been small circulation, specialized publications serving alumni groups, industry associations, clubs, professional societies, and the numerous consumer interests that have emerged. But there has been less growth in total circulation, since it takes many 25,000 and 150,000 circulation magazines to replace the mass circulation versions of *Life, Saturday Evening Post, Look,* and *Collier's*. (Although the first two have reappeared, they are all structured to survive on a smaller circulation than the six or eight million of their predecessors.)

Publishers have always been quick in sensing new interests within the public and then establishing new publications to cater to them. When the movies made Hollywood a center of attention, *Photoplay* appeared and grew into a fat fan magazine. In 1934, with model railroad hobbyists numbering in the hundreds, an entrepreneur put out *Model Railroader*, a magazine whose circulation is now near 175,000. And when, in 1951, the aqualung made underwater adventure available to skilled swimmers, an enthusiast launched *Skin Diver*, now selling 166,000 copies a month.

Whole categories have sprung up to meet new interests, and imitators have joined the successful innovators. By 1980, there were magazines for gamblers, private pilots, brides-to-be, horse breeders, home decorators and fixer-uppers, antique collectors, and followers of politics, sports, news, hair styles, and psychology. Business periodicals exist for food engineers, automotive mechanics, consumer electronics, retailers, and even magazine publishers.

For the advertiser and publisher, a consumer magazine is little more than the delivery of a market: a market for skiers, smokers, automobile buyers, furniture dusters, *ad infinitum*. A mass circulation magazine must, by its very nature, deliver a generalized market, one that is held together not by any single interest but by some vaguely defined patterns. The readers of these magazines can be identified only by toting up their demographics and trying to come up with some useful groupings. On the other hand, there are magazines that deal with a single product or concept. Moreover, this product or concept is central not only to the editorial material but also to the bulk of the advertising. Such a magazine is thus able to deliver to an advertiser a specific, highly defined audience.

For the editor and consumer, a magazine is a source of information: what it was like in Atlanta's ballpark when Aaron hit the 715th homerun, why inflation is so high, how to bake chocolate chip cookies, the latest in ski bindings. Notice that the type of information provided, however, is of two types. Much information in magazines is purely for the edification of the reader, included not to be acted on but because it is interesting or entertaining. Contrast this with information that the reader can directly utilize, or even information that exhorts the reader to act. *Tennis* has Ken Rosewall demonstrating "The Way to Improve Your Backhand," and

Apartment Life offers "Overnight Guests and No Guest Room — What To Do?"

Magazines differ not only in the types of information they provide, but also in the characteristics of the audience they reach. For the purposes of this study, the first criterion — type of information provided — can be divided into two categories: passive and active. Passive information is information intended for the reader's entertainment or general knowledge. Active information, by contrast, is intended for a specific use.

The second difference in magazines, type of audience reached, can be conveniently divided into mass audience and limited audience. Obviously, the subject matter of a magazine might appeal to a vast potential readership or to a very restricted one.

Thus, magazines can be categorized by whether their subject matter is basically active or passive as well as whether the subject is applicable to a relatively mass or limited audience.* These divisions are shown in Table 1, which also includes examples of the specific magazines applicable to each block. The term "special interest" is used here to refer particularly to the types of consumer periodicals that fit into the limited audience/active information block in the matrix. General interest magazines are considered to be those that are mass audience/passive interest in content.

Special interest magazines deal primarily with high technology, high performance requirements. A person with a casual or spectator interest in sports may read *Sports Illustrated*, but the serious golfer will likely read *Golf* or *Golf Digest* in addition to, or instead of, *Sports Illustrated*. In fact, the better or more serious an individual is at some particular skill-oriented task, the more likely he or she is to subscribe to a magazine in that field. Special interest magazines are written for the practitioner, general interest magazines for the observer. Of course, there is overlap — the tennis buff who subscribes to *Tennis* has other interests as well and might buy *Time* or *Playboy*, too.

The key is that the special interest publications demand high reader involvement — subscribers are participants in the subjects being written about. In a special interest magazine, the editorial matter centers around the activities of the readers themselves and the advertising usually is an extension of the editorial content. Thus, the special interest magazine is selling a readership of unquestionable homogeneity as related to a specific product or activity, while providing a waiting audience with sought-after information that often results in intense cover-to-cover reading of editorial and advertising content alike. The less a magazine focuses on very specific activities or products, the more it moves into a mass audience category, though it may still be activity-oriented.

Limited audience/passive interest magazines, as noted, share many of the

---

* In terms of magazine publishing economics, the major distinction is circulation size, rather than type of audience, in which case *Harper's* has more in common with *Flying* than with *Reader's Digest*.

Table I   SAMPLE MAGAZINES BY EDITORIAL CONTENT AND TYPE OF AUDIENCE

	Passive editorial content (median circulation = 668,000)	*Active editorial content (median circulation = 406,000)*
Mass audience (median circulation) = 2.1 million)	Reader's Digest TV Guide People Ladies' Home Journal Sports Illustrated Newsweek Playboy Ebony Esquire National Geographic Psychology Today	Family Circle Better Homes and Gardens Outdoor Life Apartment Life Glamour Popular Mechanics Sports Afield Popular Science
	(median circulation = 3.0 million)	(median circulation = 1.8 million)
Limited audience (median circulation = 339,000)	Saturday Evening Post Harper's New Yorker Ms. New Republic Ellery Queen Mystery Magazine Philadelphia Forbes Rolling Stone Commentary Modern Romance Gourmet	Golf Digest Trains Popular Photography Flying Yachting Ski Modern Bride Camping Journal Antiques Dirt Bike Car & Driver High Fidelity Shooting Times Trailer Life
	(median circulation = 478,000)	(median circulation = 306,000)

Note: Circulation medians derived from 1st six months, 1977 Audit Bureau of Circulation statement.

economic and logistical characteristics of the special interest publications. The crucial difference is that the former must rely on demographic data to establish their validity as useful marketing outlets for advertisers. There is no doubt that all magazines can be called special interest to the extent that they involve some concept of varying specificity, and they are limited audience to the extent that not everyone wants to read them. However defined, it is the successful development of special interest audiences that has given magazines an expanded major role and enabled them to thrive into the 1980s.

REFERENCE

1. Servan-Schreiber, Jean-Louis. *The Power to Inform*. New York: McGraw-Hill, 1978.

7 THE FIFTH ESTATE: EAVESDROPPING ON AMERICAN BUSINESS TALKING TO ITSELF*

DAVID OWEN

If you look at the magazine rack in a good bookstore you will see an almost bewildering number of magazines devoted to a bewildering number of topics. There are magazines to deal with every hobby we have, every interest, every passion — whether it is sex, politics, scuba diving, do-it-yourself brain surgery...you name it. These are all consumer magazines, which survive by attracting advertising for their particular audiences.

But there is another world of publishing that we seldom encounter, that of trade publications, devoted to providing information for people in various aspects of the business world. As you might imagine, the business world is full of people doing all kinds of things, from selling toys to running pet shops, from processing frozen foods to managing cemeteries, from running drycleaning shops to administering universities.

---

* David Owen, 1987, "The Fifth Estate." As originally published in the July 1985 issue of *THE ATLANTIC MONTHLY*.

It is this world that David Owen addresses and it is a fascinating and extremely lively world, it turns out. What you discover when you examine the trade journals is that they look at the world from a highly focused perspective, which is that of the food canner, pet store owner, toy seller, or whatever. These publications are full of information about new products, political matters that may affect the industry involved, job openings, and that kind of thing.

As students, you may find it quite instructive to look at the dominant "trade journal" for university professors and administrators, *The Chronicle of Higher Education.** It is full of articles that deal with issues and topics of interest to people in the field. The first half of the publication (which has a tabloid format) is devoted typically to articles about general topics of interest to all educators.

The journal also contains a number of features: a book review section, sections on sports, government and politics, computers, a calendar of events of interest, and, most important of all for many of its readers, a "Bulletin Board" of positions that are available. This feature varies between twenty-five to fifty pages in length. If you want to know about what is going on in higher education, you will learn a great deal by reading *The Chronicle of Higher Education.*

The same applies to all the trade journals: they are fascinating and reveal a world that you didn't know existed. But they know you exist and are passionately interested in you...and every aspect of your existence, especially your discretionary income.

"If the bird is tame," Freud wrote, "I like to place him on a stand and then, while telling him what a good bird he is, I get behind him and lift one of his feet....Birds which are not tame will generally require handling by two individuals with one holding the patient in a towel and the other doing the cutting."

There's a lot more to it than that. I'm just touching on the major points. Before trying this yourself you'd want to read Arthur Freud's entire article, "Proper Nail Clipping of Birds," in the January issue of *PSM. PSM* is a magazine for pet-store owners. Its name stands for Pets Supplies Marketing. Say that aloud a few times and you'll understand why they use only the initials.

Let's see. On August 4, 1984, nearly 300 people in Las Vegas stood up and said, "Bowling belongs in the Olympic Games, and I pledge that I will do everything I can for that goal," according to *Bowling Proprietor.* The bowling industry's Olympic aspirations are "rapidly becoming the talk of the town," the magazine says. Still, bowling linage was down a bit in 1984. Perhaps hoping to reverse that trend, residents of Indiana last year contributed $296 to B-PAC, the bowling political-action committee. B-PAC tries to entice politicians to adopt a more pro-bowling stance. One of its

* *The Chronicle of Higher Education,* 1255 23rd St. NW, Washington, DC 20037.

beneficiaries is my own congressman, Bill Green, of New York City, whose district contains exactly one bowling alley.

Here are a few of the magazines that are piled up on the table in my dining room: *Turkey World, Iron Age, American Carwash Review, National Jeweler* (edited by S. Lynn Diamond), *Fur Rancher, Lab Animal, Hosiery & Underwear, Weeds Trees & Turf* (incorporating *Golf Daily*), *Infections in Surgery, American Cemetery*. I also have *Kitchen & Bath Business, Ground Water Age, Beverage World* (the average American drank 43.2 gallons of soft drinks in 1984), *National Mall Monitor, Quick Frozen Foods, Lodging Hospitality, Hardware Age, The National Notary* ("Only in Florida, Maine, and South Carolina may Notaries join couples in matrimony"), *Meat Plant, Pulp & Paper, Pizza Today*, and a couple of hundred others.

Although according to my wife it is now impossible to sit down in our apartment without landing on a copy of *Cemetery Management*, my collection of trade and professional magazines is really just the tip of the iceberg in terms of what's available. Standard Rate & Data Service's directory of business publications, which comes out monthly and is larger than the Manhattan Yellow Pages, has more than 5,000 entries. The largest single publisher is Harcourt Brace Jovanovich, whose hundred or so titles include *Plastics Focus, Pit & Quarry*, and the brand-new *Food Sanitation*. Though little known outside their fields, such magazines can be enormously profitable. Last year Rupert Murdoch bought twelve of Ziff-Davis's trade magazines, including *Meetings & Conventions* and *Aerospace Daily*, for $350 million.

Rupert Murdoch notwithstanding, most trade magazines don't attract much public attention. When people talk about "the media," they are usually not referring to *Laundry News*. In fact, aside from the 15,387 people who receive it every month, how many Americans are even aware that there is an entire magazine devoted to laundry? (Actually, I saw in the February Standard Rate & Data directory that such magazines abound; they include *American Coin-Op, American Drycleaner, American Laundry Digest, Clean Scene Quarterly, Coin Launderer & Cleaner, Coinamatic Age, Drycleaners News, National Clothesline, New Era Laundry & Cleaning Lines, Textile Maintenance Reporter*, and *Western Cleaner & Launderer*.) The specialized focus of trade magazines assures their editors a certain privacy: they can speak to their readers with a candor that is impossible in the popular media. One could never find out from reading *Time* or *Newsweek*, for example, that people who make pretzels are considered to be somewhat boring by people who make potato chips. This is a fact that to the best of my knowledge can be found in print nowhere except in the pages of *Snack Food*.

Before I started piling up trade magazines, I had a vague, free-floating sense — derived mostly from watching the evening news — that there were only about a dozen different jobs in the United States: my job, Dan Rather's job, the President's job, steelworking, farming, banking, law enforcement, driving taxis, several others. But now I realize that the economy is almost inconceivably various and that in addition to the occupations just mentioned there are jobs involving, for example, the building of clam bunk skidders, the marketing of feller-bunchers, and the repairing of log forks (*World Wood*). I also know that 42 percent of men believe that they have sensitive skin (*Progressive Grocer*) and that the 1973 Arab oil embargo, though disastrous for almost everybody else, was about the best thing that ever happened to the people who make chain saws (*Chain Saw Age*, not to be confused with *Chain Store Age*).

Trade and professional magazines make some of the most esoteric reading in the world. They are the forum where American business talks to itself. Flipping through them is like eavesdropping on private conversations.

If keeping up with all these magazines didn't take so darned much time, I might be tempted to start a magazine of my own. It would be a sort of compilation of the best parts of all my favorite trade and professional publications. I wouldn't be able to call it *Magazine Age, Communication World*, or *Editor & Publisher*, because there are already magazines with those names. Perhaps I would call it *The Other Media* or *The Fifth Estate*. It would be filled with page after page of arresting facts. For example:

Coffee aroma consists of 100 to 200 volatile chemical compounds derived from the thermal degradation of primarily sucrose in the process of roasting the coffee bean. [*Tea and Coffee Trade Journal*]

Astronaut Sally Ride's recent space mission not only advanced the space program, but also prosthetic dentistry. Material used to make her urinary catch device is now being used to make soft denture liners. [*Dental Management*]

Some people call it polish. Others say class. We term it professionalism. Trying to sum up just what professionalism is, is somewhat like trying to define beauty or honesty. It's either there, or it isn't, but its presence adds a very special lustre. And Uniforms by Mindy has it. [*Uniforms & Accessories Review*]

Ironically, Notaries are rarely seen in modern American dramas and musicals — although this nation has more Notaries than any other and their role is an important one. The reason is that the office of Notary is viewed as an auxiliary rather than a primary vocation in modern America (except in Louisiana, with its French heritage), and characters are identified by their primary vocations — as in Arthur Miller's "Death of a Salesman." [*The National Notary*. This may be the world's most self-absorbed magazine. An article in a recent issue explained that Vanessa Williams lost her Miss America title because she "violated the morals provision of a notarized agreement."]

Finally, combining the edible with the collectible, Freelance will introduce Goofy Pops™, a lollypop on a "squiggly straw." The candy will be wrapped in a cellophane which will have a puffy sticker with rolly eyes attached to it. Extra stickers will come with the Goofy Pop. [*Giftware Business*]

Every now and then my magazine would cover certain stories in greater depth. I might, for example, consider running an entire article about Goofy Pops, which in the taxonomy of giftware are classified as "stationery." (So are Mello Smello Mini Duffles, stick-on Mello Smello scratch-and-smell tattoos, Wild & Wacky Mello Smellos, Smell & Spell fragranced message stickers, and Smellopads.)

Stationery is a category of giftware, but it isn't the same thing as a gift. Before I started reading *Giftware Business*, I was a little confused on this point. Now I understand that a gift in the giftware sense isn't something like a fishing rod, a set of golf clubs, or anything else you wish someone would give you. Rather, it is something like a pewter figurine of a scuba diver, a tiny panda sculpted from "hydrostone," a pencil sharpener in the shape of a monkey standing in a shoe, or a ball-point pen packaged with a color-coordinated lady's bow tie. It is, in brief, a thing that no sensible person would ever buy for himself or herself. It is a thing that is generally thrown away shortly after it is received.

One place where people buy a lot of giftware (according to a recent issue of *Souvenirs & Novelties*, a magazine whose readership overlaps somewhat with that of *Giftware Business*) is the souvenir shop at the Oklahoma City Zoo. (Another place is the gift shop at almost any hospital. In fact, hospital gift shops have their own trade magazine, called *Hospital Gift Shop Management*.) In an article titled "Zoo Shop Employees Create Functional Displays," Judy Rowe, the manager of the zoo shop, explains the secret of her success: "When someone walks in and asks for something penguin- or tiger-themed, we'll show the shopper whatever is currently in stock. We don't stop after showing one item. I prefer to take a few extra moments and make sure my customer is aware of everything — the plush, statues, and pictures." "*Plush*" is the giftware word for fuzzy stuffed things. According to *Giftware Business*, teddy bears led the plush list last year, "but lambs did pick up momentum."

The line between gifts and souvenirs is thin. Souvenirs are generally a bit less inhibited: a baseball cap covered with golf-ball-sized plastic peas and a huge plastic pat of melting butter; "underwear that's funtawear," from British Bulldog, Ltd.; toilet paper printed with sayings like "Show business is my life"; a pair of hat-wearing Maw and Paw 'Zarky Doodler Hillbilly Character Pens, sold in a "2-holer outhouse display-gift package"; Famous Amish Dolls; fake tomahawks made by Cherokee Indians from North Carolina ("We're on the warpath to bring you fast selling items that bring high profits for you!").

Cherokee tomahawks aside, gifts and souvenirs tend to be made on islands in the Pacific. This sometimes causes tension. An article in *Souvenirs & Novelties* discusses the perceived indelicacy of selling

Japanese-made souvenirs in American battleship museums. The problem can usually be overcome. "In the past three years I have had only one person who, after discussing this issue, still refused to buy," reports Hattie Horton, the retail manager of the gift shop at Battleship Alabama Memorial Park.

If you just bought up your local battleship museum's entire supply of Bother Me greeting cards (for example, "It bothers me when you eat with your mouth open") but don't have anyone in particular you want to send them to, you might consider buying a mailing list consisting of the names of, say, all the people who between January and August of 1984 bought the phonograph record *Floyd Cramer Piano Favorites*, "featuring World Famous Love Songs and a Treasury of Favorites." There are 59,000 such people, 90 percent of them female. Finding out who they are costs fifty dollars per thousand names.

Selling names and addresses is a very big business. Popular lists, according to recent issues of *Direct Marketing* and *Fund Raising Management*, include people in the state of California who have rented or purchased wheelchairs, canes, walking chairs, or crutches; women who subscribed to *Redbook* after responding to a sweepstakes offer; members of the Association of Handicapped Artists; Americans "concerned about the growing Soviet military threat to peace"; buyers of the Thompson Chain Reference Bible; buyers of the Perry County Pizza Kit; and "people interested in the welfare of children and who support building character, teaching valuable skills, providing adequate education and suitable housing, along with developing networks to help abused, lost, stolen, and abandoned children." (Another popular mailing list consists, apparently, of the names of people who subscribe to magazines dealing with popular mailing lists. Shortly after I began reading *Direct Marketing* and *Fund Raising Management*, I received a piece of junk mail urging me to buy three books by someone named Cecil C. Hoge, St.: *Mail Order Survival & Success, Mail Order Know-How,* and *Mail Order Moonlighting.*)

For a couple of summers when I was in college, I worked as a reporter for a trade magazine called *Milling & Baking News*. Shortly before I took the job, the magazine had come to something resembling national prominence by breaking the story on the famous Russian wheat deal — the Soviet Union's enormous purchase of American grain in 1972. For several weeks that year Walter Cronkite, *The New York Times*, and the rest of the popular media relied on *Milling & Baking News* for virtually all their information about the transaction. This information was uncannily accurate. The magazine's editor, Morton I. Sosland, was getting it from an anonymous source, who, Sosland gradually realized, was probably a Soviet official (the source always addressed Sosland as "Mr. Morton," something an American Deep Throat wouldn't do). Excitement about the wheat-deal story had mostly died down by the time I signed on, although work in the office was still occasionally disrupted by a British or Japanese television crew looking for an offbeat American feature story.

As is true of many trade publications, *Milling & Baking News* has a tiny circulation — just a little over 5,500. Even so, *The Wall Street Journal* once described the magazine as "indispensable" to its industry. Its influence derives not from the number of people who read it but from who those people are. About a fifth of the magazine's readers are the chief executives of milling or baking companies. Most of these people read every issue carefully, and advertisers pay a premium to reach them. A full-page, full-color ad in *Milling & Baking News* costs about $2,500. That's not much money in absolute terms, but it works out to nearly half a dollar per subscriber, or about what it would cost to read the ad aloud to each one over the phone. A similar advertisement in *Time*, in contrast, has a cost per paying reader of less than three cents.

It is a general rule that the more carefully a trade magazine is read by its trade, the more stultifying its content is to outsiders. Indispensable or not, *Milling & Baking News* is pretty grim reading for anyone who doesn't care deeply about milling and baking. "In the face [of] sharply higher prices last week," begins a typical article in a recent issue,

> shortening business was very sluggish. Soybean oil for nearby jumped 2½@3⅛c a lb on the heels of 1¼c gain the previous week. Deferred prices rose 1⅛@3⅞c. Virtually all other oil varieties also were considerably higher. Loose lard finished up 1½@2c and edible tallow gained 3½c....

The magazine can keep this up for pages and pages. Still, trade writing is not without its charms. *Milling & Baking News*'s use of the symbol @ in place of a dash in price ranges is, I believe, unique. The *News* is also the only publication I know of that consistently uses the word "firm" precisely. Most business writers treat "firm" as a synonym for "company" or "corporation." It is not, in strict usage. A firm, according to *Webster's Third New International Dictionary*, is "a partnership of two or more persons not recognized as a legal person distinct from the members composing it." Editor Sosland — who once had a brand of flour named after him (Big Boy) — also maintains an idiosyncratic but absolute ban on the word "however."

As a summer intern at *Milling & Baking News*, I wasn't qualified to write the dense grain-market analyses that are the heart of the magazine (I was, though, once allowed to contribute an editorial praising an astronaut who had smuggled a sandwich into outer space). My usual beat was much humbler: obituaries, new-product announcements, rewritten press releases. Most trade magazines depend heavily on press releases, often printing them verbatim. It was a matter of pride at *Milling & Baking News* that a press release was never run without our at least switching around the order of the clauses and changing all the "he stated"s to "he said"s.

New-product announcements are the most fascinating part of almost any food-related trade magazine. "*Ex-Cel*, a microcrystalline cellulose powder, adds bulk to food products without adding calories," the January issue of *Prepared Foods* reports. "When mixed with water, *Ex-Cel* forms a ribbon paste ideal for low-calorie spaghetti, macaroni, and other formed products." Another issue of the same magazine announces "a fluid, oil-based coloring" ingredient that "yields a butter color on popcorn or extruded snacks." Butter color has what the prepared-food industry calls "eye appeal." A closely related concept is that of "mouthfeel," as in "Our formulary explains how to use Avicel MCC [another cellulose bulking additive] to make a coleslaw dressing with controlled flow, cling, and improved creaminess without sacrificing high-fat mouthfeel." (Eye appeal and mouthfeel are often difficult to improve without sacrificing yet another desirable quality — "consumer labeling appeal.")

Some of the most popular new food products are ones that enable manufacturers to replace expensive ingredients. "HOW TO MILK CHO-COLATE," reads the headline on an advertisement in *Candy Industry* for Durkee's line of "coating fats," "cocoa butter equivalents," and other chocolate extenders and substitutes. A similar product is Viobin Cocoa Replacer, which, according to an announcement in the January issue of *Food Technology*, "is made from defatted wheat germ and 5% added carbohydrate which is pressure toasted to a rich brown. It is then ground to a fine powder which is similar in color and texture to processed cocoas."

Even better than new-product announcements are patents for new processes and ingredients. Here are a few garnered from recent issues of *Food Technology*:

U.S. 4,473,592...Process for producing a meatbased product having a meat core of substantially constant cross-section of relatively dense compacted meat and an outer coating of fat which is mobile in the uniform state.

U.S. 4,477,476...Method for converting salmon green eggs into a roe product in which the green egg is agitated in a saturated aqueous solution of salt containing a nitrite to impart a scarlet color, after which the salted egg is dried and agitated in a saturated aqueous solution of a malate containing sufficient nitrite to impart scarlet coloring.

U.S. 4,478,861...Method of preparing a frozen food product in which a plurality of cooked pieces is treated to remove free water to form voids after which food mass is subjected to a freezing gas to surface freeze pieces while leaving some unfrozen moisture thereon. Dry powder additives are then introduced with agitation to uniformly coat pieces, after which they are fully frozen throughout and transferred to a storage container for later reconstitution.

Most people probably think they would never eat a frozen food product in which a plurality of cooked pieces had been treated to remove free water to form voids. But in fact almost everybody cheerfully eats stuff like this. Much of the food that is served in modern restaurants traces its ancestry directly to the patents page of *Food Technology.* ''Pre-cooked,'' ''pre-browned,'' and ''portion-controlled'' frozen-food items are ''microwaved'' and either ''plated'' immediately or, in the fancier establishments, gussied up with inexpensive ''profit-makers'' like olive bits or almond slivers before being ''menued'' as expensive, ''signature'' entrées. There isn't much need for chefs anymore. Kitchen technology has advanced to the point at which a pre-browned slice of portion-controlled prime rib can be microwaved in a minute or two and then kept in a holding oven for eight hours or more without losing eye appeal.

8 *PLAYBOY'S* DOCTRINE OF MALE*
HARVEY COX

This essay, written by theologian Harvey Cox, asks an interesting question: why is *Playboy* so popular? Why does its readership exceed that of ''all the independent religious magazines, serious political and cultural journals, and literary periodicals put together?'' It isn't because of the nudes, Cox suggests, because other ''girlie'' magazines show more nudes and are more revealing.

What *Playboy* does, brilliantly and perversely, Cox argues, is give its readers (who are mostly males) something they lack and desperately need — *an image of what it is to be a male.* The family, and other institutions in society, used to take care of this matter. But as society has changed, this job has been taken over by peer groups and, in particular, the mass media. Cox quotes the sociologist David Riesman, who believes that American character has changed, from being ''inner directed'' to ''other directed.'' Instead of acting on the basis of values that we considered correct, we now look and see what other people are doing and take our cues from them.

Thus *Playboy* serves its readers by giving them a carefully integrated package of stories and articles and advertisements glorifying a certain attitude toward life — and women, in particular. To be a male (in *Playboy*'s image of one, that is), one must buy the right products and relate to women in certain ways — one must treat sex as a leisure activity and women as ''accessories.''

This means that sex is always casual and that there is no need for permanent relationships. Women, like any other consumer objects, are portrayed as ''detachable and disposable.'' After all, one cannot be a playboy (and ''play the field'') if one is involved or ''tied down'' to a particular woman.

The problem with this philosophy, Cox tells us, is that it is destructive, in

* Reprinted with permission. Copyright © 1962. *Christianity & Crisis,* 537 West 121st Street, New York, N.Y. 10027.

several ways. Men become slaves to fashion, which is always changing, and this generates a great deal of identity anxiety. And sexuality cannot be turned into a consumer item and separated from relationships and love. Thus, as its readers get older and find a need for relationships, they stop subscribing to *Playboy*. The magazine cannot help many men with a basic problem they all have, a "deep set fear of sex" and of women. *Playboy* offers an aspirin, so to speak, when something much stronger is needed…and is ultimately antisexual, in that its doctrine of how one relates to women is unreal and, worst of all for playboy types, unsatisfying. *Playboy* deals with sex and women by trying to keep them at a safe distance and by trivializing them. And it doesn't work.

Sometime this month over one million American young men will place sixty cents on a counter somewhere and walk away with a copy of *Playboy*, one of the most spectacular successes in the entire history of American journalism. When one remembers that every copy will probably be seen by several other people in college dormitories and suburban rumpus rooms, the total readership in any one month easily exceeds that of all the independent religious magazines, serious political and cultural journals, and literary periodicals put together.

What accounts for this uncanny reception? What factors in American life have combined to allow *Playboy's* ambitious young publisher, Hugh Hefner, to pyramid his jackpot into a chain of night clubs, TV spectaculars, bachelor tours to Europe, and special discount cards? What impact does *Playboy* really have?

Clearly *Playboy's* astonishing popularity is not attributable solely to pin-up girls. For sheer nudity its pictorial art cannot compete with such would-be competitors as *Dude* and *Escapade*. Rather, *Playboy* appeals to a highly mobile, increasingly affluent group of young readers, mostly between eighteen and thirty, who want much more from their drugstore reading than bosoms and thighs. They need a total image of what it means to be a man. And Mr. Hefner's *Playboy* has no hesitancy about telling them.

Why should such a need arise? David Riesman has argued that the responsibility for character formation in our society has shifted from the family to the peer group and to the mass media peer group surrogates. Things are changing so rapidly that one who is equipped by his family with inflexible, highly internalized values becomes unable to deal with the accelerated pace of change and with the varying contexts in which he is called upon to function. This is especially true in the area of consumer values toward which the "other-directed person" is increasingly oriented.

Within the confusing plethora of mass media signals and peer group values, *Playboy* fills a special need. For the insecure young man with newly acquired time and money on his hands who still feels uncertain about his consumer skills, *Playboy* supplies a comprehensive and authoritative guidebook to this foreboding new world to which he now has access. It tells him not only who to be; it tells him *how* to be it, and even provides consolation outlets for those who secretly feel that they have not quite made it.

In supplying for the other-directed consumer of leisure both the normative identity image and the means for achieving it, *Playboy* relies on a careful integration of copy and advertising material. The comic book that appeals to a younger generation with an analogous problem skillfully intersperses illustrations of incredibly muscled men and excessively mammalian women with advertisements for body-building gimmicks and foam rubber brassiere supplements. Thus the thin-chested comic book readers of both sexes are thoughtfully supplied with both the ends and the means for attaining a spurious brand of maturity. *Playboy* merely continues the comic book tactic for the next age group. Since within every identity crisis, whether in 'teens or twenties, there is usually a sexual identity problem, *Playboy* speaks to those who desperately want to know what it means to be a *man*, and more specifically a *male*, in today's world.

Both the image of man and the means for its attainment exhibit a remarkable consistency in *Playboy*. The skilled consumer is cool and unruffled. He savors sports cars, liquor, high fidelity, and book club selections with a casual, unhurried aplomb. Though he must certainly *have* and *use* the latest consumption item, he must not permit himself to get too attached to it. The style will change and he must always be ready to adjust. His persistent anxiety that he may mix a drink incorrectly, enjoy a jazz group that is passé, or wear last year's necktie style is comforted by an authoritative tone in *Playboy* beside which papal encyclicals sound irresolute.

"Don't hesitate," he is told, "this assertive, self-assured weskit is what every man of taste wants for the fall season." Lingering doubts about his masculinity are extirpated by the firm assurance that "real men demand this ruggedly masculine smoke" (cigar ad). Though "the ladies will swoon for you, no matter what they promise, don't give them a puff. This cigar is for men only." A fur-lined canvas field jacket is described as "the most masculine thing since the cave man." What to be and how to be it are both made unambiguously clear.

But since being a male necessitates some kind of relationship to females, *Playboy* fearlessly confronts this problem too, and solves it by the consistent application of the same formula. Sex becomes one of the items of leisure activity that the knowledgeable consumer of leisure handles with his characteristic skill and detachment. The girl becomes a desirable, indeed an indispensable "Playboy accessory."

In a question-answering column entitled: "The Playboy Advisor," queries about smoking equipment (how to break in a meerschaum pipe), cocktail preparation (how to mix a "Yellow Fever"), and whether or not to wear suspenders with a vest, alternate with questions about what to do with girls who complicate the cardinal principle of casualness, either by suggesting marriage or by some other impulsive gesture toward permanent relationship. The infallible answer from this oracle never varies: sex must be contained, at all costs, within the entertainment-recreation area. Don't let her get "serious."

After all, the most famous feature of the magazine is its monthly fold-out photo of a *play*mate. She is the symbol par excellence of recreational sex. When play time is over, the playmate's function ceases, so she must be made to understand the rules of the game. As the crew-cut young man in a *Playboy* cartoon says to the rumpled and disarrayed girl he is passionately embracing, "Why speak of love at a time like this?"

The magazine's fiction purveys the same kind of severely departmentalized sex. Although the editors have recently dressed up the contents of *Playboy* with contributions by Hemingway, Bemelmans, and even a Chekhov translation, the regular run of stories relies on a repetitious and predictable formula. A successful young man, either single or somewhat less than ideally married — a figure with whom readers have no difficulty identifying — encounters a gorgeous and seductive woman who makes no demands on him except sex. She is the prose duplication of the cool-eyed but hot-blooded playmate of the fold-out page.

Drawing heavily on the phantasy life of all young Americans, the writers utilize for their stereotyped heroines the hero's school teacher, his secretary, an old girl friend, or the girl who brings her car into the garage where he works. The happy issue is always a casual but satisfying sexual experience with no entangling alliances whatever. Unlike the women he knows in real life, the *Playboy* reader's fictional girl friends know their place and ask for nothing more. They present no danger of permanent involvement. Like any good accessory, they are detachable and disposable.

Many of the advertisements reinforce the sex-accessory identification in another way by attributing female characteristics to the items they sell. Thus a full page ad for the MG assures us that this car is not only "the smoothest pleasure machine" on the road and that having one is a "love-affair," but most importantly, "you drive it — it doesn't drive you." The ad ends with the equivocal question, "Is it a date?"

Playboy insists that its message is one of liberation. Its gospel frees us from captivity to the puritanical "high-hat brigade." It solemnly crusades for "frankness" and publishes scores of letters congratulating it for its unblushing "candor." Yet the whole phenomenon of which *Playboy* is only a part vividly illustrates the awful fact of a new kind of tyranny.

Those liberated by technology and increased prosperity to new worlds of leisure now become the anxious slaves of dictatorial taste-makers. Obsequiously waiting for the latest signal on what is cool and what is awkward, they are paralyzed by the fear that they may hear pronounced on them that dread sentence occasionally intoned by "The Playboy Advisor": "you goofed!" Leisure is thus swallowed up in apprehensive competitiveness, its liberating potential transformed into a self-destructive compulsion to consume only what is *au courant. Playboy* mediates the World of the most high into one section of the consumer world, but it is a word of bondage, not of freedom.

Nor will *Playboy*'s synthetic doctrine of man stand the test of scrutiny. Psychoanalysts constantly remind us how deeply seated sexuality is in the human self. But if they didn't remind us, we would soon discover it anyway in our own experience. As much as the human male might like to terminate his relationship with a woman as he snaps off the stereo, or store her for special purposes like a camel's hair jacket, it really can't be done. And anyone with a modicum of experience with women knows it can't be done. Perhaps this is the reason why *Playboy*'s readership drops off so sharply after the age of thirty.

Playboy really feeds on the presence of a repressed fear of involvement with women, which for various reasons is still present in many otherwise adult Americans. So *Playboy*'s version of sexuality grows increasingly irrelevant as authentic sexual maturity is achieved.

The male identity crisis to which *Playboy* speaks has at its roots a deep-set fear of sex, a fear that is uncomfortably combined with fascination. *Playboy* strives to resolve this antinomy by reducing the terrible proportions of sexuality, its power and its passion, to a packageable consumption item. Thus in *Playboy*'s iconography, the nude woman symbolizes total sexual accessibility, but demands nothing from the observer. "You drive it — it doesn't drive you." The terror of sex, which cannot be separated from its ecstasy, is dissolved. But this futile attempt to reduce the *mysterium tremendum* of the sexual fails to solve the problem of being a man. For sexuality is the basic form of all human relationship, and therein lies its terror and its power.

Karl Barth has called this basic relational form of man's life *Mitmensch*, co-humanity. This means that becoming fully human, in this case a human male, necessitates not having the other totally exposed to me and my purposes — while I remain uncommitted — but exposing myself to the risk of encounter with the other by reciprocal self-exposure. The story of man's refusal to be so exposed goes back to the story of Eden and is expressed by man's desire to control the other rather than to *be with* the other. It is basically the fear to be one's self, a lack of the "courage to be."

Thus any theological critique of *Playboy* that focuses on its "lewdness" will misfire completely. *Playboy* and its less successful imitators are not "sex magazines" at all. They are basically antisexual. They dilute and dissipate authentic sexuality by reducing it to an accessory, by keeping it at a safe distance.

It is precisely because these magazines are antisexual that they deserve the most searching kind of theological criticism. They foster a heretical doctrine of man, one at radical variance with the biblical view. For *Playboy*'s man, others — especially women — are *for* him. They are his leisure accessories, his playthings. For the Bible, man only becomes fully man by being *for* the other.

Moralistic criticisms of *Playboy* fail because its anti-moralism is one of the few places in which *Playboy* is right. But if Christians bear the name of

One who was truly man because he was totally *for* the other, and if it is in him that we know who God is and what human life is for, then we must see in *Playboy* the latest and slickest episode in man's continuing refusal to be fully human.

9 HAS *MS.* UNDERGONE A SEX CHANGE?*
Susan Milligan

According to the author of the article that follows, *Ms.* has undergone a radical transformation and abandoned its feminist philosophy. She writes, "Its iconoclastic message has faded; the new message is that the way for women to succeed is the same as it has long been for men: acquire money and status."

This essay is an impressionistic content analysis of *Ms.*, which compares the kind of articles *Ms.* used to carry with the ones it now carries. Content analysis is a methodology used by researchers to gain insights into what people think and believe by examining what they read (or watch on television or listen to on the radio, for example). The theory is that people tend to read material that supports their beliefs and values, so by studying these matters in magazine articles (or other media), we can get, indirectly, information about the readers.

When sociologists do content analysis, they are very precise about what they study and design their analyses so they can get data that can be quantified. Content analyses are always comparative: researchers might look at how one magazine has changed over the years or might compare several magazines for a given time period. They might also combine these methods and look at how several magazines have changed over a period of time. For example, a sociologist named E. Barbara Phillips made a content analysis of *Ms.* (and *Family Weekly*) between 1974 and 1976 focusing on the occupations of the women written about in *Ms.* and *Family Weekly*.

In looking at a random sampling of eight issues of *Ms.* and sixteen issues of *Family Weekly*, she found that 48 percent of the articles in *Ms.* focused on political life and public service while none of the articles in *Family Weekly* were on this subject. Conversely, *Ms.* had no articles on housewifery or mothercraft while *Family Circle* had 61 percent of its articles on this topic. As Phillips writes, "…not a single *Ms.* heroine is primarily a homemaker. While *Ms.* heroines may

* Reprinted by permission from *The Washington Monthly.* Copyright by THE WASHINGTON MONTHLY CO., 1711 Connecticut Avenue, NW, Washington D.C. 20009. (202) 462–0128. October, 1986.

be wives and mothers as well as writers, politicos, or professionals, this side of their lives is downplayed, if mentioned at all."

The essay on *Ms.* we are to read is not a quantitative one, but that doesn't mean it isn't correct. The main question is whether the writer has been fair in her analysis and hasn't chosen material to support her case and neglected material that would have challenged her conclusions. You will have to be the judge of this. Does she offer evidence that seems reasonable? If you want, you can examine *Ms.* yourself and see what you find.

But for the logo in the corner, it could be *Self*. "Re-Making Love," reads the July cover headline that runs over a photo of a man kissing the bare shoulder of a carefully made-up woman. Yet this is *Ms.*, the country's leading feminist magazine. So, what does *Ms.*, which claims "the most influential women in America" as its readers, have to say about the current condition of love-making?

"'Re-Making Love' was chosen as our cover story," write the editors, "because sexuality is the area of our lives where the power balance has changed the most and is likely to stay changed." And how has that balance changed? Feminists used to get angry at men who treated women as sex objects; now *Ms.* says sex objects are okay — if they're men. The authors of this article write: "Whether in 1950 or 1980, casual sex has always been *the* macho symbol, and very few men were complaining as long as they controlled the action." Now, they boast, women can control the action, too, and they applaud women such as one who told them, "I have lovers because what else is there in life that's so much fun as turning on a new man, interesting him, conquering him?" They also scoff at George Leonard, who, in a 1982 *Esquire* article, deplored the "loss of loving, nurturing, long-term" sex. Have we ever come a long way.

Claiming *"the* macho symbol" as a woman's right is just one example of how *Ms.* has come to encourage some of the very values it used to condemn. While still officially feminist, *Ms.* is a compromised version of the radical magazine it was fourteen years ago. The magazine that declared in its first issue that it wanted to be as "serious, outrageous, satisfying, sad, funky, intimate, global, compassionate, and full of change as women's lives really are" has retreated from that complexity. *Ms.* is now full of articles such as "How to Manage a Fear of Power," "Packing It In: A 10-Day Trip in a Carry-On Bag," "Toys for Free Grown-ups: A Consumer Guide to Sex Gadgets, Potions, and Videos," and "The New Computer Diet — From Chocolate Chips to Microchips." There is little anymore that distinguishes *Ms.* from other mainstream women's magazines such as *Cosmopolitan, Mademoiselle, Workng Woman*, or even magazines such as *Playgirl*.

"When *Ms.* was launched scarcely a decade ago, it was a different world," proclaims a recent trade ad. "We led the way, and we changed the world. So much so that we changed ourselves...." And so the magazine did. Perhaps the biggest change in *Ms.* is that it no longer challenges the greed, selfishness, and materialism it once claimed subjugated women and imprisoned men. Today's *Ms.* not only condones those values, but offers itself as a primer on how women can live by them.

In 1972, when modern feminism was hitting its stride, *Ms.* published its first issue, providing a forum for feminist political debate. Co-founded by Gloria Steinem and Patricia Carbine, *Ms.* was meant to fill a void left by traditional women's magazines. The first issue promised to examine the problems and hopes raised by the changing roles of women. Nearly every article questioned a cultural, political, or social norm. Even the magazine's name made a statement that women would not be defined by their roles as wives or mothers. In those first years the magazine grappled with a wide range of tough issues. Ann Crittenden Scott proposed in "The Value of Work" that housework be considered real work and that men and women have equal control over family finances. "Three Lives in Appalachia" damned stripmining and black lung disease in the hills of Kentucky. John Kenneth Galbraith wrote that American society identified "increasing consumption of goods and services with increasing happiness" and explained how it used women to build the demand for, and to manage, all those consumables. There were articles such as "A Legislative Agenda for the 93rd Congress," which proposed tax, welfare, and health insurance reforms; "Defusing the Atomic Establishment"; "Child Care Leave for Fathers"; "Economic Reality and the Limits of Feminism"; and "Abortion Reform: Never Again."

As the years passed, plenty of the women beating on the doors and windows of male-dominated institutions — many of them *Ms.* readers — succeeded in breaking in. Unfortunately, many of them are now so intent on rearranging the furniture inside to suit themselves that they've forgotten they swore to tear the whole rotten structure down and build anew. *Ms.* seems to have conveniently forgotten as well and has joined in the re-decorating. Its iconoclastic message has faded; the new message is that the way for women to succeed is the same as it has long been for men: acquire money and status.

The women *Ms.* has written about lately are almost always well paid, professional, and powerful; the female forklift driver is rarely spoken of in the same breath. In the July issue, Emily Card profiles ten women who "exert great influence" on the U.S. economy. They include a corporate vice president, a judge, a congresswoman, a commissioner of the Securities and Exchange Commission, and a member of the Federal Reserve Board of Governors. The month before Sallie Bingham of the Bingham communications empire was the focus of the cover story.

Even when *Ms.* still grasps the "correct" rhetoric, its examples often mock the effort. Last November, the cover story "For Love and Money" promised a "changed definition of success." The women profiled are described as "successful yet underrewarded, happy yet still striving and dreaming." So who are all these underrewarded heroines? First is Judith Langer, whose consulting firm probes the predilections of the American consumer — for $2,800 per session. Sessions such as this one: "The women gathered at the long table are sharing their deepest feelings about flannel sheets — feelings they may have never before known they had." Sessions that help industry exploit the way women have been encouraged to define themselves through their purchases: "Working women often develop 'two selves' in order to provide needed separation from their job. For example, some wear fancy underwear beneath their work clothes.... Others buy themselves 'treats,' anything from an ice-cream cone to a new blouse, just as a reward for making it through another week."

In the list there are two more women who run the same kind of consulting business (and gross $1.5 million per year), as well as an "executive bodyguard," an accountant, a woman who works in the Office of Consumer Affairs in Boston, two lawyers, four film directors, one community organizer who helps Korean immigrants adjust to living in New York City, and several artists. In discussing the artists, the article describes a meeting of women artists, critics, and dealers where "the women get down to the real business of the meeting — an exchange of information not often heard among artists." A thoughtful discussion of the sources of their inspirations, perhaps? No. They're more interested in "how they're getting shows, who was buying what, and for how much." Those who sell works for $30,000–$75,000 are revered, though they complain they haven't "achieved parity with their megabuck male counterparts."

Ms. has plenty of ideas on how women should use their money once they make it. It has run stories such as "New Frontiers in Jewelry Design," "The Right Shoe: A Guide to the Immortal Sole," "The New Appeal of Hotel Dining Rooms," and "Tips on Tipping," as well as articles on investing, business plans, and tax write-offs. A recent article "The Joy of Risk-Taking," plugs hiking trips in Tibet, scuba diving in the Caribbean, and skiing in Norway. *Ms.*'s reader profile says its readers "shop in gourmet stores more than anybody — even more than readers of *Harper's Bazaar*." They also buy more rum and tequila, more fine china, more lingerie, more 35mm cameras, more books, more imported cars, and more fine jewelry and gems than readers of any other women's magazine. Accordingly, *Ms.* ran an article that suggested its readers buy as gifts $75 teakettles, $50 icebuckets, and $40 high-tech corkscrews, which, it said, "reflect the way we live now."

Concern for social issues has been eclipsed by concern for "Pampering Yourself," as a February article was titled. That article confides: "Being confined to your quarters on a blustery day can make for a delightful time if you celebrate your own company as you would that of a special friend. Wear something you feel great in, take out the good china, take a bath instead of the customary shower, dab on some perfume before going to bed — whether or not you sleep alone."

Noting in the profile that its readers "cook for fun more than anybody — even readers of *Food and Wine*," *Ms.* has even found space for gourmet hints. In a July article on buying and storing fancy cheeses, the author writes: "Experts differ as to how cheese should be stored. Some say it should be wrapped in wax paper so the cheese is not suffocated. Others say that cheese should not be exposed to air and should be sealed in plastic wrap or foil. Whatever the case, a little drying usually does not affect quality." If the author seems to be straying a bit far for even the most laissez-faire feminist reader, she reins herself in by giving up a third of the next page to praise for women cheesemakers.

Larding this kind of article with leftover radicalisms is common. An April article on "Dream Houses," which catalogs reader responses to an earlier questionnaire, reveals that *Ms.* readers "had strong ideas about the 'character' of a house....Fireplaces, gardens, and lots of closet space cropped up over and over again...and virtually everybody had something to say about kitchens and laundry rooms." Sensing, perhaps, that this was getting a little too *House & Garden*, there's a brief bow towards conscience. "Some of you even expressed misgivings at thinking about a dream house. Said one: 'This was a lovely fantasy! But I feel slightly guilty because my greed is boundless, and recently I've seen and lived in Third World countries.'"

In the same spirit, in an article on buying computers, Lindsy Van Gelder writes, "How would you like to type 'RR is a MCP' and have your computer keystroke 'Ronald Reagan is a male chauvinist pig'?" Right on.

Ms. used to run articles that criticized society's emphasis on a woman's appearance. The magazine that in 1973 printed "Alice in Cosmeticland," which ridiculed the rituals of using makeup to please a man, now carries as many ads for cosmetics as any mainstream beauty magazine; fashion and grooming make up 30 percent of *Ms.* ads. In fact, *Ms.* recently announced that its entire November issue will be devoted to fashion.

That shouldn't be surprising if you saw the May "Beauty of Health" issue, which shows a woman leaning out of her bath wearing only strategically placed bubbles and perfect makeup. (There is one issue every year devoted entirely to health, though last year there were two, including an August issue on "Staying Fit For Life.") In between informative stories on women's health care centers and the National Black Women's Health Network are stories such as "Do you Have Color Anxiety?" an analysis of the fun of wearing bright colors, a story that includes information on plumping out wrinkles with collagen injections, and — the clincher for the healthy feminist — "Going for the Big 'O': Discoveries About Easily Orgasmic Women."

Ms. also now runs articles on men's appearance. In an "exclusive" interview with February's coverman Richard Gere [*Ms.* was on the right on our cover; *Playgirl* on the left], Gloria Steinem hails Gere, her "premier example" of the new "sexual and sensual" male lead, who, she says, has displaced the "ordinary looks of a Dustin Hoffman or Donald Sutherland — or a Woody Allen, Al Pacino, and others...." In reclaiming the importance of prettiness, *Ms.* has at least gone egalitarian.

You might assume that at the very least *Ms.* would refuse to encourage practices that are dangerous to one's health. Especially since the first issue of the magazine stated that a humane advertising policy was an important goal: "Obviously, *Ms.* won't solicit or accept ads, whatever the product they're presenting, that are downright insulting to women. Nor will we accept product categories that might be harmful." Moreover, a survey last year revealed that "our readers identified health coverage as the number one reason you read *Ms.*"

But just how harmful must a product be before it offends *Ms.*'s editorial board? Publisher Patricia Carbine says the only ads the magazine refuses outright are those for products such as bust developers. Yet *Ms.* regularly runs cigarette ads (and always has), even though smoking was clearly recognized as unsafe in the early 1970s and is now the leading cause of cancer deaths among women. Although tobacco companies have increasingly directed their campaigns at women, depicting smoking as both assertive and sexy, *Ms.* has only infrequently, in general articles on health, pointed to its dangers. "We write about subjects when they're news," Carbine says. "What we have done consistently in regard to smoking is to report news as it breaks."

Following a complaint from a reader that running tobacco ads in its 1985 health issue was offensive, *Ms.* editors responded that they "depend on advertising to 'pay the rent' and keep the magazine financially healthy [ad revenue was down 11.2 percent last year]....*Ms.* readers have the intelligence to make their own choices if they have up-to-date, relevant information about products...."

Vacuous articles and articles that promote the lifestyle of the powerful and well-to-do are certainly common enough in the magazine market. But one expects more of the country's most influential feminist magazine. After all, *Ms.* even refers to itself as "the magazine of record for women."

It is true that there are articles in *Ms.* about poor women, pink-collar workers, and Third World patriarchies — articles that expose serious problems. Last December, for example, *Ms.* reported the spate of miscarriages resulting from the Union Carbide plant leak at Bhopal, India. *Ms.* also was responsible for the first national survey on campus date rape, which revealed staggering statistics on its prevalence.

But this kind of story is rare. Furthermore, the analysis offered on important feminist issues is too often limited, the proposals for change too often narrow, and the space given to either, too small. While the early *Ms.* sometimes ran articles on silly subjects, they tended to be short; the bulk of the magazine was devoted to serious issues. Now the reverse is true.

Few magazines are willing to struggle with the difficult problems that still face women. Wasn't *Ms.* founded to offer more than *Glamour*, *Mademoiselle*, or *Vogue*, which, for all their fluff, have taken to running legislative updates on issues that affect women, as well as articles on sexual harassment, spouse abuse, and pay equity?

Why has *Ms.* changed so much? In large part, it seems, because its readership has. *Ms.* is proud of its nearly 480,000 regular readers, whom it describes in a recent ad: "*Ms.* stands squarely on the cutting edge, and our readers are the readers who are making it happen. They're the innovators, the opinion-makers." *Ms.*'s most recent reader profile supplies the statistics. *Ms.* readers are "much better educated than readers of any other women's magazine...better than readers of *Esquire, U.S. News, Time.* 71 percent went to college...26 percent have a $40,000 plus household income. 41 percent own stock. They have an average $88,000 each invested. More work in professional specialties than...readers of *Forbes, Fortune, Money,* and *Business Week.* 13 percent own their own business. 35 percent are in management positions." And, of course, *Ms.* readers "run, jog, swim, play tennis more often than anybody — including readers of *Self.*"

Without question, the women's movement has radically changed the boundaries of a woman's and, to a lesser extent, a man's, role in American society. And *Ms.* helped lead the way. *Ms.* urged women to attain the positions that have given them the power to make change. The tragedy is that it no longer pushes them to demand that change. Instead of challenging its readers, it panders to them: the economics of magazine marketing has taken over.

"Think of the magazine as a woman," says Carbine. "There are virtually no women of any age in the country who have not been on a sort of personal journey over the history of *Ms.*....There are many diverse things to write about precisely because of things the magazine helped set in motion....In the earlier days, we spent a lot of space examining where women really were, vis-a-vis society. It's accurate to say that we don't have to do that anymore. What's now accurate — and more fun — is the ability to look at solutions as opposed to devoting space to quantifying the problem." But instead of offering "solutions" that show women how to play by today's rules, *Ms.* would do better to build on its original ideals. The early *Ms.* certainly didn't have all the answers, and sometimes it was wrong. But at least in its groping, it challenged the worst of the status quo, and pointed to the possibility of a society where relationships could be more than conquests, where individual worth wouldn't be measured by the money one made or the prestige of the job one held.

By publishing heaps of articles on gaining traditional status jobs, on being pretty, on playing sexual power games, and on buying the toys of the entitled, *Ms.* insinuates that these are what should be important. And in that pile, *Ms.* also buries its occasional political insight — and its credibility. After all, how seriously can anyone take a story about a welfare mother trying to break out of her Chicago ghetto when the pages are perfumed with the cloying sweetness of Calvin Klein's "Obsession?" As an old feminist saying goes, "context is everything."

BOOKS

Because we have become so fascinated with television in recent years we have tended to neglect other media. We do so at our peril. For while television may dominate our leisure time and may be having a major influence on our decision making (about soaps and senators), if you take a long-range perspective, it is the book, more than any other medium, which has most profoundly affected our lives and shaped our societies.

Think, for example, of the power of the Bible. In the West, at least, it has had an immense impact upon our consciousness and our values. The stories of the Old Testament, for example, are deeply embedded in our belief structure.

Think, also, of the awesome impact of the writings of Karl Marx. His books, and the books of those influenced by him, have profoundly affected political thought and now many countries have adopted his ideas to varying degrees — from democratic socialist countries such as Sweden to communist countries such as Russia and China. The fact that there are such profound differences among Russia, China, and other communist countries such as Yugoslavia and Hungary, shows that Marxism is not monolithic and that countries often shape their Marxism to fit in with other beliefs and values they have.

Many important books seem, at first glance, to have no relation to social and political matters...but are looked upon as just great stories. If you probe a bit, however, you often find that these books also have an important ideological dimension to them. As an example let us consider *Robinson Crusoe*. It is generally regarded as a story for children but, as Ian Watt argues[1], it is much more than that. In an essay on the book, Watt points out that we tend to regard it not as a novel but more as a myth, like *Don Juan*, *Faust* and *Don Quixote*.

"Their basic plots," he says, "their enduring images, all exhibit a single-minded pursuit by the protagonist of one of the characteristic aspirations of Western man." Young children may read *Robinson Crusoe* as an adventure, but they get much more than that from it. The book, Watt suggests, "is related to three essential themes of modern civilization — which we can briefly designate as 'Back to Nature,' 'The Dignity of Labor,' and 'Economic Man.'" Western society, according to Watt, has turned this story into a myth "by retaining only what its unconscious needs dictate and forgetting everything else."

The first of these themes, which focuses on "nature," is one that plays a major role in American social and political thought. We see ourselves as living in nature (in contrast, for example, with Europe, which we see as "culture" and being institution-bound). In nature it is the individual who is basic, since there are no artificial institutions. In American thought we modified these notions and now are willing to accept some institutions, but the fewer the better. That is because we see institutions, especially government, as hampering individual initiative. Thus Crusoe becomes recreated in the figure of the American pioneer, who also lives in freedom in nature.

In a state of nature one must rely on one's own labor; in the story, Crusoe is able to live quite nicely, though he is fortunate in being marooned on an island where nature was provident and he had the use of a number of implements from civilization. The impact of Defoe's detailed description of Crusoe's labors is profound. "Eventually they fasten upon our imaginative life a picture of the human lot as heroic only when productive, and of man as capable of redemption only through untiring labor."

Crusoe is, ultimately, Watt argues, "an economic man," who is dominated by the pursuit of his self-interest and has little room for "higher emotional needs." He is capable of enormous enterprise but his life is too one-dimensional and is ultimately unsatisfying. What is important for our considerations is that Robinson Crusoe, as a culture hero, is so dominating. He crowds out other culture heroes in our pantheon of mythological figures, leaving us with a distorted and rather narrow sense of human possibility.

What Watt is suggesting is that characters such as Robinson Crusoe exert a profound influence on us, whether we realize this or not. We identify with this hero and internalize his values, which become our values. Mythic figures like Robinson Crusoe, then, play an important role for millions of people and have a significant political dimension to them. When thinking about the media, we must not underestimate the power of books. Books may not always (or even very often) have our immediate attention but they may (in subtle ways) be shaping our consciousness and our world.

REFERENCE

1. Ian Watt, "*Robinson Crusoe* as a Myth," *Essays in Criticism: A Quarterly Journal of Literary Criticism*, April, 1951, 95–119.

10 PUBLISHING IN THE '80S: FROM THE AUTHOR[*]

Patricia Holt

There is a considerable amount of controversy among scholars about how much time the typical American spends reading books — of any kind. We have some statistics about book sales that seem to be pretty accurate: sales per capita rose from 2.75 in 1970 to 4.89 in 1980. But what does this mean? Is 4.89 books per capita good or bad? And what kind of books are we talking about — romances, trashy novels, or "serious" books? Do people read the books they buy? That's another matter to think about. We really don't know.

If the average American is watching more than three and a half hours of television and listening to the radio for a couple of hours each day, how much time does that leave for reading books? Especially when you factor into the analysis statistics that indicate that on average we also spend another couple of hours per day reading newspapers and magazines.

It is with these thoughts as a background that we should read the following essay on the state of the book publishing industry in the 1980s. It is important that we recognize that books must compete with radio, television, records, newspapers, magazines, and other forms of entertainment for a share of the public's time and disposable income. (How much book reading, we might ask, is done for pleasure and is self-motivated and how much is done because it is required for courses or for the job?)

The essay is based on an informal survey of a number of executives in the book publishing industry, discussing the problems they face and the general shape of the industry. As we might imagine, opinions vary, from some who think the book publishing industry is a disaster area to others who think it is doing very well.

Editors are often torn between the need to publish books that will make money and the desire to publish books that they think deserve to be published but which are not necessarily good commercial properties. Editors must also compete with one another for name authors and must think about tie-ins (in the case of novels) with movies or television and book clubs. Most authors struggle to get published while some big name authors get millions for jotting down a plot idea on the back of an envelope. In short, the book publishing industry is a complicated, fast-moving, and fascinating one whose broad parameters are sketched out in the essay that follows. It is written by a person with a great deal of experience and knowledge and is based on interviews with industry leaders.

In a rare public appearance earlier this year (for the Afghanistan Refugee Fund and City Arts and Lectures), British writer Doris Lessing told a San Francisco audience why she recently pulled off a hoax on the publishing industry by writing two novels under the name Jane Somers.

Lessing had been concerned for some time that to the publishing industry (not her readers) the stature and celebrity of her name had become more important than the quality of her work itself. So she set out to see if an unknown writer of equal talent to Doris Lessing could publish a work of fiction successfully.

An amusing irony to her efforts, Lessing said, was that only two people guessed the real identity of Jane Somers. One was a British editor who inquired politely if the author had not been "influenced" in some manner by Doris Lessing. The other was Lessing's editor at Alfred A. Knopf, Robert Gottlieb who, in his blunt American way, "rang me up immediately and said, 'Doris, who the hell do you think you're kidding?' He thought the whole thing in excruciatingly bad taste."

Gottlieb did publish the book, however, and although generally it was not reviewed well, Lessing said that "when (a few) well-known critics rang up Knopf and asked why Knopf did not do more with the book (i.e., publicize it better), Gottlieb said, 'I could not do this because there was nothing to sell.' If you brood about that for a moment it's quite interesting. We have now reached a point where a novel is not enough, or a book is not enough. You have to have a photograph and biography and the whole personality thing."

This "oversell" or commercialism that has crept into the industry typifies what is perhaps the least interesting yet most alarming aspect of publishing — its bigness, its blockbusteritis, its boom-or-bust mentality. Because of this, Lessing said, publishing has become "a literary machine" on both sides of the Atlantic.

"It's very automatic, very mechanical, and I think...we should look at it as coldly as we look at how, say, paper is manufactured or potatoes are sold. Because that is exactly the spirit of most publishers now. They're extremely commercial, much more commercial than they were."

Just how commercial publishing has become was one of the subjects my colleague, Bill Chleboun, and I hoped to explore when we set out from San Francisco to Minneapolis, New York, Stamford (Conn.), Nashville, and Washington D.C. to talk to publishers and booksellers two months ago. The responses we received ranged from the very positive — "I think we're better (at publishing) than we were 20 years ago" (Howard Kaminsky, Random House) to the very pessimistic — "the state of publishing is a terrible mess" (Roger Straus, Farrar, Straus & Giroux).

To many publishers, though, bigness is actually something the book publishing industry has needed for years. As Alan Mirken, president of Crown Publishers puts it, "When you stop to think of the number of titles in a bookstore today, and then go back 15–20 years, you find there weren't that many titles available. We've come a long way in getting books into a lot of people's hands, and I'm grateful to the chains (chain bookstores such as Walden, Dalton, and Crown) for that."

Adds Kaminsky, chief executive of Random House's adult trade division: "Look at today's best sellers: Where formerly 100,000–200,000 copies sold was an enormous best seller, now we have books selling 500,000 or 700,000 and, in some rare cases, one million copies in hardcover. I believe all that is good: anything that encourages people to pick up a book is a good thing. It might lead them to read a more challenging book in the long run."

To Louis Wolfe, co-chief executive of Bantam Books, however, big sales figures lead to "top-heavy" publishing lists on which a handful of best sellers are favored while literary and "midrange" books are left to fend for themselves. "A few hardcover books are selling extremely well," he says, "and sure, it's nice to point to our own book, 'Iacocca,' and say that there are 1.65 million copies in print. That's wonderful, but at that number it's probably gone beyond being a book — it's a phenomenon. What happens beyond it, or beyond those first 10–12 books (on the best seller list)? Nothing." As an industry capable of reaching large numbers of people with a wide diversity of books, "we aren't any further ahead than we used to be," he says.

What really worries Wolfe and other publishers, however, is a sharp decline of mass-market (drug store racksized) paperbacks (20 percent down) and the larger-sized trade paperbacks (a whopping 39 percent down) recorded in the first two months of this year. Calling these figures "a sign of disaster," he said that "the time has come for the industry to *sell* reading as the least expensive entertainment available today...We should be doing the generic kind of campaign that the orange, milk and wool board does that says, buy X product if it has a certain industry logo. Why don't we somehow say, buy a book; it's fun?"

The other question: Does top-heaviness in sales result in top-heaviness in editorial selection? Are publishers looking for the big books to such an extent that slower-selling literary and "midrange" books are getting lost in the shuffle?

"I don't think so," responds Kaminsky. "People who are in this business are here to publish good and enduring books. No one in this business has said I'm not interested in a challenging book...We want to be excitingly eclectic." Kaminsky agrees that too many books are being published today, and that too much duplication goes on, but, like many publishers, he insists that "there isn't a book that has merit that we won't publish."

Of course, that was exactly Lessing's point. After the Jane Somers manuscript was submitted, she said, editors wrote to say "they liked it but found it too depressing to publish." This irked her. It used to be, she said, that "serious publishers did not refuse a book for this reason. If they did, they were ashamed to say so. But I have been sent a lot of letters now — rejection letters by publishers in America and in England — and I can assure you that some of the most prestigious publishers have no shame whatsoever in saying, 'We like this book but it is too depressing to publish.'"

Then, again, this is nothing new. Any industry that attempts to merge commerce and art is bound to let some works of quality slip through the cracks, especially as the system grows bulkier. "As to the number of good books coming out today," says Robert Bernstein, president and chairman of Random House, "you do not have to worry as a reader. We're still flooded with them." He's right — book reviewers can attest to the fact that good books are published in quantity every year; the problem is how to unbury them from the mountains of garbage published every year as well.

Why can't large lists of titles — many of which are going to sink without a trace within weeks of publication — be cut back? "I joined Simon & Schuster over two decades ago," says Dan Green, president of that company's adult trade division, "and we now publish four or five times what we did then, just in cloth. I think it's wonderful that we can do that, because we are able to offer the American reading public a choice. I'd be very unhappy with the notion of cutting back the number of titles published, because you know the kind of book that would be cut first, don't you? It would be the odd, idiosyncratic book, the kind that doesn't fit into existing molds but nevertheless gets published somehow."

It wouldn't be the fluff fiction, the padded-out romance, the multigenerational saga set in the wine country that reads like someone produced "Falcon Crest" in print? Wouldn't that kind of book, and all its hundreds of duplications, be the first to go?

"You're being pejorative in a way you shouldn't be," responds Green, "because there is an audience of people who want to read that kind of fiction, and why shouldn't they be allowed to?"

Many publishers responded this way when I made fun of fluff fiction — because people are reading this stuff in large numbers, it is *undemocratic* of me to criticize its quality. "I'm not saying people shouldn't be allowed to read what they want," I responded. "I'm saying that publishers are getting awfully exploitative when they publish so many titles in this genre because they think it's hot and end up chasing after their audience."

"Maybe you've got it the wrong way," Green said. "Maybe this is simply what people are reading today, and what writers are writing. I'm just saying, thank God we're not censoring ourselves, or all those odd, strange, seemingly unsaleable books that are so difficult to publish might not make it."

Another important factor here is that many publishers see bigness as an inevitable consequence of American life. They shrug at notions that corporate publishing is not good for literature. They wince at the term "blockbuster mentality" as if a foul odor had just penetrated the room, explaining patiently that, although the traditions of publishing are different from its present realities, the best of both worlds is possible.

Harper's Simon Michael Bessie takes this point of view: "The traditional feeling used to be that trade book publishing is best done in relatively small-sized units that have themselves to be responsible to, because you're dealing in an area of individual judgment in which people operate best if they can make their own bets and support them as best they can — and if those bets don't work, they lose. I think that corporate organization, which has become increasingly necessary everywhere else, is not at home with general publishing at its best. But that doesn't mean it can't work."

Bessie was one of the first to understand this dynamic when, after thirteen years with Harper, he joined forces with Pat Knopf and Hiram Hayden to found Atheneum in 1959. "For all three of us there was this niggling question: Can you call yourself a book publisher if you aren't dependent on your own judgment and your own means? In other words, if I have to go to the publishers (of my house) for yesses and nos, am I really doing it?"

Atheneum surged ahead at the outset with a best seller every year for three years, without which, Bessie says, "I think we probably wouldn't have made it." But the house could not build a backlist (an inventory of older books that would keep on selling year after year) sufficient to support nonbest-seller seasons and was finally sold to Scribner's. Bessie went back to Harper's, where he and his wife Cornelia now publish fifteen books a year at Harper under their own imprint.

How does "imprint publishing" work? "Exactly the same as with general publishing. We have a profit if we have one or more big books — those that sell more than 100,000 copies and/or have a large subsidiary rights (paperback, foreign, first serial) income. There is no profit if we publish a list that includes no such books. We can cover our costs if we can produce books that sell 6,000–8,000 copies because we carry a very low overhead."

Bessie's case is instructive because wherever you go in publishing people say that corporations moved in on publishers when (1) owners of independent houses grew old enough to want to sell out or (2) small and medium-sized houses could not keep up with rising costs and *had* to sell out. While communications conglomerates (RCA, ITT, CBS, MCA, etc.) may have made mistakes in trying to slick up or overmodernize what is essentially an industry of ideas, they did bring a creaky and arcane "gentlemen's profession" (which was just as sexist and elitist as the name implies) into the twentieth century. The problem is that business formulas aimed at generating profits did not work as well with books as with other products — retail drugs, for example, shoes, or soap.

In the '80s what we find, then, is the "house of many houses," basically exemplified by Random House, which owns Knopf, Pantheon, Fawcett, Ballantine, Del Rey, Villard, Times Books, Aventura, and Vintage, and distributes for Sierra Club, Shambhala, and others. As Robert Bernstein explains, "There is a trend toward bigness, no question about it. Publishing costs so much that when small publishers start, they can't do it as efficiently because they can't afford all the mechanics — shipping, billing, production, distribution, and so forth." Random House thus centralizes these business processes under one cost-efficient umbrella, Bernstein says, allowing each subsidiary to publish more cheaply yet still retain its editorial autonomy.

The best part, Bernstein says, is that "publishing is still an easy entry business. There are still people who are entering publishing with one, two, three books, and finding a market for them. If you had an idea today for a new *Whole Earth Catalog*, you could still get distribution from a very good publisher."

At the same time, of course, there are those who would never want to distribute their books through a major publisher for fear that the system might be *too* big. Authors who have seen their books get lost in a corporate shuffle had no recourse to do anything about it until smaller publishers came along to "republish the losers," as it were.

Ten Speed Press in Berkeley, for example, has picked up and republished "at least a dozen good quality books that larger publishers have dropped or put out of print or didn't have the patience to market for more than one season," according to company founder Phil Wood. Interestingly, by placing such books within a computerized system of its own, Ten Speed's "little" house has often increased sales from the 1,500–2,000-copy sale of the larger house to 500,000–1 million copies "and still growing," as Wood says.

Still, Ten Speed is 3,000 miles away from the corporate structure in which Bob Bernstein flourishes. "When I took over the company in 1966," he recalls, "there was Bennett Cerf, top of the Random House mountain. I decided instantly I wouldn't have the temperament or social abilities of Cerf, that I wouldn't be the outside star that he was. The reason I came was that the only way Random House could grow from there was that, instead of having a mountain, we had to have a mountain range."

But why a range that went on and on and on? You had at that point Knopf and Pantheon. Why *keep* growing?

"One reason is that you need to get more and more of an overhead base because you're paying more each year for the same process — in other words, you can be efficient and mechanized, but inflation is always a constant. So you have this expanding overhead, and you know if you don't get more sales, you aren't going to cover it. Life doesn't stand still: you either get bigger or smaller."

That was exactly the case of Times Books, the latest Random House acquisition. Once the publishing arm of *The New York Times*, this moderately successful house discovered that without a best seller every year "there was no way," says Times' Joe Consolino, "for a trade house our size to survive just the increased costs of doing business." The only possible chance to make it as an independent, Consolino said, would have been to buy *another* independent — i.e., "make an acquisition ourselves of a significant nature to be able to create the dollar volume income to be able to afford to stay in business."

Key to the future at Times Books, Consolino thinks, is "that Random House gives us our competitive position in acquiring both hard and softcover rights." This is an issue of some controversy today because it means that hardcover houses are merging with softcover houses in order to compete for best-selling authors by offering more and more money as an advance against royalties.

Simon & Schuster and Pocketbooks; Doubleday and Dell; Random House and Ballantine; Viking and Penguin; New American Library, and E. P. Dutton are some of the mergers that, combined with paperback houses starting their own hardcover lines (Bantam, Avon, Warner) result in more centralization and more bigness within the industry. Further, that cherished tradition in publishing, the paperback auction (in which many paperback houses bid against each other for mass market rights to a book) may become a thing of the past because of these mergers and, some critics fear, short-change the author in the long run.

"The fact is," says Roger Straus, "if you don't go to auction, you never know how much a book is worth. We just sold Jamaica Kincaid's novel *Annie John* in an auction for over $30,000. Now there is no way any publisher could have assumed you could get so much for that little book. So in fact the author in a hard-soft deal is being trapped."

Or as an editor who wished not to be named mused: "It's this endless cry: hard-soft deal, hard-soft deal, hard-soft deal. Realistically this is going to mean you can only buy a hardcover book that meets the terms of a softcover book. It means *hard* is the cosmetic, *soft* is the business. It means the book that's going to pay you back for that huge advance has got to appeal to a million people in paperback and 200,000 in hardcover. What kind of book is that going to be? Not the serious book. Not the midrange book. It has to be a book that is commercial by paperback standards."

To some publishers, however, hardcover editors making softcover decisions is not a bad thing. Delacorte and Dell, for example, are considered to be Doubleday's "hard-soft combination," says president Henry Reath. "Really everything that's published in Delacorte is being bought because they're going to do it in Dell." Perhaps that's why Dial Press, which Doubleday acquired along with the other two some years back, got lost in the process. "Dial had a troubled history," said Reath, "and as the focus got tighter on other publishers, it finally became the stepchild."

But disappearing imprints, the hard-soft mergers, giants gobbling up other companies (the latest: Simon & Schuster's purchase of Prentice-Hall; Macmillan's of Scribner and affiliates), top-heavy sales, the need for a best seller each season to survive, and a system of editorial selection that grows ever more capable of letting good books fall through the cracks — all of these are indications of a bigness that is reaching unheard-of proportions.

Yet even as Penguin, with its recent acquisition of no less than four publishing houses in England last month, moves with its U.S. hardcover house Viking toward a new phenomenon, worldwide publishing (one English-language edition for the entire planet), there are people in the industry who have learned to break down its bigness into manageable parts.

11

INTRIGUES OF THE STORY TRADE: HOW MEGA-BOOKS BECOME MINI-SERIES*

JAMES TRAUB

The book publishing industry has changed considerably in the last few decades. In the 1950s and in the 1960s book publishers had a sense that they were not so much businessmen as "servants" of literature and the arts. This doesn't mean that they didn't want to make a profit; but this element did not seem to be terribly dominant in their thinking. Publishing was notorious for paying low salaries but the people who went into it, as editors and publishers, often felt that they were special and that they had an obligation to society. Their function was to find good writers and publish good books.

All this has changed and book publishing is now dominated (in general) by businessmen who see books as commodities to be used to generate profits. The esthete has been replaced by the MBA and publishing has been "rationalized," in the business sense of the term. It is often the marketing director who makes the final decision about whether a book is to be published or not. Books are now products that are manufactured and sold — to people and, in the case of certain works of fiction, to television and film producers.

What these producers are looking for are "megabooks," blockbuster novels that become best sellers and have the kind of plot that makes for a good mini-series. Most of these novels have little literary merit, but that is quite irrelevant. Writers who produce this kind of book often receive million dollar contracts for their services. This is because their name alone guarantees huge numbers of readers that, in turn, often leads to lucrative contracts with television producers. That is the subject of the essay that follows.

What I've been discussing applies, primarily, to popular novels and their relationship to the mass media. It is true that the publishing industry has changed and become more businesslike, but there are still many publishing houses that bring out fine novels and important nonfiction works. In some cases, the "blockbuster" hits they publish make it possible for them to publish the other material, which may not be particularly profitable. There are also many small book publishers flourishing in America.

There is a good deal of disagreement about how many books the average American reads in a year. It is estimated that among reading-age Americans, we sell about five books per capita — but we don't know what these books are and

---

whether people read the books they buy. One thing we do know — ironically, people who see television programs and films made from books often purchase them and read them. As the ads now go, "you've seen the mini-series, now read the book."

People who spend their workdays with intrigue, glamour, and melodrama seem to get covered with the stuff, just as surely as a house painter comes home with his overalls spattered. The business of publishing best-selling books has the furious pace, the nervy confrontations, of a real page-turner. And the business of making hit TV shows — that's practically a lifestyle of the rich and famous, a world where hyperbole is the stuff of daily life. But the most melodramatic of all, the most *hot*, is the swiftly expanding business of making hit books into hit television shows — specifically, mini-series. The process radiates a heat so intense that conventional rules of behavior simply melt away. Conniving and even stealing are taken quite for granted; nobody can afford to be nice.

Owen Laster, a big literary agent at the very big William Morris Agency, takes precautions when he sends out an important manuscript to be copied. He gives it a dummy title page to thwart would-be thieves. In the past, he believes, his manuscripts have been illicitly copied at the behest of story scouts, generally well-bred young women (and a few men) who dredge the literary swamps in search of raw material for TV and movie producers.

Laster recalls he once had an especially hot property, which he decided to let no one see, just to build up the tension surrounding it. Nevertheless, maybe half a dozen story scouts had managed to finagle copies of the manuscript. One scout, who hadn't, begged him desperately to let her see it. Her job, she said, was at stake. Laster refused: he wasn't ready to show it. The story scout, he believes, soon quit her job, probably under duress.

Along the feverish frontier between books and television, tales like that are told with casual resignation. Only a newcomer with an antiquated reverence for books is shocked. Publishing used to be a modest, noble sort of affair, in which rich and cultivated men and women printed, almost as a public service, the literary fruit of poor and cultivated men and women. There were best-sellers, of course, but book publishing was no place to go if you were hell-bent on profit. In this introspective world, television was no more welcome than a drum major in a symphony orchestra.

But all that has changed. Broadcasting and publishing are now a pair of giant entertainment businesses (often under the same corporate roof) that have less and less trouble finding a common vocabulary and opportunities for common profit. Publishing has awakened, as it were, to the values on which television was built — all-out competition, a ready submission to the judgments of the marketplace, and above all, a fixation on the hit.

Publishers have become comfortable with the mechanisms of mass appeal — and that, in part, means television.

In a less drastic change, television executives have discovered the assets of the printed page. Their own obsession with the hit has led them to the mini-series, an electronic version of the best-seller in which millions of dollars are staked on the possibility of exorbitant success. (Over the last five years the average mini-series has attracted half again the audience of the average prime-time show.) And the mini-series depends almost entirely on books. Few television scripts have the immense wealth of character, action, and detail needed to supply five or ten hours of television. The made-for-TV movie, in contrast, is usually inspired by newspaper articles on fatal diseases, wife-beating, vigilantism, or the like.

Unlike the traditional series, which builds up an audience over time, the mini-series is a spectacular event requiring an equally spectacular carnival of publicity — a staged hit. Thus it needs not just a book but a hot book. It capitalizes on publicity the book has already earned, and returns it with interest. Paperbacks issued in synchrony with a mini-series have sold a million copies, or more.

Immense though it is, the mini-series occupies only one place in a larger process whose very substance is publicity. From a single manuscript climbs a vast, giddy spiral fueled by hype: book club selection, foreign publication, paperbacks, mini-series, "novelizations" of the mini-series, and hardcover sequels, which start the whole whirl again. "Everything," says literary agent Morton Janklow, "feeds on everything else."

In the beginning is the book, the thick best-seller stacked all by itself near every bookstore cash register. "A book that's 500 pages long, has a very complex plot spanning twenty years, and is written by a big-name author with a big audience — *that*," says Ellen Cotler, who ferrets out manuscripts for the Leonard Goldberg company, "is a mini-series." The characteristic ambiance of these colossi is one of incessant activity, most of it sexual, spreading across vast reaches of space and time, as if the authors were too restless and energetic to stop and reflect. Much of this action takes the form of competition and conquest — in space, in war, and, above all, in bed. Authors of contemporary "high" literature generally identify with the misfit, the loser, the anti-hero. Mega-book writers, though, have the practical sense to focus on the successful.

Not every mini-series, of course, has featured the intrigues and cat-fights of the rich, the powerful, and the attractive. One has only to think of *Holocaust*, *Roots*, or the recent *Fatal Vision* — all of which depend on the melodrama arising from a dangerous or frightening situation — or the historical epics like *George Washington*. Critics have praised some of these more "serious" mini-series, though not, by the large, very enthusiastically. Perhaps more representative of the mini-series climate was NBC's sexed-up, heavy-handed version of Ernest Hemingway's *The Sun Also Rises*, which aired last December, one of the great critical and popular disasters the form has suffered.

Owing perhaps to the limited stock of sagas with proven mass appeal, mini-series productions tend to have a distinct family resemblance. A remarkable number of them concern no-longer-young women, the group comprising the largest bloc of television viewers. (Young men, on the other hand, dominate the movie-going audience. Thus science-fiction and teenage themes do well in theaters, while *Dynasty* succeeds on TV.) The plot of Shirley Conran's *Lace*, for example, sprinted through Gstaad, Paris, London, Manhattan, and an oil sheikdom detailing the erotic and professional adventures of five extraordinary women. Leonard Goldberg is preparing to adapt Joseph Amiel's *Birth Right*, "a revenge story," according to Ellen Cotler, about a woman adopted into a Rothschild-like family who later gets chiseled out of her inheritance. And Crown Publishers is selling the rights, for what is expected to be a large sum, to Shirley Lord's *One of My Very Best Friends*. The story, according to Phyllis Fleiss, head of Crown subsidiary rights, is "a saga of two women — a gossip columnist and a cosmetic tycoon. One's a charmer, and the other's a bitch. The two women have been friendly for years, and then they both fall in love with the same man, and the cosmetic executive betrays her best friend. What could be better for a mini-series?"

The atmosphere of pressure and power, the lightning action, the women intriguing against one another — it's reminiscent of Owen Laster's story of desperate competition and deceit. Sometimes it appears as if the worlds of high-powered publishing and broadcasting are modeling themselves after their own products, or their products after themselves. The authors, after all, often dwell in the same empyrean as the big agents and executives. Judith Krantz's *Mistral's Daughter*, which was made into what the paperback cover blurb calls "an enthralling CBS-TV mini-series," opens with the beautiful young heroine stepping into an elevator full of other attractive young women "gripped in silent, fierce, and frightened concentration." CBS would barely have to modify the scene in order to insert it in an enthralling mini-series about New York story scouts. Call it *Story Girls*, crank up the hype machine, and you've got a major, major hit.

The story scout is a sort of intelligence agent for Hollywood in Manhattan's publishing world. CBS, ABC, and most of the studios each employ two or three of them to read, or know about, every book manuscript or magazine article that might conceivably make it onto the big or little screen. For most scouts it is a humble occupation, one whose existence is almost unknown within the networks. Joe Smith at ABC calls himself simply a "forward research service," or a "fielder." If he sees anything good, he calls it to his superior's attention, and then the book vanishes up the hierarchy.

It doesn't take great powers of discrimination to figure out which scripts will appeal to a TV executive. A scout knows that his or her boss wants a good story; the particular texture, the sensibility, even the setting of a book are almost irrelevant. And the story has to be "high-concept" — capable of being expressed in a seventeen-second promotional spot. "There's a rule at

ABC," says Smith. "It has to hit you in the heart or the groin." And it has to score a direct hit. Apparently on the lookout for a TV deal, money-minded authors are creating a virtual genre of books that read like *The Thorn Birds* or *The Winds of War*. As former Lorimar scout Jayne Pliner says, it's gotten ridiculous. "You've got generational sagas of a family of shoemakers, generational sagas of a family of skiers," and on and on.

Story scouts don't get paid to read books so much as to find them as early as possible. A good story scout can feel the heat emanating from a book when it's only a title on a publisher's list, and — here's the part that makes for an enthralling mini-series — knows how to get her hands on it first. Karen Everett (who was then at Highgate Pictures) learned that columnist Rex Reed was writing a novel the moment he signed a book contract. Reed's agent was a friend, and so, "as a kind of favor," he let her see Reed's outline. That was enough. It was a big, racy story by a big name. When Reed finishes the novel, Highgate will turn it into a mini-series for NBC. And that's how Everett works. "There are certain people I talk to every week," she says, "people who are the hottest, the best, who have the hottest material." She "tracks" books, she says, sounding vaguely like an officer in the Pentagon's Situation Room.

The story scout is a hypersensitive thermometer thrust into the publishing atmosphere to measure incipient heat. This heat comes from a hot book, of course, but a book can't produce the necessary excitement all by itself. Even before a manuscript appears, the atmosphere of the hit is, to use Morton Janklow's word, orchestrated. The orchestration begins with the author's agent and the head of subsidiary rights at the publishing house. Their goal is to pyramid a simple book contract into a vast multi-part deal by selling various rights to the networks, studios, book clubs, magazines, foreign publishers, and so on. (Powerful authors may retain virtually all these rights, leaving the publisher out of the picture at this point.)

Normally, representatives of film and TV producers and other suitors are allowed to see a manuscript as soon as an editor has it in final form. But not always. A climate of mystery and nervous anticipation may be preferable. Sometimes the manuscript is withheld until the moment of publication, as happened with Bob Woodward's *Wired*. Sometimes an agent will give an advance peek — an outline or a chapter or even a whole work — to a few select friends. "Sometimes," says Owen Laster, "you can use that to build anxiety" — play desperate scouts against one another, and thus heighten the frenzy surrounding the book.

The book may be the utmost dud, but at this point nobody notices; frenzy crowds out judgment. All anyone knows is that the book is hot. Jobs, reputations, and deals are on the line, or they seem to be, anyway. That's when the story scout starts stealing, or "sneaking," to use the professional jargon. The greatest potential victim of sneaking is the author, whose manuscript may make the rounds and be rejected before it's even finished, as Jenny Tripp of Telcom Entertainment points out. Unlike the outright thief, the sneak doesn't swipe the hot goods herself; she has it copied by a contact, maybe a low-level chum at the publishing house. A few years ago, one story scout was believed to be bribing the copy-machine operator at a major publishing house. "There is no end to what people will do," says Tripp, "to be the first one on the block."

Almost any scout will admit to sneaking, but not to enjoying it. "I don't like being devious," says Ellen Cotler, "but it's my job to get that book, and if the only way I can get the book is by sneaking it, then I'll sneak it." She concedes that she and her colleagues get a majority of hot manuscripts from "confidential sources." It's her job to get that book. But why? Very few manuscripts are sold to the first bidder. Getting there first, says Karen Everett, gives "a psychological advantage." But the narrow advantage hardly seems to justify the chicanery, and scouts themselves recognize something silly in their mad scramble. They are reacting, after all, to one another; to their bosses; to book clubs and magazines and foreign publishers; to the atmosphere of the hit, an atmosphere that feeds on itself and everything else.

Like all the other mega-book buyers, TV producers feed on the hit, and it feeds on them. Take Michael Korda's *Queenie*, for example. Korda's autobiographical *Charmed Lives* had sold quite well, and when Karen Everett got word that he was writing a fictionalized account of the life of his aunt, the actress Merle Oberon, who enjoyed many lovers on many continents, she began "tracking" Korda's progress. So did, over time, practically everyone else in the business. To get the television rights to *Queenie*, Highgate had to write a check for $175,000 and promise to deliver another $750,000 when the shooting began — "pick-up money," as it's called. When Highgate bought *Queenie*, the book was already a hit.

From there "the reverberations went out," said Marcella Burger, head of Simon & Schuster subsidiary rights. Television had turned up the heat. Everyone had heard that Highgate paid a giant sum for the book, which provided further reassurance that it was going to be a hit. The Book of the Month Club made *Queenie* a selection, though officials there deny that the TV deal influenced their decision. Warner Books bought the paperback rights for a startling $1.2 million, though Warner also denies that it reacted to the TV deal. "I had never seen anything go that crazy," says Burger. Everything was feeding off everything else. Foreign-rights prices went through the roof. The British bought *Queenie* for almost $190,000, the French for $60,000. Burger recently met the Dutch publisher who paid $15,000 for the rights. "He said to me," Burger recalls, "'My God, what have I done?'" He had been overcome by the atmosphere of the hit, like a man walking into a casino and forgetting his resolution of a moment before.

The variations are endless. Sometimes a story seems to bounce back and forth so quickly between book and television show that the line between the two begins to blur, and one is aware only of a non-stop process of adaptation. The era of the blockbuster commercial mini-series dates back, not to *Roots* in 1977, but to a twelve-hour adaptation of Irwin Shaw's *Rich Man, Poor Man* in 1976. The show was such a smashing success that

Universal itself dreamed up and produced a weekly series titled *Rich Man, Poor Man — Book II*, which ran from 1976 to 1977. Shaw himself then took over the job, writing his own sequel, *Beggar Man, Thief*, which begat yet another mini-series in 1977. Before ABC aired Jackie Collins's *Hollywood Wives* this past February, Morton Janklow predicted it was "going to be colossal" — so colossal, as it turned out, that *Hollywood Wives II* and *Hollywood Wives III* are already in the works, and the producer, the colossal Aaron Spelling, may spin the whole thing off into a regular series.

Janklow is the five-star general, the Zen-master, of the orchestration of rights. Janklow is pretty colossal himself, the equivalent in power to a studio head or a publishing mogul. He uses the word "control" almost as often as he uses the word "colossal." He controls, to name only a very few best-selling authors, Jackie Collins, Sidney Sheldon, Judith Krantz, and Shirley Conran. He also controls, he says, a breathtaking 100 hours of network time, a figure he derives by counting all the mini-series adapted from his authors' books and either shown in the last year, soon to be shown, or in production. His shows, he claims, have controlled "the last three or four ratings sweeps, and will control the next two or three."

One of Janklow's most impressive displays of virtuosity began when British journalist Shirley Conran sent him an outline of *Lace*. Janklow immediately recognized a colossal hit, told Conran to stick to her outline, and began kindling the fire. As soon as Conran sent him a first draft, and he saw that it was good, Janklow gathered together "four or five" major publishers to bid for the book rights. Simon & Schuster finally won the bidding at $750,000, a remarkable figure for a virtually unknown author. It was a "hard/soft deal," meaning that Simon & Schuster's subsidiary, Pocket Books, got the paperback rights.

Meanwhile, a story scout at Lorimar (the manufacturers of *Dallas*) had already snuck — or as Janklow says, "purloined" — the manuscript. Studio executives gazed upon The Sentence That Launched a Thousand Deals. This is the last line of the novel's first chapter, wherein a profoundly unpleasant but supremely famous starlet majestically demands of the four older, more-powerful-but-not-so-famous women whom she has lured into her gigantic hotel suite, "Which one of you bitches is my mother?" That sentence sold *Lace* all over Europe, according to Marcella Burger. Lorimar's Jayne Pliner calls it "the hook, if ever there was one."

Morton Janklow doesn't have to deal with story scouts. Ignoring the fact that Lorimar already had the manuscript, he called Lee Rich, the studio's president, and said, as he recalls, "Lee, I've got a gigantic mini-series for you." He sent the manuscript to Los Angeles, and two days later Rich called back to option the book.

That was only the beginning. In the spring of 1983 *Lace* appeared in paperback. By February 1984, when ABC ran the mini-series, *Lace* had sold a million copies in paperback and was what you might call a household word. Despite, or perhaps because of, the casting of a pouting, posturing, chubby adolescent, Phoebe Cates, as the gorgeous monomaniacal starlet, combined with the show's weakness for eyeball-rolling innuendo, *Lace* turned out to be the highest-rated mini-series of the year. "All anybody was saying," according to Pliner, "was 'I want another *Lace*.'" Morton Janklow, of course, was already working on one. "After the overnight ratings for the first show," he recalls, "I got on the phone to London and said. 'Shirley, we ought to be prepared to come back with a continuation of the story.'" Conran was prepared: She wrote a treatment of a script, Lorimar accepted it, and ABC will broadcast *Lace II* during "sweeps week" in May. Pocket Books meanwhile purchased rights to Conran's novelization of her own script, so that a paperback version of *Lace II* will appear several weeks before the show. The hype will be coordinated: Ads for the show will help sell the book, and the book jacket will display scenes from the mini-series and admonish readers to watch it.

It doesn't stop there; it never stops. Conran has already worked up an outline for her next novel, *The Legend*. Janklow has already sold it to Simon & Schuster and to Warner Books, and optioned it to Lorimar. Shirley Conran has joined Sidney Sheldon, Judith Krantz, and Danielle Steele, a privileged class not of mere scribblers but of blue-chip stocks, their value rising and falling with each new set of sales figures. No doubt they sit alone in their rooms, like other writers, and murmur to themselves. Yet their books set in motion a huge machine involving hundreds of people and millions of dollars. It's pointless, of course, to wish it otherwise, to wish that books be counterweights of decorum to the shouting market-mad world. Books *are* commodities. One can only be thankful that some of the people who write them refuse to see them that way.

12 MARKETING AND AGENTS: WHERE TO GO WITH THE COMPLETED SCRIPT*

SCOTT MEREDITH

A medium is a mode of transmission, a channel of communication. Television is a medium which "carries" various kinds of programs to us. We must make a distinction between the medium (plural: media) and the kinds of programs or art forms they carry. We must also be mindful of the impact that the medium has on

* Reprinted by permission of the author and the author's agents, Scott Meredith Literary Agency, Inc., 845 Third Avenue, New York, NY 10022.

the work of art. In the case of books, think of the power of design, of typefaces and of illustrations and photographs to affect our imaginations. Think, also, of the magic of words themselves. We look at some marks on a sheet of paper and can be moved to laugh or cry, to change our conception of the universe, to start a revolution....

Because so many people are fascinated by language and by the power of words to move people (and, in some cases, to make a great deal of money) we have an enormous number of people who write. It doesn't cost very much to write; all you need is a typewriter and some paper. There is a famous tale, no doubt fictitious, that is relevant. The first bit of writing ever discovered goes as follows: "children no longer obey their parents and everyone is writing books."

This is where literary agents come in. They function as go-betweens who "mediate" between authors and publishers. Agents save publishers money by weeding out nonpublishable books. In principle, if a reputable agent takes a book it is publishable; it may not be of interest to one publisher or another, since tastes and needs vary, but the book is "by definition" a viable one.

There is a kind of catch-22 in publishing: you need to publish a book to get an agent and you need an agent to publish a book. How does anyone ever get started, you might ask? The answer is that sometimes you can publish a book without having an agent and get an agent without having published a book.

Publishers make many mistakes. Every publisher has rejected manuscripts that have gone on to become bestsellers and to make enormous amounts of money. Some of these books have been rejected fifteen or twenty times before they were published. So one must realize that the book publishing industry has an element of chance (or is it irrationality) in it.

For those people who write on, despite the odds, Scott Meredith has excellent advice on how to deal with publishers and literary agents. His article is witty, entertaining, and full of good practical advice. He knows what he is talking about, since he handles many of our most important writers.

When you have finished plotting and writing and revising your scripts, you will want to know how to go about selling them. There are, of course, two methods: submitting them directly to the publishing houses, and submitting them to the publishing houses through a reliable literary agent.

Let's have a look, first of all, at the literary agent situation. I covered the subject of literary agencies pretty thoroughly in an article called "Can We Still Be Friends?" which was published in the trade journal *Writer's Digest*, and quote largely from this article in the material on agents which follows.

A few feet from my desk, off in a dark corner, there's a curious spot on the wall which looks scarred and lacerated and about to cave in. As a matter of fact, it *is* about to cave in — for it has received harsh treatment through the years. It is the section of the wall against which I beat my head.

Most of my clients and potential clients, I'm happy to report, are awfully nice. We exchange lovingly cordial letters when I get them better deals than they expected, and icily cordial ones when I have to confess that I argued for more money with an editor for two hours and he won — and when they come to New York, sometimes I buy them Scotches or martinis, and sometimes they buy champagne cocktails for me.

Sometimes, however, some of their requests and questions can, as I say, send an agent, sobbing bitterly, out of his chair to see which is harder — his head or the wall. I'd like to discuss and attempt to clarify a few of the more recurrent insanity inspirers, and in that way, perhaps, straighten out some points in the minds of those of you who are contemplating getting agents but don't quite understand their operating methods.

1. The enclosed story has been rejected by a total of forty-seven publishing companies. I know, however, that you agents have influence with editors and publishers, so please sell it for me as soon as possible.

There isn't an agent in the business who has ever sold a bad script because of personal friendship or influence with an editor or publisher. Most agents have no objection to seeing heavily rejected scripts because they feel they may do a better job of market selection than the author has done, and not because they hope that influence will turn the trick even if the script is a poor one. If that was your reason for thinking of signing up with an agent, you'd better forget about it.

The only reason an agent is able to sell a script is that the story is a good and salable script. No agent is better than the clients he represents — and no agent has ever been able to sell a poor script because he happens to be an agent.

With similar scripts of equal value, sometimes, editorial friendship will tip the scales. But if an editor begins to buy poor stuff from an agent friend, the overpowering odor of the material will soon come to the publisher's attention — and the editor will go out on his or her ear. What, then, would be the point in the carefully cultivated friendship some writers think agents spend their time building? And if the agent's friendship is with the publisher himself, even the publisher can't buy sickening stuff — or the reading public will not buy the books he publishes and will instead give their dollars to publishers who don't have an unscrupulous agent friend.

An agent, generally speaking, has three values as far as the writer is concerned: (1) If he's honest and on the level, he can furnish you with frank evaluations of your stuff, tell you truthfully and expertly about your weak points and strong points — something your family and friends will not or cannot do. (2) He spends every working day in the publishing area — visiting editors, talking to editors on the phone, lunching with editors, sometimes lugging his wife over for games of bridge with editors and their wives. Because of this, he knows the day-by-day things that go on in the field — which houses are buying heavily and which are temporarily stocked, and particular tastes and taboos and eccentricities of editors and publishers —

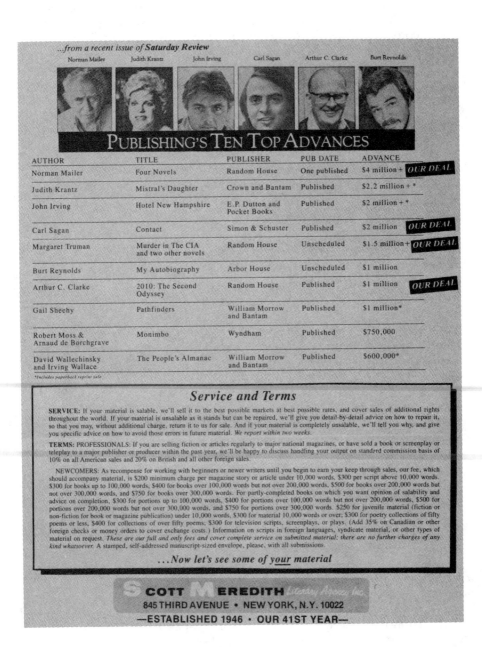

This is part of a newsletter sent by Scott Meredith.

and he can bring you better deals on your material, perhaps contracts with better houses than the ones for which you planned your scripts, and up-to-the minute trend tips. (3) Equally important, he is a third person. If you write an editor and tell him how superb your script really is, or how much you deserve a big advance, you sound conceited and may antagonize him — even if your script *is* good, or if you *do* deserve a big advance. But an agent may do this because he's not talking about his own work: if he is enthusiastic about a script or asks for more money, it's all right.

2. I don't want an agent who acts as a messenger service. Please inform me by return special delivery air mail whether or not you submit in person everything you handle.

Of course I don't — and it's about time that fond illusion is dispelled. No agent submits in person all the material he handles.

If his morning mail turns up a novel that he thinks is the best he has ever read and which he feels will become an ageless classic, there's no question in the world but that he'll telephone an editor and howl ecstatically about it, or make an appointment with an editor and go over and plug the script to the skies. If a really good nonfiction book comes in, he'll surely telephone a few editors to determine their attitude toward the subject before sending it along. Or if a script of the length and type an editor has requested comes along, or a script by a writer in whom the agent has interested an editor, of course the agent will phone and say, "Joe, I'm sending over Sam McFoop's new novel," or "Bill, I've got an appointment near your office. I'll stop by and give you a really excellent science fiction novel that's just come in."

But as far as the usual case is concerned — well, large agencies like mine employ messengers, and a few employ the same government men in gray you use when you send your material directly to publishers. If a script rates special attention or heralding of some kind, you may be sure it will get it, through an attached note, a phone call, or a personal visit — but when the script is a typical good script, just right for a house and exactly like others in that respect, there's nothing to be accomplished by personal delivery.

The value of an agent's "messenger service," of course, is that it is his business to know exactly where the script must go. The unagented writer may send a mystery to a house whose inventory is loaded with mysteries, or a nonfiction book to a house that has just contracted for or published a similar book, but the good agent, who — himself and through his staff — keeps up to the second on market information, will almost never do this. He'll know that another house is *light* on mysteries, and he'll know another house likely to snap up a nonfiction book on your subject, and you'll have a sale instead of a perhaps unexplained rejection.

3. Tell me, do you think it's true that agents who charge fees are off the level? My cousin works in a bar, and a writer who used to come in there and cadge drinks told him that a good agent doesn't charge fees.

No, kiddo, I don't think it's true. You see, *we* charge fees ourselves for reading, analyzing, and making detailed reports on scripts by unestablished writers.

During the earlier days of my agency, we charged no fees for one simple reason: we accepted only established writers with established reputations. There was no reason under the sun to charge fees to examine and report on incoming stuff: our clients had sold enough to justify the conclusion that their output was almost always salable as it stood, and we knew we'd derive our profit from the commission on sales. We knew, too, that the commissions would be regular enough to cover all overhead and pay off the butcher and baker as well.

Many agencies work that way today. They handle the top names only and won't handle you until you become a top name yourself, and they don't charge fees because, when you're added to their list, your stuff is so professional and your sales chances always so good that it isn't necessary. They've got an important and urgent place in the field — they take business worries off the hands of busy professionals.

I decided to add promising new writers to our agency list because, in the course of an expansion program some years ago, I hired several additional staff members who were fresh and bright and full of good ideas. An agency built of household-name clients is a fine thing, they pointed out, but to add only writers who have already arrived is a halfway measure. There are many fine writers who never arrive because of poor market sense or because nobody ever gets around to straightening out the technical flaws in their stuff — and if newer writers could be sifted through and the promising people *groomed* for major success, it would easily be worthwhile. This was in line with my own thinking, and I agreed, provided overhead would be covered while the grooming is going on.

That phrase — "provided overhead be covered" — is the answer to fees, and the reason so many agents charge them. Newer writers may believe they know technique backward and forward, but in many cases it turns out that they've misunderstood or misinterpreted the rules and their stuff is full of holes. These errors must be corrected: the agent and his staff must write long letters of advice and analysis, pushing the newcomer's stuff into proper channels, until he straightens out and begins to sell. And even these beginning sales mean nothing, for until the sales become steady and regular, the agent's time spent in the selling eats up the profit.

During this period, the agent must be paid for the time spent away from his arrived clients — his staff must be paid, his electricity and stationery and telephone bills must be covered. Most agents, you will find, charge fees which obviously cover only overhead — and proof of the pudding is in the fact that all agents drop fees after they make several deals for a client.

Our decision to handle new writers as well as established people, incidentally, was one of the happiest moves we've ever made, since so very many of the top writers on our list today first came to us in that way: with no sales at all to their credit. And that, of course, is the reason we now have an absolute policy of pushing a new writer's script as hard as scripts by our biggest names: we know through happy experience that the new writer, whose scripts today bring in small commissions, may well be the man or woman writing the hot, big-money properties tomorrow.

The average agency fee for short stories or articles runs five dollars per thousand words of manuscript, with a minimum fee of fifty dollars per script of under ten thousand words, and flat rates for books (generally one hundred dollars for scripts up to 150,000 words, one hundred and fifty dollars for scripts above that length). This usually includes all services — reading, detailed analysis and report, assistance and advice for necessary revisions, marketing, etc. The only additional charge is the commission upon sale of the manuscript, which is the same as that charged on scripts by established writers: ten percent on deals made with United States markets, and twenty percent on deals made with British, French, and other foreign markets. (This area of the agent's representation, incidentally, is an extremely important one, because sales possibilities are so complex and widespread today that only a specialist such as an agent can handle the job efficiently. An agent's job is only beginning when he makes a deal on your book with the American publisher. Aside from overseeing and assisting wherever possible in the various domestic areas — serialization in a magazine before book publication, advertising and promotion after book publication, the eventual paperback reprint, book club deals, motion picture and television deals, and the like — he also goes to work to arrange for publication of the book by foreign firms around the world. And on some books, separate deals can be made in thirty different countries.)

4. I understand that you handle on straight commission basis writers who have been selling regularly. I've sold $620 worth of news reporting to *Feed Grinder*, and now I want to write humorous novels. I presume you'll handle me on straight commission basis and without fee charges. What do you say?

Usually I say "No," for this fellow doesn't really understand the purpose of fees, and probably suspects agents invented them just to annoy him personally.

We charge a fee in the first place because we want our basic expenses to be covered while we're working with a writer who hasn't proved himself through steady sales — and we skip fees with a writer who has been getting published because we feel that he's proved himself sufficiently professional to take the chance of working with him without coverage of overhead and profit prior to commission on sales. But the point is that, if we're not going to charge him coverage-of-overhead fees, he must have a sales record which will justify it.

The fact that a writer has achieved considerable success in trade news reporting doesn't give any clue at all to his abilities as a writer of light fiction. He may be a dud or he may be a master; but, if he should turn out to be a dud, we can't afford to analyze his stuff and work him into fiction markets without charge simply because he's a great success in a totally different field.

If a successful genre writer wants to try to switch to mainstream novels, for example, I'm always happy to take him on, on commission — because one kind of fiction is in its elements much like all other fiction, and the two are close enough. If a popular novelist wants us to handle his unexpected book of sentimental verse, that's all right — and we'll be happy to do it, for the commissions on his novels cover the additional expense of selling a book of verse at one thousand dollars advance, or possibly even five hundred dollars, and the author's soul is at peace.

But if you've had some success in one field and want to go into an entirely different one, don't expect an agent to work his head off breaking you into the new field without payment of fees.

5. Hiss, hiss. You returned my novel, *He Done Killed Her Dead*, with a letter explaining why it was unsalable. You'll be amazed to hear that *Independent Corn-Pone Grower* has just bought the first chapter and scheduled it for their Fall-Winter issue.

My reaction to this sort of thing is generally, Great going, pal, and many more — but the *Independent Corn-Pone Grower* pays only five bucks for material.

Although some writers do not realize it, it must be understood by you that a literary agency is not entirely a benevolent association, but is engaged in making money so that the owner and his staff keep off skid row. And the commission on a five-dollar sale, I can tell you without pausing to count on my fingers, is only fifty cents — not even enough these days to buy permission to step into a restaurant and sniff deeply.

Occasionally an agent will make a sale to a very minor market because the script won't go in any of the better ones, and the writer is either a newcomer who can use the emotional stimulus of a sale, or an old-timer who can use money in any shape, form, or amount. But there is a limit to these things: obviously, when an agent has exhausted all the best markets and all the fair ones, he simply cannot afford to continue with the tiny ones — and once in a while a script sells to these tiny ones, the markets to which the agent cannot afford to submit.

Have the same consideration for the agent he tries to have for you. Don't ask him to handle your output if you plan to specialize in fliers, or religious-market material, which sell for a few dollars apiece. And don't expect him to continue trying your short story right down to the experimental journals that pay their writers with subscriptions. An agent who tries to pay his rent with 10 percent of subscriptions will quickly find himself outside his office building.

Another answer to the fact that writers sometimes sell work returned by agents is that de Lawd never quite got around to making any of us perfect. A very good agent I know received a script from a client who was a comparatively new writer, and didn't like it too much, but he sent it to a publishing house anyhow because the editors there were especially receptive to newcomers. When the house returned it with a cold comment, he decided his original opinion had been backed up, and returned the script to its author. The author sent it off to another top house, which promptly contracted for it.

When you consider, however, that this was the agent's second major error in judgment in nearly fourteen years, you've got to admit that the record isn't a bad one.

6. Please send me eleven bank references, your certificate of citizenship, and a sworn statement testifying that you have been vaccinated against inflamed gums. I was recently gypped like all get-out by an agent whose office was four blocks from your own, and I'm afraid that you may be a dangerous criminal, too.

The answer to that one is that there have been thieves and incompetents in every industry and profession from bootblacking to banking to bazooka-making to the Presidency of the United States — and it seems somewhat wildly imaginative to assume that a black hood should be placed over an entire field because one member is a bad 'un. Jack the Ripper was possibly an editor during the daytime, as a disgruntled writer once assured me, but there are still some awfully nice guys among editors.

Generally speaking, an agent who has many established professionals among his clients is bound to be honest and reliable — because writers pass the word around quickly when an agent is shady, and the shady agent's list quickly dissolves or never gets built up. There's one way to find out about an agent's clients, incidentally: write and ask him.

Occasionally, of course, an agent who has worked honorably for writers for years will suddenly go screwball and pull all kinds of stunts, as was the case with one some years ago. This is the sort of thing that no one can predict — and is perhaps caused by temporary or permanent insanity, glandular trouble, or an overdose of Serutan. It is in the class with bank tellers who are honest for twenty years and suddenly rush off with a satchelful of money, and is a chance you must take — like the chance you take when you turn in a suit or dress to the dry cleaner's. He may be gone, clothing and all, the next morning; but if he's been in business for a while and has a reputation for honesty, the chances are that he won't.

7. I sent you a script on Monday, and here it is Thursday and I haven't heard from you. What's the matter — you lose my script or something?

No, we haven't, friend. We're still working on it, so hold your horses. Most agencies begin work on material almost immediately after its arrival. After the script has been carded and otherwise registered, it is turned over to the agency head or his staff for reading, and if immediately salable is sent out to market.

Sometimes, however, it isn't. It displays certain important flaws, yet at the same time it displays a lot of good writing and some evident ability. That makes it a problem: it isn't quite right to take to market, it can't be returned for a rewrite because the fault is in the basic framework itself and that would amount to writing an entirely new script, and yet it isn't bad enough to be returned with suggestion to destroy. There's a staff meeting called; sometimes, when the script is really a puzzler, two or three meetings. All this takes time, for though the script may be enough of a hair-grayer to interest everybody, discussions and meetings on it must be sandwiched between work on other pressing matters. The average agency report is sent within two weeks, and many times (as is the case with established professionals, whose scripts can usually go out to market immediately) even by return mail, but you must realize that work is being performed for your own good even if a month passes without report.

And if a script is okayed and sent to market, the agent cannot send the writer a play-by-play description of what is happening to it, though he will, of course, inform the writer initially that it has gone out. The agent reports to the author whenever he has news — a deal, a requested rewrite from an editor, an important editorial comment, or something of that sort. He just cannot, however, inform the author each time a script has not made the grade at a market and gone to another, or he would have no time to do anything else.

Generally, for the reason of the rush-and-unrush system, plus the fact that agents who consistently send good material to editors will naturally get prompter attention, literary agents get fast reports on material they send to market. Sometimes, however, editors get bogged down with other work and take longer in their reporting; in those cases, the agent's only choice is to prod them gently as much as possible but mostly grin and bear it. And then, of course, the agent's own report to you of eventual acceptance will be slower in coming.

Just remember that the key to happiness lies in that adage laid down long, long ago: if you want to stay sane, forget about a script the moment it leaves your home, and concentrate on new material.

If you decide to submit directly to publishing houses instead of working through an agent, there are two things you must do to familiarize yourself with market needs and otherwise keep in touch with your business. First, read the published works in the field for which you're aiming, and read them carefully. And second, read the writers' trade journals.

The authorship journals are to writers what medical journals are to doctors: they serve as clearing houses for information on new techniques, new angles on old techniques, and all other technique information of value to the worker in the field. In addition, these publications report important events in the publishing world such as prize contests and the birth of new markets and from time to time publish full lists of markets and needs.

Writers' magazines may be secured at larger newsstands or at your public library, and you'll find them stimulating and helpful reading whether or not you work through an agent.

When you get your specific choice of markets down pat, there are several things to keep in mind about the marketing itself.

Try to keep yourself, first of all, from becoming discouraged and giving up on a script because it piles up a few rejections. Sometimes a script hits the right market at the right moment and sells at first submission, or within two or three submissions; other scripts just as good may take a lot of offering around before they're accepted. Almost everyone who has been in the writing business for some time can think of dozens of cases of manuscripts which had been rejected at market after market and then were finally accepted. (*The Godfather* is just one example that comes to mind; it went begging from house to house before it was finally published and became a monumental best seller.) Even more recently, my agency took on a script that was an odd sort of job and which we knew would be hard to sell, but which we liked very much, and we offered it to forty markets without acceptance or even encouragement. The forty-first market bought it gladly, paid a top price for it, and subsequently we showed an outstanding motion picture producer the book in galleys and he's bought the movie rights. Negotiations have also been concluded for the author to do the screenplay for the film, thus adding a large screen-writing fee to the healthy amounts the author has already received from the book advance and purchase of film rights.

The point is that if you have real faith in a script, keep it going to market after market until every logical possibility has been exhausted.

I might add, also, that although it is considered unethical to submit a story to more than one magazine at a time, because of the irritations and mix-ups which might occur if you sent out several copies of the same story and several different editors bought the story simultaneously, it's becoming increasingly acceptable, for several reasons, to submit copies of book manuscripts to more than one house at a time. The first reason has to do with the difference between book and magazine purchasing procedures. The process of contracting for your material is much more involved and time-consuming in the book field than with magazines, and there really is no danger that several houses could complete purchase simultaneously or even feel morally that they'd "acquired" your book. Second, as publishing houses continue to merge, sometimes growing smaller in number and staff but larger in the totals of books they publish each season, editors are having to face the fact that, with the increased number of submissions to each house, the delays in reading and reporting on submitted scripts are increasing, and the author will occasionally feel that he has to protect his interests by submitting to a few houses instead of just one. Third, and actually most important, some agencies (I'll admit that we were the first) have cleared the way for this practice by pioneering multiple submissions on our most important and hottest properties, pitting publishers against each other in competitive bidding and thereby "testing the market" and determining the best deal possible (the largest advance available, for example) on each book offered in that way.

No matter where and how you market your script, remember that it isn't wise to inform an editor that a script has previously been seen and rejected by others. However fair-minded he may be, and however much he may feel that he wants what he wants and doesn't care whether or not others wanted it, he may still form an unconscious prejudice against it.

Make sure, too, that you keep careful records of the markets to which you have submitted each script: you don't want to forget and return a script to an editor who has already seen and rejected it. The only time it is really safe to resubmit a script to a house that has already seen it is when you read in a writers' magazine that there has been a reorganization there and the staff substantially changed.

13   THE MOVIE INSIDE MY HEAD*

RICK BOYER

How is it that people become writers? Why do some people spend their lives building houses or working in shops and others playing around with words and the "movies" inside their heads, as our author puts it.

Writers, we are told, see things somewhat differently from people who don't write (I was about to say "ordinary people," but writers are ordinary people for the most part). Are they more sensitive? Are they more interested in people, their motivations, and preoccupations? Do they see things differently, for one reason or another?

Whatever the case, and creativity remains an enigma in the final analysis, writers are people who are willing to give of themselves and who have enough ego strength to feel that their efforts are valuable and will bring pleasure and insight to others. And, above all, writers are people who are willing to work hard, for writing takes a great deal of effort. The computer is a big help, since it facilitates rewriting, which is one of the keys to good writing. But a computer can only do what a writer tells it to do. So if you don't have a love of language (a kind of erotic fascination with words and their power to generate powerful emotional

---

and intellectual responses in people) and the ability to use words, computers will be of little benefit.

You must also work on something you really want to write and not do something foreign to you because you think it will be commercial. There are, of course, writers who churn out blockbuster novels that are highly formulaic and make lots of money. When our author tried to write one, he hated writing it, and the novel was ultimately rejected. You have to be true to yourself; if you aren't, it will show in the writing.

There is a correlation, also, our author tells us, between writing and reading. Writers read a great deal and with good reason: If you are going to write, you have to have something to write about. Writers also read with an eye toward craft — trying to learn more about how to write, looking at how different authors achieve their effects. For in the final analysis, and I will be somewhat reductionistic here, writing is a form of generating effects in people by using words. Sounds easy? Just remember that the odds of getting a first novel published are more than 10,000 to one. This suggests that writers also have to be courageous. Or is it foolhardy?

Recently, I was requested to appear, solo, before the board of directors of my Boston-based publisher. I have been on national television several times, including "The Today Show," "CBS Evening News," "PM Magazine," "The David Susskind Show," and similar programs. But the nervousness I felt as I entered that spacious boardroom, thirty-three stories above Boston harbor rivaled that of all the previous experiences put together. The board included such luminaries as the President of M.I.T., the Chairman of Arthur D. Little Company, The Chairman and C.E.O. of Norton, Inc. — still one of New England's largest employers — the Chairman of the Boston Federal Reserve Board...and so on.

So I waltzed in there and stood before them. The faces peered at me from over three-piece worsted suits, gazing far over the polished rosewood table that looked as big as the gridiron at Soldier Field. Bank presidents, university chancellors, captains of industry. All kinds of lightweights. And their faces, smiling though they were, seemed to be asking me silently: "okay hotshot, so what do *you* have to tell us that's so damn enlightening?"

As I said before, I was a little nervous. But hell, I thought, I'd been asked a lot of tough questions. Surely there was none too tough for a nice glib answer. I mean, I'd been interviewed by a lot of —

"Mr. Boyer," asked an attractive woman who, it turned out, was the wife of one of New York's leading politicians, and herself a major patron of the arts, "why did you become a writer?"

Oops! Got me there, right off the bat. The one question I couldn't answer. Hadn't thought about. It just seemed to have happened.

"Well..." I began slowly, "I don't really know how I got here, exactly....I mean...I think it started back when I was about fourteen years old...."

Why do people become writers? I think that's a more interesting question than *how* do people become writers. Although the two are linked in some ways, as we shall see in a little bit. But what makes somebody take up the pen or typewriter while his colleagues are content to make a secure living selling insurance, practicing law, or teaching?

I'm not sure I know. But I know there are symptoms of the writing calling, and I will briefly describe them.

A major symptom is compulsive reading. All major novelists — and probably 99-plus percent of the minor ones as well — are compulsive readers. If they will later become novelists, then they'll be reading fiction. Perhaps those who will eventually become biographers, reporters, or general nonfiction writers won't read fiction. But regardless, the potential writer is a reader, for it is reading that feeds writing. It is reading the written word, and visualizing through the reader's imagination of what is conveyed by the written words on a page, that initiates the skill and talent of writing the written word. So, in short, you must read to write. If a compulsive reader is without a good book, he'll try a mediocre one. Or he'll read magazines. I subscribe to seventeen magazines, from the *New Yorker* to *Guns and Ammo*...from *Smithsonian* and *Bon Appetit* to *Soldier of Fortune* and *Field and Stream*. If he can't find a magazine or mediocre book, he'll try soup labels. In fact, he'll generally try reading many, many things of marginal quality before he succumbs to solitaire or television. In the course of my teaching, travels, and appearances, I've had scores of people come up to me and confess their secret urge to write. I encourage these people. But often it becomes apparent that the aspirant I'm talking with doesn't read anything but *TV Guide*. Sorry, Charlie. Not a prayer. Not a snowball's chance in hell.

What about some other symptoms of this illness called "urge to write?"

Well, one is sensitivity. It's been said before that writers are sensitive people. It's a cliché — a stereotype. But like so many stereotypes, it has a basis in fact. Writers *are* sensitive. Events that slide past the average person like a warm spring breeze hit the writer full in the face like a left hook from Marvin Hagler. My writing teacher in graduate school, Kurt Vonnegut, Jr., used to say that writers — and by extension all artists — are like the canaries that miners took down into the coal mines in the old days. Canaries, being extremely sensitive to oxygen levels, would collapse and die when the air in the mine started to go bad. The birds died long before the men noticed the poison coal gas, and so saved the men. Well, Vonnegut said, writers are like those canaries: they see and feel things long before the rest of the population, and so give warning. I remember, when I was about thirteen years old, Jerry Lewis appearing on TV in support of the muscular dystrophy fund. With him was a boy in a wheelchair. During the ad, it was made clear that the boy was dying, and that nothing could save him. A boy my own age. In a wheelchair. Dying. The vision of that boy haunted me steadily, constantly, for over a month. My other friends forgot it after a few minutes. In all honesty, the vision of that boy, and all others like him, still haunts me. Things bother me. I can't help thinking about them, worrying, and wondering about them. Sensitivity. Vulnerability. Whatever you choose to call it, writers have it. Have it in spades.

A third symptom of Writer's Syndrome is a compulsive need to share experience. I remember as a boy of fifteen sailing in a sloop in Lake Michigan. I remember closing my eyes momentarily, then opening them to the scene of the boat heeled over in the waves, the sail snapping and thrumming in the wind, the boat's timbers and lines making those faint creaks and groans as she plowed through the cold blue water. "That's how this looks," I remember saying to myself. "That's what Rick's doing right now..." It was my own movie, right inside my head. *Movie inside my head.* Remember that phrase, for that's what writing fiction is all about: visualizing a movie in your head. Then the writing is simply the putting down on paper of that movie. That movie, peopled by the characters you choose, doing what you want them to, where, when, why, and how you want them to do it, is the basis of all fiction.

But how do you get that movie? Do you find it under a rock? In a hollow tree in a secret, shady glen in a spooky forest? Of course not. You must make it up. You must create it. And creativity is such an overworked, overused, vague word that it's boring. But I will say this: any writer of fiction needs, perhaps above all other things, an *active imagination*. For he must improve upon reality. His task is to make fiction more real than reality, more heightened. Albert Einstein said: "imagination is more important than knowledge." I'm not sure I totally agree, but then, who's going to argue with Albert? What a smarty pants *he* was!

So there, I think, are the basic symptoms of this rather dubious calling: this thing we call writing. First, there is the love of the written word as expressed in compulsive reading. Secondly, a desire to share with other people, to communicate, those private, often beautiful and sometimes disturbing, episodes of the movie inside your head. And you as a writer will have this movie in your head for two very important reasons, and they are the other symptoms. You will have an active, visual imagination that works overtime, providing you with clear, sometimes startling images that you can translate into the written word. And secondly, you will have that movie inside your head because, unlike most of your friends, colleagues, and loved ones, you are both blessed and cursed by an extraordinary sensitivity, a vulnerability, that *won't let it rest!*

So, suppose you've discovered the movie inside your head. Suppose that you figure you've got the urge to communicate, the love of the written word — as expressed mainly by a voracious appetite for reading — writer's sensitivity to the feelings of life, and, of course, an active imagination. If you have writer's syndrome, what then?

The answer is: you must scratch the itch. You must write. And the only way you'll truly learn to write well is by writing. Writing and re-writing. And writing and writing and re-writing and re-writing. And on and on and on and on....

What to write about? That's the hardest question of all. Two words of advice on this. One: write about what you know. And two: be honest.

Write about what you know. You can't fake a location, for example. You can't write well about a place you've never been. Audiences are sophisticated these days; they're educated and well travelled. And if not well travelled, they've been almost everywhere indirectly through television and the movies. They'll know when you're faking it. Write about things you've done, or observed, first hand. Just as you can't fake a location, you can't fake a job, an object, an attitude, an emotion, you haven't experienced. Don't worry, there are plenty of experiences there in your life. Don't be afraid to use them.

Be honest. Don't write about characters you don't believe in. Make them good; make them bad; make them in between. But you, as the author and the creator the characters, must believe in each one totally. Because if you don't, the reader never will. I know this is true, because in 1980 I began my "blockbuster" novel. You all know what blockbusters are. They're those paperback novels with big, bright covers that are set up on special cardboard display cases (called "floor dumps" in the bookselling trade) in the middle of the bookstore, up front near the cash registers. They've got *blockbuster* written all over them, literally and figuratively. The publisher has sunk oodles of loot into seeing that everybody buys and reads this "blockbuster." Everybody wants to write one because they make you rich and famous. And everybody wants that. Including especially, me.

So, I began grinding out this blockbuster. It had everything needed to become a blockbuster, too. I saw to that. It had sex; it had violence. I had Israeli spies and old, retired Nazis. It was set in the Arctic and on exotic, tropical islands. It took place in Washington and Moscow. Tel Aviv and Paraguay. You name it; the book had it.

But the further I got into this made-to-order blockbuster, the more I realized I had a major problem: the book was no fun to write. I was, literally, *grinding* it out. I didn't look forward to continuing the story; I dreaded sitting down at the typewriter to work on it. Finally, I sent a big portion of the book out to publishers for review and, I hoped, a fat contract offer. But guess what? None of them cared much for it. They all said the characters were not believable. They weren't real people; they were moving mannequins. And guess what again? I agreed with them. And then I realized why the writing hadn't been any fun. You see, I was deliberately trying to write someone else's conception of a book. I was deliberately faking it, trying to write a blockbuster. Or rather, what I thought publishers thought a blockbuster should be. But it wasn't my book. No, I was writing someone else's book. I was trying to write down the movie in *someone else's* head, and that's why it was no fun to write. And also why it was boring to read.

I guess I could re-phrase these two rules (write about what you know, and be honest) in shorter form: write from the heart. If you write from your heart, you'll write from your own experience naturally. And you will believe utterly in every person, place, and action, even if you invent some of them. Because if it's from your heart, its from *you*.

Okay, so you're busy writing from the heart, and writing and re-writing. How do you know what you are producing is any good? One way to find out is to show the WIP (work in progress) to friends and colleagues. Make sure these friends and colleagues that you choose are also literate. That is, make sure they are readers — people who appreciate books and read often for pleasure. Somebody who only reads the sports page and TV Guide might be able to make a few suggestions as to the action, but he won't be worth a damn for telling you how to improve the writing style.

It's also important that these reviewers know you well enough to be absolutely frank and candid with you about the work. Don't choose somebody who is going to say he likes the work — when he can't stand it — just so your feelings won't be hurt.

When you get the responses back (and I here inject the caveat that if you want to write, you had better develop a thick skin, and *fast*, because the criticisms can be devastating) listen to them carefully, and weigh in your own mind their validity. This is tricky. On the one hand, you must have enough basic faith in your ability and in your story so that you won't dash off and re-write the work according to everyone else's wishes. If you operate on this principle, you'll never finish the piece. And even if you managed to complete it, you'd end up with a story that makes no sense and has no style, since it, like a third-rate television sit-com, is trying to please everybody, and consequently pleases no one.

On the other hand, you *did* send the work out for comments and suggestions. You should always pay attention to intelligent criticism, and see if following the suggestions contained therein won't improve the work. I can't give you any help regarding which comments to accept and which to ignore except this one, which is a cardinal rule with me: if the comments are disparate, each mentioning a different point, you will have to pick and choose which ones to follow (if any). However, if all, or the majority of comments, make the *same points*, then you'd better follow them, and without hesitation. So look for uniformity of criticism. It's almost always a sure-fire guide.

Now, a word or two about grammar, syntax, style, and so on. The word is: we're *not* doing these. There are plenty of books out there that will tell you how to use correct grammar. There are books about how to develop a good style (whatever that is). There are books on how to write novels, how to create "memorable characters," how to sell your book, and so on. You know where to buy them.

One thing about grammar, though. Good grammar does not automatically translate into good fiction. Just because you are a good speller, use the parts of speech correctly, and know how to construct a paragraph, doesn't automatically mean you've got what it takes to be a novelist. In fact, one of the world's greatest novels — and my personal favorite of all books — is told through the eyes of a rural, uneducated, abused, neglected, outcast boy of thirteen. Huckleberry Finn is a brilliant novel, but grammatical it *ain't.*

And what is style, anyway? There are hundreds of definitions. Most experts agree that writing style is the use of words that sets an author's work apart, that identifies it as unmistakably his. Hemingway was famous for his sparse style. He told stories reporter-fashion, with few descriptive words and no wasted ones. Twain's style was down-home and on the button. Twain could describe something, be it a steamboat or an evening gown, a thunderstorm or a running coyote, better than anyone. Melville's style is eloquent and philosophical. Dickens' is highly descriptive, especially regarding his characters and use of dialect. P.G. Wodehouse's use of words is cozy and witty. Noel Coward's is flamboyant and witty. Norman Mailer's is raw and macho. And so on.

I would say that writing style — good writing style — is the use of words that is clear, specific, interesting, and genuine. Genuine means it's not faked. Genuine means, written from the heart. Genuine means *appropriate,* for the occasion, or the book. Your particular style will evolve with time and effort. It should fit you naturally.

Finding your own style is like trying on bluejeans. You keep trying on pairs and pairs of jeans until you suddenly stop, walk around, look in the mirror and say: this is it! You know you've finally got the right pair because the pants fit naturally. Don't bind in the crotch...don't sag in the seat... don't chafe at the waist, don't drag on the floor...and like that. Same with style: you'll find one that fits you when it *fits.*

So that's my version of how, and mainly *why,* people elect to become writers. Look for the signs of writer's syndrome. You may or may not be blessed, or cursed, with it. If you have it, and the urge to write that cannot be denied or postponed, then *do it!* And always remember that books about writing may help, but they are no substitute for writing and re-writing, which is the only way to really learn the craft. Remember, too, that reading feeds writing; it's the grass and clover that makes the milk. And when you read, read the best. Read works that have proven themselves over time. Life is short; don't waste time reading crud. Above all, don't give up. It's a sad fact, but oftentimes the successful writer is not the most talented one, but rather the one who is simply too stupid to quit.

So get going. And remember, develop a thick skin, and fast. And one more thing: good luck; you're gonna need it.*

So I finished my little talk and answered the questions that were asked of me by the board of directors. I went down the carpeted hallway and got into

---

* I read recently that the odds of publishing a first novel nowadays are approximately 14,000 to 1...against. Have a nice day.

the elevator for the ride down to the street. "That was brilliant!" said one of the directors who was sharing the elevator.

"Well thanks," I said. "But you know, really it isn't. It just happens, I guess." Then I shut up, closed my eyes, and watched that never-ending, crazy-quilt, mental panorama unfold. I was busy watching that *movie inside my head*...

14   BOND AND HAMMER*
Charles Winick

To understand the cultural significance and importance of heroic figures such as James Bond and Mike Hammer, it is useful to know something about mythic heroes in general. With this as a background one can make sense of heroes of all kinds, regardless of the genre, formula, or medium. What follows is a selection from an analysis made by Joseph Campbell in *Hero with a Thousand Faces* of the "composite hero" who is an archetype or model for all heroes:

> The mythological hero, setting forth from his hut or castle, is lured, carried away, or else voluntarily proceeds, to a threshold of adventure. There he encounters a shadow presence that guards the passage. There the hero may defeat or conciliate this power and go alive into the kingdom of the dark (brother-battle, dragon-battle; offering, charm), or be slain by the opponent and descend in death (dismemberment, crucifixion). Beyond the threshold, then, the hero journeys through a world of unfamiliar yet strangely intimate forces, some of which severely threaten him (tests), some of which give magical aid (helpers). When he arrives at the nadir of the mythological round, he undergoes a supreme ordeal and gains his reward. The triumph may be represented as the hero's sexual union with the goddess-mother of the world (sacred marriage), his recognition by the father-creator (father atonement), or again — if the powers have remained unfriendly to him — his theft of the boon he came to gain (bride-theft, fire-theft); intrinsically it is an expansion of consciousness and therewith of being (illumination, transfiguration, freedom). The final work is that of the return. If the powers have blessed the hero, he now sets forth under their protection (emissary); if not, he flees and is pursued (transformation flight, obstacle flight). At the return threshold the transcendental powers must remain behind; the hero

---

* Charles Winick, "Bond and Hammer" from *The New People* (1968). Reprinted by permission of Sanford Greenburger Associates, Inc.

re-emerges from the kingdom of dread (return, insurrection). The boon that he brings restores the world (elixir)."[1]

We have to update and modernize many of the matters discussed in this model; thus, instead of stealing "fire" he or she may steal "secrets" (as a spy) or kill a villain or two. But if Campbell is correct, all heroes are variations of one mythological heroic figure and Bond, Hammer, Superman, Luke Skywalker, and Rambo (to name some important ones) all are based upon the pattern sketched above. Campbell's notion that there is a basic model for all heroes is controversial. It may be that he overgeneralized but it is remarkable how well the pattern applies to our heroes, ancient and modern.

REFERENCE

1. Campbell, Joseph (1956). *Hero with a Thousand Faces*. (New York: World Publishing) pp. 245, 246.

Mickey Spillane's Mike Hammer and Ian Fleming's James Bond became extraordinarily successful at the same time as the group hero. Spillane had created the character Mike Danger for comic books. When the industry's uneasiness about censorship led to a decline in comic book sales, Spillane had little difficulty in adapting his techniques to the Mike Hammer series. Hammer is a killer who takes the law into his own hands — the first book celebrating his exploits was aptly called *I, The Jury*.

Hammer and James Bond prefer gratuitous killing to solving cases by using their wits. We have so little confidence in what lone intelligence can accomplish in the urbanized world that our two most popular detectives solve cases by the vendetta morality of murder. The Mike Hammer novels account for seven of the fifteen leading American bestsellers of all time and Bond, the professional assassin who lacks personal identity and real allegiance, is an American hero.

If there is an obligatory scene in a Spillane novel, it is one in which Hammer shoots his girlfriend in the stomach. "It was easy," is Hammer's comment after gratuitously shooting his nude fiancée in *I, The Jury*. In the film version of Fleming's *From Russia With Love*, a key scene shows a man being shot while dangling from the mouth of Anita Ekberg in a large painting on the side of a building. The best evidence of the huge audience response to such material is provided by the astonishing $150 million grossed by the first four Bond films and the more than $100 million that Americans spent on "007"-licensed products during 1966.

Sean Connery has almost agreed with *Pravda*'s description of Bond as a "sadistic rapist" in his observation that the series is successful because it is "sadism for the whole family." Like Hammer, Bond has no continuing personal relationships with women but conducts detached adventures. His major thrill seems to come from arousing women and then not making love to them, in a kind of sexless sex. In *Goldfinger*, Bond is in bed with a woman, tells his chief on the telephone that "I can't talk to you now, something big's come up" — and then ignores the woman. American audiences reserve their greatest applause for three kinds of situations: nonfulfillment, as in the *Goldfinger* scene; Bond's use of gratuitous violence; and the mechanical devices that are the films' real hero.

Several interview studies have established that the most typical American fans of Bond are men who tend to alienation, impotence, hostility toward women, and passivity, with fantasies of violence. Similar characteristics have been reported in other countries. Small wonder that many Bond fans happily hummed along with the title song of *Thunderball* about a man who knew the secret of success: "His needs are more, so he gives less."

Bond's cruelty to women has received recognition in the advertising for the "007" line of men's toiletries. The Colgate-Palmolive Company has been spending $400,000 a week to disseminate slogans like "007 for the license to kill...women." Such advertising is primarily directed at young men, whose fantasies about women, once nurtured on romance and soft music, may now be more amenable to brutality.

The Bond novels received considerable impetus from the enormous publicity afforded the Profumo affair in England. The combination of fast women, peers, weekend country orgies, Soviet espionage, an American procurer who committed suicide, a lying cabinet minister, and a famous actress made life appear to be imitating art in its corroboration of Ian Fleming's vision of reality. There was a sharp increase in the sale of Bond books during and after the Profumo publicity, suggesting that many readers may have regarded Stephen Ward's trial as a confirmation of Fleming's themes.

Bond's great popularity is less surprising in England than the United States, because the English have long enjoyed heroes who murder out of a sense of duty. T. E. Lawrence's legendary status in his own country is partially attributable to his celibacy, but largely to his enthusiasm for dynamiting trains and engaging in other kinds of brutality, while serving the Crown, just as the detailed technology of Bond's murders is presumably part of his patriotic responsibility. One reason that Bond is more of a hero in America than England could be his many resemblances to a Fascist or Nazi officer, which may stir some uncomfortable memories even in a country that shared Lawrence's relish for the minutiae of violence.

Bond is an ideal American hero because he triumphantly represents the new technology. The Bond movies would be ordinary thrillers without the complicated gadgets that make gratuitous murder such fun. When depersonalization and alienation are rife, it is easier for us to respond to Bond's machinery and unbelievable luck than to courage, integrity, and similar old-fashioned virtues.

Bond and Hammer are amoral, sadistic, misogynistic. They could encourage paranoid fantasies because the evil they are fighting can never be vanquished and is always coming up strong for the next encounter. Bond's employer is identified by code (M.) and has extraordinary potentialities for good and evil. Bond and Hammer are proponents of a lynch or vigilante morality that encourages people to take the law into their own hands. Each man implies that extant procedures for establishing order are inadequate and is an extra-legal avenger who typically ends each story by participating in a symbolic lynching. The culprit is killed instead of being turned over to the police in accordance with orderly processes of justice, as Sam Spade would have done. American enthusiasm for Bond and Hammer is especially troubling in the light of our traditional respect for law and law enforcement. No other country has any analogue to our veneration for J. Edgar Hoover and the police and T-men and G-men who have been glorified in American popular culture and are regarded as necessary evils in other countries.

Our preoccupation with vigilantes suggests the possibility that many Americans are losing confidence in the ability of reason and intelligence to solve problems. We have honored reason and intelligence ever since the Areopagus law court in Athens reminded us that public good cannot be advanced by private murders or the vendetta morality of terror. When Orestes killed Aegisthus and Clytemnestra in an act of revenge, Athena was wise enough to refer the case to jurors of the Areopagus. This early example of man's ability to think in terms of abstract Justice contrasts with Bond and Hammer, who represent the barbaric cruelty of the childhood of the human race, the archaic and unintelligible emotions of the Furies who are more interested in the blood on Orestes' hands than in how it got there.

One reason for the almost unbearably intense guilt that Americans experienced after President Kennedy's assassination was our identification with fictional and movie vigilantes who take the law into their own hands. The awful horror of what happened when this was done in Dallas was a sobering reminder of our enthusiasm for vigilante heroes. President Kennedy's widely publicized enthusiasm for the Bond books added an additional poignant note to the events of November 1963. Lee Oswald had read Ian Fleming, according to New Orleans Public Library records. Without adopting any primitive thinking about the effects of mass media, we can consider the possibility, however remote, that James bond's glorification of violence, marksmanship, and ability to kill without guilt may have been one of the many strands in Oswald's fantasies about using murder in achieving his own goals.

The close relationship between sex and violence in Bond and Hammer reminds us of the reciprocal relationship between sex and violence. Some slang words reflect the connotations of sex as an attack, and "violate" and "violence" come from the same root. A related reason for our interest in violence could be its status as one of the few remaining mysteries, now that sex has become less awesome.

We abhor the violence in which Hammer and Bond engage but are attracted by its provision of a triple respite from the boredom of everyday life. Their great popularity may reflect our desperate need to reach beyond a world of neuter people and identify with persons who assert themselves in an ultimate manner — by killing.

RADIO

In the greater San Francisco area there are approximately sixty radio stations competing for listeners. There is an important university station, KUSF, and there are several stations that play material from the Public Broadcasting System, the most important of which is KQED-FM. There is an alternative broadcasting station, KPFA, which offers "radical" news broadcasts (and a variety of other kinds of programs) and there are several all-classical music stations, such as KKHI and KDFC.

Then there is the usual spectrum of stations found in major metropolitan areas that are listed below:

Beautiful Music	Mexican Top 40
News/Sports/Traffic/Weather	Black Soul
Disco (now discontinued)	Country
Christian	News Talk
Adult Contemporary	Big Bands and Oldies
Light Rock	Top Forty
Soft Jazz, Blues, Salsa	All Oldies
Progressive Alternative	Jazz Fusion
Album Oriented Rock	Easy Listening
Free Form	Punk, New Wave

Of course the San Francisco area is the fifth largest media market in America and you might expect to find a considerable amount of variety there. Stations keep changing their formats in a desperate quest for a higher share of the listening audience and higher advertising revenues.

Radio has become increasingly specialized in the major markets, where it serves a wide variety of publics. Its success is intimately connected to something that plays a crucial role in our lives — our automobiles.

Thus Los Angeles is the second largest city in America, but it is the number one radio market. This is because there are so many cars in Los Angeles and because the people there spend so much time in the automobiles. Rush hour in Los Angeles starts earlier and ends later than in most cities. And while all these Los Angelinos are in their automobiles they are listening to their radios.

As we develop, our interests change and we use the radio for different purposes. The chart that follows offers some examples of how, I would suggest, this works.

Age	Program type	Need
youth	adventure	heroes
teenagers	rock music	love, emotions
adults	news	information
senior citizens	talk shows	participation

The boundaries separating one age group from another are not very strong and there is a good deal of overlapping. But young children (when there were adventure stories, that is) used to follow "The Lone Ranger" and the myriad other heroes with great dedication. (This function, as far as young children are concerned, has now been usurped by television.)

Teenagers and those around that age listen to rock music, which deals with their increased interest in the opposite sex and with their emotional needs. Music television has had an impact here, but radio still plays an important role.

Adults, having consolidated their identities and no longer (as a rule) having the kind of romantic involvements of teenagers, tend to be more interested in news and information about politics and events. When they listen to music, they tend to listen to music that is less strident than rock and roll — formats such as easy listening or golden oldies. Older people, statistics suggest, listen to talk shows a great deal (and participate in them, as well). These programs help older people deal with feelings of loneliness and separation.

The chart shown above offers suggestions about how people in different age groups, with different developmental needs, use radio. Statistics indicate that as people grow older, they change their listening (and television viewing) habits — presumably because of different needs they have.

The articles in this section deal with a variety of topics — with a focus on some of radio's more important programs and formats. When television became popular it was widely believed that radio would die out. That has not proved to be the case. Radio is alive and well and showing a great deal of vitality. Whether it is all it might be is another matter.

15 HELLO, YOU'RE ON THE AIR*

JEAN FRANCO

Talk shows are one of the most fascinating kinds of programs, for the "anonymity" of the radio seems to facilitate all kinds of remarkable revelations on the part of those who call in. The talk show is a general category; within this we find many different kinds of talk shows, ranging from general discussions of political events to psychiatric shows, in which people talk about their problems (many of which turn out to have a sexual component to them).

Approximately ten percent of the AM dial is devoted to talk shows. These programs appeal to an older and often less affluent audience, people who are between thirty-five to sixty-five years old. (Some estimates place half the audience for radio talk shows at above sixty-five years of age.) Since the American public is aging, it would seem likely that talk shows will be growing increasingly important.

What do these talk shows tell us about American society? On the immediate level, they tell us what people are interested in and excited about. That is, they tell us a good deal about opinions people have. When you listen to a number of talk shows, you find that there are all kinds of people in America, and that many of them have some pretty remarkable (one might say bizarre) ideas.

Many people use these talk shows as a forum — that is, a means of getting their ideas and their opinions broadcast. There are "one-issue" callers who call a given station a number of times in a given day. There are members of organizations who use their calls to spread its views and make its existence known to people. These people use talk radio as an electronic form of a "town meeting."

There are many talk shows that are very specialized — and which deal with everything from making and taking care of money to chatter about sports or the problems of minorities. Some talks shows, then, have an educational thrust to them, using the term "education" very broadly.

One of the most important uses people make of talk shows is to find companionship and company. These shows help people who are isolated and lonely obtain partial relief from these feelings by being able to listen to others and, for those who phone in, talk to others. The talk shows, then, help people keep in contact with other people…even if this contact is electronically mediated.

The article we are to read focuses on the talk show hosts on a radio station in San Francisco and how they relate to audiences. It is a fascinating picture and a perspective that is not common in studies of talk radio.

---

* Jean Franco, "Hello, You're On The Air." From *Tabloid* Magazine, Winter, 1982, No. 5.

"The new media are egalitarian in structure. Anyone can take part in them by a simple switching process….Potentially, the new media do away with all educational privileges and thereby with the cultural monopoly of the bourgeois intelligentsia. This is one of the reasons for the intelligentsia's resentment against the new industry."
(Hans Magnus Enzenberger, *"Constituents of a Theory of the Media,"* The Consciousness Industry)

"Do the media's various genres and formats, which divide up 'the public' into fragments and partition off different areas of knowledge, do anything other than reproduce social divisions intrinsic to bourgeois society?"
(Armand Mattelart, Mass Media, Ideologies and the Revolutionary Movement)

Critics who believe that the media have deprived people of their voice often imagine an alternative of magical mass participation. The "people" will be transformed into cultural producers. No longer passive receivers of media messages, they will busy themselves in non-stop communication. Curiously these critics don't hear what is within earshot or pay attention to a form of participation that already exists — the radio talk show.

You're on the air.

Compared to the lavish attention given to television, radio has attracted very little comment and talk shows practically none at all. Yet there's hardly a minute of the day when you can't call into some program or other to ask for advice, give advice, make a public confession or talk about yourself and the government. Ronald Reagan called a talk show in Texas when he wanted to give his economic policy an airing. In *Private Benjamin* Goldie Hawn phones in to a talk show for advice and gets recruited into the army. Do you want to set someone straight on ERA, or tell the caller before last what you think of his damnfool ideas, do you want to tell someone about the funny thing that happened on the way to your honeymoon or get advice about acne? Call in. You might have to wait for an hour and a half before you get on the air, and you have to go through a producer who screens what you have to say — all of which rules out the spontaneous overflow of powerful feeling, but is good for slow burners and patient watchers in the night. Let's face it, there's a hell of a lot of us around.

The whole country is blanketed with talk. There are hundreds of talk shows going on at any one moment in the United States, some of them for twenty-four hours a day. You'd need a thousand years to get a balanced view of it all. Radio talk is as varied as talk itself.

KGO's midnight to dawn audience outdistances most other stations' overall performance. What does that mean to you as an advertiser? I'll tell you. Our listeners tonight are your customers tomorrow. If you enjoy playing "Everything is Coming up Roses" on the cash register, this is the place to write the music. (Russ Coughlan, KGO, San Francisco)

Radio talk defies statistics too. How can you tell who's listening or when? Or how many? Listeners are always changing, always on the move, always being cut off or switching stations. After all, talk shows came in during the sixties at the height of television prime time compulsive watching when radio was supposed to curl up and die. Instead radio reached places that television couldn't get to — the inside of cars, the workbench, the counter — and many of the best talk shows were late at night when television had closed down or was showing old movies. If there's a classic place for listening to talk shows, it is driving long distances at night, or when you're waiting for the traffic lights to change at rush hour.

OK. The light's red, you're waiting for the green arrow, and here's someone calling in to KGO worried, of all things, about *dichotomies*.

...Now to my belief, dichotomies began in the Garden of Eden. As a Believer, I have decided that nuclear bombs and dichotomies, although scientific, they're not good, Russ.

Anyway, have a nice day tomorrow.

As you wait in the supermarket, you hear an anxious voice from a transistor,

No, that's the problem. Poland's not allowed in,

Oh, O.K.

No, no, no. That's the whole point — that Poland's not allowed in. We should quit playing politics with people's lives.

Snatches of rap. This kind of listening appeals to those of us who creep after tour groups in museums, eavesdropping on their conversations. It's the ear's equivalent to the keyhole. It's rap rhythm. You can almost dance to it. Rap records use heated up talk shows. And they're better than muzak.

Rap snatches are like subauditory appetizers that make you ready for a whole show. That's when you sit down and listen to the people who call in. You begin to recognize regulars who have preferences for certain talk shows and the patience to hold the line at 2AM. In public broadcasting call-ins, all the callers seem to be regulars, thus enhancing the impression of a cosy club. But the true talk show audience is composed of invalids, insomniacs, and verbal exhibitionists like the people who call Bill Bassett in San Diego with their sex talk. Bill's gravelly voice has the effect of making every conversation into a seduction scene.

Haven't we talked before?

Studio at KNBR Radio, San Francisco. Photo courtesy of KNBR.

No, this is my first time.

You don't sound terrified at all, my darling. Are you married, pumpkin?

Listening to Bill Bassett is like hearing public confession and he does not fail to remind his listeners that they can be heard all over southern California. Callers give their first names (which can easily be fictional), but they also have both the anonymity of the confessional and the publicity of an exhibitionist.

The regulars are mostly night people. On KGO in the Bay Area, there is a dividing line between day shows and night shows. Day shows are often advice shows. The hosts invite guests. X-spurts, as one lady caller called them. "X is an unknown quantity and spurt is simply a drip under pressure." Well, so the X-spurts — astrologers, psychics, human relations counsellors, politicians, and sex therapists, but also vets, real estate agents, carpenters, and car repairmen attract a lot of calls. But this kind of show simply duplicates the communication of knowledge in society at large, carrying out the transmission and acquisition of techniques which enable people to deal with cars, manage bank accounts and human relations, preferably by using the same devices. The rules for all categories are the same: look after your property, give it a regular check up, proceed in an orderly way and don't rush into anything without taking professional advice.

The real talk show, however, is quite different. It is a free flow affair with Jim Eason or Russ Coughlan quoting something they read in the paper or sounding off about bureaucracy or the med fly. The calls come rolling in the minute their shift starts. This is public opinion in the raw, the absolute contrast to the "expert." And best of all, it is mostly political talk. At a moment when political decisions are increasingly being reserved for the experts (e.g. MX missile sites), the talk show remains one area in which it is legitimate and good to have opinions even when you know nothing at all about whatever it is you're talking about.

Keep on jogging, I'll be back....

"You're a mature adult lady and I can tell that by your voice." (Russ Coughlan on KGO)

The talk show recognizes the supremacy of the expert, then, but at the same time and especially at night, it also accommodates that public opinion that just floats around without any party or institution to accommodate it. Opinion is, by definition, not informed or specialized and information must not be allowed to get in its way. Whereas conversation with the expert is unequal — the caller is asking for guidance, the free flow talk show starts from the assumption that everyone is entitled to an opinion. The host must give the impression that other people's opinions are as legitimate as his own. He can't lecture from an obvious position of superiority, he can only argue from sources that are available to everybody — newspapers, television, radio news. So at the very least, talk shows are good ways of gauging what opinions are around at any given time. Of course there is endless confusion and misquotation. That is why the predominant tone of the talk show host (almost invariably male in the political talk shows) is emphatic and assertive, especially when he is on shaky ground. Talk shows are not about hard facts. They are about holding and defending opinions. What you are testing when you call is not the truth of your information, the validity of experience, or even your grasp on reality, but the ability to hold your own. That's why the talk show host can't afford to be consistent. If the callers are against hand gun control, he leans toward it. Russ Coughlan believes as a matter of principle in going whichever way the wind blows.

It has a lot to do with societal pressures at the time, and I think what society ought to do and what we ought to do is to adjust to whatever the condition is at the time. There might be a lot of times we ought to be right-wing. There might be a lot of times when you say "I have a Barry Goldwater attitude to that thing and we ought to go in with 8 million bombers" and then there's another time when you're going to say "What! You're going to take food from poor people!" And what we can't do is to get so constricted in our thinking that we're not able to change as the condition of the time changes.

Women rarely host political talk shows perhaps because they are too deferential to the listeners. You have to be both patient and abrasive to make it work. KGO in the Bay Area runs twenty-four hours of talk, much of it is free flow, and has a regular team that includes Owen Spann, Jim Eason Ray Taliaferro, and Russ Coughlan. They each have their different styles. Eason is the bullyboy, a "quasi-libertarian" according to his own description of himself. Taliaferro is a more liberal counterpart, but inclined to be too brusque with callers. "Thank you so much for your call" is out of his mouth even before the listener has caught breath. Russ, on the other hand, lets talkers go on and on. He's on the night shift from 11 till 1 a.m. when lonely people begin to feel their loneliness.

> I don't make a million and a half a year like that phony left-fielder for the Yankees who catches three fly balls a night. I sit here three hours a night, five nights a week — fifteen hours, listening to you insane people talk to me.

It is true that the host has an advantage over the listeners. He has his producer, who screens calls. He can use the bleeper to eliminate obscenities. He has a sheaf of newsclippings to back up whatever line he wants to plug on that particular show. But the important thing is that his information comes from sources that are available to everybody — from newspapers, popular TV shows or radio news flashes. If you have ever had the feeling that the Left is out of touch with what people think you should listen to one of the talk shows precisely because it is a barometer not of accuracy or detail, but of common knowledge. Here for instance is Russ brazening out his ignorance of Irish history with a caller with an Irish accent who has challenged him to explain what he means when he says that there are two IRAs:

> Well the IRA was originally formed to fight, as I recall, the Black and Tans during the Black and Tan times of the English in Ireland. They were a revolutionary organization to fight that kind of oppression by the British. The IRA grew and grew and all of a sudden in the later years as more young people came into it with different political ideas there was an arm or group of people within the IRA that were Marxists, avowed Marxists because they wanted a revolution, you know, because of their Marxist attitudes and not because of the original idea that the IRA was formed for. And on the basis of that the IRA withdrew from that militant group and formed the provisional IRA and Marxist group which is the IRA which is running around throwing the bombs and starving themselves to death in prison are based upon the Marxist lot.

Well of course this is quite wrong as history. It has more the air of a fairy tale. The IRA, like Jack's beanstalk, just grew and grew and grew. Russ has mixed up the non-Marxist left, which has a militant wing (the Provos) with quite a different group, the INLA, the Irish National Liberation Army.

The point of all this is not to show that the talk show host is mistaken — you could spend a lifetime correcting just one evening's errors — but rather to demonstrate that this represents "common knowledge" i.e. the knowledge that is going around at any given time. In this case it becomes clear that Russ has got it all from a current best-seller, Claire Sterling's *The Terrorist Network*. The caller is able to counter with two best-sellers of his own which give the IRA view of things.

A persistent caller with special knowledge can get the better of the host in this way, but it is often a slender victory, especially for people with strong ideological convictions. One of the purposes of the talk show is a constant and ever-fluctuating sifting process whereby such people are labelled as crazies and others, in contrast, are made to feel safely "inside". Those on the inside agree to exchange opinions, unlike those crazy people who suddenly become Marxists and then go around throwing bombs and starving themselves to death.

Keep on jogging, I'll be right back.

> If you support the right, the natural tendency is for the other extreme, the far left to come into power, and by and large, they're just as bad or even worse than what they got rid of. By and large, it seems to me, what we should be doing and not just in El Salvador, but in any other troubled nations, nations with whom we have dealings is to try and encourage people who are more towards the center, who are more moderate. (Russ Coughlan)

> You're really crazy. You're all fired up and going crazy. (Russ Coughlan)

Opinions, like the stock market but unlike "rigid ideologies" fluctuate. The market is, indeed the economic model on which the talk shows are based. Hence the worst transgression is for the consumer to sabotage the system by refusing payment or by slamming down the phone. A caller admitting that she had to declare bankruptcy in order not to lose her home during a spell of unemployment brought on an outburst of denunciation, for it was considered a transgression of the whole market system, and as such had to be proved immoral.

> Big business is not *bad* business, guys. They're getting stuck a lot....Come on, if you owe, you owe. That never changes. If I was in a craps game, in the army, and one of you guys owed me, you owed me.

Business, Russ explains, is there to keep things moving.

What we deal with in television and radio is moving goods and services and what makes the economy of the United States is moving goods and services and that isn't moving goods and services to people who are going to stick you. And I tell you that's what the free enterprise system is about, so don't condemn us because we advertise. And our advertisers are good guys, they give you value for whatever it is.

The talk show is like the economy because it keeps things moving. It mustn't stick or worse, get stuck. That's why it follows rules that are rather different from those of everyday conversation. In everyday conversation there are implicit conventions for when it is appropriate to intervene or change the subject, and for when the ball can be passed from one speaker to the next. But the talk show rules are quite different since one speaker (the host) has so much power. Moreover, the impression of movement can only be kept up by constant interruptions ("Hey, Phil, I've got to run, thanks for your call") which are made necessary by commercial breaks, by news and weather reports as well as by the host's sense of when a caller has had his or her two cents worth. ("Thank you for letting me put in my two cents worth," says a caller to Ray Taliaferro.) Because only the host has the right to interrupt, the power in a talk show is quite unequally divided, just as the power between business and the customer is unequally divided. The caller's only defense in this situation, especially if he or she holds an unpopular position, is to hang up — only to expose themselves to instant condemnation. A lady who accuses Russ of being a pharisee and immediately slams down the phone, for instance, aroused the following diatribe:

What I'd like to ask is what is her morality. Don't bring up a lot of obtuse kinds of conditions to talk about whether we should pay our bills or not. Come on. What we are talking about, we're not talking about that. And that terrible moral lady who hung up. I'd like to ask where *her* morals are. Her morals are probably only talking about people who have difficulties not doing anything about it.

You know you are really lucky to live in California. Your life style is the envy of people all over the country. One of your favorite pastimes is showing your bodies around the beach and around the pool and your only problem is having a little too much body to show off. Well, that's where the Diet Center comes in....(Ad on KGO)

Russ Coughlan once compared the individual's relation to society to a marriage in which people can change as long as they're loyal to one another. "If we accept the hard line on things and never change from that then we're divorcing ourselves, or not being married to the situation that society is." But unlike marriage, speakers in talk shows cannot talk to one another, only to the host, who far from acting as a marriage broker must keep the extremes apart, disconnect them. On one night a supporter of the

Nicaraguan revolution calls in and Russ responds by rejecting his entire statement as propaganda. Any country that doesn't have the confidence of business, he says, must have something wrong with it. A little later a former mercenary in Nicaragua calls in and Russ leans the other way. The purpose is not to let these people begin an argument with one another, but rather to let them demonstrate, by their very extremes, the pluralism of the talk show.

The paradox is that to keep the show moving, some extremists are needed. That's what makes people listen and get indignant and call back. Indignation is one indication of the strength of opinions (even if they're always fluctuating). Now in a not very subtle way, talk shows are always drawing boundaries between what is crazy and what is good normal American. Because talk show hosts differ among themselves and because these boundaries are always changing, the line between crazy and interesting is often pretty tenuous. In fact, what has been fascinating over the last few months has been to observe how the pious liberal morality that won instant approval some time back now has become downright eccentric, a "bleeding heart" morality.

Jim Eason is adept at putting his listeners into the crazy camp. During the hostage crisis, a program regular called and wanted to send the Shah back in order to ward off the threat of a third world war:

EASON: I am telling you if you send him back to Iran you are a firm believer in capital punishment without a trial.

CALLER: Not without a trial.

E: One point at a time now. You have never heard me advocate capital punishment without a trial?

C: They say they'll give him a trial.

E: Listen the Ayatollah says no trial. He'll be killed.

C: I want to ask you one more question. Would you have us keep the Shah and involve us in a third world war?

E: Let me ask you a question in return.

At this point the caller puts down the phone, a tactic that nearly always sends the talk show host into a frenzy. Jim Eason goes into a long monologue about sending the Shah back "to be killed."

Now that's a radical stance, and it's a profoundly unAmerican stance. We don't believe that just because someone calls himself the head of the Islamic world, just because he wants the Shah killed and his family killed and all of the other people killed, we don't believe that in this country it is foreign to the American way. However, there are a couple of folks apparently who are so concerned about the forty-nine hostages that they are willing to have someone killed, a sacrificial lamb [i.e. the

Shah!]. Let them kill him to get our forty-nine people back. I say to hell with that! I would say send him back, but he's not going to get a fair trial, he's going to get killed probably as soon as he steps off the plane. You hear people advocate not only capital punishment but murder. Apparently some folks favor that. I just think you ought to remember though that last May 13 that Ayatollah said it the way it is and for that reason I'm saying don't send the Shah back, never, never, never send the Shah back because if you do, you have his *blood on your hands*. Now if you're willing to accept that, if you say, well on certain occasions we are happy to deliver him over to be killed, fine, that means someone like the last caller in the 30s and 40s when Jews were trying to escape to this country would say pack up and send them back. No trial is necessary. I don't think we ought to say that.

The "bleeding heart," afraid of a third world war has suddenly become responsible for the holocaust. Still, there are holocausts and there are holocausts:

EASON: I don't care if the Shah was the worst mass murderer in history, surpassing Hitler and Mao Tse Tung, you don't grab our embassy.

The problem with Eason's tirades is that there is always some crazy out there who can go over his limits. During the hostage crisis, he got this helpful suggestion from a caller:

CALLER: Just give them 72 hours and launch all 64 fleet ballistic missiles and just totally annihilate them. Our people are not going to make it out. There's no way those forty-nine people are going to get out, I think.

EASON: Well I think they will if the United States crawls on its hands and kisses Khomeini's feet and bargains and gives him everything he wants, we'll get those forty-nine people out.

C: Right. Now this is the straw that broke the camel's back. This has been going on for too long. Just push the button, no American lives lost and totally annihilate them if we have to.

E: Well, that's a little further than I am willing to go.

C: Well it'd make an ideal refugee camp for the Cambodian refugees.

Thank you so much for calling.

Hullo, Line 2, speak up or forever hold thy…

…Good to talk to you, crazy.

Listening to talk shows you soon realize that being American is a source of anxiety. The very pluralism of the talk show (and even the constant interruption, the coitus interruptus) practically guarantees this anxiety. Someone is always being labelled a crazy. For instance, ERA supporters, "with all their stomping and screaming and their anti-Phyllis Schlafly attitude...." In part this arises from the talk show structure itself. Callers are always on their own, or at least they never mention having someone else with them. They are on the air to exhibit themselves and their views. Yet at the same time there is often a nostalgia for community, for solidarity, which can only be thwarted. This anxiety often becomes crystallized around the issue of who belongs to the community. A worried caller asks Russ about a Datsun ad showing a native American (described as a creepy-looking guy) buying red, white and blue Datsuns for his reservation. Surely that's un-American. But no, Russ doesn't agree. A lot of people make money out of selling Datsuns and making money can't be unAmerican.

The labelling of certain callers as crazies is a way of drawing a line around community. It is always a fluctuating, tenuous line so that people constantly need to enquire about it (rather like the weather). Yesterday's in-group is tomorrow's candidate for the booby-hatch. It is in fact a prime example of how people are constituted as subjects by feeling themselves to be hailed by a mode of address that implicitly excludes others. (We adult, mature people...) In other words, the talk show lets us see ideology at work. At the same time it once and for all destroys the notion that ideology is a monolithic or unchanging thing. On the contrary, it is as fluctuating as a hi-fi needle. However, it also shows how hard the feeling of exclusion is on people and how anxious they are to get back on track — which is the strong card of any dominant ideology.

Yet even in the limited sphere in which it can operate today, the talk show has tremendous potential. We can detect this as soon as some topic or event occurs in which the callers have more authority than the host. When, that is, people draw on the authority of their own experience, when their opinions are no longer based on newspaper and television ads. At the end of August, there was a gas leak in San Francisco which released dangerous PCB fumes into office buildings in a downtown area. The authorities acted in a typical cover-up, "no danger to health" fashion. A caller not only told it like it was, but at the same time revealed what cannot help being thrust to the fore — the system's total indifference to human beings:

CALLER: One o'clock, I think it was when a hysterical voice came over the loudspeaker saying, practically screaming, to evacuate the building, don't use the elevators, so we all went out and there was no announcement not to smoke, just go down the stairs and as we got down lower and lower, the gas got thicker and thicker, it was just filled with gas, the stairway.

COUGHLAN: Could you smell the gas?

CALLER: Oh, it was terrible. It was terrible. It was really just filled with gas, but there was no announcement at any time, not to smoke. In my office, on the ninth floor many people smoke. It's my understanding that the building could have blown at that time.

The disembodied voice that doesn't give them essential information reveals the chaos behind the appearance of a system. The chaos is confirmed by the caller when he goes to work next day, now extremely suspicious of the bosses. His headache is so bad he can't work.

CALLER: It's my opinion that those filters are full of PCB and no one has changed them. The PCB is splattered all over that side there, the windows are all coated.

The system is quite indifferent to people, that much has become clear. In a sense, the talk show's dynamic comes from this very indifference and hence, for the need, for some personal contact out there. But it's also the irony of the situation that the talk show — except on special occasions — only personalizes that very indifference. And that, after all, is the function of the host.

Hey sorry, I've got to run....

"Why couldn't you build a little community somewhere like that?" (Russ Coughlan, on Disneyland)

16   RADIO: WHAT ONCE MADE IT OURS AND OURS ALONE*

GEORGE E. STEINER

It is difficult for people who are part of the television generation and are used to seeing incredible special effects in films like *TRON* or *Star Wars* to understand the power that radio used to have. Radio was once the dominant entertainment medium (before television arrived on the scene) and millions of people spent their evenings almost "glued" to the radio set.

* George Steiner, "Radio: What Once Made it Ours and Ours Alone." This article was written especially for this volume. Copyright © 1987 George Steiner.

For young people, in the radio age (1930s and 1940s) there were any number of programs to listen to: "The Green Hornet," "Jack Armstrong" ("the All-American boy"), "Counter-Spy," "The Shadow," and certainly, one of the greatest, "The Lone Ranger."

"The Lone Ranger" used to be broadcast three times a week and listening to it was a ritual, slavishly observed, by millions of young boys and girls. Young children liked the program because there was action and excitement and because the good guys always won. And parents liked the program because there was a minimal amount of violence and the stories always had a strong moral flavor.

If you move up a level, from that of the story line and its moral principles to that of the social and political messages generated by the series, you find, so Marxist critics argue, something quite different. For one Marxist critic, Ariel Dorfman, "The Lone Ranger," while it entertained children with action and adventure, did something else, which was quite insidious. It glorified (that is, brainwashed children with) the values of a "bourgeois capitalist society" by reproducing the myth of social mobility. This myth is the so-called American Dream, which argues that in an egalitarian society anyone can succeed who has enough willpower and determination.

As Dorfman writes about the famed masked-man:

"In the 'Lone Ranger's' case, the hero starts from below zero. He starts with an apparently insurmountable hurdle, which would discourage anyone else. Let this be an invigorating example…Your handicap doesn't matter. It doesn't matter if you're an outsider, if they treat you like a criminal, a dangerous element, or if they don't have any faith in your ability and intentions. Your qualities will be proved in time. Meanwhile, just like the Ranger, you must earn the right to success. You can overcome natural or artificial limitations as long as you're bold and good and are sure of the fairness of your actions." The negative side of this, Dorfman points out, is that if you don't make it, you must assume it is your own fault. Ultimately this philosophy supports the status quo and leaves many people feeling bitter and full of self-hatred.

Why is it that so many older Americans today still have nothing but praise for the radio they knew when growing up? Was the radio they experienced really that good, that different, that special?

The development and acceptance of radio in America during the 1930s and the 1940s was due to a number of special circumstances that were present in our society then and only then.

Radio was the first electronic entertainment medium to enter the American home. One could hear and listen to all kinds of people speak from all around the world and one imagined what they looked like. Radio became one's ear to the outside world. An ear to the world doesn't seem too significant until one realizes that the ear is extremely credulous and that it believes what it hears. The same cannot be said for the eye. The eye is unwilling to make concessions to the imagination. Perhaps this is why Steve Allen was credited with the observation, "Radio is the theater of the mind; television the theater of the mindless."

In those early years if a person could not afford the cost of a manufactured five-tubed radio set, he could build his own starting with the simple crystal set and moving on up to the one vacuum tube receiver. Individuals of all kinds, not just the technically inclined, could and did participate in this technological development and they were rewarded by being the first one on their block to actually hear an opera star sing or to listen to election returns. Those who could afford to buy a radio set became the envy of their neighborhood, because they often invited their close friends over to their house for an evening of listening. Being an owner of a radio set gave one a social status.

Likewise, without the dedication and discoveries of such men as Heinrich Hertz (radio waves, 1887), Guglielmo Marconi (wireless telegraphy, 1894), John Armstrong Fleming (the vacuum tube, 1904), Dr. Lee De Forest (audion vacuum tube, 1906), the United States Navy (ship-to-shore communications), and the radio set manufacturers, the radio medium could not have made the move toward becoming an electronic mass medium. In addition, had not the U.S. Government passed the early Radio Act of 1927, which was followed by the Communications Act of 1934, which established the Federal Communications Commission (FCC), radio broadcasting licenses and broadcast policy would not have had order, direction, or control.

The remaining elements that gave broadcasters the motivation to move their broadcasting equipment from roof tops into carpeted and sound-balanced radio studios as well as improve the quality of their programming was commercialism. Program time on radio could be sold to a sponsor who paid money in order to have his product mentioned on a broadcast. Program quality did improve and the radio listening audience accepted the radio medium with open arms.

As radio programming continued to develop and improve, listeners found the "Adventures of _____" or the "True Life Story of _____" as a means of escape from a day-to-day world that first went through a depression and was then concerned about what Hitler was doing over in Europe.

Radio programs gave listeners something to talk about and discuss with friends, neighbors and relatives. It wasn't, however, until the beginning of World War II, that radio took on another program dimension seriously, the reporting of the news.

Radio had a lot going for it and unless one actually listened and heard it and experienced it then, its role with today's older American generation cannot be understood or fully appreciated. It was a first in the home — you could make your own set. Individuals as well as the U.S. Government helped develop it technically. Selling air-time provided a source of income which helped stations improve their facilities (as well as their programs) and America listened, because radio took peoples' minds off of their problems and encouraged them to fantasize and dream a little.

It would seem that of all of the above factors that made early radio listeners today's old radio fans, it was the programs and the stars on them that are still remembered and often talked about. It was also true that those responsible for the radio programs helped develop a widespread public taste for music, comedy, and drama and it was done in that order.

If such was the case, then it would seem appropriate to review in general terms the simple programming types that were first heard and then describe the highly structured format that one program, "The Lone Ranger," used in order to hold onto its large audiences for some twenty years.

Musical programming comprised nearly half of all radio programming in the early thirties. Live orchestras in radio studios would provide the music for their regular schedule of programs, but they would also have to "fill in" for other programs whenever talent failed to show up. The late Cy Trobbe, who played violin in a number of radio studio orchestras during this early period of broadcasting, referred to his music as "rather bland, quiet and soft, with no surprises." It wasn't always possible to broadcast 78 rpm records created for home use on radio stations. The American Society of Composers, Authors and Publishers (ASCAP) prohibited their use for broadcasts because they were afraid that if people heard the records over the airwaves they wouldn't buy them for their home use. Obviously there has been a total reversal in their position today, because playing a record for broadcast promotes the sale of that record.

As time went on local stations not affiliated with the networks could lease a library of musical transcriptions complete with scripted introductions and identified selections. "It's Music for Tuesday," was typical of the way this type of program was introduced. No surprises here!

The network stations and their affiliates had the advantage of broadcasting "live" big name bands like Benny Goodman, Tommy Dorsey and Russ Morgan. Classical music, as well as what is now termed "Country and Western" could be heard if one made a serious effort to locate it on a program schedule ahead of time or if people switched their radio dial around until they found it.

Had early radio confined its programming solely to musical presentations, it is doubtful that radio would have attracted the large audiences it needed to satisfy the commercial sponsor's goals in terms of sales. It is difficult to know if musical programming alone would have fully satisfied the individual listener's needs at that point in time.

No one seems certain as to the reason why comedy type programs and comedians became radio's next programming fare. Whoever made that initial decision was right, for not only did Americans like to listen to comedians, the programs became big business for broadcasters. Top comedians were earning thousands of dollars for each broadcast they did. In order to pay out that kind of money for a talent fee, one can be assured that sales for the product being advertised on the comedians' program were bringing in thousands upon thousands of dollars.

According to an article in *Variety* back in the 1930s, "Radio's axiom for comedians is to be simple and be funny or be fancy and lousy."[1] The axiom was accepted by most of the successful radio comedians and it worked, because Americans needed and wanted to laugh and they did at the antics of Ed Wynn, Jack Benny, Joe Penner and of course at Amos 'n Andy in their situation comedy whose story centered around the activities of their Fresh Air Taxi Company. The program was an immediate success and became so popular that department stores would play the program over their public address system and movie houses would stop the showing of a film and set a radio set on their stage so that their audiences could listen to Amos 'n Andy. Had these merchants not provided for this listening arrangement, many of their in-store customers would have gone home earlier. Surveys taken at the time of their popularity indicated that over half of the potential listeners available across America had their radio dials set for the Amos 'n Andy program. Some authors have indicated that by capturing the full attention of our nation, they, Amos 'n Andy, turned radio, a popular medium, into a mass medium. With a listening audience for a particular Amos 'n Andy program segment estimated at nearly forty million listeners, the radio medium ceased to be an experiment.

The success of the radio soap opera, the daytime dramatic serial broadcasting every fifteen minutes from 9AM until 5PM on either network or network affiliated stations, led the way for new dramatic series that were broadcast during prime time hours in the evenings. Mysteries, westerns, and at times more "serious" dramas coming from such programs as "Lux Radio Theater" and "Mercury Theater on the Air" were performed in the evening prime time hours. Old radio fans would be upset if such programs as "One Man's Family" (1932), "I Love a Mystery" (1939), "The Shadow" (1936) and of course "The Lone Ranger" (1933), were not listed as the type of radio program that they will never forget.

The brief listing and overview above of some of the early radio program offerings does not give a reader, former radio fan or not, a sense of what radio writers, producers, and directors did within their individual programs to not only hold onto their current listeners, but to continually attract new ones. I was a graduate student at Wayne State University in Detroit, Michigan in the late forties and early fifties, when the Director, Assistant Director and head writer for "The Lone Ranger" program taught undergraduate classes in their area of expertise. I also was a part-time actor on each of the three programs that originated from Detroit — "The Lone Ranger," "The Green Hornet," and the "Challenge of the Yukon" — and what follows will detail what it took to keep "The Lone Ranger" alive and in his saddle for some twenty years.

No doubt many of the older "Lone Ranger" radio fans will remember and recognize the techniques used by the program producers of "The Lone Ranger" once they are brought to mind. If some of this information brings back fond memories, as well as helps clarify the reasons why so many listeners became faithful fans of "The Lone Ranger," then the writing of this article is well served. Of this one thing all can be certain: "The Lone Ranger" pioneered in the development of effective production techniques and these same techniques are still being used, as applicable, in today's successful television programs.

PROGRAM TYPE

"The Lone Ranger" program was one of the first Western-type programs to be broadcast. It appealed to the young as well as the old. It was always broadcast "live" and the problem facing "The Lone Ranger" was resolved within one-half hour's time. It could be heard across the country at either 7:00PM or at 7:30PM (depending on where you lived) every Monday, Wednesday, and Friday night. The only time you would not have heard it was on the day that President Roosevelt died and on VE Day (end of World War II in Europe). The producers knew that the 7:00 PM hour was an excellent time to reach all of the family members in their homes and those family members could always depend on hearing the program, because the Lone Ranger was always there just like an old and trusted friend.

PROGRAM IDENTITY

The opening theme music of "The Lone Ranger" throughout its long history was always Rossini's "William Tell Overture." It is difficult to identify any other musical program theme that became so synonymous with a program. Even today it is hard to separate the two. Walter Poole who at one time was the conductor for the Detroit Symphony, absolutely refused to schedule the playing of the "William Tell Overture" in any of his concerts. It seems that the one time he did so the audience kept shouting "Hi Yo, Silver" and it ruined the concert.

Generally the same program opening and closing announcement was read by the same announcer in the same way every time the program was broadcast.

Program identity or "signature" was the one element most radio producers sought for their programs, because by having it you could be assured that the minute the theme music was heard by a listener, whatever room he or she happened to be in, he or she knew exactly what the program was. It was almost unnecessary for a listener to hear the announcer in order to identify the program, but when one did hear the announcer's particular speech patterns and intonations in the opening announcement of "The Lone Ranger" no doubt could possibly remain.

ACTION ORIENTED

Some dramas can become boring after a while, if there is very little movement or action in a scene. This type of criticism could never be leveled at "The Lone Ranger," because the producers understood that if they kept the listener's ear busy and believing, he or she couldn't become bored, but would instead become even more involved by letting go and being a part of the action whether it was a fight in a bar or chasing an outlaw down the canyon. "The Lone Ranger" was loaded with action — sound action, mind action. To create the effect of action, every fight in a bar, for example, involved one actor grasping the arm of another actor and pushing and pulling the other with accompanying grunts and groans. Sound men in a separate sound room would do the shoe scuffling sound to add further to the reality of the scene. When the Lone Ranger and other actors were supposed to mount their horses, they would jump up in the air and land on one leg in order to simulate the effort. They also expressed this effort vocally. Whenever two actors were supposed to be riding their horses while carrying on a conversation, they would beat their upper arms against their torsos to the beat of a horse's gallop. Again, the sound men would add the "live" horses hoof beats to the scene. On "The Lone Ranger" no actor just stood in front of a microphone and read. He had to be verbally and physically alive.

THE LONE RANGER ACTOR

Among those who were a part of "The Lone Ranger's" early program development, the debate as to who played the Lone Ranger's role on radio still continues. The exact number of Lone Rangers on radio also continues to be controversial.

Since the real purpose of this article is to illustrate the overall effectiveness of the total program on its listeners rather than detail the history of those who played what, when, the remarks that follow will be confined to those years when the late Brace Beemer played the part of the Lone Ranger, 1941 to 1954.

The actor who played the part of the Lone Ranger had the starring role — of that there was no doubt. It is quite possible that some listeners thought that the Lone Ranger even wore his black mask and costume in the radio studio as he read his lines from a script. This of course was not true, but it is true that he was never to be seen in public without wearing both the mask and costume. There was a problem with the idea of the mask in the programs themselves, but everyone concerned somehow managed to live with the problem. Charles Livingstone, the director of the radio program approved of it, because he said, "When he (Lone Ranger) wears the mask he can even be more human."[2] Mr. Fran Striker, one of the original writers for the series expressed other concerns:

…and the mask is difficult to work with. You put that together with no drinking and no sex and it's very limiting for a writer. He can't go into town wearing the mask, because people will see him and wonder, "Why is he wearing a mask?" The mask is a constant source of trouble for law men who have always associated a mask with the bad guy.[3]

Obviously the reason for the mask was to blank out the full identity of the man playing the part. By so doing a child and even an adult listener could vicariously be the Lone Ranger as he listened. Although radio listeners could not see what the Lone Ranger looked like while he was playing his role on radio, reference to the mask was always made throughout the programs in order to reinforce the concept that the Lone Ranger was not one man, but an "everyman."

Rarely were any visitors either young or old allowed in the studios to watch the broadcasts. The producers of the program wanted to protect the myth they had created and apparently it worked in those days.

The accredited creator of the Lone Ranger idea, the late Mr. George W. Trendle, identified his mythical creation as follows:

I am often asked the why's and wherefores that make my mythical creation a perennial. His continued acceptance by parents and others, I am convinced, can greatly be attributed to the fact that he (Lone Ranger) is a composite of all men who uphold the laws of God and man.[4]

Another dimension to the Lone Ranger character was identified by Dan Battie, one of the staff writers of the program.

The Ranger's motivation is the good of the West. He wants to see the country expand. Sometimes the President of the United States calls upon him for a special assignment sort of thing. He works outside the law so much because he can get more done that way. The sheriffs aren't stupid or anything like that. It's just that the Lone Ranger is so much smarter than they are.[5]

THE OTHER ACTORS

The Lone Ranger's trustworthy companion was Tonto, an Indian. His real name was John Todd and he played the role of Tonto for twenty-one years. The origin and meaning of Tonto's famous expression, "kemo sabay" has also been a source of controversy over the more recent years. According to some sources, the phrase meant "trusted friend" or "good scout." Others said it was just an expression that came from the name of a summer camp for boys in Northern Michigan. An anthropologist, Dr. Martha Kendal, a specialist in Indian languages, concluded in her research on tribal roots of the phrase, that "Tonto and his masked friend are mythical characters, and as such, they do not have to be fixed in historical reality."[6]

Reality, historical or otherwise, would certainly have been distorted in Tonto's case had listeners been allowed to see what the actor playing the part of Tonto looked like.

> The front office wants to maintain the illusion that I'm a real Indian. Can you imagine the reaction if children saw me with my pot gut. I'm one of the reasons they keep the kids out of the studio.[7]

The other actors that made up the cast for the program ranged in age from young adults up to middle age and beyond. Some of the actors started out as juveniles and over the period of time that the program was on the air became adult heavies.

A listener to "The Lone Ranger" could always be assured that shortly after the program started he or she would be hearing from the good guys as well as the bad guys. Fran Striker, one of the original writers, was very clear in his mind how the good guys as well as the bad guys should be presented:

> Now, when you get your good character, give him something to make people like him. I mean he loves a dog, or maybe he can't walk. And the villain has to be as bad as the other guy is good. We don't have time to show WHY he's bad. So what you do is you open with "Scar" throwing a baby out of the window, or beating his horse or something so that people will immediately see that he is bad. We don't have any time to go into the psychology of all this. Anyhow, if you explain WHY a man is bad, he's likely to get sympathy. I mean if you show a drunken bum and then you explain that the reason he's drunk is that he has incurable cancer, he gets sympathy.

> It's instinctive to choose sides. And people want to have good and bad guys. Like if you go to a game you hate, like basketball, for example. You don't even know who's playing and really don't care. Suddenly one of the players gives another player a low blow. Immediately you choose the side of the good guy. But remember the bad guys feel justified in being bad. Like the guy who hates the railroads, because some railroad man threw a bomb into his house when he was a kid.[8]

The "bad" guy was not only easily identified by what he said he was going to do, but even his name sounded hard and not "good." Here are just a few of the "bad" guy names that were listed on the cover sheets of the actual scripts: Slade (smooth crook), Buck Canton (tough killer), Blacky Pierce (tough crook), Adobe Dodge (heavy), Jake Markel (tough gunman), Mort Slinger (smooth killer), and finally Tucson Thorpe (smooth, quiet-talker, outlaw leader).

THE WRITERS

There were a number of people involved in the writing of the Lone Ranger scripts. However, for the purpose of this essay, the discussion of the writing phase of the program will be confined to the thoughts and ideas of Mr. Fran Striker who was employed as the head writer. It is believed by this writer that it was Mr. Striker who contributed most to the "imaging" on the Lone Ranger programs. He was a very nice man, a good teacher, and one who worked very hard at his job.

Author David Rothel in his book, *Who Was That Masked Man?*, talked about Mr. Striker's output.

> It was estimated that in 1939 Striker was pounding out approximately sixty thousand words every week of the year. Someone figured that it was equivalent of a bible every three months. Each year, Striker, with the assistance of a small staff of writers, wrote 156 "Lone Ranger" radio adventures, 365 newspaper cartoons. Striker was putting in fourteen hour work days in 1939 for his ten thousand dollar salary.[9]

As a result of attending two semesters of Mr. Striker's writing classes at Wayne University in Detroit, some thirty-seven years ago, this author not only learned a considerable amount about writing in general, but was privy to the writing techniques that were used by Striker and the other writers in turning out some 2,500 Lone Ranger scripts over the years. About plots in stories, Striker was very specific.

> There are no new plots and this includes the writings of today's top writers. Plots never change. Don't rack your brain for new ones. Hang new ornaments onto the old ones, use unusual devices and gimmicks. Try to be original with an old plot. Avoid freaks and give your character a true-to-life personality.[10]

Perhaps one of the first "new ornaments on old plots" was the one where the trader sold the guns to the Indians without the gun's loading pins, which made them useless. The listener wasn't in on this until the Indians discovered that their trader friend had tricked them. Up to that point in time everyone thought that the Indians would have an easy time of killing all of the settlers and this concern added to the empathy the listeners had for the settlers.

Mr. Striker's position as to what kind of story "The Lone Ranger" was is most evident in the following quote:

> This story is a formula story and it follows the pattern of Horatio Alger. You know what I mean. The good guy always wins and the bad guy always loses. It's been a very successful pattern for an awful long

time. With the Ranger, he's fearless, and strong and clean living and he chases horses, not women; that's about the only difference.[11]

It should be noted that in order to turn out three half hour "Lone Ranger" scripts every week of the year for nearly twenty or so years, some sort of writing method had to be used in order to help the writers come up with acceptable scripts. This mass media demanded mass production of programs. This demand on writers is as evident today as it was in those earlier years.

What now follows is a part of what Mr. Striker designed as his formula for writing "The Lone Ranger":

I can tell you exactly how I write a show. And I'll never run out of plots. We have these eight elements:

1. Establish a character.
2. Give him a problem he can't solve.
3. Explain why he can't solve it and that involves the villain.
4. The Lone Ranger learns about the situation.
5. The antagonist learns that the Ranger is going to interfere.
6. The antagonist plots to kill the Ranger.
7. The Ranger outwits or outfights the crooks and survives.
8. The Ranger solves the situation.

Now you don't have to do every show in just that order, you can shuffle them around if you like. About one out of every five shows we do conforms exactly to the pattern. So here's what you do. Under the eight elements you list the possibilities:

1. *Establish a character.*
   Old man, young man, old woman, young women, etc.
2. *Give him a problem he/she can't solve.*
   He's going to lose his ranch.
   He's going to lose a gold mine.
   She can't marry someone.
   He's falsely accused of a crime.
3. *Explain why he can't solve it and that involves the villain.*
   He can't find any witnesses.
   The people in town don't trust him.
   He's a coward.

You do the same thing for all of the remaining points. So when you take them in all of their possible combinations you have 8 to the 10th power of possible plots. The thing could go on forever.[12]

Another advantage of using the formula system was that it kept the plot consistently in the minds of the listeners, because each formula segment followed another in a logical order. In addition to the consistency of story line, there was little opportunity to spend too much time on one plot segment and as a result the program moved dramatically from one point to the next without the listener ever realizing what was being done for the theater of his mind.

NARRATION

Narration was used extensively on "The Lone Ranger." It was written to describe the action that was taking place in a scene, as well as to prepare the listener for what was coming up. Musical bridges as well as sound effects were used behind narration. When used all together, these production elements helped to keep up the dramatic intensity that was established early in the program and throughout the scenes that followed.

Many established writers are critical of dramas that use narration. They refer to it as a "cop-out" or "crutch" which dramatic writers use when they can't tell the story in straight dialogue.

Narration was widely used in many radio dramas. Despite the criticism of it, it was an efficient and effective production device, because there were times when it was the only way the story could be clarified. The narrator on "The Lone Ranger" was an outside observer and even though his presence was constant he was never considered as an interruption, but rather as means for moving the scene along which helped to strengthen the overall structure of the program.

Having the same narrator on most of "The Lone Ranger" during the time of the program's popularity up to the end of its "live" broadcasts in 1954, gave its listeners a continuity they looked for and expected in their radio heroes.

SOUND EFFECTS

On "The Lone Ranger" sound effects played a major role in developing the action in a scene. In most instances sound complemented what was happening. For example, a fist hitting the palm of the hand in order to simulate the sound in a barroom fight along with a wooden chair crashing to the floor and at the same time an actor yelling, "Take that you no good bum," can be very effective and would sound very realistic.

Although sound-effects recordings were available as time went on, a good number of the sounds heard on "The Lone Ranger" were done "live," because sound-effects libraries were limited to general or background sounds. One could probably have located the sound of a dog barking on a recording, but not the sound of a dog growling as he pulled the trouser leg of the bad guy. To create this effect the actor playing the part of the dog would put a handkerchief in between his clenched teeth and as he pulled vigorously on the cloth he also growled loudly and produced the desired effect.

Gun shots were almost always a part of a western program on radio. "Live" gun shots from starting guns (blank pistols) did not pick up well on a microphone. No one except those who were actually involved in the production of "The Lone Ranger" knew how the special recordings of gun shots were especially developed for the program. They did sound like real gun shots and that added to the believability of a scene.

Horses' hoof beats were done "live." The sound men either used halved sections of coconut shells or rubber toilet plungers. A variety of ground surfaces were confined to small flat–boxed containers. These surfaces would act as the base for the sound man as he hit them with his hand-held coconut shell or bathroom plunger. In some instances he would have to move his hand-created gallop from one surface to another in order to get the effect of a horse slowing down and crossing a bridge. Most sound effects were never done without being accompanied by a dialogue between actors or a description of the scene by the narrator.

The following story illustrates how important a role sound effects played in "The Lone Ranger." It seems that the actor playing the Lone Ranger made a personal appearance along with a white horse (Silver) at a local Detroit theater. After the Ranger's appearance was over the theater manager proceeded to auction off the "Lone Ranger's" horse. The theater manager was taken to court and the attorney for The Lone Ranger Enterprises is reported to have said as he held up two bathroom plungers in front of the judge, "Your Honor, this is the Lone Ranger's horse. It's only a sound."

BRIDGE MUSIC

On radio, bridge music was used to make the transition or bridge from one scene sequence to another. For "The Lone Ranger" the bridge music was taken from classical musical recordings. There were certain advantages to using classical music as the source for bridges. First of all the melody was not easily recognizable and the selections used were up-beat in nature and seemed to fit the mood and excitement needed to lead the listener from one scene to the next. Charles Livingston, the program's director, insisted that no piece of bridge music would ever be used twice in one program. This requirement did give each "Lone Ranger" a uniqueness that also added to the program's effectiveness.

CONCLUSION

"The Lone Ranger" was the type of program that not only set the standards for other radio programs that have followed, but did at the same time make millions for its owners even before it was sold to the Jack Wrather Corp. for $3 million.

Contrary to what a former actor who played the Lone Ranger role on television would want you to believe, the Lone Ranger wasn't just one man, but was a composite of all men. The major attraction and devotion to the Lone Ranger character began and ended with radio, because he was a mythical creation and never really existed except in the "mind's" eye. And so that is why near the end of the program when the sheriff would ask, "Say, who was that masked man, anyway?" we would tune out the sound coming from the radio speaker and would answer that question ourselves, "Why, don't you know, I was that Masked Man."

It was because of programs such as "The Lone Ranger" and the many, many other programs like it that were broadcast during the 1930s and 1940s that the medium of radio was ours and ours alone.

NOTES

1. *Variety*, May 7, 1930, 76.
2. Charles Livingston, Class Lecture, Wayne State Univ., Detroit, Michigan, Spring Semester 1950.
3. Fran Striker, Class Lecture, Wayne State Univ., Detroit, Michigan, October 4, 1949.
4. "Lone Ranger Creator Reflects on Radio's Golden Age," (article) Author and source not identified.
5. Dan Battie, Staff Writer, Interview, September, 1950.
6. Martha Kendall, "Hi Yo Silver Away," *The Smithonian*, September, 1977, 113.
7. John Todd, Actor, Interview, September, 1950.
8. Fran Striker, Class Lecture, October 4, 1949.
9. David Rothel, *Who Was That Masked Man*? (New Jersey: A.S. Barnes & Co. Inc.,) 1976, 40.
10. Fran Striker, Class Lecture, October 4, 1949.
11. Striker, *loc cit.*
12. Striker, *loc cit.*

17   MAKING RADIO COMEDY *

DAN COFFEY

Woody Allen's film *Radio Days* has sparked a return of interest in the radio comedy shows of the 1940s. This period was the golden age of radio comedy, when there were a number of brilliant comics and comedy shows: Jack Benny, Fred Allen, Edgar Bergen and Charlie McCarthy, The Great Gildersleeve, Burns and Allen, Amos and Andy, Bob Hope, and Fibber McGee and Mollie, to name some of the more important ones.

In those days, radio was a kind of obsession with people, and the stars were great celebrities. And people "grew up" listening to these shows, whose characters were almost like members of the family, it seemed. (As far as para-social relationships are concerned, in which members of the audience tend to feel that they "know" stars of programs — they were much more intense with radio, I would argue, than with television, because radio left so much up to our imaginations.)

Woody Allen has described this period in loving terms:

> …it was a wonderful time. The country was extremely patriotic and America was pulling together in a way it really didn't after that time. We had no television. The popular culture of the day was movies and radio, and it was a very glamorous age.[1]

Radio had a tremendous hold on the nation. People still listen to the radio now, but the medium does not have the central role it had in the 1940s and is only a pale imitation of what it once was.

And there is not very much comedy on the radio, either, which is a shame, because radio lends itself to comedy very well. It is easy and cheap to produce radio comedy — but because people use radio differently now, there is little interest in putting on comedy shows. People get their comedy from television, mostly. And most of what they get is pretty banal and second-rate: formula-written situation comedies.

Most week days, on public radio, comedy lovers can get a brief ninety-second "fix" as "Dr. Science" answers questions and offers his whacky explanations of science. Dan Coffey, who plays "Dr. Science," ("he has a master's degree in science," and "knows more than you do") offers some thoughts about radio comedy in the essay that follows.

Why do we laugh? How do we make people laugh? The greatest minds throughout history have wrestled with these problems and offered many theories

---

* Dan Coffey, "Making Radio Comedy." This article was written especially for this book. Copyright © 1987, Dan Coffey.

and explanations. There are questions that "Dr. Science" (his first name is "Doctor") is well qualified to answer... To the extent that he is qualified to answer any question, that is.

REFERENCE

1. Avery Corman, "Why Allen, Simon Return to Their Youth," *San Francisco Examiner and Chronicle*, February 15, 1987.

I make radio comedy and enjoy it more than anything else I do. It is a major source of my income, and it doesn't feel at all like work, so I consider myself to be very fortunate.

Most of what I do is with Duck's Breath Mystery Theatre, a group of five former graduate students from Iowa City, Iowa. We moved to San Francisco in the spring of 1976 and have been slugging it out ever since. Although we started out strictly as a stage group, we evolved into radio and quickly realized the publicity benefits of working in a mass medium.

We began by submitting short topical pieces to National Public Radio's "All Things Considered." From the moment they were played we realized the tremendous power of being "nationally known." Even though we obtain almost no income directly from National Public Radio, the fallout from such work is immense.

Due to the efforts of our manager, Steve Baker, we were able to obtain grants from the now-defunct Satellite Program Development Fund, the National Endowment for the Arts, and most lately, from the Corporation for Public Broadcasting to produce a series of ninety-second comedy spots we call "Duck's Breath Homemade Radio."

We began recording these at the humble studios of KQED-FM in San Francisco. This is where we have recorded most of our pieces for "All Things Considered," where we recorded "Dr. Science" back when it was still "Mr. Science," and where until last year we recorded almost everything. Two-track mono. Usually mixed with music from a turntable, with a sound effect or two from another turntable. Every once in a while we'd EQ a voice or add reverb if the Lexicon weren't out on location.

When we started to get grants we started to pay KQED for our time there. Since their rate was not in the least bit competitive we took our business elsewhere, to a studio in the avenues, closer to where most of us lived. This place had compressor/limiters, multi-track machines and the ability to isolate the microphones! Good-bye hollow sound! So long fly by the seat of your pants mixing!

It paid off. Our album, "Born to Be Tiled" on Rounder Records, got reviewed in the *San Francisco Examiner,* and among other praise, was said to have "high production value." No one had ever said that about Duck's Breath before.

The challenge in coming up with comedy radio is to keep it simple. You can't hear more than two or three things at once. Most people are doing something else, like driving or cooking breakfast when they listen to us on the radio. The densely produced radio piece that one listens to with headphones is not for us.

From my point of view, the success or failure of a piece boils down to the following ratio: Writing — 90 percent, performance — 5 percent, clever use of the medium — 5 percent. That's why I like radio so much. Because I think of myself first as a writer.

Another thing I like about radio is that, compared to other media there are very few variables. A small variation in one of the parameters means a great deal. There's less to go wrong and more to be gained by elegance. There's the way you get the audience on your side by asking them to participate in the theatre of it. "Close your eyes please, and imagine with us," instead of "Look at this! Haven't we made up Randy Quaid to look just like LBJ?"

I've never met an actor who didn't enjoy acting in a radio play. Having been an actor in all four media, I know that radio acting is a piece of cake compared to the sweating out, hanging around, and suffering through that is required of stage, television, and film.

I'm not sure how radio comedy differs from radio drama in general. I know you have to get to the point pretty quickly in comedy. There's a lot more room for slack in "art." I find myself getting pretty judgmental when I listen to someone speaking through a vocal processor and pretending that makes it "art." Pretentiousness is the last refuge of the unimaginative. The naive often confuse obscurity with profundity. These facts I remember from my graduate student days. I too was guilty of running around in black leotards to electronic music (or even worse, had someone else do the running while I puffed on my pipe and contemplated my efforts from afar).

I'm not very much into satire. I have the same problem with satire that I do with guerilla theatre. Either your audience already agrees with you and you're engaging in a kind of group approval session, or you're preaching. I think that the contract I have with my audience is one where I can pretend to be a fool and invite them to laugh at me. But I don't think of myself as a satirist. Mort Sahl is a satirist.

I can't wait to see what the future will bring for comedy radio. Hopefully, what we're doing is part of that evolution. Already much of our work for public radio is available in cassette via Newman Books on Tape. These are sold in bookstores, and are packaged in plastic shrink-wrapped packages that are the same size as small paperbacks, so they fit in the same racks as paperback books. As more people have cassette players in their cars, more of these will sell to people who seek some variety to morning drive time radio.

I wonder why there is so little home grown dramatic radio production.

It's always been puzzling to me that more people don't take advantage of the fact that nowadays it is incredibly cheap to produce broadcast quality audio. For a couple of hundred dollars you can buy an excellent cassette player and microphone. These things were comparatively much more expensive even a few years ago. And yet I don't hear much home produced radio theatre. I think the equipment is there, but most people never use their tape recorders for anything more ambitious than dubbing albums. You can buy a PZM microphone at Radio Shack for $30. Get your friends to stand around it, throw a few sleeping bags over the chairs to dampen the room sound, and well, you've got yourself the audio quality that Jack Benny had at his disposal when he made his radio shows. Pop a metal cassette in the deck, switch on some noise reduction and you too could be a radio producer.

Of course you have to have ideas. Every cab driver, waiter, and parking lot attendant in Los Angeles has a screenplay he's trying to peddle. I suspect that it isn't the chance of having their ideas realized and shared with an audience that is the driving force, so much as the money they might make if a film is made. That kind of money simply isn't made in radio, nowadays.

Even though the budgetary requirements are less, there is still no guarantee that everything you produce will find an audience. I don't have any suggestions as to how to get stations to play what you produce, other than the shorter the better, and if an idea hits, make a lot of the same thing. Satellite distribution has taken the drudgery out of getting the program to the stations, but just because you uplink something doesn't mean that anyone's recording the downlink.

Duck's Breath has been lucky to have already established an audience, albeit a small one, via our stage performances. We're also lucky to have been able to stick together as a group for twelve years. It took a lot of time to build our reputation and our audience. Now every time we go into the studio, we know that the final product will be listened to by tens of thousands of people. Not the tens of millions that television reaches, but enough.

18 PLAYING THE QUICK CHANGE GAME*

ERIC ZORN

We know that radio stations are, in the final analysis, businesses — run by people who are interested in making profits. That is true of all media, of course…but most media cannot make rapid changes in formatting the way radio can. Newspapers evolve over a period of years, for instance. Magazines can be created rather quickly, when a new market opens up (such as computers) but relative to radio, newspapers, magazines, and other media move like turtles.

It is not unusual, however, to wake up one morning and find that your favorite rock and roll station has "gone" country western or disco — or whatever. Radio stations are frenetically chasing audiences and changing formats to appeal to them — and one audience, in particular — the target audience of people between twenty-five and fifty-four, who have a good deal of income. Remember that radio stations make money (like television stations) by "delivering" an audience to advertisers. The larger the audience and the more affluent it is, the more radio stations can charge to air commercials.

The dominant format in radio in the mid-1980s is adult contemporary, a combination of pop hits, hits by mainstream artists, and some album cuts played in loose rotation. (This means, you only hear the songs a few times during the entire day instead of hearing some songs over and over again.) It is a rather bland mixture of ingredients that suggests that radio, for the majority of listeners, is now a kind of background noise.

Radio, the data suggests, appeals to an older audience. At one time, the prime target was people in the eighteen to forty-nine range. Now the target is twenty-five to fifty-four…with the core of the population located, broadly, in the twenty-five to forty range. Attracting these people means a great deal of money. It is estimated that in the larger markets, for example, a difference of one point in annual audience share means $2 million in revenues from advertising; so the competition is intense.

It is rather ironic that a medium that once produced great comedy, wonderful adventure programs, and that is capable of doing so much has become so conservative. And as the price of radio stations keeps escalating, market forces push radio into mainstream formats and the medium becomes less interesting. The radio industry, once dominated by people with broadcasting backgrounds, is now full of people with business backgrounds who play "the quick-change game" or any other game they can, to maximize profits. The question we must ask

---

is this — are they killing the goose that has been laying the golden (not oldies) eggs?

Radio, like other ancient species, survives and thrives by adaptation. Thirty years ago it responded to the threat of television by adopting narrow program formats. Now it adjusts to the most minute changes in public taste by throwing out one format and trying another.

The current scene in radio is one of almost crazed format-switching. "Contemporary hit radio" (CHR) continues to dominate the airwaves, but an older format, "album-oriented rock" (AOR), is making a comeback. "Personalities" are in; heavy metal is out. Formats are fragmenting into ever tinier pieces. CHR has spawned a sub-genre known as "adult CHR"; several AOR stations have shifted to "eclectic-oriented rock" (EOR). An entire roster of new formats has been developed to prop up faltering AM stations.

The whole process suggests profusion and variety, yet the standardization of formats and the increasing use of satellite programming have in fact homogenized the sound of many stations.

MARKETPLACE

There are some 8,400 commercial radio stations in America, with still more on the way (the Federal Communications Commission issued some 588 construction permits in 1985 and authorized the licensing of 700 new FM outlets). Yet because of radio's profitability, demand for frequencies still so greatly exceeds supply that stations are selling for eye-popping sums. A Los Angeles AM/FM combo — KTNQ–AM and KLVE–FM — went for more than $40 million in 1985, and brokers predict that, for the foreseeable future, prices will continue rising faster than the inflation rate. And radio advertising revenues are growing at the annual rate of 14.5 percent during the first half of 1985. Unfortunately, listeners rarely if ever profit from escalating station prices; programmers and general managers have become notably more conservative in an effort to keep the cash flowing.

Numerous stations adopted CHR after consultant Mike Jacobs used it to revive the CBS-owned FM stations group in recent years. As of mid-1985 almost 900 stations — or 10 percent of all commercial radio stations — played CHR, according to Maurie Webster, president of the Radio Information Center in New York, a major source of radio statistics. The highly disciplined format offers a list of top songs shorter than was typical in the late 1970s — often accompanied by humorous deejay banter.

Other trends in the 1982–85 period indicate radio's growing effort to recruit the Yuppie listener. The "golden oldies" format, which appeals to

Percentage of listeners

Adult Contemporary	19.0%
Rock/Contemporary Hit	17.0%
Album-Oriented	10.5%
Easy Listening	10.4%
Country	9.7%
News/Talk	6.6%
Urban Contemporary	4.9%
Middle-of-the-Road/Nostalgia	4.8%
Black/R&B	3.9%
All-News	3.5%
Spanish	2.2%
Golden Oldies	2.1%
Religious	1.6%
Classical	1.5%
Soft Contemporary	1.2%
Variety	0.6%

Format Wars — Who's listening and what they're listening to in the 100 largest U.S. radio markets (AM and FM). Source: Radio Information Center's analysis of Arbitron's spring 1985 ratings in the top 100 markets.

children of the sixties, was up, while the fifties rock format, now known as "nostalgia" radio, dropped 45 percent, according to Webster. Other observers note that rock sounds aimed at younger listeners are fading from the radio airwaves; while the older listeners' enchantment with clever and sardonic chatter has made stars of such radio personalities as Don Imus at WNBC-AM in New York. MTV and other music-video services are now the place to hear tomorrow's hits today, especially for the teenagers radio is disenfranchising.

FM remains the band preferred for music by listeners under forty. AM stations outnumber FM stations but attract only 29 percent of listeners; they continue to drop music for talk, and to try out such novel programming ideas as the Children's Radio Network, which aims at young children and their mothers. More and more of the talk shows are syndicated or network-originated, because they are cheaper than programs produced in-house. Indeed, 83 percent of stations, both AM and FM, are using syndicated, satellite-delivered music and talk programming.

TECHNOLOGY

Smaller portable stereo radios, some the size of a credit card, have made the medium more pervasive than ever (more than 12 million walkaround sets are in circulation). Stations are using compact-disc players in their studios, but the consequent great improvement in sound is barely noticeable to the listener due to garden-variety FM noise. Help should arrive soon in the form of an improved noise-reduction system from CBS Laboratories.

AM stereo continues to have problems. The number of stereo-equipped AM stations has increased from 300 to 400 in the past year, and more than 1.5 million AM-stereo radios are now on the market. Yet consumer resistance is still high, perhaps prompted by the dearth of good music programming on the AM band. Incompatibility among competing transmission systems remains a hindrance, although the field has recently narrowed from the original five systems to the two offered by Motorola and Kahn Communications.

REGULATION

In 1985 the FCC lifted the rules that prohibited the purchase and rapid resale of broadcast properties, opening the market wide for speculators and investors. Formerly, almost all station owners had broadcasting backgrounds, but the field is now crowded with venture capitalists and big-money interests looking for tried-and-true formats and low operating costs.

Deregulation, which started in a big way in 1981, will continue as the FCC attempts to clear away what it calls the "regulatory underbrush" of niggling rules (for example, stations couldn't broadcast the sound of sirens until this year). Broadcasters, however, aren't relaxing: They are currently fighting efforts to ban beer and wine advertising on the air, as well as attempts to outlaw sexually explicit, violent, and profane rock lyrics.

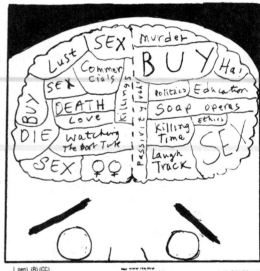

TELEVISION

Television is the medium everyone loves to hate. The statistics on television are staggering. It is estimated that the average person in America watches more than 3½ hours of television each day. The television set is on in the typical American household something like seven hours per day. Children raised in America now have seen around 17,000 hours of television by the time they graduate from high school. They watched thousands of killings and perhaps 500,000 (give or take 100,000) commercials.

Much of the programming on television is, so the media critics tell us, rubbish. That is, most of the television shows are boring, junky, silly, and trivial from an aesthetic (taste) point of view. Television has been described as a cultural "wasteland" and one of the slang terms we use for television, "the boob tube," is most revealing.

Of course one might ask, what if television were good? If people watch more than three and a half hours of rubbish, how much time would they spend watching television if there were good programs on it? An interesting question. As you might suspect, scholars have devoted a great deal of attention to this phenomenon. There have been thousands of research papers published on the medium, and an astronomical number of analyses and criticisms of the medium, its programs, and the television industry that creates these programs.

Television is a medium that broadcasts a wide variety of popular art forms or genres (that is, kinds of programs). Thus television carries commercials, news programs, game shows, soap operas, action-adventure programs, situation comedies, sports shows, religious shows, documentaries, educational programs, dramas, talk shows, and so forth. All of these popular arts are not terribly popular with critics, we must remember. This is nothing new. Critics and people with "elevated" tastes have never thought much of the entertainments of the common people, and still don't. And popular taste, the record indicates, has never been "elevated." So there may be an element of elitist scorn behind the judgments of television critics (and all media critics).

But we also find that many psychologists and sociologists have nasty things to say about television, and they are not concerned with taste but with how people use television and, conversely, how television uses people. We make use of television to serve a number of needs. Lonely people find it brings a kind of companionship; bored people use it to kill time. This matter of how we use the medium is dealt with in one of the essays in this section.

A fascinating essay, on the way "Dallas" is perceived in Germany, offers an interesting thesis. It turns out, as we might have suspected, that Germans "decode" or interpret "Dallas" in terms of German values and beliefs and thus see the program considerably differently from Americans. It might be argued, of course, that there is a difference between the way people from western societies are affected by television as opposed to those from third-world countries, whose cultures are presumably more fragile.

I have also included an essay on the medium of television itself; how does television generate its effects, what powers do the aesthetic aspects of television (lighting, shot angles, etc.) have? This essay suggests that if the medium isn't the whole message (McLuhan suggested it is), it is a very important part of the message.

Television is, above all, a dramatic medium and one of the selections deals with this fact in considerable detail. It provides us with more clues about why this medium has such an impact on people's emotions and, presumably, other aspects of their lives. It also teaches us something about analyzing television programs. Programming is also dealt with in chapters on formulaic aspects of situation comedies and dramas.

In addition, one of the most popular television series, "Star Trek," is analyzed in terms of the values it reflects and its psychological significance. If a series is popular, it must be because it offers important gratifications to people and reinforces values and beliefs that they feel strongly about. This analysis considers the main characters in the program and discusses how they relate to the human psyche.

Most of us assume that television is important and that it is powerful. That is why researchers investigate it and we watch it so much. But might we be wrong? Is television nothing more than moving wallpaper, popcorn for the mind? These are questions you will have to resolve for yourselves. It may be, of course, that television (and all media, to a greater or lesser extent) have powerful effects, but we have not been able to prove this...yet. Of course, television does take up a lot of our time and this, in itself, is a matter of some significance.

Whatever the case, television, more than most media, intrigues us, fascinates us, and worries many of us.

19 DRAMA AS COMMUNICATION*

MARTIN ESSLIN

"The appeal of television is, at the most basic level, an erotic appeal," according to Martin Esslin. This is so, he argues, because television is essentially a dramatic medium and "drama is basically erotic." How does he justify this assertion?

First, he suggests that television feeds upon our interest in other people, and that there is an erotic aspect to this interest. He writes, "Actors give the spectators who watch them a great deal of pleasure by being interesting, memorable, or beautiful specimens of humanity." There is, then, a sexual element to our television viewing, especially because television is a close-up medium, and thus, the most intimate of our media. (This is because, in part, the close-up most nearly approximates direct contact with others.)

Another consideration involves the fact that television is a "daydream" machine that brings an endless number of collective daydreams and fantasies to us. This leads to a "blurring of the distinction between fact and fiction, the real world and fantasy, on the screen," and thus facilitates our often unconscious erotic feelings about the people whose images we see on the television screen.

What television transmits, Esslin tells us, is essentially personality and this is a significant insight because people have an insatiable curiosity about others. This is the heart of our craving for stories. Fiction is, in the final analysis, gossip that is given dramatic form for use on television.

There is a term in psychoanalytic literature that deals with people who derive an unusual amount of sexual satisfaction from looking at others — *scopophilia*. "Scopo" means looking (as in periscope, telescope) and "philia" means "love of" as in Philadelphia, the City of Brotherly Love. We often use the term "voyeur" for such people. Television viewers are not scopophiliacs, but there is an erotic aspect to watching television that we must recognize.

And the fact that we watch so many dramas on television in a typical week must have some impact upon our sense of reality. It is widely held by critics that when we watch drama there is a willing "suspension of disbelief" that occurs; we accept characters as real and identify with them. Because we spend so much time with the alternate realities of television dramas we may end up with a permanently suspended attitude of disbelief which has important social implications.

* Excerpted from *The Age of Television*. Copyright © 1982 Martin Esslin. Used by permission of W.H. Freeman and Company.

Drama can be discussed from a number of different viewpoints: literary, artistic, or technological. It can also be examined simply as a technique of communication, different — in some respects more efficient, in some less so — from other ways in which human beings convey messages to one another. There may be messages drama can convey better than any other form of communication, others that it may not be able to handle well at all. What then are the main characteristics of drama, its strengths and weaknesses as a method of communication?

NARRATION VS. DRAMA

Let us begin with a concrete example, by comparing the way a novelist and a director of a dramatic performance communicate the equivalent content to their respective audiences. The novelist might, for instance, introduce a new character into his story in the following manner:

> And then a young woman of remarkable beauty entered the room. She was tall, had honey-colored hair, a round face, deep blue eyes, a firm, full mouth above a well-rounded yet energetic chin. She wore a dress of pale blue velvet, elegantly cut in a slightly old-fashioned style, with white lace trimmings. The expression on her face was serious, not to say melancholy, and yet, at times, the shadow of a mischievous smile seemed to hover around the corners of her mouth....

And so on at some length. What the novelist has to communicate over a considerable period of time through the accumulation of a number of distinct items of information, the director of the dramatic performance can convey in a single moment, simply by having an actress of the desired appearance and dress enter upon the stage. Whereas the reader of the novel has to keep each item of information in his mind while the others are added one by one, line by line, to build up the complete picture, the spectator of a dramatic performance receives them as one image and with a correspondingly more immediate emotional impact. The information conveyed by the linear, discursive method of the novelist has to pass through the reader's consciousness before it can coalesce into a picture in his mind. By contrast, the spectator of a dramatic performance will get the picture at the outset, though most of the components of the impression will remain below the threshold of full consciousness.

The novelist can control the features he includes in his description and he will select them carefully. The director of the dramatic performance will try to do the same: he will select an actress whose appearance corresponds to the author's description; he will choose a dress intended to convey the qualities required by the character and the situation in which she finds herself in the scene; he will rehearse the expression with which she is to enter the room. But the actress will possess an almost infinite number of other features and characteristics that the director cannot control. Which of these features the spectator will consciously become aware of will depend on his or her own personal reaction, talent for observation, mood, and any number of other factors that are equally beyond the director's control. One spectator may detect a resemblance between the actress and his own sister; another might notice her costume and recognize the designer who created it — an item of information perhaps unknown to the director himself and one that he may never have intended to convey!

The novelist's description may also evoke subconscious associations in the reader's mind. But in the dramatic performance there are an infinite number of items of *concrete information* conveyed to the spectator at every moment. In this respect drama — which can best be defined as a mimetic reproduction of the world — mirrors the situation in our "real" lives: we are constantly confronted with people and situations we have to view, recognize, and interpret; we are compelled to select the information we need by concentrating on a few significant features and rejecting the bulk of data that continuously bombard our senses. Nevertheless there is an essential difference between a dramatic performance and the world of "reality": reality occurs spontaneously and unrepeatably, whereas the dramatic performance has been deliberately engineered to produce in us an intended emotional and intellectual response. Although drama necessarily shares many of the features of reality, it is of course only a simulation of reality and is, above all, simplified, compressed, reordered, manipulated, reversible, and repeatable.

There is a commonplace of dramatic production that in the course of rehearsals, during the endless discussions between the director, designer, writer, and cast concerning the psychology of the characters and their appearance and environment, someone invariably will interject that such discussion is futile because the audience will not notice these fine points of detail. To which, equally invariably, the director will respond that though the audience may not notice such details consciously, subliminally they will take them in and their responses will be affected. And this is undoubtedly true. What is also true, however, is that many things that were not discussed and not intended will affect as strongly the conscious or unconscious reaction of individuals in the audience, each of whom will have to come to terms with what he or she has seen and heard.

DECODING DRAMA

Because the communication in drama occurs not in a linear sequence but in tightly bundled clusters of data that bombard the senses, the spectator's task of decoding a dramatic performance is very different from the reader's task of decoding a novel. To return to our initial example: the entrance of the beautiful woman on the stage will produce an immediate emotional effect (provided, that is, that the director has skillfully focused the attention of the audience upon that entrance). But few members of the audience will be able to say subsequently why they found the woman beautiful: whether it was the shadow of the mischievous smile that played upon her otherwise melancholy countenance or the lace trimmings on her well-cut dress or her deep blue eyes — if indeed they *did* find her beautiful, which some may not have. Those who did may merely remember a sense of mystery and elegance. Some may, either during the performance or afterward, try to analyze the beauty of the woman as they remember particular features in detail. But almost certainly the features they call to mind will be different from those the novelist used to build his picture. And most of the audience will remain unaware of all these distinct details and their interaction.

But, it may be objected, our example concerns a purely visual image, the *appearance* of a character on stage before that character has uttered a single word. Is not drama, like the novel, primarily made up of words and therefore subject to the same mechanisms of expression and understanding as any other verbal form of communication, whether it be a novel, a newspaper dispatch, or a scientific treatise?

Drama does contain an element of the linear and abstract, but everything that is said on the stage emerges from human beings who are perceived primarily as images and, accordingly, what they say is merely a secondary function of those images. The verbal element will of necessity either reinforce or contradict the primary message of the image to which it is subordinate. If, say, Iago assures Othello of his affection, but has an expression of burning hatred in his eyes, the verbal element will clearly be devalued. It is what the characters do, not what they say, that matters in drama. In the famous final scene of Samuel Beckett's *Waiting for Godot* one of the two weary men says "Let's go" but the stage direction — and the action of the two characters — is what matters: "They do not move." In either case the primacy of the visual, situational, concrete element — the image — over the abstract content of the verbal element is inescapable.

It is a cliché of the theater that a good director could fascinate an audience by staging a reading of the telephone directory: such a director would invent intriguing images that would make the audience forget that the words they hear are only a list of names. But no one who needed a number from the phone book would find it expedient to seek it in a dramatic performance. There follows from this a very simple but critical insight: drama is not the most effective way to communicate abstract or purely verbal content or information. If the content is primarily abstract or verbal, it can better be conveyed by silent reading or by recitation, without the full spectrum of means available to stage or screen.

In a dramatic performance on a stage or on a television or movie screen the number of sign systems (i.e., systems of significance) involved is extraordinary. The full range of verbal language (on which the novelist must rely) and the full gamut of voice expression (which so powerfully augments whatever is read on the radio) are enhanced by a vast array of other sign systems. Not only does the appearance of the actor's face and body convey an immense amount of information, but his gestures and movements are signs as well in a complex system of body language. Costumes form another complete sign system, that of dress and its meanings. To this is added the visual sign system of the setting — whether painted or three-dimensional, as on the stage, or photographically conveyed, as on the screen — as well as the elaborate system of significances contained in props: the furniture of a room or the architecture of a building. There is also the system of signs in the lighting plot and that in the musical background that underlies most movies and many television shows. Still another sign system in both movies and television is the variation of shots (long, medium, close) and their montage — the juxtaposition of long-shots to closeups and the cutting from one scene or shot to another. It is impossible to assign each of these sign systems a rigidly maintained rank on a ladder of rising priorities, but one point should be evident: *in drama the complex, multilayered image predominates over the spoken word.*

ASPECTS OF PERSONALITY

Drama is about people in social interaction; the primary interest of the spectator of drama is attached to the personalities involved, their appearance and character, their effects on each other. The linguistic element, insofar as it is concerned with the transmission of abstract ideas, may often come very far down our ladder, after gesture and movement, after costume, even after the impact of the setting.

In drama, at any given moment, the spectator receives a complex of information that coalesces into a general impression, an *image* with an emotional impact, which consists of numerous elements that will remain below the threshold of consciousness but will always be focused upon a human personality, a character. The brightness of the sunshine, the airiness of the lovely buildings on the square, the lively rhythm of the background music, the vivid colors of the costume the actor wears, the springiness of his steps all contribute to the spectator's impression that the young lover he sees in front of him is supremely happy, but few in the audience will be aware of the many elements of information that come together to produce this impression. Drama is always action; its action is always that of human beings. In drama we experience the world through personality.

When we are presented with abstract ideas on the printed page, we may overlook or forget that they are the product of the thought of the individual who has written the text; we may thus receive these ideas as abstract truths. But in drama what we hear is always spoken by a specific individual and has value only as his or her own pronouncement. When we see *Hamlet*, we may accept the words of Hamlet himself or Polonius or Horatio as containing abstract moral or philosophical truths or insights, or we may not. Nothing in the play constrains us to believe the words spoken represent more than the thoughts of the characters — thoughts influenced by their personalities and motives. We are merely informed what this or that character is saying, not necessarily even whether he himself believes what he is saying or whether he is trying to deceive his interlocutor.

Whenever attempts have been made to introduce abstraction into drama — as in morality plays of the late Middle Ages and early Renaissance in which virtues and vices appeared as emblematic figures: Faith, Good Works, Gluttony, Lechery — the figures of these abstractions inevitably turned into individualized characters. And, paradoxically, the vices, by appearing more human, usually more effectively captured the sympathy of their audiences. In the abstract, Faith or Chastity may have been preferable characteristics; on the stage, individualized and humanized, Avarice or Lechery were easier to identify with, more amusing, and therefore more attractive. Allegorical characters have by no means disappeared. They thrive in our time in television commercials, as exemplified, say, by the demons of dirt and grime infesting clogged drains.

The element of personality in drama appears in a highly complex form. When we see Olivier or Gielgud as Hamlet we are interested and involved not only in the fictitious character of Hamlet, but also in the real personality of Laurence Olivier or John Gielgud. The two, character and actor, are fused almost inextricably, so that it is difficult to say which it is that mainly attracts or interests us. Yet it *is* possible to say that we like Olivier's Hamlet better than Gielgud's, or even that we were fascinated by Gielgud's but utterly bored by X's portrayal.

LITERATURE AND DRAMA

At the same time, we know that the character of Hamlet himself as he exists in Shakespeare's play is one that will always be intriguing. This consideration highlights another essential point about the nature of drama as a method of communication: plays that are merely read are literature, and they adhere to the same principles of perception as the novel. If we read *Hamlet* the process of communication we experience is the same as that when we read *War and Peace*. The difference is merely that the descriptive passages in the play — the stage directions — are shorter and the dialogue passages more numerous than in the novel. But in reading *Hamlet* we are, as in reading *War and Peace*, transforming the signs on the page, word by word, line by line, into mental images that coalesce into something like the equivalent of a performance. Seeing a play performed reverses that process and is — with respect to the act of communication that is taking place — totally different.

Those exceptional dramatic texts that have achieved over time the status of literature provide powerful evidence of the essential difference between literature and drama as methods of communication. In performance a dramatic text can convey very different meanings each time it is presented. A performance of *Hamlet*, to stick with our example, is totally different today from a performance of the same text a hundred, two hundred, or three hundred years ago. Not only have the words themselves been uttered in different styles of pronunciation and expressiveness from century to century, not only have costumes and the spatial and visual configuration of the stage changed but, because of the many additional sign systems superimposed in performance upon the basic blueprint of the written text, different sorts of communication are taking place at each performance and very different meanings are being conveyed.

There is of course an essential *core* to such a play: the basic structure of its plot, the interaction of its characters, and the imagery contained in the language. But apart from the obvious differences in acting style, stage technology, and directing, there are also fundamental differences between a performance, say, for Elizabethans who believed in the physical existence of ghosts and one for an audience today that will regard the play's ghost as, at best, a metaphor for Hamlet's subconscious fears or suspicions. The fundamental characteristic of a play-text that remains performable over a period of centuries is that it lends itself — thanks to the durability of the language and depth of the attitudes intrinsic to it — to the production of an almost infinite number of different styles, evoking as many different meanings. A look at the repertoire of theaters throughout the world shows how relatively rare texts of this kind actually are.

Applying these considerations from the history of classical stage drama to the proliferation of drama today in the mass media, we can immediately sense their force. How much of the fictionalized drama seen every day on commercial television could bear translation into written texts and come to be regarded as literature by generations hence? Indeed, how many scripts of even highly successful movie "classics" could be considered literature? Of course, in movies the dramatic performance and the text have been inextricably fused by the process of mechanical recording. Thus we can now look back on some eighty years of such recorded performances. Even after so relatively short a lapse of time, however, it is clear that few of even the most outstanding movies (such as the greatest Garbo, Dietrich, D.W. Griffith, Chaplin, or Marx Brothers films) survive the passage of the years without a profound modification of their impact and meaning. When we view an old movie today, for example, elements such as the fashions of the period, commonplace and hardly noticed at the time, become valuable items of historical interest and may overshadow either the plot or the performance of the principal actors, which were, originally, major features of the film. The meaning of the text itself may also change over time: it can become a period piece as language evolves and as the concepts and conditions it describes change.

What all these considerations highlight once again is that a performance,

San Francisco University Audio-Visual/ITV Center

whether live (and thus subject to variation in each presentation) or mechanically recorded (and thus fixed once and for all), will carry a richer, more complex package of meaning-producing systems than will the written word alone. This multilayered dramatic package will produce an emotional impact the elements of which remain largely subliminal. And the abstract, purely intellectual content of a performed dramatic work will tend to be subordinate to its emotional impact, which is principally the outcome of the interaction of characters and human personalities.

Like the stage and the cinema screen, television deals primarily in images — not only the explicitly dramatic programs broadcast but *all* of television. It is impossible merely to transmit a text on TV unless it is being shown as a silent caption (in which case it is really a means of distributing the printed word). The moment an announcement is read by a speaker on camera a multitude of dramatic sign systems are unleashed. The intention may be only to let us know that "today is Wednesday the twenty-third of May," but we are being informed as well that these words are spoken by a good-looking male of about thirty-five years of age with a blond moustache, that the studio in which he is sitting has a window with a view of midtown Manhattan, that the young man is wearing a tie with blue stripes, that he has a wedding band on his left hand and a wart on his right cheek. We are getting one line of information from the text he is speaking, but at the same time a flood of data is being released about him and his environment. Whether he intends it or not, he has become a *character* in the primary dramatic sense.

DRAMATIS PERSONAE

The frame of the television screen turns everything that happens on it into a stage and everything that is seen or heard upon it into a sign. What is more important, everything that takes place upon that stage has an emotional impact. For instance, we probably respond to the young man announcing the date either favorably or unfavorably. The emotional charge that powers our response in this case may be mild or even subconscious. But in the long run our attitude toward him or one of his rivals may determine which station we select when we watch the news. An awareness of this fact will lie behind the decision of the network's or station's management when it chooses its anchors. It will also shape the anchors' decisions about how to dress and how to conduct themselves, in other words, about what kind of character they will try to present to the viewers.

In a television game show the contestant's answer to a question is less important than his reaction to his success or failure in finding the proper answer — his visible distress if he has failed, his jumping for joy if he has succeeded. In the political interview, however important the personality being questioned may be, however momentous the topics upon which he is speaking, our real interest springs from watching his or her reaction to the sharp searching and provocative questioning to which he or she is being subjected. We are not primarily getting facts; we are getting drama, which is to say we are getting information about the character we are watching rather than about the subject under discussion.

As a method of communication, therefore, drama is highly effective in conveying *human character*, and much less effective in communicating ideas or abstract thought, simply because in drama every abstract idea has to be incarnated as the utterance of an individual and that individual tends to occupy the foreground and to overpower, at least to some degree, the impact of the ideas he or she is voicing. Moreover, as our reactions to individuals are differentiated by our tastes, memories, and fantasies, ideas communicated via television tend to be judged in the light of our reaction to the personalities conveying them. Whether we respond favorably or unfavorably to the multitude of subliminal signals that make up the total impact of such personalities will largely determine whether we accept or reject the ideas they purvey — insofar as we take these ideas in at all.

Since actors are the pivotal point, the central and sole essential ingredient of drama, the effectiveness of television performers of all kinds will derive from their ability to project personality, in other words, from their talent as actors. In this respect it is interesting to note how miserably most inexperienced speakers appear on television, speakers such as one occasionally sees in the spots the stations provide for reply to their own editorial opinions. The expressionless faces of the people on these spots as they tonelessly read a prepared text points up the demands on the usual television performer, to be not only a professional but a professional with acting talent. What these untrained speakers have to say rarely has any impact on the viewers. On television a message delivered by a person without acting talent is hardly noticed at all.

The situation is entirely different when television catches actual participants in news events at moments of high emotion: the relatives of a murder victim, hostages who have been released, eyewitnesses to an accident, and so on. The emotional intensity of the situation — its drama — turns such neophytes into effective performers able to project an intense state of mind and genuine passion. The participants in game shows are in a similarly excited emotional state, which tends to transform them too into effective actors (though they have, in addition, been carefully pretested for their natural acting ability, attractiveness, or quirkiness of character).

The ability of TV to transmit personality is, undoubtedly, the secret of its immense power. For human beings are insatiable in their interest about other human beings. Once, when traveling through a remote region of then-colonial East Africa and seeing the villages of grass huts without shops or electricity or roads or any other amenities, I asked an African friend what the local people did during the long dark hours after nightfall, which at the equator comes early the whole year round. Without hesitation my friend replied, "They gossip. They tell each other about the love affairs and sicknesses of their neighbors." Indeed this seems to me one of the basic human drives. Next to the satisfaction of the drives for food, shelter, and procreation, the satisfaction of the drive to gossip about the experiences of others must be one of the central concerns of all human existence. It is the source of all fiction and storytelling, and the source too of drama. Hearing about what has happened to other people, how they have coped with crises in their lives, is of the utmost importance to the survival of the individual and of the species; it is part of an endless learning process.

Herein lies the source of humanity's insatiable craving for stories: all fiction is ultimately gossip. Television, with its unending stream of characters conveyed dramatically (whether fictional or "real"), is the most perfect mechanized conveyor of that gossip. Being essentially dramatic rather than discursive in nature, moreover, television satisfies this craving in a uniquely effective manner; it not only retells stories *about* other people, it actually transports these other people into our own living rooms. The attraction of gossip, of course, contains at its root one of the most powerful human impulses. Our interest in other people contains of necessity a strong erotic element. It is this which constitutes one of the basic characteristics and magnetic powers of drama: drama is basically *erotic*. Actors give the spectators who watch them a great deal of pleasure simply by being interesting, memorable, or beautiful physical specimens of humanity. Quite apart from their artistic and intellectual accomplishments, actors are people who, for money, exhibit their physical presence to the public. We all know that great stars derive their special magnetism from sex appeal. But what applies to the big stars contributes as well to the attractiveness and success of the lesser lights. In a sense all actors are exhibitionists: they enjoy being seen, being found appealing and worth looking at. Conversely audiences of drama are also, in a certain sense, voyeurs.

Though this is true of all drama, it is especially true of television. Television is the most voyeuristic of all communication media, not only because it provides more material in an unending stream of images and in the form most universally accessible to the totality of the population, but also because it is the most intimate of the dramatic media. In the theater the actors are relatively remote from the audience and the dramatic occasion is public. In the cinema, also a public occasion gathering a large audience into a single room, the actors are nearer to the spectators than in the theater, but in close-ups they are larger than life. Television is seen at a close range and in a more private context. The close-up of the television performer is on a scale that most nearly approximates direct human contact.

THE DAYDREAM MACHINE

The appeal of television is, at the most basic level, an erotic appeal. TV brings other human beings into close proximity for detailed inspection. The people we view in close-ups on the television screen appear to be as near to us as our sexual partners during an embrace. And yet they are glimpsed behind a glass screen, through a window that cannot be opened. The television screen is a stage, a frame for the display of images, but though so near, the world it brings to us is also beyond our reach, a world of inaccessible phantoms. The world it shows us on its stage, behind that window through which we can see but cannot grasp or touch, is essentially a world of fantasy.

Thus television is closely akin to the daydream. The essential feature of daydreams is that they are outside our conscious control. Their charm lies precisely in the spontaneous images they flash before our mind's eye, to which we surrender passively and with pleasure. Television images are received in this same way. Hollywood earned for the movie industry the tag "dream factory" in its early years of mass-entertainment production; in a similar way the television industry has engineered a product that can be called the "daydream machine," for TV brings an uninterrupted procession of collective daydreams, collective fantasies, into our homes. It is this essential characteristic of television that accounts for the blurring of the distinction between fact and fiction, the real world and fantasy, on the screen.

Our daydreams, after all, also concern themselves with the real world; through them we may even reach important decisions, evolve plans, and devise strategies for future conduct. Daydreams nevertheless remain fantasies; they are experienced as intuitions to which we surrender passively rather than as processes of consciously directed, inductive reasoning. Even the most "real" features of television, such as the news, contain the element of fantasy, and of erotic fantasy at that. There is the appeal of the anchorman or anchorwoman and of the reporters, the appeal of the political personalities and other subjects of news broadcasts — hostages, beauty queens, criminals, and victims of crime. And there is the sensationalistic, even sadomasochistic, appeal of the scenes of violence, war, and disaster that make up so much of the material presented on TV news: demonstrators being beaten by police; prisoners being executed in a war or revolution; the smoldering debris left in the aftermath of a plane crash. The undoubted element of "reality" contained in the news is thus, by being broadcast on television, automatically transmuted into the stuff of fantasy and daydream — drama — into a story told in images laden with emotional overtones and sometimes hardly distinguishable from fiction.

All drama depends on that "suspension of disbelief" that will make us, for a brief time, accept the characters we see on the stage as real human beings so that we can identify with them to experience their joys and their sorrows, the whole range of their emotions. Television protracts the suspension of disbelief. What distinguishes TV from the theater and the cinema is sheer quantity of material: the continuousness of TV and the vast amount of material it spews forth enlarge and intensify the traditional characteristics of the other dramatic media so immensely that the increased *quantity* of material broadcast on TV becomes a new *qualitative* characteristic. We may have believed, for the span of three hours, that Hamlet was a real person, but then we are left to reflect on his character with detachment and analytical insight. The character in the soap opera, on the other hand, is with us almost every day over a period of years and becomes so familiar that detached reflection is inhibited or never occurs at all. Disbelief may become permanently suspended.

It is the constant presence of this alternative world that is both real and fictional — a fantasy yet an immensely real factor in the lives of whole populations — that makes the explosion of the dramatic form of communication on television such a revolutionary development.

20   TV FORMULAS: PRIME-TIME GLUE *

Joyce Nelson

A great deal of what we see on television can be described as being formula written. A formula, as we use the term in discussing narratives, is a conventionally structured story with easily recognized character types and widely accepted resolutions. Many genres of programs found on television are based on formulas.

Think, for example, of the typical western. It takes place at a certain time in our history, at a certain place, with characters who usually wear certain kinds of clothing. There are numerous conventional characters and events in westerns: the lone cowboy hero, the blonde schoolmarm, the inept sheriff, the nasty villain and his henchmen, the chase scene, and the eventual fight between the good guy and the bad guy. These conventions are not always followed slavishly, but are common enough so that audiences can recognize, very quickly, that they are seeing a western and can have some degree of confidence about the kinds of things that will happen in the story. The same applies to other genres such as detective stories, science fiction adventures, spy stories, soap operas, and situation comedies.

There are a number of reasons why formulas play such an important role in the mass media and in television in particular. First, television needs a tremendous number of stories and it is easier to use a formula than invent something new and original. And second, audiences would find it difficult to understand new kinds of stories all the time. With formula-based stories, the audience has an understanding of what to expect and the writers don't have to worry too much about explaining everything. The audience knows, in a very general way, how things will turn out; it doesn't know how a particular story will be resolved, however. So there is room for creativity and surprise in formula-based stories.

This essay compares and contrasts crime stories and situation comedies on television in terms of how they are shot, where the action takes place, the kinds of characters involved, and their attitudes toward authority, among other things. And from this comparison the author draws certain conclusions about the messages people may be getting from each of these program types and how they may be socializing people.

It is useful to take the concept of the formula and apply it to other kinds of programs and to take the author's method of analyzing what formulas mean to people and see what you find in examining soap operas, spy stories, and other popular genres. There may be some interesting revelations.

---

* Joyce Nelson, "TV Formulas as Prime Time Glue," reprinted by permission IN SEARCH, Department of Communications, Canada. (Fall, 1979)

Channel-hopping on a cable convertor can give us a false sense of plenitude. With all those stations to choose from, the cabled world of television offerings appears to be a veritable supermarket of viewing. A closer look reveals otherwise.

According to several recent studies in both Canada and the U.S., the long-term trend in commercial broadcasting has been toward less diversity of programming and greater homogeneity of network schedules. In other words, fewer and fewer types of programs are taking up increasing amounts of broadcast time. Currently, the two staples of commercial prime time are the sitcom and the crime series. Much as soap operas and game shows have tended to dominate daytime hours, these two formulas are the backbone of prime time. A convenient (but tired and misleading) argument is that this is "what the public wants." But a reading of Erik Barnouw's latest work, *The Sponsor: Notes on a Modern Potentate* (Oxford University Press, 1978), provides convincing and detailed evidence of the power of advertisers in determining programming fare. Basically, the sponsor always plays it safe: avoiding controversy, opting for the familiar, relying on the tried-and-tested formulas which will provide the innocuous context for their ads.

Given that sponsors have supported the rise of the sitcom and the crime series for recent prime time, it is useful to look more closely at the conventions at work in these two formulas. What emerges from such scrutiny is that the sitcom and the crime series are closely interconnected. In an important sense, they build on one another, deriving added meaning through combination. In many cases, the gaps in one formula are filled in by the conventions of the other. These two predominant program types together ritualistically reiterate a world view, a zeitgeist of prime time which is fascinating to explore. The conventions of sitcoms and crime series function as a set of oppositions which mutually reinforce an ideology that is particularly well-suited to the advertiser's message.

WHAT'S IN A NAME

Titles of formula shows are themselves revealing. Crime series have names like "Kojak," "Mannix," "Baretta," "Delvecchio," "Starsky and Hutch" — using the last name of the hero to convey authority, formality, power. Sitcoms use central characters' first name in the program title — "Julia," "Nancy," "Rhoda," "Laverne & Shirley," "Bob Newhart Show" — to suggest informality, personable qualities. Another grouping of crime series uses titles that refer to milieu: "Streets of San Francisco," "The Naked City," "Sidestreet," "N.Y.P.D.," "Hawaii Five-O" since setting is important to this formula. While sitcoms often utilize the pretense of urban settings — Minneapolis for "Mary Tyler Moore," Milwaukee for "Laverne & Shirley," Chicago for "Bob Newhart Show" — their titles rarely refer to setting.

Instead, another set of sitcoms uses titles that indicate the importance of the family unit for this formula: "Eight Is Enough," "All in the Family," "Three's Company," "Brothers and Sisters," "The Jeffersons," "Harris & Company."

Of course, there are occasional exceptions, but usually the titles themselves conventionally signal which formula is at work.

HARD FILM AND SOFT VIDEOTAPE

Another convention of crime series is that they are shot on film rather than being videotaped. While filming is a more expensive way of making programs, the choice definitely contributes to the desired look of this formula. In comparison to the videotaped image, the filmed image is considered to be more crisp and to have more depth, so that objects and movement in both foreground and background are clearly visible within the same shot. The sharpness of image also contributes to the so-called hard-edge qualities we have come to expect from crime series: the stark outlines and the definite areas of shadow, for instance.

An image in depth is also important for the kind of action taking place in this formula. According to Brian Walker, producer for "Sidestreet," the directors are asked to "make sure that the action moves toward the camera. The camera is always being pushed by the action coming into the foreground, rather than moving away from the camera. The former is obviously more dramatic." This movement from background into foreground creates a sense of urgency, especially when speed is involved. A car chase, or running figures, would not be nearly so involving if the action were shot on the horizontal plane, with movement from left to right on the screen. Thus, the scope of the action and the depth of the image are important conventions of the crime show formula.

Sitcoms, however, are usually videotaped with a four-camera setup in a studio. Some sitcoms made by Grant Tinker's MTM enterprises, notably "Mary Tyler Moore," have been filmed, but in general, the resulting crisp image in depth is not considered important for this studio-bound formula. Since story action is confined to small interiors of a stage set, the actual movement of figures and objects never achieves the scope found in crime shows. The dramatic movement from background into foreground is simply not important to this formula, which relies on small gestures, facial expressions and relatively restricted bodily movement for its action.

Videotape, too, has its own look, one which viewers have come to expect from sitcoms. The taped image is essentially flat, without much depth, and the contours of figures are softer than on film. A keen eye can readily distinguish between film and tape, which has prompted the makers of "King of Kensington" and some other sitcoms to re-do their opening outdoor "signature" sequence, changing it from a filmed sequence to a taped one in order to give unity to the look of the entire show. This relatively flat image is in keeping with the predominant movement of the actors in sitcoms.

Because they are shot on the proscenium stage of a studio set, sitcoms are characterized by action along the horizontal plane. Camera distance is typically medium shots and close-ups, with camera movement restricted. Such a shooting style contrasts with that of crime shows, where extremes of camera distance are common (from extreme long shots to tight close-ups) and camera movement is often quite elaborate, encorporating dollies and cranes and extensive tracking shots at times.

INTERIORS, EXTERIORS

Sitcoms rarely, if ever, use location-shooting. Except for a brief introductory signature sequence, where we see the parks and city streets of Minneapolis for "Mary Tyler Moore" or the stalls and crowds of Kensington Market for "King of Kensington," for example, this formula uses the convention of setting a milieu which is then never seen again during the rest of the episode.

In crime series, however, urban milieu is central and location-shooting takes full advantage of the recognizable features of a particular city. Chase scenes are often choreographed to contain familiar landmarks and areas such as Central Park, Wall Street, Grand Central Station in New York, Fisherman's Wharf, Telegraph Hill, the docks and bridges of San Francisco, the Yonge Street "strip," CN Tower and City Hall in Toronto. Rather than disguise the city or ignore it, this formula relies on its identifying features, making the setting much more than a backdrop. In fact, "Sidestreet's" Brian Walker considers Toronto "another star of the show."

Of course, urban milieu is important to the recurring and central theme of this formula — the battle between good and evil involved in crime. Even with the recent tendency of series to veer off into fantasy, programs like "The Incredible Hulk," "Wonder Woman," "Bionic Woman," "$6 Million Man" are still crime-centered. Whether the main character is male, female or mutant, openly uniformed or secretly disguised, the power of the Law is always behind him/her/it. This is true not only for characters who are police ("Baretta," Sidestreet," "Police Woman," "Kojak"), but also for private detectives ("The Rockford Files," "Barnaby Jones"), the more fantastic super-heroes with secret identities and even for the more marginal characters in terms of the legal system, such as local reporter "Mrs. Colombo." In every case, a sense of righteousness, personal moral principle, the Law backs up the hero's action and provides the clear-cut motivation for the decisiveness of the main characters.

Interestingly, this aspect of the formula coincides with shooting style. "We've got to feel that the main characters are basically ahead of the story," says the producer of "Sidestreet," "that they have a better understanding of it, at least as policemen and hopefully as human beings, than the people involved in the situation. The main thing is that they are not lumbering along behind the action, but are instead forcing the action. This has to do with the style of shooting as well: people moving towards camera, pushing the camera back." The central characters of this formula use quick and effective gestures, take decisive action and are forceful figures of authority. Even a crippled law-enforcer like Raymond Burr's "Ironside," confined to a wheelchair, is suitably, bizzarrely hard-edged.

LOVABLE LOSERS

These conventions are in obvious contrast with those of sitcoms. The recurring, central theme of situation comedy is the simple frustration involved in inter-personal relationships. The small, daily problems associated with family units or close-knit groups provide the basis for story-lines and jokes in this formula. New neighbors move in next door, an old boy friend appears on the scene, a difference of opinion develops between friends: such incidents provide the typical conflict on which an episode is based.

Sitcom characters aren't particularly decisive or effective. In fact, much of the humor is based on their ineffectiveness as they struggle to solve some simple problem or as they vascillate among alternative ways of dealing with a situation. This is perhaps particularly true of characters in the MTM stable, characters such as Mary Richards, Rhoda, the psychiatrist played by Bob Newhart. They are lovable because they are indecisive and unsure of themselves. "King of Kensington's" Larry is played this way, as well. Other sitcom characters, especially those developed by Norman Lear, may seem more angry, stubborn, authoritarian, but these traits are themselves the basis for comedy and the source of personal and humorous frustration. In the course of the half-hour, a character learns some lesson in compromising, softening, relenting momentarily. A third group of sitcoms is in the Garry Marshall stable — "Happy Days," "Laverne & Shirley," "Blansky's Beauties," programs with slightly bizarre characters engaged in wacky horse-play intended to endear us to their bumbling personas.

John Leonard, TV critic for the *New York Times*, has nicely summarized the conventions for sitcome characters in the U.S.:

What is allowed in U.S. sitcom, even according to the people who do the best ones, is quite constricting. The characters have to be vulnerable, and to a certain extent they have to lose week by week. There is a kind of "Hollywood-Universal City-TV sitcom-abstract principle" that to be funny, you can't be wise. I mean wise in the sense of wisdom, not in the sense of being a "wiseacre". You can't be wise, you have to have somehow stumbled through to the right solution so that you are not presented as being better than anyone else. I sat in on discussions with the best writers in the business and they said the public doesn't like to feel that people on TV are better than they are.

This last remark should be qualified by reference to the crime show formula, where by convention the central character is wise, ahead of the story, forcing the action, powerful. Unlike sitcom characters, the main characters of crime series are rarely what one could call family types. Marriage, children, the nuclear family unit are, for them, either something in the past (as in "Sidestreet" and, I seem to recall, "Police Woman") or they are an implied hindrance to their life-style, which mainly revolves around work. In fact, in this formula, work is the "raison d'être," the central personal commitment. Time-off may be alluded to (Rockford's fishing, Baretta's swinging), but it is rarely shown. Instead, the hour-long crime show centers upon work (the solving of the crime) done effectively and without compromise.

In contrast, we usually see sitcom characters during their leisure hours, off work. Jobs may be referred to (Laverne and Shirley work in a brewery, the Fonz is an auto mechanic, Archie Bunker runs a tavern), but the work is by no means central to this series. When the job provides the situation for the comedy, as in "Mary Tyler Moore," "The Bob Newhart Show," "Barney Miller," work is used to reveal frustration, daily problems and small compromises humorously made. The characters aren't the dedicated and successful workaholics found in the crime series.

TAPED BEFORE A LIVE AUDIENCE

One obvious convention of the sitcom formula has not been mentioned so far. Sitcoms are taped before a live studio audience. This standard practice, which at first glance seems trivial, is actually quite important to the pacing and feel of a show. The actors rely on audience response to judge the timing of jokes and the quality of their performance. Usually, a show is taped twice, in front of two different audiences. Selections are made of the better scenes from both tapings and a final mix is made, including pickups (individual shots re-done or cutaways added) and an augmented laugh-track. This latter element, an important convention in the formula, is a carefully orchestrated sound-track mixing of some of the laughs from the live studio audience with selections from the pre-recorded library of snickers, chuckles and guffaws.

Structurally, this augmented laugh track corresponds to the musical track of the crime show. Music is never used in a sitcom, aside from its recurring theme song over the opening and closing credits. However, music is an important element in the crime show formula. Interwoven carefully with the sounds of squealing tires, shouts, gun shots, the music track almost works subliminally to establish mood and pace and to underline dramatic moments. Not only are there often layers of foreground and background sound, but usually the level of the music track is brought up into the foreground to heighten a dramatic climax, a kind of audial depth in keeping with the visual look.

Another audial difference between these two formulas is in the kind and amount of dialogue. Sitcoms generally use rapidly paced and plentiful dialogue. ("Mork & Mindy" is a good example, where a verbal joke usually has at least one "topper" and most of the humor is in the dialogue.) Canadian director Norman Campbell, known for his ballet specials in this country, has worked on most of the popular U.S. sitcoms. He says, "Dialogue very much dictates the cutting of a show. I could almost look at a script once and tell what the camera cutting would be on it because if you're dealing with comedy, you can see where the jokes are, whose face you want to be on, and when you want to cut to a reaction. Quite often the reaction is more important than the person saying the joke line. The person getting the butt of the joke is perhaps the more preposterous figure."

Crime shows, because they are more action-oriented, usually involve far less dialogue than a sitcom and in this formula cutting highlights movement. Perhaps as a hold-over from the strong, silent Western hero who believed in less talk and more action, the crime show hero doesn't waste words. If energy in sitcom is located in the dialogue, energy in a crime series is located in action.

Structurally, we can place many of the conventions of these two formulas as a set of oppositions such as the following:

Crime show formula	Sitcom formula
film	videotape
sharp, in-depth image	soft, flat image
large-scale movement	confined movement
action-centered	dialogue-centered
musical track	laugh track
public urban setting	private interior
work-oriented	leisure-oriented
loners	groups
wise, effective authority figures	bumbling, ineffective common folk
powerful figures	powerless figures
hour-long	half-hour long
uncompromising	vulnerable
winners	compromising losers
formal and heroic	informal and unheroic

NETWORK NEWS FORMULA

Interestingly, two other evening formulas pick up some of these conventions as well. The national network news show resembles the crime show formula in several ways. The anchorman (whether male or female) must exude authority, certainty and a sense of calm wisdom in the face of complex and often disastrous events being reported. Like the crime show hero, he or she must be ahead of the story, on top of the action, organizing it effectively.

The news items themselves are usually about other powerful people — politicians or leaders involved in the ritualistic display of authority, or the items deal with action-centered trouble-spots around the world. According to the conventions of news shows (as Canadian critic Morris Wolfe has written), an item that involves some action-footage (a fire, a demonstration, an airplane, a disaster) will usually be selected over an item that is simply a "talking-head." Like the crime show formula, exteriors and action are important to the news show. The anchors and reporters aren't meant to be viewed as family-types with personal lives. Instead, they are job-oriented, mobile, decisive loners. The dialogue in news is spare, lean, to the point.

The celebrity talk show shares some of the conventions of the sitcom formula. It, too, is videotaped completely within interiors, involving the confined movement possible on a studio set. It is, of course, dialogue-centered with a studio audience providing laughter and applause. There is a sense of informality, with host and guests on easy terms with one another, trying to come across as just plain folks. Talk is personal, leisurely and concerned with family, hobbies, jokes and anecdotes. The set is intended to be like a livingroom, where people hold drinks, smoke, relax and are informal. While power and authority usually accompany celebrity, such topics are in bad taste on the celebrity talk show. Instead, this formula, like the sitcom, centers on human foibles, small idiosyncrasies, the vulnerabilities of host and guests who are supposedly no better than we are.

THE FORMULAS BENEFIT THE ADVERTISERS

A curious ideology arises from the formulas of the sitcom and crime series in combination. Wisdom, authority, decisive action, and leadership qualities are rarely associated with the characters who most closely resemble us in our living rooms. Instead, those qualities are reserved for people who are set apart: the law enforcers and event-explainers, a small group of authority figures who nightly re-enact their expertise. As well, the outside world, the world beyond the confines of the home, seems one of danger, crime, disaster and complexity that only a select few can cope with. The majority must bumble through their small, daily frustrations and personal problems, never questioning or mentioning the bigger events, the larger forces at work in society.

We begin to see how these standard commercial program formulas work to the benefit of the advertisers who sponsor them. The kinds of products advertised and the pitch given in the commercial messages for the products, both are suited to the ideological environment provided by the programs. Many products are associated with the fear of heightening interpersonal problems. Mouthwashes, toothpaste, deodorants, soaps, shampoos, cosmetics, foot powder, even liquor are often attached to this fear. Other products are associated with the desire to be effective and competent: laundry soap, aerosol sprays, polishes, foods are often pitched to us this way. Other products are associated with power: cars, equipment, tools, for instance; while some ads refer to the dangers and complexities outside the home: lost or stolen travellers' cheques, accident insurance, credit cards, even garbage-bag spray to keep away roving animals. The people in these ads (who are supposed to be "just plain folks") appear decisive, sure of themselves and their purchases, and on top of whatever used to be a problem.

The over-all message of commercial prime time seems to be that while there is little room for decisive and effective action on our part, either in world events or daily life, we can at least become competent, informed consumers, making choices in the marketplace between one brand and another. On commercial prime time, our wisdom is supposed to be product-knowledge and our leadership qualities are to be shown in fervent brand loyalty, daring attempts to squeeze the toilet paper or even the great good fortune of writing our own commercials for a laundry detergent.

21 "DALLAS" AMONG GERMAN VIEWERS *

Herta Herzog Massing

In 1941 Herta Herzog Massing wrote, under her maiden name, an important essay on radio soap operas, "On Borrowed Experience."[1] It was based on personal interviews with 100 women living in the Greater New York area (mostly housewives) and concerned itself with the functions these programs had for their listeners. Massing concluded that soap operas appealed to the insecurity of the women and offered them "remedies of a substitute character." She suggested that listening to these programs offered the following gratifications:

1. An emotional release
2. A wishful remodeling of the listener's drudgery
3. An ideology and recipes for adjustment.

She discussed each of these gratifications in detail.

Thus, the women who obtained an emotional release from the soap operas said these programs gave them an "outlet for pent-up anxieties" and a "chance to compensate" for their own hardships "through aggressiveness against other people." Some women said the shows gave them a chance to cry. As Massing explained it, "the sketches, in their specific sad content, serve as an outlet for the unspecific anxiety" of some of the listeners.

In some extreme cases, the women identified very strongly with the characters in the stories. "In the most radical form of identification," Massing tells us, "the listener escapes into the story quite consciously. She makes use of the stories to superimpose upon her life another, more desirable life." Women switched from story to story to obtain the gratifications they were seeking or because they thought the story lines were too boring or improbable. In most cases the women selected various aspects of the stories "to fit into their lives to make them more interesting or more agreeable." Thus they used the stories to compensate for what they felt were deficiencies in their own lives.

Finally, the listeners used the stories as recipes for making adjustments to life and as models of behavior for coping with various kinds of problems. The stories, Massing suggested, explained things by providing labels for them and placed a kind of structure on the random and eventless quality of their everyday lives.

Massing concluded that the soap operas become "an integral part of the lives of many listeners. They are not only successful means of a temporary emotional release or escape from a disliked reality…they seem to have become a model of

* Published by permission of Transaction, Inc. from "Decoding Dallas," by Herta Herzog Massing, *Society*, Nov./Dec. 1986, pp. 74–77. Copyright © 1986 by Transaction, Inc.

reality by which one is taught how to think and how to act." It is useful to apply Massing's work on radio soap operas to contemporary television soaps, such as "Dallas" and consider how they function for their audiences.

REFERENCE

1. Herzog, Herta, 1941. "On Borrowed Experience." *Studies in Philosophy and Social Science*, IX.

The highly successful television development of primetime serials started off by "Dallas" has been of interest for various theoretical and disciplinary orientations. Several focus on the text and the hypothesized spectator-text relation. In the tradition of literary analysis and film theory "Dallas" has been studied as melodrama in its serial form and nonclosure structure which also characterizes daytime "soaps." Soap opera analysis has stressed the gender differences and implications for the day and evening versions.

Another major focus has been the reading of the text in the context of and as a symptom of popular culture. Critics of popular culture, and of things American in particular, have concerned themselves with the question of whether the worldwide diffusion of programs such as "Dallas" made possible by the growth of the new media technologies may eventually result in worldwide cultural assimilation at the expense of indigenous diversity. Until recently, however, little was known empirically about the qualities of audience response to "Dallas" or any other of the prime-time soaps, in the United States or abroad. This pilot study was a first attempt to examine the meaning of "Dallas" for German television viewers.

Audience analysis today still lacks a broad theoretical framework. Considerable discussion, notably on the concept of audience gratification, has mainly served to highlight the complexities of viewer response. As pointed out recently, progress is being made in a convergence of content-oriented analysis. The "reading" of the import "Dallas" on the part of German television viewers has been one task of this study. The second concerns selected aspects of the multifaceted meaning of the program, particularly the possibilities for the projection of various sociopsychological interests and needs in their cultural-ideological context.

The German field work for "Dallas" was carried out in November 1982. It consisted of intensive qualitative interviews, supplemented by a brief projective personality test with a small sample of fifty-one viewers of the middle and lower middle class, divided equally by sex and age group (16–25 and 45–60 years of age), living in large and small towns in various sections of Germany. It consisted both of people who had watched the program from the very beginning and other less regular viewers. In the spring of 1985 a comparable group of control interviews was carried out with fifty-one "Dallas" viewers living in various sections and cities of the United States.

As postulated by our theoretical stance, the milieu of "Dallas" turned out indeed to be a very important element of its appeal for German viewers. While interestingly foreign, it still conforms to what they think of or are willing to accept as typically American. Viewers are impressed with the physical environment such as the Southfork ranch, the big highways, the city traffic and skyscrapers of "Dallas" as well as with the lifestyle of the Ewings for whom "money does not matter." The Ewings display some strange habits, it is noted, such as wearing a cowboy hat to the office, the "eternal drink in their hands," or the dining out "at every occasion." But life is generally easier in America, one has heard, money there is made more easily and therefore probably also spent more easily. Rich people anywhere, it is reasoned, do not lead ordinary lives. Germany has its rich people too, although "they do not show their wealth" like the Ewings, a point noted with some condescension as well as appreciation for the "insights" afforded. The plot is not altogether far-fetched, German viewers concluded; the story could happen in Germany, at least in relation to the kinds of problems faced by the Ewings.

FAMILY AS A BRIDGE

The three-generation Ewing clan is a bridging element, tying the story together for German audiences. Fitting with the hierarchical concept of the traditional German family structure, it helps the viewer to relate to the characters of "Dallas."

Jock (the character had not yet died at the time of the interviews) is an important person for the German viewer. In the spontaneous listing of the characters of "Dallas," Jock was nearly as often mentioned in first place as his son J. R. Jock is perceived as the patriarch of the family, founder of a business which he built through hard work. He is judged tough in his business dealings but never shooting from the hip, determined to defend his business interests even against his wife whom he dearly loves. Miss Ellie fits the stereotype of the good mother: she is always working for peace, trying to hold the family together. Some of the older viewers are impressed that she dares to show independence even against her husband when her moral principles are involved.

To the younger viewers, Bobby is the "kid brother of J. R.," while the older viewers see him as the "younger son of Jock." Generation differences also show in the perception of Sue Ellen, wife of J. R. The older viewers see in her the woman ruined by her husband. The younger ones tend to see her as a somewhat unstable person (she has some extramarital affairs and a drinking problem), badly treated by her husband but unwilling to pass up the Ewing riches. Sue Ellen is her own problem, they say.

J. R. THE SCOUNDREL

J. R. is the one truly melodramatic character of "Dallas" who does not fit cultural mores. He is perceived as "a scoundrel the like of which has never before been shown on German television." In his unscrupulous mad quest for more wealth and more power for and through Ewing Oil, he establishes an "interconnection between business and family life" which intrigues some of the male viewers. J. R. does not stand for the threats of business as an institution as has been surmised from an American point of view. German viewers see in him an individual scoundrel of excessive dimension, responsible for problems that can happen in every family. He is the unpredictable devil ex machina; without him there would be no story. His laugh always "signals the next outrageous incident."

A remarkable facet of this scoundrel is his success: J. R. never fails. He is masterful in his plots (a *Koenner*), successful with women he merely uses and with his dirty business machinations. He always finds a way out (*Hintertuerchen*) in contrast to his counterpart Cliff Barnes who is unanimously seen as the "eternal loser." For some viewers in the group — not nearly as many as suspected by the German press — J. R. is indeed the reason for their enjoyment of "Dallas." He sparks their admiration for a macho ideal. They would like to dare being as unscrupulously cunning and aggressive and get away with it as he does. They are not like him but wish they were.

A sizable number of viewers in this case study recognize in the story and its characters other aspects of their own often barely understood or accepted longings and problems. In a variety of ways "Dallas" provides them with a temporary release through projection. Here are a few examples, as indicated by the verbal statement of the viewer and supported and further illuminated by the test material:

A sixteen-year-old high school student struggling to reconcile his childhood dependency needs with his strivings for masculine maturity is quite outspoken in his negative assessment of Miss Ellie (very rare in the total group): She is a "grandma-type," he says, and he does not like her. He admires, however, Dusty, the friend of Sue Ellen. Although a cripple physically, he says, he is able to give her the manly support she does not get from her husband.

A young dental assistant from a very modest background identifies with Pam, wife of Bobby Ewing. "She is not a *real* Ewing yet she made it," being loved by her husband and successful in her independent business activities.

An older housewife sees in the "disparity between the splendid facade of the Ewings and their inner turmoil" a replica of her own situation. As shown also in the test data, she is troubled to maintain a social front despite inner feelings of inadequacy and insecurity.

For viewers having a hard time to maintain control of themselves "Dallas" provides a chance to let go emotionally. A retired government employee with marked sadomasochistic tendencies he controls with great difficulty says: "I am looking forward to this weekly sprinkler." It is of course "mindless night entertainment," he stresses yet he furnished unusually detailed descriptions of many of its incidents, mostly the catastrophic ones. The process of watching is for him the opportunity to experience feelings, to emote, something he ordinarily does not permit himself.

The patterns of projection were varied. They would depend on and be limited by the possibilities inherent in the story.

In the case of "Dallas" the multitude of projections of more or less accepted feelings is facilitated through the person of Miss Ellie. It helps that she (the actress Barbara Bel Geddes) "looks German." The main reason is her role in the story. As matriarch of the family, with her continuing efforts for a peaceful family life, she asserts and reaffirms the superego and so re-assigns the viewer's projection to its properly disengaged, denied, or sup-pressed stage.

DAYDREAMS WITH DALLAS

This second major type of viewing satisfaction is readily recognized and articulated. Daydreaming is a type of enjoyment typical for soap operas generally. Yet the daydreams of German "Dallas" viewers have a unique feature. The viewers love to participate in the exciting life of the Ewings who can afford every luxury. But the Ewings also have enormous problems. Theirs is not a safe or sane or happy world (keine heile Welt): "Of course you dream with them about having that much money...but you also see that money alone does not make you happy" [female, 24 years old, social worker]. Thus the viewer does not feel so badly off after all, being less burdened with comparatively lesser problems than those the Ewings have to face all the time: "I'd love to have their money, have a big car like every one of them has. I would have a horse and ride over my ranch! And my husband is really not as considerate as Jock — but he is not as mean as J.R. either. And I do not know anyone like him among my friends or neighbors. I really would not want to be in their shoes" [female, 46 years old, wife of a business man]. For the German viewer the daydreaming escape into the life of the Ewings contains the return ticket to reality. It is doubly rewarding, being experienced as a dream and as confirmation of the viewer's everyday life.

Some viewers, mostly in the young age-group, seemed to watch "Dallas" without much personal involvement. It is available on a free night in their weekly schedule, and program choices are limited as the German viewer has as a rule only one other national and one regional channel to choose from. They rate "Dallas" a "superb spectacle." With its multiple plot structure they can "count on something to happen every time." They are curious about what new ideas will come up. "Dallas" is always good for a mild arousal that is not upsetting because its incidents occur in a familiar structure.

The United States interviews were conducted a couple of years after the German ones. Interestingly, the story development does play a role in viewer response. Certain observations of difference, however, can be made quite reliably.

For the viewer in the United States, the mise-en-scène of "Dallas" concerns a rich or very rich Texan Oil family in its business involvements and private lives, both interrelated and both short on morals. As in the German interviews, the emphasis on these points varies some from one viewer to the other. The United States interviews generally show a broader emphasis on the business setting compared with the German emphasis on the geographic setting and way of life. It is "big business after-the-dollar without scruples" for United States viewers, a situation they do not consider unfamiliar or particularly unrealistic. The threat of the big corporation, which they decode to show that money can buy anyone's silence or service, is softened because the unscrupulous greed and power strivings are shown as infights within the family. Thus the average person — the viewer — does not feel threatened. Moreover, the presentation of socio-ideological conflict in terms of familial conflict is considered typical of the soap opera. "Dallas" is perceived to be the evening version of this familiar genre with its many story lines. (It must be more extreme because it is aiming for millions of viewers and high ratings.) Soap opera style also emphasizes lust and immorality which is how the United States respondents tended to characterize the various conflicts, problems, and intrigues detailed by the German viewers in their description of the show.

A second major difference relevant to program impact concerns the United States viewer's tendency to constantly switch between an objective stance of technical interest and the subjective viewing experience, their emotional relating to the program. The United States viewers, for example, referred to the story characters frequently in terms of the actor's name and specialty, such as "Howard Keel, he is Farlow, Miss Ellie's second husband, but he does not sing." They keep abreast of the business contracts of the show's stars and consider the resulting implications for plot development. Mark, for example, might not really be dead (he crashed into the ocean but his body was never found) but will be "kept in" for Pam for when Bobby's character leaves the show. Thus, the stance concerning presumed production needs influences the Unites States viewer's response to the various characters as well as the program's personal meaning for the viewer.

For the United States audience, J. R. is clearly the key character of the show. Responsible for all the tricks, he is not so much the macho ideal as he is the rat, sneaky, cunning, the underhanded guy necessary to keep the show going. He is "mean but he plays his part very well," one viewer explained, Cliff Barnes, on the other hand, is not the eternal loser that he is to the German viewers, but the really bad guy who tries to steal everything the Ewings have.

The Ewings are not perceived as members in a hierarchical family structure by United States audiences, as they are by German viewers, for whom the hierarchical structure reflects their own cultural tradition. Rather, they are seen by United States viewers as individual agents, brought in or taken out and replaced as needed. The family serves as a construct, a frame of reference for all soap operas. The Ewings "stick together," it is said, which gives the story its frame and may also be a reading reflecting the looser family structure seemingly characteristic of American society.

The script-writer stance of the viewer also has a bearing on the nature of the personal meaning of "Dallas" for the United States viewer. For the German viewer the projection and temporary release of subjective psychological needs is a major reason for program enjoyment. This type of response seems to be far less important among United States viewers. They either tended to share the German viewers' day-dreaming reaction (albeit in a somewhat different form), or they indulged in "kicking the plot around," exercising their own predilections in competition with the producer of the show. Such musing over possible story development, often with other family members or friends watching the show, was mentioned by German viewers as a by-product of viewing activity, but is a main form of relating to the program for the United States viewers.

The fantasizing of the United States viewer appears to be more realistic and lacking the pronounced masochistic aspects of German "daydreams" surrounding "Dallas." United States viewers find it fascinating to watch the glamour, the beautiful women, the handsome men. The women in particular stress enjoying the gorgeous clothes. Said one, "these women wear things to take a shower which are nicer than we see worn to the nicest restaurants in Iowa." Male viewers enjoy playing around with the idea of having that much money available or having those million-dollar tax problems, or going to bed with one of the sexy women. The program offers an escape from their ordinary situations. They fantasize about winning the lottery, one respondent noted. They talk about being envious: "sometimes I think why can't I have all these gorgeous clothes" or "I wish I had that money and a good figure." They do not tend to draw the typical German response that all these riches are not worth having after all because of myriad problems accompanying them.

Part of viewing satisfaction in the United States is a participatory response to the incidents in which the characters are involved. A sizable number of viewers described their main satisfaction in terms of trying to outguess what is going to happen in the show "after the commercial" as they watch it, or what might happen the next time, and how they feel about it. They try to see how close they come in their guesses. They laugh and joke and enjoy feeling superior ("how stupid can she [Lucy] be!"). They follow with concern about the cruelties shown to characters they like. They hope that J. R. will be taken down a peg or two — not too much because J. R. "makes the show." United states viewers are pleased when their predictions are right and when they correspond with their own values and prejudices. "Dallas" demonstrates and proves some viewers' negative concepts of the "wheeling and dealing of high finance," their opinion that "being rich is bad because you can do anything if you are rich." It also shows positively, particularly in the person of Miss Ellie, that a family should be fiercely loyal. For the American viewer, Bobby is a "nice All-American boy" and Pamela "the independent woman of today who can handle a responsible job."

United States viewers decode "Dallas" as a "seamy soap opera" which permits them to fantasize and to exercise their creative ingenuity and attitudinal predilections. Their response lacks the cathartic element found among German viewers, a difference which in part is due to the greater experience with the soap opera genre among United States television viewers. The answer to my initial question — do viewers in different countries read popular culture differently? — must be answered affirmatively.

READINGS SUGGESTED BY THE AUTHOR

Cantor, Muriel and Pingree, Suzanne. *Soap Opera*. Beverly Hills: Sage, 1983.

Feuer, Jane. "Melodrama, Serial Form and Television Today." *Screen 25* (1984).

Mander, Mary S. "Dallas: The Mythologie of Crime and the Occult." *Journal of Popular Culture* 17 (1983).

Zillman, Adolf. "Anatomy of Suspense." In Percy H. Tannenbaum, ed. *The Entertainment Function of Television*. Hillsdale, N.J.: Lawrence Earlbaum, 1980.

22   THE NATURE OF TELEVISION NEWS*

DAN NIMMO AND JAMES E. COMBS

We all take news for granted. Once, when we were all quite innocent, we thought that news was simply a record of what happened. Indeed, Walter Cronkite, one of the most famous network TV news anchors, used to end his program with the statement, "And that's the way it is." We know now that what we see on a news program is *not* necessarily "the way it is." Instead, the news we see on television is what someone thinks it (that is, reality) is.

What I'm suggesting is that there is the element of interpretation that we must take into consideration. News isn't so much a report of reality as a form of "created reality." Of course what we see on the television screen when we watch news is, quite literally, a picture of reality. But someone is aiming the camera and the reality we see is the one someone thinks we should see.

The argument is not that news directors, camera operators, and reporters are trying to dupe us; with rare exceptions, these people are talented and honest. It is just that we must always remember that the reality we see on television is a mediated one and, thus, someone's interpretation of reality. Each medium has, scholars suggest, a kind of logic inherent in it and news people (without necessarily being conscious of this) are profoundly affected by the medium they use.

Think of the difference between a television and radio report of an event. The television report would be essentially visual and the radio one completely auditory. Each medium has its own strengths and weaknesses and people who work in a given medium quite naturally, try to exploit each medium's strengths to the maximum.

We now have begun to see television news stories, our authors tell us, as dramas — or to recognize that journalists cast a dramatic form upon stories, which leads to interesting questions about what news is and how it functions. When we see news as a narrative or story, news no longer seems to be a simple report about reality. The fact that news stories have a strong dramatic aspect to them may offer an insight into why so many people seem to be almost addicted to news programs. News is also important for local television stations because they make an enormous amount of money from their local newscasts. And it is important to viewers, because they derive a number of gratifications from watching news. News, we now recognize, is not just information; it has become a form of theatre.

---

* From Dan Nimmo and James E. Combs, *Nightly Horrors: Crisis Coverage in Television Network News.* Copyright © 1985 by The University of Tennessee Press.

"News is real. It is not imagined. It is not fantasy. News is not what might have been — it is the way things were." So wrote the editors of *TV Guide* in the "As We See It" commentary in the February 13, 1982, issue of that widely sold and popular weekly. The statement is reminiscent of how former CBS anchor Walter Cronkite signed off the "Evening News": "And that's the way it is." The editors of *TV Guide* and Cronkite were far more confident about the realities underlying television news than many press observers have ever been about TV news or news in general. For example, in his classic work, *Public Opinion*, published in 1922, Walter Lippmann took great pains to distinguish between news and truth. They are "not the same thing." he wrote, for "the function of news is to signalize an event, the function of truth is to bring to light the hidden facts, to set them in relation with each other, and to make a picture of reality on which men can act" (p. 358). Hence, "journalism is not a first hand report of raw material," but a "report of that material after it has been stylized" (p. 347). And, unless it can be clearly demonstrated that news deals with "accomplished fact, news does not separate itself from the ocean of possible truth" (p. 340).

Lippmann's views remind us that news is a form of knowledge that is but tenuously related to some abstract notion of reality. But if news cannot be likened to truth, then what are the roots of its appeal? In recent decades the idea has evolved that the social roots of newsmaking are rhetorical, stemming from the ancient and universal impulse of human groups to explain reality by telling stories. The philosopher George Herbert Mead noted that since journalism reports "situations through which men can enter the attitude and experience of other persons," news possesses elements of drama that pick out "characters which lie in men's minds," then express "through these characters situations of their own time but which carry the individuals beyond the actual fixed walls which have arisen between them" (1934, p. 257). For Mead the bulk of news was not "information" journalism but "story" journalism that presents accounts to generate gratifying aesthetic experiences and to help people relate events to their everyday lives (Diamond, 1982).

As communications scholars have explored the nature of news in the electronic age, especially the character of television news, the distinctions made long ago between news and truth, and between information and story journalism, have proved useful. Scholarly literature increasingly refers to the "created reality" of the news media, particularly to the realities constructed by nightly network TV news (Epstein, 1973; Altheide, 1976; Tuchman, 1978; Hawkins & Pingree, 1981; Iyengar, Peters, & Kinder, 1982). The realities formulated through journalism conform to the logic inherent in each medium, or what Altheide and Snow term "media logic," i.e., the "format" of "how material is organized, the style in which it is presented, the focus or emphasis on particular characteristics of behavior, and the grammar of media communication." So conceived, write Altheide and Snow, "format becomes a framework or a perspective that is used to present as well as interpret phenomena" (1979, p. 10). Media logic suggests that different kinds of news stories can be told about identical events, depending upon which medium does the telling. It may not be that "The medium is the message," as Marshall McLuhan said (1964) but rather, to borrow Lippmann's phrase, the stylizer of the message.

In recalling Mead's emphasis upon the dramatic character of story journalism, media logic may be viewed as the logic of drama. The choices of format for reporting news in a given medium are choices of dramatic presentation. Certainly TV news exemplifies a logic that favors the portrayal of happenings in dramatic ways, making reported events sometimes larger than life (Berg, 1972). Reuven Frank, at the time executive producer for the nightly news programming at NBC, wrote a memo to his staff when they moved from a 15- to a 30-minute format in 1963. According to Epstein (1973, pp. 4–5) it read:

> Every news story should, without any sacrifice of probity or responsibility, display the attributes of fiction, of drama. It should have structure and conflict, problem and denouement, rising action and falling action, a beginning, a middle and an end. These are not only the essentials of drama; they are the essentials of narrative.

News accounts thus serve as what Walter Fisher calls "real-fictions," i.e., rhetorical compositions that concern the actual world of experience (they are about "real" things) but cannot be demonstrated true or false in detail (are fictional). Writes Fisher (1970, p. 132),

> Although its aim is to express a reliable guide to belief and action for one's daily deeds, it ultimately is a fiction since its advice is not, in the final analysis, susceptible of empirical verification. The fiction is not hypothetical; its author wants and intends that it be accepted as the true and right way of conceiving of a matter; and if he is successful, his fiction becomes one of those by which men live.

Real-fictions select and organize experience into an intentional unity that might not otherwise exist. Thus, the world evoked by TV news as a series of real-fictions is a dramatic pseudo-reality created from an ongoing flow of happenings "out there" but transformed into an entertaining story that conforms to the logic of the medium while assisting people to relate those events to their everyday lives.

Viewed in a dramatistic light, then, all news is storytelling, be it print or electronic (Darnton, 1975). Or, as Schudson (1982) contends, the accepted conventions of news in both print and television are narrative in form. The TV news format, as Sharon Sperry argues (1981), is a narrative employing imagery which is both verbal and nonverbal, both aural and visual, to construct a real-fictional world. In this sense the reporting process is a literary act, a continuous search for "story lines" that goes so far as to incorporate the metaphors and plots of novels, folk traditions, and myths

(Knight & Dean, 1982; Breen & Corcoran, 1982). Indeed, Lawrence and Timberg (1979) argue that TV news stories often appeal to broadcasters and viewers alike precisely because of their "mythic adequacy," i.e., the degree that they are deeply rooted in cultural mythology and exploit appealing aesthetic qualities.

Drawing upon narrative theory, Sperry constructs a framework for exploring the nature of TV news. She notes that there are three elements in any narrative — teller, tale, and listener. The teller, or narrator, is an authority who relates the real-fiction; the ultimate narrator of any network's nightly news telecast is the anchor, assisted by correspondents of lesser stature. As Sperry points out, the anchor frames each story, reading brief reports, introducing and reviewing filmed, packaged reports from correspondents. The anchor-correspondent-anchor format, ingrained in nightly newscasts, identifies the anchor as clearly in command of storytelling. The anchor's words, says Sperry, "move the program along, linking story to story according to some larger pattern of meaning, as if the stories of the half-hour were thoughts from a single mind, ordered and moving in rational progression" (p. 299).

The anchor-narrator element of TV news links the other two, tale and listener. The tale is narrated not merely to provide information "but also to affect the listener in some way: to persuade or change him, to evoke an emotional response, or simply to interest him" (p. 298). The viewer-listener accepts the news-tale as only an approximation of truth but suspends belief willingly to share in the real-fiction spun by the narrator. The credibility of the tale, not truth or falsity as such, is the key; it increases to the degree that it conforms to standard mythic plots, especially that of a hero struggling against the odds.

Sperry quotes Av Westin, former president of ABC News, to the effect that he expected viewers to come to his news programs asking, "Is the world safe, and am I secure?" (p. 301; see also Westin, 1982). The hero motif, according to Sperry "man's simplest and most pervasive myth," offers a standardized news formula responding to Westin's question, namely, "Men muddle through life as best they can, but when tragedy strikes, they require and seek a leader, a single individual of superior worth and superior skill, who will meet the problem and conquer the evil" (Sperry, 1981, p. 300). In TV news the heroic figures need not always be cast as saviors. Demonic hero, foolish hero, plain folk hero, even bumbling but well-intentioned hero — each enters the cast of televised news dramas.

The narrative logic of TV news directs TV anchors, correspondents, and producers to select (consciously or not) a melodramatic format, conforming to an heroic plot line, in their search for mythic adequacy (Bargainnier, 1980). Weaver (1976), for example, described how the "melodramatic imperative" informs and guides televised news coverage of presidential primary campaigns, a view developed even more systematically by Swanson (1977) in an analysis of press coverage of the 1976 presidential campaign.

Since news is only an aspect of the more general fare in television programming, it is not surprising that TV news draws from the same tradition of production values that pervades the entertainment medium. Adventure, mystery, romance, pathos, and nightmare fill children's programming, sports coverage, soap operas, situation comedies, docudramas, and other shows. We should not be surprised if we find variations on these formats adapted to crisis coverage as well. Crisis reporting offers opportunities for what is known in the trade as a "continuing story," one that runs night after night, simplifies complex details around a few easily grasped symbols, and becomes almost a mini-series. When continuing stories strike a responsive chord among viewers, the possibilities for successful delivery of the audience to advertisers are increased.

Regardless of the values informing the content of nightly network television news, however, each narrative is a real-fiction contributing to the emergence of a symbolic reality created and transmitted by newsmaking, interpreted and shared by large audiences. Such realities Walter Fisher calls "rhetorical visions" [1970]. Whether rhetorical visions grow out of televised crisis reporting and whether differing networks construct different visions are questions that this study addresses.

According to the conventional wisdom expressed in introductory textbooks in American politics and in mass communication, the three major networks transmit similar messages in similar styles. Dye and Ziegler, for instance, say, "There is very little diversity in television news. The three networks present nearly identical news 'packages' each evening" (1982, p. 133). Altheide's study of network coverage of the Iranian hostage crisis produced a similar view (1982). Yet Walter Karp (1982) — in an admittedly impressionistic examination of the 1981 crisis in Poland — charts provocative differences: NBC communicates interpretations in keeping with traditional Midwestern Republicanism, CBS transmits a view of Cold War liberalism, and ABC follows a style Karp associates with the political right wing. Confirmation that the major networks do not always package stories in similar ways comes from a more empirically based analysis, that of oil crises in the 1970s (Theberge, 1982). We believe that this study may shed more light on shared and contrasting patterns in TV news coverage of the rival networks.

If television news cannot be likened to truth, as Lippmann's seminal work before the dawning of electronic journalism implied, with what can it be associated? One answer is real-fictions and the rhetorical visions that derive from such real-fictions. This raises another question, how does one go about examining such real-fictions?

REFERENCES

Diamond, E. *The Tin Kazoo*. Cambridge, MA: The M.I.T. Press, 1975.

Epstein, E. J. *News from Nowhere*. New York: Vintage Books, 1973.

Fisher, W. R. "A native view of communication." *Quarterly Journal of Speech, 56*, 132–139.

Lippman, W. *Public opinion*. New York: Macmillan, 1922.

Mead, G. H. *Mind, Self, and Society*. Chicago: University of Chicago Press, 1934.

Sperry, S. "Television news as narrative." In R. P. Adler (Ed.), *Understanding Television* (pp. 295–312). New York: Praeger, 1981.

23   THE HIDDEN MESSAGE: SOME ASPECTS OF TELEVISION AESTHETICS*

HERBERT ZETTL

For a long time television, as a medium, was looked upon as an agent of transmission, a "distribution device," and little else. One function of a medium is to connect, to "transport" various kinds (or genres) of programs. Thus, on television one finds a wide variety of programs: news shows, situation comedies, sport programs, commercials, religious programs, game shows, talk shows, action-adventure programs, and one could go on and on. What is remarkable is that the medium that carried these programs was ignored as irrelevant.

Except, of course, by Marshall McLuhan, who had argued that "the medium is the message" and that it was the programming that was irrelevant. McLuhan's argument may have been extreme, but it did have the virtue of pointing out to people that the medium of television played an important role in things. A medium affects, in profound ways, the programs or "texts" it carries.

Think, for example, of the difference between the film image and the television image. The film image is a photograph, a snapshot; a television image is a collection of dots that is constantly shifting. This, Zettl argues, makes a difference, in rather profound ways. When we watch a film in a theatre, we see these images projected on a huge screen. When we watch television, we see very small images on a small screen.

This means that when we watch long shots on film, the figures are still large;

---

think of a western with a figure riding off toward the mountains. If we watch that film on television, the same shot, on a television screen, has a tiny little figure — perhaps hardly visible. For this reason, many have argued that television is essentially a close-up medium and that extreme long shots on television don't "work" the way they do in films. In television it is the Z axis, the axis to and from the camera, that is critical.

And, Zettl points out, there are many other factors involved in the medium of television such as the lighting, the special way television relates to time and motion, the use of color, and the use of sound. These aesthetic factors enable television directors to generate various kinds of emotional responses in the viewers and to give viewers particular notions about the nature of reality. Think, for example, of the significance of the instant-replay camera and the effect this has had on television broadcasting.

After reading this essay, you will be much more aware of the power of television as an aesthetic medium and will understand the role that medium plays in shaping the message.

Pretend for the moment that you want to show your favorite car on television. What car is it? What color does it have? Do you see it moving or standing still? Where do you see it? On a city street, open road, your driveway?

If you now had to do the same thing with a late-model Chevrolet Corvette and then a classic Rolls Royce, would you "see" them both the same way? For example, would they both have the same color and would you photograph them the same way in the same location? Probably not. If not, what did you do differently and why? For example, we may picture the Corvette as a red car, traveling at high speed along a winding country road, and the Rolls Royce in black or silver, patiently waiting for the elegantly dressed couple in front of a fancy hotel or mansion. We could add to the Corvette scene the familiar cadence of high revolution engine sounds while shifting gears, and to the Rolls Royce scene the subdued, fleeting sounds of big bands and small talk. But why? Could we not reverse the scenes and have a red Rolls Royce speed along and a silver Corvette in front of the hotel?

You probably find it much harder to state the precise reasons why you pictured each of the two cars in a specific way than to imagine the television scenes in the first place. That happens to all of us. We usually perform such translation processes from tentative idea to screen image rather intuitively and uncritically, drawing on our vast repertoire of television and film images stored in our memory. But when challenged to come up with the most effective television scene we need to apply critical judgment. This means that we must have certain criteria available, a checklist if you will, which tells us before we ever pick up a camera or microphone how to frame a shot, or what colors and sounds to use in order to affect the viewer in a specific way. The same checklist should also enable us to analyze and judge the non-verbal aspects, the so-called production values, such as camera work, lighting, or sound, of existing television programs.

The field that provides us, among other things, with such checklists is called *media aesthetics*.

WHAT IS MEDIA AESTHETICS?

Traditional aesthetics concerns scholarly arguments about what is beautiful and not, and various theories of art. It is usually limited to the discussion of the traditional fine arts, such as painting, sculpture, music, dance and theatre. Photography and some of the classic films are sometimes included, but not yet fully accepted as a legitimate aesthetic category.

Media aesthetics, on the other hand, concerns itself specifically with mass media, such as television and film. It takes its cue from the original meaning of aesthetics — sense perception — and investigates the various elements and techniques with which we can influence, if not manipulate, what people see and how they feel when watching television and film. It differs significantly from traditional aesthetics in several other ways:

1. It does not stress the analysis of existing television shows or films, but is more concerned with the discussion and analysis of the fundamental aesthetic image elements — light, space, time-motion, and sound.
2. It divorces itself purposely from content in order to focus on the non-verbal codes.
3. It shows how the individual image elements can be used in order to influence the viewer's perception in a predictable way. A red Corvette racing through the tight curves of a country road certainly feels like a "hotter" sports car than a silver-colored one sitting peacefully in front of an elegant hotel entrance.
4. It stresses our responsibility as communicators toward our audience, especially since our precise, calculated application of the fundamental image elements often go unnoticed by the unsuspecting public. All the viewers can do is to have faith in our good intentions. They have no easy way of verifying the world we create on television.
5. It includes rather than excludes the technical medium requirements and their integration with the aesthetic elements. For example, the way we light a scene for television is very much dependent on how well the television camera can see in the dark.
6. It stresses the interdependence of the various aesthetic elements. The sounds of a high-performance engine pushed to its limit intensifies the power of the red Corvette, but would seem rather comical when used with the Rolls Royce.

7. Finally, it facilitates formative evaluation, the constant checking and evaluating of production elements and processes before the entire show has been completed.

AESTHETIC FIELDS

The following discussion is limited to the fundamental image elements of *television aesthetics* (including all other forms of video): (1) light and color; (2) two-dimensional space; (3) three-dimensional space; (4) time and motion; and (5) sound. These image elements are discussed in the context of aesthetic fields that, while separate and distinct from one another, interact freely with one another in an actual television production (Zettl, 1973).

The First Aesthetic Field: Light and Color

The television picture is created by a rapidly scanning electron beam or series of beams that light up tiny little phosphorous dots, meticulously plotted on the inside of the television screen. These beams constantly fluctuate in energy, sometimes hitting their designated spots rather hard, at other times hardly at all. These fluctuations we perceive as different degrees of brightness (from light to dark) and varieties of colors.

Contrary to paintings, photographs, or even film images, the television picture is always in flux. Its thousands of picture dots light up and decay depending on how often and how hard they are hit by their respective electron beam. In effect, we perceive the television image as continual variations of light and color. Therefoe, the control of light, which we ordinarily call lighting is one of the more important factors in television aesthetics.

Lighting purpose and functions.   The basic purpose of lighting is the articulation and manipulation of the perception of things and our environment. Lighting makes us see and feel in a particular way. Through specific lighting, we can for example emphasize or de-emphasize the wrinkles in a performer's face, show whether it is day or night, and make a person look normal or mysterious. While we may think that such manipulations are the result of careful illumination, it is the control of *shadows* through which we achieve such effects. As a matter of fact, you will find that you need many more lighting instruments for shadow control than for basic illumination.

Chiaroscuro and flat lighting.   The two basic types of lighting commonly used in television are chiaroscuro (light-dark) lighting and and flat lighting. They both fulfill important aesthetic functions and differ basically from each other by how the shadows are controlled.

In *chiaroscuro lighting* (which is modeled on the works of the famous chiaroscuro painters Caravaggio and Rembrandt), we use highly directional light that produces prominent shadows. These shadows emphasize the three-dimensionality of things and render the scene highly dramatic. You are probably quite familiar with such chiaroscuro scenes that show a dimly lighted staircase with long shadows on the wall, a selectively illuminated street at night where people move from dark to light areas, or a sparsely illuminated restaurant with lighted candles on the tables. The deep and prominent shadows define for us the various shapes (such as the stairs) and areas (the various restaurant tables or lighted parts of the street); they provide us with a basic "outer orientation." More so, they are primarily responsible for setting a mood, for influencing our emotions (inner orientation). The dimly lighted street with its prominent shadow areas, or the staircase with its looming shadows most likely provoke in us a slightly uneasy feeling, especially when supported by equally unnerving sounds. The chiaroscuro lighting in the restaurant, on the other hand, may trigger a sense of warmth and coziness.

Flat lighting is done by highly diffused floodlights that produce such soft, transparent shadows that we often fail to see them at all on the television screen. It is called "flat" because the absence of shadows make three-dimensional objects look oddly deprived of their depth dimension. However, flat lighting can be quite useful. Flat lighting is abundantly used in commercials that stress the smoothness of a woman's skin. The absence of shadows renders any wrinkles which may have survived make-up invisible. The flatness of the lighting is then often camouflaged by excessive back-light. Flat lighting has also become fashionable on the news set in order to keep the newscasters forever young and virile. Flat lighting triggers in us a feeling of cleanliness and efficiency. Large supermarkets, department stores, and hospitals are all illuminated with flat light. But when the scene shifts to corporate computing or word processing centers, flat lighting can also signify mechanization and depersonalization.

Let us now apply some of these theories and assume that you must light the set of a hospital corridor in such a way that it first suggests to the viewer that the hospital is dirty and run down, and then that it is clean and highly efficient, without changing anything in the set itself. Which type of lighting would you use for the run-down hospital, and which one for the clean and efficient one? Yes, chiaroscuro lighting is the right choice for the first, and flat lighting for the second assignment. Why? Because the many prominent shadow areas that stripe the corridor inevitably provoke in the viewer a feeling that (1) the hospital is so poor that it cannot afford adequate lighting; (2) it is old because it has few and small windows; (3) it lacks adequate ventilation; (4) it is most likely untidy and dirty; (5) it is a fire trap because we can't see where we are going; and (6) the rest of the hospital, including its staff, must be equally antiquated. When flat lighting is applied, however, everything changes. Due to the profuse amount of shadowless illumination and increased visibility, we now feel that (1) the corridor and with it the entire hospital is clean and germ-free; nothing is hidden behind dark corners; (2) it has big windows and is, therefore, modern throughout; (3) it is easy in which to find your way around; and (4) its staff and doctors must be equally bright and efficient.

Color.   Most of us see the world around us in color. It adds excitement and brings joy to our environment. It also helps us identify and distinguish between things, as between green and red apples, for example. Amazingly enough, all the various colors we see on television are combinations of the three primary colors of red, green, and blue. Even if we watch a black-and-white show on our color television receiver, we actually watch a carefully mixed red-green-blue show.

Like music, colors trigger an immediate emotional response in us. For example, we probably would be hard pressed brushing our teeth with black or purple toothpaste, even if we had ample scientific proof that black toothpaste is more effective than white. On the other hand, a French perfume packaged in black or purple seems perfectly appropriate, if not alluring. A red Corvette suggests speed, and fun; a red Rolls Royce bad taste.

While bright colors are often used to enhance a high-energy scene, such as the red Corvette racing along the country road, they can also keep us from getting caught up and involved in a quiet and intimate screen event, such as two people expressing their love and concern for each other. In this case, you may want to reduce the color strength (saturation), tint the whole scene with a low-energy color (beige, light blue), or eschew color altogether in favor of a subtle black-and-white rendering of the scene. In contrast to loud, high-energy colors that intensify external events, a subdued color palette invites participation in internal events.

Now, even with this small dose of color aesthetics, you should be able to shed some light on the popular argument about colorizing films that were originally shot in black and white. Putting aside for a moment important ethical considerations of infringing on a work of art, we may defend the colorizing for films if they are basically external in nature, that is, if they portray basically external events such as landscapes, galloping horses, space shots, car chases. However, if the movie deals with character rather than plot, with inner rather than outer action, color seems not only inappropriate, but could well prevent the viewer from any empathic involvement in the internal event.

The Two-Dimensional Field: Area

The two-dimensional field is defined by the borders of the television screen. It gives us a new, precisely delineated picture field in which we must present the world to our viewers. No easy task, by any means, considering that the largest television screen is many times smaller than even a home movie screen. The early television pioneers thought this size limitation to be a serious handicap, and called it a "stupendous obstacle," that, "above all other factors, has most seriously impeded the development of a fully fluent and evocative medium." (Miner, 1944, p. 587). But the relatively small size of the television screen is now an aesthetic asset and one of the principal factors that contributed to the development of a unique television style.

Inductive approach. Because of the small screen size, the vistalike overviews that are so impressive on the large movie screen are rather ineffective on television. What we must do, therefore, is *build* an overview inductively with a series of close-ups. The actual vista is rarely, if ever, shown on television, but usually triggered in the viewer's mind. Many commercials are inductively shot (a series of close-ups that lead to an actual or imagined overview), rather than deductively in the usual large-screen film style, in which we move from overview to close-up detail. More and more, this style is also used in soap operas and other television drama genres. Through tight shooting, a scene projects unusual intensity. The disadvantage of the inductive approach is that, if sloppily done, a scene remains a series of fragmented and meaningless shots.

Psychological closure. Take a small break from reading and look around you. You will notice that there is no object that you can see in all its dimensions. Most of the items are partially covered by others, or positioned in such a way that you can see only parts of them. In fact, we actually see only a small fragment of our world around us. The other parts we simply imagine to be there. We automatically supply the missing parts in our mind to create a sensible and stable configuration. This filling in of missing parts to complete a partial figure is called psychological closure, or closure for short. If we had not this (probably inborn) (see Rock, 1984) facility for psychological closure (or simply, closure), we would be in deep trouble, especially when viewing close-ups or an inductively shot television sequence. In a close-up, we need to project outside the television screen to complete the figure (Figure 1). Fortunately, your many hours of exposure to television and films have given you a certain amount of visual literacy that facilitates such psychological closure. But you must be careful in how you frame a close-up. As Figure 2 shows, the tight framing of the head suggests the very stable structure of a circle. Consequently we are not urged to project beyond the frame. The head seems bereft of its body — an uncomfortable condition even for a television image.

Vectors. One of the strongest forces operating within the screen are directional forces that lead our eyes from one point to another within, or outside of, the television screen. These forces, called *vectors*, can be as coercive as real forces.

In media aesthetics, we have three principal vector types: (1) graphic vectors, which are created by stationary objects or lines that lead our eyes from point to point within the screen (Figure 3); (2) index vectors, which point unquestionably in a specific direction (Figure 4); and (3) motion

1. Proper framing of a tight close-up

2. Wrong framing of a close-up

vectors, which are created by people or things moving in actuality or on the screen in a particular direction. Obviously, motion vectors cannot be represented by a still picture.

A simple line, a row of packages or houses, a street, or the edges of your book are all examples of graphic vectors.

Index vectors and motion vectors are quite explicit as to direction. Examples of index vectors are arrows, or somebody pointing or looking at something. A motion vector is created by somebody running, a moving car — anything that actually moves or looks as though it is moving on the television screen. Vectors not only influence greatly the framing within a

3. Graphic vector

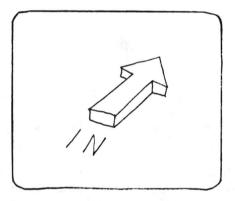

4. Index vector

shot, but also influence subsequent shots. For example, if you shoot close-ups of two people talking to each other, you must not only give the people sufficient "nose-room" to prevent the index vectors from crashing into the screen edges, but pay particular attention that the index vectors are converging, that is, that the people seem to talk to, rather than away from, each other (Figure 5). Such vector considerations are especially important if you shoot your scenes out of sequence for postproduction editing.

Point of view.   Besides vectors and field of view (ranging from extreme long shot to extreme close-up), we have a whole array of additional techniques

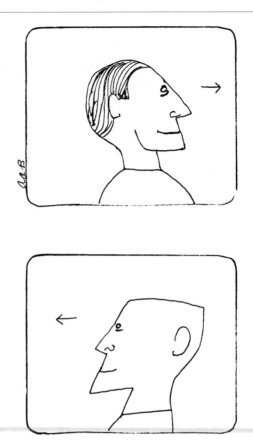

5. Shot series of converging index vectors

that help us intensify a scene and supply the shot with special meaning. One such technique is to vary camera point of view so that the camera is either looking up at a person or looking down on him. For some time now, kings, preachers, and judges have known that sitting up high had important psychological effects. They can look down on us, and we have to look up to them. A below-eye-level camera creates the same image; it makes the person so photographed quite powerful and superior by suggesting that we, the audience, are in the inferior position. The opposite is true when the camera looks down on somebody. This aesthetic device is as powerful as it is obvious. But you would be surprised by how many people actually are unaware of such blatant nonverbal persusasion techniques.

The Three-Dimensional Field: Depth and Volume

In painting, as in all photographic arts including television, we must project our three-dimensional world on a two-dimensional surface. In television,

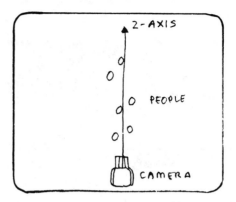

6. Articulated Z-axis

this surface is defined by its screen, the x-axis (width) and y-axis (height) of the Euclidean model. Depth (the z-axis) is strictly illusory. Nevertheless, the z-axis turns out to be by far the most important and flexible dimension in television. Because the width and height of the television field have real, highly delimited dimensions, the z-axis stretches merrily all the way to the horizon (theoretically to infinity). If, therefore, you need to show a great number of objects or people on the screen all at one time, you can space them along the z-axis, the imaginary axis toward and away from the camera (Figure 6). Such an articulation of the z-axis has become as much the trademark of effective television production as the use of the close-up.

How long we actually perceive the z-axis depends to a large extent on the type of lens used. If you zoom all the way out to put your lens in a wide-angle position, the z-axis seems greatly elongated. Small rooms look larger, hallways, streets, and buildings longer than they really are (Figure 7). Consequently, objects placed along this elongated z-axis look farther apart than they really are, and z-axis motion (cars or people moving toward or away from the camera) appears accelerated. In the narrow-angle lens position (zoomed in), the z-axis appears much shorter than when seen by a normal lens. Long hallways look short and plump, and buildings and people oddly squeezed together (see Figure 8). Motion along the shrunk z-axis reflects a sense of futility; cars traveling toward or away from the camera obviously move, but don't seem to make any perceptible progress. Z-axis motion, when shot with a narrow-angle lens, takes on a sluggishness, quite distinct from the more graceful slow motion.

Let's see now whether such aesthetic considerations can help you solve some actual production problems. What, for example, would you suggest if the dance teacher of your school asked you how to choreograph her ten dancers so that we can see them on camera most of the time and that their leaps look especially fast and dramatic on television, despite the rather small dance studio? One of the obvious answers would be to have the

7. Wide-angle lens Z-axis

8. Narrow-angle lens Z-axis

dancers move as much as possible toward and away from your camera, with the lens in an extreme wide-angle position. Such a z-axis blocking would keep all the dancers on camera, with the wide-angle lens exaggerating the dancers' speed as well as the size of the dance studio.

Your second challenge is to cover the rush-hour traffic in one of the main streets of your city for a documentary aimed at finding transportation alternatives. Yes, by shooting the oncoming traffic as close to the curb as possible with your lens zoomed all the way in, you create a shortened z-axis that shows the cars not only dangerously close together, but not getting anywhere.

A warning bell must be sounded at this point. Have you not just now purposely deceived an unsuspecting public with your aesthetic devices for our own specific ends? Yes. Is such a blatant manipulation of the audience ethical? This question is obviously much harder to answer. For example, did you really create something with your camera that did not exist when you were covering the events, or did you simply use your aesthetic techniques to intensify these events for the audience? Were the two communication purposes (to show how well the dancers do and how awful the traffic situation has become) not culturally and socially laudable? While you may not always be able to give universally true and valid answers to such questions, you must continually ask yourself whether your aesthetic manipulations are in the best interest of the public and in line with the basic ethics by which our society abides. At least, you should be cognizant of the potential dangers of such types of deliberate nonverbal persuasion. Ultimately, the answers depend on how you want to reconcile your own personal value system with the relative values and benefits of your message.

Aerial Perspective.   You are most certainly familiar with a scene in which the camera follows somebody walking down a crowded street. This person is kept in sharp focus throughout her walk, with all the other people, cars, and so forth, more or less out of focus. Or you may see close-ups of two people, with the focus changing from one to the other, indicating some connectedness between them. Both examples apply aerial perspective. Like in a foggy day, in which we see some things sharper than others, aerial perspective is used to create a figure-ground relationship, in which we emphasize the figure against the contextual and environmental ground (Koffka, 1935, pp. 177–210; Rock, 1984, pp. 113–118; Zettl, 1984, pp. 263–264). Such effects are only possible in a shallow depth of field, which means primarily that your camera is zoomed in as much as possible so that the lens is in the narrow-angle position. Like a series of close-ups, aerial perspective renders the images purposely low-definition (with few details) to entice the viewer to apply closure, to participate in the event by mentally filling in the missing detail (McLuhan, 1964, pp. 309–320). But you must be careful with such aerial perspective effects. They are often so conspicuous that they act as aesthetic sledgehammers rather than subtle cues.

The Four-Dimensional Field: Time and Motion

In television, time has attained existential reality. Time is the major structural agent in television programming, and it is bought and sold as thought it were a real commodity. One second of advertising time can cost as much as $30,000, especially if it happens to fall into a high-priority time slot within a high-rated show.

Live and Recorded Television.   Television is presently the only medium that can look at an event, clarify and intensify it, and distribute it to practically everyone on this earth while the event is taking place. This capacity of transmitting an event live has long been heralded as the essence of television. Why, then, are so few telecasts live? Besides the obvious economic, program, and production advantages of recorded television, are there any aesthetic reasons why we should not have more live telecasts? Live telecasts, however exciting, seem to be most desirable if the event is a one-time special whose outcome is not known at the beginning of the telecast and whose event details are equally unpredictable. Sports, some special concerts, news conferences, and momentous happenings such as the landing on the moon or President Kennedy's funeral are typical examples. However, if the event has been carefully prepared, scripted, and rehearsed, the immediacy of live television seems less urgent. After all, we know scene by scene what is going to happen, and we know in the beginning of the mystery that the butler did it. The production control afforded by videotaping and postproduction editing by far outweighs the occasional thrill the audience may receive from something going wrong during a live production.

We are in a strange predicament when we videotape a live event for later rebroadcast in a different time zone. What if you don't know that the telecast has been recorded and you view it as a true live broadcast? What if we later find out that we had been cheated, and that the telecast originated from a videotape?

The broadcasters feel strongly enough about such time distortion that they usually tell us when something is no longer live. We have all seen the small disclaimer on the screen that tells us that the whole thing was "recorded earlier," while hearing the announcer proudly tell us that the telecast is live.

Subjective Time.　When we sell time on broadcasting, we sell objective or clock time. But there is another mode of time that is just as important, but is never up for sale. This is subjective time, the duration we feel. Why, for example, do some scenes seem to drag hopelessly, even though there is plenty of action, while others with far less action move at a brisk pace? Apparently subjective time depends not on how much is going on in a scene or how long it actually runs, but by how relevant the event is to us. The more interested and involved we are in an event, the faster it seems to move for us. When trying to figure out a specific computer problem, we may literally forget time and need the clock to tell us how long we have been at it. But when waiting for something to happen, subjective time seems to go agonizingly slow. Why? Because waiting lacks involvement; all we do is look forward to getting involved. Subjective time, therefore, is a quality rather than a quantity. We control it not by the clock or stop watch, but by how much we can involve the viewer.

Motion.　In television, as in film, we deal with three principal motions: (1) primary motion, the movement in front of the camera; (2) secondary motion, the camera movement including the zoom "motion;" and (3) tertiary motion, which is the rhythm created by editing. Of all, primary motion is indeed of primary importance. You should always be more concerned about how people and objects move in front of the camera than with camera or editing motion. A wildly moving camera that pans incessantly from object to object is a sure giveaway for the novice director or camera operator. However, under certain circumstances, camera movement can be a powerful way of intensifying a scene. For example, a slow pan from one juror to the next can reflect much more the agony of the defendant than a series of quick cuts. A fast zoom to a ringing telephone immediately implies an important call.

Editing.   We can edit live shows and recorded shows. When switching from camera to camera in a live show, we are engaged in some form of editing. But generally, editing refers to the assembling of a screen event from a variety of recorded shots. In practice, editing means to throw out anything that does not directly and positively contribute to the intended message, and to put together the remaining shots in such a way that they make sense to the viewer. Editing is the one activity where you have the best opportunity to clarify, intensify, and interpret a story for the viewer. But this is also the place where you can most easily distort a story to suit your or your employer's specific communication goals. It is obviously difficult to condense a seven-hour hearing into a twenty-second news story without sacrificing some important information. Nevertheless, we must try to reflect the gist of the story. One of the safeguards against irresponsible editing is to use as selection criteria the essence of the story rather than the relative spectrum of available shots.

Another editing challenge is the proper sequencing of shots. You need to see that your individual shots cut together properly, which means that they should show continuity of graphic, index, and motion vectors. If, for example, you follow up a long shot of a wide receiver in a football game with a close-up, the player needs to continue in the same direction (Figure 9). Or, if you show close-ups of a conversation between two people, the index vectors must be converging, otherwise they will be talking away from each other (see Figure 5). Such obvious editing practices become much less obvious when sitting in the editing room with myriad choices. By applying some simple vector principles, however, you can save an enormous amount of time and effort. Under certain circumstances, you may violate such continuity editing, and reverse index and motion vectors in order to show somebody's external or internal disorientation. This type of cutting is called complexity editing.

The Five-Dimensional Field: Sound

Television is a visual medium. Right? Wrong. It is an audio-visual medium in which audio should be spelled in capital letters. The main reason why

9. Continuing motion

sound has remained the stepchild of television for so long is that the audio portion is easier to set up and control than video. But sound fulfills so many aesthetic and communication functions that silent television could simply not make it on its own. Here is why:

1. Television sound supplies essential information. A sound failure during a newscast readily reminds us of that fact. Contrary to popular belief that a picture is worth a thousand words, in television a word is often worth a thousand pictures. Just think how many pictures it would take to communicate this simple message: "Please meet me tomorrow at 10:00 A.M. in front of the coffee shop."
2. It establishes a mood and adds aesthetic energy. Sound is, next to lighting, the quickest way to evoke a specific mood. Music and sound seem to be able to bypass our *ratio*, our perceptual filters and critical

facilities, and affect our emotions directly. By switching from happy to ominous music while continuing to show a happy scene, we can override the visual message and forewarn the viewer of an impending disaster. Even more direct than lighting, sound can supply the frame of reference in which to interpret the visual imagery. Sound is also a relatively simple way to underline or boost the aesthetic energy of a scene. Similar to the flute players who were called on stage from time to time to get things moving again and to shake up the audience during theatre performances in ancient Greece, we now use music and sound effects to energize all sorts of television scenes, from dancing cereal boxes to a police chase along Main Street. To learn just how much music and sound effects are used, listen to a show that has plenty of outer action without watching it. Cartoons are a good example of shows that need music and sound effects for their very existence. Without the high-energy music and the many hisses and boings, cartoons would feel strangely empty and their dazzling visual display comically excessive.

3. Most importantly, sound supplies or supplements the rhythmic structure of a scene. The tertiary motion created through cuts, dissolves, wipes and other modes of transition, or through vector control, is often too subtle to reveal any kind of unifying rhythm. Very much like the drummer in a band that dictates the basic beat and keeps everybody in step, highly rhythmic music can makes us perceive the various shots as an organic, properly structured, whole. Even silent films could not do without music. The accompanying organ or piano music was essential to add aesthetic energy to the pictures and to give the various picture sequences structure and cohesion.

We should assume, therefore, that the introduction of stereo audio for television would be a big step forward. Unfortunately, this is not the case. Though eagerly embraced by audio-sensitive people who had deplored bad television sound for quite some time, high-fidelity stereo audio did not fulfill their hopes. Suprisingly, it brought about some unexpected problems. When enveloped in high-fidelity, high-volume sound, the television pictures seem to lose personality and shrink to insignificant images. They seem overwhelmed by the high-definition soundscape, and simply refuse to stand their ground. Another problem with stereo sound in television is that split sound tracks often remain separated and only converge screen center (as the third phantom channel) if we happen to sit in exactly the right position. Otherwise, we perceive the on-screen dialogue as oddly displaced and divorced from the sound source. While we see the people talking on-screen, their voices seem to become independent and flip back and forth from one side of the screen to the other. Also, the small width of the television screen (x-axis) rarely makes the channel separation wide enough to define the left and right off-screen space, so that, for example, we would hear people coming from the left or right before seeing them on the screen.

The spatial displacement of sound through stereo and the high-fidelity, high-volume sound makes sense only if the television screen size is large enough to stand up to this high-energy audio. The large screens of high-definition television projections, for example, not only tolerate but require high-energy stereo audio for proper audio-video orientation and balance.

CONCLUSION

Although we discussed the five aesthetic fields independently, you should think of them as interacting at all production phases. For example, when considering the lighting of a scene, you also need to think of a sound track congruent to the aesthetic treatment of the lighting. The same goes for the proper aesthetic analysis of a show. You need to be especially aware of how and to what extent the various aesthetic elements interact and complement one another. Finally, you should realize that the basic criterion for aesthetic choices is, and should always be, the basic communication intent of the production, the meaning of the message — what you want to say to the audience. This message can then be clarified, intensified, and interpreted through the various aesthetic nonverbal codes. Television aesthetics can give to significant vision significant form. If properly understood and applied, it can act symbiotically between idea and image, and help the audience achieve that degree of emotional literacy necessary for the peaceful and especially joyful coexistence of the people on this earth. If misused, it can lure an unsuspecting public into irrational actions. The only safeguard the audience has against such irresponsible persuasion is your personal ethics, your social responsibility, and finally, your respect and love for your fellow human beings.

REFERENCES

Koffka, K. (1935). *Principles of gestalt psychology.* New York: Harourt, Brace, and World.

McLuhan, M. (1964). *Understanding media.* New York: McGraw-Hill.

Miner, W. (1944). Post-war preambles: A producer's view of television. *Theatre Arts, 28* (October), 586–590.

Rock, I. (1984). *Perception.* New York: Scientific American Library.

Zettl, H. (1973). *Sight sound motion: Applied media aesthetics.* Belmont: Wadsworth Publishing Co.

Zettl, H. (1984). *Television production handbook.* Belmont: Wadsworth Publishing Co.

24   THE SOCIAL USES OF TELEVISION*

James Lull

We have already established that people watch television more than 3½ hours a day. But how do they "use" television? Lull employs a research methodology known as "uses and gratifications" that asks, in the words of Elihu Katz, one of the most distinguished proponents of this perspective, "not what the media do to people, but what people do with the media." To find out how people use television, Lull, and his students, visited 200 families in their homes and observed, first-hand, how people used television.

Lull developed a sophisticated methodology to obtain useful data and discovered some extremely interesting things. For one thing, television facilitated conversation. It provided family members with things to comment on, talk about. It also was used to entertain guests in the home, since it provided the guests with the opportunity to engage in "television talk."

Television also facilitates "togetherness" or its opposite, avoidance. Some people used television as an excuse not to talk with one another, while others used it in an opposite manner. It was used by some, Lull says, for psychological relief — generating an alternate reality that many people found comforting.

The medium was also used for "social learning" by many viewers. Some parents used the themes and values implicit in certain television shows to transmit these values and beliefs to their children, and reinforce them. Thus television has a socializing influence that is, it would seem, consciously recognized by many parents.

Television also was involved in demonstrations of competence and dominance. Some parents, for example, regulated the television viewing of their children, reinforcing, in their minds, their view of themselves as "good parents." In some cases, such as in single-parent families, a television character took on the role of a missing parent for children.

In certain cases, viewers "assaulted" the characters in stories or commercials and the veracity of the newscaster. This kind of action, Lull points out, is made possible due to the one-way nature of television broadcasting. Some families use information from television to argue with one another and assert positions of dominance.

Thus, people relate to television in rather complicated ways and it is neither an all-powerful, dominating medium that prevents any kind of response other than

---

* James Lull, "The Social Uses of Television," *Human Communication Research*: 6 (3) Spring, 1980, 198–209. Copyright © 1980 by Sage Publications. Reprinted by permission of Sage Publications, Inc.
Author's note: The essay is part of the article that appeared in *Human Communication Research*; it has been slightly rewritten for the purpose of this book.

complete and passive attention nor is it moving wallpaper, that people learn to take for granted. It is useful to keep these findings in mind when we make generalizations about television.

Television has become a special member of the family in homes all over the world. Many households in the more developed countries are equipped with more than one television set, a cable hookup, and a video cassette recorder (VCR). People in the world's less materially-developed countries are likewise infatuated with television. In China, for instance, television is regarded as a personal status symbol for families, a primary source of entertainment in an environment where leisure-time alternatives are few, and a sign that the country is becoming "modern." For better or worse, television is the universal essence of contemporary popular entertainment and there is no likely replacement in sight.

The popularity of television, however, does not result solely from the medium's compelling ability to capture the attention of audiences by feeding them endless amusements. The "family member" status that television occupies signifies a far deeper involvement in the textures of human communication than that of a simple provider of stories and information. Television is *used* by people in many creative and important ways in order to help them achieve a variety of personal and interpersonal objectives in their daily lives. Television is a *resource* that people employ to help construct their everyday worlds in ways that they believe benefit them. "Watching television," therefore, actually means much more than just viewing and enjoying programs.

One interesting way to study some of the implications of television in society is to look closely at how family members communicate with each other interpersonally at home. In doing so, we quickly recognize the pervasiveness and importance of television as a part of everyday family interaction. Indeed, it is difficult to imagine anything else that penetrates so deeply into the substance of normal, everyday life as television and the VCR. Of course, there are differences among families in the ways they integrate television into their everyday realities. Families living in various parts of the world, for instance, have culturally distinctive patterns in their communicative behavior, including their uses of television (Lull, 1988).

The paragraphs that follow describe some of these "social uses of television" as they have been observed and documented in research conducted in the homes of American families. The emphasis here is on the relationship between interpersonal communication and the mass media. Since television has become such an influential presence in American homes, *all* communication is affected by it in one way or another. We are interested here not only in the ways in which television's *content* is used by viewers, but how the *medium* itself is accommodated into the routines of

Table I	SOCIAL USES OF TELEVISION

Structural
Environmental (background noise; companionship; entertainment)
Regulative (punctuation of time and activity; talk patterns)

Relational
Communication Facilitation (experience illustration; common ground; conversational entrance; anxiety reduction; agenda for talk; value clarification)
Affiliation/Avoidance (physical, verbal contact/neglect; family solidarity; family relaxant; conflict reduction; relationship maintenance)
Social Learning (decision-making; behavior modeling; problem solving; value transmission; legitimization; information dissemination; substitute schooling)
Competence/Dominance (role enactment; role reinforcement; substitute role portrayal; intellectual validation; authority exercise; gate-keeping; argument facilitation)

everyday life. The social uses of television are of two primary types: structural and relational. The focus of this brief article is on the latter category, but a discussion of the former is helpful for clarifying different uses of the medium.

THE STRUCTURAL USES OF TELEVISION

Television is employed as an environmental resource in order to create a flow of constant background noise that moves to the foreground when individuals or groups desire. It is a companion for accomplishing household chores and routines. It contributes to the overall social environment by rendering a constant and predictable assortment of sounds and pictures that instantly creates an apparently busy atmosphere. The activated television set guarantees its users a nonstop backdrop of verbal communication against which they can construct their interpersonal exchanges. Of course, it always serves its timeless environmental functional as a source of entertainment for the family.

Second, television has the structural characteristic of being a behavioral regulator. Television punctuates time and family activity such as meal time, bedtime, choretime, homework periods, and a host of related activities and duties. Patterns of talk are affected by viewing routines. External family communication is similarly regulated by television. Taking part in community projects, recreational activities, or outside entertainment are directly influenced by the scheduling of television programs.

Television viewing takes place in social units other than families. Viewing in various settings can be free and selective, as it is in college dormitories, or it can be parceled out as a reward granted by the proper authorities. Children in nursery schools are allowed to watch television after they pick up their toys. Girls in a California reform school can view only when their rooms pass inspection and when they complete their evening chores. Television in a retirement home is an attractive alternative to sitting alone in a private room. Under all these conditions, television viewing contributes to the structuring of the day. There is a time for viewing. That time is often related to other responsibilities and activities in which the individual is involved.

RELATIONAL USES OF TELEVISION

The relational uses of television are far more numerous and complicated than the "structural" uses described above. They involve coordination of various types between people. The four categories described below are presented in order of their complexity, beginning with the simplest.

Communication Facilitation

Television's characters, stories, and themes are employed by viewers as abundant illustrators that facilitate conversations. Children, for example, use television programs and characters as primary known-in-common referents in order to clarify issues they discuss. Television examples are used by children to explain to each other, and to their parents and teachers, those real-world experiences, emotions, and beliefs that are difficult to make transparent in verbal communication.

A child often uses television in order to enter an adult conversation. When a child is ignored during conversations held by adults, he or she can gain entry to the discussion by using a television example that illustrates a point being made by one of the adult interactants. If participants in the conversation are familiar with the television example, the child has introduced a common referent in order to gain access to the conversation from which he or she was otherwise left out.

The viewing experience itself can be facilitative. Conversational discomfort is sometimes reduced when the television is turned on and in view of the interactants. The uneasiness of prolonged eye contact is lessened since the television set ably attracts attention during lulls in conversation. Also, the program being watched creates an immediate agenda for talk where there may otherwise be none.

The medium is used as a convenient resource for entertaining outside guests in the home. To turn on the set when guests arrive is to introduce instant common ground. Strangers in the home may then indulge in "television talk" — verbal responses to television programs that allow audience members to discuss topics of common experience that probably have little personal importance. Television viewing under these circumstances provides an opportunity for abundant talk with little substance — an exercise in conversational form for the interlocutors. In this way, viewers become better acquainted but invest minimal personal risk. Television also helps some family members clarify interpersonally their attitudes and values, especially in recent years since the medium has presented more controversial programming.

Affiliation/Avoidance

A fundamental social use of television is its potential as a resource for the construction of desired opportunities for interpersonal contact or avoidance. The nature of audience positioning in front of the television set is often used to advantage by young children who desire to engage physically or verbally their admired older siblings. Some adults orchestrate rare moments of physical contact in front of the television screen, an intimacy which need not be accompanied by conversation. An entertainment medium, however defined, is useful for this purpose. In one family which was observed in our research, the husband and wife touched each other only twice during a week. The first time the man playfully grabbed his wife and seated her on his lap while his daughter, acting as kind of a medium, told a humorous story about something that had happened at school that day. The other occasion for physical contact during the week took place one night while the couple watched television. The man was a hard-working laborer who nearly always fell asleep when he watched television at night. He dozed as he sat in a recliner rocking chair with his shoes off. He snored loudly with his mouth open. His wife, who had been sitting on the floor in the same room, pushed herself along the floor until she was close to his chair. She leaned back until her head rested against his bare feet and smiled as she created this rare moment of "intimacy."

Television viewing is a convenient family behavior which is accomplished together. The medium is used to provide opportunities for family members or friends to communally experience entertainment or informational programming. A feeling of family solidarity is sometimes achieved through television-induced laughter, sorrow, anger, or intellectual stimulation (Katz & Foulkes, 1962). Confirmation of the family as a unit of interdependent personalities is made by the attempts of viewers to predict consensually the outcomes of television shows while they watch or by the creation of on-going discussions of the details or implications of the televised stories. Audience members also use television as a family relaxant whereby group viewing promotes a family harmony by reducing interpersonal discord, at least during the viewing period.

Television can lessen the demand for the manufacture of talk and the exchange of thought by providing a sustaining focus for attention which can be employed as a kind of social distractor, rendering less intense the communicative formalities which might otherwise be expected. Since television is used by the viewer as a focus for attention, creating "parallel" rather than interactive viewing patterns, it also becomes a resource for escape — not just from the personal problems or responsibilities of the individual viewer, but from the social environment (Walters & Stone, 1975). Anthropologist Edmund Carpenter (1972) reported that a U.S. Army official in Germany blamed the high divorce rate among his troops on the lack of an English-language television station in the area where they live. The officer said, "That means a soldier and his wife have got to talk to each other in the evenings and they suddenly discover that they really don't like each other." A blue-collar family that was observed said it was grateful for television since it occupies so much of the grandparents' time in the evening thereby keeping them away from their home that is located just three doors away. This young couple preferred not to be bothered by their parents. Television limits unwanted visits.

Television functions as a social resource in a unique way that helps married couples maintain satisfactory relationships. Unlike print media that transmit bits of information, television can provoke a vicarious, evanescent fantasy world that serves for some the psychological purpose of a desirable, if temporary, occupation of an alternative reality.

Psychological transformations triggered by program viewing become resources put to use by the inventive social actor. An example is revealed in the case of a farm woman who resigned her premed scholarship to a major midwestern university, married her high-school boyfriend, and attended vocational school in order to become a medical secretary. Her first child was born one year following her marriage, causing her to quit her job at the medical office.

The only television shows watched by this woman during the research period were programs that featured settings and themes directly related to the medical profession. When these programs were aired, she engaged in a continual and intense commentary about the nature of the story, particularly as it related to medical consideration. She remarked about the appropriateness of operating room procedures. She evaluated the work of subordinates and always referred to the doctors by their formal titles. She praised medical work well done and found fault with mistakes made by the staff. The Caesarean section of quintuplets during one melodrama fascinated her as she remarked instructively about the importance of quickly trimming "all five cords."

During an interview probe following a week-long observation period conducted by the researcher, the woman said:

I've always been interested in anything medical, anything to do with the medical field. So, that's what I like...I usually find that their (medical) information is pretty accurate for their diagnosis of disease and so forth...so, I enjoy it because I worked around a lot of that and it just kinda keeps me in the business, I guess.

Her husband appeared to recognize the desirability of using television as a fantasy stimulant for his wife. Although his wife knew full well what time her favorites were televised, he reminded her of these and encouraged her to watch. He even changed the television channel from "Monday Night Football" in order to insure that she watched a medical program that was presented by a competing network at the same time. His encouragement of her participation in the dream world that their marriage and child raising denied her may have helped him dismiss whatever guilt he harbored for having been, in part, responsible for curtailing her vocational opportunities.

Social Learning

Television is widely regarded as a resource for learning. Of special interest here are the social uses made of the many opportunities for learning from television. Much information for daily living is available from the electronic media. Obvious examples are consumer product and political commercials that provide an agenda for decision making, actions that have important implications for the society, the family unit, and the individual. But more subtle learning experiences have been noted as well. Early studies of soap operas, for instance, demonstrated that these melodramas provide practical suggestions for social interaction that are widely imitated by audience members (Lazarsfeld & Stanton, 1949; Herzog, 1944). These imitations may be useful in the solving of family problems that bear resemblance to difficulties resolved in television dramas. At the very least, television provides an abundance of role models that audience members find socially useful.

Parents encourage their children to watch television game shows, public television, or network specials as substitute school experiences. Themes and values implicit in television programs are used by the parents to educate their children about the topics being presented in accord with their own view of the world. In this way, the value system of the parent is transmitted to the child and attitudes already in place are reinforced.

Scholarly research on how individuals learn from the mass media, then pass the information along in predictable interpersonal diffusion patterns, dates back more than forty years. The *two-step flow* and the *multi-step flow* theories implied that opinion leaders, who are heavy media consumers in their areas of expertise, learn much about their specialities from television and other media. These informational experts then transmit their knowledge to a network of human acquaintances.

In accomplishing the information-dissemination task, opinion leaders use information from the media to not only educate their friends, acquaintances, or coworkers, but also to assert themselves as valued members of society. The opinion leader uses television and other media to help create and then fulfill an interpersonal role that may have the effect of demonstrating personal competence in a particular area.

Competence/Dominance

There are a variety of ways in which television provides unique opportunities for the demonstration of competence by means of family role fulfillment. The regulation of childrens' television viewing by a parent is one means for accomplishing this objective. For those adults who desire to supervise closely or restrict the flow of unwanted external information into the home, the methodical and authoritative regulating of television viewing is useful as an occasion for the undertaking of a gatekeeping function. In doing so, the parent, often the mother, makes observable to the children and spouse a correct role-determined and rule-governed action that confirms the individual as a "good parent" or "good mother." Successful enactment of the television regulatory function directs media experiences of the children into forms that are consistent with the parent's moral perspective. Simultaneously, the parent asserts an expected jurisdictional act that confirms proper performance of a particular family role.

The symbolic portrayal of roles by television characters may confirm similar roles that are undertaken by audience members. When behavior by an actor or actress on television resembles the way in which the viewer behaves under similar circumstances, the experience may be useful to the viewer as a means for demonstrating role competence to the other audience members. Similarly, a family member may use television in order to learn acceptable role behavior, then imitate this behavior in a way that results in acceptance of the role enactment by other family members.

The role of a missing parent can be played by a television character. It is convenient in some single-parent families for the adult who is present to encourage the watching of particular television programs where a favored image of the missing parent is regularly presented. Implicitly, the role of the lone parent can be preserved or clarified as the substitute parent's complementary actions are portrayed on the screen.

Some viewers capitalize on the one-way nature of television by verbally assaulting the characters, newscasters, or commercials. One man who was observed constantly disagreed out loud with the evening news reports on television. He clarified the reports and chided the announcer for not knowing the "real facts." Vocal criticisms of programs or commercial announcements also serve as ways for viewers to reassure one another that, despite the fact that they are now watching, they know how bad television is, a self-promoting evaluation.

In another case, a housewife who majored in French in college repeatedly corrected the poor pronunciation of French words uttered by an American actor who attempted to masquerade as a Frenchman. Gans, in a study of poor Italian families in Boston, found that his subjects received attention from other viewers when they noticed that activities on the screen were technically unfeasible or when they pointed out "anachronisms or mistakes [that] appear in the plot" (Gans, 1962, p. 194).

A television viewer may or may not use the medium to demonstrate competence for purposes of dominating other family members. But, cases in which this occurs are often found in ethnographic research. For instance, family members may use television as a validator of contested information, thereby demonstrating intellectual competence. In one family, for example, the capture and arrest of two famous criminals was a topic of conversation on the evening they were apprehended in San Francisco. There were conflicting reports among family members as to whether or not a third party had also been captured. The highly authoritarian father had heard an early radio report that only the first two had been arrested. He had not learned the later news that the third person had been taken into the custody of the police as well. His wife and daughter both told him that they had heard on the car radio that all three had been arrested. He arrogantly denied the validity of their reports and said that the family could find out the "true situation" by watching the news on television. The husband later was embarrassed to discover on the news that the third suspect had indeed been apprehended, a turn of events that falsified his version of the incident. "See," his wife said emphatically when the news was revealed. "We were right! I told you that she had been caught and you wouldn't believe me." The medium had confirmed her and disconfirmed him on the issue. A few minutes later television provided an opportunity for him to recapture his dominant position. During a commercial message, he voiced an opinion about some attribute of the product that was being promoted. His wife disagreed. Seconds later the announcer on the commercial gave information that supported the husband. He quickly and defiantly turned to his wife and said, "I don't talk much. But when I do you should listen."

Men, women, boys, and girls use television to communicate to each other attitudes toward the appropriateness of male and female behavior with respect to sex roles. Teenaged boys we observed shouted criticism at female detectives with their sisters in the room. The program provided an opportunity for the boys to vocalize their negative feelings about the qualifications of the television actresses for doing "men's work." Similarly, adolescent girls competed to correctly identify wardrobe fashions of various historical periods during a program which featured this topic. The girls tried to identify the periods before the announcer on the program did so. Correct identification gave status to the girl who guessed right, validating her as a relative expert on women's fashions and placing her in an esteemed position in the eyes of her peers.

Interpersonal dominance strategies involve television in other ways. Television viewing in many homes is authoritatively granted or taken away as a reward or punishment. Adults and children argue to decide who will watch what programs, thereby creating an opportunity for the airing of personal differences. For family members who are angered by each other, television viewing (the program decision-making process or the viewing experience) provides incessant opportunities for argument, provoking possible dominance struggles among family members.

More subtle uses of the medium are made by some viewers to influence other audience members. In one case, a married couple watched a television program in which the lead actor passionately embraced a young woman. The husband at home asked his wife during this scene if the two on the screen were married. She answered, "Do they look married to you?" They both laughed quietly without taking their eyes off the screen. By coorienting and commenting on the television program, these family members spoke to each other indirectly, but made their positions about relational matters clearly known.

CONCLUSION

The illustrations given in this brief article indicate clearly that television is a powerful resource available for use in human communication, especially in family interaction. Several researchers in the United States and elsewhere are now trying to understand more fully the implications of television in society by living with families in order to study them like an anthropologist would. This is an exciting development in the field of mass communication research where all kinds of research methodologies need to be employed in order to document the powerful, yet often subtle, ways that television influences our everyday lives.

REFERENCES

Carpenter, E. *Oh! What a Blow that Phantom Gave Me.* New York: Holt, Rinehart and Winston, 1972.

Gans, H. J. *The Urban Villagers.* New York: Free Press, 1962.

Herzog, H. "What do we really know about daytime serial listeners?" In P. Lazarsfeld & F. N. Stanton (Eds.) *Radio Research: 1942–1943.* New York: Duell, Sloan, and Pearce, 1944.

Katz, E. and Foulkes, D. "On the use of mass media as 'escape'," *Public Opinion Quarterly* 4, 377–388.

Lazarsfeld, P. and Stanton, F. N. (Eds.) *Communications Research: 1948–1949.* New York: Harper, 1949.

Lull, J. *World Families Watch Television.* Beverly Hills, CA.: Sage Publications, 1988.

Walter, J. K. and Stone, V. A. "Television and family communication." *Journal of Broadcasting* 4, 409–414.

25 "STAR TREK": A ROMANCE OF INNER SPACE*

Arthur Asa Berger

"Star Trek" is one of the most enduring television programs yet created…it continues on in reruns endlessly and it has generated an extremely successful series of motion pictures that build upon the original characters and situations. This analysis of "Star Trek" uses psychoanalytic concepts in an attempt to explain why this series has been so popular.

The thesis in this essay is that the three main characters in the series, Captain Kirk, Mr. Spock, and Dr. McCoy, function as components of the human psyche. Freud has suggested that the human psyche is composed of three parts: the *id* (or drives), the *ego* (or rationality), and the *superego* (or guilt). The essay argues that Kirk is, in essence, a superego figure — and his name, Kirk, or "church" in German, as well as his behavior supports this thesis. Mr. Spock, the pointy-eared Vulcan, is an ego figure, who has no emotions and functions the way the ego does, mediating between the demands of the id and the superego. The third figure, McCoy, is essentially an id figure, guided by feelings and emotions more than anything else.

If you put these three characters together, each representing one facet of the psyche, you get a complete person. It may be the degree to which each of these characters represents an aspect of the psyche that makes them so easy to identify with and the series so appealing to people. Viewers may not realize how the characters function, but they still are affected by them.

Interestingly enough, Leonard Nimoy, who plays Spock, made a comment to this effect in a recent television interview in San Francisco, where the fourth *Star Trek* film was made. He said that people seem to recognize that the three main characters really form one character.

The remainder of the essay deals with the important themes found in an episode of "Star Trek," "The Alternative Factor." The episode also has a psychoanalytic center to it, focusing on a character who has a dual nature, a split in his psyche between good and evil aspects. And there is a socio-political theme involved as well, namely the matter of a good society being "invaded" by an evil force, a theme connected to American attitudes about our society being pure and innocent and in danger of contamination by alien forces. These latter feelings, described as a kind of diffuse paranoia, are still with us, many would argue.

---

* Arthur Asa Berger, "Star Trek: A Romance of Inner Space" was first published in Arthur Asa Berger, *The TV-Guided American*, Walker & Co., 1976.

"Star Trek" is a classic space opera, the most interesting science fiction program television has created, and one which, remarkably enough, has refused to die. Though it is no longer being produced, its reruns are very popular and a vast audience of "Trekkers" exist, who relish these programs and put pressure on stations to carry them. The Trekkers even have a fan organization and publish a journal for aficionados of the program. It has taken on the characteristics of a cult.

The program deals with the adventures of the crew of the starship *Enterprise* on a five-year mission in outer space to explore new worlds, to seek out new civilizations, to "boldly go where no man has gone before." The word *enterprise* has a number of meanings. According to the *Webster's Seventh New Collegiate Dictionary* it involves: (1) a project or undertaking that is difficult, complicated, or risky; (2a) a business organization; (2b) systematic, purposeful activity; (3) readiness to engage in daring action. The program actually comprehends all of these meanings, though the emphasis is upon adventure and risk.

Although the *Enterprise* is a starship (spaceship) and part of a vast fleet of such vehicles, it also is a self-contained little world; all ships are. It is commanded by Captain Kirk, a man of action and courage. He has two colleagues who are dominant in the series: Mr. Spock, the half-human, half-Vulcan science officer who represents "pure rationality," and "Bones" McCoy, the ship's physician, who represents feeling. The three form a triumvirate containing all the necessary ingredients for a heroic personality, except that they are distributed in three persons. Each of these figures is deficient in an important way, though as a team they are a formidable combination. The powers and deficiencies of these characters are charted below:

Chart I POWERS AND DEFICIENCIES OF CHARACTERS

Character	Powers	Deficiency
Captain Kirk	action	reason, feeling
Mr. Spock	reason	action, feeling
Dr. McCoy	feeling	action, reason

Ultimately, Kirk has to make decisions and take action, based upon knowledge and information from Spock and impressions from Dr. McCoy.

And what is remarkable is that despite the panoply of technology and all the gadgets and gismos on the *Enterprise*, it is human courage that is ultimately decisive. The difference between Kirk and the various robots, presences, monsters, forces, whatever you will, that attack the starship and crew, is that humans have willpower and courage. When this is allied with superior information (from Mr. Spock) it must always triumph.

"Star Trek," then, is not about science but rather human courage and boldness, working within certain parameters set by science and technology. Machines and technology form the backdrop, against which stories involving emotion, risk, madness, destructiveness, and courage are played out. Technology is a facilitating factor, but it does not really dominate men. It can't, otherwise aliens with superior technology would triumph, and that would be that. The division or dissociation of the psyche into three mutually exclusive (generally speaking) components is rather interesting, and suggests that each of our heroes is a manifestation of one component or part of what Freud calls our "psychical apparatus."

The following definitions (of the *id*, the *ego* and the *superego*) are taken from *The Random House Dictionary of the English Language* (The Unabridged Edition). First the *id*:

> The part of the psyche, residing in the unconscious, that is the source of instinctive energy. Its impulses, which seek satisfaction in accordance with the pleasure principle, are modified by the ego and the superego before they are given overt expression.

The second component of the psyche, the *ego*, is a portion of the *id* that undergoes special development, according to Freud. The *ego* is defined as:

> The part of the psychic apparatus that experiences and reacts to the outside world and thus mediates between the primitive drives of the id and the demands of the social and physical environment.

Freud said, in *An Outline of Psycho-Analysis*, that the ego has control of voluntary movement and the ego's task is self-preservation. It stores up experiences in the memory, it avoids excessively strong stimuli by flight, it deals with moderately strong stimuli by adaptation, and it brings about changes in the world by activity.

The *superego* is defined as follows:

> The part of the psychic apparatus which mediates between ego drives and social ideals, acting as a conscience which may be partly conscious and partly unconscious.

Freud believed that this was formed during childhood and that the superego represents "a special agency in which...parental influence is prolonged."

The superego has traditionally been identified with conscience, but it is much more than that since the superego functions on both a conscious and an unconscious level and passes judgment not only upon actions we intend to take, but also upon actions we do not recognize we intend to undertake. For our purposes we must stretch the concept of the superego slightly and suggest that it represents not only a moral judgment of what is acceptable, but also an intellectual assessment of what reality is like. We must split off the last part of the ego, as Freud described it above, and give this function to the superego — namely, acting in the world for the sake of survival.

If we do this, then we find that we can — without too much distortion — connect Kirk, Spock, and McCoy with the three components of the psyche, the superego, the ego, and the id:

Chart II

COMPONENTS OF THE PSYCHE AND CHARACTERS

Component	Meaning	Realization	Character
super-ego	conscience	action	Capt. Kirk
ego	reason	intelligence	Mr. Spock
id	instinct	feeling	Dr. McCoy

All charts represent oversimplifications and perhaps a bit of stretching, but I believe this chart does portray, graphically, the relation that exists between each character and the three components of the psyche, as Freud described them.

The fact that none of these characters is a "whole" man is important; we do not have a complete hero, a rounded man. Instead, we find aspects of the complete hero *dissociated* into three persons, each of whom represents one quality and is deficient in others. It may very well be that part of the popularity of the program stems from its delineation of characters who are radically flawed, who are not integrated, who are deficient in some important aspect, and in whom we recognize ourselves.

We are given good reason to understand why Mr. Spock is the way he is; he is half-Vulcan and therefore can be excused for lacking affect — or can he? He is, after all, half-human and as such should have some element of feeling. As a symbolic hero, he is most significant. He represents the emotional cripple, the mechanical man, the man who has such control of himself and his feelings that he seems to be a robot. As such he represents millions of people who find themselves in the same situation; *we are afraid to have emotions, we suppress our feelings because we fear that if we do have feelings we must, inevitably, act on them, and these actions could be destructive.* In essence, we are afraid of going out of control and hurting people, since we identify feelings with aggression a great deal of the time. Consequently, we suppress our feelings, or our capacity to have feelings, and become robots. We also can get hurt if we have feelings, so we avoid rejection and hurt from others, though we are grievously doing damage to ourselves by bottling up our emotions.

Americans have many historical influences that have produced this character trait, or at least helped induce it. Our Puritan heritage certainly is important here, with its stress on self-restraint and the internalization of prohibitions. There is a great deal of discipline in the Puritan mind, and a narrowness, which has been distorted somewhat in evangelical movements that canalize emotion in very narrow channels. The feelings and emotions found in religious frenzy do not apply to interpersonal relations, generally speaking.

Spock, pure rationality, would find his counterpart in the Puritan saint, pure sanctity — and both would be freaks, monsters, whose ties with humanity would be most negligible. Neither Spock nor the Puritans attain the purity and narrowness they are identified with, however; Spock has human blood in his veins and the Puritans never were quite able to transcend their human limitations, though perhaps they would have liked to have done so. It is not much of a leap from the Puritans to the self-made man, who also has one goal — success — and who pursues this with such passion that there is little to his life but the pursuit. The self-made man represents a secularization of the Puritan ethic, but the psychological dynamics are similar. The Puritan, the success-seeking zealot, and Spock are all the same — one-dimensional men, men without qualities but with one quality alone, that dominates them and gives them their identity.

There is but one area where the person who is not in touch with his or her feelings (this "person" may be the typical American, as a matter of fact) does allow him or herself the luxury of having emotions — romantic love, and, ironically, it may even be that our experience of romantic love is what convinces us to strangulate our feelings everywhere else. In contemporary American society we believe that romantic love is irresistible and all powerful, that it takes us where it will and we cannot control it. This belief, which sociologists have demonstrated to be sheer mythology, has two effects, both harmful. First, we concentrate too much of our emotional life on romantic love, which cannot stand up to the burdens placed upon it. We expect too much from it, because we have no place else where we feel free. Secondly, our belief that it is overpowering leads us to fear our emotions, to fear that they will get out of hand and will become devastating. (Unrequited love is painful, and emotions, in general, are dangerous.) Thus we become monsters of self-control and retreat into ourselves. Some, who are hurt in romantic love, become doubly convinced of the danger of emotions; they fear being hurt again and they fear hurting others.

What I have been describing represents a rather extreme situation, but I do believe that large numbers of Americans have problems with their emotions and fears of aggression and hurt. It is probably exacerbated here in America, where the Puritan influence is still so strong and where Americans suffer from a general lack of sensory stimulation. The combination of sensory deprivation and unifocal psychic development poses enormous problems. We have little sense of our bodies, we have meager sensory stimulation (touch, smell, texture), and we avoid our feelings. *In extremo*, we are all Mr. Spocks, intelligence without emotion — except that not being Vulcanian we feel bad, somehow.

I have focused my attention upon Mr. Spock because he is the most interesting of the characters as far as his being "defined" is concerned. The Captain and Dr. McCoy are less focused and a bit more rounded, though they each symbolize a component of the psyche, as I have suggested. Mr. Spock, the human-Vulcanian, is a classic or textbook case, and his dilemma has similarities to that of the typical American who is afraid to get in touch with his emotions but unhappy because he finds his life unpleasant and drab.

At this point I would like to turn away from the psychological constellation in the characters (to a degree we have been dealing with inner space in outer space) to the subjects or themes found in the programs. I make a distinction between the plot of an episode and the theme or topic dealt with — which might be guilt or identity or retribution, for example.

I will deal with a typical episode, "The Alternative Factor," as an example of the significance of themes in "Star Trek." Generally speaking, interesting and important themes are raised in the program — in this case the theme is "duality." The story starts with the *Enterprise* being subjected to forces that Mr. Spock cannot explain. It turns out that the entire universe has also been subjected to some kind of "cosmic winking," and Captain Kirk is ordered to investigate. A human presence is detected on an abandoned planet near the starship and when members of the crew beam down, they discover a small spaceship and a wild man, Lazarus, who screams "you've come...there's a chance to stop him...." With that he faints and topples from a cliff. He is taken to the *Enterprise* and given medical attention. When he wakes he explains that he is devoting his life to chasing an evil *humanoid*, who lives only to destroy, who represents death, antilife, and must be stopped, for he has the capacity to annihilate universes at one stroke.

It turns out there are two Lazaruses — a good one who struggles with his alternative universe or, to be more precise, a parallel universe to our own. the *Enterprise*, which will enable him to destroy the universe, and the good Lazarus is constantly fighting to prevent this. The battles between Lazarus and his other nature are shown by using negative instead of positive prints...and Lazarus alternates between evil and goodness, as one or the other elements within him takes command.

The explanation of how the two Lazaruses exist and how the evil one can annihilate the universe is rather complicated. It turns out that there is an alternative universe or, to be more precise, a parallel universe to our own. Ours is matter and the other universe is antimatter. If Lazarus can bring the antimatter universe into contact with the regular universe, matter and antimatter will cancel themselves out. The cosmic winking involved a rip in the universe and represented a corridor, so to speak, between the alternative universes. Ultimately, with the aid of Captain Kirk, the evil Lazarus is forced into the corridor where he will spend eternity locked in struggle with the good Lazarus, and both universes will be preserved.

Obviously this is a rather complex story, both in terms of the physics involved and the themes dealt with. The most important theme is that of man's dual nature: we are all Lazaruses, with evil and goodness as constituents of our personality. And, it is implied, just as Lazarus had to come to grips with his evil nature, we must come to grips with ours, otherwise our world and our moral being will be annihilated. If we cannot do good, at least we can prevent ourselves from doing evil. We must, then, find a way of reconciling conflicting components of our personality; hopefully our goodness will triumph, though we cannot be certain of this.

This split between alternative selves is related to the problem we find symbolized by Mr. Spock — that of the man who fears that he cannot let himself go, cannot dare to feel, lest his evil nature be released and annihilate him. We are dealing with a theme that was brilliantly characterized in Stevenson's *Dr. Jekyll and Mr. Hyde*. As Martin Grotjahn says in *Beyond Laughter* (p. 149):

> We live in constant dread that our unconscious may find its way to consciousness and overwhelm our controls: then Mr. Hyde would overpower Dr. Jekyll and would do all the bad things we had hoped were safely repressed a long time ago.

In the episode we have been discussing these alternative selves were given form in the two Lazaruses, but the message is clear: we all have two natures and we must resolve the conflict between them in order to survive and maintain our sanity. The alternatives we face are a kind of schizophrenia or a deadened, emotionless, mummylike existence.

There is also a social theme in this episode, as well as a psychological one. I am talking about the notion of invasion, of the infection of the paradisical society by foreign elements. The starship *Enterprise* can be seen as a Utopian social and political community. It is racially and sexually integrated and international, a perfectly functioning social order. As it soars through the outer limits of space it is continually subjected to attempts by various entities, forces, beings and such to enter and take control of it, for a multitude of nefarious reasons.

The members of the crew represent, symbolically, a rather idealized picture of the typical American — clean-cut, efficient, courageous, and somewhat mechanical. They are portrayed pressing buttons, reading dials, manipulating gadgets, and almost as appendages to their marvelous machines. It is almost a parody of contemporary American society, full of clean-cut, semimechanical functionaries. The individuals are all good democrats, but the system is quasi-totalitarian, though that is to be expected in a military ambience. This smoothly functioning society is penetrated by some force, evil or good, and some kind of a solution is found in which the foreign elements are controlled, one way or another. The *Enterprise*, as a system, resists contamination and flies on to new adventures.

This theme is a central organizing myth in the American imagination. We have traditionally seen ourselves as Adamic innocents in a garden and have defined ourselves as non-Europeans, non-Asians, people who have escaped from history. History, in our mind, is identified with institutions, such as the Roman Catholic Church, royalty, a professional military caste, and so forth. This phenomenon was described by R. W. B. Lewis in *The American Adam*, which discussed the American mind of the mid-nineteenth century (p. 5):

> The new habits to be engendered on the new American scene were suggested by the image of a radically new personality, the hero of the new adventure: an individual emancipated from history, happily bereft of ancestry, untouched and undefiled by the usual inheritances of family and race; an individual standing alone, self-reliant and self-propelling, ready to confront whatever awaited him with the aid of his own, unique and inherent resources. It was not surprising, in a Bible-reading generation, that the new hero (in praise or disapproval) was most easily identified with Adam before the Fall. Adam was the first, the archetypal, man. His moral position was prior to experience, and in his very newness he was fundamentally innocent.

Given the belief that we were new Adams in a New Eden, our fundamental task is evident: we must keep the new Eden innocent, we must protect it from contamination...either by foreign bodies (immigrants) or foreign ideas (Catholicism, and Marxism, for example) and, we must maintain our own innocence.

Thus the adventures on "Star Trek" reflect this fundamental belief that we must maintain our innocence and protect ourselves from foreign influences. Ultimately we find man in a state of siege: he cannot allow that which is in him to escape, lest his aggressive impulses destroy those whom he loves (to the extent that he can love), and he must be on eternal guard against invasion and contamination from forces outside him. We find, then, a diffuse social paranoia, in which the fear of contamination creates a sense of danger from without, and a fear of danger from within. There is no place to turn.

Of course I have been dealing with extreme cases and with beliefs (in our Adamic innocence), which are unwarranted, though which have shaped our behavior. The fact that "Star Trek" is based upon a ritual reenactment of our central organizing myth means that it is still with us, though it is buried deep within our unconscious, and is camouflaged. It may even be that our need to preserve our innocence, on an individual basis, is what is behind our lack of affection and fear of our feelings. If that is the case, we must face the consequences of our innocence — rather our belief in our innocence — and find a more salutory myth around which to organize our lives.

BIBLIOGRAPHY

Freud, S. *An Outline of Psycho-Analysis.* New York: W.W. Norton, 1949.

Grotjahn, M. *Beyond Laughter: Humor and The Subconscious.* New York: McGraw-Hill, 1966.

Lewis, R. W. B. *The American Adam: Innocence, Tragedy, and Tradition in the Nineteenth Century.* Chicago, Il: The University of Chicago Press, 1955.

Stevenson, R. L. *Dr. Jekyll and Mr. Hyde.* New York: Bantam Books, 1981.

FILM

It wasn't too long ago that film was regarded as little more than vulgar entertainment. Now film, or in its elite manifestations what we now call "the cinema," is considered an important art medium that has produced a number of masterpieces. There are, of course, many terrible films; in fact, most films are mediocre at best. But the same applies to any medium. Think of print — we find everything in print from comic books and "girlie" magazines to plays and novels of genius.

This suggests that it is not fair to blame a medium for its worst productions but to consider, instead, what the medium is capable of doing. Even if we take a genre, such as the novel, we find the overwhelming percentage of novels, throughout history, have been unimportant and unremarkable. The novel, too, I should point out, was once considered a trivial art form.

Now we realize that film is a very complex medium; it is not as simple as one might imagine. There are a number of different ways of approaching film, depending upon one's interests and one's audience. These are sketched out below.

1. *Film Reviews.* These are found typically in newspapers and magazines and vary from short articles that focus on the plot and the performance qualities of the film, to longer essays that might say something about the relation of the film to societal concerns. The audience of film reviews is primarily interested in knowing what the film is about, whether it is a good show that is worth seeing.

2. *Film Criticism*. This kind of writing is not primarily evaluative. It is scholarly and often extremely erudite and uses various modes of interpretation (psycho-analytic thought, Marxist thought, semiotic analysis, historical perspectives) to deal with the film in as profound a manner as possible. Film criticism does not arise spontaneously. Critics generally have certain beliefs and metho-dologies that they use in making their criticisms.

One of the most influential techiques used by film critics is psychoanalytic thought. According to this perspective, people who view films are generally not aware of the significance of what they are seeing. They do not recognize, for example, that *King Kong* is, at the deepest levels, about Oedipal struggles we all allegedly have. Audiences may not recognize such things but are af-fected by them. Thus psychoanalytic critics are interested in the "hidden content" of films and how this content may be affecting viewers. *Star Wars* also has an important Oedipal component to it, though this is not apparent. (It may account, in part, for its success, however.)

Historians are interested in how the film relates to historical events when it was made or how it portrays society if it is a period film. The historian often uses the film as an historical document and is not as concerned with aesthetic matters as other critics. There are also film historians who deal with the history of film as an art form and with matters involved in the production of a given film and how the film relates to the director's other work.

3. *Film Theorists*. These scholars are not concerned with particular films but, instead, with how film itself works. The most important methodology employed by film theorists in recent years is semiotics (and its other manifestations, semiology and structuralism). The basic question the film theorist asks is "how does a film generate meaning?"

Semiotics is the science of signs — a sign being something that represents or stands for something else. For example, a facial expression represents an emotion or a kind of hat (top hat) reflects status or a kind of lighting (very powerful lighting) is used to generate some kind of a powerful emotional experience (as in horror films). Signs function in rather complicated ways and semiotics is both a powerful and revealing methodology for interpreting the world and a complex, even mystifying one. A film, for a semiotician, is a system of signs. Semioticians ask what codes we must know to interpret signs in a film (which they call a "text") and suggest that understanding a film is very much like "reading" a book.

Criticism is something we "turn on" when we want to understand a film; ordinarily, when we see a film, we just relax and enjoy it. Just as psychoanalysts don't psychoanalyze everyone they meet, critics don't automatically analyze every film (or other text) they see. But when you want to analyze a film, knowing something about critical techniques enables you to make more profound interpretations of them.

26 "I DREAM FOR A LIVING"*
RICHARD CORLISS, *TIME* MAGAZINE

There are a number of different focal points we might consider when dealing with the media. There is, for example, *the work* itself (in current jargon called a "text") which can be interpreted in a variety of different ways. Then there is *the audience* of that text. Sociologists and other social scientists spend a great deal of time studying audiences and trying to understand how these audiences make use of texts and the effects texts may be having on people. Thus, there are numerous studies of violence on television and its alleged effects on viewers.

A third focal point is *the society* in general; the media and the art forms they carry are connected to the societies in which they are found in very important ways. Thus, American society and culture form a background that must be considered in dealing with the media: our economic and political beliefs shape the media, in general, and our values permeate the films and television programs we see and all the other media that play such an important part in our lives.

Finally, there are *the artists* who create the works we find in the media. In the case of books, we generally find a single author/artist figure who has created what we read. Film, on the other hand (and television as well) is a collaborative medium, and a given film involves numerous creative individuals: writers, directors, actors and actresses, musicians, film editors…the list goes on and on. Film theorists generally agree now that the one person most responsible for giving a film its look and shape is the director (the so-called "auteur" or author).

If we believe (as I do) that the medium, itself, is important, we end up with five focal points that might be considered when dealing with the mass media and the texts they carry. To help you remember these I have used alliteration and designate them as:

> *Art works* (that is, the "texts")
>
> *Artists* (who create the "texts")
>
> *Audiences* (who go to films, watch television, etc.)
>
> *America* (the society that forms the background for the media)
>
> *The Medium* (which carries and shapes the "texts").

The essay that follows examines the life of an important artist/auteur or, as we might put it most simply, film-maker — Steven Spielberg. It is an excellent example of biographical criticism, which shows how an artist's background and experiences shape that person's work.

All is darkness — as dark as a minute to midnight on the first day of creation, as dark as a movie house just before the feature starts. Then the movement begins, a tracking shot down the birth canal of a hallway, toward the
mystery. Suddenly, light! A bright room filled with old men in beards and
black hats: sages, perhaps, from another world. At the far end of the room,
on a raised platform, is a blazing red light. The senses are suffused; the
mystery deepens. There is only one persuasive explanation for this scene. It
must be from a Steven Spielberg movie.

Well, no. And yes. It is Spielberg's earliest memory, from a day in 1948
when he was taken in a stroller to a Cincinnati synagogue for a service with
Hasidic elders. "The old men were handing me little crackers," Spielberg
recalls. "My parents said later I must have been about six months old at the
time." What a memory; and what profitable use he has found for his
memories and fantasies. If this synagogue scene has never made it into one
of the director-producer's movies, still the mood and metaphor it represents
— of fear escalating into wonder, of the ordinary made extraordinary, of the
journey from darkness into light — inform just about every frame Spielberg
has committed to film.

He is, of course, the world's most successful picturemaker. *E.T. The
Extra-Terrestrial* (1982) has earned more money than any other movie in
history. *Jaws* (1975) is fifth on the all-time list, *Raiders of the Lost Ark*
(1981) seventh, *Indiana Jones and the Temple of Doom* (1984) eighth, *Close
Encounters of the Third Kind* (1977) fifteenth and *Gremlins* (1984), which
he did not direct but developed and "presented," seventeenth. Only his pal
George Lucas, with whom he collaborated on *Raiders* and *Indiana Jones*,
approaches that patch of box-office ionosphere; and Lucas, at least since
Star Wars eight years ago, has delegated the directing of his films to other
hands. Spielberg is very hands-on; as Director Martin Scorsese puts it,
"Lucas became so powerful that he didn't have to direct. But directing is
what Steven has to do." Spielberg admits, "Yeah, I'm a mogul now. And I
love the work the way Patton loved the stink of battle. But when I grow up,
I still want to be a director."

This summer, as director and mogul, he has more than enough work to
keep him happy. Two new comic adventures bear the "Steven Spielberg
Presents" imprimatur. *The Goonies*, directed by Richard Donner from a
Spielberg story, earned a healthy $41.4 million in its first twenty-four days'
release; *Back to the Future*, a spiffy time-machine comedy from Director-
Writer Bob Zemeckis, opened last week to positive reviews and audience
acclaim. But that is just for openers. Next week *E.T.* will beam back down to
1,500 theaters for a saturation rerelease. At Amblin Entertainment,
Spielberg's studio-within-a-studio on the Universal Pictures lot, he is
shepherding another pair of pictures, *Young Sherlock Holmes* and *The
Money Pit*, toward Christmas premieres. September will see the debut of
Spielberg's NBC anthology series *Amazing Stories*. He is directing four of
the first season's twenty-two shows, and has written the stories for fifteen.

Last month he took two giant strides toward answering critics who say he refuses to grow up, artistically or personally. On June 5 he began directing *The Color Purple*, an adaptation of Alice Walker's stark, poetic novel about Southern blacks. Eight days later, his live-in love, actress Amy Irving, presented him with 7-lb 7½-oz. Max Samuel Spielberg, whom the proud father describes as "my biggest and best production of the year."

That will sound like gentle facetiousness to anyone who does not realize that Spielberg's movie productions are his children too. He can be criticized for photocopying the boy-meets-his-better-self wonder of *E.T.* in his more recent films; the copy is rougher and darker in the comic nightmare *Gremlins*, a bit crumpled and smudged in the fun-house frenzy of *The Goonies*. But the films' very limitations are identity badges on a body of work as personal, even as obsessive, as that of Ingmar Bergman, David Lean, or any other monarch of cinema academe. Spielberg the director is supposed to be a movie machine, and if that is so, fine. We need more artisans with his acute eye and gift for camera placement and movement, lighting, editing and the care and feeding of actors. But he is also a compulsive teller of stories about himself as he once was and still is. Each new film he directs or oversees is like another chapter in the autobiography of a modern Peter Pan.

The self-referential touches start with jokes on his own name. As Critic Veronica Geng has noted, *Spielberg* translates from the German as "play mountain." The hero of *Close Encounters* finds his way to the starship by molding a mountain out of a dirt hill. At the beginning of both *Raiders* and *Indiana Jones*, the hilly Paramount Pictures logo dissolves into other fantasy mountains. More directly autobiographical is the genesis of several of his films. *Close Encounters* was born one night when young Steven's father woke the six-year-old and drove him to a large meadow to see a meteor shower. *E.T.* and *The Goonies* find their wellsprings in the need of a young outcast for a playmate, real or imagined. *Poltergeist*, which Spielberg describes as being "all about the terrible things I did to my younger sisters," also emerged from a spooky encounter (ethereal figure, shivery bedroom, car that wouldn't start) that the filmmaker experienced in 1972. Each picture has allowed him to remake his own childhood, then to generalize it so it touches millons of once-again kids.

Take the word of another eternal youth Michael Jackson. For years the pop megastar was rumored to have been chosen by Spielberg to play Peter Pan in a new adaptation of the James M. Barrie tale. It was not to be, and at the moment Jackson is working with Lucas on a project. But the reclusive young thriller declares it "my honor" to speak about Spielberg. "I must have seen *E.T.* around forty times, and *Jaws* a good hundred or so," Jackson says. "You feel loved in his films. Steven never sleeps, never rests at ease. Last year, during the Victory Tour, I was on vacation with him in the Hamptons. But instead of vacating like everybody else, he found a Betamax and we made movies. He put a plastic bag around the whole camera, taped it up and shot underwater scenes in the swimming pool. I worked the lights. He is constantly creating, because making movies is like playing. He will always be young. I love Steven so much, it almost makes me cry. He inspires me more than anybody on earth today."

Hear, from the other end of the age scale, the evidence of David Lean. The director of *Lawrence of Arabia* and *A Passage to India* had seen Spielberg's 1971 TV movie *Duel*, released as a theatrical feature in Europe, and "immediately I knew that here was a very bright new director. Steven takes real pleasure in the sensuality of forming action scenes — wonderful flowing movements. He has this extraordinary size of vision, a sweep that illuminates his films. But then Steven is the way the movies used to be. He just loves making films. He is entertaining his teenage self — and what is wrong with that? I see Steven as a younger brother. I suppose I see myself in him. I have rarely felt so at ease with anyone. Curious thing, that."

Or maybe not so curious. Spielberg has that tonic effect on a lot of people. Prowling the bustling *Amazing Stories* set in his blue baseball cap, brown leather bomber jacket, salmon-colored jeans, pink socks, and gray running shoes with SPIELBERG stamped on the heels, the Mogul of Magic looks just old enough to be the classmate-coach at a college touch-football scrimmage. He has time for everyone, with a few jokes in between: "TV stands for Tender Vittles. That's what we're givin' 'em, folks, Tender Vittles." Spielberg's noncombative vitality infects everyone he works with. Says Richard Donner: "Steven is over your shoulder the whole time. He always bows to you because you're the director, but he's got so many good ideas that you want to grab every one of them. It's as if he's 17 going on 18. Next year he's going to learn to drive."

The drive is there already, four on the floor, nonstop. "I dream for a living," Spielberg explains. "Once a month the sky falls on my head, I come to, and I see another movie I want to make. Sometimes I think I've got ball bearings for brains; these ideas are slipping and sliding across each other all the time. My problem is that my imagination won't turn off. I wake up so excited I can't eat breakfast. I've never run out of energy. It's not like OPEC oil; I don't worry about a premium going on my energy. It's just always been there. I got it from my mom."

Mom is a stitch. At 65, Leah Adler still has enough vim to run a kosher restaurant in West Los Angeles with her second husband Bernie while moonlighting as an extra in the *Amazing Stories* episode directed by Clint Eastwood. Back in the early '60s, though, in the Pheonix suburb of Scottsdale, Leah Spielberg could summon just enough energy to ride the roller coaster called Young Steven. "He was my first, so I didn't know that everybody didn't have kids like him," she recalls with a happy shrug. "I just hung on for dear life. He was always the center of attention, ruling his three younger sisters. And me too, actually. Our living room was strewn with cables and floodlights — that's where Steven did his filming. We never said no. We never had a chance to say no. Steven didn't understand that word."

Spielberg's memories of his childhood are as dramatic and fantastic as you might expect from a master fabulist. Could real life have been nearly so much fun? "It was creative and chaotic at our house," says Steven's father

Arnold, 68, a computer executive with twelve patents to his name. "I'd help Steven construct sets for his 8-mm movies, with toy trucks and papier mâché mountains. At night I'd tell the kids cliffhanger tales about characters like Joanie Frothy Flakes and Lenny Ludhead. I see pieces of me in Steven. I see the storyteller."

In every Spielberg "family" film since *Close Encounters*, the mother figure is the repository of strength and common sense; Dad is either absent or a bit vague, less in touch with the forces of wonder. As described by Steven, Arnold was neither a hero nor a villain, but a hardworking perfectionist. "Steven's love and mastery of technology definitely come from our father," says Steven's sister Sue, 31, a mother of two who lives outside Washington. "Mom was a classical pianist, artistic and whimsical. She led the way for Steven to be as creative as he wanted to be. We were bohemians growing up in suburbia. And everything was centered on Steven. When he was babysitting for us he'd resort to creative torture. One time he came into the bedroom with his face wrapped in toilet paper like a mummy. He peeled off the paper layer by layer and threw it at us. He was a delight, but a terror. And we kept coming back for more."

Why not? Each evening alone with big brother meant a new Amazing Story. The youngest, Nancy (now 29 and a jewelry designer in New York City), remembers: "We were sitting with our dolls, and Steven was singing as if he was on the radio. Then he interrupted himself 'to bring us an important message.' He announced that a tornado was coming, then flipped us over his head to safety. If we looked at him, he said, we'd turn to stone." Nancy played a featured role in Steven's minimum opus *Firelight*, a sci-fi thriller made when he was 16 and she was eight. "I played a kid in the backyard who was supposed to reach up toward the firelight. Steven had me look directly at the sun. 'Quit squinting!' he'd shout. 'Don't blink!' And though I might have gone blind, I did what he said because, after all, it was Steven directing."

The fateful day when this movie-mad child got close to his Hollywood dream came in the summer of 1965, when 17-year-old Steven, visiting his cousins in Canoga Park, took the studio tour of Universal Pictures. "The tram wasn't stopping at the sound stages," Steven says. "So during a bathroom break I snuck away and wandered over there, just watching. I met a man who asked what I was doing, and I told him my story. Instead of calling the guards to throw me off the lot, he talked with me for about an hour. His name was Chuck Silvers, head of the editorial department. He said he'd like to see some of my little films, and so he gave me a pass to get on the lot the next day. I showed him about four of my 8-mm films. He was very impressed. Then he said, 'I don't have the authority to write you any more passes, but good luck to you.'"

The next day a young man wearing a business suit and carrying a briefcase strode past the gate guard, waved and heaved a silent sigh. He had made it! "It was my father's briefcase," Spielberg says. "There was nothing in it but a sandwich and two candy bars. So every day that summer I went in my suit and hung out with directors and writers and editors and dubbers. I found an office that wasn't being used, and became a squatter. I went to a camera store, bought some plastic name titles and put my name in the building directory: Steven Spielberg, Room 23C."

Two years later, Spielberg enrolled at California State University, Long Beach, but it is safe to say he matriculated at Universal U. Cramming 15½ units into two frenetic days of classes a week, he was able to spend three days on the studio lot, asking executives to watch his films. "They were embarrassed when I asked them to remove their pictures from the wall so I could project my little silent movies. They said, 'If you make your films in 16-mm or, even better, 35-mm, then they'll get seen.' So I immediately went to work in the college commissary to earn the money to buy 16-mm film and rent a camera. I had to get those films seen."

Obsession and addiction: successful careers are built on these qualities, whether or not they are accompanied by talent. Spielberg had felt the craving ever since his first day on the Universal lot: "I was on the outside of a wonderful hallucination that everyone was sharing. And I wanted to do more than be a part of the hallucination. I wanted to control it. I wanted to be a director." And so, bankrolled by a young friend with hopes of being a producer, he wrote and directed, in ten days, for $10,000, a short film called *Amblin'*, about a boy and a girl hitchhiking from the desert to the Pacific Ocean. The day after Spielberg showed the film at Universal, he was called in by Sidney Jay Sheinberg, head of TV production, and offered a seven-year contract to direct Universal TV series. He was 20 years old. "I quit college," Spielberg says, "so fast I didn't even clean out my locker."

Today, after twenty summers on and off the Universal lot, the erstwhile trespasser practically owns the place. He might deserve to: *E.T.* and *Jaws* have grossed $835 million on a $19 million investment. Moreover, Sheinberg, now president and chief operating officer of Universal's parent organization, MCA, has maintained a paternal relationship with Spielberg. So, according to Sheinberg, "when Steven called me about two years ago and said, 'I want to come home, I said, 'When?' and 'How much space do you need?'" In this fashion the man who saw a boy's film called *Amblin'* determined fifteen years later to build that boy the movie industry's most sumptuous clubhouse as headquarters for Spielberg's Amblin Entertainment. The building is reputed to have cost between $4 million and $6 million to construct and furnish. Spielberg says he doesn't know, and will never ask, the price tag, and Sheinberg won't snitch. "It would be like telling how much the birthday present cost," he says.

Playpen and sweatshop, summer camp and botanical gardens, Amblin is where Steven Spielberg dreams for a living. The two-story stucco building, on a far corner of the Universal lot, looks like Walt Disney's Frontierland as it might have been designed by a very hip Hopi. The studiously roughhewn walls and ceilings refuse to form right angles; instead they bend and breathe, going with the architectural flow. Native artifacts are everywhere. A cave painting ornaments one wall in the steam room; in the courtyard a pink marble bust of an Indian madonna with children stands guard over an abandoned plastic tricycle. The staff bustles about, casually garbed in jeans and boots, like cowpokes at home on an impossibly opulent reservation. You are reminded that in more than one Spielberg movie, insensitive white folks get their comeuppance when they build their homes on sacred Indian ground. Amblin means to lift the curse: it is a big happy tepee erected on the real estate of infidel Hollywood.

Inside and out, state-of-nature merges with state-of-the-art. In the brick-lined conference room, a massive oak chest conceals fancy video equipment that glides up pneumatically with the push of a button. Across the path from the front entrance, a giant weeping willow shades a wishing well out of which Bruce, the *Jaws* shark, pokes his snout. Behind the high-tech kitchen, and over the wooden bridge that crosses a stream fed by a rushing water-fall, is a clear-water pond stocked with fat fish, black and silver and gold Japanese koi. As you walk through the voluptuous gardens, a golden re-triever named Brandy trots up to you and, no kidding, smiles. She is the genial cerberus of Amblin, the mascot that welcomes you inside Spielberg's paradise.

Without family, paradise is a house but not a home. So the suburban boy has assembled a professional tribe remarkably like his own in Scottsdale. The roles of his kid sisters are taken by a sorority of doting, efficient junior staff members. And Steven's "parents" are his fellow Amblin bosses, Kathleen Kennedy, 32, and Frank Marshall, 38. They share executive-producer credits on the films he presents; they keep four sharp eyes on a dozen or so film projects; they grease the tracks that connect Steven with the studios and the press; they act as a DEW line to monitor the unguided missiles of his imagination. Notes Kennedy: "Ten times a week Steven will rush into my office and say, 'Kath, I have a great idea.' And sometimes I feel like, 'Oh, not another one.'" In private life, Kennedy and Marshall live together. Brandy is their dog.

Spielberg has gone his original nuclear family one better. In Screenwriter Chris Columbus (*Gremlins, The Goonies*) and the writer-producer-director tandem of Bob Gale and Robert Zemeckis (*Back to the Future*), he has found the younger brothers and bright playmates he never had. Columbus is now writing the third Indiana Jones film, which Spielberg will shoot next summer. Of *Back to the Future*, says Spielberg: "My main contribution was making Bob Zemeckis aware of his own best work and getting him to do it" after the script had been rejected by just about every studio in town. "I'm not the bank," he cautions. "Sometimes I'm the guy holding the flashlight, trying to show filmmakers where the holes are so they don't fall in." Zemeckis faced a gaping crevasse when he realized that the performance of his star, Eric Stoltz, was too intense for the picture's comic-romantic mood. After five weeks and $4 million spent, Stoltz was fired and Michael J. Fox signed to replace him. Spielberg calls this "the hardest decision I've ever made."

Tough calls come with the territory of moguldom. Spielberg insists that

"George Lucas has an empire; I just have a small commando operation." Yet Amblin is producing almost as many feature films this year as Lucas has in a decade. Often Spielberg will wait till the last minute before deciding whether he will direct a film or not. *The Goonies*, for example, was "a film I didn't want to direct but I did want to see, so I asked Richard Donner to do it. I've always been very zealous about directors' rights. I retain final-cut privilege, but I won't exercise it unless the director has a complete nervous breakdown, tries to burn the set down and is found one morning in the corner eating Ding Dongs."

Still not busy enough, Steven? How about masterminding an anthology series for TV? *Amazing Stories* won a unique guarantee from NBC: the network agreed to buy forty-four shows, or two years' worth instead of the customary six to twenty-two weeks, and to pay a record-breaking license fee of $800,000 to $1 million an episode. Spielberg explains the series' origin: "I get too many ideas, and I want to act on them all. *Amazing Stories* is a foster home for ideas that will never grow into adulthood, that aren't strong enough to stretch beyond twenty-three minutes." Spielberg has hired Eastwood, Scorsese, Peter Hyams, Paul Bartel, Bob Clark, and Irvin Kershner to direct segments. (Eastwood says his involvement is the result of "part friendship, part lark.") Spielberg has also anointed four young film school grads for their big-time directorial debuts.

Amazing Stories may not be an instant hit; with the exception of the Walt Disney series, no anthology show has finished in the Nielsen Top 25 since *Alfred Hitchcock Presents* a quarter-century ago. But it could blaze trails, or at least reopen them. With this show Spielberg is attempting to transform the weekly series from a comfortable habit to an event worth anticipating and savoring. Each Sunday night at 8, a new baby movie, with a spooky story, feature-film production values and, often as not, a distinctive visual style. One of Spielberg's own episodes, an hourlong drama called "The Mission," envelops its suspense in a visual style that suggests Rembrandt on Halloween. More important, it finds a new twist for the Spielberg credo: the miraculous power of the artistic imagination. This story of a World War II gunnery ace who, in the author's provocative words, "literally paints himself *out* of a corner," is a fairy tale for the technocratic 20th century. It should be the first movie that Mom and Dad show to Max Samuel Spielberg.

Fall in with Spielberg and you fall into a Spielberg movie. Such is the testimony of Amy Irving, 31, as she sits in the lavish Coldwater Canyon home they share (they call it "the house that *Jaws* built"). In 1979 Irving had broken up with the filmmaker after a four-year affair. Then in 1983 she was on location in India and "one night, in front of three friends, I made a wish. I said, 'I wish I'd have a visitor, and I want it to be Steven.' Later that night my assistant came to me and said, 'Steven arrives in the morning.'" Irving then surprised Spielberg, who was in India scouting locations for *Indiana Jones and the Temple of Doom*, by meeting him at the airport. Says she: "From that moment, I knew. Now we're really in love. And here I am with the Prince of Hollywood. I guess that makes me the Princess."

Turn a page of the storybook and see Steven and Amy walking hand in hand through the rain toward Claude Monet's house in the Paris suburb of Giverny. "Just as we arrived," Irving recalls, "the rain stopped, so we were able to walk around the gardens. When we walked inside, it started pouring again. Then, during lunch, a double rainbow appeared outside our window. It was very magical, and then I threw up. That was the first time I realized I was with child." As a memento of their visit, Spielberg bought a Monet, which hangs on their living room wall. In the den is the original Rosebud sled used in *Citizen Kane.*

As for the discipline of fatherhood, Spielberg will let history be his guide: "My mom spoiled me. I'll spoil the baby. Amy will be strong with Max, and I'll be the pushover." But he promises a change. "Until now Amy and I have looked elsewhere for our 400 cc of real life — spell that *r-e-e-l*. I'm great with a movie camera between me and reality. But with the baby, I have an excuse to finally look real life in the eye and not be afraid of what I discover."

Undoubtedly, tens of millions of moviegoers hope the filmmaker stays the precocious little boy he seems to be. Only the Hollywood graybeards and a flank of film critics feel like shouting, "Steven, grow up!" Whichever path he chooses, there are dangers. Walt Disney kept recycling the magic of his animated fables until the gold turned into dross. Charlie Chaplin got serious and lost his audience. Spielberg, who says, "I want people to love my movies, and I'll be a whore to get them into the theaters," means to have it both ways: to mature as an artist while retaining his copyright on adolescent thrills and wonder, to blossom as a director while he diversifies as a mogul.

Scorsese, who has known Spielberg since 1971, detects "a pressure in Steven to top himself. The audience sees his name on a project and expects more and bigger. That's a tough position to be in." And Spielberg, who boasts that "I can dump on me better than anybody else," confesses that "I find my leg stuck in the trap I built. To have directed a movie like *Young Sherlock Holmes* would have gnawed that leg right off."

He hardly needs to be told that fables about know-nothing adults and feel-it-all children are not the only tales worth spinning; that adults must face such plot twists as pain, exultation and emotional compromise; that there is drama to be found in the grown-up compulsions of power and, dare we say it, sex. Sure, Spielberg knows there is life after high school. "But after *E.T.,*" he says, "people expected a certain kind of film from me, a certain amount of screams and cheers and laughs and thrills. And I was caving in to that. I knew I could give it to them, but I realize it made me a little arrogant about my own style. It was all too easy. The whole titillation I've always felt about the unknown — of seeing that tree outside my bedroom window and shutting the drapes till morning — was taken away from me. And I got scared. I don't want to see where I'm going."

Enter *The Color Purple*, an epistolary novel about incest, sexual brutality, sapphic love and the indomitable will to survive. It did not seem the sort of material Steven Spielberg would touch with a ten-foot wand. Which is precisely why he went for it. "*The Color Purple* is the biggest challenge of my career," he proclaims. "When I read it I loved it; I cried and cried at the end. But I didn't think I would ever develop it as a project. Finally I said, I've got to do this for me. I want to make something that might not be everybody's favorite but, this year at least, is my favorite. *The Color Purple* is the kind of character piece that a director like Sidney Lumet could do brilliantly with one hand tied behind his back. But I'm going into it with both eyes wide open and my heart beating at Mach 2."

Perhaps *The Color Purple* will bring Spielberg the one triumph that has thus far eluded him: an Oscar for Best Director (though Clint Eastwood wonders if the industry may not think Spielberg is "a little too young and too successful. He has done so well, it may be a long time before anyone bestows on him any brassworks for the fireplace"). But even with that statuette, one suspects that Spielberg would still be restless. He would still crave those moments when he can spin amazing stories for himself, his kid sisters and a world of children in the dark. To demand that he revoke his inexhaustible thirst for wonder would be like asking Dickens to be Dreiser, or Peter Pan to settle down and become complacent old Mr. Darling.

But Spielberg has surprised us before: as an auteur prodigy, as the thrill-master of *Duel* and *Jaws*, as the savvy director who could reinvent the movies' innocence. The man is only 37 now, and his toughest audience is himself. You needn't be a child to believe that this movie magician still has astonishments in store.

---

27 THE FASCINATING KING NAMED KONG*

Mark Rubinstein

In order to understand the grip that *King Kong* has on people we must delve into psychoanalytic theory. It is the most useful way, our author argues, to understand why this story about a gigantic ape and a beautiful blonde woman has so much power and why people are endlessly fascinated by it.

The argument is that this story speaks to us in remarkable ways and is, it turns out, much more than a story about an ape and a woman. *King Kong* is, to put it bluntly, directly connected to Oedipal anxieties we all have buried in our psyches

---

* Reprinted with permission from *Psychology Today* Magazine. Copyright © 1977 American Psychological Association.

and this is the source of its power. To understand *King Kong*, then, you have to know something about the ideas of Sigmund Freud.

The Oedipus complex draws upon the Greek myth of Oedipus, who unknowingly, killed his father, married his mother, and blinded himself when he discovered what he had done. According to Freud, all people, when they are young children around three years of age, pass through a stage in which they form strong libidinal attachments to parents of the opposite sex and are hostile to parents of the same sex. This process is unconscious and normally the Oedipus complex is repressed and resolved in a satisfactory manner. If not, it becomes, Freud suggested, the core of neurosis.

In a famous letter Freud wrote (to Wilhelm Fliess, in 1897) he states, "I have found love of the mother and jealousy of the father in my own case too, and now believe it to be a general phenomena of early childhood, even if it does not always occur so early as in children who have been made hysterics....If that is the case, the gripping power of Oedipus Rex, in spite of all the rational objections to the inexorable fate that the story presupposes, becomes intelligible...the Greek myth seizes upon a compulsion which everyone recognizes because he has felt traces of it in himself. Every member of the audience was once a budding Oedipus in fantasy, and this dream fulfillment played out in reality causes everyone to recoil in horror, with the full measure of repression which separates his infantile from his present state."

King Kong, from this perspective, is a recasting of the Oedipus myth. The creators of this film, according to a psychoanalytic point of view, did not consciously attempt to do this at all. They just wanted to make an exciting film, but in doing this they drew upon elements in their psyches that had Oedipal aspects to them.

Freudian theory is quite controversial and some scholars consider it to be sheer nonsense. If this is so, how does one explain the remarkable power this fantastic story has?

Nearly forty-three years after its release in 1933, Hollywood is remaking the film classic *King Kong*. It may seem odd that such a blatant fantasy should succeed so admirably where others of the same genre have failed. But *King Kong* touches us as few films can, for its dreams are deeply embedded in the individual and collective human psyche.

The ease with which the film draws the viewer into its surreal world is partly due to its technical wizardry. *King Kong* was the first good film to animate miniature models by means of stop-motion photography, and to use rear-process and superimposed images. The film's use of Arnold Bocklin's macabre painting, "The Isle of the Dead," to represent Skull Island, the home of Kong, accentuates the dreamlike quality. So does Max Steiner's lush musical score.

But the key to the film's immense popularity is that its various elements combine to form a colossal, universal myth about human history, religion, society, the family, and sexuality. It is a myth that Sigmund Freud helped elucidate as long ago as 1913.

The film opens as Carl Denham, an entrepreneur and filmmaker, is searching for a woman willing to join him on a voyage to a remote corner of the world where they will make a mysterious film. He happens upon Ann Darrow, whom he rescues from an angry fruit-vendor whose wares she has just tried to steal.

Denham feeds her and promises stardom, and she becomes a ready partner in his scheme. Denham's ship and its adventurous crew set off for a desolate and forbidding part of the world, where everything familiar is lost behind rolling banks of mist and fog.

THE BEAST-GOD

They drop anchor off Skull Island, which looms out of the sea to the accompaniment of throbbing native drums. The explorers discover that the natives are engaged in a primitive and frightening ritual — the sacrifice of a young woman to the great ape Kong. These sacrifices seem to propitiate the beast-god, but whether he devours the women or makes them his brides, no one seems to know.

The natives worship and fear Kong. They dress themselves in ape costumes, mime him, and chant and dance ritualistically. Evidently Kong does something for them in return: he refrains from breaking down the massive wall the natives have erected between him and their village. The film also implies that Kong protects the village from other large predators (dinosaurs, pterodactyls) that inhabit the island.

The natives clearly regard Kong as a totem animal, and it is here that the heart of the mythology of *King Kong* resides. Freud, in his book *Totem and Taboo*, speculated that aboriginal man lived in small hordes or clans within which the oldest and strongest male took as many wives as he could, and jealously guarded them against other men. By driving out or killing the others, this jealous father established himself as head of the horde. The younger males then wandered off, and, by finding partners from other clans, were able to prevent inbreeding. Freud borrowed this idea, by the way, from Charles Darwin, who emphasized its biological aspects.

At some point, Freud suggested, the expelled sons banded together to murder and eat the primal father, thereby ending the father-dominated horde. Devouring the father also allowed each son and brother to identify with the father, to share a portion of his strength.

But the murder of the patriarch posed a new problem. Once the brothers identified with the father, they were all rivals for the women. This impractical and dangerous situation could have destroyed their new social organization. And so, to insure group harmony and survival, they prohibited marriage to women within the clan. Marriage could only take place outside the extended family. Sexual relations with women of the same clan were now considered incestuous and forbidden.

RELIGIONS ARE AMBIVALENT

The members of the clan also needed to assuage their sense of guilt for having slain the father and to insure that his spirit would not seek retribution. They therefore created a totemic system by which some animal was chosen to be a substitute for the slain leader. The animal's life would be protected and treated as sacred. Eventually, the totem animal and father would become a tribal god.

Totemic religions and their derivatives attempt to assuage guilt and appease the primal father through obeisance. As Freud pointed out, however, religions are ambivalent. The sons' sense of guilt at their defiance was never obliterated and, according to the deeply rooted law of retaliation, the murder could be atoned for only by the sacrifice of another human life. In Christianity, for instance, man's original sin was an offense against God the Father, and man could redeem himself only by the sacrifice of Christ, God the Son.

Freud maintained, then, that human society was founded on a common criminal deed (the murder of the primal father) and on subsequent prohibitions against incest and aggression. Similarly, religion developed from the need to expiate the common sense of guilt. The whole process, tragic and violent as it may have been, served to promote the survival and increasing civilization of the society.

One further element in this theory is essential. Freud held that each individual repeats part of the collective experience in relation to his or her own parents. Just as in the ancient horde, the child wants to possess the parent of the opposite sex to the exclusion of the rival parent of the same sex. Later, by renouncing such Oedipal strivings and coming to terms with the impracticality of such incest, the child comes to identify with the same-sex parent and seeks marital fulfillment with a spouse who may resemble the originally desired parent.

Thus each person's development reflects or copies part of the social development of the human family, and each one of us must deal with some of the same issues in the nuclear family as did the members of the primal horde.

It should be clearer now, at least to those who have seen the movie of 1933, why the story of King Kong has the power to move us the way it does. It not only retells certain basic myths of human society and religion, but it also recounts stories of our own childhood passions and development.

As the story unfolds, the high priest of the Kong totem clan offers to make a trade with the explorer Denham in order to possess the "golden woman," Ann Darrow. Denham refuses, and so the natives steal aboard the ship and seize her. They offer her in sacrifice to the totem beast-god, trussing her to two large stakes within the confines of the wall. Then they summon Kong by beating a large gong.

We hear a thunderous roar and Kong appears. He leers at Ann Darrow and makes off with her to the remote regions of the island.

PROTECTIVE AND POSSESSIVE

The music races as Denham, Ann's lover Jack Driscoll, and other crew members give chase beyond the wall, and as the action progresses it becomes apparent that we are somehow moving backward in the stream of time — that Skull Island is a dreamlike land where time stands still. Kong battles a Tyrannosaurus rex, a giant snake, and a pterodactyl. The ape's Cyclopean size and power, and his absolute determination, make him a godlike and indomitable figure in his primeval world.

During this part of the narrative, Kong saves Ann from the snake and the pterodactyl. He is protective and possessive. But while Kong is battling the pterodactyl at the entrance of his cave, Jack rescues her, and they make their way back to the native village. Wild with rage, Kong thunders after them and shatters the door of the wall that has separated him from the village for so long. He destroys everything in his path before Denham finally overcomes him with a gas bomb.

Modern technology has conquered god and beast.

Denham removes Kong from the pre-history of Skull Island to modern-day Manhattan Island, a move that spans millions of years. Once safely back in civilization, he decides to display his prize for all to see. Kong is chained to a great chromium cross, and the crowd gasps at his sinewy, helpless form. This crucifixion is clearly reminiscent of the crucifixion of Christ. Suddenly, thinking that the photographers with their flashbulbs are hurting Ann Darrow, Kong strains against his bonds and tears himself free. He smashes his way through the building and emerges in the streets of Manhattan. Once again the natives scatter as Kong bursts through the wall.

But Manhattan is not an island where time has stopped, and his battles, though similar to the ones on Skull Island, are with machines instead of with Mesozoic creatures. He pummels an elevated train as he once did the snake. He finds Ann Darrow, abducts her, and takes her to the highest peak on the island — the Empire State Building. (In the remake of the film, he will straddle the twin towers of the World Trade Center, the newest temple of technological achievement.) But steel birds that spew fire and bullets mortally wound the giant ape. He manages to tear one of the planes apart, as he did the pterodactyl. But with his strength ebbing, Kong looks longingly at Ann Darrow and carefully places her aside. It is the most touching scene of the film. Surrounded by the buzzing planes, he flails at them until he plummets to his death.

As in Freud's version of this universal myth, the savage primal father becomes deified. The tyrant of Skull Island, bent on the abduction and possession of the woman, is martyred before our eyes at the top of the modern world. He emerges as a godlike and unbegotten giant whose fate is that of crucifixion, encirclement, and slaughter. Our sympathy is real. So is our contrition, which may account for the T-shirts emblazoned with the message, "King Kong Died For Our Sins."

COLLECTIVE SIN

This film distills centuries of developing religious myth. On Skull Island we are in a primitive totemic world of sacrifices to the primal father. On Manhattan Island, although Kong is still the totem animal and again represents the slain father, he is also something more. He becomes the sacrificial object itself — the God-Son whose martyrdom is meant to atone for the original collective sin against the father. This progression from Skull Island to Manhattan Island reveals mankind's relationship to the primal father and the evolution of his religion.

It should not perplex anyone that this creature represents at different times the primal father, the substitute totem animal, and finally the son. Multi-faceted symbolism of this sort is typical of mythology, fable, dream, and religious allegory. *King Kong* is all of these. The issues of sacrifice and obedience, power and possession, sin and atonement all converge in the same timeless dreamscape. In a hallucinatory condensation of time and place, the film portrays man in both primitive and contemporary form, in the primal jungle and in the modern city, endlessly struggling with the massive archetype, King Kong.

As with all myths and fables, *King Kong* has other layers of meaning than the one I have described. Some critics see it as a tragedy of human beings unleashing environmental forces they do not understand. Both men and nature are almost destroyed in the process. Others interpret this Depression-era film as social criticism. Thus the capitalist Denham, in his greed for profit, endangers Ann Darrow, exploits nature ruthlessly, upsets the primitive harmony of Skull Island, and nearly destroys Manhattan when his captive rebels. A somewhat similar theory depicts the film as an allegory of racism.

All these interpretations are worth thinking about. None of them actually contradicts the Freudian theme.

There is at least one other interpretation of this cinematic myth. The apocryphal Arabian proverb that precedes the film reads: "And the Prophet said — And lo! the Beast looked upon the face of Beauty. And it stayed its hand from killing. And from that day it was as one dead." The screenwriters are implying that Kong's downfall is due to his interest in a woman, an interest that will render him impotent and lifeless. This interpretation, I believe, is based on the ancient fantasy that sexual intercourse will deplete a man of all his powers, as in the Samson and Delilah myth. We should remember, though, that Delilah consented willingly to Samson's advances; in fact she wanted to beguile him. This is not the case with Kong and Ann Darrow. She never consents to his advances and he never succeeds in satisfying his sexual interest in her.

His interest, by the way, is certainly sexual. This is apparent in the original version of the film. On Skull Mountain, before battling the pterodactyl, Kong was shown peeling off Ann Darrow's clothing and sniffing the shreds of her garment. Several years after the film's release, the scene was snipped by the censors because it was considered too overtly sexual. Kong is not depleted of his strength by his love. It is his primal fate to battle for the woman and to be defeated by men who individually could never match him.

At bottom, King Kong is the myth of the primal father, his struggle, and his death. It grips adults as tightly as it grips children because it goes to the core of our individual and collective experience. The new version of this popular myth will resurrect Kong to live through his agony once again. The crowds will no doubt be large, and each of us will bring to the theater that portion of inner being in which the small child still lives, and where Kong's struggle still smolders.

28 BLACK SHADOWS*

John Fell

We've had films for more than ninety years in America, so the medium is very useful for historians and others interested in using it as a means of tracing our attitudes and values. Films do more than entertain us; they record life as we see it or want to see it. And they capture life in terms of powerful images, gripping figures, and exciting stories.

This article, on stereotypes of blacks in films, makes an important point. The way movies have stereotyped blacks has been a "shameful" one, and what makes things even worse is the fact that, in general, these films have only reflected the values and attitudes of the general public.

The bitter fact we must face in thinking about our attitudes toward blacks —

* John Fell, "Black Shadows." This article was written especially for this book. Copyright © 1987, John Fell.

and we might add Jews, women, various ethnic groups, the aged, and continue on ad infinitum — is that we used to stereotype people in terrible ways in our early history. The case of the blacks in film demonstrates this. We were more open and naive then, I might add — or should I say innocent or less sophisticated. Our arts reflected our values directly and with little camouflaging. Generally speaking, it is no longer possible to present images of blacks (or other groups) the way we used to, but there is some question about how much progress we have made.

For one thing, blacks are still stereotyped in the media — though the stereotypes are less obvious and not as hostile or negative as they used to be. In some cases, black moviemakers perpetuated stereotypes, driven, it would seem, more by the desire to make money than by anything else. (It is rather ironic that the Cosby show has been received so well; Cosby and his writers use the power of the program to counter stereotypes of blacks and, have had the character Theo like school and be positive about it. Cosby was, in 1986, the top hero for teens in America according to one opinion poll.) Some critics argue, I might point out, that the Cosby show is a sellout that has little to do with the typical black family.

We might also think about whether Americans have changed their values and attitudes toward blacks and other groups. Do people keep their attitudes hidden; that is, we may be keeping negative feelings and stereotypes of blacks and others to ourselves rather than expressing them. Even if this is the case, it seems that racism and all the other "isms" are no longer acceptable to most Americans. We have progressed — but much remains to be done.

Overall, the movies' relation to American blacks has been a shameful one, only mitigated if at all by the truism that film has restated the popular perceptions of its mass audience. How far motion pictures enlarged and refined these stereotypes is largely the subject of this essay.

Some of the earliest black appearances on turn-of-the-century nickelodeon screens were untypical because they were "newsreel" footage, showing black U.S. Army troops disembarking in New York harbor for the Spanish American War in 1898 and black soldiers staging drills and maneuvers. Other, staged "actualities," as non-fiction footage came to be called, were more common and more predictable. *Dancing Darkey Boy* (1897) shows a small boy performing on a table, surrounded by a clapping audience, mostly white, one or two in blackface. *Watermelon Eating Contest* (1900) poses four young men consuming watermelon slices at breakneck speed with unbelievable good humor. *Laughing Ben* (1902) is a closeup of a near-toothless old man in spasms of hilarity. *Comedy Cakewalk* (1903) has several costumed couples performing the dance.

In this early period of motion picture exhibition, programming consisted of a series of very short pieces, shown in little storefront theaters, music halls, and sometimes travelling shows. The entertainments that were fiction, that is, "made up," gradually came to be composed of several shots, rather like a sequence of panels in a comic strip, and indeed movies and comics shared a good deal of similar material, jokes and depictions. Among other discoveries, anyone who researches turn-of-the-century comics and political cartoons in metropolitan newspapers will find depictions of blacks, Orientals, Irish, Italians and Germans very like what appear in films. Much of it survived, too, in theatrical melodramas and in the music halls as well as vaudeville.

For our purposes, a capsule description of a few selected story films will suffice. *What Happened in a Tunnel* (1903) and *A Kiss in the Dark* (1904) use the same joke: a young white man tries to steal a kiss from a white girl; instead, she substitutes her black maid. In *How Charlie Lost the Heiress* (1903), a black woman persuades a white man to watch her two children momentarily. Charlie's fiancée, the heiress, passes by and runs off, indignant at what she sees. Charlie faints. In *The 'Gater and the Pickaninny* (1903), a large alligator consumes a small boy who is fishing in a swamp. The boy's father hurries in, cuts open the animal and frees his son. Finally, *A Nigger in the Woodpile* (1904) betrays an out-of-the-ordinary sadism. In his farmyard, a white man saws wood, piling it in cords nearby. A second white arrives, carrying a box of dynamite. After drilling a hole in a log, they hide one stick of explosive, returning the wood to the pile. Later, two blacks help themselves to some firewood. The thieves put their loot in a cabin stove, which of course blows up. In the last scene, the two whites appear at the ruined cabin, enjoying the sight of their victims.

In trying to unravel the matter of why such stereotypes were perpetuated, several factors need to be balanced against one another. While slavery itself was half a century past, social segregation and economic servitude among this country's black population existed as a fact of everyday life. One way for the rest of the country to rationalize such inequities, as some of the states had rationalized slavery, was to imagine the victims to be, alternately, undeserving and uncaring. Laughing, prancing, watermelon-eating darkies were obviously unconcerned about ignorance and poverty. The deluded vision often drew its images from a rural world of alligators and farmyards: simple problems with simple answers. And to the extent that such people were jovial, they were unthreatening; they didn't resent their lot.

Much of the myth about black sensibilities had developed out of the traveling minstrel shows whose songs, dances, and jokes had entertained both rural and cosmopolitan America since the 1840s. Minstrel troupes eventually institutionalized comic figures like Sambo and jokes about purported black weaknesses like chicken-stealing and dice. Eventually a commercialized nostalgia toward life in the Old South was further perpetuated by popular songs about rivers like the Swanee and the Mississippi and the contentments of country life.

Finally, we need to admit to one more thread in Victorian American culture — its cruelties. From prizefights to gang warfare in the decaying cities, violence was as American as apple pie. If blacks were ridiculed, so too were pigtailed Chinese, women, children, old people, the lame, the deaf, and the blind. In *A Bucket of Cream Ale* (1904) a black woman has a glass of beer thrown in her face, then retaliates by dumping a bucket of it on her assailant. Her action is justified because he's a Dutchman. In *The Fights of Nations* (1907), different nationalities display their ethnic peculiarities in a barroom. Spaniards fight with knives. Scots wear kilts and duel with swords. Jews bicker and gesture. The Irish drink and brawl. Blacks fight with razors.

Probably the earliest black character to show up in a movie story was played by a madeup white man, the slightly portly actor who masqueraded as Uncle Tom in a 1903 version of *Uncle Tom's Cabin*. "Tom Shows" were a regular feature of post–Civil War America, and although the character originated by Harriet Beecher Stowe in her pre–Civil War novel was courageous in his beliefs as well as loyal to white masters, it was the loyalty that survived in adaptations as the years passed: a Southern plantation owner's version of slavery in which blacks lived in loyal gratitude to their benevolent owners. In the movies' next years, slaves either marched behind Confederate banners with their masters — *A Slave's Devotion* (1913), *Old Mammy's Charge* (1914), *Old Mammy's Secret Code* (1913) — or else they assumed the family's care with, of course, due deference.

This country's first publicized film director, D. W. Griffith, himself a Southerner, told such stories in *His Trust* (1911) and *His Trust Fulfilled* (1911). "Feature" films at this stage ran one-reel lengths (ten to twelve minutes) and Griffith's two titles were an early effort to broaden the form, for they were sequential parts of a single narrative. In them, another black-faced white plays Old George, who vows to protect his master's family. The father dies in battle. Old George first saves everyone when the mansion catches on fire, then spends his meager savings to provide the daughter a seminary education. She marries an English cousin. The last scenes are described by the Biograph production company's bulletin.

> Old George at a distance views the festivities with tears of joy streaming down his black but honest cheeks, and after they depart for their new home, he goes back to his cabin, takes down his master's saber and fondles it, happy in realization that he has fulfilled his trust.

D. W. Griffith's great Civil War epic appeared in 1914, a two-hour film whose magnitude had never been witnessed before. *The Birth of a Nation* stunned viewers with its battle scenes and infuriated racially sensitive audiences in its depictions of rapacious and criminal black soldiers and freed slaves. In its melodramatic conclusion, a besieged cabin of white Northerners and Southerners is rescued from a mob of crazed black militants by the Ku Klux Klan. For all its ambition and skills, *The Birth of a Nation* was, and still is, attacked by civic groups. Screenings in Boston led to race riots, followed by unsuccessful efforts to revoke exhibition licenses. In response, the recently formed National Association for the Advancement of Colored People issued a pamphlet, *Fighting a Vicious Film*. Griffith revived his spectacle throughout the 1920s. Its road show appearances often coincided with recruitment rallies of the Klan, which experienced a massive revival during the same decade.

One consequence of controversies engendered by Griffith's film were the first efforts by black Americans to film their own story. *Birth of a Race* (1919) was conceived in idealistic fanfare, but its final version suffered sadly from squabbles among the several factions who finally figured in its execution. It was an abject failure. Organized in 1916, the Lincoln Motion Picture Company of Los Angeles looked to middle-class blacks for financing. They produced features over a six-year span. Little of the work survives, but *By Right of Birth* (ca. 1921) sets a mold and a mood for many subsequent black productions: a hero or heroine aspires to genteel, middle class values, patterned by blacks on white society. In process, the main character must free himself from the temptations of lower-class life. The basic plot translates Horatio Alger into an ethnic world. For example, *The Scar of Shame* (1928), made by The Colored Players (an integrated production unit) tells a similar story.

Black films made by blacks posed special sorts of problems. A major one was distribution, for most movie houses were either controlled by Hollywood studios or located in white neighborhoods. Indeed, the existence of segregated audiences made a strong argument for blacks producing their own work. To publicize the results, the Lincoln Motion Picture Company devised a scheme of working with entertainment editors of cosmopolitan black newspapers like the *Chicago Defender*, but the genius at producing, financing and distributing black features soon appeared in the person of Oscar Micheaux.

Micheaux's first film was *Body and Soul* (1924), which introduced a young, talented singer and actor — Paul Robeson. Unlike upward-striving stories like *By Right of Birth*, Micheaux played a Hollywood game of sex and sin. Robeson was a preacher gone bad, who drank heavily, seduced a parishoner, and stole her money. Only it turned out all to be a dream! Besides writing and directing his productions (*Body and Soul* is a very well-constructed silent film), Micheaux assumed personal responsibility for their exhibition. This involved working closely with what finally amounted to about four hundred black movie theaters, but also roadshowing the films when no theaters were available. Roadshowing had first been demonstrated by Griffith with *The Birth of a Nation*. It amounted to renting an exhibition hall for the screening, then producing sufficient advance publicity so that an audience might be assured. Drawing on his past experience, Micheaux could compute a film's production costs very closely, and he continued to make films up to the time of World War II, although their character grew increasingly exploitative, so that movies like *God's Step Children* (1938) were themselves denounced for perpetuating black stereotypes. Micheaux's work was finally acknowledged by Hollywood at the 1987 Academy Awards.

Following Oscar Micheaux's example, other entrepeneurs made motion pictures exclusively for black audiences through the 1930s and 1940s. Most were white-financed and worked with white crews, while the casts were exclusively black except for an occasional policeman, nightclub owner, or underworld boss. Many such films were exploitative. In large measure they were take-offs on Hollywood formulas: westerns, crime stories, comedies and musicals. Several star performers mirrored white counterparts. There was a black Valentino, a Negro Jean Harlow, a black Rita Hayworth, a black James Cagney. The band singer Herb Jeffries became a singing cowboy like Gene Autry or Roy Rogers. Boxing champions like Henry Armstrong and Joe Louis were featured in autobiographies. Such films sometimes reflected and sometimes, if rarely, commented on caste snobbery in the black community.

In mainstream Hollywood film where most employment, if there was any for blacks, rested, the advent of sound had proved to be a short-term blessing. Dating back to the mid-twenties, many short, experimental sound films now constitute the single existing visual documentation of some black artists. These include the team of Eubie Blake and Noble Sissle, and the great blues singer Bessie Smith who survive otherwise only in memory and on phonograph records. Many other artists were captured at high points of their success: Duke Ellington, Louis Armstrong, Cab Calloway, Fats Waller, Ethel Waters, Billie Holiday, and the Nicholas Brothers among them.

Performers like these were sought out because their popularity promised some attendance guarantee in a new medium that no one knew quite how to use. Many silent movie stars had voices out of keeping with their images. There was even a rumor that black speech recorded better than white. Often musicians and singers were encouraged to perform material of proven success, so that the line between what was "staged" and what was "documented" becomes a very fine one. Thus in a short titled *Black and Tan* (1929) we can not only hear the music of Duke Ellington when he was enjoying his initial success, we also see dancers and costumes that clearly reproduce actual performances from New York's Cotton Club nightclub in its heyday. [Logical extensions of filming performances were productions like *Jazz on a Summer's Day* (1960), *Monterey Pop* (1968) and *Woodstock* (1970).] Sound's early days saw two Hollywood-produced all-black features, *Hallelujah-* and *Hearts in Dixie* (both 1929). Although both were white visions of a black world, they showcased some effective performances, particularly *Hallelujah!*

Henceforth, except for periodic appearances in musicals, most black performers soon found themselves relegated to the old, cliched roles as sound film became increasingly predictable in its output. Of course, almost all Hollywood's formularized product penned its characters with highly conventional strokes, but black actors and actresses found themselves even more constrained than others.

The most common role was a comic one, built around the old notion of an ignorant, shuffling, rural darkey, bug-eyed with fright at any danger and lazy beyond measure. It was epitomized by a man who named himself Stepin Fetchit, after a racehorse; for years he was the most famous black actor in films. Stepin Fetchit appeared in everything from high-budget features to B-picture Charlie Chans. Seeing him now, the viewer may find himself slightly ill at ease: righteously indignant over so crude and distorted an image of mumbling, ineffective stupidity while at the same time feeling a tinge of guilty amusement, for Lincoln Perry, the actor, played a continuous character — picture to picture — with a marvelous invention and economy of gesture and speech, far better at what he did than the inferior darkey versions that were played by other actors like Willie Best and Mantan Moreland. Distinctions like these posed dilemmas for black audiences of the time. Should they shun films in which blacks portrayed such demeaning people? Or ought they to support performers in whatever work they found, applauding the acting skills? After all, Stepin Fetchit was not real. He was a character, like Jack Benny or W. C. Fields.

Another ritualized performance was the maid's, usually fat, sometimes quite subservient (like Louise Beavers), sometimes sassy (like Hattie McDaniel), invariably cheerful. Hattie McDaniel was the first member of her race to win an Academy Award, that for Best Supporting Actress in *Gone With the Wind* (1939) and was said always to employ a white maid for herself. Billie Holiday was enraged to learn she'd been cast as a maid in *New Orleans* (1947). Ethel Waters turned the role into that of a wise counselor in *Member of the Wedding* (1952).

A masculine equivalent of the maid was Bill Robinson's servant role, an updating of Old George in *His Trust*. Robinson was one of the great dancers of his era, but he is probably best remembered now for following Shirley Temple's childish orders in *The Littlest Rebel* and *The Little Colonel* (both 1935) with devastating geniality.

The plight of the light-skinned black beauty provides striking evidence of Hollywood's unyielding obedience toward patterns of social constraint. Nina Mae McKinney was outstanding as a passionate young temptress in *Hallelujah!*, but no subsequent good parts followed. She spent much of the rest of her life performing in Europe or appearing in minor, inferior movies. Freddi Washington starred with Paul Robeson in *The Emperor Jones* (1933) and then played the daughter of Louise Beavers who tried to pass for white in *Imitation of Life* (1934), but never found another good part. Attractive young black women could play neither maids nor clowns, and unless the story was all-black, there could be no love interest for them.

Lena Horne was customarily spotted by M-G-M musicals in isolated performances, beautifully gowned, exotically attractive, and vulnerable to being cut out of the films in Southern states where her adjacency to white performers might be considered some sort of danger. The two wartime all-black Hollywood musicals were *Cabin in the Sky* and *Stormy Weather* (both 1943). Lena Horne appeared in each, a temptation for Eddie Anderson (best known as Jack Benny's "Rochester") in the former, a love interest to Bill Robinson in *Stormy Weather*. Robinson was 65 at this point, Horne 23.

Dorothy Dandridge finally received feature billing ten years later in *Carmen Jones* (1954). Her own star status coincided with Hollywood's timid adoption of integration as a plot theme. Subsequent films like *Island in the Sun* (1957) and *Tamango* (1959) cast her in love affairs with white males, customarily with tragic consequences. Dandridge committed suicide in 1965, her screen roles long run out. One last stereotypical role was gingerly approached by motion pictures, because it more openly represented anxieties held by the dominant culture. This was the sexually powerful black male. He appears, if at all, as animal-like and criminal. Southern white America's fear that black males lusted after white women found its archetypal expression in *The Birth of a Nation* when Gus, a renegade soldier, pursues a young Southern girl to the edge of a cliff from which she flings herself, preferring death to a fate worse than the plot itself. Such events were understandably infrequent thereafter. Perhaps the closest variation takes place in *They Won't Forget* (1937). There a black janitor finds a murdered blonde student in a Southern classroom building. He is terrorized by police interrogation and nearly commits perjury in the courtroom out of fear for his safety.

World War II began to witness occasional appearances of sympathetic black characters, usually male, in dramatic stories. Several of these were war combat films in which an endangered military unit had its token black soldier along with a boy from Brooklyn, a tough sergeant, and a Pole from Pittsburg named Kowalski. Although they received relatively little distribution, the military filmed *The Negro Soldier* (1944) and *The Negro Sailor* (1945) to applaud (and to encourage) black contributions to the war effort. In *Home of the Brave* (1949), a psychologically debilitated black private is cured by an Army psychiatrist through reliving racial incidents that had triggered his crackup. *Home of the Brave* had originally been built around anti-Semitism, but at this juncture, Hollywood was undertaking a series of productions dealing with intolerance toward blacks. Others included *Lost Boundaries* (1949) about a black family who had passed for white in a New England town for twenty years, and *Pinky* (1949), which concerned a light-complexioned black girl who starts to pass, then changes her mind. The featured role was played by a white actress, Jeanne Crain. Freddi Washington was thought too old for the part. Ethel Waters played Granny, and Nina Mae McKinney was a tough, slum figure.

Henceforth, black roles expanded in conception, gradually embracing possibilities for courageous stands against racial injustice. To do this, an actor (parts were customarily male) first had to be impressively virtuous (Harry Belafonte, Sidney Poitier) and sometimes self-sacrificing; Poitier died for the sake of his white buddy in *Edge of the City* (1957) and in *The Defiant Ones* (1958). After passing through a perod of superhuman goodness (*Guess Who's Coming to Dinner* in 1967, *Lilies of the Field*, 1963), Poitier finally descended to levels of ordinary heroism in movies like *They Call Me MISTER Tibbs* (1970) and *Buck and the Preacher* (1972) with Belafonte.

Freed from stigmas of subservience, black actors in films of the seventies and eighties assumed characters that sometimes combined an exuberant sexuality with life styles bordering on the edge of illegality. These past two decades have also marked a period when the average age for movie attendance has fallen dramatically, so that characters like Shaft, a cynical black detective, and Super Fly, a Harlem cocaine dealer who finally leaves the business, are also calculatedly gauged to appeal to young audiences. Dedicated to "...all the Brothers and Sisters who had enough of the Man," *Sweet Sweetback's Baadasssss Song* (1971) took the rebellion all out. Sweetback (played by Melvin Van Peebles, who also wrote and directed) is a picaresque, sexually superhuman savior in a world peopled by malevolent whites and defeated blacks. The term "blaxploitation" came into use at about that time, describing this and similar films.

Where *Sweetback*, *Shaft* and *Super Fly* customarily operated out of urban settings, another view of black experience turned to rural environments, or if not the country, the kind of family life that found itself pressured and often torn apart by city dissonances. In such stories, a man's challenge is not so much to survive melodramatic dangers as it is to find strength enough to withstand, day to day, the indignities of ordinary existence. *Nothing But a Man* (1964) illustrates this motif especially well. *The Learning Tree* (1969) evokes farmland Kansas in the 1920s, where a young boy is slowly initiated into such truths of black life.

More often, though, tales such as these gave new options and opportunities to black actresses, usually as centerpieces holding firm against family stress. Adapted from a prize winning play, *A Raisin in the Sun* (1961) looks at a Chicago, working class family. On the father's death, they are paid a $10,000 life insurance policy, only to split asunder as each person considers how the money might resolve his or her frustrations. In *Sounder* (1979), a Louisiana sharecropper is consigned to a chain gang for stealing from a white man's smokehouse to feed his family. Facing awful poverty and terrible workloads to maintain the farm, the family survives because of the wife, played by Cicely Tyson. *The Autobiography of Miss Jane Pittman* (1974), a film for television, provided Tyson another opportunity to portray a woman equipped not only with enduring strength, but a kind of joyful resiliency as well.

By the time of Steven Spielberg's *The Color Purple* in 1986, serious and reasonable questions were raised about the film's faithful representation of its source book's values and intentions and about the accuracy of the actors' and actresses' renditions of their parts. But perhaps what was most significant was the fact that discussion took place in a forum where racism was the subject rather than the ammunition of the arguments. Blacks in film had moved a long distance from *Dancing Darkey Boy* and *Watermelon Eating Contest*, which is not to say that there wasn't some distance for both blacks and for films to go.

RECOMMENDED READING

Bogle, Donald. *Toms, Coons, Mulattoes, Mammies, & Bucks: an Interpretive History of Blacks in American Film.* New York: Viking, 1973.

Cripps, Thomas. *Slow Fade to Black: The Negro in American Film, 1900–1942.* New York: Oxford, 1977.

——. *Black Film as Genre.* Bloomington, IN; Indiana University Press, 1979.

Leab, Daniel. *From Sambo to Superspade: The Black Experience in Motion Pictures.* Boston: Houghton Mifflin, 1975.

Mapp, Edward. *Blacks in American Films: Today and Yesterday.* Metuchen, N.J.: Scarecrow, 1972.

Murray, James P. *To Find an Image: Black Films from Uncle Tom to Super Fly.* Indianapolis: Bobbs-Merrill, 1973.

29 *STAR WARS* AND *THE WIZARD OF OZ*: STRUCTURAL AND PSYCHOLOGICAL ANALYSIS OF POPULAR AMERICAN FANTASY FILMS*

CONRAD PHILLIP KOTTAK

This essay on *Star Wars* makes use of the ideas of the famous French anthropologist Claude Lévi-Strauss, one of the most important members of a school of thinkers known as structuralists. The structuralists are concerned, as their name suggests, with the way things are structured (myths, stories, kinships systems) and, in particular, with their most elementary components and the way they are organized.

A myth, for example, would be made up of a series of "mythemes" (elements) which can be combined in various ways to show us what a myth is really about — as contrasted with what happens in the story. Lévi-Strauss starts with the fact that human beings find meaning in the world by making binary oppositions. This is the most fundamental operation of the human mind according to many thinkers.

---

* From *Researching American Culture* by Conrad Kottak Copyright © 1982 by The University of Michigan. Reprinted by permission of The University of Michigan Press.

Computers work on a binary principle: off/on. And the human mind functions in a similar way, because, many linguists think, meaning is always relational. What does the term "rich" mean? Nothing, unless there is "poor." Thus the mind always searches out oppositions, for any topic, to make sense. As Ferdinand de Saussure, a famous linguist, said, "Concepts are purely differential and defined not by their positive content but negatively by their relations with the other terms of the system." To which he added, "the most precise characteristic" of concepts "is in being what the others are not." So we make sense of things by finding differences between them, and the most important of these differences is the polar opposition.

Just as these polar oppositions help us make sense of concepts, they also help us make sense of narratives such as stories and myths. What Lévi-Strauss argued (and I am simplifying things a bit) is that buried in narratives are sets of polar oppositions that can be elicited. These oppositions give the real meaning of the narrative — a meaning which is not obvious to us.

Myths also undergo processes of transformation in which the major elements switch from one pole to another. What Kottak argues in this essay is that "*Star Wars* is a systematic structural transformation of *The Wizard of Oz*." Not only does Kottak assert this to be true, he also offers persuasive evidence to support his contention. He then argues that *The Empire Strikes Back* is a reversal or negation of the original *Star Wars* story, and offers evidence to support this idea as well.

Kottak's essay helps us recognize the essentially mythic nature of *Star Wars* and why it achieved such immense popularity.

One of the main assumptions of anthropologists who study contemporary American culture is that techniques originally developed to analyze cultural features of small-scale societies can also be applied to industrial societies like our own. For example, the structural analysis that Claude Lévi-Strauss (1967) has applied to the myths of Native Americans and other nonindustrial populations can also be used with contemporary forms of narrative expression. People who live in small, unspecialized societies share a common fund of knowledge, acquired through enculturation. A rudimentary division of labor may, for example, assign the role of myth-teller to men, in which case expertise in myth will be shared by many or most men in that society. Or, knowledge of a culture's narratives may be widely shared among most adults.

Americans, too, share knowledge through our common enculturation. We learn national myths in elementary school; every child knows what kind of tree George Washington chopped down, and what he said when asked about his mischievous deed. But our most widely shared experiences with narratives come through the mass media, particularly television. The average American watches several hours each day. (The popularity of the microwave oven may be based as much on its resemblance to a television set as on quick cooking in homes where both spouses work. People can have the illusion that they are cooking in their TV.) Consequently, I have found that one of the most effective ways of teaching contemporary college students how to diagram kinship relationships is to use televised situation comedies to illustrate changes in family patterns. I contrast the nuclear families of the 1950s, as depicted on "Leave It to Beaver," "Ozzie and Harriet," and "Father Knows Best," with the more complex and blended families shown in more recent programs like "The Brady Bunch," "My Three Sons," "Soap," and "Dallas."

I also gather information on the enculturation that today's college student has experienced by asking a series of questions: How many have never been in a Roman Catholic church in the United States, in a Protestant church, in a Jewish temple? The number of students who respond positively to these questions is always much greater than those who have never eaten at McDonald's, or attended a baseball game, rock concert, or Walt Disney movie. Recently I found that all the students in a class of eighty had seen *The Wizard of Oz* (telecast annually for more than a decade) and all but one had seen *Star Wars*. This provided a basis for their general understanding of the following structural analysis of the two films.

Lévi-Strauss, pursuing the study of cultural universals, has argued that there are basic similarities in the way people think all over the world. There are, he contends, universal structures of the human mind or brain, and these show up in the products (including creative expression) of all known cultures. He asserts that people everywhere have a need to classify, to categorize their own experiences and the world around them, and that one of the most common ways of doing this is by binary opposition. Thus, things and qualities that in nature are continuous, that really differ in degree rather than in kind, are treated as discrete and opposite. For example, the continuum that runs from tall to short is dichotomized simply into "tall" and "short." Good and evil are similar polarizations of contrasts that are not actually so clear-cut.

Lévi-Strauss has applied his assumptions about classification and binary opposition to myths and folk tales, showing that these narratives are often made up of simple building blocks, elementary structures, or "mythemes." Examining the myths of different cultures, Lévi-Strauss shows that one tale can be converted into another through a series of simple operations; for example, converting the positive element of one myth into its negative, reversing the order of the elements, replacing a male hero with a female, and preserving or repeating certain key elements. As a result of such operations, two apparently dissimilar myths can be shown to be variations on a common structure, i.e., to be transformations of each other. One example is Lévi-Strauss's (1967) analysis of the "Cinderella" story, a widespread tale whose essential elements vary from one culture to its neighbor. (To understand that fairy tales have a series of different versions, think of the several endings of "The Three Little Pigs" and of "Little Red Riding Hood.") Eventually, after a sufficient number of reversals, oppositions, and negations as the tale is told, retold, and incorporated into the traditions of successive societies, "Cinderella" becomes "Ash Boy," with a series of simple contrasts related to the change in hero's gender. (For other examples of this, see Lévi-Strauss 1969; but see also Marvin Harris's [1979] important critique of the limitations of structural analysis.)

I will argue in this essay that *Star Wars* is a systematic structural transformation of *The Wizard of Oz*, even more obviously (to American natives) than "Ash Boy" is a transformation of "Cinderella." To round out the following analysis and extend it a bit farther, to *Star Wars's* sequel, *The Empire Strikes Back (TESB)*, I will also use techniques developed by neo-Freudian psychoanalyst Bruno Bettelheim.

In his book *The Uses of Enchantment: The Meaning and Importance of Fairy Tales*, Bettelheim (1975) urges parents to read or tell folk fairy tales to their children. He chides American parents and librarians for pushing children to read "realistic" stories, which often are dull, too complex, and psychologically empty for children. Folk fairy tales, in contrast, permit children to identify with heroes who win out in the end, offering confidence that no matter how bad things seem now, they will eventually improve. They offer reassurance that, though small and insignificant now, the child will eventually grow up and achieve independence from parents and siblings.

Related to Lévi-Strauss's focus on binary oppositions is Bettelheim's analysis of how fairy tales permit children to deal with their ambivalent feelings about their parents and siblings. Children both love and hate their parents. Bettelheim tells of one girl who, when scolded and yelled at by her mother, developed the fantasy that a Martian was temporarily inhabiting the mother's body, as an explanation for her change in mood. Fairy tales often split the good and bad aspects of the parent into separate figures of good or evil. Thus in "Cinderella," the mother is split in two, an evil stepmother and a fairy go(o)dmother. And Cinderella's two evil stepsisters disguise the child's hostile and rivalrous feelings toward his or her real siblings. A tale like "Cinderella" permits the child to deal, guiltlessly, with hostile feelings toward parents and siblings, since positive feelings are preserved in the idealized good figure.

According to Bettelheim, it doesn't matter much whether the hero is male or female, since children of both sexes can usually find psychological satisfaction of some sort from a fairy tale. However, male heroes typically slay dragons, giants, or monsters (representing the father) and free princesses from captivity, whereas female characters accomplish something and establish a home of their own.

The contributions of Lévi-Strauss and Bettelheim permit the following analysis of the visual fairy tales that contemporary Americans know best. I cannot say how many of these resemblances were part of a conscious design by *Star Wars's* writer and director George Lucas and how many were manifestations of a collective unconscious that Lucas shares with us through common enculturation.

The Wizard of Oz and Star Wars both begin in arid country, the first in Kansas, the second on the desert planet Tatooine (see Table 1). Star Wars changes The Wizard's female hero into a boy, Luke Skywalker. As in fairy tales, both heroes have short, common first names, and second names that describe their ambience and activity. Thus Luke, who travels aboard spaceships, is a Skywalker, while Dorothy Gale is swept off to Oz by a cyclone (a gale of wind). Dorothy leaves home with her dog Toto, who is being pursued by, and has managed to escape from, a woman who in Oz becomes the

Table I   STAR WARS AS A STRUCTURAL TRANSFORMATION OF THE WIZARD OF OZ

Star Wars	The Wizard of Oz
Male hero (Luke Skywalker)	Female hero (Dorothy Gale)
Arid Tatooine	Arid Kansas

Luke follows R2D2
    R2D2 flees Vader
	Dorothy follows Toto
	    Toto flees witch

Luke lives with uncle and aunt
    Primary relationship with uncle
    (same sex as hero)
    Strained, distant relationship with
    uncle
	Dorothy lives with uncle and aunt
	    Primary relationship with aunt
	    (same sex as hero)
	    Warm, close relationship with aunt

Tripartite division of same-sex parent
    2 parts good, 1 part bad father
    Good father dead at beginning
    Good father dead (?) at end
    Bad father survives
	Tripartite division of same-sex parent
	    2 parts bad, 1 part good mother
	    Bad mother dead at beginning
	    Bad mother dead at end
	    Good mother survives

Relationship with parent of opposite sex (Princess Leia Organa):
    Princess is unwilling captive
    Needle
    Princess is freed
	Relationship with parent of opposite sex (The Wizard of Oz):
	    Wizard makes impossible demands
	    Broomstick
	    Wizard turns out to be sham

Trio of companions:
    Han Solo, C3PO, Chewbacca
	Trio of companions:
	    Scarecrow, Tin Woodman,
	        Cowardly Lion

Minor characters:
    Jawas
    Sand People
    Stormtroopers
	Minor characters:
	    Munchkins
	    Apple Trees
	    Flying Monkeys

Settings:
    Death Star
    Verdant Tikal (rebel base)
	Settings:
	    Witch's castle
	    Emerald City

Conclusion:
    Luke uses magic to accomplish goal
        (destroy Death Star)
	Conclusion:
	    Dorothy uses magic to accomplish
	        goal (return to Kansas)

Wicked Witch of the West. Luke follows his own "Two-Two" (R2D2), who is fleeing Darth Vader, the witch's structural equivalent.

Dorothy and Luke both live with an uncle and aunt, but because of the gender change of the hero, the primary relationship is reversed and inverted. Thus Dorothy's relationship with her aunt is primary, warm, and loving, whereas Luke's relationship with his uncle, though primary, is strained and distant. Aunt and uncle are in the tales for the same reason. They represent home (the nuclear family of orientation), which children must eventually leave to make it on their own. Yet, as Bettelheim points out, disguising parents as uncle and aunt establishes social distance; the child can deal with the hero's separation (in *The Wizard of Oz*) or the aunt's and uncle's death (in *Star Wars*) more easily than with the death or separation of the real parents. Furthermore, this permits the child's strong feelings toward his or her real parents to be represented in different, more central characters.

Both films focus on the child's relationship with the parent of the same sex, dividing that parent into three parts. In *The Wizard*, the mother is split into two parts bad and one good: the Wicked Witch of the East, dead at the beginning of the movie; the Wicked Witch of the West, dead at the end; and Glinda, the goodmother, who survives. *Star Wars* reverses the proportion of good and bad, giving Luke a good father (his own), the Jedi knight who is dead at the film's beginning; another good father, Ben Kenobi, who is ambiguously dead when the movie ends; and a father figure of total evil. It is easy to note the phonetic resemblance of Darth Vader to "dark father." In a *New York Times* interview (May 18, 1980), just before the opening of *The Empire Strikes Back*, Lucas claimed that he chose "Darth Vader" because it sounded like both "dark father" and "deathwater." As the goodmother third survives *The Wizard of Oz*, the badfather third lives on after *Star Wars*, to strike back in the sequel.

The child's relationship with the parent of opposite sex is also represented in the two films. Dorothy's father figure is the Wizard of Oz, initially a terrifying figure, later proved to be a fake. Bettelheim notes that the typical fairy tale father is either disguised as a monster or giant, or else (when preserved as a human) is weak, distant, or ineffective. Children wonder why Cinderella's father permits her to be treated badly by her stepmother and siblings, why the father of Hansel and Gretel doesn't throw out his new wife instead of his children, and why Mr. White, Snow White's father, doesn't tell the queen she's too narcissistic. Dorothy counts on the wizard to save her, finds that he is posing seemingly impossible demands, achieves significantly on her own, and no longer relies on a father who offers no more than she herself possesses.

Luke's mother figure is Princess Leia Organa. As Bettelheim notes, early-Oedipal boys commonly fantasize their mothers to be unwilling captives of their fathers, and fairy tales frequently disguise mothers as princesses, whose freedom the boy-hero must obtain. In graphic Freudian imagery, Darth Vader threatens Princess Leia with a needle the size of the witch's broomstick. By the end of the film, Luke has freed Leia, vanquished Vader, and the princess seems destined to become Ms. Organa-Skywalker.

There are other striking parallels in the structures of the two films. Fairy-tale heroes are often accompanied on their adventures by secondary characters who personify virtues needed in a successful quest. Dorothy takes along wisdom (the Scarecrow), love (the Tin Woodman), and courage (the Cowardly Lion). *Star Wars* includes a structurally equivalent trio — Han Solo, C3PO, and Chewbacca — but their association with particular qualities is not as precise. The minor characters are also structurally parallel — Munchkins and Jawas, Apple Trees and Sand People, Flying Monkeys and Stormtroopers. And compare settings — the witch's castle and the Death Star, the Emerald City and the rebel base (filmed at Tikal, in verdant Guatemala). The endings are also parallel. Luke accomplishes his objective on his own, using the Force (Oceanian *mana*, magical power). Dorothy's aim is to return to Kansas; that she does, tapping her shoes together, drawing on the Force in her ruby slippers.

I have previously argued (Kottak 1978b) that these resemblances help explain *Star Wars*'s huge success. It is likely that all successful cultural products blend old and new, draw on familiar themes, rearrange them in novel ways, and thus win a lasting place in the imaginations of whatever culture creates or accepts them. *Star Wars* successfully used old cultural themes in novel ways, and it came along at an optimistic time, a time for heroes, in American culture. It drew on *The* American fairy tale, one that had been available in book form since the turn of the century. The movie version of *The Wizard of Oz* was not immediately successful when it was released in 1939, the same year as *Gone with the Wind*, which found a much larger immediate audience. *The Wizard*'s popularity had to await happier years, and annual telecasting that brings it into every home. Our familiarity with this narrative therefore comes more from television than from movies.

In 1980 *Star Wars*'s sequel, *TESB*, rivaled the success of the 1977 film. Was *TESB* a structural transformation of any previous work of American culture? I considered *Gone with the Wind* and *Casablanca*, two popular old films with stereotyped and memorable characters, but I found only minor parallels. I soon did discover the source of *TESB*'s structure in a previous film — *Star Wars* itself. In the case of *Star Wars*'s transformation of *The Wizard*, most of the structural contrasts were simply those that logically followed from the change from female to male hero. There were only a few structural inversions (two parts bad to two parts good, and goodmother versus badfather lives on). *TESB* transforms *Star Wars* differently, but also through a series of simple operations. Rather than the gender change, there is a partial shift in perspective from young hero to old villain, and a series of elements are converted into their opposites. (Note that being opposite or inverted is not the same as a gender change, since a male is not really the opposite of a female, though our culture sometimes considers them as such.) *TESB* is a negation, accomplished through a fairly consistent series of simple structural inversions of elements of the original. The trilogy awaits conclusion in the next film, to be, in dialectical terms, the negation of the negation, the synthesis of the thesis (*Star Wars*) and the antithesis (*TESB*).

But let us look at *TESB*. There are some important general oppositions. First, in *Star Wars* Luke was preoccupied with freeing the mother figure; here he is absorbed in relationships with father figures. Second, Darth Vader dominates the second film much as Luke dominated the first. Third, Vader becomes more human in *TESB* (for example, through a quick shot of his pink head as his helmet is lowered, and through his emotional invitation to his son to join him in ruling the galaxy). Luke simultaneously becomes less clearly good as he flirts with the dark side of the Force (killing Vader's image which turns out to have his face, and becoming partially bionic like his father). Note that Luke is shown upside down several times in *TESB*, symbolically suggesting the overall turnaround. That inversion (Table 2) is marked from the very beginning, the opening shot of a tall, spindly, dark, imperial robot landing on a cold, wet planet — the opposite of the *Star Wars* opening, in which a short, squat, light, rebel robot (R2D2) landed on a hot, dry planet. Luke is almost immediately hung up by an ice creature, as if to say at once that everything here is upside down. In *Star Wars* Luke saw an image of the mother figure that propelled him on his adventures. Here an image of Ben (an aspect of the father) serves the same function. In the first film Luke was gradually joined by a party of companions. Here they split up.

Yoda's inclusion offers structural balance to several elements of the *Star Wars* plot. As a dramatic presence he replaces Ben Kenobi. As an intelligent, alien, cartoonlike nonhuman, he substitutes for the aliens in the celebrated cantina scene of the first film. Most important, he fills the gap in the tripartite division of the father into two parts good and one bad when Darth Vader reveals himself to be Luke's real father, previously thought dead. In addition to his role as triple structural equivalent, Yoda is, in Lévi-Strauss's terms, a mediating figure par excellence, since he links Luke, Ben, and Darth Vader, having taught all three. He also links the positive and negative sides of the Force, which his students have used for good and for evil.

The two films proceed through a similar order of events, which are often simple inversions of the original structure (e.g., good father becomes bad father, dead father becomes live father). Occasionally the parallel parts of the plots are similar in content. Thus, in *Star Wars* the Millenium Falcon emerged from hyperspace amid the rock fragments of Alderan's destruction, whereas in *TESB*, unable to enter hyperspace (an inversion), the Falcon must dodge other rocks — asteroids. And there are some structural equivalents. The giant worm that swallows the Falcon in *TESB* replaces the garbage snake-monster of *Star Wars*. The heroes eventually converge on the City in the Clouds, which takes the place of the Death Star. They encounter Lando Calrissian, who eventually substitutes for Han Solo.

Many of the most striking oppositions come at the end. For example, in *Star Wars* Han's premature departure was resolved; he returned to help Luke in the final battle. But here his departure is unresolved; he provides no

Table 2   *THE EMPIRE STRIKES BACK (TESB)* AS A STRUCTURAL NEGATION OF *STAR WARS*

The Empire Strikes Back	Star Wars
Tall, spindly, dark imperial robot lands on cold, wet planet	Short, squat, light rebel robot lands on hot, dry planet
Image of Ben starts Luke on adventures	Image of Leia starts Luke on adventures
Luke separates from companions	Luke is joined by companions
Vader gradually disposes of assistants	Luke gradually acquires assistants
Yoda replaces...	Ben, as dramatic presence
Yoda replaces...	Cantina scene, as nonhuman
Yoda replaces... (real father alive and evil)	Luke's dead good father (real father dead and good)
Luke experiences dark side of The Force	Luke experiments with good side of The Force
No hyperspace drive — rocks	Out of hyperspace — rocks
Giant worm	Garbage snake
City in clouds	Death Star
Han departs prematurely; doesn't return	Han departs prematurely; returns
Lando Calrissian replaces...	Han Solo
Luke's real father alive and evil (told late in film)	Luke's real father dead and good (told early in film)
Young, good figure battles evil, gives up; undergoes (emotional) transformation	Old, good figure battles evil, gives up; undergoes (spiritual) transformation
Luke rejects bad father's life	Luke rejects good father's death
Bad father deprives Luke of light saber	Good father gives Luke light saber
Leia saves Luke	Luke saves Leia
Luke indentifies with bad father (telepathically and bionically)	Luke indentifies with good father (telepathically and spiritually)
Vader wins	Luke wins
Luke (temporarily defeated) leaves in ship	Vader (temporarily defeated) leaves in ship
Companions split	Companions assemble
Vader isolated	Luke social

support for Luke's climactic battle. In *Star Wars*, the old good figure (Ben) battled evil, gave up, but underwent a transformation, to become spirit; here the young good figure (Luke) battles evil, gives up, and undergoes an emotional transformation by confronting his parentage. After *Star Wars*'s duel, Luke yelled "No!" rejecting the good father's death. Here he yells

"No!" rejecting the bad father's life. In *Star Wars* Ben presented Luke with a light saber (symbolic identification with the father), but here Vader slashes off Luke's saber, along with his hand. In *Star Wars* Luke used the Force to destroy evil; here he uses the Force to call Leia. He saved her in *Star Wars*; now she saves him.

In *Star Wars* Luke partially mastered the good side of the Force and became spiritually like the goodfather. In *TESB* Luke flirts with the dark side of the Force and by the film's end has become mechanically like his bionic badfather. There he drew on Ben's spiritual presence and telepathic contact to destroy the Death Star; here he is telepathically touched by the darkfather. At the end of *Star Wars* Vader left in a ship; here Luke does. There the companions came together; here they split up.

Star Wars concluded with Luke's triumph against seemingly impossible odds. Here he doesn't win; he simply escapes, like Vader in the original, to strike back in the next episode. At the end of *Star Wars* Luke Skywalker and the loyal companions he had gradually assembled during the film celebrated together. But by the end of *TESB*, Darth Vader has systematically disposed of his three assistants, admirals who have failed him in reaching his objectives. Vader's isolation and alienation from other people stands in sharp contrast to Luke's identity as a social person. Thus, at the end of *TESB* Vader stands alone, without a son, as Luke was without a father at the beginning of *Star Wars*. My prediction for the trilogy's conclusion, for the negation of the negation: both Luke and Vader will be social and together, reunited as reformed Jedi and equal son.

Many other elements could be mentioned to demonstrate that *Star Wars* and *TESB* are structural transformations of one another, but I leave that to other analysts. My intent here has been to use three extremely popular products of the electronic mass media to show that techniques developed to analyze the expressive forms of simpler societies can also be applied to our own. Use of structural analysis and of Bettelheim's research on the nature of fairy tales and their psychological significance helps uncover the enduring cultural meaning of these films. It also confirms Lévi-Strauss's finding, from the myths of non-Western societies, that narratives that on the surface seem very different may share a deeper structure that is not very different at all. *Star Wars* used a gender contrast, structural equivalents, and a few inversions to transform *The Wizard of Oz*. *TESB* uses inversion, structural equivalents, and reversal of outcome to transform *Star Wars*.

Consider this final structural twist, a last major similarity between the *Star Wars* films and *Oz*. The literary sequel to *The Wizard of Oz*, *The Land of Oz*, also patterned itself on the structure of the original, using such simple operations as a gender contrast and substitution of structural equivalents to accomplish the transformation. Instead of Dorothy, *The Land of Oz* has a male hero, Tip. A sawhorse replaces Toto, and a trio composed of Pumpkinhead, Wogglebug, and sofa-creature stand in for Dorothy's three companions. However, in one of the most psychologically curious outcomes in children's literature, the hero doesn't save the princess, but turns into a princess himself (into Ozma, the "girlish" ruler of Oz). That transformation probably explains why the *Oz* books never underwent the kind of movie serialization that the *Star Wars* story is undergoing. It shows as well that even similar structures can't produce success when, in content, fundamental cultural assumptions are violated. Boys, after all, should turn not into girls, but into men.

BIBLIOGRAPHY

Bettelheim, Bruno. *The Uses of Enchantment: The Meaning and The Importance of Fairy Tales*. New York: Alfred A Knopf, 1975.

Harris, Marvin. *Cultural Materialism: The Struggle for a Science of Culture*. New York: Random House, 1979.

Lévi-Strauss, Claude. *Structural Anthropology*. C. Jocobson and B. G. Schoepf, transl. Garden City, N.Y.: Doubleday, 1967.

30   PICTURE WINDOWS*
RICHARD ZAKS

How is it that many films that "bomb" at the box office in America still make money? The answer is, our author tells us, that films, like cats, have more than one life. Naturally, film producers love to have success at the box office, but a goodly number of films are not well received and don't do very well with the original movie-house audiences to which they are directed. If the reviews are bad and word-of-mouth (what people tell their friends about a given film) is also bad, then generally speaking films don't make money in theatres.

But the box-office is just the beginning, and most film producers are aware that theatre revenues may not be very good. As Zaks writes, "Nothing has been more dramatic than the decline of the local movie theatre — the first window through which all films pass." The second window is home video, and the statistics here are incredible. "In 1980, studios collected $20 million from worldwide sales of videocassettes; in 1985, nearly $2 billion — more than any other window except theatrical." As more and more people purchase VCRs, the revenues from sales and rentals of videocassettes will grow.

Another window is pay-per-view cable broadcasting. This area has not

---

* Copyright © 1986, *CHANNELS* Magazine. Reprinted with permission.

developed greatly yet, but its potential is enormous and it is likely, Zaks says, that film producers will put their films on pay-per-view before releasing them on videocassettes.

Perhaps the most common outlet for films is television. Pay Cable television uses a great many films, but the development of VCRs is now throwing a shadow on that window. The television networks have a need for "product," but movie producers are reluctant, in many cases, to put their films on television since that kills box-office draw. Now the networks are making their own made-for-television movies and doing very well with them.

There are now 225 independent stations and they are all desperate for "product." So syndication has become one more window by which film producers churn revenue out of their films. These independent stations generally broadcast old television programs and films, since they seldom have the capacity to produce very much in the way of programming.

We must also remember that Hollywood movies are shown all over the world, so we must factor international sales into our figures. Given all of these windows, it is easy to understand why films make money, even if they are not box-office successes. The major actor in the film business is now the videocassette; it is reshaping the film business not only in America, but all over the world.

In Hollywood, the kingdom of fantasy, it's not just sunshine that pours through windows — it's money. Vast amounts of it. Windows are opportunities. When NASA first used the term "window," it referred to the period during which a rocket could successfully blast off. Hollywood appropriated the jargon to refer to something much more mundane: a limited exposure in a given medium.

In the early 1970s, there were only a few windows. After making its debut in the theaters, a film that did well might be re-released some months later. By the second year of its life it would move into the "broadcast window." Networks paid top dollar for movies because popular pictures paid for themselves in higher ratings. Three or four years later the final rite of passage began — through the syndication window, which allowed for repeated screenings on independent television stations.

Those days are gone. Thanks to cable television and especially the videocassette recorder, a well-launched movie no longer flies straight out of the theaters and onto the networks. Instead, the trajectory takes it first on a detour through a multitude of new and immensely profitable windows that have opened in the 1980s. The most important are home video, pay-per-view, and pay cable. Together, they have not only transformed the viewing habits of audiences, but restructured the way movies make money.

Nothing has been more dramatic than the decline of the local movie theater — the first window through which all films pass. In 1978, according to investment bankers Goldman Sachs & Company, the theatrical window supplied 80 percent of a film's total earnings; by 1985, the box office take had plunged to 43 percent, an all-time low.

Even that was a struggle. Two years ago, studios typically released their movies to 900 theaters across the country. But when revenues declined, they adopted a new strategy, "bursting," under which films are distributed to more theaters (1,200) for shorter amounts of time. With marketing costs for a new film having jumped from $4 million to nearly $10 million since 1978, studios want to assure a high return. This sounds logical, only it isn't working: theaters sold 12 percent fewer tickets in 1985 than they did in 1984. One consequence of this saturation exposure has been the slow strangulation of second-run and drive-in theaters.

Nonetheless, when a movie does score, it can still score big (thanks largely to steady increases in the average price of a ticket): *Beverly Hills Cop*, for example, took in $232 million at the box office. But successes like this are increasingly rare, and a major culprit is home video.

The statistics are incontrovertible: In 1980, studios collected $20 million from worldwide sales of videocassettes; in 1985, nearly $2 billion — more than any other window except theatrical. The first figure represented one percent of a movie's total revenue; the latter, 34 percent.

Movies haven't lost their appeal, they've simply sailed through the home video window and into the 27 million homes with videocassette recorders. Films that perform poorly in the theaters enter the home video market as soon as three months after their release, but most are delayed at least six months. Big hits can take a year or more. A few, like *E.T.*, may never arrive at all.

Steven Spielberg's reluctance to release *E.T.* on videocassettes is one response to the central paradox of the home video window: Once a movie passes through this portal, the distributor cannot retrieve it. Purchasers of cassettes won't give them back. This reduces potential revenues from other windows, and makes theatrical re-release (once a source of great profits for companies like Disney, which dusted off its classic hits every seven years) almost impossible.

Spielberg's plans for *E.T.* are unknown. But Disney has diverged from its founder's policy of hoarding titles for theatrical re-release. The company's new management is rushing its vast film library into home video, aiming to sell as many cassettes as possible before putting the titles into syndication.

Although the home video window has grown enormously over the past few years, it is likely to face increasing competition in the future. The seeds of this threat lie in the "First Sale" Doctrine, under which studios can only collect a fee when they sell a cassette. Many of the sales are to stores, which rent tapes to customers for a small fee. Studios see none of these revenues. Goldman Sachs estimates that 90 percent of all videocassette transactions are rentals rather than purchases, and predicts that this year, for the first time, people will spend more on videocassette rentals than they do at the box office — meaning that studios will get less and less of the money people spend on movies. As a result, the view through the pay-per-view window is looking brighter than ever before — at least from Hollywood's vantage.

Showtime launched Viewer's Choice, a pay-per-view service, in November 1985, narrowly beating Request Television's competing PPV system. Subscribers to Viewer's Choice pay $4 or $5 to watch a movie, which is available to them the same day it is released to the videocassette market. When it started, the service reached 140,000 cable subscribers; by mid-1986, it should have about 500,000 signed up.

The growth of pay-per-view has until recently been blocked by several obstacles: First, the failure to get movies before they pass through the home video window. Although most titles are released simultaneously in the home video and PPV windows, only Columbia, of all the studios, actually preempts home video by turning first to PPV. Second, only a limited number of homes are reached by pay-per-view. At the end of 1985, only eight million homes had addressable converters, which enable cable subscribers to receive and pay for programs.

These problems are likely to be resolved, because PPV offers studios something they don't get from videocassette rentals: a share of the take (as high as 50 percent). Once enough homes (around 20 million) receive PPV, the film industry will increasingly seek profits from this window before putting its films into home video.

Responding to this prospect, the nation's largest video store chain, National Video, has voluntarily agreed to forsake the protection of the First Sale Doctrine. Under an experimental arrangement called pay-per-transaction, studios are supplying tapes to ten National Video stores at $6 apiece (enough to serve all customers who want to rent hit movies as soon as they're released); the stores will split rental revenues 50-50 with the studios.

As recently as 1983, pay cable — especially HBO — seemed on the verge of devouring Hollywood. The industry's overall revenues had increased elevenfold since 1978, when pay cable accounted for just 2 percent of a movie's total take. By 1983, the share of revenues from pay services had jumped to 12 percent, and HBO was virtually dictating what it would pay for Hollywood's movies.

Most films enter pay cable six months after home video and stay there for twelve to eighteen months (during that time they can only be shown a total of fifteen to eighteen days). But in the past few years, the shutters on this window have begun to close. "If the studios are trying to retain value," complains Steve Scheffer, executive vice president of film programming at HBO, "they're certainly skinning the movie cat too many times."

Translation: films are passing through too many other windows before they get to Scheffer's. By the time movies reach pay cable, many of the people who used to watch them on HBO, Showtime, or The Movie Channel have already rented the tape. As a result, the pay services are having trouble signing up new subscribers, and their share of movie's total revenue is less now than it was in 1983. Goldman Sachs expects revenues to decline 4 percent in 1986.

Not long ago, when the networks were buying almost any film produced by the major studios, every night was a night at the movies on broadcast television. No more. In 1979–80, NBC showed thirty-five theatrical films; in 1984–85, it aired only thirteen. Since 1978, the network window's share of revenues has fallen dramatically. The network window (which allows movies to be shown twice in three years or three times in four years) does not open until two and a half years after theatrical debut.

Instead of showing the studios' overexposed movies, the networks are commissioning more and more of their own. CBS plans to air fifty made-for-television movies this year. These cost only $2 million each, and tend to get better ratings than rerun movies. Since the networks often retain distribution rights to the films they finance, they can get further profits from other windows, such as pay television and the international marketplace.

With the network window all but closed, studios are looking eagerly toward the one that has taken its place: syndication.

This market is booming: The number of independent stations has soared from less than 100 in 1978 to 225 this year. And they all need "product." Increasingly, they're buying theatrical film packages from studios.

"In syndication, you don't talk about runs," says Michael Gerber, senior vice president of Viacom International, which has accumulated 1,000 films for syndication. "I get unlimited usage; it's mine for twenty-five years." Films that don't go to the networks reach Gerber two and a half years after their release; those that do arrive an additional three or four years later.

The pick of Hollywood's litter sometimes enters a second-pay window after airing on broadcast television or in first-run syndication. This period lasts for six months and includes eight exhibition days, according to Showtime/The Movie Channel. After leaving this window, films go back into syndication.

In the risky movie business, where the cost of making and marketing films has tripled since 1978 and profitable ventures are an exception, studios need profits from every possible window. Yet for every new window that opens, another one shuts: just as pay television once reduced the value of the network window, home video is now hurting both the pay and the theatrical windows. The greater the number of windows, the more fiercely they will all compete.

RECORDING

The phonograph evolved out of Thomas A. Edison's "talking machine," which was patented in 1877. Edison thought, originally, that this machine would be used only for business purposes. It took more than a decade for the device to develop into the modern phonograph — the first ones were sold in the 1930s and were, as you might imagine, very primitive. Since then, phonographs have evolved a great deal and it is now possible to purchase audio systems that cost thousands of dollars.

The most advanced accessible technology for recording music is the compact disc, a very popular and increasingly dominant form of recording. There are criticisms that have been made of the sound quality of compact disks and I have provided an article in which the author tests these criticisms by means of ingenious comparisons he makes of compact disks and long playing records.

Another essay deals with the work of Laurie Anderson, her fascinating song "O Superman," and the whole phenomenon of what is called "performance art." It is difficult to define "performance art." Many artists have turned their attention away from creating objects (painting, sculptures, installations, etc.) to giving performances. Anything goes with this genre; it isn't so much new as newly popular and some of it is pretty wild. Anderson is one of the most important of the performance artists and has become quite popular (even appearing on television from time to time). Her work is often difficult and offbeat, but it has a curious appeal to it, and she has an authentic style.

I have included two essays on the rock world and its use of sex and violence...especially as manifested on MTV. The first essay quotes a psychologist and several psychiatrists who have very negative opinions about the impact rock music has on young people; especially Music Television. Joyce Brothers, the psychologist, suggests that young people "have not fused the idea of love and sex, so when you teach them that violence and sex are related, it is extremely dangerous for their future behavior." And psychiatrist Thomas Radecki argues that "the message is that violence is normal and OK, that hostile sexual relations between men and women are common and acceptable, that heroes actively engage in torture and murder of others for fun."

I also have an article on "The Battle of the Sexes on MTV" which deals, in great detail, with the way MTV portrays women and with the way it degrades them. This article, written by a film critic, examines a number of music videos. It also deals with the fact that MTV is really a form of advertising; the videos are, in actuality, commercials for rock bands.

These points have relevance to an analysis made by a political scientist, Andrew Hacker, in an essay in the *New York Times Book Review*. He says, "If there is anything that shapes and expresses the current consciousness of young people, it is the music that looms so large in their lives from a very early age. When we examine rock or its sundry variations, we find that the music's message is implicitly subversive, invoking a dissociation from adult society. This is not to say that they think in revolutionary terms, simply that there is a lot of disaffection out there. A Marxist analysis might view these young people as constituting a class without an economic role apart from consumption. This would explain their alienation and their search for sensual gratification." (May 8, 1983)

Let me quote one other person who deals with the power of music — the philosopher Plato. He writes, in *The Republic*, "...musical training is a more potent instrument than any other, because rhythm and harmony find their way into the inward places of the soul, on which they mightily fasten, imparting grace, and make the soul of him who is rightly educated graceful, or of him who is ill-educated ungraceful."

What is important, says Plato, is the rhythm and harmony, not the lyrics. We might question that assertion when we consider contemporary rock lyrics — some of which range between being uncouth and being scandalous. When we are dealing with MTV, of course, we are dealing with the translation of lyrics into narratives, and must consider the power of images as they are wedded to music — a very potent combination. One thing is certain — records are a big business and a means by which young people often "define" themselves. And MTV is a new genre that deserves to be taken very seriously. Plato would no doubt have been shocked at the kind of "education" MTV provides — with good reason, too, many would say.

31 VIOLENCE, SEX FLARE IN ROCK WORLD*

BARBARA JAEGER

What signficance does rock and roll have in the lives of the people who listen to it so much of the time? Is it merely some kind of a noisy background to the lives of young people (and a good way for them to "bug" their parents) or or does it play a more important role in shaping their attitudes toward life, politics — and, in particular, sex?

There seems to be good evidence that as people get older their tastes change and the young people who are so crazy for rock and roll find themselves listening to much blander kinds of music when they reach their thirties and forties. If this is correct, being crazy about rock and roll is something young people do at a particular stage in their development. The question is, does rock and roll have a long-range impact on those who listen to it (and watch it on MTV)?

The author of the article that follows is quite negative about the rock music/MTV phenomenon. Here are a few quotes from her essay that set the tone:

> Every day on cable television's Music Television (MTV), children as young as 5 regularly watch women in chains and people being tortured and shot.

She quotes some promotional material from an album by Motley Crue:

> "We're the American youth. And youth is about sex, drugs, pizza, and more sex. We're intellectuals on a crotch level."

She quotes Vince Neil, the lead singer of this group, discussing its erotic encounters with groupies:

> "We like the fat ones best...because they'll do anything."

What has happened, suggests the author, is that rock and roll, which always has been "a counterculture art form, emphasizing sex and rebellion against authority...has turned cruel and vicious and, possibly, dangerous."

She cites a number of psychiatrists who have rather negative things to say about what this music teaches young people about life, and, in particular, sexuality. Is rock and roll merely a kind of theatre, a kind of absurdist entertainment, or is it, instead (or also), a form of instruction about life and sex? And even if young people consider rock a bit of a joke, is it not possible that they still internalize (that is, without being aware of it, make it part of them) its values and perspectives and

---

* Reprinted with permission from *The Record* (1984) Hackensack, N.J. 07602.

are affected by it in profound and destructive ways? These matters trouble educators, politicians, and parents.

On a recent Saturday night in Passaic, N.J., rock star Billy Idol stood at the edge of the Capitol Theater stage and encouraged two young girls to fondle him. A couple of weeks before, at the Brendan Byrne Arena in East Rutherford, Vince Neil, lead singer of the heavy-metal group, Motley Crue, peppered his between-song patter with sexual vulgarities and a description of the group's erotic encounters with groupies. ("We like the fat ones the best," boasted Neil, "because they'll do anything.") Many of the 13,000 fans in the audience were no more than 11 or 12 years old, and had been ferried to and from the arena by their parents.

Every day on cable television's Music Television (MTV), children as young as 5 regularly watch women in chains and people being tortured and shot.

Rock 'n' roll has always been a counterculture art form, emphasizing sex and rebellion against authority. Recently, what had been merely suggestive has turned cruel and vicious and, possibly, dangerous.

"Teenagers have not fused the idea of love and sex," says psychologist and nationally syndicated columnist Dr. Joyce Brothers, "so when you teach them that violence and sex are related, it's extremely dangerous for their future behavior."

That the music industry sees sex and violence as a marketable commodity is evidenced by a recent press release sent to pop music writers by Elektra-Asylum Records. The promotional material described the latest album from Motley Crue as "dripping with impure and adulterated lust."

The release began by quoting the group's bass player, Nikki Sixx: "We're the American youth. And youth is about sex, drugs, pizza and more sex. We're intellectuals on a crotch level."

Also detailed in the four-page release was the band's run-in with Canadian customs officals, who confiscated "a herdful of black studded leather, a metal shop's worth of chains and spikes, and a handful of hard-core porno magazines."

The executives at Elektra-Asylum, a division of Warner Communications, refused to comment on the band or why the company would publicize the group in this manner.

Motley Crue is by no means an exception.

At Idol's Passaic performance, the 28-year-old British rocker wore tight, black leather pants slung low on the hips, a sleeveless black and red shirt that looked as if it went through a paper shredder, a studded black leather gauntlet, and an Iron Cross.

His costume was tame compared with his banter and mannerisms. With an arrogant sneer, Idol taunted a young girl trying to climb up on the stage.

"Just try to get those big breasts up here," he shouted. After introducing Judi Dozier, his female keyboard player, Idol, in a lewd aside, alluded to her sexual availability.

When his fist wasn't raised in the air, it was groping his crotch. At one point, he writhed on the floor, a microphone shoved down the front of his pants, while two girls — who looked no older than 16 — bent over him.

These kinds of performances are no longer restricted to concert halls and theaters. They are now being piped into homes daily.

"Kids today are media kids in the truest sense of the word," says disc jockey, Pete Fornatale, a 15-year veteran at New York rock radio station WNEW-FM. "They can't remember a day in their lives without television. Because of the seductiveness of the tube, in the same way that I view 'Sesame Street' to be seductive in a positive way, I view some of the music videos in a negative way. One is teaching them their ABC's and one, two, threes and the other is teaching them to bring knives to concerts and to defile as many women as they can in the shortest time possible.

"Kids are being exposed to the grossest kind of behavior as if it were acceptable. If it can be done in public, if it can come into your living room via the television set, the message is that it is OK...it's not OK."

MTV, the 24-hour rock music channel, has come under heavy fire by such groups as Women Against Pornography (WAP) and the National Coalition on Television Violence (NCTV). In a recent report, the NCTV said more than half of the videos shown on MTV feature violence, or strongly suggest violence.

Among the videos cited by the NCTV are Michael Jackson's *Thriller*: "features a very appealing young hero having fun terrorizing his girlfriend with horror violence"; the Rolling Stones' "Undercover of the Night": "features intense automatic weapons violence...including a violent lawless execution"; and Idol's *Dancing with Myself*; "filmed by the producer of *The Texas Chainsaw Massacre*, has a naked woman struggling in chains behind a translucent sheet."

Says Dr. Thomas Radecki, NCTV chairman and a psychiatrist on the staff of the University of Illinois School of Medicine: "The message is that violence is normal and OK, that hostile sexual relations between men and women are common and acceptable, that heroes actively engage in torture and murder of others for fun."

Fornatale, the father of three sons, ages 4, 8, and 12, agrees. "What disturbs me about the state of current music video is that I wouldn't want my kids to think or to get their attitudes about women, about sexuality, or about violence from the content of a large percent of these videos." He worries that they are attractively done and often sophisticated, while their values are worthless or, worse, dangerous.

In a statement, MTV replied: "MTV is not pro-violent and we're not advocating violence. And at this point in time, it's not an issue we're willing to debate in the press."

In fairness to the cable channel, its management has rejected videos for violence and nudity — a scene from the Rolling Stones' *She Was Hot* was deemed as going "beyond the bounds of good taste," an edited version is now airing — and MTV has pulled other videos following a public outcry — Van Halen's *(Oh) Pretty Woman*, which featured, among other things, bondage and fondling.

Evelina Kane, a member of WAP, says the most disturbing aspect of rock videos is the amount of violence directed toward women.

"The message of most videos is about sex and sex roles and the perpetuation of the myth of men as active and women as passive," Kane says. "With the prominence of scanty costumes and the dominance of men, what's being reintroduced is the idea of women as either good girls or whores."

Idol disagrees. According to his publicist, Ellen Golden, Idol says critics of his videos are "missing their points." He says the theme of *Dancing With Myself* is the struggle for freedom and the chained woman represents Oktobriana, a symbol of the struggle for liberation in the Russian Revolution — on his left arm, Idol sports a tattoo of Oktobriana. And in *White Wedding*, when he jams a wedding band on his bride's finger, drawing blood in the process, Idol says, he is illustrating men's cruelty to women.

Nevertheless, violence and sex are prevalent — and explicit — in many of today's rock lyrics. In "Dance with Me," the Lords of the New Church sing "Let's dance little stranger/Show me secret sins/Love can be like bondage/Seduce me once again…The way I wanna love you/Well, it could be against the law."

Kiss' latest album is "Lick it Up." In addition to the title track, it includes such songs as "Not for the Innocent," "Young and Wasted," and "Gimme More" ("Like a dog to a bone, make you sweat make you moan/Love is sweet so insane, come on lick my candy cane").

Album covers routinely feature women in bondage ("Vices" by Waysted depicts a woman in handcuffs and chains), bizarre creatures (Ozzy Osbourne as a werewolf on "Bark at the Moon"), and violence (the Scorpions' "Blackout" shows a man in a straitjacket with forks stuck in his eyes).

The names of some groups — particularly those of punk rock bands — are just as controversial. Among the current crop are the Dead Kennedys, Alien Sex Fiend, 3 Teens Kill 4, and Woman Haters.

The Stones were also the target of a demonstration and a national press conference staged by a group of Southern California women because of a billboard advertising the album "Black and Blue." The ad featured a woman in chains with bruises on her face and legs, and the caption read, "I'm black and blue from the Rolling Stones…and I love it."

While the billboard was removed, the Stones have chosen not to address the latest criticism. An assistant to Paul Wasserman, the Stones' publicist, says the group has no comment regarding its video "Undercover of the Night."

"What young people are seeing and hearing is a distortion of what life is all about," sums up Dr. Gladys Halvorsen, a Tenafly, N.J., child and adolescent psychiatrist. "And this distortion can have damaging effects. At this impressionable age, young people need strong role models and they're not getting them."

32   THE BATTLE OF THE SEXES ON MTV *

MARSHA KINDER

The essay that follows is the second half of a long essay by Marsha Kinder titled "Phallic Film and the Boob Tube: The Power of Gender Identification in Cinema, Television and Music Video." The essay focuses upon sexuality in the media and the way women are portrayed as objects (and men are shown as subjects). This portrayal, Kinder argues, both deprives women of their humanity and deludes men into thinking they are "naturally empowered by their gender."

In the portion of the essay that I have used, Kinder suggests that it is on television that the "decisive battle" over gender identification will be played out, and the most suitable arena for analyzing this phenomenon is MTV — Music Television. She makes a number of interesting points about MTV and television:

1. It can be argued that commercials are the most important part of television and the actual programming is of secondary signficance. (This argument has been made by a film scholar, Nick Browne.)
2. The programs and the commercials form a "supertext" that must be considered when analyzing television.
3. MTV is one big commercial and erases the illusionary boundaries between programs and commercials.
4. The stylistic conventions of advertising (in particular the commercial) dominate MTV. It uses the techniques found in commercials, which explains why the videos look so much like commercials. The term scholars use for works that borrow from (or are affected by) other works is "intertextuality."
5. This intertextuality has radical implications. It suggests that individualism (associated with conservative political and social philosophies) is simplistic. The argument would go as follows: just as all works are made up or affected by other works, so are individuals part of something greater than themselves and the notion that individuals are "self-made" is an illusion. Every work of art is

---

* Reprinted with permission of ONETWOTHREEFOUR Magazine and the author (1987). This essay was adapted by the author for this volume.

related to every other work of art and every person is connected to (and in a sense responsible for) everyone else.
6. MTV has "coopted" the radical potentiality of intertextuality, which it uses for its own purposes.

The essay then discusses a number of rock videos in terms of these and related issues. It is a very "high-level" essay and some of the terminology used is difficult, but it is worth the effort because of the value of the insights.

Television began to challenge cinema during the post-war era of the late forties and fifties when American women fresh from the factories were forced back into the home where they would become the daytime audience for soap operas and game shows. Perhaps this historic dimension helps explain TV's metaphoric gender identification as female, particularly in contrast to the earlier medium of cinema, which is usually discussed in phallocentric terms.

Like Eve being made out of Adam's rib, television is seen as derivative of and subordinate to the cinema, thus deserving a subordinate metaphor — a less potent part. Yet television has considerable powers, even if they have been misused. Many TV historians assume it may be less capable than cinema of reaching artistic or intellectual heights, yet it offers more seductive and debilitating pleasures. In Melanie Klein's terms, it has been primarily perceived as "the bad object," "the bad breast" — an idea that is carried in the popular phrase "the boob tube." This pun implies that TV is a technology that is both female and stupid: it's female because it's stupid, and it's stupid because it's female.

Beverle Houston has thus far offered the most powerful explanation of TV's metaphorical identification with the female breast.

> In its endless flow of text, it suggests the first flow of nourishment in and from the mother's body, evoking a moment when the emerging sexual drive is still closely linked to — propped on — the life-and-death urgency of the feeding instinct....It is no accident that the main textbook in American television studies is called *The Tube of Plenty*."[1]

Television's endless flow is not limited metaphorically to the mother's breast, but can also be extended more generally to female sexuality with its multi-climaxes, particularly when contrasted with the big-bang structure of male sexuality. While the masculine structure is analogous to the single dramatic climax of the well-made play and film, the endless female flow is the ideal narrative model for women's shows like soap opera as well as for most television programming.[2]

Television's metaphoric identification with female sexuality can also center on vaginal receptivity. Once you own a TV set, you identify with the equipment, for you, too, become the basic receiver, the passive consumer who is so hotly pursued by the competing suitors — advertisers, stations, and stars — who boldly express their desire in direct address and who keep reminding you of what you lack. You, in turn, are trained to desire everything television has to offer — not only the goods being advertised, but all the latest TV hardware to compensate for your sense of inadequacy and loss. As in the automotive industry, obsolescence and rapid technological improvement are made to seem inevitable. The steady stream of innovations that define technological progress distract our attention from the steady state of ideology they carry, which limits rather than extends our choices and pushes us deeper into the role of passive consumer.

Satellite technology has now extended this receptivity to cosmic proportions. We now have the Super Dish capable of absorbing the world — and of reinforcing TV's metaphorical identification with females. In the most remote villages of India, millions of Third World spectators are receiving government messages and American soaps via INSAT, an Indian satellite that was launched to achieve national unity (probably at the expense of cultural diversity) and that has been described as the prime political legacy of the matriarchal Indira Ghandi.

The increased receptivity of the TV spectator need not be seen totally in negative terms, though this has been the prevailing tendency in the discourse on television, partly because in Western culture receptivity is associated perjoratively with passivity and weakness — so-called feminine traits. In a quite different context, Wilhelm Reich tried to reclaim vaginal receptivity as a highly positive value, associated with flexibility and strength, and providing an alternative resource for human progress and the social formation of human subjectivity. As Juliet Mitchell explains in *Psychoanalysis and Feminism*:

> "For Reich vaginal receptivity came possibly to represent a meeting of the self and the world in universal love; he postulated that it was a new and higher stage on the evolutionary road from beasthood to godhead. In women's sexuality perhaps mankind would at last rejoin the natural."[3]

Yet underlying this optimism we still find the essentialist metaphorical identification of woman with nature and man with machines — only their position and values have been reversed on the evolutionary scale.

A CHANGE OF SEX FOR THE TUBE?

Now in the eighties when television has become the dominant mass medium, usurping the position formerly held by phallocentric cinema, the question is: will TV retain its gender identification with the female, the so-called subordinate sex, or will it have to undergo a sex change? The seventies saw the rise of women's liberation, so the timing was right for the rise of television; but the 1980s brought a backlash and the false media construct of "post-feminism," and we can already see signs of an effort to reclaim this victorious technology for mankind.

Beverle Houston has theorized television as the site of the family struggle. She argues that, not only does its constant flow of images promise feeding off the mother, but it also carries the Name-of-the-Father.

> In a scenario of their early months and years together, the mother's eyes are drawn to the shimmering set, and very soon the eyes of the infant as well. The television text intervenes with enough force to prohibit the child's desire to be the exclusive desire of the mother. In their very bedroom, the infant is forced through her to confront this third term, the television and its representational practices. Thus the television substitutes itself partly for other institutions and discourses which constitute the Name-of-the-Father." (p. 185)

This identification of television with the intervention of the father is also present in *Blue Velvet*, David Lynch's grotesquely comic transplant of the Oedipus story deep into the Edenic heartland of the small-town American family. In the climactic scene, set in the womblike apartment of the mysteriously masochistic mother/whore, when all of the opposing daddies are wiped out before the voyeuristic gaze of our young perverted/detective hero, a smashed television set is prominently featured among the array of decimated patriarchs.

It's easy to envision the patriarchy performing a sex change on the "tube of plenty" — switching its referent from breast to phallus. This process is already well under way in movies about television. In *Death Watch*, Harvey Keitel plays a TV camerman who has a lens implanted in his eyes, literally transforming him into a walking video camera who can document Romy Schneider's death on live TV and thereby fuse soap opera with video verité. In another sci-fi thriller, *Videodrome*, access to certain X-rated video tapes displaying the rape and torture of women causes brain tumors in male spectators. In turn, these tumors cause video hallucinations that transform the protagonist (the owner of a cable station featuring pornography) into a killer phallus. At first, his hand turns into a gun; then, his whole body is fetishized. What is the effect of these programs on the female spectator? The heroine played by rock singer Debra Harry (also known as Blondie) is a media star who gives advice to the lovelorn. The deviant videodrome programming intensifies her inherent masochism, causing her to offer herself as a willing victim.

Naturally, this sci-fi vision presents an exaggerated version of what the filmmakers think TV is already doing to our brains and sexuality. In the historic battle of the media, cinema portrays television as the "bad object" — a pattern we can see in many other films outside the sci-fi genre, such as *Network, Poltergeist*, and *King of Comedy*.[4] But what is most important to my argument here is that in both *Death Watch* and *Videodrome*, it is the man's body that fuses with video technology, while woman provides the spectacle through her suffering and death. The battle between the media is metaphorically reinscribed as a battle between the sexes, a reinscription that may remind us of Henry Adams's use of "The Dynamo and the Virgin" to describe another "sequence of forces" at the turn of the century.[5]

INTERTEXTUALITY, THE DOMAIN OF MTV

The decisive battles over TV's gender identification will undoubtedly be played out not in movies, but on television. There is no more suitable arena than MTV — the 24-hour national cable station whose rock video programming has proved so lucrative and popular, especially with adolescents for whom gender identification is so crucial and for whom it is identified with a rebellion against parents. Though it supposedly offers alternative programming, MTV actually provides a model that highlights through exaggeration the unique aspects of television, particularly those that distinguish the medium from cinema.[6] Thus it conflates the three battles-of the sexes, the generations, and the media — and wages all three in the advertising arena. Like the Friday night video fights on MTV, no matter who loses the battle, the sponsor is always the winner.

Like all television, the primary function of MTV is to sell products. While this goal is fairly visible on MTV, it is disguised in most conventional programming on commercial television. Nick Browne has argued that while the television program is presented as the primary text and the commercials that temporarily interrupt it as secondary, the opposite is true, for the main function of the program is to provide a suitable environment for the commercial message. The actual television text is "a super text that consists of the particular program and all the introductory and interstitial material — chiefly announcements and ads."[7] MTV exposes the "supertext" by erasing the illusory boundaries within its continuous flow of uniform programming and reveals the central mediating position of advertising by adopting its formal conventions as the dominant stylistic. In fact, *everything* on MTV is a commercial — advertising spots, news, station ID's, interviews, and especially music video clips.

This erosion of boundaries can be seen as a special form of intertextuality

— a modernist convention with radical potential that undermines bourgeois individualism by decentering individual works, revealing that all texts are made out of other texts. Yet as Fredric Jameson has argued, in the context of postmodernism, this parodic convention is stripped of its subversive potential and transformed into *pastiche*.[8]

The cooptive powers of music video may rival those of the fetish. It has succeeded in absorbing not only intertextuality, but other modernist conventions with radical potential like reflexiveness, parody, surrealism and even androgyny — turning them into potent cooptive mechanisms that, like the oozing characters of addiction in William Burroughs *Naked Lunch* or the cancerous monsters in *Alien*, *The Thing*, and *Invasion of the Body Snatchers*, first invade the rival by feigning likeness and then transform the Other from within until all functional difference or resistance is eradicated.

Music video has even made its way into children's TV programs such as "Sesame Street" (where charismatic monsters and cows perform music videos that parody parodies) and onto the Disney channel, which has developed a G-rated version of the MTV format. Using current pop hits as a sound track, DTV (as it's called) re-edits and recycles classic Disney images to make them more appealing to "rad" kiddies of the eighties. In a one-hour special called "Romancin'" (which was broadcast on a major commercial network), DTV made Madonna, the Eurhythmics, and Lionel Richie reaffirm wholesome heterosexual mating, clearly-demarcated gender lines, and the traditional nuclear family by pairing their songs with scenes of chipmunks singing, angels matchmaking, and Bambi and friends coupling. It's hard to be very enthusiastic about this development, unless one is connected with MTV. For those who are primarily concerned with the values promoted on children's programming, this quixotic attempt to coopt MTV may backfire, for in cultivating in tiny tots (whose parents probably prevent them from seeing the real thing) a taste for the MTV format, it grooms them as future viewers. On the other hand, if one takes the competition for higher ratings in the youth market as the real battle, then one sees the so-called "non-commercial" PBS and Disney channels striving to adopt whatever format sells and another line of resistance and functional difference evaporates. In either event, DTV was based on the shrewd perception that music video tends to trivialize words and music by riveting the spectator's attention to the fast-changing flow of visual images. It is this dimension — along with its extraordinary profitability — that has helped music video rival not only other modes of television, but also radio and cinema.

Significantly, MTV uses intertextuality as one of its main devices for enunciating the battle between cinema and video. The range of intertextuality and its relation to the three battles of media, sexes and generations can be illustrated by examining four specific music videos: Duran Duran's *A View to a Kill*, the Power Station's *Some Like It Hot*, Tom Petty's *Don't Come Around Here No More*, and Cyndi Lauper's *Goonies*.

Duran Duran's *A View to a Kill* centers on the competitive struggle between film and television for male dominance over spectatorship. From the perspective of the film industry, this video clip of the title song from the James Bond movie was merely one component in an elaborate promotion for the film that also included straight forward TV ads (featuring some of the same images used in the video clip), a short documentary film broadcast on cable that showed how the Bond film was made, and an exclusive MTV interview with Roger Moore telling how Duran Duran came to do the title song. For the filmmakers, Duran Duran is one of many groups of recording artists who have done title songs and promotions for the successful Bond series, and television is merely one advertising medium being used to sell tickets to their movie.

From the perspective of MTV, the film and its title song were sources of free programming, provided by the film and music industries in exchange for free air time. Whereas most other TV stations usually have to pay for the programs that the commercials interrupt, MTV originally had no such overhead. But once the phenomenal success of MTV generated competition, the record companies started charging the stations for the use of their videos — especially for exclusive rights to preview the clip for the intial period when it would generate the most excitement and therefore have the greatest selling power. This situation highlights the main business of every TV station — not to generate programs, but to deliver viewers at the lowest cost per thousand to advertisers who normally have to pay both for the commercials and the time it takes to air them. Since everything on MTV is a commercial, the Bond movie could triple as ad, news, and exclusive new clip. In this sweet business arrangement, both advertisers and station make a killing, so long as the viewer watches and buys. Each sees the other as a tool being manipulated to serve its own lucrative venture — as *A View to a Kill*.

The competitive edge comes out in the interview when the handsome young video jockey wistfully quips about the middle-aged Roger Moore, "He'll always be the Saint to me!" In this innocent remark, the VJ not only reclaims Moore as a TV star (the Saint), but implies he watched him as a kid and that the TV images of machismo imprinted him more strongly than those projected on the silver screen.

This line of media rivalry is elaborated in Duran Duran's performance. From the perspective of the band, this clip is one more work in their reflexive cannon of music videos that explore how media images, both from film and television, construct our subjectivity. In *A View to a Kill* the singers thrust themselves and their hardware into one of Bond's most spectacular sequences and capture the film space for video. Duran Duran tries to outdo the Bond film, not only in reflexiveness, but also in spectacle and male dominance. At the opening of the clip a womblike eye containing Bond is abruptly displaced by the phallic image of the Eiffel Tower, the setting for the scene that Duran Duran has chosen to invade. As if this setting were not sufficiently phallic, the band members blatantly fetishize their own video camera, detonators, and guns, which fit right into the Bond mythos where the male always controls the gaze and where all technological toys represent the powers of the phallus.

They also thrust themselves into the middle of a violent confrontation between Bond and one of his formidable antagonists, played by statuesque rock singer Grace Jones. As a powerful non-male, non-white symbolic Other, Jones may appear biologically suited to arouse castration fear, yet her punk stylization seems designed to transform her into a reassuring fetish. In their video take-over, not only do Duran Duran displace the fetishized Grace Jones as Bond's key rival, but they also choose a scene in which her role is played by a stuntman. As if that double displacement weren't enough, when we consider that the filmmakers chose Duran Duran to do the title song rather than Jones, we see that at the very moment that Jones was taking a big step forward in her career from rock to film star, the black woman proved to be doubly restricted in both media. This subordination of women is also echoed in the dramatic business introduced in the scene by the band. One singer poses as a fashion photographer taking shots of a female model, but this heterosexual encounter is exposed as merely a deceptive cover for the *real* battle between the male media stars.

After watching this video, we are left wondering how we are to read the band's relationship to Bond? Clearly Duran Duran is parodying his machismo, yet this reading is problematic because the spy thriller is already reflexively parodic in its own right. In all Bond movies, the spectator's passive act of surreptitious looking is glamorized by being associated with the adventurous occupation of spying. From the opening shot of the eye at the beginning of the titles (which also opens the clip), *A View to a Kill* eases us into voyeuristic pleasure through an all pervasive reflexiveness, which makes the video clip appear to be merely an extension (rather than a parody) of its tactics and vision.

Thus, instead of functioning like the radical reflexiveness of a Brecht or Godard, which breaks emotional identification by demystifying the nature of representation and the way it carries the dominant ideology, Duran Duran's brand of reflexiveness is that winking complicity so pervasive in postmodernist *pastiche* and so popular in music videos and TV commercials — the kind of reflexiveness that leads us to accept deception or sadomasochism as harmless so long as we can see through it with humor but that simultaneously encourages us to identify with its perpetrators.

The specific image from the clip that comes to mind is the young singer on the tower who is disguised as a blind man. Is he pretending to be blind to Bond's corruption while really performing a critique, or is he actually blind to his own complicity in the action? Then there's the other young man with the earphones who pushes the buttons and plays with Bond's identity. At the end of the clip, when he identifies himself as Simon LeBon, he links himself to a different culture, technology, and generation, but, despite his *goodness*, he positions himelf as the true inheritor of Bond's macho media legacy.

SOME LIKE IT HOT

The title of the Power Station's clip, *Some Like It Hot*, immediately introduces an intertextuality both with the children's nursery rhyme and with the Billy Wilder comedy from the repressive 1950s. Wilder's film subverted the boundaries both of genre — by fusing romantic comedy with a parody of the male-dominated gangster film — and of gender — by having Marilyn Monroe do a self parody and by putting Tony Curtis and Jack Lemmon in drag so that they could join an all-girl band to escape from the patriarchal gangsters who wanted to punish them for surreptitiously watching the St. Valentine's Day massacre. At the end of the film when the eccentric millionaire (who has been hotly pursuing Lemmon) learns that his fiancee is really a man, instead of rejecting him in anger he tolerantly reaffirms his desire, quipping, "Nobody's perfect!" The punch line not only subverts the patriarchal law of sexual difference on which both Oedipal conflict and romance are built, but also gives the last word to the kind of vaginal receptivity and deviant taste that are affirmed in the nursery rhyme, "Some like it hot, some like it cold, some like it in the pot, nine days old."

By reprocessing this title, the Power Station foregrounds the current usage of *hot* within the lingo of the teen subculture and the survivability of Monroe as a popular icon of female masochism, yet the video works to restore the same repressive sexual stereotypes that Wilder's film was interrogating. The clip depicts women as painted constructions — either as a stylized animated drawing that may evoke Monroe and that assumes X-rated postures suggesting dance, sex, and torture; or as *live* fragmented figures costumed in spiked heels, pointy phallicized breasts, and fluorescent bondage. In this video, all the power sources are male — whether it's the all-boy band who generates the words and music while situated next to a phallic three-pronged cactus; or the feminine paraphernalia — lipstick, blow-dryer, razor, nail polish brush, sun lamp — all blatantly fetishized to signal that they are energized by the absent phallus. This clip condemns female spectators to a masochistic aesthetic by glamorizing the ball and chain, and coopts female icons by claiming they emanate from a male power station. Both the name of the group and their visual images reassure this Pepsi generation that the remote source of control for all TV broadcasting still lies safe in the laps of the patriarchy.

DON'T COME AROUND HERE NO MORE

In *Don't Come Around Here No More* by Tom Petty and the Heartbreakers the intertextuality is even more compromising. It presents a comic video version of the mad tea party from Lewis Carroll's Victorian verbal dream text that has been so widely adapted in film, both in animation and live action, that inspired in the 1960s the classic psychedelic album by the Jefferson Airplane called *Surrealistic Pillow*, and that has recently been read by Teresa DeLauretis in *Alice Doesn't: Feminism, Semiotics and Cinema* (one of the most sophisticated theoretical texts to emerge from recent feminist film studies) as "a parable suggesting...the situation, the predicament, and the adventure of critical feminism."[9]

In earlier versions of *Alice in Wonderland*, despite the linguistic traps set by the patriarchy, females still boldly grabbed their share of the discourse — whether it was the persistently questioning Alice, the castrating Queen of Hearts, or even the assertive lead singer of the Airplane Grace Slick. But in this music video version Petty captures all the power for himself and forces the silent Alice to "give it up." Playing the Mad Hatter, he's the one who dominates the discourse and who gives all the orders — as the title confirms. His phallic mushrooms literally bowl Alice over and make her spread her legs, transforming her into a passive victim within his surrealistic vision. When Alice is drowning in a cup of tea, even the vaginal donut proves impotent as a life-saver. In the process of video adaptation, there is a transfer of power, not only from female to male, but also from word to image. Just as the original Alice had challenged male supremacy over the Symbolic, Petty seeks dominance over the female realm of the Imaginary.

It is here in the visuals that the clip demonstrates the superiority of video software technology in achieving, at relatively little cost and effort, surrealist imagery — a stylistic that has become fairly commonplace on MTV. In one scene Petty transforms Alice into a baby Miss Piggy, not only infantilizing her, but also extending the intertextuality beyond Carroll's tale to the Muppets on commercial television. The clip uses surreal trickery to manipulate Alice's size and finally to turn her into a pastry that Petty can devour. This image of cannibalism implies not only that music video feeds on intertextuality, but that adaptation is another form of consumption.

Like Duran Duran's brand of reflexivity, the surrealism we see on MTV must be distinguished from its historic roots in modernism. Best represented in film by Luis Buñuel, the surrealist movement of the 1920s used dream rhetoric as a radical strategy to undermine the power of bourgeois ideology, particularly as it was manifest in the fine arts. In contrast, this postmodernist pop surrealism uses dream images to cultivate a narcissism that promotes our submission to bourgeois consumerism.

These three clips all show the process of masculinizing video technology as television usurps the dominant position formerly held by cinema. We also see this gender identification in the iconography of one of MTV's oldest and most popular station ID's: the phallic rocket, the man on the moon, and the male technician at the video control panel.

Is there no female voice on MTV to challenge this mastery? We might hear Madonna harnessing the male dynamo to reclaim the lost powers of the Virgin. Or Bananarama parodying the cooptive fruits of the male fetish. Or Tina Turner mythologizing the survival power of female sexuality. But the female opposition on MTV is probably best represented by Cyndi Lauper.

THE GOONIES

By flaunting bad taste, Cyndi Lauper reconnects the new wave aesthetic to the naive "shlumpiness" of "lovely peasants" who genuinely love wrestling, melodrama, and other forms of pop trash. She deliberately positions her work in opposition to the snobbish "high art" pretensions of cinema. The object of her satire is never bad taste, for she finds strength in the lowbrow and the cliché, which are "good enough" for her. Thus, the intertextuality of most of her videos mediates between movies and commercial television. For example, in *Time After Time*, the vision of her banal romance is shaped by a Bette Davis tearjerker watched on TV.

The intertextuality is much more elaborate in *The Goonies* (*Good Enough*), which is from the sound track of a youth-market film "presented" by Steven Spielberg. The clip breaks the boundaries of many conventions by mixing genres (thriller, melodrama, comedy) and media (TV and film) and by presenting itself as Part I in a series of cliff hangers.

While working successfully within the structures of patriarchy, Lauper subverts them from within by exposing male power as a sham. The male authority figures in the clip are all bumbling comic figures. The political heavies ("cheating creditors" and "filthy rich customers") are played by TV wrestlers, whom Lauper has regularly challenged on commercial television. Her repeated victories remind us that the posturing machismo of these veterans of early TV history was no more authentic than their wins or losses and that their gender identification was always in question (remember Gorgeous George?). Since the villains of *The Goonies* come from commercial TV, it's only fitting that the good guy hail from Hollywood. He's a deus ex machina played by the master of money-making movies, Steven Spielberg — the executive producer of *The Goonies* film and the director of the blockbuster *Raiders of the Lost Ark*, which Lauper's clip parodies. When Cyndi is poised at an impasse threatened by goony villains wielding comically cumbersome swords, she plays helpless female and cries, "Steven Spielberg, how do I get out of this one?" Though he is positioned at the control panel of a moviola on which her image and narrative are being manipulated, he sheepishly admits, "I don't know." In this subversive clip, no god or hero comes to the rescue.

The clip also reaffirms the resourcefulness of what is normally defined as subordinate on both registers of class and sex. Her family's Mom and Pop gas station provides the setting and fuel for her rebellion and closes the generation gap; Lauper refuses to be distracted from the class struggle by the battle of generations. The power of the breast and the womb as sexual icons and as the original referents for the fetish is comically developed when she bottle feeds a mobile cow, generating two kinds of super fresh milk, and when she displaces the image of her patriarchal grandpop in order to discover a hidden vaginal cave which provides access to a rupture in both the clip's style and narrative.

The real strength in Lauper's challenge of male dominance comes in the recognition that the sexual struggle must be waged, not only reflexively and metaphorically in terms of the rivalry between the media and their technology (a battle that can be as distracting as the generation gap), but economically where patriarchal power has always been materially based.

Such readings of music videos do not encourage one to strive for sex changes in the gender identification of the mass media or for simple power reversals within the patriarchal coding of sexual difference. Rather, they demonstrate the futility of such projects and the necessity for resisting the reification of sexual metaphors that so easily entrap both women and men in essentialist definitions and that so readily restrict the human potential of technological change — whether it be in cinema or in video.

NOTES

1. Beverle Houston, "Viewing Television: The Metapsychology of Endless Consumption," *Quarterly Review of Film Studies*, IX, 3 (Summer 1984), p. 184.
2. For an elaboration of this argument see my essay on *Scenes from a Marriage* in *Film Quarterly* (Winter 1974–75), 48–53, and Tania Modleski's "The Search for Tomorrow in Today's Soap Operas," *Film Quarterly* (Fall 1979).
3. Juliet Mitchell, *Psychoanalysis and Feminism: Freud, Reich, Laing and Women* (New York: Pantheon Books, 1974), p. 201.
4. Beverle Houston has been doing germinal work on movies about television. Though most of this material is contained in papers read at various conferences and not yet published, one pivotal essay in print is "King of Comedy: A Crisis of Substitution," *Framework*, 24 (Spring 1984), 74–92.
5. Henry Adams, "The Dynamo and The Virgin" (1900) in *The Education of Henry Adams* (Boston: Houghton Mifflin Co., 1961), p. 384.
6. I have argued this position at greater length elsewhere. See "Music Video and the Spectator: Television, Ideology and Dream," *Film Quarterly* (Fall 1984), pp. 2–15.
7. Nick Browne, "The Political Economy of the Television (Super) Text," *Quarterly Review of Film Studies*, IX, 3 (Summer 1984), p. 176.
8. Fredric Jameson, "Postmodernism and Consumer Society," in *The Anti-Aesthetic: Essays on Postmodern Culture*, Hal Foster, ed. (Port Townsend, Washington: Bay Press, 1983), pp. 114–115.
9. Teresa DeLauretis, *Alice Doesn't: Feminism, Semiotics, Cinema* (Bloomington: Indiana University Press, 1984), p. 2.

33 SILENT WARNINGS*
GREIL MARCUS

Laurie Anderson is somewhat of an enigma. She is often described as a performance artist (whatever that is) and is generally thought of as somewhat "avant-garde." Yet she has appeared on television and even had a hit record in England — "O Superman," the subject of the article that follows.

Performance art asks us to look at art in a new way. We used to think of art in terms of "objects" such as paintings or sculptures or works of architecture. That is, there was something physical and lasting about works of art. Then, along came performance artists who suggested that "concepts" were the significant thing and that a performance itself might also be seen as a work of art.

The problem with art is that it is difficult, or perhaps impossible, to determine when one is dealing with a serious artist and when one is being put on by someone who may be deficient in imagination and talent…but very audacious and egotistic. It is this "anything goes" aspect to avant garde art forms that is so disturbing to people.

Laurie Anderson is one of the most accessible and interesting of the performance artists, and makes use of new technology to create many of her songs and performance pieces. Greil Marcus describes the way she starts her performance of "O Superman" as follows:

> Playing Farfisa organ, filtering and electronically distorting her voice against a never-flagging tape of "ah…ah…ah…," the interjections seemingly timed to a cricket's chirp, Anderson sets comedy against fear: here, the object of deconstruction was nothing less than the United States itself.

The article then deals with the rest of the song and what it reflects (broadly speaking) about American culture and society.

Marcus contrasts Laurie Anderson's work with that of Yoko Ono. She writes, "In contrast to Anderson, Yoko Ono is precisely the sort of intellectually effete, aesthetically decadent post-dada artist I was talking about earlier — a maker of art by fiat." Ono, we are told, uses her definition of herself as an "artist" to do drugs, and ultimately, anything she wants to do, a conceit that Marcus finds "amazing."

We face a dilemma…art must evolve, but where and how do we draw the line between charlatans and poseurs and legitimate artists? There may be no answer to this dilemma except to wait for the test of time.

* Permission to use the following copyrighted material is gratefully acknowledged: "Silent Warnings" by Greil Marcus first appeared in *California*, Dec. 1981, pp. 131–133.

Laurie Anderson's emergence from the ghetto of avant-garde performance art into the domain of the international pop star is one of the remarkable stories of the year. But while we're going to be seeing her picture everywhere over the next months, a line Anderson recently offered is worth keeping in mind, both as a description of her aural/visual constructions and as a frame for her coming status as media celebrity: "What you see is not what you hear."

Anderson, 34, grew up in the Chicago area and now lives in New York. She trained as an Egyptologist, but for more than ten years she has been performing in the live conceptual art tradition that began with Filippo Marinetti's first Futurist Evening in Trieste in 1910. The form became legend with the dada performances at the Cabaret Voltaire in Zurich in 1916, where the artist's implicit promise to reveal the meaning of life was turned into a vaudeville show in which all the acts appeared at the same time. Hans Arp reports from the scene: "Total pandemonium. The people around us are shouting, laughing, and gesticulating. Our replies are sighs of love, volleys of hiccups, poems, moos, and miaowing of medieval *Bruitists*. Tzara is wiggling his behind like the belly of an oriental dancer. Janco is playing an invisible violin and bowing and scraping. Madame Hennings, with a Madonna face [the Cab Volt performers often wore primitivist masks that presented distorted versions of their real faces], is doing the splits. Huelsenbeck is banging away nonstop on the great drum, with Ball accompanying him on the piano, pale as a chalky ghost." The next year the craze captured Paris with the epochal *Parade*, a full-scale production by Jean Cocteau, Erik Satie, Pablo Picasso, and Léonide Massine.

Just as cubism and photomontage subverted the claims of the fixed image, live art used noise to subvert music, costumes that overwhelmed those who wore them to subvert the actor, chance and absurdity to subvert dramatic narrative, and the street to subvert the stage. The result was an enormous sense of possibility — now, anything could be "art." The last bastion of mystification, it seemed, had been overthrown.

As happened with other twentieth-century avant-garde movements, performance art inverted itself. It led to a situation in which anything could be Art with a capital *A* — and for that matter an *R* and a *T*. The decadence of the tradition can be seen in much of the American performance art of the last decade. The most paltry gesture (the artist masturbating and recording the event on video) could be cloaked in the sort of authority that radical live art had meant to destroy. The concept became more important than the performance that was meant to test it, to bring it to life — because in truth the performance was only meant to preserve the integrity, which is to say the sterility, of the concept. Concept was no longer an opportunity for the live exercise of imagination; it often became a way of disguising, through the authority a performer assumes over an audience — even an imaginary, "conceptual" audience (so much the better!) — the fact that no imagination was present. Someone setting up a game of three-card monte in an "art space" was doing performance art — in more ways than one. But in

Anderson's work that combination of vaudeville and the artist's promise to reveal the meaning of life still makes itself felt.

While various Anderson pieces have appeared on obscure new-music anthology LPs over the years, Anderson released a record of her own for the first time this spring: "O Superman"/"Walk the Dog," a seven-inch, fourteen-minute disc drawn from her *United States (Transportation, Politics, Money, and Love)*, a multihour performance that has yet to be presented in its entirety. Issued on the tiny New York independent label One Ten, "O Superman" was also Anderson's first real venture into a new art space — the market, the pop process.

The 5,000 copies One Ten originally pressed slowly began to appear in the more adventurous record stores and to be heard on a few of the nonprofit FM stations you find jammed onto the far left end of the dial. The record played mostly late at night, when the line between dreaming and waking is thinnest — and it's just that line "O Superman" means to dissolve.

The record found its way to Great Britain's John Peel, an eclectic BBC disc jockey whose anarchic show is beamed to the entire country four days a week. He spun "O Superman," and the response, as they say not more than once a year, was unprecedented. Within weeks, "O Superman" was the most talked about record in the nation. Even Capitol Radio, London's closest equivalent to an American Top 40 station, was playing it, though there was hardly a copy to be had anywhere in England — or, by this time, in the U.S.A. The London independent label Rough Trade picked up some of One Ten's second pressing of 5,000 copies; they went fast, and Anderson entered the U.K.'s independent singles charts. Swiftly, Anderson cut a deal with Warner Bros., and by mid-October, just a fortnight after the major shipped 125,000 copies of the disc, "O Superman" reached number two on the British pop charts.

Warner Bros. has just made the record available in this country, and you should be able to find it in almost any store. Whether it will become any kind of hit on our timid airwaves is another question. Eight-minute AM hits in the United States are almost unknown; not even commercial FM stations still play long pieces — and, length aside, "O Superman" is a very strange record. It is, I discovered this fall, an even stranger performance.

I saw Laurie Anderson at the cinema in San Francisco — the debut production for the venue's new management. For a place set up mainly to present internationally known postpunk bands, it was an interesting bill: Anderson plus William Burroughs and poet John Giorno. But Anderson was the reason the 1,200-seat converted movie theater was jammed. The previous day (when the Warner Bros. signing was only a rumor), I had heard people in three different record stores asking, rather desperately, for "O Superman" — no luck.

Anderson took the stage in a black satin jacket, black shirt, black tie, black pants, her eyes made up to look like those of an emissary from the Village of the Damned, her hair chopped and spiked into a punk do, and immediately defused the expectations of the crowd with a bit of rambling, deadpan patter. She mimed with her neon violin, set a few tapes rolling to no apparent purpose. Having broken the context of artistic seriousness that had greeted her, she faded into "O Superman."

Little else Anderson did that night came close to this piece. Much of her work — combining music, props, sound effects, movement, talk, and projected images — fell somewhere between noodling and academic deconstruction: "Closed Circuit," nominally a skewed blues, came off as a riff seeking a subject. But "O Superman" — on record impressive partly for its commitment to craft and appealing partly because of its seemingly blithe toying with sound and myth — was an act of prophecy. Playing Farfisa organ, filtering and electronically distorting her voice against a never-flagging tape of "ah...ah...ah," the interjections seemingly timed to a cricket's chirp, Anderson set comedy against fear: here, the object of deconstruction was nothing less than the United States itself.

"O Superman" begins with the recorded leave-a-message instructions of an answer phone. Mom checks in ("Are you coming home?"), and then an anonymous voice: the voice, you come to think soon enough, of the nation's future — or its fortune-teller.

"Well, you don't know me," the voice says, "but I know you" — Anderson suddenly lifts and curls the line out of speech and into music, bringing you into a conversation that a moment before you were only overhearing — "And I've got a message/To give to you/Here come the planes...." This last word is drawn out electronically, giving you time to think about it, to form an image, even to helplessly glance up at the roof of the theater. The word carries over into the next verse, and the voice goes on: "So you'd better get ready/Ready to go/You can come as you are/But pay as you go."

It's a good joke, but by this point only that anonymous voice can afford to laugh. The voice creates the sense that one has incurred a debt without knowing it and that one must now make the debt good. The piece is absolutely terrifying, and the voice turns playful, or sadistic, with a prim little lilt: "They're American planes/Made in America/Smoking — or Nonsmoking." The woman whose machine has picked up the call now picks up the phone herself, but the voice continues with its riddles: "Neither snow nor rain/Nor gloom of night/Shall stay these couriers/From the swift completion/Of their appointed rounds." The voice is gentle, ageless, magically summoning the shared American memory of old catch-phrases, old certainties — but these couriers are not delivering the mail. There isn't a note, a tone, a word, an inflection that is out of place, that doesn't have its purpose in advancing the awful, revelatory mood of the piece — in moments you can almost hear Anderson crouching behind a line, hear her back off from another even as she delivers it.

The song drifts away. The voice departs, and the woman is left to make her peace with its echo: "When love is gone/There's always justice/And when justice is gone/There's always force/And when force is gone...there's always Mom (Hi, Mom!)." What is left, really, is retreat, because the mystery, solved, is implacable. In a weird but by now inevitable merging of technological authority and the yearning for a love that need not be earned, Mom becomes America, and the woman we are listening to wants only to surrender to its arms. And so she does.

Were we to hear "O Superman" on the radio every day, as, presumably, the British are — were we to hear it waking up, driving the car, without warning — both Anderson's concept and its execution would be tested. Then we would find out how strong this work really is.

In contrast to Anderson, Yoko Ono is precisely the sort of intellectually effete, aesthetically decadent postdada artist I was speaking of earlier — a maker of art by fiat. It has been a year since John Lennon was shot to death — a year during which Ono has performed as something like a professional widow (on her "Season of Glass" LP, not at all badly) — but now it is time to blow the whistle.

Recently, *Rolling Stone* interviewer Barbara Graustark pressed Ono on the subject of her and Lennon's heroin use in the late sixties. Ono finally owned up, and then produced this extraordinary statement: "But we were taking it in celebration, not out of depression. We were artists. We were celebrating ourselves. It was beautiful to be on a high....You know, when you think about people who take drugs, you think of weak people who can't help themselves or get off. But that's when I realized what a powerful person John was. Once he decided, he would just say, 'Okay, this is the last one.' And then he would go through withdrawal, and I would, too. He had willpower that was amazing."

It's the central conceit of these comments that is amazing: *we were artists*. Throughout almost all of Ono's conceptual artwork from the early sixties on — her Duchamp imitations, bag acts, bed-ins, noise albums, one-note films — one can find this theme: whatever the artist does is sanctified. (Even murder can be sanctified, as Chris Burden has labored to prove, so far unsuccessfully — he once took a shot at an airplane and labeled the act an art statement.) Dada wanted to smash the sanctity of art; the New York neodada tradition out of which Ono has worked tries to make the artist into God.

What Ono was trying to tell Graustark was that she and Lennon were special: better than you and me. This is a spiritually repressive message — and her *Los Angeles Times* ad soliciting "plants, rocks, and/or stones" to decorate the Central Park lanes where "John and I took our last walk together" is of a piece with it — but the effect of Ono's comments on smack will be concretely destructive. Can anyone imagine a statement more likely to encourage heroin use among people who identify with John Lennon? Among high school and college students who think of themselves as "artists" (who will be led to think that "willpower," which we all believe we have and which is part of the self-image of the driven artist, is all it takes to get off heroin)? Among those who think that sensitivity is dispensation?

Yoko Ono's comments about heroin are not just personal, not just one more example of the sentimentality and mindlessness that have characterized her discourse with the public over the years. They are part and parcel of a tradition that meant to liberate both art and life, and which, in certain hands, now enshrines the falsification of the former and the suppression of the latter.

34   CD OR NOT CD?*
ALLAN ULRICH

It may seem a bit far-fetched to suggest that there is something sexual about audiophiles. But if you define them as people with an almost overwhelming passion for perfect reproduction (of sound), you can see that there may be a sexual element to this phenomenon. Audiophiles are, literally, "sound lovers." And many of them are willing to go to incredible expense to obtain high level reproduction of music — an experience that is (literally) sensual. Since the sensual and sexual are closely connected, it is not too difficult to see that there is a sexual dimension to this matter. The phenomenon might be described as involving audial sexuality.

I am not talking about the person who puts together a good audio system for $500 or $1000 here. What I have in mind are the people who spend tens of thousands of dollars for their systems — who seek perfect sound and are willing to pay almost anything for it.

In recent years, the most important development in the field has been the invention of compact discs — small, 4.7-inch records that can hold up to two hours of music and which are "read" by lasers, generating distortion-free music. Compact discs have all kinds of advantages: they last indefinitely, you can program which selections to hear on a given record easily, and because the sound is reproduced digitally, it is more spacious and more detailed than sound reproduced analogically (on long-playing records).

Critics of compact discs argue that they "break" the sound when they record and that they don't capture overtones as well as long-playing records do. So there are trade-offs involved in using compact discs. They are also much more expensive than long playing records and require fairly expensive compact disc players (though the price of these players has fallen a great deal in recent years).

The argument about compact discs may be irrelevant, however, since a new process has come on the market that threatens to make compact discs an old technology. This new development is called the Digital Audio Tape — it involves

---

* Allan Ulrich, "CD or Not CD?" Reprinted from SAN FRANCISCO FOCUS magazine (May, 1986).

the same digital recording technology as the compact disc, but you can record music with DATs and get incredible sound. Digital Audio Tape cassettes are much smaller than conventional audio cassettes and can record up to three hours of music. When this system becomes popular and starts being mass produced, its costs will come down and it quite likely will be the dominant system in the future.

First, you have to accept the hard, immutable truth: no manner of recording will ever replace the live experience of the concert hall. Nothing ever devised by the human mind will replace the extreme range of frequencies, the pinpoint direction of instrumental sound, the thrill of hearing a piano chord bounce off the walls of the auditorium and resonate in your skull.

Nothing will ever replace the nonmusical, ritualistic aspects of concert-going, either. Nothing will replace the smell of wet fur on a rainy winter evening, the sight of a percussionist's satisfied face after executing an extended solo — or the annoyance of a bored child kicking at the back of a seat during a heart-stopping solo violin passage.

None of these obvious generalizations has stopped technology from trying to improve on the enduring science of acoustics. Within some of our lifetimes, we have passed through the era of single-sided acoustical recording (made by playing or singing into a large, morning-glory horn); the advent of the electrical process and fragile double-sided records; and the switch from the format of (approximately, but not always) 78 revolutions per minute to the hardier, generally unbreakable longer-playing records, which were either seven, ten or twelve inches in diameter and played at a speed of either 33⅓ or 45 rpm.

Now, to the demonstrable pleasure of the prime movers in the recording industry and to that of many listeners, and to the chagrin of a small but articulate minority of sound experts, we have finally witnessed the dawn of the digital age. We have witnessed the rise of compact discs.

Do CDs sound better? Do they (as proponents say) represent music as it should be heard? Or is the CD merely a nefarious plot toward the gradual and calculated obsolescence of conventional equipment, a devious strategy to prop up a sagging industry by introducing new hardware and the corresponding software?

Curiosity, rather than any of the above questions, led me to take the plunge last year. I have now lived with a compact disc player for six months and, at the risk of receiving a spate of letters, I can say I am ready to accept it as another component of a sound system, not as a replacement for cassette, tape or conventional turntable.

The physical advantages of the CD seem obvious and make the medium a most attractive lure for the consumer. CDs come in only one size, 4.7 inches diameter, and information on them is decoded in a uniform way. (That's a sure sign the industry is seeking rapid universal acceptance. There will be no formatting confusion of the sort that spawned the war of VHS versus Beta in the videocassette recorder field.)

CDs can accommodate up to approximately seventy-five minutes of music on one of their reflective aluminum sides, and rumor has it that the 120-minute disc will appear on the market within the next couple of years. Pioneer has already marketed a CD changer, which means that you can now savor every note of *Parsifal* on four discs without moving from your armchair. If our parents had wanted to listen to Wagner's last opera, all five hours of it, they would have been forced to tote around thirty separate 78s weighing upwards of twenty pounds (fortunately for that generation, nobody had then recorded *Parsifal* complete).

Leaving aside their potential use as miniature Frisbees, CDs are just about unbreakable; they will never deteriorate with repeated play and are *relatively* impervious to damage through either willful or accidental mishandling. The important information on CDs is embedded within the metal and protected by a clear, hard surface. So, generally, CD's will arrive free of the scratches, nicks, abrasions, warps, off-center pressings, pitch variations and those deposits of crackling static electricity that plague conventional records.

But, occasionally, one will acquire a faulty CD. The imperfections will be perceptible on first hearing, and they will be the devil to deal with. You will hear a click, and then either a passage of music will be repeated, or, often, the sound will jump about ten pages forward or back in the score.

Since there's no stylus or cartridge involved, you can't simply lift the turntable arm a fraction of an inch and hope the problem will disappear. You can either clean the disc by rubbing it (from the center out only) with a soft, dry, lint-free cloth, or (the most extreme method I've encountered) by repolishing the surface with toothpaste on the end of a Q-Tip. Or — the most direct solution for resolving the dilemma — you can return it to the dealer for replacement.

CDs should be handled only by the edges and kept away from extremes of heat, the manufacturers warn. They are acting perhaps with excessive caution in issuing their caveats. On a CD, nothing touches the encoded surfaces, which are "read" by a laser, as the record spins rapidly (up to 500 rpm).

You pick out a particular selection by setting a counter, so that the light scans the disc at a certain point. Most CD packaging lists the various selections, and, in some cases, there are indexing cues within those bands. If you're dying to have that stunning horn passage repeated instantly, many CD players have the capability of moving the beam back or forward moment by moment. Sophisticated playback apparatus also allows you to program the selections in any order you desire, which means you can skip over bits you don't care to hear. A friend of mine who absolutely adores the music in Mozart operas but can't abide the harpsichord-accompanied recitatives between numbers thus considers CDs the ideal solution to his problem.

Some listeners will bask in the more spacious, more detailed sound in the new format. This revolution really began in 1978, with the advent of large-scale digital recording. Until then, engineers captured sound on disc much the same way they captured Enrico Caruso almost eight decades earlier. The grooves of a record were filled with minute wave forms that were "analogs" to the waves that sound physically produces in the environment. The master tapes were middlemen in this process.

Digital recording transforms everything into a series of numbers. The constant sound waves are "sampled" at regular intervals, and the music is coded numerically in a binary on-off fashion. With conventional grooved LP recordings, that data was reconverted back to analog. But with CDs, the information can be embedded in small pits, and the process of digitalization is complete. You can manufacture CDs from analog masters, but the listener will always be aware of the residual tape hiss. On purely digital CDs, the background is so silent the listening experience is almost eerie.

Arguments against CDs revolve, to a great extent, around the sampling process, which results in subtle breaks in the sound. As long as the sound is discontinuous, it simply can't compare to the uninterrupted flow of analog recording. The only solution is state-of-the-art conventional equipment, which can set the consumer back as much as $50,000 for a system, beyond the reach of most music lovers. And while the nay-sayers may be correct, most people simply do not hear those breaks and do not succumb to the fatigue that is supposed to afflict them after listening to CDs for long periods. And no amount of logic will convince people that they're hearing something when their ears tell them otherwise.

Everybody should test CDs for themselves. I did, and listening at home on moderately priced equipment provided me some fascinating contrasts. You may even get better results at a well-stocked audio shop (but not at one of those hi-fi supermarkets).

It helped to compare CD and LP versions of music recorded at Davies Symphony Hall. CD is reputed to bleach out a natural hall acoustic, and certainly two Telarc discs featuring the auditorium's Ruffatti organ — the Joseph Jongen *Symphonie Concertante* for organ and orchestra, with Michael Murray and the San Francisco Symphony conducted by Edo de Waart (CD-80096/DG-10096 in the LP format); and Murray in a solo recital (CD-80097/DG-10097) — created a sonic ambiance quite unlike that experienced in the auditorium itself (not entirely a curse). There was just that much more air around the notes in the CD; there was no hint of any artificial bass, to which many LPs are prone. And the sound in the midrange acquired an unearthly clarity. That midrange, unfortunately, is exactly where the Ruffatti organ's reeds lack ideal color and expressivity. The verdict: despite that curiously disembodied sensation, these are a couple of sonic blockbusters.

De Waart's affable recording of Grieg's incidental music to Ibsen's play *Peer Gynt* (Philips CD 411 038–2/LP 6514 378), with soprano Elly Ameling and the San Francisco Chorus and Symphony, provided more answers. The CD opened up brilliantly at the top. In "Song of the Church-goers," the chorus stood out amidst the orchestral forces, as did Ameling in her solos. When your ear searched for a clarinet, you could pick it out without difficulty. You didn't have to accept a trombone cadence on faith. There it was. And where Grieg called for percussion ("In the Hall of the Mountain King"), the thumping and thwacking gave an almost visceral thrill.

Recordings by the symphony's new music director, Herbert Blomstedt, leading his former orchestra, the Staatskapelle, Dresden, have appeared in stores recently. Blomstedt's traditional, solid performance of Bruckner's Symphony No. 7 in E Major in the Japanese Denon label (CD: 38C37–7286/LP: OB-7375/6 ND) offered illuminating moments in both formats. The tremendous dynamic range of Bruckner's style, from whispering *pianissimos* to massed *fortissimo* choirs, was more shatteringly captured on CD. But reverberation in the LP format seemed just that fraction more natural; on CD, the chords echoed into infinity with uncanny abruptness.

Detractors claim that you lose those all-important overtones on CD. A comparison of a recent operatic release was a good test: London's superb new recording of Verdi's *Un Ballo in Maschera* (CD: 410–210–2/LP: 410–210–1) boasts tenor Luciano Pavarotti and sopranos Margaret Price and Kathleen Battle in remarkably fresh estate and Georg Solti conducting the National Philharmonic with a wit and warmth one would hardly have suspected beforehand. It's probably the best recording of the opera now available.

The CD of *Ballo* sounded that little bit fresher, and the separation between channels proved just that mite more gripping, than on the LP. But the overtones — those ascending frequencies in the harmonic series that are often felt rather than heard, and that impart a unique character to a musician — seemed a trifle lacking. I can't say that Pavarotti and Price sounded drained of life. Their recorded counterparts just didn't always remind me of those singers' triumphs in the opera house.

But one simply can't yield to generalizations. CD has been said to bestow an unappealing glassiness to the sound of a modern grand piano. Then you turn to a performance by Alfred Brendel, whom analog recordings never seemed to represent satisfactorily. You listen to his recent CD (Philips 412 227–2) of shorter Beethoven works — "Für Elise," the *Eroica* Variations, Six Bagatelles, Op. 6, and Six Ecossaises — and you suddenly detect a sensuousness of tone to match the fabled intellect of this important artist. So it will be every pair of ears for itself in the world of CD.

Right now, American converts should find themselves in an ambiguous position. The format first made an impact on the domestic market in 1983, and prices have plummeted in the past three years. Now, the equipment is available; CD players start at under $200 and range upwards to at least $1500 for all kinds of features. But where are the CDs themselves?

Look in any of the catalogues, and you'll find treasures comparable to what LP offered in its infancy. You will find operas by Salieri, motets by Lully, sonatas by MacDowell. Then, try finding them in the stores. Production of the discs has simply not kept up with the supply of players.

Manufacturing a CD is a much more complex process than turning out a conventional record. Most American companies have their product pressed in plants overseas; the companies must wait their turn, and even then there is no guarantee they will get all they request. The shortage is passed on to your local record store.

But by the middle of next year, industry people predict more stateside pressing plants will be on line. When that happens, the price of CDs, which runs 50 to 100 percent more than for LPs, should come down.

Right now, it's a seller's market. Too few companies have shown the willingness to capitalize on the new format by offering as much music as a CD can contain. Paying fifteen dollars for a Beethoven Fifth Symphony (all thirty-five minutes of it) seems like a minor swindle. The good news is that some manufacturers are adding inducements to CD (that Michael Murray recital contains an eight-minute bonus, Messaien's "Dieu parmi Nous"). The better news is that it's now possible to press many operas in the standard repertoire on two CDs, as opposed to three LPs (the Pavarotti *Ballo in Maschera* was issued that way), and, while you won't save a lot of money, the expenditure hurts a little less.

There's no doubt that CD is here to say. Some American companies (like Delos) have dropped LPs. Many imports arrive from abroad only in CD format. And this revolution has proved a gold mine to firms with enormous catalogues of material. Reissues of recordings, many long out of print, are appearing at premium prices. CBS has launched a massive re-release program devoted to conductor Bruno Walter. EMI has begun to recycle its monaural Wilhelm Furtwängler classics, and Philips has its Wilhelm Mengelberg treasures coming this year.

Genuine collectors will not junk their LPs wholesale. They've spent far too many years tracking down those priceless performances, defending the old masters against the Ludwigs-come-lately and carting their hoards from apartment to bungalow. So bring on the CDs. I'll keep listening, but I'll also keep my records of Alfred Cortot playing Chopin, Elena Gerhardt singing Wolf, Richard Strauss elegantly conducting his own works. The fidelity may be low, but, in their own way, they are the most constant friends a record collector ever had.

ISSUES AND THEMES

Many people think that historians are people who write books that tell what happened in the past. That is not quite accurate. Historians are people who write *interpretations* of what happened in the past and, as you might imagine, different historians offer varying descriptions and explanations of what happened (and more particularly why things happened the way they did). Thus historians may all agree about the dates for the Civil War but offer many different explanations of why it occurred and what its significance was. All of these historians, I might add, are dealing with the same events. It is the weight or importance they give to certain matters that lead to their differing views.

In the same light, scholars in the communication field differ on many matters. They differ on what communication is, how it works, and how it should be studied. (They also disagree on whether the media have a significant effect, as we shall see in a different section of this book.)

These differences are signifiers of several things. One thing they reflect is that communications is a relatively young discipline. There have been schools of communication at our universities for only the past few decades or so, and many of our older and most prestigious universities still do not have schools of communication (or even departments of communication). As a young discipline, it might be expected that there would be a great deal of disagreement about methods of study and divisions on theoretical issues.

Another thing signified is that communications is a vital and dynamic discipline; thus all the controversy or "ferment" about communications should be seen in a positive sense. A number of scholars feel very strongly about communications and there is room in the field for all kinds of people with many different methods of analysis to conduct research and make important contributions.

In this section we deal with a variety of topics. There is an essay on the Marxist perspective on communications (and, in particular, the mass media). It is the political impact of the media that interests the Marxists and they offer some interesting and provocative ideas for us to consider. The Marxists believe that the mass media are a crucial tool used by "the ruling class" to maintain control. For Marxists, the economic institutions (the base) shape, in complicated ways, all other institutions, such as the Church, education, the arts, and the legal profession (the superstructure). The mass media play a crucial role in shaping people's consciousness, Marxists claim, so they pay a great deal of attention to them. There is a considerable amount of disagreement among Marxists, I might point out, about how to interpret and understand the media.

We also have a discussion of the Fairness Doctrine, a ruling that has had a great deal of impact on the broadcasting industry and which is under attack by some people, who suggest that the fairness doctrine has done more harm than good. And there is an essay on the way the mass media "educate" us. It is possible to make a distinction between "instruction" and "education." "Instruction" is what we experience in schools, institutions that supposedly are staffed by trained people who have our best interests in mind. "Education," on the other hand, refers to everything else we learn as a result of our experiences. And the media are a large part of our everyday experience of life.

The question is, how good an "education" are we getting from the media? We used to believe in the "liberal arts," a broad, humanistic education that supposedly prepared us for life — in contrast to the training we get nowadays in many disciplines...and via many media.

There was one sector of television that was originally designed to be educational. This mission was broadened and educational television became public television. There still remain a number of questions about public television. What should it do? How should it be financed? To whom is it responsible? These questions are discussed in an essay by Anthony Tiano, the president of the public broadcasting station in San Francisco, KQED.

This section deals with theories and issues and provides us with some important concepts and methods, as well as a glance at some of the major issues in the field of mass media studies. History is a very old discipline, yet it is full of disputes by historians with different points of view about almost every topic conceivable. There is no discipline that is vital that is not alive with controversy. This is to be expected. And the analysis of the mass media is full of controversy (and sometimes invective). The important thing for us to do is to look at these issues as a very fine means of learning about the central concerns of mass media studies.

35   LIBERAL EDUCATION IN THE INFORMATION AGE*

GEORGE GERBNER

We often come across the term "liberal" in the media. The term has two
meanings: in politics, it deals with people who generally favor having the
government play a major role in looking after the needs of citizens. Thus we talk
about liberals and conservatives. When we use the term referring to education, as
in "the liberal arts," we refer to something else — the role education and the arts
have in giving people a more profound understanding of the societies in which
they live and a better understanding of themselves, so they can lead richer, more
fulfilling lives.

Gerbner suggests that television can play a liberating role, but the power
television has to "free" people is connected to the power television has to
"enslave" them. He starts this essay pointing out that we now live in an
information age (a greater percentage of our Gross National Product comes from
activities involving the creation and exchange of information than from
manufacturing products) and that the media play an increasingly important role in
socializing people. The messages and images we absorb from the media affect our
culture and, because our culture has an enormous influence on the way we
develop, the media affect each of us profoundly — whether we realize this or not.

The media give us roles to follow, models to imitate, and personalities to
identify with...all of which are highly significant for us, as individuals, and for
society in general. Human beings, Gerbner suggests, are storytelling creatures.
And the stories we tell, about how things work (fiction), about what things are
(news and documentaries), and what we should do (values) have much more
impact on us than we might imagine.

Gerbner offers us an interesting analogy to use when thinking about television,
our most powerful medium. Television is like a tribal religion: we use it in highly
ritualistic ways and it shapes our behavior and view of the world. If you look at the
content of television, Gerbner says, you find that television offers a highly
distorted picture of society that seems to be giving those who are heavy viewers of
the medium a number of sexist, racist, and ageist ideas. We cannot turn television
off, he says, so we must learn how to cope with it...and learn how to change it, so
it can achieve its promise and become a truly "liberating" agent.

Gerbner does a fine job of raising the question: what kind of an "education"
are we getting from the media? Is it "liberal" in the best sense of the term...or is it
something else?

* From *Current Issues in Higher Education* (1983–1984). Published with permission of the
American Association for Higher Education.

The challenge of an information society in the telecommunications age is not only a challenge to education but also to the very process of humanization, the process that makes human beings out of Homo sapiens. In order to address that challenge, we need to take four steps:

- The first is to reflect on the unique and distinctive aspects of the humanization process.
- The second is to sketch how these aspects have shaped us and brought us to where we are.
- The third is to identify the mission of a liberal education in that process.
- And the fourth is to try to develop a strategic conception of what we are up against in pursuing that mission.

HOMO SAPIENS: THE STORYTELLERS

Scottish patriot Andrew Fletcher once said that if he were permitted to write all the ballads, he need not care who makes the laws of a nation. Ballads, songs, tales, gestures, and images make up the unique design of the human environment. All animals react to things but humans act in a world of towering symbolic constructions that we call culture and includes art, science, law, religion, statecraft, and all other storytelling. Culture is that system of messages and images which regulates social relations; introduces us into roles of gender, age, class, vocation; gives us models of conformity and targets for rebellion; provides the range of personalities, temperaments, and mentalities said to be our "characteristics"; helps us rise to selfless acts of courage and sacrifice; and makes us accept (or even perpetrate) repression and slaughter of countless unknown people assigned to the appropriate categories of barbarians and other enemies. In other words, culture is that symbolic organization which socializes us and cultivates our fantasies about a world we do not experience directly. It is a system of stories and other artifacts, increasingly mass-produced, that mediates between existence and our consciousness of existence, and thereby helps shape both. As we encounter something new we hold it up to that fantasy. If it fits we call it real. Of course, that does not *make* it real; it only makes us behave as if it were. Therefore, it is all the more important to obtain accurate knowledge, to make warranted assertions, to develop ways of making statements that are relevant, valid, and true, to know what stories are and do, and most of all, to study how and on whose behalf we tell the stories that reflect, express, and shape our reality.

There are basically three kinds of stories. The first are stories about how things *work*. They illuminate our all-important but invisible network of relationships. They depict facts and people and set them in action so that the hidden dynamics of their interplay can be seen and explored. We call this type of story fiction, drama, poetry, etc. Only artful creations can incorporate a full and compelling human vision of how things really work.

The second are stories about what things *are*. They provide some verisimilitude to the larger mythology of how things work. They fill in that synthetic framework with selected facts — news, anecdotes, descriptions, explanations — to provide confirmation of a society's fantasy of its reality. Sometimes they undertake the difficult and risky task of challenging the mythology.

The third are stories of *value* and *choice*. They are as if to say: if this is how things work and what things are, then what should we do about them? What are our choices and what set of priorities should we follow? These are the exhortations, sermons, and instructions of all times. Today, most of them are called commercials. They present the styles of life to be desired and the choices to be made to attain them.

THREE CULTURAL EPOCHS

These three kinds of stories have been woven together in different ways in different cultural epochs.

First, of course, is the preindustrial way of providing explanations of how things work, what things are, and what to do about them. The preindustrial way is face-to-face. It depends on memory and on ritual. It requires a great deal of repetition and the accumulation of a limited set of stories about the origin of the Universe, about the meaning of life, and the ways of proper conduct. The leaders of the tribe can reach and tell or interpret the stories for each small and stable total community.

Then comes the industrial transformation. The first machine is the printing press. The first industrial product stamping out standardized commodities is the book. That paves the way for the transformations to come. It breaks up the ritual and the face-to-face community. Printed stories are movable packages of consciousness that can be taken across hitherto impenetrable or closely guarded boundaries of time, space, language, religion, status. The book lifts people from their traditional moorings as the industrial revolution uproots them from their communities and cultures; it frees them from historic dependence on the ministrations and interpretations of their local chiefs and priests. The book can now be given to all who can read (a new class) to interpret as they wish.

Meanwhile people engage in long and costly struggles to tell stories and thus shape reality from their own points of view. The struggle is necessary for the formation of new identities and interests as the industrial age breaks the community into different and conflicting classes, mixes together religious and ethnic groups, and restructures the process of humanization heretofore confined by geography and relative stability. The way to achieve some control over the newly differentiating consciousness in a situation of unprecedented mobility and flux is to gain the right to select and write and publish stories (and thus create publics) stemming from radically different conceptions of reality existing in the same society. Notions of individuality and class consciousness are rooted in this era. The publication of different types of stories creates and cultivates mass publics — those loose aggregates of people who share some consciousness without ever meeting face-to-face. Mass publics are necessary for self-government and much of economic, eductional, religious, and cultural life in the print-industrial epoch. Ever since the industrialization of storytelling, human consciousness is increasingly the product of a system of symbol mass-production.

Next comes the second industrial transformation. We enter the telecommunications era. Its mainstream is television, superimposed upon and reorganizing print-based culture. Television has its own characteristics. It is a centralized ritual, distant and pervasive and yet seemingly personal and face-to-face. It turns out and disseminates a limited number of stories about how things work, what they are, and what to do about them, along with the stars, scenes, social types, and other myths that make an otherwise diverse audience into a new kind of community: the modern mass public. In terms of its essential socializing functions, television is more like tribal religion than like any other selectively used medium preceeding it.

In the average American home, the television set is on 6 hours and 48 minutes a day. Most people do not watch television by the program but by the clock. The majority do not even decide what to watch until they turn on the set. The viewing pattern follows the style of life of the family. If that is rich and diverse, television has a lesser role in it. Otherwise, television practically monopolizes cultural participation and dominates the cultivation of common consciousness as local parochial culture did before the print era.

LIBERATING EDUCATION

Now to liberal education. I prefer to define it as "liberating education." I believe that its traditional role is to liberate the individual from an unwitting and unquestioning dependence on the traditional local and parochial cultural environment.

Liberation begins with putting the individual in touch with the great art, science, and philosophy of humankind. But if liberal education is liberation from dependence on an impoverished local and parochial cultural environment, then what role does it have today? Our cultural environment is anything but impoverished.

Television alone has abolished the old provincialism and parochialism. No one is out in the sticks anymore, culturally speaking. One can be very young or very old, far from the center of things, lying in a hospital or locked in a prison, and still live in the same cultural mainstream of the world of television as do most others more able, mobile, or fortunate.

For the first time in human history, the resident of the penthouse shares a great deal of the common culture with the inhabitant of the ghetto. The famous and the infamous, the celebrities and the criminals, the politicians, the spies, and the cops, and the parade of other culture heroes and villains that makes up the common mythology are now in the home and available to everyone. Television is the cement of cohesion in an otherwise diverse and divergent society. The world it presents even encompasses more of the great art and science and philosophy than a whole nation has ever shared before. So what are we to be liberated from?

To answer that question, we have to review some evidence. It bears upon the reversal of the trend toward differentiation of consciousness according to individual and group interest, and the rise of a common environment of stories, ritualistically used, presenting a world according to television.

THE WORLD OF TELEVISION

We have moved away from the historic experience of humankind. Children used to grow up in a home where parents told most of the stories. Today, television tells most of the stories to most of the people most of the time. This electronic pulpit and faithful messenger would be the envy of every Emperor and Pope who ever lived. Children do not have five or six years of relatively protected development within the family and the neighborhood before emerging into the outside culture of school and reading. By the time they can speak, let alone read, they have absorbed hundreds of thousands of stories — programs, news, commercials — produced on the television assembly-line to the specifications of adult tastes and industrial needs. The pervasive mass ritual blurs, when it does not short-circuit, social distinctions rooted in a subcultural and class membership, blends community consciousness into its mainstream, and bends that in the direction of its own institutional interests.

How does that work? What is the world according to television like? To discover its main features and functions, we have to look at familiar structures in an unfamiliar light. Rituals rationalize and serve a social order. They make the necessary and inevitable appear natural and right. In conventional entertainment stories, plots perform that rationalizing function. They provide novelty, diversion, and distraction from the constant reiteration of the functions performed by casting, power, and fate. The main points to observe, therefore, are who is who (number and characterization of different social types in the cast); who risks and gets what (power to allocate resources including personal integrity, freedom of action, and safety); and who comes to what end (fate, or outcomes inherent in the structure that relates social types to a calculus of power, risks and relative success or failure).

When observed in that way, as the Annenberg School of Communications has been doing for over fifteen years on an annual sample basis, the world of television drama is found to be one in which men outnumber women at least three to one; young people comprise one-third and older people one-fifth of their true proportion of the population, and all other minorities have less than their share of the action but more than their share of the risks. The lessons learned from that, as we have found by surveying light and heavy viewers in otherwise similar groups, are those that tend to cultivate and confirm rather than challenge or change some of our stereotypic inequities and prejudices.

We have found that the heavier viewers (matched with light viewers by income, education, sex, age, and so on) are less likely to believe that women are as capable as men for responsible positions, more likely to be opposed to open housing, more likely to view older citizens as a vanishing breed, and are generally more likely to respond to our surveys in a way we would call sexist, racist, and ageist.

The world according to television also is one in which violence occurs at the rate of six acts per hour in prime time and twenty-five per hour in children's weekend daytime programming.

Violence is essentially a demonstration of power. It shows who can get away with what against whom. Exposure to violence cultivates a sense of relative powers, of one's risks and place in the social hierarchy, and a sense of heightened anxiety and insecurity about a world that is shown to be much meaner and more dangerous than anyone has directly experienced. Insecurity leads to demands for protection, dependence on authority, and acceptance of repression if it comes in the name of security.

In the world of television, most people are professionals. Service and blue collar workers who occupy about 60 percent of our population occupy only 10 percent of the television population. The average viewer of prime time television sees a stable cast of about 300 characters a week. Of those, about 44 are engaged in law enforcement and about 21 are criminals. The restoration of law and order is a chief feature of the ritual. And the most general characteristic of heavy viewers compared to similar groups of light viewers is a certain rigidity and resistance to change.

Despite the overwhelming presence of professionals on TV, the process of educating plays a small and ambivalent role. Surveys show that the more children and adolescents watch television, the lower their school and IQ test scores and educational aspirations seem to be.

THE TASKS OF LIBERATION

These are a few of the many features and functions of the television mythology that have been studied. But just as important as the individual findings are the results that show television reducing or eliminating differences in people's consciousness of the world around them, and absorbing them into its synthetic and homogenized mainstream. The vast majority of stories that make up the world according to television are made to uniform specifications of institutional service and sales. Relatively rich and attractive though it may be, the world of television acts to screen us from, rather than to mediate, the rapidly changing requirements of equity, justice, and survival.

Liberation cannot be accomplished by turning it off. Television is for most people the most attractive thing going any time of the day or night. We live in a world in which the vast majority will not turn it off. If we don't get the message from the tube, we get it through other people.

The strategic conception calls for action on three fronts: as educators, as parents, and as citizens. We can use the skills and insights employed in teaching the humanities and social sciences and apply them to the everyday cultural environment from which all our students learn. Media studies and critical viewing curricula which develop an analytical and critical stance toward mass-produced culture and its television mainstream should be at the center of liberal education.

Teaching students how to be parents in a television culture is also a part of liberation. Participation and discussion rather than proscription or prescription is the best way to put the person, and not the set, in control of the message.

Teaching citizenship in the television age involves the struggle for public access to and real participation in the institutional decision-making process affecting the humanization of our species. This includes a broader resource base enabling the medium to address a greater variety of interests and needs than the middle-majority consumer market. Only then will television be able to create a world of stories fit for all groups in our diverse society.

As teachers, parents, and citizens we can work for a fresh approach to liberal education aimed at liberation from the mass-produced dreams that hurt.

These, at least, are the dreams that heal!

36   MASS CULTURE, POLITICAL CONSCIOUSNESS, AND ENGLISH STUDIES*

Donald Lazere

In order to understand this essay on Marxist cultural theory as it applies to the mass media, it is useful to review a few central concepts of Marxist theory for those who may not be familiar with his ideas. (Let me mention, in passing, that many scholars in the critical tradition of media studies are not Marxists and that many Marxists do not approve of the kind of societies found in Russia and its Eastern European satellites.)

1. *Dialectical Materialism.* Marx believed that the economic system or "mode of production" found in a society shaped, in complicated ways, its beliefs and values...and thus, human consciousness. As Marx wrote, "The mode of production of material life determines the general character of the social, political, and spiritual processes of life. It is not the consciousness of men that determines their being, but, on the contrary, their social being determines their consciousness." Ideas, then, are products of society. In Marxist terms, the economic system is called the base and the legal, political, religious, and other institutions are called the superstructure.

2. *Class Conflict.* All societies are divided into classes and history is the record of class conflict. Marx wrote, "the history of all hitherto existing society is the history of class struggles." Marx hoped to abolish classes and by so doing abolish conflict. Those who owned the factories, etc. were called by Marx the "bourgeoisie." The rest of society, the workers, he called the "proletariat."

3. *False Consciousness.* Marx believed that the ruling class is able to impose its ideas about things upon the masses. He wrote, "the ideas of the ruling class are, in every age, the ruling ideas: i.e. the class which is the dominant material force in society is at the same time the dominant intellectual force." If the ruling classes can convince the masses to accept the status quo and that class differences are good or natural (that is, its ideological views) there will be no problem of revolution or strife, and the bourgeoisie can continue to exploit the proletariat.

The media, then, are important because they are a fundamental means of generating false consciousness in the masses. And the Marxist critics focus, then, on the ideological content hidden in the media and try to expose it. Much of this ideology is spread by people who actually believe it — that is, Marxists do not argue that the media is manipulative and spreading ideology consciously. It is the fact that ideology is so taken-for-granted that makes it so dangerous.

The critical tradition that has dealt most fully with the politics of mass culture is Marxist cultural theory. Many people still make the outmoded association of Marxist theory with Stalinism and simplistic notions of socialist realism, but the most valuable recent Marxist criticism has been written in vehement opposition to these notions. (See the November 1972 *College English* issue on new Marxist literary criticism.) Nor does one need to espouse Marxism whole to take it seriously as an intellectual discipline and to find value in its analytic methods, as many critics have done in the past and, increasingly, in the present — critics including non-Marxist socialists and independent leftists; some of the contributors to this issue, for example, would not call themselves Marxists, but most draw to a greater or lesser extent from Marxist theory.

Applied to any aspect of culture, Marxist method seeks to explicate the manifest and latent or coded reflections of modes of material production, ideological values, class relations and structures of social power — racial or sexual as well as politico-economic — or the state of consciousness of people in a precise historical or socio-economic situation. In this issue, for example, Fredric Jameson finds in the relations between the characters (and actors) in the film *Dog Day Afternoon* a complexly symbolic expression, probably unintended by the filmmakers, of individuals' sense of powerlessness in today's age of impersonal, multinational-corporate rule. The Marxist method, recently in varying degrees of combination with structuralism and semiology, has provided an incisive analytic tool for studying the political signification in every facet of contemporary culture, including popular entertainment in TV and films, music, mass circulation books, newspaper and magazine features, comics, fashion, tourism, sports and games, as well as such acculturating institutions as education, religion, the family and child-rearing, social and sexual relations between men and women — all the patterns of work, play, and other customs of everyday life. The English critic Richard Hoggart has provided a good model for this kind of analysis in *The Uses of Literacy*; Roland Barthes has devoted a book, *Système de la Mode*, to the semiotics of fashion; and Stanley Aronowitz can do a minute explication of children's games,[1] methods of painting a door in different countries, or the sexual-political folkways of a San Francisco billiards bar. The most frequent theme in Marxist cultural criticism is the way the prevalent mode of production and the ideology of the ruling class in any society dominate every phase of culture, and, at present, the way capitalist production and ideology dominate American culture, along with that of the rest of the world that American business and culture have colonized. This domination is perpetuated both through overt propaganda in political rhetoric, news reporting, advertising and public relations, and through the often unconscious absorption of capitalistic values by creators and consumers in all the above aspects of the culture of everyday life.

The preeminent importance in the twentieth century of ideology as a means of political control was emphasized early in the century by Georg Lukács in *History and Class Consciousness*, where he analyzed the false consciousness imposed by capitalist ideology on the working class that caused them to accept beliefs that are against their own self-interest, and by Antonio Gramsci in his formulation of "ideological hegemony" whereby the interests of the capitalist class are made to appear to all other segments of society as the natural, immutable order of the world. By the 1930s the role of modern mass culture as a key agency of ideological hegemony became a central concern of the "Frankfurt School," which included Max Horkheimer, T. W. Adorno, Erich Fromm, Leo Lowenthal, and Herbert Marcuse, all of whom emigrated to the United States after the rise of Hitler and subsequently focused their attention on American mass culture. The Frankfurt School critics perceived that in the twentieth century mass culture has surpassed the church and challenged the family and the state (with which it has increasingly merged) among the most influential socializing forces. They also saw certain similarities between all modern mass societies, whether in totalitarian dictatorships or capitalist democracies; whereas fascism and communism use police state repression and blatant propaganda to control the masses, in ostensibly free countries like the United States mass production and communication have created the less heavy-handed and brutal but little less efficient weapon of cultural conditioning, whereby the capitalist class is able to regiment mass consciousness and perpetuate what Marcuse terms "the systematic moronization of children and adults alike by publicity and propaganda."

Similar critiques of mass society were, of course, made through the forties and fifties by Orwell in *1984* and Huxley in *Brave New World Revisited*, by C. Wright Mills, Fromm (preeminently in *The Sane Society* in 1955, a book whose value has been underestimated), and "the New York intellectuals" associated with journals such as *Partisan Review*, *Politics*, the early *Commentary*, and *Dissent*, among whom the critics of mass culture included Dwight Macdonald, Clement Greenberg, Edmund Wilson, Paul Goodman, Leslie Fiedler, Irving Howe, Mary McCarthy, Norman Mailer, and James Baldwin. Thus the views on mass society of the New York intellectuals and the Frankfurt School dominated the monumental collection *Mass Culture* edited by Bernard Rosenberg and David Manning White in 1957. Most of the New York intellectuals, however, with the exception of Goodman, Baldwin, and (to some extent) Mailer, by the fifties had backed away from their earlier Marxism and somewhat muted their criticisms of capitalism and the United States under the exigencies of Cold-War anti-Communism; they now, like the elitist cultural conservatives,

tended to hold the masses themselves, rather than their capitalistic manipulators, responsible for their benightedness. In rejecting the manipulation thesis, they prepared the way for the popular culture school, which,
with McLuhan as mediator, simply focused on the positive rather than the
negative aspects of what McQuade and Atwan accept as the "common culture" between commercial producers and consumers.[2]

Marcuse's *One Dimensional Man* in 1964, then, added little that was
radically new in theory to the various earlier critiques of mass society and
culture. The catalytic effect of that book and Marcuse's subsequent works
resulted from their coinciding historically with the civil rights, anti-
Vietnam War, and (later) feminist movements, and with the reawaken-
ing awareness among the young after the virtual moratorium on criticism
of capitalism during the earlier Cold War — of the manipulativeness,
dishonesty, and increasingly monopolistic power of American state and
corporate capitalism. The growing concern among critics since *One
Dimensional Man* over the extent of mass-cultural throught control in the
United States and other Western democracies is indicated in the titles of
several recent books: Hans Magnus Enzensberger's *The Consciousness
Industry*, Guy Debord's *Society of the Spectacle*, Herbert Schiller's *The
Mind Managers* and *Communication and Cultural Domination*, Stuart
Ewen's *Captains of Consciousness*, Stanley Aronowitz's *False Promises:
The Shaping of American Working Class Consciousness*, Robert Sobel's *The
Manipulators: America in the Media Age*, and Kevin Phillips' *Mediacracy*.
(All of these authors except the last two are leftists. Sobel and Phillips
represent a movement by conservatives to coopt the leftist critique by
locating power in media personnel themselves, without considering them as
agents of corporate capitalism, and by focusing on the points of opposition
between media and the state rather than of collaboration.)

The French situationist Debord's notion of *la société du spectacle* has
become central in New Left cultural criticism. As Norman Fruchter puts it,

> The spectacle is the continuously produced and therefore continuously
> evolving pseudo-reality, predominantly visual, which each individual
> encounters, inhabits and accepts as public and official *reality*, thereby
> denying as much as is possible, the daily private reality of exploitation,
> pain, suffering and inauthenticity he or she experiences.[3]

The conlonization of leisure time in the twentieth century, the manufacture of mindless distraction to fill people's every spare moment, is a more
pervasive means of keeping the masses diverted from critical political consciousness than any bread and circuses devised by earlier ruling classes —
even though the culture industry's immediate motivation may not be
political mind control so much as profits. The majority of Americans are
probably more knowledgeable about and emotionally involved in "Kojak"
and the Super Bowl than about their society's gravest problems. Another
aspect of the spectacle is that in our time politics is show business and show

business is politics. Secretary of State Kissinger is interviewed by Howard Cosell on the telecast of the baseball play-offs and fervently declares, "I've been a Yankee fan all my life." All political sectors, from the President to the SLA, have learned every trick for getting maximum media exposure. One of the Croatian nationalists who skyjacked a jetliner to publicize their cause summed it up when he surrendered and broke in half the fake stick of dynamite with which he had terrorized the passengers, cracking, "That's show business." For the television generation, the lines have become blurred between reality and make-believe, between news, drama, and salesmanship. The events of Watergate did not have the full stamp of authenticity in the public's mind until they were aesthetically shaped on film as *All the President's Men*; the real Woodward and Bernstein now look like second-rate imitations of Redford and Hoffman.

The professional consultants who developed the format of rapid-fire, "top forty stories" local newscasts justified it by claiming, "People who watch television the most are unread, uneducated, untraveled and unable to concentrate on single subjects more than a minute or two." The fragmented discourse, the mixture of the important with the trivial, the deadening of sensitivity by the glut of senseless violence in TV and film "entertainment," the sheer overload of media messages tends ultimately to leave people in a state of confusion and apathy, unable to make critical distinctions and paralyzed from meaningful political action. The article by Aronowitz in this issue discusses the cumulating psychological effects of mass culture as an influence in the inertia of college students in the seventies, in declining reading and writing skills, and in what more and more teachers are perceiving to be a drastic deterioration in students' cognitive and reasoning capacities.

Some recent leftist critics like Enzensberger, Gitlin, and Aronowitz (in *False Promises* and elsewhere) have argued that the Orwellian-Marcusean vision of an irremediably stupefied society is based on an overly pessimistic, undialectical analysis. They claim that the bureaucratic agencies of state and corporate control are too cumbersome to be fully effective, that indigenous expressions of cultural autonomy, especially among the industrial working class, will always resist regimentation, and that the media inadvertantly generate oppositional forces. Now, no one except the most paranoid leftists and rightists believes that the media are monolithic in intent or effect. If television was largely responsible for the selling of President Nixon and of the Vietnam War, it was also later responsible for their unselling. And the most inane features of mass media can backfire on their producers. The insertion of commercials in the telecasts of *Roots* — especially one showing a suburban woman taking Rolaids to ease her upset stomach during an exciting furniture auction, which followed the harrowing depiction of an eighteenth-century slave auction — probably nullified the impact of the latter for some viewers, but for others it brought home the grotesqueness both of commercial sponsorship and of the contrast between affluent middle-class society and the degradation of blacks past and present.

It is also true that freedom of cultural expression in the United States has tended to expand since the dismal period of the 1950s, although this is somewhat cyclical (we still have not fully recovered from the cycle of repression during the Vietnam War and following the black power and campus movements), has had to be fought for, and varies from medium to medium. (The monopolization of ownership in print media is one regressive tendency; by the time this appears, Rupert Murdoch may own *College English*, along with the *New York Post, New York, New West*, and the *Village Voice*.) It is encouraging that TV shows and films critical of American society like *Roots, Return to Manzanar, Fear on Trial*, and *The Selling of the Pentagon*, or *Network, The Godfather* (especially Part II), *The Front, Bound for Glory, Chinatown, One Flew Over the Cuckoo's Nest, Catch-22*, and even *King Kong*, can be made and reach a wide audience today, which they could not have twenty years ago — even though they all have their ideological limitations, mainly in portraying purely individualistic rather than organized revolt against the corporate state, revolt that ends in either the escape or crushing of the hero, which in either case leaves the sociopolitical status quo unchanged.

On the other hand, the Marcusean critic can argue that cultural control has been so highly developed that the ruling powers can allow opposition culture a fairly loose rein, thus perpetuating the semblance of a free, pluralistic society, while still remaining able to insure that it lacks sufficient force to break through the overall constraints of the society of the spectacle. The countercultural "revolution" of the sixties was quickly coopted and commercially debased. Provocative as ABC-TV's *Roots* was, one wonders why it could not have been produced twenty-five years ago, when its impact might have changed the whole course both of American race relations and of television quality. (Moreover, if *Roots* had not first been shown in mid-winter but in summertime, it might very likely have sparked ghetto riots.) When white viewers exclaimed, "We never knew" the true meaning of slavery before *Roots*, one could take it as an affirmation of the political power of art, but one could also ask, why *didn't* you know? Slavery is not exactly an obscure episode in American history, and TV must bear a large burden of blame for previously obscuring not only black history but the whole sense of history in general for a generation of Americans. The current crop of popular anti-1950s blacklist films, TV shows, and books, as well as the Woody Guthrie revival in *Bound for Glory* and elsewhere, are other cases of too little too late. In 1960 I submitted an article to the liberal *New York Post* attempting to gain some recognition for Guthrie, who was slowly dying in poverty and obscurity in a state hospital. Although the article mentioned nothing about his politics, it was rejected because the editors learned that Guthrie was an unregenerate communist.

Whatever degree of freedom and effectiveness opposition culture has in the United States, its ultimate constriction is the muting of any widely circulated, fundamental questioning of the capitalistic economic system or advocacy of socialism as an alternative. Throughout most of the Cold War, until quite recently, it has been virtually unheard of for any Democratic or Republican politician, any mass circulation newspaper reporter or commentator, any Hollywood film or TV show to say anything favorable about even non-communistic forms of socialism over "free enterprise." The most effective way this constriction is imposed is through a semantic ploy whereby in every phase of American public discourse capitalism as an economic system is confused or equated with political democracy, freedom, and patriotism, so that advocates of any variety of socialism (most of whom in fact believe that a socialist economy can be more conducive than capitalism to these political values) get defined into being anti-democratic and un-American. Thus even social democrats in the United States get labeled as "radical" or "extremist," while in most other democracies today they, along with more militant socialist parties, form a majority of the population and have a respected place in political, cultural, and academic life. And only in America are communists and anti-communistic socialists lumped together in the public's mind.

Because American political debate is parochially confined to the terms of liberalism vs. conservatism or the Democratic vs. the Republican party rather than the terms of capitalism vs. socialism, capitalism is simply taken for granted on all sides, to the point where it is virtually invisible as a political entity or issue. Favoritism toward capitalism is not perceived as a form of political partisanship. Hence newspeople, entertainers, or teachers can extol (or simply not question) the free enterprise system and still believe themselves to be "neutral" and "objective." In the same way the Advertising Council, which as William Lutz argues in this issue is in effect a propaganda agency for corporate capitalism, can ingenuously assert that its public service announcements are "non-commercial, non-denominational, non-partisan politically, and not designed to influence legislation." The obituary for Walt Disney in the *Los Angeles Times* claimed, "His characters knew no politics, and received affection from the young at heart of whatever political persuasion or ideology." Compare this judgment with Michael Real's analysis, in his just published book *Mass-Mediated Culture*, of Disneyland, which he finds to be a microcosm of capitalist ideology, or with Dorfman and Mattelart's book *How to Read Donald Duck*, which sees the Disney comics distributed in Latin America as filled with propaganda for American corporate imperialism. When Real hypothesizes a communist version of Disneyland or when, in this issue, Robert Cirino presents a scenario for an American socialist TV newscast (or, as he does elsewhere in his book in progress, *We're Being More than Entertained*, for "Kojak," "Marcus Welby," "The Waltons," *Jaws*, and *Reader's Digest*) readers are apt to snicker at what they perceive to be blatant propaganda. And yet, isn't it an indication of how acculturated we have been that we do not normally recognize the actual products as equally blatant propaganda for capitalism? These examples perfectly illustrate Marx's definition of ideological hegemony, the capacity of any ruling class "to represent its interest as the common interest of all the members of society, put in an ideal form; it will give its ideas the form of universality, and represent them as the only rational, universally valid ones." Indeed, as the only *conceivable* ones.

Even the kind of immediate politico-economic problems whose understanding is a necessary precondition to the ultimate questioning of capitalism have been played down in news reporting and every other form of American culture since the Cold War began. The continued existence of gross extremes of wealth and poverty, the role in foreign policy of international finance and corporate competition for markets, monetary policy, inflation and unemployment — nothing influences our lives so directly, yet is so little understood, so negligibly reported on, analyzed, or dramatized in popular media. The inner workings are mystified: "It's all too complicated for us; only the President and Arthur Burns can understand it."

Nevertheless, the political, economic, and environmental crises that have shaken the United States in the last decade have generated a resurgent sense throughout the country that socialism may be the only viable long-range means of solving these problems. There is a movement supported by socialists like Michael Harrington and William Domhoff to establish an openly socialistic wing in the Democratic Party. Several independent socialist general circulation publications have been started in the last year or so, including *Seven Days*, *In These Times*, and *Working papers for a New Society* — although *Ramparts* folded and the survival of any publication not subsidized by capitalist advertising dollars is precarious. More articles advocating socialism have appeared recently than at any time since the outset of the Cold War in liberal (but not socialist) journals like *Harper's*, *The Nation*, and the *Village Voice*.[4] The most significant sign of a socialist renaissance is that such bulwarks of capitalist ideological hegemony as the Advertising Council, *Time* (in a cover article), and *TV Guide*[5] have recently been compelled to acknowledge it and print defenses of capitalism — thereby making the momentous concession that capitalism is a contestable entity, not invisible and inalterable as the air we breathe. When Nixon had to drop his facade of blithe obliviousness toward his attackers and attest, "I am not a crook," you knew he was in big trouble.

The basic problem of mass culture under capitalism is that most major media of public information are owned by businessmen and supported by advertisers whose need to maximize profits works against artistic integrity and freedom of expression. They are going to be naturally inclined to restrict ideological content to that which favors their particular interests and those of capitalism in general. Defenders of capitalism argue that if an opposition movement, even for socialism, becomes so widespread that it becomes profitable to cater to it, the culture industry will do so, thereby proving that the profit motive guarantees free expression. One can agree with this in theory, but still point out a catch in practice: the long range self-interest of capitalists is likely to motivate them to use their control of media to keep oppositional opinion from ever emerging in the first place, so that if opposition does survive, it is in spite of, not because of, the profit motive. And it remains to be seen just how far corporate capitalism will go in publicizing a movement for its own abolition.

Few American socialists would want to replace capitalism with bureau-cratic state monopoly and Soviet-style commissars in culture or any politico-economic area — although this is what many Americans have been misled to think socialists believe in. The model for a democratic-socialist communications system would have a pluralistic structure something like that envisioned by Cirino in this issue, or one in which a diversity of non-profit media would be financed by local communities (like WNYC in New York), public corporations like BBC and PBS, direct support from listeners and viewers (Pacifica Radio, pay-TV), universities and school systems, workers' and consumers' cooperatives, trade unions, and other interest groups. Most sober-minded socialists recognize that instituting such a system would entail its own problems and that once instituted it would undoubtedly have its own flaws; there is no certainty that it would even necessarily be an improvement in every respect over the capitalistic system, but it can provide in its theoretical structure plausible *possibilities* for improvement precluded by the structure of capitalism.

NOTES

1. *False Promises* (New York: McGraw-Hill, 1973), pp. 61–69.
2. The decreasing emphasis on capitalism as a factor in mass culture that characterized "end of ideology" criticism during the Cold War can be seen in the revisions in attitude and vocabulary between Dwight Macdonald's "A Theory of Popular Culture" in *Politics* (1944), "A Theory of Mass Culture" in the Rosenberg-White *Mass Culture* (1953), and "Masscult and Midcult" in *Partisan Review* (1960), and Macdonald's *Against the American Grain* (1962) — although Macdonald remained more critical of capitalism than most Cold War liberals. A similar rejection of the manipulation thesis is apparent in David Riesman's *The Lonely Crowd* (1953) and Daniel Boorstin's *The Image* (1962). Boorstin, after a brilliant exposition of mind-manipulation by business and government, concludes, "While we have given others great power to deceive us, to create pseudo-events, celebrities, and images, they could not have done so without our collaboration. If there is a crime of deception being committed in America today, each of us is the principal, and all others are only accessories....Each of us must disenchant himself, must moderate his expectations, must prepare himself to receive messages coming in from the outside." (New York: Harper Colophon Books, 1964), p. 260.
3. "Movement Propaganda and the Culture of the Spectacle," *Liberation* (May 1971), pp. 4–17, followed by commentary from Todd Gitlin and Lee Baxandall.
4. Robert Lekachman, "The Specter of Full Employment," *Harper's*, February 1977; Robert Bellah and Michael Harrington, "Coming Around to Socialism," *The Nation*, December 28, 1974; Pete Hamill, "Socialism: America's Great Fear May Be Our Only Hope," *The Village Voice*, January 13, 1975.
5. "Can Capitalism Survive?", *Time*, July 14, 1975; Edith Efron, "Television News' Invisible Issue: Socialism," *TV Guide*, August 21, 1976.

37   # THE IMAGE FREEZING MACHINE*
STANLEY MILGRAM

There's more to a photograph than meets the eye, as this essay on photography points out. To supplement Milgram's ideas, let me offer some quotations from an important book on the subject, Susan Sontag's *On Photography*.[1] These quotations and the essay that follows should help you think about photography in a different way. And you can apply the insights you gain from this material to advertising, graphic design, film, television, and any other area where photographic images are found.

1. In deciding how a picture should look, in preferring one exposure to another, photographers are always imposing standards on their subjects. Although there is a sense in which the camera does indeed capture reality, not just interpret it, photographs are as much an interpretation of the world as paintings and drawings are. (pp. 6, 7)

2. ...There is something predatory in the act of taking a picture. To photograph people is to violate them, by seeing them as they never see themselves, by having knowledge of them they can never have; it turns people into objects that can be symbolically possessed. Just as the camera is a sublimation of the gun, to photograph someone is a sublimated murder — a soft murder, appropriate to a sad, frightened time. (pp. 14, 15)

3. In a world ruled by photographic images, all borders ("framing") seem arbitrary. Anything can be separated, can be made discontinuous, from anything else: all that is necessary is to frame the subject differently. (Conversely, anything can be made adjacent to anything else.) Photography reinforces a nominalist view of social reality as consisting of small units of an apparently infinite number — as the number of photographs that could be taken of anything is unlimited. (p. 22)

4. A capitalist society requires a culture based on images. It needs to furnish vast amounts of entertainment in order to stimulate buying and anesthetize the injuries of class, race, and sex. And it needs to gather unlimited amounts of information in order to better exploit natural resources, increase productivity, keep order, make war, give jobs to bureaucrats...

---

* Published by permission of Transaction, Inc. from "The Image-Freezing Machine," by Stanley Milgram, *Society*, Nov./Dec. 1976, pp. 7–12. Copyright © 1976 by Transaction, Inc.

Cameras define reality in the two ways essential to the working of an advanced industrial society: as a spectacle (for masses) and as an object of surveillance (for rulers). (p. 178)

REFERENCE

1. Sontag, Susan, 1973. *On Photography*. New York: Delta Books (Dell).

The habit of taking pictures is now so widespread that we forget how recent it is. At the beginning of the nineteenth century only a talent for drawing or painting would allow a person to visually record what he saw. At the end of the century anyone could do it with the aid of a simple rectangular box. He looked into a small ground glass window, framed the picture he wanted, then pushed the shutter. Kodak did the rest.

EVOLUTIONARY DEVELOPMENT

The best way to grasp the human significance of photography is not to think of camera, film, and tripod as something external to human nature, but as evolutionary developments as much a part of human nature as the opposable thumb. A deficiency existed in the way our sensory and information-storing capacities functioned. They had limits, and photography was one way to overcome those limits. The limit in human functioning is simply that although we can see things very well, we cannot store what we see so that we can reliably bring up the image for repeated viewing. Instead, visual images are incompletely stored in memory — often in a highly schematized form — and subject to decay and distortion.

Moreover, memory is private. It resides in the neural structure of the individual and does not directly take the form of an external object that others can see. And when the person dies all the images stored in his brain vanish, along with all the other information he possesses.

The perishability of our visual experience led men to seek to fix it by externalizing it, by placing it on something more permanent and more available to public scrutiny than the brain. A first solution to this problem evolved through the development of skills in painting and drawing. Man had the capacity to depict what he saw by representing those forms and colors on an external surface. But this act required a special talent, which only a fraction of men possessed.

WHAT DID PEOPLE RECORD?

An optochemical means for recording visual images was achieved in the nineteenth century: photography allowed anyone to freeze a moment of visual experience and thus to augment his memory, to preserve it beyond his own lifetime, and to show others what he saw. To a psychologist this new capacity to fix and externalize visual experience is intriguing, for it immediately raises the question of what people chose to render into permanent photographic images.

In principle the camera could be used to record any visual event. But the fact is that people overwhelmingly wanted to record images of themselves and their loved ones. The growth of portrait photography in the nineteenth century absorbed photography with a voracious thirst that revealed the extraordinary need for an image-freezing machine. The process was scarcely known before 1839; within twenty years commercial studios had sprung up in New York, London, Paris, and Basle. A hundred thousand daguerreotype portraits were made in Paris in 1849. By 1860 New York City claimed more than fifty photoportrait studios. It is true that some photographers could make a living taking pictures of faraway places and selling them; but the business end of the enterprise rested overwhelmingly on photoportraiture.

AUDITORY VERSUS VISUAL

To understand how special this fact is, consider that when later in the century the technical means for recording not visual but auditory events became possible, there was no such rush to record oneself. Indeed, while people wanted pictures of themselves, they wanted sound recordings not of their own voices but of impersonal cultural objects — above all, music.

So the recording of the visual and the auditory aspects of experience are skewed in enormously different ways. Even today there are hundreds of record stores in which we shop for sound recordings of musical groups. But picture stores, in which we shop for recorded images, are not to be found on anything like this scale.

We need to dig a little deeper into the contrasts between visual and auditory recording. The recording of sound depends on a performance, while visual recording does not. The photographed person may remain passive and still be recorded.

This contrast between the passivity of photography and activity of sound recording reaches down to the very origin of the physical energies underlying the two processes: the energy for a voice recording originates in the activity of the speaker, but the energy for a photograph of him is external in origin, merely light that has bounced off him. You can photograph a corpse but not record him on a casette. The potentially passive nature of the object photographed colors the entire process; it means that the camera captures what one is, a state of being. One does not have to do anything for it. It merely soaks you in. Perhaps for that reason voice recording studios, which require performance, have never developed on anything like the scale of photographic studios.

PHOTOPORTRAITURE

The phenomenon of photographic portraiture is even more revealing when we consider the stereotyped nature of portraiture. After all, even if a man wants a visual record of himself, he may want a record of himself doing something worthwhile (such as giving money to a beggar, helping a lame animal, or lending a tool to a neighbor). Instead, we find men and women seated before the cameras, in general not doing anything but looking, at most aided by a prop of a book or surrounded by other family members. People did not want a photographic rendering of themselves performing a specific action as much as they wanted a general statement of their character.

The sources of this attitude are not hard to find. To some extent they derive from traditional oil portraiture, and the camera was merely a cheap way to acquire the equivalent of an oil painting. Then, too, the early technology of photography did not permit action shots, and it was to the photographic entrepreneur's advantage to do all his work in the studio. But most of all it was a desire to have not specific actions but one's general likeness recorded for posterity. Although the subject knew that he had nothing to do but sit and be photographed, he realized that the full burden of a multitude of moods and moments would be represented by that single exposure of the camera. The burden placed on that moment was very substantial, and motivated the subject to work for an optimal image: he posed.

We all make some adjustment as we take account of the person we are dealing with. Even half-consciously we are able to adjust ourselves to act in a manner appropriate to the specific situation. But the problem of a photograph is that, although it is taken in one situation, it may be seen by many people and in many situations. How then are we to adjust to the camera? How can we create a facial expression that is generically useful, and not merely useful for a narrowly defined occasion?

The most typical strategy, particularly when photography was first coming into general use, was to use a socially conventional face and express as much civic virtue as possible in the exposed moment, an attitude that — together with the technical necessity of holding a stationary position for a matter of minutes — led to the bland, stilted photographs that were the typical product of nineteenth century daguerrian studios.

There was one human experience that all human beings had known in the nineteenth century and that led them to underestimate the truthful-

Snapshot of Stanley Milgram and Arthur Asa Berger

ness of the camera. I am not speaking of portraits by artists, which were limited to the well-to-do, but a more mundane experience: the mirror. If you had never had a photograph taken of yourself, the best clue to what it would look like was based on what you had seen in the mirror. And that is where the surprise came in. For individuals almost never reject what they see in the mirror, but hundreds of daguerreotypes were angrily denounced by men and women who knew they were more comely than the photograph showed.

They should have learned that the psychological preparations made before looking into a mirror are such that we do not affront our own self-image. Even today individuals are constantly rejecting unflattering snapshots, firmly believing that they could never look as bad as the photograph shows. But such reactions rarely come upon looking into a mirror. Perhaps the old saying "a mirror offers us a thousand faces; we only accept one" contains the relevant wisdom.

The camera, by freezing our faces at a particular moment and from a particular viewpoint, often gives us one of those faces we would prefer not to accept. But, unlike the mirror, we cannot make those instantaneous adjustments — turns of the head, lowering of the eyelids, search for the exact angle — that defuse the offending image. Rather, we rely on the photographer to function as an ego supporter and photograph us as we would like to be presented to that generic constituency which is the audience of all photographs.

PHOTOGRAPHIC ART

Photography is a way of recording the visual aspect of things for further scrutiny. Only one other sensory modality, hearing, has been similarly susceptible to recording. We do not as yet have adequate technologies for recording experiences of smell, touch, or taste; and we do not feel much need for developing them. But of the need to have a visual record there can be no doubt, as the growth of a vast photographic industry attests.

But it is not only capturing a likeness that is the essence of photography. We know that life masks can be made that depict the person's physiognomy in three dimensions, or at least in bas-relief. Yet such techniques never acquired the popularity of photography. Of course there is the greater convenience of photography. But beyond that matter, the reduction of the image to the two-dimensional plane is the crucial element.

Consider that stereoscopic photographs were available as early as the mid-nineteenth century, yet play only a minor part in photography. Color film has found a secure place in photography; but though of high technical excellence it has not supplanted black and white, which continues to exert an attraction to millions of photographers (particularly those of artistic bent). The abstracting quality of the black-and-white two-dimensional photograph appeals to many photographers over the greater verisimilitude of stereoscopy and color. It remains to be seen whether the recently discovered hologram, with its uncanny shifting parallax, will force a fundamental change in emphasis. History suggests that although holograms may develop a significant niche of their own, they will not supplant the ordinary black-and-white print.

TRADE-OFF

The act of taking a picture, like the act of seeing itself, occurs in a broad range of human situations and always involves some sort of exchange. There is the trade-off between the passive enjoyment of a unique moment and the active process of photographing it. The man who sees a beautiful scene, and has his camera, stops to take a picture; but the photographic act may interfere with his fully savoring the experience. There is not only the minor inconvenience of carrying a few pounds of camera equipment, but the interruption of a fully spontaneous set of activities by the need to stop to take pictures and divide his attention between enjoyment of the scene and the mental set needed to photograph it. The photographic act devalues the moment, as he trades the full value of the present instant for a future record of it.

The very meaning of human activities, such as travel, becomes transformed by photographic possibilities. We seek out places not only for their beauty, but because they are suitable backgrounds for our pictures. A group of tourists, Nikons hanging about their necks, sees its arrival at the Eiffel Tower as the consummation of a photographic quest. The place becomes subordinate to its photographic potential. The value of our vacation will depend not only on what we experience at the moment, but on how it all comes out in the pictures. This contamination of the pleasurable present by the photographic urge is prompting growing numbers of vacationers to leave their cameras home.

But if the photographing act is best seen as an exchange, this view is most clearly present when we photograph other people. What kind of exchange is it? The English language is blunt: a photographer *takes* a picture. He does not create a picture or borrow one, he *takes* it. A camera bug travels to a foreign country, sees a peasant in the field, and takes a picture of him. Now why does the photographer think he has the right to snatch the image of the peasant? It is true that the photographer invests time, film, and effort into taking the picture, but it is hard to understand wherein he derives the right to keep for his own purposes the image of the peasant's face.

Photography is an exchange, obviously unfair; and the native who once allowed himself to be photographed, just to be pleasant, in time may realize that he is giving away something — his image — for nothing. There is, of course, the pride he may feel of having been deemed worthy as a subject of a photograph; but in the long run this type of glory wears thin, and the native may decide to charge the photographer (as boys in the Caribbean do with increasing frequency). The relationship becomes a professional one.

PHOTOGRAPHER-SUBJECT RELATIONSHIP

Naturally it is convenient for photographers to carry on their activities with the assumption that individuals, tacitly at least, give their assent to being photographed. (I am referring now not to the use of the photograph — which is bound by legal constraints — but to the act of photographing others, which is considerably less controlled by law). But how do people feel about giving away their image? How many people would actually agree to have their picture taken by a stranger for some unspecified purpose?

To study this subject my students and I recently went into the streets of midtown Manhattan. Camera in hand, each of us asked a stranger, "May I take your picture?" If asked to explain his motives, the student answered simply, "I'm interested in photography." We posed the question to more than one hundred people in Bryant Park and on 40th and 42nd streets.

In the street 35 percent allowed us to take their picture, while 65 percent refused. Hands went up over the face, people scowled or walked hurriedly — reminding us that the act of photographing has given rise to a whole set of gestures that never existed before the camera: gestures of the photographer, gestures of the subject allowing or refusing to be photographed. Photography has created an entirely new choreography of human body movement.

In Bryant Park itself the population divided evenly between those who assented and those who refused. Females were less willing than males to have their picture taken. The willingness of people to have their picture taken interacts subtly with mood temperament and the exact pose and circumstances of the potential subject. Of the six people we approached who were lounging on the grass, five agreed to have their picture taken — an impressive proportion.

We have only begun this sociopsychological inquiry into the act of photographing, but one point is already clear. The culture of photography is so widespread, and the normality of taking pictures so deeply rooted, that everyone understood what it meant to be photographed and took the request in stride.

The importance of this fact can only be understood in comparison with other requests we might make. For example, a few years ago our class went into the New York Subway. Each student stood in front of a seated passenger, and asked, "May I have your seat?" However trivial the request may seem, it is extremely difficult to utter and, for some, impossible.

But the act of asking if we might take someone's picture is not nearly as difficult; it flows naturally and is self-justifying. It is part of a shared culture. Perhaps in our culture we are profligate with our image because we feel that the photographer does not really take it from us but simply reproduces it, a form of visual cloning in which the original is not diminished even while multiples of itself are created. Degrees of camera shyness vary among cultures, and who knows where wisdom resides? Maybe the custom of letting strangers take our pictures bespeaks an inexcusable indifference to our own image.

But now we are slipping into insubstantial fantasies when a far more significant question remains in the relationship between the photographer and his subject. This question concerns the capacity of some photographers to render portraits of greater artistic depth than others. Some critics attribute this capacity to the superior selectivity of the master photographer: he seeks out faces of potential interest, then selects the right moment to snap the shutter. No doubt this search is part of the process.

But when we examine photographs of Diane Arbus, for example, we begin to understand that the psychological consistency in the faces of many diverse individuals must in part be due to the photographer's capacity to induce a certain attitude or expression in the subject and that a subtle psychological relationship exists between photographer and subject in which the photographer — or at least some photographers — play a part in creating the faces they photograph.

PSYCHOLOGICAL PROCESSES

The job of the photographer, and that of the psychologist interested in photography, are very different. The photographer seeks to capture a particular moment on film; the psychologist tries to explain why the photographer is taking the picture and how motives, perceptual processes, and emotional factors come into play. He tries to do so through research, conducting experiments, and formulating questions open to inquiry. It is odd that Eastman Kodak spends vast sums of research in film chemistry, but that so little research has been conducted on the larger social and psychological processes of photography.

Consider, for a moment, not the history of psychology, but its history within a single individual. An important set of psychological questions concerns the way in which a person learns to take photographs. Although children, for example, are reported to have a clear, naive vision of things — imbued with wonder and freshness — there are few great child photographers. Perhaps we have simply not placed the camera in the child's hands at a sufficiently early age; but, having seen large numbers of photographs taken by my own children, I am skeptical of this argument. On the whole, the freshness and even artistry we often find in children's drawings do not translate into their photographic view.

Psychologists have studied children's drawings for many years; they find that the drawings change systematically with age, and can often tell us a good deal about the mental processes of the child. But can photography be used in this way? What if we gave every two-year-old a camera and studied the pictures he look over the span of a lifetime? What would we learn about the child and about the growth of photographic skill as he matures? Perhaps there are Piagetian stages of development that will be revealed through a study of children's photographs. Is there a systematic shift in what and how he photographs comparable to systematic stages in the use of language and thought?

There is another side to the relationship of photography and human development. The individual learns not only how to take pictures, but also how to appear in them (that is, to pose). Infants are not self-conscious about cameras. They do not know what the camera is for, and this innocence allows us to capture their naive actions. But the child learns very quickly, and by the age of five or six he may not be able to stand in front of a camera without grimacing and feeling ill at ease. In most individuals this awkward feeling is gradually brought under the control of an adjustive response (a pose). Studying how poses change over time, in different social classes, in different cultures, and through the growth and maturation of the individual, is a first-class research problem.

The photographic process itself may help in analyzing this aspect of photography. Eadweard Muybridge used the camera to obtain a sequence of pictures of humans and animals in action so that he could better analyze the components of locomotion. We could do well to apply Muybridge's technique to the act of photography itself as a way of better understanding it. How might it be used to study, for example, the pose?

Here is one possible scenario. A person comes to a portrait studio to have his picture taken. From the moment he or she enters the studio a camera covertly takes a series of pictures of the person, perhaps one every ten seconds or so. The photographer performs his normal functions, poses the subject as he usually does, and snaps a series of portraits. By examining the portraits in the longer sequence taken by the hidden camera, it becomes easy to see how the official pose differs from the unposed pictures. It will help us understand the adjustments the individual makes to the camera. The method would be particularly instructive when a master portrait photographer is at work, for we would then be able to trace photographically the means by which he brings his subject to the desired appearance for the portrait.

This technique is easy, but some questions are hard to answer even through ingenious experiments. Why, for example, are some people photogenic and others not? Is it a matter of the perceptual effects in that certain three-dimensional forms translate more flatteringly into flat photographs than others; or do some people come alive before a camera, and relate to it with a radiance and warmth elicited by no other stimulus, while others twist their faces into anxious masks? Both factors are probably at work.

PSYCHOLOGY OF THE PHOTOGRAPHER

One of the most challenging questions deals with the psychological characteristics of the professional photographer. Certainly some kind of visual intelligence is needed for this type of work. But beyond that level the forms of activity are so varied that different constellations of motives and abilities are probably at work in different domains of the photographic profession.

As to why people become photographers, the answers are probably as dependent on chance and circumstance as they are in any other occupation. But are there any "hidden" motives underlying the practice of the photographer's craft? Freudian psychology might say that the profession of photography is a sublimated form of voyeurism, and that underlying every lifelong commitment to photography is some remnant of the desire to catch a glimpse of the primal scene (i.e., sexual intercourse between parents). Like the little boy peeking at that special scene, the photographer positions himself to view an event — not to intervene in it, but to passively register it.

We need not seriously accept this interpretation in order to acknowledge that a good photographer does require an extraordinary balance of passive and aggressive tendencies. He needs the aggressiveness to intrude himself into a situation where he is often irrelevant and sometimes unwanted. Photographs of funerals, accidents, and grief-stricken moments are not generally offered up to the photographer; they are taken by him, as a thief snatches diamonds. At the same time, there is a passive component to photography, for the photographer must keep himself receptive to the images presented by the environment and let them enter his camera.

Photographs can constitute an important psychological document about an individual. Robert U. Akeret's sensitive book *Photoanalysis* (1973) shows how far we can go in interpreting the psychological meaning of individual snapshots. But we can also use the aggregate of photographs in an individual's possession as an index of his psychic life. People ordinarily photograph only what interests them. If we examine the photographs a person has taken during his lifetime, we will be able to discern the things that were and were not important to him. It is probably as good a measure as we have of his enduring lifetime cathexes. Stuart Albert has suggested that we examine the entire content of family photo albums to see which events are recorded and which are not. He believes that we photograph mostly during periods of rapid change and growth, thus explaining the preponderance of photographs of children in their period of rapid maturation.

Through the family photo album the family constructs a type of fairy tale. Only the happy moments tend to be shown. Families construct a pseudonarrative that highlights all that was life affirming and pleasurable, with a systematic suppression of life's pains. However imperfect, for most contemporary families the album is the only narrative available of its history, having supplanted the family Bible — where, in earlier times, a record of births, deaths, and marriages was maintained.

Photography is ready for an invasion of psychologists and experimentalists who will not be satisfied to hear that there is something called the "decisive moment"; they will want to show how long it is, and find out what would happen if Cartier-Bresson were saddled with a camera whose shutter snapped unpredictably from five to thirty seconds after depressing the release button. Would he miss all the good shots? The psychologists will want to know whether the immediate feedback of a Polaroid system facilitates learning photographic skills, and whether certain personality types among photographers prefer color to black and white. The psychologists will want to probe into the enormous credibility of photographs. They will want to know who in the family takes the photographs and examine the pattern of photographs a person takes during a lifetime.

CREATING REALITY

But perhaps the most interesting set of questions concerns the photographs themselves and the socioimagistic reality they create. Photographs are often treated as compelling and incontrovertible evidence that the events depicted in them actually happened. This belief is overlayed by the fact that the photograph constitutes a reality, valued in and of itself. The pictures constitute a reality of their own and evoke emotions, attitudes, and convictions. Photographs, therefore, not only depict realities; they create a new plane of reality to which people respond.

There is a universe of events that we smell and a universe that we hear; there is also a universe of events whose existence is embodied in photographs. Thus each year we eagerly await the official Chinese Communist May Day photograph to see who is photographed alongside the chairman and who has been displaced. The official photograph is not only a reflection of the political reality, but itself solidifies that reality and becomes an element in it. The question, therefore, is to what degree events that exist in photographs exert an effect outside the photograph. Does a photograph act back on and shape the real world?

Events happen not only in the real world, but in photographs as well; and this new focus of action may exert a devastating power. House detectives have known this fact for years. A photograph showing a political candidate shaking hands with a Communist party official can ruin his chances for reelection, even when the photograph is fake.

Or consider a more typical case. An aspiring young lawyer sees the president for five minutes. A photograph is taken of the two men chatting; the lawyer proudly hangs it behind his desk. The image-freezing machine has done its work. Clients see the photograph, are impressed, draw inferences. The lawyer need never mention the photograph. It resoundingly speaks for itself, a powerful new element in the lawyer's career. The lawyer has learned through personal experience what prophets of photography have long suspected: a photograph not only records events, it creates them.

READINGS SUGGESTED BY THE AUTHOR:

Akeret, Robert U. *Photoanalysis: How to Interpret the Hidden Psychological Meaning of Personal and Public Photographs.* New York: Wyden, 1973.

Arnheim, R. "On the Nature of Photography." *Critical Inquiry* 1 (September 1974): 149–61.

Becker, Howard. "Photography and Sociology." *Studies in the Anthropology of Visual Communications* 5 (1974): 3–26.

Newhall, Beaumont. *The History of Photography.* New York: Museum of Modern Art, 1964.

Scharf, Aaron. *Art and Photography.* Baltimore: Penguin Books, 1974.
Sontag, S. "Photography." *New York Review of Books*, 18 October 1973; 13 November 1973; 18 April 1974.

38   PUBLIC TELEVISION: A SYSTEM OF COMPROMISES*

Anthony Tiano

There are two television publics in America. One, which is huge, watches commercial television; the other, which is relatively small, watches public television. The first group numbers well over 90 percent of the American public, which doesn't leave too many people for the second group.

But this second group tends to be, from a socioeconomic perspective, an elite. It is better educated than the general public, and made up of large numbers of professional people who are affluent. Many of these people are opinion leaders in their communities and they wield influence and power considerably out of proportion to their numbers.

Public television, as it currently exists, is a kind of narrowcasting that broadcasts programs that are not always designed to appeal to the so-called "lowest common denominator." There is, quite obviously, a need for this kind of programming. The question is — does public broadcasting do as good a job of serving its audience as it might?

The situation is complicated by a number of factors. What is the mission of public television? People disagree on this topic. Some who work in public television feel that having an audience of such a small percent makes them irrelevant. Others think that selectivity means, of necessity, relatively small audiences.

How should public television be supported? Traditionally, it has received a major amount of financial support from the government, but in recent years (and in an era of budget deficits) this support has been waning. How does one solve that problem?

Critics of public broadcasting suggest that it is very dull, full of nature films and dramas bought from the British Broadcasting Corporation. They claim it has not contributed anything particularly interesting to television, with the possible exception of Sesame Street and a few other programs.

This essay, specially written for this book by Anthony Tiano, the president and chief executive officer of Public Television Station KQED, gives a perspective from someone in the field who operates one of the more important stations in the system. It offers us some revealing insights about public broadcasting, in general, and the operation of a public broadcasting station, in particular.

"EDUCATIONAL TELEVISION"

The men who designed educational television in the United States made decisions about the role local educational broadcast stations would play in networking, funding, program production, and government support, which set the stage for a noble experiment in American media.

These men were educators — thinkers and dreamers, not businessmen — so educational television made very little sense from a business perspective. The agreements leading to the creation of The National Educational Television Network (NET) in 1961 made NET simply a film and tape distribution center with no power or authority over local stations. Because it might control programming, any national association was viewed with suspicion.

NET was created because programming was scarce and it allowed stations to share programs by shipping films and an occasional videotape from station to station with NET at the hub. Each station was sovereign and could accept or reject programming distributed to it and would vote on all programming decisions, leaving no central programming power.

With program voting power in the hands of local stations, the decisions were difficult to predict. The philosophies that bound these men to educational television were vague. The policies of the State of South Carolina were not necessarily consistent with those of the Board of Education in Denver; nor either of those with the decisions of the Board of Regents of the University of Wisconsin. Education was important but the philosophies about education were diverse and the use of this new medium in its support was very different from one local station to another. In fact, it seemed that the only glue for the system was the crushing scarcity of programming and funding that permeated every aspect of every decision. In these early days, there was not enough money, so there was not enough high-quality, attractive programming.

The stations licensed to universities and school boards were trying to increase or maintain their budgets by citing classroom advantages like extending the impact of a high-quality teacher, while other stations not operated by such institutions had begun to experiment with new sources of funds: voluntary public contributions, auctions, and philanthropic support by corporations and local businesses. KQED, a station licensed to a group of community volunteers in San Francisco, was the first station in the country to hold an annual broadcast auction. It was conducted out of the back of a Volvo station wagon and sold goods and services donated by local merchants. The first auction raised $8,000, which was enough to operate the station for nearly two months. The strongly held views on auctions and other means of community fundraising divided stations into philosophical camps for years.

If there was a common set of beliefs within the industry, local operators believed that their highest mission was to produce local programming to serve the local area. This was a noble belief but had the result in many communities that funds were wasted on undernourished local programs that attracted pitifully small audiences and therefore had virtually no impact on either the population or the issues of the day.

In some cases, of course, local stations would produce programs for their own communities and then share them with others first by kinescope film recording and later by electromagnetic videotape. There was little money changing hands because the school board or university that owned the station considered this an opportunity to promote their services or to recruit students or faculty. The University of Wisconsin offered "The Friendly Giant," The University of New Mexico made "TV Kindergarten" available, and KQED offered "Folk Guitar." Since the programs were sent by mail, there was no discussion about a consistent schedule — and no acknowledged need for one. Each station decided on its local program productions based upon its own priorities and there was no centralized program production decision-making apparatus in place. This left most stations capable only of deciding to air or not to air programs produced by others but unable to create high quality programs themselves.

It was the scarcity of funds and programs that finally led to a controversial federal government funding initiative. There was a clear need for a stable and predictable source of funds to support this non-commercial medium. Advertising was scorned, and since the government had created this patchwork of local transmitters, it seemed appropriate for it to pony-up the needed dollars. By the mid-1960s, there was a full-blown movement enlisting the services of university presidents, superintendents of public education, and well-known journalists from across America. This movement has been successful in generating small amounts of funding from our government, but with public television's growing emphasis on news and current affairs programs, some difficult questions regarding the role of government in America's free press have emerged.

By 1965, when the first Carnegie Commission met, the evolution of educational television from the classroom to a force in the local community had begun. In the process, virtually all of the problems that confront the industry today were present: local autonomy prevents the development of a consistently planned national program service and leads to waste and inefficiency; duplication of public television stations serving the same market with limited programming and resources wastes federal funds and confuses audiences; fundraising that is offensive to audiences and insufficient; and consistent initiatives by some in government to control the system's program content.

PUBLIC TELEVISION

There were far fewer than 100 stations in the system exchanging films and an occasional videotape by 1965. Each station's process for program screening and selection was done independently and, for the most part, was unsophisticated. Programs were aired in one community or another based upon the particular philosophies of the television operators. "Age of Kings" played almost everywhere because it was non-controversial Shakespeare. Interestingly, from the vantage of the 1980s, the U.S. Army's "The Big Picture" was also a tradition on educational television.

But programs that contained questionable language were scrapped in some areas and those that carried a theme supporting the civil rights movement were rejected in others. The philosophy was local: the icons were local broadcast coverage area maps; the mantra was local responsiveness; and each station manager was a high priest with absolute authority over what the people in the local area saw and heard on the educational channel. It was difficult to argue with the decisions of this local nobility complete with earned title that bestowed credibility and wisdom. That these men cared deeply was clear, but the underlying philosophies that drove and united them were muddled and confusing.

Even the most adamant local practitioners recognized the need for quality programs that could only be produced by sharing the costs. Stations in the large cities began to take control of productions for national distribution because this was where the creative talents and financial resources could be marshalled. They led the way into a new era not just of instructional television, but an exciting effort to bring the highest quality programs to the American people from wherever they might be produced. It was this idea that members of the 1966 Carnegie Commission titled "Public Television."

In large cities like New York, Boston, Washington, San Francisco, Dallas, and Los Angeles the stations were owned by local citizens groups that formed into non-profit corporations to hold the Federal Communications Commission-granted license. These were independent "community-licensed" stations that did not have the luxury of appealing to local universities or school boards for funds. Their independence forced the enormous responsibility of finding the money needed for operational costs directly upon the volunteer board and staff. The funds had to come from grants and other gifts. They had begun to raise needed operating funds from the most diverse sources imaginable — televised auctions, on-air appeals for viewer support and local community events. But in the early days, with the program schedule weak and with only limited ability to widely promote a program series, it was rough going at best. The leaders of these stations realized that the future of this experiment depended upon convincing the stations (and later corporations) to aggregate funds for the purpose of producing programs for the entire country. A few visionary members of this group recognized that unless the system was to become simply another commercial television outlet, even that would not be enough. They needed another funding source that would provide stability and time to plan for each season's schedule.

Some suggested that, like the British, Americans had a right to expect high culture and an independent journalistic voice supported in part by their government. The proposal was that the federal government would provide funds that matched those generated locally through the fundraising activities of the stations. It was difficult to design a mechanism that allowed receipt of funds without encouraging the dreaded hand of government at the editor's table. The decisions made in the middle 1960s pulled the system together around some common themes and directions and the success of some programs made the industry more tangible and respected. Most of what was put in place in the late 1960s is still with public broadcasting today.

HOW PUBLIC TELEVISION WORKS

The Public Broadcasting Act of 1967 created the Corporation for Public Broadcasting (CPB), which receives funds appropriated by the Congress. CPB is required by law to distribute the funds according to a formula. About 50 percent of the funds go directly to the local public television stations in the form of "Community Service Grant" designed to extend service in the local area. About 20 percent goes to radio stations and radio program production. The remaining 30 percent is used in several ways: a portion goes to fund a small CPB Program Fund directed at projects that are unlikely to be funded by the stations or other government agencies or corporations. Another amount is used to fund the national interconnection system — an impressive system of up- and down-links that send or receive signals from a communications satellite. Smaller percentages fund copyright payments, and some other non-administrative costs.

The discretionary money available to CPB covers administrative, planning and training functions. A small amount is set aside for the development of programming with clear social goals and for projects developed by minority and independent producers.

The Public Broadcasting Service (PBS) was created to replace the earlier NET program service. PBS was not allowed to produce television programs in order to protect many large market television stations that had become accustomed to and adept at the management of the large grants required for such projects. These stations did not want PBS as a competitor. Thus, PBS became responsible only for program scheduling. Today, it is the role of PBS to lead by consensus not edict; to innovate only after all 170 licensees see the need; and to respond to the needs of the system as a clearinghouse, technical operator, and occasional flack-catcher.

In addition to CPB and PBS there are a number of other national and regional organizations: National Public Radio (NPR); The National Association of Public Television Stations (NAPTS), which has responsibility for television system planning and representation before Congress and other federal agencies; The Eastern Educational Television Network (EEN); The Southern Educational Communications Association (SECA); The Central Educational Network (CEN); and The Pacific Mountain Network (PMN). The regional networks provide a range of services to the local stations in their area. The largest of the regionals is EEN, which also operates a small alternate network service that feeds programs not suitable for PBS distribution, either because they carry unacceptable credits or because the program is of interest to a smaller number of stations throughout the country.

Public television was, and still is, a convoluted and confusing set of initiatives but it represents a masterful set of compromises over the past thirty years. Since 1967 there has been an occasional call for a massive overhaul. Some politicians have attempted to strengthen the role of government, while others within the industry have tried to make it more efficient and responsive. The stormy tenure of Sonja Landau, as a member and then chairperson of the Board of CPB, led many long-time station managers to call for the elimination of CPB entirely in 1985. Mrs. Landau was instrumental in ousting of Ed Pfister, then President of CPB, at the industry's annual meeting in San Francisco in April, 1985. She and her colleagues hand-picked Martin Rubenstein as his replacement. In the following year several members of the CPB Board were forced to leave as their terms expired. Rubenstein remarks wryly that he had only two meetings with his Board of Directors: "The one where they hired me and the one where they fired me." Rubenstein left CPB eleven months after he started. As a commercial radio producer and executive, Rubenstein found the system byzantine and its practitioners consistently making decisions not in their own best interest.

But it is not likely that there will be a massive restructure of public broadcasting. The attendant opportunity for elimination of all federal funding sobers the most vehement desire to improve on the status quo.

The best argument for the existing system is its programming record. In every season of public television since 1975, there has been at least one program of spectacular success. Others have, over the years, become important in many households. From the early beginnings rooted in classroom music and science, the system has brought some of the most memorable and important programming to American television screens. "Masterpiece Theatre" began the miniseries concept. "Great Performances" has become a nourishing fountain for the most notable dancers, singers, and actors of our time. "The MacNeil/Lehrer Newshour" provides quality, in-depth news and discussion on the day's issues. "Nova" and the *National Geographic* specials have redefined quality in science and nature documentaries. Over 50 percent of the television households in the United States turn to public television for its coverage of science, nature, medicine, and current as well as cultural events each week.

The list of important public television offerings is long and growing as its successes build upon themselves. As the programs have improved, the audiences have grown and the funding has followed. From limited funds and adversity have come innovation and entrepreneurship. In 1986 the system raised nearly half of its available funds from individual contributions, auctions, and other local sources. The balance of the funding came from universities, school boards, state authorities, and about 20 percent from the federal government. The total revenue from all sources in 1986 was slightly less than $1 billion each year and public television programs now attract the best creative minds of the twentieth and twenty-first century. One billion dollars is small in comparison to the commercial networks, but public television is growing.

INTERNAL WEAKNESSES

Those close to the public broadcasting industry know that it is a fragile, uncontrollable association plagued by problems created by itself and the federal government:

1. The fierce local independence that was necessary to the system when it was almost entirely local and funded by institutions remains today. As the system grows in size and importance, the need for clear program-decision making authority and leadership in editorial, technological, political, and economic issues is critical. While the station must remain the predominant, basic unit of the system, some decisions must be delegated to the national program service, PBS. Fears of a strong national network make the stations continue to resist any loss of control, no matter how trivial. PBS has not been successful in trying to launch a new cable television network, in building a series of new businesses to help fund the system, or in providing leadership in program development. So the system continues to select its programs by vote, not by expert opinion, and we lurch from one season to another with no clear program strategy.

2. The strong belief in local programming and autonomy resulted in the creation of a system in which large cities and small towns could participate in the development and distribution of programs nationwide. As the expertise for major production began to be centralized within the larger cities — New York, Boston, Los Angeles, Pittsburgh, Washington, and San Francisco — these station operators wanted no centralized

program production decision-making aparatus. Rather than a system-wide programming head, there is a sort of clearinghouse function at PBS that serves only to direct the traffic of programs once produced rather than order programs for a specific opportunity in the schedule.

3. The efforts to provide local programs detract from the funding and production of high-quality, domestically produced product that is vital to the future of the system. It is significant in 1987 that the typical public television station spends between 10 and 15 percent of its budget on its national programming, while commercial independents spend between 40 and 60 percent. Attempts to increase the proportion devoted to national programming meet with fierce resistance.

The growth of autonomous producing stations and the reluctance of local stations to fully fund the national program service has caused serious problems:

1. Many of public television's most important programs are selected by leaders in large corporations, not by public television professionals themselves. The exhausting process of developing a concept and seeking funding from OUTSIDE the system make corporate public information officers more powerful in public television than most people at the producing stations. They decide to fund a program based upon their corporate goals and it appears on public television in place of other projects that did not receive funding through the same process.

2. There is no single editor for news and current affairs efforts in the system. In early 1987 when Bill Moyers returned to public television, it was to a cold dash of reality. He proposed to offer a series of two- to three-minute nightly comments following the events of the Constitutional Convention of 1787. What he found was that intra-family battles prevented him from the obvious inclusion of this material within The "MacNeil/Lehrer Newshour". MacNeil/Lehrer and WNET are solely responsible for the content of their programs and Robin MacNeil said no. At NBC or CBS the decision would be made on the basis of the good of the system rather than what was good only for "The Nightly News." MacNeil/Lehrer is independent and can simply reject an idea if they do not see it in their best interest. A further example of individual versus system interest is that PBS has fed both the "NacNeil/Lehrer Newshour" and "The Nightly Business Report" for several years. It is clear that ten minutes of business news included with MacNeil/Lehrer each night would be sufficient, but WPBT in Miami would lose an important contract with Digital Equipment Corporation and the "Newshour" would have to relinquish some precious time. The same editorial independence is true for "Frontline" and "Nova."

3. Because the public television system has been unwilling to fully fund projects, it has been unable to secure full rights to the programs it funds and produces. The result is a serious migration of public television's

most popular programs to commercial independent television stations. The *National Geographic* specials are now programmed on commercial independents to compete, on the same nights, with the new programs offered to public television in 1987.

4. Federal funding for a broadcasting service is anathema to the concept of a free and independent press that can and must be critical of the very hands that feed it. The history of the federal government's role in public broadcasting is a turbulent one. Johnson's people created it; Nixon's Office of Telecommunications Policy tried to eliminate all funding; Carter promised great things but delivered virtually nothing; and Reagan vowed to withdraw all funds but was able only to effect a brief reduction. And still, the underlying problem of federal funding without federal control remains. It is amazing how well the system has prospered by the support from its audiences while battling to maintain its federal funds.

5. Finally, it is crucial that public television maintains a look and a feel that is different from the commercial stations if it is to prosper in the future. The differentiation must exist in both programming and funding. Public television must resist the temptation to re-form the system into a quasi-commercial network through greater enhancement of the existing underwriting credit.

The system is not without bright spots. The public television viewer now understands that there is something different about watching this channel. Not just that it has no commercials, but that it is more serious and wide-ranging. At 8:00 P.M. on a given night there will not be a sitcom or action/adventure series. Instead, the viewer will be transported to real people and places in Africa, India, Moscow, or the Nile. The venue is the universe, and the goals remain as lofty as ever. These are programs that challenge, excite, and expand our imagination and understanding.

After thirty-three years of service in large and small communities in the country, the public television service has become a force. Its programs are recognized for quality, and its fundraising, while annoying and dull, is successful. So, while the problems within the system are serious, they have not prevented delivery of a quality product to the American consumer.

THREATS FROM THE OUTSIDE

The mid-1980s will be remembered for the dramatic impact of regulatory, marketplace, and court-ordered alterations to the mass media and tele-communications industries.

The Federal Communications Commission, in efforts directed at de-regulating the broadcast and cable industries, opened new channels for broadcasting in the United States: low-power television was approved in the early 1980s and new stations began to operate by mid-decade; a microwave based multipoint distribution system was expanded with new data and video services offered to the public and to industrial users; and changes in requirements and minimum holding periods for broadcast owners resulted in many new independent television stations and a concentration of ownership.

This proliferation of television stations, along with the growth of advertiser-supported cable television, created a dream marketplace for program syndicators by 1986.

The price of program product climbed so high that some commercial independent television stations were forced into bankruptcy, unable to meet the heavy payment schedule demanded by program syndicators. Where one independent station had bid on a product in each market, now three and even four entered bids for the same off-network and new syndication offerings. What had been a safe, glamorous business became a somewhat marginal investment.

The combined revenues of the twenty-five largest players in the electronic media in 1986 exceeded $22 billion. According to *Channels* magazine, "the industry had become so concentrated, and the companies so assiduously purchased other firms among their competitors, customers and suppliers, that the twenty-five biggest now include owners of: all three TV networks as well as Fox Broadcasting Company network; nine of the ten TV station groups with the greatest potential audience; seven of the ten most extensive cable system holdings, serving more than a third of U.S. cable subscribers; eleven of the top fifteen syndicators of TV programming; and seven of the top ten publishers of pre-recorded videocassettes with two thirds of sales." Between 1984 and 1987 all three networks changed ownership. Cap Cities, an owner of major market television stations, purchased ABC and its seven Owned and Operated Stations; General Electric purchased NBC; and Leonard Tisch of Loew's, who had been a member of CBS's Board, took control of CBS.

In each case, the new network owners began to examine the costs associated with programming and news production. At NBC, Robert Wright decided to cut all departments by an equal 2 percent bringing howls of protest from all department heads. Lawrence Grossman, who came to NBC News from the financially strapped PBS, simply refused. At CBS, Van Gordon Sauter was ceremoniously fired and replaced by a new maven at cutting costs. At ABC the layoffs at the locally owned and operated stations was dramatic with 25 percent of the staff reportedly forced into the streets.

But it was probably the decision by the U.S. Appeals Court in Washington, D.C. that rocked the industry the most. In a case involving a Quincy, Ill. cable operator, the U.S. Court held that the operators of cable television systems must be subject to the same protections under the First Amendment to the Constitution that applied to newspaper publishers. This specifically rendered long-standing rules that required carriage of all local broadcast stations unconstitutional and illegal. These "must-carry" rules had required cable operators to devote one channel to every local broadcast station within 35 miles of their operation. In the early days cable operators were all too happy to carry the local stations since it was the improved reception of these stations that prompted people to subscribe.

HOME BOX OFFICE and other "premium" channels that offered movies and sporting events changed the economics of cable. Operators now advertised new services instead of improved reception. As the number of subscribers for HBO climbed after a decade of operation, other services sprang to life. CINEMAX, THE MOVIE CHANNEL, PLAYBOY CHANNEL, THE ENTERTAINMENT AND SPORTS PROGRAMMING NETWORK, USA NETWORK, and THE HOME SHOPPING NETWORK, began to compete for the limited channel capacity of the local operator and for advertising dollars as well. In areas such as San Francisco where operators were bound by law to carry as many as four public stations and a total of 18 local channels, they could only sit by and watch potential revenue evaporate. The Quincy decision was an exquisite moment for the cable industry — and the beginning of a panic for local independents — commercial and non-commercial. A count by The National Association of Public Television Stations reported that over fifty public television stations were dropped or reassigned to a different channel within weeks of the decision. In major markets from New York to San Francisco, there was talk of moving local stations from their existing channel location in order to favor "satellite delivered" services.

In early 1987 the cable operator finds him- or herself between the audience and the broadcast station in nearly 50 percent of American homes. Decisions to alter the channel line-up, create new program services, and supply traditional entertainment are being made more extensively than ever by the cable television operator. The singular dominance of the broadcaster has passed.

Ownership of local cable television operations has become more centralized as the FCC now allows greater ownership here as well as on the broadcast spectrum. Tele-Communications, Inc. is the largest multiple system owner in the country controlling access to over 6 percent of American homes with aggressive plans to grow further. Even "market-force" preachers have begun to ask questions about the control of the media and the "free-press" in the U.S. Americans have been successful in preventing an "official government press." Will we be able to escape from the one tyranny only to fall prey to a massive corporate editor? The growth of Gannett, Hearst, ABC/Cap Cities, General Electric, and Metromedia (not to mention Rupert Murdoch's FOX Network) will leave most Americans subject to the news interpretation of a few newspaper, radio, television, and cable editors.

As the Reagan Administration deregulated the commercial media, it had limited success in 1983 in reducing funding to public broadcasting. The reduction of $35 million was small in terms of total industry revenues, but it had a serious impact on planning for the national schedule in 1985. The reduction was evident in the 1985–86 season. Reagan succeeded mostly in providing public broadcasting with a battle cry of "reduced federal funds," which proved very compelling to a growing army of local supporters. It was not a serious blow. Local stations did experiment with efforts to raise funds from corporations willing to "underwrite" the costs of programming. A new array of "enhancements" for underwriters was explored...and one by one they were rejected by corporations as not going far enough down the road of product sales. With the increasing menu available to the advertiser, public broadcasting simply did not have the appeal to increase its share of corporate expenditures.

The local stations turned, once again, to their communities. In some markets the emphasis was on increasing support from the corporate community, in others it was on traditional support by viewers. In the years from 1980 to 1987 revenue for public television and radio stations grew dramatically with subscriber activities playing the most important part in the growth. It is possible that the Reagan revolution made viewers feel more inclined to support, or that the growth of cable made viewers more aware of the need to "pay" for some television. For whatever reason the growth was remarkable and necessary.

AN OPTIMISTIC VIEW OF THE FUTURE

With nearly a full generation behind it, public television has grown and matured into a service that now reaches over 60 percent of the American people each week and nearly 90 percent during each month. Public television's "share" of the audience is growing from year to year, while the commercial networks decline. The increase of channel hopping caused by a proliferation of new services and improved remote control technology in television sets, has been a boon to public broadcasters. More people "stumble" on public television and find something they like. About one in ten is a supporter of the local station. As public television's audience has grown, so has its underlying base of subscriber support. There are more people supporting public television in the United States today than any other charity. There are nearly 8 million members of local public television stations nationwide.

It is this support that probably represents the best long-term source of funds for public television. If the programs are of quality and interest, and if public television is clearly different from its commercial counterparts, people will support it. If not, the viewers will have scores of other choices.

At KQED in San Francisco, the strategy has proven very successful. Viewer support is considered "pay television — on the honor system." A concerted effort over a five-year period doubled the audience, tripled the members, and increased revenues by nearly 400 percent. Local voluntary support is a daily operation to keep a message in front of the viewers to constantly remind them why they are a necessary part of public television.

This may be the only solution to the funding problems that have plagued public television since its beginnings in Houston in 1953. After years of struggling with variant philosophies within and hostile competitors and environments outside, the stations and the program suppliers are finding increasingly successful models for survival and success. If public television can maintain its differentiated programming image, grasp control of its program production and distribution activities, and increase its willingness to support a national program service of high-quality and expensive programs, it has a very bright future indeed. Each of these solutions are possible and there is a growing sense of self-determination within the industry.

In many ways the public television industry has all the inefficiency and messiness of American democracy. It is not the simplest way of doing things but it may well prove to be the best.

39 VISUALIZING STEREOTYPES*
BERNARD RUBIN

A stereotype is a generalization that people share. This generalization is about some group or category of people such as blacks, gays, Arabs, southerners, professors, women, Jews, athletes, Italians...one could go on and on. Stereotypes focus upon matters such as racial, ethnic, national, sexual, or occupational identity.

Stereotypes can be positive (the kindly professor), negative (the dishonest Wall Street broker), or mixed (the dedicated but "sexless" old maid schoolteacher). Whatever the case, stereotypes are misleading because they oversimplify and overgeneralize. They suggest that all members of a given group or category are alike in certain respects, which minimizes individual differences and is not true.

The term was made popular many years ago by Walter Lippmann who adapted it from its original usage in the printing industry. Stereotyping is particularly problematical in the mass media because writers generally don't have time to develop characters yet must supply viewers and listeners with a means of understanding the motivations of these characters. In such situations it is easy to rely on stereotypes. Hence the cheap Scot or drunken Irishman.

In recent years, as the identity ideal of the WASP (White, Anglo-Saxon Protestant) has withered and people have become proud of their ethnic and racial identity, things are changing. Ethnic and racial groups have put pressure on the

* Reprinted by permission of the publisher from *When Information Counts*, edited by Bernard Rubin. Lexington MA: Lexington Books, D.C. Heath and Company, Copyright © 1985, Associates in Research for Public Reporting.

media to stop stereotyping them and the amount of stereotyping has slightly diminished. There is also the matter of increased competition. As new technologies develop, people have access to many different kinds of entertainment, and if they find programs or films that, they feel, stereotype them, they will take their business elsewhere.

For the moment, however, stereotyping still remains a problem — especially on television, which is our dominant entertainment medium. Studies have shown that sexual and racial stereotyping still exists on television, though it may not be quite as overt as it used to be. (In its camouflaged form it may be even more insidious.)

The question we must ask is whether television, and other media to varying extents, can ever avoid stereotyping. Allied to that is the matter of why stereotypes endure the way they do. Stereotypes generate unrealistic and negative images of groups of people, which impact on our social and political lives. As such, stereotypes in the media pose an important problem for American society — one that we have yet to solve.

SCRATCHES ON THE SCREENS

The most grave charge leveled at the managers of the motion picture and film industries is that they have consistently been guilty of depicting powerless or downtrodden or struggling groups erroneously. Most public imagery of such groups has depended upon stereotyping, and that stereotyping has provoked bitterness and suspicion and hatred.

Consistency is no virtue when social harmony is regularly thwarted by creative people. While much of the problem has been documented, there is not enough appreciation of how much carryover of bad habits is to be noted in recent and current work.

Racism has been and is promoted or prompted through film and television imagery. The approximately 12 percent of the population of the United States that is black has endured much vilification on the screen from the first days of the movie industry. Conversely, most of the issues and circumstances faced every day by blacks are absent from motion pictures or television schedules. The "Buckwheats" of the *Our Gang* comedies have remained more fixed in the screened constellations than have the *Roots*-type attempts of television to depict black history and circumstances. There are few parts for black actors that command attention from vast audiences. Television's "The Jeffersons" or "Benson" deserve comedic plaudits at the same time that they deserve adverse criticism as reductions of the experiences of millions of people to the slapstick vaudeville level.

In a recent issue of the British journal *Screen*, Robert Stam and Louise

Spence stress stereotyping by commission and omission through the years.[1] Examples: *King of Jazz* (1930) "paid tribute to the origins of jazz...completely bypassing both Africa and Afro-Americans." And where, they ask, were blacks in Hitchcock's 1957 drama, done in "documentary-like" style, *The Wrong Man?* "The subways and even the prisons" in the New York City of that film are "totally devoid of blacks."

Shaft (1971), in their view, merely plays a substitution game to cater to egos of a black male audience. The black here is simply a substitute for whites in similar films. They critique television's "Mod Squad," which has persisted into the 1980s through reruns. Placing black characters as law enforcers creates positive images that have less than substantial reinforcements for ordinary blacks every day.

Roots, the television series that commanded more mass attention to black origins than any previous television effort, is, for Stam and Spence, exploitive imagery. One may argue with their conclusion, but would the counter argument be influenced by the desire not to cast a bad reflection on a production that rose so far above others? Students of stereotypes are sometimes so anxious to fight denigration of individuals and groups that they have a kind of blind spot on the subject of positive-tending stereotyping works. Stam and Spence label *Roots* a cooptive version of Afro-American history...a film which cast blacks as just another immigrant group making its way toward freedom and prosperity in democratic America. It is hard for this observer to be as harsh, knowing that history is more saga telling than the professional historian will admit. Each generation reframes the old sagas to suit its purposes. Was *Roots* positive cooption? Should it have concentrated on realistic stereotypes that hard evidence would show more accurate? To illustrate, *Roots* is built on the nuclear family concept ("retrospectively projected onto Kunta's life in Africa"[2]). How would another creative producer have handled the problems that are posed? We are reminded: "Questions of image scale and duration...are intricately related to the respect afforded a character and the potential for audience sympathy, understanding and identification."[3] Mass communicators are obliged to reach beyond evidence of stereotyped products of the media, to understand the central issue of their complicity.

Because symbolism is so vital to human beings, the symbols transferred by television and films may be more important than any review of specific story themes or general contents. This point is repeatedly made by theoretical analysts concentrating on the mass media. Perhaps it is useful that an appreciation or interpretation of the usage of the word *theoretical* be given here, slanted to the author's perspective. The theoretician depends upon specific knowledge, but has the determination to struggle beyond what is commonly termed data to a conclusion that makes sense of all the evidence at his disposal. That evidence consists of hard data and circumstantial material that helps reveal some underlying truth.

It is easy to be trapped into prolonged citation of specific data from television and film worlds without asking what is basically happening. We are closer to posing the question after applying some theoretical conclusions drawn by careful scholars.

In *Road of Propaganda: The Semantics of Biased Communication*, Karin Dovring, the Swedish journalist and mass communication scholar, reminds us of the pertinence of identity relationships between slogans and key symbols:

> The more identification symbols are used, and the more these are already well known to the public, the faster the slogan, supposed to comprehend the public demand, becomes a key symbol itself. It penetrates the areas of interests and demands and rises to the level of identification with the established community myth. As a part of the ideology it can even be used for attention-calling since its communication is already accomplished.[4]

One perceives that real progress against deleterious stereotyping will not be made until we mass communicators understand that most symbolic identification of groups represents community consensus at any given time. Democracy is inevitably tied up with consensus achievement by politicians and by mass media influentials. It must be true that so much protest against unfair stereotyping has led to such puny industry efforts to combat such denigration, because many leaders of the communications world are among the least anxious to go ahead of the social status quo. Controversial mass media products are avoided unless categorized as necessary showpieces in an almost totally bland schedule of presentations.

Social uplifting of groups has always been marginally interesting to television and motion picture moguls, so long as audiences don't complain that they are instigators of radical change. Most moguls prefer to live within the precincts of the society they accept as conventional.

Artists, investigative reporters, political activists, social worker reformers, and the like, on the other hand, complain that for all the innovative films and television programs of any calendar year, worthwhile because of contents that combat antidemocratic stereotyping and that fight against the blind spots in our social and political life, the tendencies and the effects of the total effort are predominantly negative. Surveyed in that light, the battle against unfair stereotyping doesn't seem to be going too well.

Lippmann himself is at the heart of the dilemma. Critics of the media were mesmerized by his rendition of stereotype theory when he first evolved his arguments. What most analysts have failed to recognize is how dated some elements of Lippmann's approach are. Throughout his career, he was an essentially nineteenth-century analyst (both as a novice reporter and as the sagacious old pundit interviewed on television at length each year by Eric Sevareid). He looked at the world through the printed word and was hopeful that "experts" would learn enough from each other, largely through printed reports, to lead the world.

In nineteenth-century style, Lippmann counted heavily on leaders influencing events. Despite the fundamental and dramatic shifts in his lifetime, Lippman believed that intelligent leaders would prevail over the forces of irrationality, brutism, and banal evil. Perhaps that is why he ignored (or preferred to consign to an inner recess of his subconscious) the Nazi-perpetuated genocide!

This man of print grappled with one issue of television — its limited offerings — but never saw deeply into the problem. In the worlds of the printed word through which he traveled intellectually, one could always count on some forum for any subject. A book, or an article in a learned journal, or a newspaper report, or a critique in an obscure intellectually oriented magazine could always be found to delve into the subject or segment of a subject in which he was interested. In a sense, Lippmann could popularize stereotypes and thrive on the ways his peers considered the dangers, because he was inwardly sure that the intellectual shorthand stereotypes represented would always be followed up with more complete, fair, and representative portraits.

He did not entertain the thought that stereotypes could be dead ends. Even though, at times, Lippmann manufactured dead-ended imageries of groups, he felt intellectually secure that some other expert would convert his dead ends into open intellectual highways if the facts warranted.

When Lippmann surveyed television, he saw the fact of its comparatively few channels stifling public interests. In 1951, commenting on the televised Kefauver inquiry on interstate crime, he observed:

> With television, an event is broadcast or it is ignored: either it is in enormous headlines or it is nowhere at all. This power to choose what the great mass of the people shall see…is altogether too great to be left to the judgment of a few television companies and to private arrangements made by committees and commercial sponsors."[5]

Television, for Lippmann, was far too limited an instrument to carry on intellectual progress in the fashion of the print media.

If leaders of television are so slavishly devoted to the status quo, as a general rule, and if Lippmann was both innovative and somewhat antiquarian when it came to reliance on the powers of ideas transported through print, how has television handled the problem of stereotypes? The answer is deceptively simple. *Television has carried on the tradition of the forerunning motion picture industry and has concentrated primarily on evocations that have an instant visual impact.*

Portrayals of three-dimensional quality only serve as highlights superimposed on a darker area. Lippmann never fully accepted that true literacy might be gained through pictorial communication, via the film or television industries. Leaders of those industries have been subdued by peer judgments that communication of nuances surrounding individuals or groups is always difficult and often dangerous. A creed has grown up around the notion that only *artists* can conjure up full-fledged depictions of individuals or society that emphasize more than surface values. Those managers have seen themselves as manufacturers of ready-made, one-size-fits-most-customers mental clothing. Most are as antiquarian and print-oriented as Lippmann was. He wanted mankind led by experts; most television and film industry managers don't really want to lead at all and prefer to separate art from the everyday commerce they engage in.

For every television product that shows a person or group as a psychological, sociological, economic, or philosophical whole, there are scores that rely on cosmetic cartoon characterizations. Until we all admit that we haven't achieved more than Lippmann — indeed, much less, since he showed us the basic geography of the stereotype — we will go on lamenting reliance on superficiality in mass communication. Stereotyping contrary to democratic goals of fairness will prevail so long as we agree with Lippmann that television is inherently second-rate in comparison with print. That just isn't so!

With all deference to the beauty and powers of the print media, we are on the verge of a new era of mass communications. In a few short years, video cassettes have become like library books in the Third World, not only for the dominant classes, but also for those whose literacy is more visual than print-oriented. What most people of the world learn of happenings, art, politics, science, and so on, will soon depend upon some version of motion pictures, transmitted by television. The average product that is prepared for television audiences will have to rise above the trite and superficial, or we shall continue to pay for ignorance and disinformation, facing up to the costs of suspicion and bitterness.

In technologically advanced regions, the challenge is no less profound. If television's products continue to take advantage of gullibility, false notions, and prejudices via one-dimensional depictions, the effects upon the body civil and politic will not benefit our democratic goals. One must be pessimistic if depictions of the poor, the rich, blacks, children, Orientals, the aged, religious groups, and so forth, continue along present lines.

The complaints are so routine, and come from so many segments of society that one wonders if they can be met with complacency by leaders of the industry. Today's leaders of conventional television must be wondering if a new kind of television revolution impends because of the pressures from technological changes and public demands.

Because it is clear that television will become more personally valuable to individuals as a means for virtually limitless accessing of information from recordings or from numerous cable, satellite, or conventionally broadcast channels at home and abroad, one is tempted to conclude that we could be offered fairer pictures of each other. The predominance of unfairly drawn stereotypes could diminish in proportion to the variety of sources to be drawn from. Just as stereotypes are more easily handled in print simply because there are so many descriptive choices for the curious about any group or person, so they could be more manageable for television's consumers. Those consumers will be less subject to propaganda that goes counter to their own inclinations.

Lippmann's basic theory of stereotypes is correct, but he erred as driven by his own ego. The coming age of individualistic electronic communication, to follow what we now signify as television, will allow most perceptive persons to have the same opportunity to be right or wrong. Providers of programming aimed at millions of people at a single showing will have to be more mindful of the competitive situation. If the consumer doesn't like this news or that news, there will be other choices a-plenty. If the creator of a product wants an audience in the new age of electronic communication, he will have to act more like an author or publisher in the book or magazine businesses of today. Acceptance of products will be selective and personal to a degree not yet reached.

Until the golden day of predominantly three-dimensional television dawns, we will have to contend with growing dissatisfaction among the industry's consumers. Complaints about unfair stereotyping are ever louder and more numerous and emanate from virtually all organized groups. Taken together, they constitute an indictment against the mass media on the charge that stereotyped *shorthand* communication generally runs counter to the objectives of true education. Instead of being molded from a sweepingly descriptive composite of the pictured individual or group, the message goes beyond distortion to lies.

One fascinating aspect is the range of those demanding redress. Some of the most powerful economic elements in the country share in the plaintiff's indictment. To illustrate, the Mobil Oil Corporation, through its advocacy advertisements (primarily placed in print organs), has for some time hit upon those influential television news presentations and entertainment offerings that, it claims, simplify issues and events and personalities to the point of disinformation. Three of the myths Mobil's public affairs department would have us beware of are "1. The myth of the villainous businessman"; "2. The myth of the informed public", and "3. The myth of the crusading reporter":

> A 1980 study by the non-profit, research-oriented Media Institute... found that "two out of three businessmen on television are portrayed as foolish, greedy or criminal; almost half of all work activities performed by businessmen involves illegal acts; and...television almost never portrays business as a socially useful or economically productive activity."
>
> TV's myth of the villainous businessman could...in the long run, undermine the public trust in the basic exchange relationships that form the underpinnings of our free enterprise system.[6]

In "2. the myth of the informed public", the Mobil conclusion is that, on television, "anyone whose role is directed toward profit-making is a 'bad guy' — just as he is in a TV adventure show." Mobil declares that theme is a "basic scenario for television newscasts on economic issues," featuring "the following mythic cast of characters":

> *Liberal politician:* Defender of consumer interests and environmental protection.
>
> *Conservative politician:* In the pocket of big business.
>
> *Social activist:* A "public interest" representative. Has unruly hair and wears folksy clothes.
>
> *Business executive:* Motivated by greed for more profits, unwilling to put the country's good ahead of his company's.[7]

Finally:

> Among the upcoming journalists, members of the "TV generation", only one-quarter of the Columbia School of Journalism students interviewed [by Professors Stanley Rothman of Smith College and Robert and Linda Lichter of George Washington University]...believe that the private enterprise system is fair and almost 40% advocate public ownership of corporations.[8]

Lippmann would have understood the Mobil complaints, but he probably would have interpreted those complaints in the light of television realities. Aren't myths and stereotypes created, in part, to overcome the difficulties of trying to reach masses with intellectual arguments or analyses? While Mobil objects to one set of myths, that corporation doesn't try to grasp the reality that it may be demanding a more accommodative set of myths and is not as concerned with presenting objective reality to the general public. In regard to the conflicts of opinions and the data that shape opinions, Lippmann observed:

> The mind...was evolved as an instrument of defense and for the mastery of specific difficulties: only in the latest period of human development have men thought of trying to comprehend a whole situation in all of its manifold complexity....In actual affairs they have to select isolated phenomena, since they have only limited energy and a short time in which to observe and understand: out of the infinite intricacy of the real world, the intelligence must cut patterns abstract, isolated and artificially simplified. Only about these partial views can men think. Only in their light can men act.[9]

Lippmann contemplated "partial views" from this perspective in 1937, but his remarks are directly linked to his elitist comprehensions of public opinion in 1922. By 1955, he had refined the problem, tracing another aspect of "the democratic malady" in his segment of *Essays in the Public Philosophy* entitled "The Decline of the West." As against the experts he advocated so faithfully, he saw democratic politicians paying a price for success. Being "insecure and intimidated men," with "exceptions so rare that they are regarded as miracles or freaks of nature," the "decisive consideration is not whether the proposition is good but whether it is popular." The "men under them who report and collect the news come to realize in their turn that it is safer to be wrong before it has become fashionable to be right."[10]

We have to ask ourselves whether complaints against stereotyping can be met by honest television entrepreneurs. Or is Lippmann correct, and must we reluctantly conclude that the stereotypes manufactured are not used by accident but deliberately, primarily by television creators and managers who are another breed of politicians? If they were to come down hard for television products based upon reason, truth, impartiality of researchers, and a profound search for fairness, would they not defy the realities of *mass media?* Would they not have to reassess the entire scope and meaning given to the word *entertainment* and strive for programming that both attracts and educates? Would they not have to finally deal with Lippmann's conclusions that mass man can only grasp a little at a time, while they are faithful to the goal of raising or at least sustaining rational exchanges between individuals and groups? Would they not have to contend with the substantial problem that, if Lippmann is right, the politicians have so framed the setting for discourse to their publics that crude popularity has become the be-all and the end-all of society? To really mount a creative counterattack against unfair stereotyping through good works, they would have to be prepared to stand by works that were *both fair to the subjects and unpopular.* The unpopularity would stem from public resistance to images that were clear and contrary to accepted distortions.

Women, ethnic groups, the elderly, the physically or mentally handicapped, and other categories of people would be reflected by new, cleaned mirrors. To clean those mirrors, television leaders should recognize that their problems are in part distinct from those common in the motion picture or print media industries. The reasons are simple. First, the film industry's products are typically independent treatments of subject matter, no matter how much any film or genre is a copy of another. Television, on the other hand, has from its beginnings relied upon formats to the degree that, at any one period, the public receives substantially the same range of products from all commercial networks. Even when public television introduced novel ideas such as the miniseries to develop new audiences, the concepts too often degenerated into formulas. Once the concept was understood by commercial network leaders and galvanized by the popularity of new programs, the formula was adopted and made up into a popular brew.

Action for Children's Television, an organization headquartered in Newton, Massachusetts, gives us insights into ordinary daily fare uncovered by researchers recently:

Only 3% of all characters are in the 65-and-over group; a dispropor-
tionate number of these are male....Men outnumber women 3 to 1...
TV women are more passive and less achievement oriented than
men...the proportional representation of minorities in TV comedies
and dramas has actually declined over the last decade....In 1981 it was
reported in a study dealing with commercial television specifically
aimed at children that out of a total of 1145 characters in the programs
studied only 22% were female...; only 3.7% of all characters were
black...; of all characters with speaking parts, 57.5% were white and
33.8% were animals, robots or other non-humans.[11]

Documentation on inaccurate stereotyping is extensive, and much of it is
in book-length research devoted to impacts on specific groups. Among the
impressive works are Ralph E. Friar and Natasha A. Friar, *The Only Good
Indian: The Hollywood Gospel* (1972)[12]; William B. Helmreich, *The Things
They Say Behind Your Back* (1982)[13]; and Leonard C. Archer, *Black Images
in the American Theatre* (1973).[14]

Lippmann's suspicions about aspects of democracy in this country and
the intellectual force of public opinion under democratic systems of government anywhere are substantiated. Archer documents the persistence of
antisocial stereotyping of blacks in television shows that attracted huge
television audiences. "Amos 'n' Andy," the carryover from the original
radio format, was strenuously denounced by leaders of the National Association for the Advancement of Colored People. Writing in 1951, Walter
White, NAACP executive secretary, was most direct: "If the television
industry and advertisers who are eager to sell their goods and services in a
$5,000,000 Negro market had previously presented Negro characters as
'normal human beings' and as an integral part of the American scene, a
series like 'Amos "n" Andy' and "Beulah"could be taken in stride." After
thundering against television's then-habitual depictions of blacks (doctors
— charlatans and thieves; women — cackling hens and tempestuous
shrews; all Negroes — allergic to toil) White declared: "Unhappy the system
of segregation in the United States that permits far too many Americans no
opportunities to know Negroes except through the medium of television."[15]

We have come a long way in twentieth-century time and circumstance
since "Amos 'n' Andy." Today's television viewers with long memories
or access to reruns might recall "Sanford and Son," "Good Times," and
"That's My Mama," a trio of series that carried on the racist tradition
against which Walter White struggled. They might also remember the
episodes in the *Roots* saga and such programs as "The Autobiography of
Miss Jane Pittman" as more elevating and impressive efforts to get at the
inner dignity and backgrounds of blacks. The two latter programs depended
upon stereotyping in part to further the story lines, but the stereotyping was
designed to increase the knowledge and strengthen the humane inclinations
of audiences.

Less easy to categorize is the currently running series "The Jeffersons."

Slick, produced by people who know every entertainment trick attractive to mass television audiences, and well acted, this series projects beyond the common experiences of most blacks in the United States, portraying financially successful blacks and reverse-discriminatory sentiments in conflict with socially good relationships between friends black and white. According to William A. Henry III, the Pulitzer prize-winning television critic, the programs reinforce "what television has already taught Americans, and what they yearn to believe: that a social revolution has been won." The main character, George Jefferson, is a reverse Archie Bunker:

> He is too mean spirited and too much a bragging buffoon to be admired for his character....His business acumen is so little in view that his wealth seems merely a stroke of luck....he seems uninterested in the plight of less lucky blacks. He does not live in the ghetto, he spends little time there, he devotes scant energy to black causes...he behaves like a nouveau-gauche white....He is not an inspiring role model to black youth.[16]

The native American has been as maligned by motion pictures as much as any group, and television picked up on the approaches and themes that had prevailed in the film industry since the earliest silent movies. In television's early years, as many old films as could be acquired cheaply from the Hollywood studios found their way onto the black-and-white TV screens. They are still a television staple, with little counterstereotyping work challenging the imageries of the "red man," the "savage," the "scalphunter." The native American, oppressed in real life, was not often depicted with dignity or understanding but was usually the foil to the courageous settlers or cavalry soldiers in the frontier west. Vitually no understanding of native tribal ways or cultures was or is communicated. If the roles were good, whites usually played Indian parts in such films. The end result of decades of stereotypical indoctrination was massive public indifference to native Americans, supported by massive public ignorance. The classic portrayals of the brutal savages in the westerns constitute a great bulwark for racism in this country."[17]

Television's own products have not often been celebrated for accuracy or sympathy for the native American. In "The Lone Ranger," transferred from radio to television, his companion Tonto was one of the small screen's noble Indians who appear from time to time as exceptions to prove the rule about stereotyping. Typical of television stereotyping was the "Wagon Train" series. In many episodes, Indians were shown as drunken, cowardly outlaws. Another series, "Riverboat," is said to have depicted the "Indians as inhuman fiends." In the series "Wanted — Dead or Alive," "a typical program showed Apaches massacring a group of whites in the desert." Series such as "Laramie" and "Overland Trail" are similarly criticized.

When television replays Hollywood's Indian epics, it acts as an agent for bigotry in the opinion of many native Americans. The following comments from young Indians polled in 1971 about particular films were published in the *Akwesasne Notes* by The White Roots of Peace, Mohawk Nation:

Soldier Blue (1970) — The only good part...was the massacre of the Indians by the Cavalry. That saved it because it showed the truth. The rest was junk....*The Stalking Moon* (1967) — The Indian was shown as a totally primitive animal who'd kill anything....*Little Big Man* (1970) — Chief Dan George was great and Dustin Hoffman was bad. But the picture actually showed some things realistically....*A Man Called Horse* (1970) — Same old savage stereotype. White actors playing cigar store Indians.[18]

After tracing the histories and analyzing the contents of prominent stereotypes (examples: Jews — "the Jewish mother," "shrewd business-men"; Italians — "belong to the Mafia," "talk with their hands"; blacks — "violent criminals," "great rhythm"; Japanese — "sneaky," "women servile and obedient"; Poles — "dumb," "racists and bigots"; WASPs — "hard-working industrious, and thrifty," "cold and insensitive"), William B. Helmreich concludes that we should not assume antistereotyping positions that deny elements of truth in the shorthand descriptions:

It turns out that approximately one-third of the stereotypes can be said to have a good deal of truth to them....Bigots will not, however, find much support for their prejudices from the relatively high number of valid stereotypes...because most of the stereotypes for which support can be found are positive or flattering to the group involved, whereas those that seem highly inaccurate tend by and large to be negative.[19]

Television's leaders will find little comfort from Helmreich's conclusion, because the industry does too little to counter the inaccurate stereotypes. In 1979, the U.S. Commission on Civil Rights, in its study *Window Dressing on the Set: An Update*, reported:

Television drama continues in its failure to reflect the gender and racial-ethnic composition of the American population....Minority males are disproportionately seen in comic roles....Minorities, regard-less of sex, are disproportionately cast in teenage roles; in contrast white male characters are disproportionately cast in adult roles.... Minorities, regardless of sex, are less frequently portrayed in an identifiable occupation than majority characters.[20]

Discrimination against women by televison was rampant. As of 1979, sex stereotyping presenting a composite picture of women counter to real life was the norm. According to Louis Nunez, the Commission's acting staff director, the distortions were legion:

We found 40 percent of female characters on TV in the 21 to 30-year-old bracket, while only 20 percent of the male characters were in that bracket....Female minority characters have no identifiable job 46 percent of the time....Forty percent (of white female characters) have no identifiable occupation....To the extent that television serves as a creator or reinforcer of beliefs about the kinds of occupations that are appropriate for people, we thus found it plays a negative role in regard to women.[21]

In November 1982, further negative news about women's roles in television news organizations appeared. The absence of female anchors on any of the major networks (except for week-end roles) was noted. In a study funded by Gannett, Knight-Ridder, and the American Association of University Women, Jean Gaddy Wilson, the project director, reported that, in addition to the implications of the shortage of women as network anchors:

In the local markets, the news team is usually led by a man, with a woman in a deferring role; on the corporate level very few women rise above middle management....General managers and news directors, producers and directors are usually male. Promotion directors, community affairs directors are usually women.[22]

In the summer of 1983, Christine Craft, a former co-anchor on the nightly news on KMBC-TV in Kansas City, Missouri, was awarded $500,000 in a suit she brought alleging that she had been demoted because she was "too old, unattractive and not deferential enough to men." The facts are that Ms. Craft is in her mid-thirties and is as acceptable in appearance as anyone could wish. Her victory, though not final, should be celebrated by all reporters, regardless of gender.[23]

Sexism on television, abetted by reliance on stereotype portrayals, is still pervasive. Television advertising plays a major role in promoting sexist imagery. Successive studies since the 1950s have reached similar conclusions, asserting that the data show that women as sex objects highlight the selling pitches for numerous products. Again, women are infrequently portrayed in professional roles. The National Advertising Review Board report of 1975 provided numerous illustrations of the sexist theme. The National Airlines "Fly me" campaign was perhaps no worse than the Continental Airlines "We really move our tail for you" advertising.

Sex-biased advertising takes many forms. A 1978 study analyzing 367 television commercials and concentrating on product representatives found that "81 percent of the women were portrayed with domestic products, while 19 percent of the women and 64 percent of the men were portrayed with non-domestic products."[24]

Effects on children of television's stereotypes have also been explored frequently. One 1979 study found that "adolescent girls exposed to a heavy dose of beauty commercials were more likely than a control group of girls not exposed to the commercials to believe that being beautiful is an important characteristic and is necessary to attract men." Another study relates the benefit of counter-stereotyping against the type of propaganda just described. A 1975 investigation "revealed that children who were shown a commercial featuring a female judge were more likely than a no-exposure control group to rate the profession as an appropriate one for females."[25]

BETTER STEREOTYPING?

Throughout his professional life, Walter Lippmann provoked his colleagues in the worlds of journalism, politics, and scholarship, trying to make them see beyond headlines to where issues precipitate events and to how sentiments and emotions run a constant race with facts. Those who tangle with dilemmas of juggling what we now like to term *data* with less solid circumstantial evidence never had a better wordsmith to describe connections between ideas grasped and those just beyond clear comprehension. One of his major achievements was to champion reason in an illogical framework of human relationships. He preferred the sane, thoughtful comprehension of a problem to the quick and easy pronouncements that too often pass for solutions.

Snared by his own adherence to the elitist-based intellectual potentialities of humankind, he sometimes had difficulty dealing head-on with perversion and cruelty. Lippmann wanted his colleagues to truly assume the mantles of leadership he himself felt comfortable with.

Even in explaining how stereotypes work, he tried to resolve the issues of how the press ought to deal with such shorthand fairly. To understand Lippmann, one ought to accept the fact that his own passages into unfair stereotyping came about because he had too little tolerance for cultural diversity and was too ready to believe that tyrants could be weakened by truths revealed about their viciousness.

Nearing the zenith of his career as television was emerging from its electronic womb, Lippmann was accepted by news and public affairs managers of the networks as a model pundit. Right from its beginnings, television was best at presenting broad outlines of social, political, and economic happenings. Lippmann, as always, was ready and eager to summarize after tending to the tasks of research on his own. His first appearance on television (later to become an annual ritual) took place in early July of 1960, when he was interviewed at length on CBS-TV. *Television: The Management Magazine of Broadcast Advertising* treated the interview in the prominent article "Television and Politics" in its July 1960 issue as something of an event of tremendous consequence. Opposite the first page of text was a full-page photograph of the great man facing his interviewer, seated in a lawn chair in the verdant surround of his garden. The videotape camera is pointed squarely at him.

> At left is Walter Lippmann. He has never been a political candidate. He has been on television only once. But in this one telecast may well lie the key to television's true strength and significance in politics. To most observers, political function reached its zenith in the recent nominating conventions. Millions upon millions of people were able to watch prospective candidates for the nation's highest office in action....The basic question is, what can television contribute, by way of information and opinion, to the electorate's political enlightenment? In this direction, one of the most important breakthroughs was the recent telecast with Walter Lippmann....Here a significantly large audience, again numbering many millions, had the opportunity of sitting down, watching and listening to the sage comments of one of the most respected observers on the political scene. Controversial but enlightening, and of immediate political pertinence, were Lippmann's discussions of the role of the Presidency, of the qualifications for leadership, of recent history.[26]

Television's capacities to deal with stereotypes in a socially progressive manner have not grown much since Lippmann passed the torch of criticism to others, despite the medium's tremendous potentials. News programs have become so important that, since the mid-1950s, more people rely on television for the news than on print media. Documentaries on television, although always a scarce commodity, have also done much to add to the luster of the small screen. Election reports, beginning with the opening nominating highlights at the start of each electoral season, have won high praise for immediacy and liveliness. For all such achievements, the medium does its best work on its own terms.

Usually, subtleties are lost because of the concentration on showmanship. The historical backgrounds to important stories are routinely sacrificed altogether or reduced to gross summarizations. Analysis, always difficult to depict pictorially, is never a preoccupation of television's public affairs people. Stereotypes were and remain a mainstay.

We all try to answer important questions about stereotypes with which Lippmann struggled as well. Why, for example, are stereotypes so enduring, especially in their perverse forms? Why are stereotypes so impervious to personal experience and hard facts? How can television and the other mass media budge them with democratically affirmative work?

Is Jacques Ellul correct when, in his provocative analysis of the roles of propaganda, he concludes, "propaganda is principally interested in shaping action and behavior, and with little thought"?[27] Is television so dominated by the advertising fraternity and its influences that it has become more interested in getting commercial propaganda over than it is in provoking any other consumer reactions?

Are we soon to enter a period of better stereotyping because of the new devices of this electronic age? Will diversity of opinion and of message, fostered by cable transmission, satellites, home player-recorders, and so forth, introduce more media fairness, or will technical novelties increase in number as the levels of true intellectual stimulation plateau or fall?

According to one estimate, the average American watches television for 1,300 hours a year.[28] Many of our less socially beneficial stereotypes, in basic formats, predated Lippmann's earliest inquiries and are still with us now. Television is the greatest instrument for the transmission of quick and impressive information that the world has seen. Can we light up the blind spots behind its most visible stereotypes?

NOTES

1. Robert Stam and Louise Spence, "Colonialism, Racism and Representation," *Screen* (March–April 1983), pp. 2–20.
2. Ibid., p. 9.
3. Ibid., p. 17.
4. Karin Dovring, *Road of Propaganda: The Semantics of Biased Communication* (New York: Philosophical Library, 1959), p. 113.
5. Lippmann quoted in John Luskin, *Lippmann, Liberty and the Press* (University: University of Alabama Press, 1972), p. 156.
6. See Mobil Corporation advertisement, "1. The Myth of the Villainous Business-man," *Time*, August 29, 1983, p. 4.
7. See Mobil Corporation advertisement, "2. The Myth of the Informed Public," *Boston Globe*, August 29, 1983.
8. See Mobil Corporation advertisement, "3. The Myth of the Crusading Reporter," *The New York Times*, September 1, 1983. Also, for particulars about distortions Mobil complains about relative to the energy situation in the United States, see Public Affairs, Mobil Corporation, *The Energy Crisis and the media: Ten Case Histories* (New York: Mobil Oil Corporation, 1983).
9. Walter Lippmann, *The Good Society* (Boston: Little, Brown, 1937), p. 31.
10. Walter Lippmann, *Essays in the Public Philosophy* (Boston: Little, Brown, 1955), pp. 26–27.
11. *Fighting TV Stereotypes. An ACT Handbook* (Newtonville, MA: Action for Children's Television, 1983), fifth page.
12. Ralph E. Friar and Natasha A. Friar, *The Only Good Indian: The Hollywood Gospel* (New York: Drama Book Specialists, 1972).
13. William B. Helmreich, *The Things They Say Behind Your Back* (Garden City, NY: Doubleday, 1982).
14. Leonard C. Archer, *Black Images in the American Theatre* (Brooklyn, N.Y.: Pageant-Poseidon, 1973).
15. Walter White, "Negro Leader Looks at TV Race Problem," *Printers' Ink*, August 24, 1951, p. 31.
16. William A. Henry III, "The Jeffersons: Black Like Nobody," *Channels*, March–April 1983, pp. 62, 64.

17. See Robert F. Berkhofer, Jr., *The White Man's Indian* (New York: Knopf, 1978).
18. Friar and Friar, *The Only Good Indian*, pp. 260–261, 166.
19. Helmreich, *The Things They Say Behind Your Back*, p. 244.
20. *Window Dressing on the Set: An Update* (Washington, D.C.: U.S. Commission on Civil Rights, January 1979), pp. 60–62.
21. Louis Nunez, "TV Image of Women: Distorted," *Chicago Tribune*, January 25, 1979, Sec. 3, p. 4.
22. "Jean Gaddy Wilson Offers Preliminary Look at Major Study...Women in News Media," *Media Report to Women*, March–April 1983, p. 4.
23. "Judge Upholds Award to TV Anchorwoman," *New York Times*, September 1, 1983. After award overturn, legal battles continued into 1985.
24. See a report of the study in W. O'Donnell and K. O'Donnell, "Update: Sex-role Messages in TV Commercials," in Matilda Butler and William Paisley, eds., *Women and the Mass Media* (New York: Human Sciences Press, 1980), p. 74.
25. See Robert M. Liebert, Joyce N. Sprafkin, and Emily S. Davidson, *The Early Window: Effects of Television on Children and Youth* (New York: Pergamon Press, 1982), p. 167.
26. "Television and Politics," *Television: The Management of Broadcast Advertising* July 1960, p. 47.
27. Jacques Ellul, *Propaganda* (New York: Vintage Books–Random House, 1973), p. 278.
28. Jean-Louis Servan-Schreiber, *The Power to Inform* (New York: McGraw-Hill, 1974), p. 213.

media

MEDIA EFFECTS

In this section we deal with the problem of media effects. It is an important topic and a controversial one. We all spend a great deal of time watching television, listening to the radio, reading magazines and newspapers — and yet, so many media researchers tell us, the effects of media on individuals seem to be trivial.

There is also the matter of how one studies media effects. You will discover there are numerous theories about how media affect people and that there are periods when scholars seem to agree that media effects are powerful and other periods when they tend to think that media effects are weak. It all seems to depend upon which theories of how the media work are in vogue with the social scientists who study the media. Theories arise, seem to be useful, are tested and generally found wanting in some respect, and are replaced by other theories.

It is almost like being on a rollercoaster. In recent years there has been an increase in the influence of a group of critics who believe that the media are powerful — the Marxists. These thinkers use concepts from Marxist thought to interpret the media and deal with its role in society. Being a Marxist does not mean that they are "Communists" who want to violently overthrow the American government; most of them do not think too much of the Soviet Union and its Eastern European satellites or any totalitarian society. There are numerous divisions within Marxist thought, I should point out; Marxists disagree with one another on many issues, though they all use and adapt Marx's ideas as the basis for their critique of the mass media in America and western society.

One important thinker in this camp, who is famous for having a number of criticisms of the politics of "the left" is the East German poet, writer, and media theorist Hans Magnus Enzenberger. He has written an essay, "The Industrialization of the Mind," which offers a number of ideas that we might think about relative to this matter of media effects. Enzenberger is concerned about our notion that we have effective control over our minds. Here are a few quotations from the essay, reprinted in *The Consciousness Industry* (New York: Seabury Press, 1974), serve as an excellent point of departure for our investigation of media effects:

1. All of us, no matter now irresolute we are, like to think that we reign supreme in our own consciousness, that we are masters of what our minds accept or reject. Since the Soul is not much mentioned any more, except by priests, poets, and pop musicians, the last refuge a person can take from the catastrophic world seems to be his or her own mind. Where else can he or she expect to withstand the daily siege, if not within him or herself? Even under the conditions of totalitarian rule, where no one can fancy any more that his or her home is his or her castle, the mind of the individual is considered a kind of last citadel and hotly defended; though this imaginary fortress may have been long since taken over by an ingenious enemy.

   No illusion is more stubbornly upheld than the sovereignty of the mind. It is a good example of the impact of philosophy on people who ignore it; for the idea that men can "make up their minds" individually and by themselves is essentially derived from the tenets of bourgeois philosophy...We might do worse, I think, than dust off the admirably laconic statement that one of our classics made more than a century ago: "What is going on in our minds has always been, and will always be, a product of society."

2. The mind industry's main business and concern is not to sell its product: it is to "sell" the existing order, to perpetuate the prevailing pattern of man's domination by man, no matter who runs the society, and by what means. It main task is to expand and train our consciousness — in order to exploit it.

3. The self-appointed elites who run modern societies must try to control people's minds. What each of us accepts or rejects, what we think and decide is now...a matter of prime political concern: it would be too dangerous to leave these matters to ourselves. Material exploitation must camouflage itself in order to survive; immaterial exploitation has become its necessary corollary. The few cannot go on accumulating wealth unless they accumulate the power to manipulate the minds of the many.

Enzenberger assumes, then, a powerful media — a media that has already, he tells us, industrialized our minds. And this is made easier because we all have the illusions that we maintain sovereignty over our individual minds. There are problems with Enzenberger's analysis: he offers no evidence for his assertions but merely tells us that our minds have been industrialized. And if we don't believe him, so his argument suggests, it may be because we have all been victimized by bourgeois individualistic philosophy. Still, he provides us with a good starting point from which to consider the whole question of media effects. He raises the problem of how much control we have over our minds and how susceptible we are to being influenced (if not manipulated) by the media.

40

WHO'S AFRAID OF THE BIG BAD MEDIA?*

WILLIAM J. MCGUIRE

This essay asks a very provocative question and gives a most remarkable answer. The question it asks is "Can we prove that the media have a significant impact on individuals and upon society in general?" The answer it gives is "No, we can't!" This answer stems from an exhaustive search of articles and books dealing with the effects of media. The evidence, which seems to be overwhelming, suggests that whatever effects media might have on people are trivial and not significant.

Or, to put it somewhat differently, nobody has been able to prove that the media have the effects they are reputed to have.

Is it possible, then, that the hours and hours we spend in front of the boob tube, soaking up violence, being bombarded by commercials, watching heroes and heroines with whom we identify and villains we loathe…have no important impact on us? If that is the case, why do corporations spend billions of dollars for advertising? Why do educators plead to have parents limit the amount of television they allow their children to watch? Why do people cry at films? Why are books banned and burned?

Common sense, of course, tells us that the media are powerful. But common sense, as a wit once noted, tells us that the world is flat. A number of people have a stake in the notion that the media are powerful. Advertising agencies must believe in the notion — otherwise it would make no sense to spend $100,000 to make a thirty-second commercial and millions more for air time to show it. And researchers have a stake in a powerful medium, otherwise it would be a waste of time and effort (and money) to study the media as a major socializing force.

William J. McGuire, author of the essay that follows, has made a major study of the question of media effects and has discussed the matter in an authoritative essay, "The Myth of Mass Media Impact: Savagings and Salvagings."[1] He concludes this essay with a challenge to those who believe that the media are powerful. The burden of proof lies on your shoulders, he tells them, and you'd better redesign your research programs if you want anyone to take you seriously.

The essay you will read was specially written for the book and contains many of the most important points in the original article, without some of the detail (due to space limitations). It flies against our intuitive feelings that the media have powerful impacts and raises important questions about the role of media in society.

REFERENCE

1. W. J. McGuire. "The Myth of Massive Media Impact: Savagings and Salvagings." In G. Comstock (Ed.), *Public Communication and Behavior* (vol. 1, pp. 173–257). Orlando, FL: Academic Press, 1986.

Television and the other mass media have been credited with — and blamed for — having a variety of major effects on the public. The high-consumption life styles portrayed in the media and encouraged by the advertisements they carry are accused of creating insatiable wants and a materialistic value system in the public. The violence pervading television shows has been blamed for the increase in crime. The media's biased depiction (or non-depiction) of low-power groups purportedly contributes to their stereotyping (or invisibility) in the public mind. The superficial political ads presented during election campaigns are said to have trivialized voters' decision-making. The media's pre-empting of most of the public's leisure time is blamed for the decline of family life, of social interaction, and of the pursuit of higher culture. The passivity and agitated animation to which television accustoms the young are accused of lowering their level of attention and educability.

The widespread agreement that the mass media, and especially television, have enormous impact on the public should itself lead us to question this belief on the principle that any judgment on which everyone has agreed should arouse our suspicions. Unanimous acceptance often reflects, not that support for the position is overwhelming, but that the interests of diverse factions are served by its being accepted and so it has become agreed dogma because absence of an adversarial constituency has spared it from critical scrutiny.

ORIGINS OF THE BELIEF IN LARGE MASS MEDIA EFFECTS

On the issue of mass media impact, it is in the interest of each of the many contending factions to support the assertion that the mass media have large effects. Self-interest compels the managers and owners of television channels and other media to insist that their messages have sizable impact because the economic basis of most mass media is the sale of the time and space to advertisers who must be convinced that ads sell. These advertisers in turn, who buy the time, have their own reasons for being true believers in massive media impacts: it would take heroic virtue for marketing and other executives who spend billions of their companies' dollars each year on advertising to confess that ads are ineffectual and so they have been wasting all this money. The enemies of the media are equally compelled to insist on massive impacts because their criticisms and urging for regulation of the media assume, not the ineffectualness but the massive malevolent impact of the media. Even those supposedly neutral students of the topic, the basic researchers who study media effects, would have much to lose by reporting that the media are ineffectual and so the topic of their investigations is unimportant. Hence, all of the contending factions are loathe to question the truism that the media have massive impact.

To claim that the media have little effect on the public would violate not only this implicit conspiracy of silence but also a number of common sense informal observations that suggest that the media, especially television, must be having vast influence on the public. For example, the amount of time spent being exposed to the media is so great that it must be producing considerable effect: The average American spends more than three hours a day, 20 percent of his/her waking life, watching television; the average child sees 20,000 ads and 10,000 acts of violence each year on television and reaches age 18 having spent more time in front of the home television set than in front of the school teacher. Surely all this watching must be having a formidable effect? And consider the pervasiveness of commercial advertising: Hard-headed business executives, who must know the value of a dollar even if not of much else, spend 50 billion of them a year on mass media advertising. They must know what they are doing and if not able to document the effectiveness of such a vast investment would they not have been fired by their companies or eliminated by market forces? And must not television violence be inciting the viewer to violence considering that there is so much of it and that the advent of television in the 1950s was quickly followed by the sharp rise in crime, riots, assassinations, etc., through the 1960s, to a level that frightened people off the streets at night?

Considering the general agreement and the a priori plausibility of the claim that the media have massive direct impacts on the American public, it is surprising how little support the contention receives from empirical research. This paucity of evidence does not derive from lack of research, of which there has been plenty. Neither is it due to the inadequacy of the research: While most of these evaluation studies leave considerable room for improvement, we often find the higher the quality of the research, the less impact it finds. Effects occasionally reach the conventionally accepted .05 level of statistical significance but are slight in magnitude, accounting for only a few percent of the variance in the dependent-variable behavior of buying, aggression, or whatever. These modest results do not disprove the existence of any impact (or even the possibility of considerable impact) but the pervasive paltriness of the demonstrated effects should shake the confidence of those who assert that the media have massive direct impact and should prevent them from claiming that research offers clear support for this assertion.

WEAKNESS OF THE EVIDENCE FOR MASSIVE MEDIA IMPACTS

Evidence in support of the claim that the media have sizable direct impact on the public is weak as regards each of the dozen most often-mentioned intended or unintended effects of the media. The most commonly mentioned intended effects include: (1) the influence of commercial advertising on buying behavior; (2) the impact of mass media political campaigns on voting; (3) public service announcements' efficacy in promoting beneficial behavior; (4) the role of prolonged multimedia campaigns in changing lifestyles; (5) monolithic indoctrination effects on ideology; and (6) the effects of mass-mediated ritual displays on maintaining social control. The most often cited unintended effects of the mass media include: (1) the impact of program violence on viewers' antisocial aggression; (2) representation on the media as a determinant of social visibility; (3) biased presentation on the media as influencing the public's stereotyping of groups; (4) effects of erotic materials on objectionable sexual behavior; (5) modes of media presentation as affecting cognitive styles; and (6) the impact of introducing new media on public thought processes. Space limitations here will allow us to discuss evidence regarding the purported impacts in only a couple of these dozen areas: We shall focus on the first-listed effect of each of the two classes, the intended effect of commercial advertising on buying behavior and the unintended effect of program violence on viewer aggression, because these two effects have received the greatest amount of research attention.

Effects of Television Ads on Buying Behavior

The ultimate payoff variable for whether American advertisers are getting their dollars' worth for the 50 billion spent each year is how much goods and services the ads sell relative to their costs. Much of the evaluation research uses some convenient approximations of buying, such as reported liking for the brand or awareness of its existence. Whatever the criterion, there are four research strategies used to measure advertising impact; two involve "macro" or "econometric" studies, those that use brand-share, and those that use total product-class sales summed across consumers as their effectiveness criteria. The other two strategies involve "micro" or "behavioral" studies that measure the buying by individual consumers, either in field or in laboratory situations.

Econometric (Macro) Research on Advertising Effectiveness.   Macro-level research includes both brand-share and product-class research. Brand-share studies involve tracking the comparative performance of several competing brands of a product (for example, several brands of soft drinks or several makes of cars) over successive time periods and, for each brand, measuring (a) its share of the industry's total advertising budget and (b) its share of the total sales of the product. These two measures are obtained for each of the brands for an extended time period, for example, monthly over a two-year time span. The researcher can then estimate the efficacy of the advertising by analyzing whether rises and falls in a brand's advertising share lead to rises and falls in their share of the product's total sales. Such brand-share studies typically find surprisingly little effect, often not even a modest statistically significant effect, much less a sizable impact that demonstrably exceeds the cost of the advertising. This discouraging appraisal seems indicated even by reviews sponsored by the advertising agencies themselves (Albion & Farris, 1981).

The other subtype of macro-evaluation research, product-class studies, yields equally discouraging results. This type of study tracks a whole product class over time without distinguishing among individual brands; for example, the total ad budget of all the major beer manufacturers and the total beer sales might be measured for twelve successive three-month periods spread over three years. Ad efficacy can then be measured by analyzing whether fluctuations in the industry's total advertising leads to fluctuations in total beer sales. Results usually furnish little support for belief in massive advertising effects. For example, the Federal Trade Commission study (Murphy, 1980) on cigarette smoking found that annual fluctuations in cigarette advertising (or indeed, in anti-cigarette advertising) had little relationship to annual cigarette sales. It is not that such studies are too insensitive to detect any effect or that cigarette smoking is too ingrained to be affected by any manipulation because the research does find sizable "price elasticity" effects on smoking, that is, raising the price of cigarettes results in a major reduction in the amount of cigarette sales.

Behavioral (Micro) Research on Advertising Effectiveness. Micro-level or "behavioral" studies evaluate advertising effects on the level of the individual person, in either field or laboratory situations. Particularly well investigated by field studies is how exposure to television ads for over-the-counter drugs affects the viewers' use of legal and illegal drugs, a relatively well-studied topic because of the high level of advertising by pharmaceutical companies and the high level of public concern about drug use. The general indication from a dozen respectable field studies (e.g., Milavsky, Pekowsky, & Stipp, 1975) is that exposure to TV drug ads accounts at most for a few percent of the variance in legal drug use and even less in illegal use of drugs. These field studies typically involve monitoring the TV viewing of a group of adolescents for an extended period to measure how many drug ads they have been exposed to during successive time periods and monitoring concurrently the drug use of these adolescents, to determine statistically the relationship between number of ads seen and subsequent level of drug use.

A typical laboratory study might involve dividing children randomly into two equivalent groups and then exposing the two groups to television programs in which contrasting ads have been inserted. The children are then offered payment for their participation in the form of commodities that include the products advertised in their own program versus the competing products advertised in the other group's programs to determine if they choose more of the products they had seen advertised. These laboratory studies tend to show positive effects but are inconclusive because of weak methodology and artificiality.

All of these four types of advertising evaluation research have thus yielded surprisingly weak support for the contention that advertisements have large direct impacts on the consumers' buying behavior or even on their liking for or awareness of the product. Evidence is equally weak for large impacts on the other intended media effects among the half-dozen listed above. For example, the effects of media campaigning on election outcomes or of public service announcements on prosocial behavior (McGuire, 1986) are found to be quite modest or nonexistent.

Effects of Program Violence on Viewer's Aggressive Behavior

As regards unintended effects purportedly produced by the mass media, of the half-dozen we mention above by far the best studied has been the possible impact of watching violent television programs on the viewer's subsequent antisocial aggressive behavior. By the 1960s television had spread to most U.S. households and the average American was spending several hours a day watching its programs, which were often violent. Not long after, the U.S. crime rate began rising dramatically. Many observers were putting 2 + 2 together and charging that TV violence was to blame for the rise in crime and other antisocial aggression such as riots and assassinations (just as violent comic books had been so charged in the 1950s [Wertham, 1955], and violent films before that). The premise that television programs are saturated with violence is easy to demonstrate: Primetime shows average a half-dozen acts of violence per hour and Saturday morning children's programs three times that level; the average person sees 10,000 acts of violence per year on television. The violence counts raise controversies about what is to be scored as violent and how units are defined but, however such issues are resolved, the daily body count on television is appalling. It must be admitted that the violence level is even greater in popular novels and films and that throughout history people have sought out violent spectacles (Goldstein, 1983).

But the prevalence of televised violence is only one premise of the argument that television is responsible; the other premise is that viewers emulate what they see on the TV screen and so are provoked to aggressive behavior by watching violence. It is this second premise of the argument that is debatable theoretically and poorly supported empirically.

Theoretical Analyses of Violence Effects. Most theories predict that viewer aggression does go up with violent television watching but there are a minority of theories implying that exposure to television violence could actually be negatively related to viewer aggression. Theoretical conjectures about a relationship between exposure to TV violence and viewer aggression usually assumes that it is the former that affects the latter. Four such theories predict a positive and two a negative relationship. The four predicting a positive relationship include social learning, disinhibition, arousal, and mood theories. Social learning theory, the most popular of these views, asserts that people will model their own behavior after behavior they witness in others, especially when they see that behavior being rewarded. Disinhibition theory asserts that as violence is shown pervasively it comes to be perceived as banal and even as condoned socially, which perception lowers a viewer's natural inhibition against hurting other persons. Arousal theory posits that violence depictions are exciting and so multiply the vigor of viewers' responses, including aggressive ones. Mood theories say that exposure to violence induces anger and other negative moods in the viewer and that such moods provoke antisocial behaviors. Two other theories, the catharsis and the time-monopoly positions, predict a negative relationship. Catharsis theory states that watching violent programs allows the person to release aggressive tensions in fantasy so that he or she will be less aggressive in overt behavior. Time-monopoly theory asserts that spending a lot of time watching violent (or other) shows on television reduces the amount of time available to the viewer for going out on the street and perpetrating mayhem.

Other theories predict the reverse causal flow, such that the person's level of aggression affects the amount of televised violence to which (s)he is exposed. Two such theories, ostracism and predilection, predict a positive relationship and one, conventionality, a negative relationship between aggression and television exposure. Ostracism theory has it that antisocial aggressive people are shunned by others and so have little else to do but sit home and watch television with its predominantly violent shows. Predilection theory maintains that the more aggressive the person is, the more violent is his or her personality, and thus he or she seeks out violent shows for enjoyment. Conventionality theory predicts a negative effect of personal aggressiveness on exposure to televised violence on the grounds that the conventional, unaggressive person tends to stay home watching television (and its high proportion of violent shows) while more aggressive types are out clobbering people so that they have relatively little time left for watching television and little desire for so passive an activity.

Twice as many of all these theories predict positive as predict negative relationships between exposure to TV violence and viewers' levels of antisocial aggression. However, we shall see in the next section that despite the weight of common sense and of these theoretical explanations, the empirical evidence is weak that exposure to violent television accounts for a great proportion of the violence in society.

Empirical Evidence for Violence Effects. Research to test the impact of televised violence has been carried out in both laboratory and natural-world situations. The laboratory studies have typically used either young children or college students, two populations readily available for such experimentation. Two groups of matched children might be shown a violent television cartoon versus a comparably exciting but nonviolent cartoon. The children are then put in play situations where they can emulate an adult model by kicking an inflated clown doll as a measure of aggression. Or two matched groups of college students might be shown a violent prizefighting film versus a nonviolent but equally exciting sports film, and the students' subsequent aggression measured in terms of how much electric shock they administer when immediately afterwards they participate in a learning situation where they are encouraged to train a learner by giving him shocks when he makes an error. In these laboratory studies the group exposed to the more violent material often scores significantly higher on aggression, especially if they are persons predisposed to violence or pre-angered when they enter the study; but the modest effect size and the artificiality of the conditions, particularly as regards the aggressiveness measures, raise doubts about the validity of generalizing these laboratory findings.

Violence-evaluation research carried out in natural-world situations include concurrent and retrospective subtypes. Concurrent studies of a correlational subtype might investigate a junior high school population repeatedly over several years, measuring their reported television watching to calculate the amount of violence to which each child has been exposed in successive time intervals, and also measuring for each interval the child's aggression as indicated by peer or teacher ratings, by delinquency records, etc. Statistical analyses are then done to determine the extent to which later aggression levels can be predicted from earlier levels of violence exposure. An alternative, manipulational subtype of concurrent study is to divide an institutionalized population into equivalent subgroups and manipulate the amount of violent television watched by the several subgroups and then measure the amount of aggression in each subgroup and analyze if the subgroup shown more violent television later exhibits more aggressive behavior.

The retrospective (or "archival") type of natural-world research might study the time periods around each of a series of highly publicized violent spectacles (such as championship prizefights) versus control time periods in which the media were not reporting a great deal of violent news. The national reports on the amount of violent crime are then analyzed to determine if the crime rate increases from before to after the prizefights but not in the matched control periods. Findings in some natural world studies, both concurrent and retrospective, (Huesmann, Lagerspetz, & Eron, 1984; Milavsky, Kessler, Stipp, & Rubens, 1982; Phillips, 1986) indicate a significant positive relationship but the magnitude of the effect is surprisingly weak relative to the general belief about massive media impacts.

The bottom-line effectiveness indications for the half-dozen other types of unintended media effects mentioned above (amount of exposure on television as it affects social visibility, exposure to vivid television material as it affects viewers' cognitive style, etc.) are as modest as in this case of television violence, which was just discussed in more detail simply because it has been the best studied of the purported unintended effects. Research on the other five types of unintended effects also shows at most a slight positive effect, only occasionally attaining the conventionally-accepted .05 statistical significance level and even then of too small a magnitude to support the common belief that the media have massive impacts.

EXCUSES FOR KEEPING THE FAITH IN MASSIVE MEDIA IMPACTS

So far we have argued that the results of empirical research do not provide strong support for the common belief that mass media have large direct impacts on the people exposed to them, but here we turn to argue for caution in rejecting the belief in massive impacts. Even though studies to date on a dozen intended and unintended types of purported media impacts show only small to vanishing effects, it would be premature to rule out the possibility of massive effects. The theoretical foundations of empirical science include the principle that the null hypothesis cannot be proven, that is, that negative results do not prove that there are no effects. Below we shall mention briefly five types of excuses that argue for keeping the faith regarding massive media impacts even though they have seldom been found in past research.

Methodological Weaknesses May Obscure Effects

A first type of excuse is that massive effects do occur but are missed because the evaluation research is so methodologically flawed. Any informed student of media evaluations will be aware that the research has serious flaws, including crude measures of the independent variables (such as the amount of exposure to specific types of ads or to violence) and of the dependent variables (such as the amount of the viewers' purchases or of their antisocial aggression), poor statistical models for estimating the relationships between the two, poor controls for extraneous variables, poor manipulations of the independent variables, possible experimenter biases, etc. All research is somewhat flawed and this media evaluation research is at best only average in methodological sophistication. But these inadequacies are a poor excuse for the failure to obtain evidence for massive media impacts because improvements in methodology seem more often to reduce than increase the size of the impact.

Environmental Conditions May Obscure Media Impact

A second type of excuse is that the mass media potentially have vast impacts but they have to operate under conditions that obscure their true effectiveness. For example, it may be that people selectively avoid messages with which they do not already agree and so are seldom exposed to the disagreeing media material that would have converted them had they received it. Another such excuse is that the media transmit opposed sets of messages from rival politicians, or from competing brands of a product, etc., that mutually cancel one another's effects. Still another excuse of this type is that media messages come in obscuring environments clouded by advertisement clutter, by more interesting entertainment programs, by distracting situations in the life of the viewer, etc. Granting that such conditions exist and could have an obscuring effect, it would follow that the media could have large impacts in some hypothetical world where these conditions were absent. But in the world that is, such conditions would tend to reduce the hypothetical media effects even more substantially than they do in research situations.

Circumscribed Effects May Be Missed in the Search for General Effects

One fallback position is to argue that even if the media do not have large effects always and everywhere, they may have sizable impact in special subdomains, in which circumscribed effects are lost in the typical evaluation study that looks solely for overall effects. For example, media campaigns may do little for familiar products or known candidates but do help new ones get an initial hearing; or the media may not convert the opposition but may serve to keep the faith of those already convinced; or the media may have sizable effects only on highly involving issues (or only on unimportant ones); or the media may not have much impact by themselves but may multiply the impacts of other factors like personal experience; or the media may affect the timing of a response like buying or aggression, even if they do not affect the amount of the response in the long run. Some or all of these circumscribed effects are plausible although none has been firmly established by research (except possibly the greater media impact for a new product or candidate). In any case, they all represent a considerable fallback from the earlier assertion of generally massive media effects.

Effects May Be Confined to Especially Susceptible Subpopulations

An alternative fallback strategy is to argue that even if the media do not have large effects on everyone, they do sizably affect certain highly susceptible subpopulations, the focused effects on whom get lost in the typical evaluation study designed to detect universal effects. Among the subpopulations suggested as being especially susceptible are children, certain personality types, elites who monitor the media carefully and serve as opinion leaders, those who have not yet had time to become jaded with a new medium, etc. Where there is some supporting evidence that a special subgroup is more susceptible than is the general population, the demonstrated effect size tends to be modest even among these susceptibles.

Indirect Effects May Be Missed in the Search for Direct Impacts

Another way of defending the hypothesis of massive media impact is to argue that sizable effects occur but operate only indirectly and so are lost in research designed only to pick up direct effects. A number of well-known theories use this defense strategy. The two-step flow theory asserts that the media may not directly effect the general public but do affect highly attentive opinion leaders who monitor the media and who later convince the general public to adopt the media position. The agenda-setting theory argues that the media do not change the public's stands on issues but do determine which issues are salient to the public when they make their decisions. The spiral-of-silence theory asserts that the media do not convert the public but by stressing one side on an issue silence the opposition by giving them the impression that they stand alone. Another theory of indirect effect is that even if the media do not have great direct impact, the general belief that they do changes institutional practices in ways that indirectly make them effective, as when political parties choose photogenic candidates, or the candidates and elected officials change their style of behavior on the mistaken assumption that television charisma has been shown to have sizable effects on voting behavior. Evidence is available that supports some of these conjectured indirect effects (for example, see Iyengar & Kinder, 1987, on agenda setting) but the effect size continues to be unimpressive. In any case such indirect effects would leave unexplained the lack of evidence for the generally-believed sizable direct effects of the media.

CONCLUSION

Although the general public and the diverse groups who are professionally involved with the media may be convinced that the mass media have vast direct impacts on the public, a considerable amount of empirical research on the topic has provided surprisingly little support for massive impact. Rather, the interim bottom line to which the existing research findings add up is that media effects can occasionally be detected statistically but are usually quite small in magnitude. This does not prove that massive effects do not occur: Empirical research is unsuitable for proving the null hypothesis and there are many types of excuses to explain away these failures to confirm large media effects as we have described above. However, even if the failures to confirm do not definitely disprove the assertion that mass media have sizable direct effects on those exposed to them, they make it improper to claim that the empirical results support the general belief. For the present, a Scotch verdict of "Not Proven" seems indicated on the proposition that the mass media have vast direct impacts on the public exposed to them.

ACKNOWLEDGMENT

The writing of this chapter was greatly aided by research grant number MH 32588 received from the Interpersonal Processes and Problems Section, Behavioral Sciences Research Branch, National Institute of Mental Health, U.S. Department of Health and Human Services.

REFERENCES

Albion, M. S. & Farris, P. W. (1981). *The advertising controversy: Evidence on the economic effects of advertising*. Dedham, MA: Auburn House.

Goldstein, J. H. (Ed.). (1983). *Sports violence*. New York: Springer-Verlag.

Huesmann, L. R., Lagerspetz, K., & Eron, L. D. (1984). Intervening variables in the TV violence-aggression relation: Evidence from two countries. *Developmental Psychology, 20*, 746–775.

Iyengar, S. & Kinder, D. R. (1987). *News that matters: Television and American opinion*. Cambridge, MA: Harvard University Press.

McGuire, W. J. (1986). The myth of massive media impact: Savagings and salvagings. In G. Comstock (Ed.), *Public communication and behavior* (Vol. 1, pp. 173–257). Orlando, FL: Academic Press.

Milavsky, J. R., Pekowsky, B., & Stipp, H. H. (1975). TV drug advertising and proprietary and illicit drug use among teenage boys. *Public Opinion Quarterly, 39*, 457–481.

Milavsky, J. R., Kessler, R. C., Stipp, H. H., & Rubens, W. S. (1982). *Television and aggression: Results of a panel study*. New York: Academic Press.

Murphy, R. D. (1980). Consumer responses to cigarette health warnings. In L. A. Morris, M. B. Mazis, & I. Barofsky (Eds.), *Product labeling and health risks* (Report No. 6, pp. 13–21). Cold Spring Harbor Laboratory, NY: Branbury Reports.

Phillips, D. P. (1986). The found experiment: A new technique for assessing the impact of mass media violence on real-world aggressive behavior. In G. Comstock (Ed.), *Public communication and behavior* (Vol. 1, 259–307). Orlando, FL: Academic Press.

Wertham, F. (1955). *Seduction of the innocent*. London: Museum Press.

43   ON CONCEPTUALIZING MEDIA EFFECTS: ANOTHER LOOK*

Elihu Katz

How have scholars attempted to explain the effects media have upon people? Let us assume, for argument's sake, that media do have signficant effects (even though there is a considerable amount of debate on this matter). What we discover is that there have been a number of different theories about media effects, and Katz offers a survey of these theories and shows how our thinking about media effects has evolved.

There are two concepts, he suggests, that help us understand all of these theories. These concepts are *selectivity* and *interpersonal relations*. Selectivity is defined as the sociopsychological processes that shape the way individuals are exposed to the media, perceive it, and recall it and its messages. The principle of selectivity suggests that individual differences matter and that what we choose to watch on television, for instance, and how we make sense of it and think about what we've seen is a very complex matter and is tied to individual personality.

Interpersonal relations involve the various social groupings and networks that people belong to, which "intervene in the flow of mass communication." That is, our use of the media is affected by our families, friends, and organizations we belong to; it does not take place in a social vacuum, and the way others talk about a film or television program we've seen is significant.

We are selective, then, about what media we use and recall and we are affected by social considerations.

Katz then describes the way work on media effects has progressed, starting with early studies of political campaigns, which found that the impact of the media was not very powerful. This, in turn, led to studies of "diffusion research" (how ideas spread) and "uses and gratifications research," (how people use media and what gratifications they get from them). Next came "knowledge-gap" research, which focused on the difference that being part of the information society (and having access to information) made on people's lives. These theories were followed, in turn, by work on "agenda-setting," "technological impact," and "ideological" analysis (Marxism, primarily). And work on other theories continues.

This essay provides an excellent overview of the way theories about media effects have evolved from the earliest investigations to the present. It provides us with "the big picture."

---

* Elihu Katz, "On Conceptualizing Media Effects: Another Look," pp. 32–42, *Applied Social Psychology Annual*, Vol. 8. Edited by S. Oskamp. © 1987. Reprinted by premission of Sage Publications, Inc.

These remarks are addressed to several different audiences: to broadcast media workers, to communication researchers, and to interested individuals who wish to appraise the findings of communication research. In this presentation I will mention a number of themes or points that have come up in other studies and then I will describe some of the attempts by communication researchers to conceptualize the effects of mass communication. Finally I will examine some of the problems of such conceptualization.*

ISSUES IN MEDIA RESEARCH

One interesting issue that arose was how we should study media content. Should we study content quantitatively by counting or averaging, or are there critical moments that grab you and have an effect far beyond any of the regularly repeated stimuli, which we normally quantify and assign each an equal weight? This is a famous issue in content analysis. It was expressed by Bradley Greenberg as the difference between the drip-drip view of media effects and the drench view.

Another issue is, where should we seek the communication's message or value? Where does it inhere: in the text, in the program, in the genre, in the medium? What about the structure or the pacing of a program? Is that a message? Is that a value?

Indeed, how do we study values? How do we determine the values in a program? Who does the reading or interpretation of those values? Is it the researcher or the viewer?

Also, how should one characterize the viewer? Is he or she seated before the television set in a role we might call "television viewer"? Is he or she in the role of a family member, or of an active consumer, or of a passive recipient after coming home tired at night and turning on the set? Are there special roles which change people's response to the media?

Another issue that has been discussed is: Does television present reality? And who wants it to? I submit that nobody wants it to. It shouldn't, and it doesn't, and it can't.

Also, does television lead or follow social change? Does it retard social change? Should some portion of it try to advance desirable social changes?

Finally, what about television research? Are its methods adequate? How can it help us to answer some of the above questions? Those are some of the main issues that I'll try to address at least briefly.

There's a joke that's brought to mind by all the conflicting views of media effects. It's about the two psychiatrists who meet, and one says: "I have a patient with a split personality." The other says: "What's so unusual about that?" The first one replies: "You don't understand; both pay." The same

* I wish to thank the editor, Professor Stuart Oskamp, for his assistance in transforming a chatty talk into a printed paper. Nevertheless, the reader should be aware that this is an edited and improved transcript of a talk and cannot claim to be a formal paper.

thing is true for media research. We researchers get paid and rewarded in various ways for saying the media are totally ineffective, and we get paid and rewarded — even by the same people — for saying that the media are omnipotent, they're all-powerful, they're to blame for everything.

If you read the reviews of the research you generally find conclusions of "no effect." Researcher W. J. McGuire has seriously reviewed almost everything — not just the area of violence — and he finds only trivial effects. So if that's right, which some of us have challenged and some of us have agreed with, you'd have to say that the only thing that keeps mass media researchers going is trying to reconcile our gut feeling that there are major effects with the fact that we can't find them.

This really is an interesting problem. And it's enough of a mystery to keep people going. Fortunately we're not alone in this. Students of the effects of education and students of the effects of psychotherapy haven't gotten any farther and yet, as McGuire says, that doesn't stop them from getting up early in the morning to go to their analysts, and it doesn't stop them from sending their children to school. According to McGuire, all the ad agencies should close, politicians should spend their money in more effective ways, and so on.

HISTORY OF RESEARCH ON MEDIA EFFECTS

Now I want to review quickly the history of efforts to conceptualize mass media effects.* We began mass media research with a study of campaigns, i.e., an assessment of short-run attempts to influence or to change opinions, attitudes, and actions. That research didn't show any dramatic results — nothing like the results that early students of mass communication had anticipated. As political scientists, as sociologists, as social psychologists, they were interested in the process of remote social control, but they didn't find very much of it in the study of campaigns.

What they did then was to open the black box and ask, "What's going on inside?" They came up with a set of intervening variables, factors that come between the message and the hoped-for response, to try to explain where the message is stopped or thwarted, and why it sometimes gets through and has an impact. The two intervening variables that seem to me most interesting, and which I've devoted a lot of time to myself, are the variable of selectivity, which is central to much of social psychological research, and the variable of interpersonal communication, the fact that people talk to each other.

Selectivity is interesting because it suggests a more active audience than does the original mass-society theory from which communications research

* I draw heavily in what follows on Katz (1980). For full bibliographical references, see that paper.

was derived. Whereas mass-society theory posited an atomized society made up of powerless and passive individuals, the idea of selectivity indicates that the audience is more active in negotiating with the message. Similarly, the idea of interpersonal relations opposes the image of the atomized, alienated, disconnected individual with the notion that people are (still) connected to others in their primary groups. As a result, we began to reconceptualize the notion of media effects in terms of their interaction with interpersonal networks and interpersonal norms. There arose traditions of research, some bigger and some smaller, which have taken up questions different from the issue of how the media tell us *what* to think.

One such question is typical of diffusion research, which may be thought of as conceptualizing the media as showing us *when* to think — when a particular view will be fashionable, so to speak, or when it is our turn to adopt it. Diffusion research posits that influence takes time and moves through mass media and interpersonal channels. Gratifications research, on the other hand, builds on the idea of selectivity. It doesn't really deal with media effects directly, but rather with the idea of choosing from among a menu of media offerings those which can serve one's own needs. A third research tradition, knowledge-gap research, suggests that communication on a certain issue — trying to overcome the starting gap between two classes or two groups, one of which is more advantaged than the other — may result in the advantaged group being still *more* advantaged, even though both groups progress in their knowledge. That tradition of work seems to be asking the question *who* should think, not *what* to think, and not *when* to think. Finally, socialization research is really asking the question what to believe, which is as close to the issue of what to think, but socialization research looks at a much longer time span in conceptualizing the effects of messages and training. These research traditions are all studying limited effects, because they each take account of the intervening variables of selectivity and interpersonal relations, in trying to explain the effects being investigated.

There have been three contenders in recent years for *powerful* effects, for the idea that earlier research has been misleading and that media effects can be reconceptualized and shown to be powerful. One was the so-called agenda-setting tradition (McCombs & Shaw, 1972), which stresses that effects research should study, not the role of the media in *what* we think, but in what we think *about*. A second contender for the notion of powerful effects is what I call a media-effects or technological tradition. Consider McLuhan (1964), who proposed that the media tell us not what to think, not what to think about, not when to think, not who should think, but *how* to think. That viewpoint suggests that the different media differentially affect the functioning of our brain, and thus the effect of mass communications resides in the medium and not in the message. Third, perhaps the most interesting contender for revival of a theory of powerful effects derives from an ideological tradition. It stems from the so-called critical school of Horkheimer and Adorno, the Frankfurt school, but it only recently has found some expression in empirical work. The two major examples, which I'll discuss shortly, are George Gerbner (1979) and Elisabeth Noelle-Neumann (1974).

Looking at these three traditions that have proposed a revival of the idea of powerful effects, I will make a few state-of-the-art comments about each. One can say that agenda-setting has retreated and become another tradition of limited effects; it has very quickly had to take account of selectivity and interpersonal relations in trying to explain how the mass media put an issue on the agenda of society. The media-effects viewpoint is still around, but it's very unresearched, and it's very difficult to operationalize McLuhan for social-psychological research. It is very difficult to study the role of the mass media in affecting cognitive processes of the deepest kind — activating one hemisphere of the brain at the expense of the other, for example — particularly in the short run. Consequently this theory has been very little studied; but notice that it is the classic example of what I mean by a powerful effect, in that it doesn't require recourse to intervening variables such as selectivity or interpersonal relations to explain media effects.

Turning to studies from the ideological viewpoint, in recent years we've had attempts to operationalize some of the critical thinking of the Frankfurt school. George Gerbner's (1979) work is perhaps the best example. He says, in effect, that mass-society theory is more applicable today than before because television shuts people into their homes — he says they're afraid to go out anyway — and, disconnecting them from direct access to other people or to direct experience of their environment, it sends them a distorted message about reality, of which television itself is the only witness. Moreover, it has a monopoly, in that all of television is sending a set of messages that are essentially the same, leaving little chance for selectivity. And it's talking to atomized people, connected to the television set but not to each other.

Noelle-Neumann (1974) in her theory is slightly more sociological, but it's the same formula, except that the conspiracy she perceives is of the left. Noelle-Neumann thinks of the media not as a rightist mafia but as a leftist mafia, trying to promote unwanted change — and incidentally, preserve the myth of an opposition — whereas Gerbner is talking about the status quo desired by the powers that be. Her theory suggests that journalists collude with each other monopolistically in order to distort reality, thus reducing the possibility of any kind of individual selectivity because they provide no variety to choose from. By shutting people off from each other, the media become the sole reference group. People look to the media to scan the distribution of opinion in society, and they find their own opinion to be either popular or unpopular. Since they are without recourse to other interactions or other reference groups, the scanning tells them whether to speak or not. The decision not to speak is thus a function of the extent to which they expect to be rejected by public opinion as reflected in the mass media. People may hold to an unpopular opinion, but if the media represent their opinion as unpopular, they won't *express* it, according to Noelle-

Neumann. They won't speak out and won't recruit others to their position — thus creating a spiral of silence.

According to the ideological effects tradition, the media do not tell us what to think, or how to think, or when to think, or who should think, but rather what *not to think*, or in the case of Noelle-Neumann, what *not to say*. This accords well with the Frankfurt school tradition, which suggests that the media influence us not to think about certain subjects which the elite would not like us to think about. For example, we should not have thought that women's place is anywhere but at home, as the mass media depicted it for so many years. How social change nevertheless takes place, such as the one we've seen in women's roles, is a question that rightly troubles the critical tradition, because theories of hegemony don't provide for such changes.

In an article that I wrote on this topic (Katz, 1980), I tried to show how the two variables, selectivity and interpersonal relations, not only help to define limited effects and powerful effects, but also are a thread that can tie these varied research traditions together. Thus the idea of selectivity, central as it is to the study of campaigns, takes us to the active audience of uses-and-gratifications research, and from there into knowledge-gap research, which posits a selectivity based on people's prior cognitive frameworks and differential capacities to absorb new information. Similarly, the idea of interpersonal communication leads from the study of campaigns to the study of diffusion to the study of the role of the media in socialization, and it continues into agenda-setting research and so on.

Under the influence of mass-society theory, mass communication research seemed very different from other areas of communication. However, when tempered by the concepts of interpersonal relations and selectivity, study of the effects of mass media can be reconnected with some of the classical concerns of other humanistic and social disciplines — for instance, how Christianity was spread in the first century, or how an archaeological artifact or cultural pattern moves from one society to another, or how the folklore of children spreads around the world without benefit of mass communication. The reintegration of these different disciplines is a healthy development.

RECONCILING MEDIA RESEARCH FINDINGS
WITH OUR GUT FEELINGS

By and large, as McGuire has summarized, the research findings to date have not provided clear demonstrations of powerful media effects. So researchers must continue to struggle with the question of how to reconcile the research findings with our gut feeling that there are big effects — still the same question. The only answer seems to be to open the black box once more, to look at processes within the individual, and to accept the complexity that commonsense and research tell us is there. We simply must accept that complexity, however messy, however difficult it is to do. At the same time we have to consider a lot of questions about how to think about communication. What is the text? Where do values inhere? Who is the viewer addressed by the text? Who is the viewer in fact? What role is she or he playing? What is the immediate viewing context? What is the nature of the society within which the viewer is decoding the message?

In an effort to conceptualize these last thoughts, I want to propose the concept of "involvement," relating to the varieties of viewing experience and the roles assumed by viewers. This is not a clean-cut concept, since it obviously incorporates the concepts of selectivity and interpersonal relations, yet it is more than both of these. It contributes a social context to these abstracted intervening variables. The expectations of television, and the viewing experience implicit in the social roles and social contexts in which viewers find themselves, are important determinants of television effects.

Effects, of course, need not be limited to the cognitive effects discussed so far. Indeed, a badly-neglected effect in research on mass communication is that the media may tell us how to *feel*. And they may situate us in certain *roles* — family members, consumers, students, farmers, or citizens. For historical reasons, mass communications research has been mostly about cognition. It is partly because of its roots in propaganda studies, in the interests of advertisers or politicians, and in the interests of researchers in cognitive opinion and attitude change, that we have largely neglected the idea of feeling, of emotion, of affect (whether as a prerequisite to cognitive change or as an impressive effect in itself); and of role. If television can make hundreds of millions of people feel something, that's a powerful effect — and one that's very neglected in our research. An example is the integrative effect of mass communication — the way in which the mass media can sometimes make the society feel as one. These points aren't original; I didn't invent them; but they are neglected conceptualizations of effect.

I want to illustrate this notion of "involvement" or "role" in two studies on which I have been working over the last few years. I believe that both of these projects lead in the direction of more powerful effects, albeit via the intervening variables of viewer involvement, context, and role. They are not necessarily representative of everyday broadcasting, for they involve deviant case analysis — that is, studying the exception in order to understand the rule. One of these is a cross-cultural study of "Dallas" and the other is a study of historic media events.

The studies of "Dallas" (Katz & Liebes, 1985; Liebes & Katz, in press) are the poor man's cross-cultural study. We show an episode of "Dallas" to focus groups containing three couples of homogeneous ethnicity, meeting in a home. Ten groups each were drawn from four ethnic communities in Israel — Arabs, Jews of Moroccan origin, new immigrants to Israel from Russia, and kibbutz members. Another ten groups were drawn from second generation Americans in Los Angeles. After the episode is shown, we ask them first to retell it in their own words as if they were going to tell it to somebody the next morning. Then we ask them what motivates the characters, and what does it say about America? We ask them, "Are they trying to tell us something, and if so, what?" and so on. These are questions not about media effects but about understanding: What is the message? Who is the viewer? Does the message get decoded the same way in different cultural settings? Is it understood at all? (It's subtitled in Israel, by the way, in two languages, Hebrew and Arabic.) Or is the message only the pretty pictures and the pretty girls?

The answer, briefly, is that *a* story is understood, but not the same story. There are interesting differences among the ethnic groups. It's almost as if the decoding were a process of what has been rightly called negotiation between what I bring to the story and what the story brings to me. Also, there's a lot of mutual aid in decoding, with people looking to each other. In each of these six-person groups there seems to be an archivist, who says what happened, where a particular character came from, or what happened in the episode before. There's a lot of conversation about the program, not only within our constructed groups, but also in everyday life, as we know from asking background questions about when and how and with whom they discuss the program. There's an active comparing of the viewers' own situations with what they see on the screen — a constant mental commuting between the fictional television and real life.

People are *very* involved in the program. But a finding that is relevant to this discussion is that there seem to be two patterns of involvement. One pattern is an involvement with the reality of the program, and the other is an involvement with the program as a construction, as a work of art, as something that somebody planned and wrote and produced.* The more traditional groups see the program as more real, but even the critical groups relate to the program as real to a large extent. However, the latter, more Westernized groups also tend to see the program as an artistic construction.

Thus, if you ask viewers, "Why all the fuss about babies?" some people will say, "because those are very rich people, they need heirs, and what's the use of making all that money unless you have somebody to give it to," and so on. Other people — or sometimes the same people wearing a critical hat — will tell you, "Babies are very good for conflict between parents, and conflict is very good for a soap opera." Thus there are two wholly different ways of looking at the same thing. It is interesting from a cross-cultural point of view to see the ratio of those different kinds of statements within each of the groups, and also the way in which the more critical viewers, the viewers who see it more as a construction, play with it "ludicly" (Stephenson, 1954) — that is to say, they take roles. "If my son were a bank

---

* This distinction between "real" and "critical" follows Jakobson's (1980) distinction between "referential" and "metalinguistic." Neuman's (1982) terms "interpretive" versus "analytic" are analogous. Obviously, we should settle on some agreed nomenclature.

robber, would I drive the getaway car?" asked a woman rhetorically in response to J. R.'s attempt to enlist Miss Ellie in his scheme to kidnap his baby back from the ranch to which he had been abducted.

I'm suggesting that we need to look at patterns of involvement. In re-opening the black box, we need to look at the way in which people get involved in particular roles, with particular identities, with the text as they read it, and in particular social situations. Then one must raise the question of the relationship between involvement and effect, the answer to which is not obvious. Some researchers have suggested, Herb Krugman (1971) for example, that people are most affected by mass communication when they are *least* involved, when the stimulus is mostly in the background rather than directly badgering them. On the other hand, you might argue that a playful, ludic kind of involvement, a poetic kind of involvement if you will, is in itself so engaging that it makes the involved person vulnerable, perhaps even more so than those who treat the program as real. However, the best bet, I feel, is that the people who treat a story as real are most affected by it.

This argument speaks to the hypothesis of cultural imperialism. At first glance, it may seem a ridiculous hypothesis, but if you think about the infiltration of alien values, even through media that are merely intended as entertainment, a case can be made that those most culturally remote from the locus of the program in Dallas, Texas, are more likely to think of the program as real. As a result, they may become involved in a kind of negotiation wherein they question themselves by comparison with the presumed reality of the program, and in the process allow the alien values — or at least the alien issues — to drip into their cultures. That's one example of research on a potentially powerful media effect.

The other example comes from studies on the live broadcasting of historic occasions (Katz & Dayan, 1985). "The high holidays of mass communication" is one of our subtitles. These media events include Sadat's coming to Jerusalem, the Pope's pilgrimage to Poland, the astronauts landing on the moon, the Kennedy funeral, the Olympics, the Watergate hearings, and other "historic ceremonies" in which the media interrupt the flow of our lives. They say, "Stop everything! We take you away from your regular schedule of living, away from our regular schedule of broadcasting, to something you can't afford to miss." People do stop and watch when these programs are on, and they expect others to do so. What's more, they dress up (rather than undress) for the occasion. They celebrate, they invite friends, they respond affectively, they serve refreshments. They do all of the things that some theorists would suggest are not typical of everyday television viewing. They're not tired, not boozy, not otherwise occupied, not just letting the programs flow onward. They're intent, they're concentrated, they are with others, they are discussing, they contemplate values which the event brings into focus. The Challenger explosion would be a recent example. In addition, viewers take a role as they participate: the role of citizen, the role of mourner at the Kennedy funeral, the role of fan at the

World Cup or the Olympics, the role of loyal subject at the Royal Wedding, and so on. They were participating, not just as television viewers, not just as family members, not even as consumers, but in socially definable roles which have a quality of mindfulness. They participate in a role, at the very least, to say "amen." To Jews a blessing isn't complete unless somebody says "amen," and this is the same idea.

The three crucial partners in a ceremony — public opinion, broadcasters, and organizers — are equally involved in the making of a media event. In his book *Adventure, Mystery, Romance*, John Cawelti (1976) calls this process a "contract" — a contract among authors and audiences to make a particular genre move, be successful, have an effect.

If you look at these two research programs as possibly dealing with deviant cases, you have to take a position as to what everyday television is like. Is the typical experience of viewing like that? If not, how are these experiences different? It's clear in these two cases that people are really *watching programs*, not just receiving a continuing media flow. They're concentrated, they are with others, they are playing roles, and they are participating in ways that are rather different, we think, from everyday television. It is possible that these conditions may obtain only rarely.

Here I would suggest that we need to move closer to the humanities to try to get another hold on theory that can augment the social science approach to mass communication. We can learn something from students of cinema and students of literature.

God divided the world such that he gave cinema to the humanists and television to the social scientists. And that means that the humanists, students of cinema and of literature, are concerned with texts, whereas the empirical study of television only rarely looks at texts. We count acts of violence or role portrayals or the use of bad language or whatever, as if these *were* the text. But the idea of the text as a narrative, as a story, is often neglected. And it's only because God divided the world this way that television is defined by social scientists as an agency of influence, involving cognitive effects, rather than as an agency of affect and involvement. If you go out on the street and ask anybody what television is about, they will *not* tell you that it's about changing opinions, attitudes, and actions. They will tell you that it's about entertainment, about pleasure. The psychoanalytic study of cinema — since cinema theory is informed by psychoanalytic theory, for better or worse — is all about pleasure, about regression, about positioning the viewer at some prior point in his or her psychogenetic development, which allows him or her to watch the film in a particular way. Whether you like that idea or not (and I suppose many of us social scientists might not like it), the idea of finding a role that is typical for audience members, and in which the text helps position you, is part of the heritage which we now have from cinema studies (e.g., Houston, 1985). Now that cinema researchers are moving into television, because mainline cinema has now moved into television, we may both get and give some new ideas about involvement, affect, role, and effects.

SUMMARY

What can be learned from all this? First, we should study television not only as a medium of influence but also of entertainment. Second, we should study the interaction between viewers and texts as a complex process in which social roles are implicated. We should examine microscopically the types of readings of different texts that occur for viewers in different roles. Third, we should study patterns of involvement, study emotion, study the sense of integration, of belonging, of identity — not just changes of opinions, attitudes, and actions — both in themselves and as elements in the process of media effects.

Fourth, we should be aware of the usefulness of converging evidence from different types of theory. I mentioned cinema theory, and I want to mention another hopeful reconciliation between different types of theory. We are, I think, witnessing an interesting convergence between the so-called dominant paradigm in mass communications theory and the critical paradigm. The dominant paradigm — let's use the gratifications expression of it — is that the viewer is so sovereign that there is virtually no text. The text is like a projective test, into which the viewer reads his needs and in which she or he finds gratifications. That is really ridiculous! For instance, it says that the *New York Times* is just as good to read for pornography as for anything else. Such "vulgar gratificationism," I hope, is now expiring, and a more sophisticated awareness of the text and the interaction between the viewers' needs and the supply of messages is occupying gratification researchers. For instance, Blumler (1985) points out that if you watch a political campaign as a spectator sport, you will learn something different than if you watch the same campaign in an attempt to reach a decision, or in an attempt to get ammunition to use in arguing against the other side.

On the other hand, critical research has been interested only in texts and not in audiences. This was not because they weren't interested in message effects on audiences, but because they thought they could *read* effects from the text itself and know what the effect would be just from their own content analysis. If the message is clear, they felt, why bother to study effects empirically? Hegemonic messages impose themselves relentlessly on defenseless viewers — that has been the view of critical research until just lately. But now some leading critical researchers are actually watching real viewers decode television news, and they're looking at readings that they call "dominant" versus readings which they call "oppositional."

The interesting thing is that there's a convergence: The gratificationists are becoming interested in texts and their influence, not only as messages but as ways to position viewers in roles, at the same time as the critical theorists are becoming interested in actual readings, in real viewers. Why they are interested in this is itself an interesting question. One reason may be because you can't predict or explain any kind of social change using a hegemonic theory; so if indeed there has been a change in the image of women in the media, as our researchers have told us, that is a reason to get interested in how people decode hegemonic messages oppositionally, and how their opposition perhaps then feeds back to the program makers. You can't predict a revolution on the basis of critical theory, because it cannot explain how the leaders of the revolution could have seen through the dominant media texts and realized that they are a manipulation. And if the researchers can see that, why can't some others in the audience see it also?

That brings me to my last point about conceptualizing media effects: Don't underestimate the viewer. Viewers in the "Dallas" study were very good at making critical statements, often not less sophisticated than those you can read in the press or hear in academia about the construction of the program and about its message. For example, the Russian Jews, coming straight from Russia to Israel and learning that in order to be Israelis they have to watch "Dallas," were asked, "What is the message of the program? Are they trying to tell us something?" Together with the other groups, they say "Yes, they're trying to tell us that the rich are unhappy." "But," they add, "don't believe it; it's a manipulation; it's what they want us to believe."

REFERENCES

Blumler, J. G., Gurevitch, M., & Katz, E. (1985). Reaching out: A future for gratifications research. In K. E. Rosengren et al. (Eds.), *Media gratifications research: Current perspectives.* Beverly Hills. CA: Sage.

Cawelti, J. (1976). *Adventure, mystery, romance.* Chicago: University of Chicago Press.

Fajes, F. (1984). Critical mass communications research and media effects: The problem of the disappearing audience. *Media, Culture and Society*, 6, 219–232.

Graber, D. A. (1984). *Processing the news.* New York: Longman.

Gross, L. (1985). Life vs. art: The interpretation of visual narratives. *Studies in visual communication*, 11, 2–11.

Houston, B. (1985). Television: The metapsychology of endless consumption. *Quarterly Review of Film Studies*, 8.

Jakobson, R. (1980). Linguistics and poetics. In R. deGeorge & F. deGeorge (Eds.) *The structuralists: From Marx to Levi-Strauss.* New York: Anchor Books.

Katz, E. (1980). On conceptualizing media effects. In T. McCormack (Ed.), *Studies in communication* (Vol. 1). Greenwich. CT: JAI Press.

Katz, E., & Dayan, D. (1985). Media events: On the experience of not being there. *Religion*, 15, 305–324.

Katz, E., & Liebes, T. (1985). Mutual aid in the decoding of "Dallas." In P. Drummond & R. Patterson (Eds.). *Television in transition* (pp. 187–198). London: British Film Institute.

Krugman, H. (1971). Brainwave measure of media involvement. *Journal of Advertising Research*, 3–9.

Liebes, T., & Katz, E. (in press). Patterns of involvement in television fiction: A comparative analysis. *European Journal of Communication*, 1.

McCormack, T. (1984). *Content analysis: The social history of a method.*

McGuire, W. J. (in press). The myth of massive media impact: Savagings and salvagings. In G. Comstock (Ed.), *Public Communication and Behavior* (Vol. 1). New York: Academic Press.

Morley, D. (1980). *The "nationwide" audience: Stucture and decoding.* London: British Film Institute.

Neuman, R. (1982). Television and American culture: The mass medium and the pluralist audience. *Public Opinion Quarterly*, 46, 471–487.

Stephenson, W. (1954). *A play theory of mass communication.* Chicago: University of Chicago Press.

42   THE POISONED CHALICE: INTERNATIONAL TELEVISION AND THE IDEA OF DOMINANCE*

MICHAEL TRACEY

This essay deals with a topic that has generated a great deal of heat (and not too much light, some would say) among media researchers. There has been a good deal of interest in the one-way flow of television programs (and other media) from what our author calls "North Atlantic culture" — that is, the United States, the United Kingdom, Western European countries — to Third World countries.

The question is…what impact does this flow have upon these cultures? The reason for the flow is quite simple. It costs too much to produce television for most of the Third World countries, but it costs them relatively little to purchase already-made programming. Thus these countries are full of American entertainment shows, and these programs, so many analysts argue, are having a devastating impact on allegedly more fragile cultures. These programs are carriers of Western values and life-styles, and more insidiously, so the cultural-domination theorists claim, of bourgeois capitalist values.

Tracey challenges the idea that the media are agents of domination. He suggests that the cultural domination theory is too simplistic and lacks evidence. It does not recognize, for instance, that people in different cultures generally interpret a given television program in terms of their values and beliefs. There is not one "legitimate" way to understand a television show. The notion that western television can "destroy" a native culture is, ultimately, premised on a

* Reprinted by premission of *Daedalus*, Journal of the American Academy of Arts and Sciences, "The Moving Image," Vol. 114, No. 4, Fall 1985, Cambridge, MA.

theory of media that is unsupportable (the so-called "hypodermic" theory) and that has been discarded.

There is a considerable amount of disagareement, also, Tracey points out, on the effects of media (in general) on people. We now recognize that the way people "process" media is a very complicated matter. Indeed, some media theorists argue that media have no significant effect upon people — or at least that effects cannot be proven.

Tracey's conclusion, then, is that North Atlantic media may be all-pervasive but they are not all-powerful. Scholars who argue that television is dominating and destroying Third-World cultures and imposing Western values and capitalist ideology, are prisoners of their own theories, Tracey suggests. The theories might sound plausible but they are not based on evidence.

A 1953 UNESCO publication (*TV, A World Survey*) made the statement: "International cooperation is beginning to open up new fields for television and it is increasingly recognized how effective it can be to bring about greater awareness about each other among nations differing in language and character." The same report spoke of how television could make the "treasures of man's civilization" available, and of TV as a means of "global peace and understanding." Bliss was it in that dawn. The view of global television now espoused within the chambers of UNESCO is that it is a distinctly poisoned chalice.

By 1972, the General Conference of UNESCO was suggesting that there was a danger that the mass media could become vehicles for "the domination of world public opinion or a source of moral and cultural pollution," and that the one-way flow of television from a small number of countries threatened "the cultural values of most of the remaining countries." In 1973, at the meeting of the heads of state of non-aligned countries, there were calls for the "reorganization of existing communication channels that are the legacy of the colonial past, and that have hampered free, direct and fast communication between them." It was added that "cultural alienation and imported civilization, imposed imperialism and colonialism, should be countered by...a constant and determined recourse to the social and cultural values of the population which define them as a sovereign people."

And so on, as large parts of the international community have become anxious about the adverse effects of foreign television on their countries. This is not just true of the developing countries; many important and influential voices can be heard throughout Europe expressing concern over the implications of "foreign" television. It is admittedly not an anxiety overly present in American society — which in terms of the penetration of anything foreign and visual remains in a state of *virgo intacto*. International television and cultural dominance have, however, become an important issue of international politics. On that agenda, it is taken as given by most societies that adverse effects do follow from their populations' cultural appetites, as expressed in the TV they watch.

Equally influential sections of the academic community have argued vociferously about the alleged powerful influences of international television. Cees Hamelink, for example, in his most recent book, speaks of how in recent years the delicate process by which developing societies evolve and adapt is being increasingly threatened by the advanced industrial states' large-scale export of cultural system to Third World countries. As a result, he suggests, the survival of autonomous cultural systems in many areas of the Third World is very much in question. He adds: "It is the argument of this study that cultural autonomy is essential for a process of independent development. However, cultural autonomy is virtually impossible in a system that attempts to integrate the weak and poor countries in a global community that serves best the interests of only the rich and powerful. This autonomy has to be secured through the formulation and implementation of national policies based on international *dissociation*, which encourage self-reliant development and the cooperation of developing countries among themselves."

The general effect he suggests, however, is for cultural "synchronization" — the eradication of diversity, and its replacement with "a single global culture" in which the cultural traffic is overwhelmingly one way, with the result that the "whole process of social inventiveness and cultural creativity is thrown into confusion or is definitely destroyed. Unique dimensions in the spectrum of human values, which have evolved over centuries, rapidly disappear."

Hamelink offers little in the way of substantial or rigorous evidence to support his case. In those areas where he draws on a significant body of research, however, he handles the evidence in a curious way. For example, in pointing out that international television flow consists of news as well as entertainment, he states: "The role of international news in transferring values should not be underestimated. The selection of news by the few large international news agencies undoubtedly reflects the values of metropolitan countries. Most developing countries are dependent on this choice for their information on events outside their country. They receive international news as well as news about themselves via the news centres in New York, Paris, or London." He then quotes an unnamed government official: "In the absence of a national news agency in Thailand, India receives only the American or British version of events in that country. How that keeps Thailand and India from understanding each other more deeply and readily is for those who know how to judge."[1]

The most recent and comprehensive research now available presents a much more complicated picture — one, moreover, that Hamelink ignores. At the end of the 1970s, UNESCO and the International Association for Mass Communication Research (IAMCR) sponsored a report on an international study of news coverage by press, radio, and TV in twenty-nine countries. The author of the main report (the result of work by several different but coordinated research teams) notes: "If ever it was clear that good evidence doesn't prove a case, that is true of the international research project *The World of the News....*"[2]

The study involved thirteen teams in different countries, plus the accumulation of information from a range of other countries. Covering broadcasting and the press, it examined twenty-nine media systems in all. What was perhaps most notable about the findings of the limited quantitative analysis was that, although the participating nations reflected different levels of development and a variety of political perspectives, the overall pattern of attention paid to certain kinds of events was remarkably similar. While politics dominated international news everywhere, the study also revealed the prominence of regionalism. Every national system devoted most attention to people and events within its immediate geographical region. This focus characterized between 23 and 63 percent of all international news in every system. Thus, Nigeria was most concerned about African affairs and African actors, Argentina featured Latin American news, and so on.

The final report of the study states that there are many questions left unanswered, but that "the validity of our quantitative findings is supported by and in turn reverberates the general findings of many other such studies conducted over the past decade."[3] For example, a look at the geographic emphasis of international news from the data of forty-two countries (culled from ten separate empirical studies) reveals a strong, consistent, and simple pattern. Regional news is emphasized in the media of all countries. After the dominance of one's own region comes news from North America and Western Europe; the "invisible" parts of the world are Eastern Europe and the developing world.

One reviewer of the report observes: "Let us begin by noting what this study does *not* show. It does not show that Western media and news agencies ignore the Third World. It does not show that they single out the Third World for unfair negative coverage. It does not show that they see the Third World through a filter of cultural bias. It does not show that the Third World media are hostage to a Western news monopoly. It does not show that the socialist and Third World media systems that claim to represent an alternative model operate much differently than their Western counterparts."[4]

A rule that seems to emerge is that the less developed a nation, the more its media use geographically proximate stories. Thus, foreign news from the immediate geographic region is 26 percent in the U.S., 56 percent in the Ivory Coast, and 63 percent in Malaysia. Assertions that the Western media and news agencies ignore the Third World are simply untrue. About a third of foreign news stories in northern media systems originate in the Third World; in the Third World, about 60 to 75 percent of all foreign news is from other Third World countries. The big gaps in world news are not the absence of Third World news in the Western media, but news about Eastern Europe in all other areas of the world and non-regional Third World news within the Third World.

What emerges from what is probably the most detailed piece of research on international news flow is that many of the charges against the Western media and news services lack evidence to support them; that the sameness among media of very different political systems argues against the theory of cultural imperialism; and that much of the rhetoric addresses outdated questions. Stevenson concludes: "Too much of the NWIO [New World Information Order] debate has focused on assertions that were probably never true and certainly are no longer true. This study helps clear the air of the pseudo debate." The study also potentially provides a very important perspective on the key suppositions that have underlain the patterns and consequences of other forms of international communications, such as the distribution of television programs.

Herb Schiller has also become well known as a theorist of communication as cultural domination. In his first and most influential work, *Mass Communications and American Empire* (1969), he states: "Mass communications are now a pillar of the emergent imperial society. Messages 'made in America' radiate across the globe and serve as the ganglia of national power and expansionism. The ideological images of 'have not' states are increasingly in the custody of American informational media. National authority over attitude creation and opinion formation in the developing world has weakened and is being relinquished to powerful external forces....Everywhere local culture is facing submersion from the mass-produced outpourings of commercial broadcasting."

Fourteen years later, the tune remained essentially the same. In a paper on "Electronic Information Flows: New Basis for Global Domination," Schiller develops, in a somewhat polemical manner, his analysis of the evolving political economy of the industrial societies and the enormous power of a small number of multinational corporations. Nothing wrong with all that, apart from the occasional touch of hyperbole (at one point he talks of the welfare state as "already mostly a memory" — this, a set of institutions that take up a huge part of the gross domestic product!). Where I part from Schiller's analysis is when he slips into such phrases as "a vast extension in cultural control and domination to say nothing of economic and political mastery" and "saturating the cultural space of the nation."[5] Let me ask again: what does that mean, and, at the risk of being accused of outrageous positivism, where's the evidence? Certainly, he provides none.

What, then, about the idea of *domination*? A whole library of works exists on cross-national influences, trans-border data flow, the economics of cultural imperialism, TV flows, and so on. Hamelink and Schiller are just two of the more prominent members of an extensive school of thought.[6] Each tends to be loaded with sets of assumptions about cultural influences, about meanings and the shaping of consciousness. Yet each equally tends to hold those views in the abstract, outside of any grasp of their place within the life of a society. As the late Ithiel de Sola Pool observed: "There is, in fact, remarkably little research of any kind on international communication. There is a great deal of essay writing about it. But by research I mean studies in which data is collected to establish or refute some general proposition....The two topics regarding international communication that have been most extensively studied, and very badly, I must say, are the balance in the flow of communication among countries, and the cultural biases in what flows. These are topics on which there have been a few empirical studies, though by far the great bulk of that literature consists of polemical essays unenlightened by facts."[7]

Look, for example, at a book such as *National Sovereignty and International Communication* edited by Schiller and Nordenstreng in 1979, which contains little that is based on traditional social science research studies. It offers little or no empirical or historical analysis, and as Pool puts it: "What does exist is not serious social research, but assertions wrapped in rabid tracts full of ideology and with the occasional numbers out of context."[8]

Since its first appearance on American television in 1978 and its subsequent export to many foreign countries, "Dallas" has become the exemplar of the global influence of American television, the apparent embodiment of the theory of cultural imperialism, a metaphor for an entire argument. Clearly, at one level "Dallas" fits the stereotype: it is available in many different countries and is always sold at a lower price than any home-produced equivalent. What has been almost totally ignored, however, is the relationship between the program and the various audiences that, for whatever reasons, in whatever circumstances, with whatever consequences, actually sit down and watch it. Any exploration at that level, no matter how cursory, provides some important qualifications to the imperialism thesis. For example, in most countries "Dallas" is not as popular as home-produced soaps, and it is completely ignored in countries as diverse as Brazil and Japan, which nevertheless have well-established and highly popular domestic dramas as part of their main TV offerings. In New Zealand, other kinds of shows from other countries are more popular than "Dallas" and its ilk. While a number of researchers *have* recognized the need to understand the different audience responses to programs such as "Dallas" — e.g., Elihu Katz and Tamar Liebes in Israel, Jean Bianchi in France, David Morley and Dorothy Hobson in Britain[9] — these efforts have, to date, unfortunately been inhibited by a lack of real resources.

It is, in fact, simply untrue to say that imported television programs, from the U.S. or other metropolitan countries, always have a dominant presence within an indigenous television culture. Certainly they do not always attract larger audiences than homemade programs, nor do they always threaten national production.

In Brazil, for example, which is the sixth biggest television market in the world, the level of imported television material *fell* by 32 percent between 1973 and 1982, largely due to the activities of TV Globo, which captures between 60 and 80 percent of the television audience. Between 5:30 P.M. and

11:00 P.M., 84 percent of the programs offered are in-house productions. In August 1983, the top ten programs were all Globo productions, including three "telenovellas." As Richard Paterson points out, in Brazil one sees "a television devoted to national culture. TV Globo has fully utilized the possibilities created by these circumstances to develop a different sort of television. The development of an indigenous television puts into question Schiller's thesis about the inevitability of traditional drama and folk music retreating before the likes of Peyton Place and Bonanza."[10]

"Dallas," by the way, in 1982 occupied 69th position in the Brazilian ratings and 109th in Mexico.[11] In the very different context of Britain, however, while successful, it has never seriously challenged the domestically produced dramas "Coronation Street," "Crossroads," and "Emmerdale Farm." Another illustration of how indigenous populations do not respond to imported material in stereotypical ways can be seen in South Africa. There, TV1 carries such imports as "Dallas" and "The A-Team," with vernacular services on TV2 and TV3. In December 1983, however, Bophuthatswana Television, broadcasting from the capital of Mmabatho, began to broadcast in English but with increasing amounts of material of a local nature in Setswana. More and more of the black population of South Africa turns to this channel. Indeed, the success has been so great that President Mpepha of the tiny republic of Venda has now announced that he wants his own television service, Radio Television Thohoyandau.[12]

In Singapore, where the government's Singapore Broadcasting Corporation runs three channels broadcasting in English, Mandarin, Tamil, and Malay, and where 60 percent of the programs are English-language (the bulk of which are imported), Chinese programs, particularly from Hong Kong, are consistently the most popular. In Ireland, which imports 65 percent of its total output and where the BBC and ITV are readily available to most of the population, the most popular programs for many years have been "The Late, Late Show" on Saturdays, hosted by Gay Byrne, followed by the home-produced drama series "The Riordans," "Bracken," and "Glenroe." In countries such as New Zealand and Sweden, where the local broadcasting services face enormous problems that necessitate the importation of foreign television, home-grown programs nevertheless compete in popularity. In New Zealand, in fact, there is evidence that the bulk of the population actively dislikes the American shows they see on their screens. In Zimbabwe in 1982, locally produced programs such as "The Mukadda Family" had much higher ratings than the imported "Dallas," "Dynasty," and "Falcon Crest." One author writing about television in Bangladesh observed: "Imported programmes are popular, but do not dominate BTV. In the 1980s some would say that the 'Incredible Hulk' does sit uneasily between 'Shilpo-O-Shahilya' [a series on art and literature] and 'Jalsa' [a programme on classical music]. 'Dallas,' 'Charlie's Angels,' and 'Chips' are cheaper for BTV to transmit than any local dramas — but local productions challenge them in a way few outsiders would believe possible."[13]

One could go on. This is not to say that imported programs are *not* an important part of the total structure of many countries' broadcasting, nor, indeed, that in some cases they are not very popular. It is merely to observe that even a limited glance at the available evidence — such as it is — about the most simple facts of television viewing, indicates that the picture of the role of television in any society is far more complex than is often allowed for. As far as we can tell, audiences discriminate and tend to prefer home-produced television, rather than slavishly pursuing imported programs.

The point of this Cook's tour, then, is actually quite simple: it is to show that a rather more discrete, subtle, and empirical approach is necessary before we can begin to understand the actual experience of the flow of international television, and thus the notion of television dominance. The question this in turn raises is: what model can best explain cultural influences in the lives of a given society, and where can we find the methodology to test that model?

The problem with the old model is that it took a not very good inventory and pretended it was an analysis. One can say nothing of influences, of how those programs engage with a society simply on the basis of a surface description; and yet that is all we have tended to have so far. As a former colleague of mine quite rightly argued:

> The development of theories about the ill effects of the importation of American television programmes depends on the measuring devices of imports/exports and the income earned from such sales for their substantiation. Unfortunately these measures, although useful, do not focus on the size and responses of the audiences who eventually see such programmes. There is an assumption that American TV imports do have an impact wherever and whenever they are shown, but actual investigation (or verification) of this seldom occurs. Much of the evidence that is offered is merely anecdotal or circumstantial. Observations of New Guinean tribesmen clustered around a set in the sweltering jungle watching "Bonanza" or of Algerian nomads watching "Dallas" in the heat of the desert, are often offered as sufficient proof.[14]

On the basis of what we know — *really* know as opposed to imagine we know — what then can be said about the notion of dominance by international television? What is the argument? What is the problem? Let me begin not with some humble, underdeveloped, exploited nation, but with a huge, wealthy, powerful one: Canada. Canada apparently has one overwhelming problem when it comes to the culture of television, and that is its proximity to an even more powerful, wealthy, and huge society, the United States. In a recent account of the development of cable TV in Canada, Tim Hollins made the following point:

> Over 80 percent of the Canadian population lives within one hundred miles of the American border, and the realities of this situation have

had a greater impact than somewhat abstract cultural aspirations. Although regulation has been imposed to promote both Canadian broadcasting and production, the Canadians themselves have consistently demonstrated a strong interest, even a preference for material from the United States. Consequently, the Government has had to find a path between accepting the reality of the U.S. cultural imperialism and forcing a Canadian cultural chauvinism which appears antithetical to the rights and wishes of its own citizens.[15]

The first, and rather tricky, problem for government leaders, intellectuals, reformers, and political evangelists (who may also be academics) around the globe is that, as Hollins suggests about Canada, populations do have this unfortunate habit of choosing television programs that are not "good" for them. Indeed, one might construct the first law of international communications: that which is bad for them, they *will* insist on watching.

I am, you will detect, a touch less worried than some about this situation — described in endless meetings of UNESCO and kindred bodies, and enough books and articles to threaten the existence of tropical rain forests — partly because I suspect that assumptions about the extent of exposure to "foreign" material are overstated, and mainly because I believe that the assumptions about their "effects" are certainly overstated, and devoid of decent evidence and good theory. It is difficult, for example, to take too seriously the assumptions behind a phrase such as "the Dallas-drugged viewers," which I saw used recently in the context of a discussion of Italian television. Nor the sentiment, however well meaning, in this observation: "For the survival and development of important human values, the study of intercultural communication may be one of the critical areas of communication research. One has only to witness 'Kojak' and 'Starsky and Hutch' bouncing off satellites *into the intimacy of minds and homes* [my emphasis] in cultures of India and Thailand to realize this."

Such, however, is the power of the orthodoxy on these matters that I write these words with a feeling of guilt, a certain trepidation in waiting for the howls of scorn that one can doubt something so self-evident. Indeed, it seems to me that the Western writer, from within the comfort of his wealth, faces a difficult problem in addressing objectively issues of dominance and cultural imperialism. On the one hand, he is in danger of either assuming uncritically the notions and sentiments uttered by Third World leaders and their Western acolytes out of a wish for them to be right. On the other hand, if he challenges those arguments, questions them, suggests that maybe they are not totally correct, that perhaps they are self-interested or just plain innocently wrong, he is immediately open to the accusation of having a mealy-mouthed, uncaring attitude towards the problems of developing societies. Yet, in all honesty, one has to say that it is possible that, within the realms of international communications, a poverty of thought has emerged to match the real poverty of resources that afflicts developing societies.

In seeking to understand international television, then, one has to ask: What evidence is there? What can we say? What do we know? In researching this article, I constantly returned to these questions and to the simple statement: "It is claimed that this mass of material coming in from outside is both erasing traditional cultures and inhibiting the emergence of authentic cultural changes. There is no clear evidence that this is in fact happening, nor indeed any that it is not."[16] In the heart of darkness, which is the image offered by the many views of the adverse consequences of imported television, there is a vacuum: an absence of evidence and good theory. In this context, I was struck by a comment made by Wilbur Schramm in an interesting article called "The Unique Perspective of Communication: A Retrospective Review."[17] He was saying, or at least he seemed to me to be saying, that for all its effort, all its worth, over decades communication research really had not *said* very much. He asked, "Has it produced a central, interrelated body of theory on which the practitioners of a discipline can build and unify their thinking?" Good question. And the correct answer: "I am afraid that it has not....In a similar vein, we must ask whether we have produced only *ingredients* of communication theory. Are the pieces of a general theory of communication lying around us ready to be assembled? Or, for some reason, is a central theory of communication beyond our capability at this time?"

The question to pose is not what is the nature of cultural domination or imperialism, with all the assumptions of intellectual, psychological, and emotional influence. The real question is why such simple, impressionistic analyses have come to hold such sway in the debate about the character of communications in international as well as domestic life. Why have such analyses — paradoxically dripping with human concern — become so divorced from any human contact?

There is a marvelous little article by Irene Penacchioni about the viewing of popular television in poverty-ridden northeast Brazil.[18] It is a fine example of the view that the role and use of television ought to be viewed ethnographically from *within* a culture, rather than condescendingly from without. She pulls no punches: "In my opinion...the investigations into television which are carried out by sociology are informed by the amused condescensions of intellectuals towards mass culture and by their dark fear of the alleged power of images....Intellectuals use the written word to protect themselves from television as though it were a cross to protect them from vampires." She writes of the popularity of the telenovella with the local people:

> It is important to understand the pleasure of following a fiction from day to day over a long period of time; pleasures associated with the "to be continued," of curiosity and expectation about the unpredictable, which will make itself heard again. What next? What will happen to our hero? The genealogy of pleasure, this joy related to the telenovella, has to be sought in the occidental history of folk poetry....Television

seems to correspond to a cyclical and everyday representation of time as found in folk poetry....The phenomenon of television cannot be comprehended here without a systematic investigation of the cultural context, and its different aspects, in the Northeast of Brazil.

One of the moments she describes is of a group of people sitting around a TV set in the town square, not just watching telenovellas, but laughing uproariously at the exploits of Charlie Chaplin. When I read this, another very familiar image came to my mind.

I was born in a working-class community called Oldham, in the north of England. Before the First World War, Oldham produced most of the world's spun cotton. It is a place of mills and chimneys, and I was born and raised in one of the areas of housing — called St. Mary's — built to serve those mills. I recently heard a record by a local group of folk singers called the Oldham Tinkers, and one track is about Charlie Chaplin. This song was apparently very popular with local children in the years immediately after the First World War. Was that early evidence of the cultural influences of Hollywood, a primeval moment of the imperialism of one culture, the subjugation of another? It seems almost boorish to think of it that way. Was the little man not a deep well of pleasure through laughter, a pleasure that was simply universal in appeal? Was it not Chaplin's real genius to strike some common chord, uniting the whole of humanity? Is that not, in fact, the real genius of American popular culture, to bind together, better than anything else, common humanity? This is all terribly heretical, and yet I am more and more tempted in this little excursion to propose that the cultural imperialism thesis be stood on its head, and to suggest instead an analysis, not of exploitation, but of service — of the proffering of cultural imagery that is absorbed by more deep-seated cultural strata. That leads me, not to ask about the thesis, but to pose questions about those who proffer it. There has to be an explanation why such an intellectually undernourished theory holds such sway.

I also ask why it is that the ubiquity of the likes of "Dallas" is held in such contempt, whereas the ubiquity of, say, the Beatles or Chaplin himself is, one senses, held in awe. Perhaps we need an alternative way of looking at the general popularity of much television around the globe. George Steiner recently published an interesting book about Sophocles's *Antigone*,[19] in which he asked why this Greek tragedy has continued to haunt European culture over the past two centuries. He looks at the way in which such nineteenth-century thinkers as Hegel and Kierkegaard treated issues raised by the story — for example, the conflict between the demands of the state and private conscience answerable to a higher law. For Steiner, this embodies the wider question of why the central themes of Greek mythology exercise such a powerful hold on the European mind. Why, after two thousand years, do we still speak of narcissism, the labors of Hercules, the Oedipus complex, the Minotaur? Steiner himself flirts briefly with Jung's theory of archetypes — certain themes, situations, and figures basic to the inner realities of human experience which Greek mythology embodied in a uniquely direct way. Is it possible that in order to understand, at least in part, the popularity of the television of the North Atlantic basin one has to understand the ways in which it successfully employs certain themes, situations, and figures, rather than just pricing-mechanisms, pace, glossy sets, exotic locations, or whatever? Is the interesting thing about television, in short, perhaps not what it *imposes* but what it *taps*?

We need also to get back to basics, to consider how we assess the position of the individual in a theory of influences of communication. In the past ten to fifteen years, communications research has left behind any ideas of the "hypodermic needle" model of attitudinal and behavioral changes, and moved towards a greater emphasis on audience dispositions and intentions examined within the context of broader collective, system-wide processes. It is increasingly recognized that it is simply inadequate to treat audiences as a uniform mass, and message reception as a unidimensional process.

The demand for forms of analysis that allow, not for the uniformities, but for the divergences of human response has come from anthropologists such as Mary Douglas, with her analysis of taste as a function of the experience of group identity, hierarchy, and institution, as well as from mass-communications researchers and theorists. Douglas suggests that audience research must be able to account for the reasons that certain messages (such as comedians' jokes) "reach right through the class structure."[20] She suggests that vertical taste groups exist which cut through class, that the taste of bureaucrats will be the same at the top as at the bottom of a bureaucratic structure. This is clearly potentially relevant to any analysis of the reasons why products of one particular cultural context cut across what are ostensibly a whole range of contexts having different histories, sociopolitical orders, and so on.

Whatever the individual merits or faults of these notions, it seems clear that the one-dimensional view of the audience that was encapsulated within the mass-society theory, and to a certain extent within the cognitive and instrumental bias of the uses and gratifications approach, needs to be replaced by engagements with audience experience. These take into account the variable contexts within which messages are received, and the complex manner in which individuals ascribe meaning to these messages. The difficulty is that there has been, in the whole field of the mass media, precious little such empirical analysis.

However, even in those areas of communications in developed societies where there has been a good deal of work, there are important differences between the theoretical and empirical conclusions that have been drawn. That most researched area, the effects of televised violence, is a veritable minefield of conceptual and methodological uncertainties. In 1983, the United States National Institute of Mental Health (NIMH) published its report *Television and Behavior*. In this review of social research conducted over the past decade on the effects of television, the conclusion was drawn that, whatever the uncertainties that might have previously existed about the evidence of the effects of television, the answers were now known. It stated that the "consensus among most of the research community is that violence on television does lead to aggressive behavior by children and teenagers who watch the programs....The research question has moved from asking whether or not there is an effect to seeking explanations for the effect." Dr. David Pearl, the principal author of the report, added that "while there is some evidence which is not completely congruent with our conclusions, nevertheless, reasonable researchers have considered all of that and have concluded really that there is very little question left any longer."[21] The problem with this statement is that there are many reasonable researchers who quite seriously question the conclusions.[22]

The basic premise in George Gerbner's long-standing study of cultural indicators, in which he has mapped the manner in which television portrays American life, is that, as a leisure activity, television cuts across educational and income lines, providing the symbolic environment and world view of the majority of Americans. At the same time, Gerbner argues that, because of its links with state and industry, television has become an agency of social control for the status quo. As did the Church in the Middle Ages, television systematically cultivates in its viewers a world view and values that support the established power structure. In short, television does to the *American* people what it is held to do — by certain authors — to the rest of the world.

NOTES

1. Cees Hamelink, *Cultural Autonomy in Global Communications* (New York: Longman, 1983).
2. Annabelle Srebeny-Mohammadi, "The World of the News Study," *Journal of Communication*, Winter 1984.
3. Ibid.
4. R. L. Stevenson, "Pseudo-debate: A Review of World of the News," *Journal of Communication*, Winter 1984.
5. See Herbert Schiller's *Mass Communication and American Empire* (New York: Kelley, 1969); and his "Electronic Information Flows: New Basis for Global Domination," paper given at conference at the Institute of Education, London, July 1984.
6. Colleen Roach, "Annotated Bibliography on a New World Information and Communication Order," *Media and Development*, 1/1985.
7. Ithiel de Sola Pool, "The New Structure of International Communication: The Role of Research," in *New Structure of International Communication: The Role of Research*, papers from the 1980 conference in Caracas of the International Association for Mass Communication Research (IAMCR). Published by the IAMCR, 1982.
8. Pool, loc. cit.
9. Elihu Katz and Tamar Liebes, "Once Upon a Time in Dallas," *Intermedia* (London), May 1984.

Jean Bianchi, "Comment comprendre le succès international des séries de fiction à la télévision? Le cas Dallas," Ministère de l'industrie et de la Recherche: action concertée Communication Audiovisuelle, July 1984.

David Morley, The "Nationwide" Audience: Structure and Decoding (London; BFI Publishing, 1980).

Dorothy Hobson, Crossroads: The Drama of a Soap Opera (London: Methuen, 1982).

10. Richard Paterson, Brazilian Television in Context (London: BFI Publishing, 1982).

11. G. Lealand, American Television Programmes on British Screens (London: Broadcasting Research Unit, 1984).

12. Richard Paterson, ed., International TV and Video Guide (1985) (London: Tantivy Press, 1985).

13. Ibid.

14. Lealand, op. cit.

15. Timothy Hollins, Beyond Broadcasting: Into the Cable Age (London: Broadcasting Research Unit, 1984).

16. R. Hoggart, "The Mass Media and One Way Flow," in An English Temper (London: Chatto and Windus, 1982).

17. Wilbur Schramm, "The Unique Perspective of Communication: A Retrospective Review," Journal of Communication, Summer 1983.

18. Irene Penacchioni, "The Reception of Popular Television in Northeast Brazil," Media, Culture and Society, Oct. 1984.

19. George Steiner, Antigones (Oxford: Oxford University Press, 1984).

20. Mary Douglas and Karen Wollaeger, "Towards a Typology of Audiences," in Future of Broadcasting, ed. R. Hoggart and J. Morgan (London: Macmillan, 1982).

21. Interview with author during course of radio program "Torturing the Data," BBC Radio 3, Jan. 19, 1984.

22. P. Hirsch in Communication Research, Oct. 1980 and Jan. 1981.

D. M. Wober, "Televised Violence and Paranoid Perception: The View From Great Britain," Public Opinion Quarterly, Fall 1978.

A. Doob and G. E. McDonald, "Televised Viewing and Fear of Victimization: Is the Relationship Causal?" Journal of Personality and Social Psychology, Jan. 1979.

Berger

ADVERTISING

In the American media, advertising is the most ubiquitous and, some would say, most important of genres. Newspapers and magazines are full of advertisements — ranging from simple messages in print to very elaborate fashion advertisements, shot by top photographers. We also find a particularly powerful (or so it seems) form of advertisement in the electronic media: commercials on radio and on television. It is the function of advertisements to "deliver an audience" and advertisers pay for the quality, or spending power, of an audience as well as for its size. Many of the critics of the mass media in America argue that our particular system of funding the media, by print advertisements and commercials, has had a negative effect and transformed the media into little else than servants of the business community.

Advertising agencies claim that they can produce results; if advertising doesn't work, why spend millions on campaigns? On the other hand, when media critics or governmental agencies argue that some advertising campaigns are having negative consequences, the agencies claim that they are powerless and that advertising can't make people do what they don't want to do. "We only give people what they want," say the networks that carry the programs that "deliver" the audiences to the advertisers. "And we can't make people do what they don't want to do" say the advertising agencies and companies that use them. (The standard practice is to use the term "advertisement" for messages in print and the term "commercial" for messages on the radio or television.)

Advertising is attacked on a number of fronts by critics who argue that (1) it distracts our attention from social and political problems and focuses it on our own private wants and desires; (2) it is sexist and uses women basically as sexual objects, exploiting their sexuality to sell products and services; (3) it generates anxiety and self-hatred in people who cannot afford to live in the style pictured as "normal" in advertisements and commercials; (4) it often misleads people about what to expect from products; and (5) it teaches people to equate happiness with buying something and thus trains them to consume as a means of obtaining happiness or pleasure.

Advertising is defended by supporters who argue that (1) it pays for the periodicals we read and programs we see (which otherwise would be much more costly); (2) it lessens the price of many products through economies of scale; (3) it provides consumers with valuable information about products and services; and (4) it may attempt to persuade but it can't force anyone to do anything.

One of the essays in this section deals with Hal Riney, a famous advertising executive who heads a large agency in San Francisco. He has created many important commercials and talks about how he works and about the industry in general. (Many of the people who work for advertising agencies are extremely talented and even critics of advertising admit that ads and commercials are often highly entertaining and brilliantly conceived works.)

We are all aware of advertising as a persuasive force but we seldom give much thought to packaging. But packaging is also a powerful kind of communication and I have included an article that shows you something about how packaging works and how it can make a difference in consumer decision making. Packaging has evolved into a highly complex industry, based on a great deal of research into consumer behavior.

It is unlikely, given our system, that advertising and its sister industries will be restricted to any great extent. Given that, how do we deal with these industries so their energies are used in the most constructive and positive ways? And how do we "insulate" people against the dangers that some people feel they pose to our well being?

As the power and influence of advertising grows and spreads — it now plays an important role in our politics — we must find better ways of understanding how it works and determining what, if anything, should be done about controlling it. For the Marxists, advertising plays a central role in Capitalist societies, since it is the main instrument by which the "ruling classes" motivate people to work hard (so they can afford the "good things in life") and to accept the political order. Thus Marxists (and many other non-Marxist critics of advertising) assume advertising is a very powerful force in society; in that sense, they critics agree with the people who run the advertising agencies. Many critics focus upon the values that advertising champions. It is not enough to look at surveys about what people recall after a night of watching television, they argue. One must look at the long-term impact of this institution on our value system in general.

And so the debate continues. As a result of reading these essays you should be able to "see" advertising in a different light and gain a better understanding of how it works.

43 THE AD WORLD'S WHIMSICAL WIZARD (HAL RINEY)*

Michael Robertson

Hal Riney is generally considered to be one of the most creative and influential figures in the advertising world, and has been the subject of numerous articles. He heads an important agency in San Francisco, Hal Riney & Partners, and has made many famous commercials, such as the ones for Henry Weinhard's Private Reserve Beer and Bartles & Jaymes Premium Wine Coolers. He has won fourteen Clios (the advertising world's version of an Academy Award) and numerous other prizes. And he has been described as leading a revolution in advertising — emphasizing the creative aspects of the field and paying less attention to market research.

Here are some descriptions of the man and his work.

1. "If you've ever read Jung, you realize right away that Hal is a classic Jungian archetype: the Coyote. He's aggressive, manipulative, scheming, and, at the same time, godlike. He's able to appropriate people's interests like nobody else."[1]

2. "Riney succeeds by rejecting advertising's conventional wisdom. In a world of grab-the-viewer-by-the-neck-and-shake commercials, Riney's trademark is soft-selling through understatement and wry humor. He figures those virtues, being rare, will stand out. As advertisers increasingly use shorter commercials to cut costs, moving from 30-second to 15-second spots, Riney thinks he can win a lot more attention with longer commercials."[2]

3. "…Hal Riney's patent mixture of small-town realism and shrewdly soft wit are redefining a business known previously for its hard-sell tactics and its obsession with market research…On the flip side, advertising that uses realistic people to appeal to genuine human emotions may be even more manipulative than the harsher, louder ads of the past. But Riney claims that he is drawing honestly from within himself to create his advertising. 'Writers are interesting people because they have a sensitivity to feeling,' he said. But, he added, 'We are advocates. And I think we use whatever tools we have to make that sale.'"[3]

This last quote raises an ethical question (the manipulation of people by whatever tools are available) that is dealt with in the article that follows and that we might keep in mind when we think about advertising in general.

REFERENCES

1. Sharkey, Betsy. (1987). "World Class." *San Francisco Magazine*.
2. *Fortune*, 1987.
3. Kleiner, Art. (1986). Master of the Sentimental Sell. *The New York Times Magazine*.

If Charles Schulz ever lets Charlie Brown grow up, he will look like Hal Riney: soft, sad eyes crinkled at the edges like an old piece of Saran wrap, little wisps of Buck Henry hair thatching down over the worry lines in his forehead.

Hal Riney is an ad man. He makes the commercials that make the whole world buy. And he is unnervingly likeable. His voice is soft. He looks into some vague personal distance as he talks. His manner does not insist that you like him or believe him.

If someone must have entree to the riotous mysteries of the consumer's heart, well, why not Hal Riney? Like one of his ads, he seems Too Good To Be True.

Hal Riney is creative director and managing director of the San Francisco office of Ogilvy & Mather. A veteran of two highly productive decades in the endless journey to Oz also known as the San Francisco ad world, he started the local Ogilvy-Mather office in 1977.

He began with $1 million in billings. The agency projects $40 million in billings for the coming fiscal year. "That's really amazing," he explains. "Agencies don't grow that fast."

Riney not only makes money, he wins prizes: four Clios (the Oscars of advertising); two Gold and two Silver Lions from the Cannes Film Festival; Seven Gold Medals from the San Francisco Society of Communicating Arts; an Academy Award nomination for a short film he knocked together on his own time.

He acts a little embarrassed when he offers up his resume which lists all these things, "but I know you need this kind of stuff."

What's an apparently nice guy like Hal Riney, a country boy born in the shadow of Mt. St. Helens who still has the grace to show a little discomfort over the fact both his marriages have ended in divorce, doing in a place like this? Isn't advertising a propaganda game where ethics get edited out and morals end up on the cutting room floor?

"I wish," says Riney, "that advertising were more influential than it is. The easy answer to your question is, yes, we can get someone to buy something once. But you can't get people to continue to buy what doesn't fit their needs or their image, either real or imagined.

"The government seems to see advertising as some sort of misleading editorial material. It's actually a sort of advocacy that consumers perceive

How now, Hal?

Hal Riney, founder and creative leader of Hal Riney & Partners, San Francisco—one of the nation's most respected creative agencies. Trained as an art director, he's been hailed as "the best copywriter I've ever known" by David Ogilvy. Here, from a recent conversation, are the thoughts of the man who's created some of America's most thoughtful advertising.

On beginnings:
I met my strongest influence in Seattle, Washington—on the day I was born. My father was extraordinary. He drew, he wrote, he sold things, he was an actor. I wanted to do everything he did and only advertising offered the opportunity. So that's what I wanted to do, early on. After majoring in art and taking some journalism courses at the University of Washington, I became a news writer with the U.S. Army in Italy and Austria. When I returned to civilian life, I joined BBDO/San Francisco as a mailroom boy at $250 per month. It wasn't much money—not even then—but it was a start.

On finding a path—and starting an agency:
I wanted to be an account executive, although I didn't really know what one was. Then I became a junior account executive, found out what an account executive is—and decided I didn't want to be one. So I became an art director; then head art director and, later a writer and creative director. In 1972, branch office frustrations led me to quit and take a job as creative director at a smaller agency, Botsford-Ketchum. It was just a $12-million shop. Four years later, with billings at $50 million, I left and started Ogilvy & Mather/San Francisco. We began in a garage with four people. Ogilvy gave us a free hand—and Blitz-Weinhard gave us its business.

On today's audiences:
People today are adwise. They know what we're trying to do. They've seen millions of ads, have been exposed to every approach—so they're almost *immune*. In the old days, you could simply tell people what was good about your product, and what you wanted them to do. Now, it's tough to get their attention. Look at any list of the best-remembered ads. It's mostly a matter of money. You need an incredible budget—or real news, and that doesn't come along often. In *most* categories, for *most* products, it takes a lot of money just to maintain brand awareness, much less get people to change their perceptions or habits.

On budgets:
Many clients' expectations exceed their budgets. Creative innovation is a necessity, but you still need a lot of exposure. This is especially true with television. It's no longer the magic medium it once was, probably because most of us see over a hundred commercials a day. I think we should use print a great deal more than we do. It's more efficient in reaching specific audiences. You can produce a dozen ads for what a single TV spot might cost. And you have a chance to offer more complete, more convincing arguments. Have I convinced our clients of that? Not nearly as often as I would like.

On aiming your advertising:
I'd rather sell 10% of the people 100% of the way than sell 100% of the people 10% of the way. Spread your budget across too many media, and you won't hit anyone. It's the same as hunting quail. You look up when a covey takes flight, and you think you'll hit *something* by just pulling the trigger. But you discover you have to choose a target—or you won't hit anything. Trying to sell anything to *everyone* isn't a strategy. It's wishful thinking.

On art vs. copy:
Art and copy aren't mutually exclusive. An art director should be something of a writer, and a writer something of an art director. I think it's simpler to visualize the ad *and* write it, although many don't agree. I operate—more than I should, no doubt—as a one-man band. But I can't just *write* an ad. I care how it *looks* as well as what it says.

On overnight success:
People look at our work, and they say, "Wow, those people are doing terrific stuff. How did *that* happen?" But we've been doing good advertising—by most people's standards—for years. The catch was that they didn't see it in New York and Chicago. So, for all practical purposes, it didn't exist. Once we started working for larger national clients, our work began to be seen everywhere. It wasn't a revolution, but a *revelation*—at least to those who had not seen our work before. Which proves that it's easy to succeed overnight; it just takes 20 years to do it.

On copy and the common product:
The experts say people won't read long copy about common products; for example, beer. But we keep writing long copy about beer, and people keep reading it. You *can* entertain people in print. You *can* make print emotional. And you can *sell* your product. Print copy can cover all the small differences that add up to a big reason for buying a specific brand.

On the balance of power:
When I started in the business, account executives were the "idea people." They'd figure out the problem, and the solution. Then the creative people would execute it. Today? Smart agencies give their creative people *the problem*. Creative people who've been in the business for years are pretty astute about the *business of business*, not simply the business of making an ad. It isn't efficient to have both your account people and creative people sitting around trying to solve the same problems. So the problem solving is drifting more and more to the creative side.

On clients and communications:
You can't tell an account executive to tell someone else, who'll tell someone else, without getting the problem distorted before it reaches the people who actually do the work. Clients like to talk to creative people who can listen. We make creative people the problem solvers, and account people the managers. You need account managers to *manage*

the business—creative people are seldom good managers.

On New York:
Traditionally, when major advertisers have looked for an agency, they've looked to New York first, then Chicago and Los Angeles. But good work isn't the exclusive property of Manhattan. And today, more and major clients are looking at the entire country; putting *solution* ahead of *location*.

On doing great work:
You can't do your best work unless you deal with someone with the authority to say *absolutely yes*. The overwhelming majority of all good advertising is done by agencies that deal with the individual who makes the ultimate decision—someone who cares, who's concerned, who can approve it with no ifs, no buts, no maybes. In the agency, there has to be a sense of creative contribution to the solution. People who think they're just a cog in a machine won't make much of a commitment. And without commitment, you won't have excellence. The more inventive work has always come from smaller agencies. There are fewer layers—and more involvement by creative people. That's an advantage we've had. The idea is to build billings without building obstacles.

On taste and style:
Advertising based on insignificant product differences won't provide significant leverage. Today, some important differences are simply in *taste* and *style*; not just what the advertising says, but *how* it says it. That's why David Ogilvy has had so much influence on my work. His work has exhibited taste and style. David would deny that. He says advertising should *sell*. But taste and style are often at the heart of selling.

On solutions:
I don't know *where* solutions come from. I just keep thinking about the problem, turning it over in my mind, letting my subconscious work on it. Sometimes, something happens. Sometimes, it's good.

On The Wall Street Journal:
I want to see our advertising in a medium where *it stands out*. If you're in a thick magazine where it's almost impossible to find your ad, what good are demographics, or theoretical reach, or any of the other media measurements? That's why I like to see our ads in The Wall Street Journal. Certainly it's the most respectable, most thoughtful, most tasteful publication you can imagine. But it's also a terrific creative environment. Your ads stand out. And the ability to reach influential people in a medium where your advertising will be seen provides a special kind of leverage. Sure, the people who read The Journal are successful, intelligent, tough. Which makes them like a lot of clients for whom I've worked. The key, whether you're working *with* them, or writing *to* them, is to have high standards. But isn't that what business is all about?

The Wall Street Journal.
It works.

as just that. To say we mold opinion is not very respectful of Americans. Advertising reflects society rather than creating attitudes. We follow behind rather than lead.

"I can't think of any instance where we've had to worry about the ethics of our products. But as a large agency we deal with national companies of good reputation."

Riney says there are so many safeguards — "the FTC, our attorneys, their attorneys, the boards within the industry" — that any given ad is scrutinized 5 to 10 times. "The chance of our being misleading, if our own ethics would let us — it just can't happen."

His eyes crinkling into a positive fit of good humor, Riney recalls a "most charming and wonderful thing" in the ad biz, one of those times when the watch dogs, in their zeal to protect the American public, took a piece of humor too seriously.

Riney once did a motorcycle commercial in which a rural type warned of the cougars and bears that inhabited the nearby mountains. He told of a cyclist who some years ago went into the wilds on a motorcycle other than a Yamaha and hadn't come out — yet.

One of the major TV networks didn't want to run the ad, says Riney, because "it implied you would be eaten by a wild aninal if you didn't buy a Yamaha. If anything, the public is in some ways overprotected."

Then there are Riney's recent commercials for Henry Weinhard's Private Reserve beer, one of which won Riney his most recent Clio (see accompanying story). These commercials are based on actual events, such as a burglary in which the Oregon beer was the only thing stolen.

Two of the major TV networks insisted that Riney put a statement at the beginning of each spot acknowledging the incidents were rooted in reality. "I thought that might be misleading," says Riney. "The actual instances were pretty dull, so we had elaborated, as we ordinarily do."

Then the third major network saw the spots and insisted the agency take the claim off the versions that network aired.

But what about the fundamental ethical problem of pushing beer in a culture in which alcoholism is a major health problem?

"Go back to the Assyrians," says Riney. "I believe they were drinking beer, and there was no advertising. We do not create a need for beer. We just recommend our brand."

To most TV viewers the question of whether or not Riney's beer commercials are immoral pales next to their undeniable delightfulness. For so many commercials, whether print, TV or radio, are just plain bad.

Riney says he "despises" that quality of ad when he sees one, "when I happen to turn on my TV, which isn't often." But he understands why it happens.

Take something like toilet paper, a product whose ads are almost uniformly insulting to the intelligence of the American consumer. Riney says that these products are often of such a "terribly low interest level — people would really rather not think about them — that you may have to do something abrasive to attract attention."

Such hard sell is becoming more common because it produces "results." According to Riney, "Clients like some form of measurement of the effectiveness of their spending, and there is no universally accepted form of measuring our efforts. You can't measure persuasion without spending lots of time and lots of money. So we test for 'day-after recall,' which doesn't measure persuasion.

"It does measure memory of having seen something. Usually, the more intrusive the things you put in the commercial, the higher the score.

"I believe the long range value of talking nicely to people is immense, although it can't be measured. But it's safer to be intrusive on the theory people will eventually buy something from you if you bother them enough."

A commercial, Riney insists, can be a piece of art, one of the most highly creative things a person can do. "We create a dimension of emotional feeling. We communicate with people in almost no time at all.

"But to the business community, we're businessmen just like them. And no one would like to concede their money is being spent on anything as frivolous as art. At its best a commercial is an art form."

How many attain that level? Maybe one in a hundred, Riney would guess.

HOW A COW-TOWN AD BECAME BLUE RIBBON STOCK

The commercial begins with a telex banging out the news that the "Kingsley Ranch" has a "stock" of "Henry Weinhards" coming in on the next train. One of the old codgers on the station platform starts filling in his cronies about his own experience with Henry Weinhards.

"Kinda like a Hereford," he explains. "Come from Germany originally. Purebred stock. Used to run *Henry Weinhards* out around Saragosa. Longhorns they was...or was they shorthorns... sorta medium-size horns?"

The beer arrives, and the camera cuts back to the codger: "Used to drink Henry Weinhard's out around Saragosa..."

Hal Riney, creative director of Ogilvy & Mather's San Francisco, created and wrote the ad. Jerry Andelin was art director. It has been awarded a Clio by their fellow ad men as the best beer commercial in the 1980 industry-wide competition.

It is a commercial that takes chances, and Riney says not every client would have bought it. Beer, after all, is an "image-related" product.

According to Riney, "the client **could** have said, 'The old guy represents the consumer, and we want a young person to be drinking our beer.'"

But, Riney argues, that would have been short-sighted. Since Henry Weinhard's Private Reserve is a "premium," higher-priced product, the assumption is that it appeals to a comparatively sophisticated market.

Thus Riney's indirect approach. "I started with the word 'stock,' and that generated the idea of confusion about what it meant. The best kind of situations are those reminiscent of what we've seen or known in our own lives. And we've all known someone like that who has nothing better to do all day but sit around and make up stories."

But where does that droll, throwaway dialogue come from?

"What you do is what you do," says Riney. "It's whimsey. How do you know ...?" He shakes his head over "the arrogance and wishful thinking" involved in hoping people will laugh.

"But these commercials are not just funny for the sake of being funny. They are built on what we know are the needs of beer drinkers. They say indirectly that the beer is special. One mistake of advertising is to tell the viewer directly.

"We're being a little bit humble in these commercials, and people appreciate that. There's so much bull —— all the time."

Since on a cost-per-minute basis, commercials are the most expensive things on TV, the best of them are filled with a density of detail that tantalizes the eye. Take, for instance, the authen-

tic "Texas and Southwestern Cattle Raisers" sign on the train station, which was actually located in eastern Oregon.

In another Henry Weinhard's commercial, Riney made up a bumper sticker for a truckload of bloodhounds. It read, "When dogs are outlawed, only outlaws will have dogs."

It didn't show in the final cut. Still, Riney routinely spends a day "propping" a set with odds and ends that give it an authentic feel. "You never really see it all," says Riney. "It becomes a tapestry of things."

Is it worth the effort?

"Hell, no. But where do you stop?"

44   THE CASE OF THE CLOSET TARGET*

Martin Solow

Advertising is one of most fascinating and problematic genres of communication. Does advertising "work"? If so, how? And what do we mean by "work"? Can people avoid being influenced by it or are we all, whether we admit it or not, susceptible to its powers?

Marshall McLuhan was a media critic who was fascinated by advertising — and someone who, we might say, in his later years was co-opted by the industry. The material that follows was taken from his classic study of advertising, comics and popular culture, *The Mechanical Bride* — published in 1951. In this passage, McLuhan speculates about the way advertising works:

The ad agencies and Hollywood, in their different ways, are always trying to get inside the public mind in order to impose their collective dreams on that inner state. And in the pursuit of this goal both Hollywood and the advertising agencies themselves give major exhibitions of unconscious behavior. One dream opens into another until reality and fantasy are made

* Martin Solow, "The Case of the Closet Target." Reprinted with permission of *Madison Avenue* Magazine, © *Madison Avenue* Magazine.

interchangeable. The ad agencies flood the daytime world of conscious purpose and control with erotic imagery from the night world in order to drown, by suggestion, all sales resistance. Hollywood floods the night world with daytime imagery in which synthetic gods and goddesses (stars) appear to assume the roles of our wakeaday existence in order to flatter and console us for the failures of our daily lives. The ad agencies hold out for each of us the dream of a spot on Olympus where we can quaff and loll forever amid well-known brands. The movies reverse this procedure by showing us the stars…descending to our level.…

The advertising agencies and Hollywood generate, ultimately, a kind of collective novel "whose characters, imagery, and situations are an intimate revelation of the passions of the age."

Advertising (along with Hollywood) is not something trivial and irrelevant but is, instead, a means of understanding important aspects of society — for those who know how to interpret things. We might keep McLuhan's ideas in mind when we think about advertising. The selection that follows deals with the power of advertising. It is written by an advertising executive who points out that we generally deceive ourselves about advertising's effectiveness. McLuhan's ideas suggest we might look at advertising in a slightly different way…as a key to unlocking many of the secrets buried in the public mind.

Every time I see a survey on why people buy the products they do, I'm amused. The survey might be based upon personal interviews, telephone interviews, guarantee cards — whatever. But the answer patterns are invariably the same. Nobody but nobody (OK, almost nobody) buys anything because of advertising. Well, if we believed those surveys we'd close down a multi-billion dollar business.

So why do people buy the particular brands of toothpaste, automobiles, paper towels, etc., that they do buy? Here's what they're inclined to say on surveys:

- Recommended by a friend. (That's a big one…now if we only knew where the friend got the scoop.)
- Recommended by the store. (Perhaps it's the brand the store carries, was on special, discounted, etc.)
- Recommended by a salesperson. (Suddenly, the salesperson, often reviled as an ignoramus, hustler and con artist, is held up as the consumer expert of all time.)
- *Consumer Reports* said it was the best buy. (If this one were true, and the number of people who answered this way were projected onto the total population, we'd have consumer publications with circulation

into the billions.) Incidentally, I'm sure that favorable coverage will sell merchandise but if *CR* disappeared tomorrow I doubt it would cause more than a ripple in the sale of mass merchandise to the American people.

"People," a psychiatrist friend of mine said, "are funnier than anybody. They like to project positive images even when they answer anonymous questionnaires. Deep down," he said, "they probably believe that the mysterious person circulating those questionnaires knows who they are anyhow and is 'judging' them." The point is, says the psychiatrist, that many people desire an ideal self image. And why not? Therefore, whenever they get the chance to enhance that image — like boasting of plays they've seen, books that are *au courant*, TV shows they don't watch (and I'll get to that) and advertisements they ignore — they give rose-colored answers. How easy it is in this measured, pre-packaged, containerized world of ours to put on a box of intellectual cachet and boast of eschewing advertising.

I was struck with that particular phenomenon — the advertising eschewers — after I left *The Nation* where I was assistant to the publisher, and became an advertising copywriter. I began to be treated in some of my former circles as an apostate and learned to suffer the slings and arrows cast by outraged friends with other fortunes. Advertising, they'd sneer...nothing could induce them to be persuaded by the moronic materials of advertising.

Take an incident.

My wife and I are guests, for the first time, at a lovely home in Nassau County, near where we live. The hostess, tall and gracious in her hostess gown, moves gracefully among her guests. Someone mentions that I'm in the advertising business. "Oh," she says, brightly, "what do you do?" I mumble a few things.

"I'm sorry," she says, "I never watch TV commercials, I can't stand advertising...any advertising." Chimes of approval and assent from the small group around us. I throw up a few defenses, because I know the syndrome: "How do you buy the products you buy?" I want to know. I get a patronizing smile. She buys what she considers best; what *Consumer Reports* tells her; what she **knows** (and **how** does she know, I murmur to myself) to be the best. I excuse myself and ask, since it is a large house, for a roadmap to the bathroom. Once in the large bathroom, the door safely locked, I open the medicine cabinet and survey the contents: Colgate toothpaste; L'Oreal hairspray; Trac II shaving cream and the new Gillette Trac II razor; Ban Roll-On Deodorant (for him, I guess) and Arrid Extra Dry (for her — or maybe vice-versa); Bayer aspirins; (*Consumer Reports* would drum them out of membership since they say all aspirins are alike, only the price is different and Bayer costs a lot of money); Dristan tablets; Contac; assorted Estee Lauder cosmetics (well, maybe she saw it at the department store counters and liked the way they were packaged and smelled); Protein 29 Hair Spray (for him); Head and Shoulders; Johnson's Baby Oil; Q-Tips; Scope mouthwash and the list could go on.

I close the medicine cabinet, wash my hands, saunter back into the living room and refrain from asking how come out host and hostess use the products they do....But I knew.

Back to TV itself: There's another proposition worth noting. Namely: If all the people who claim to watch Channel 13 really watch it, it would be the number one channel in the metropolitan area. Many people make "13" into a coffee table channel. It's not the station's fault, not with such programs as "Theatre In America," "Monty Python," "Masterpiece Theatre," etc. (I happen to think the "Adams Chronicles" a bore.) Because "13" represents a degree of excellence, people feel guilty about not watching, though their hearts belong to "Baretta" or "All In The Family." Therefore, they feel they should pay lip service.

The link between these comments and the "non-watchers" of TV commercials? Coming up.

The man is from Scarsdale, complete with bulging waistline, clinging turtleneck and turquoise and silver Indian neckwear, and he is busy putting down TV and TV commercials with some vehemence.

"What," I wanted to know, "did he watch?"

"Thirteen, of course; it's the only ball game in town."

"What did he like on Channel 13?"

He particularly liked "The Ascent of Man" and "Civilization." He thought they were "marvelous," "creative," "TV at its best."

"Ah." I said, "how did you like the sequence in 'The Ascent of Man' where the black monolith is viewed as a deity?"

He loved it; thought it was one of "TV's finest hours ever."

It was indeed one of somebody's finest hours: namely Stanley Kubrick's in his movie, "2001."

I have, I confess, been forced into this sort of badinage by a built-in, lack of tolerance device, and years of listening to people boast that they neither watch TV nor the commercials.

Out of it all, I have developed Solow's First Law: Those who claim they don't watch TV are much more vulnerable to commercials than those who unashamedly do. The "non-watchers" guard is up, as boxers keep their guard up. And because their guard is up and they're paying *attention*, they are vulnerable to punches that can slip through, especially if the punches are skillful. When you're relaxed and unconcerned with your self-image, you can slip the punches with much greater ease; get up and go to the kitchen to start a hero sandwich. Real TV watchers, I'm convinced, sew, read books, newspapers and magazines, do macrame, talk and maybe fornicate.

Let's face it, we use products because we're trained to use products. We use products because we get a message, not because the drugstore clerk told us that one medicine is better than another. (That clerk is the kid you wouldn't trust to locate your baby's mouth with a nipple, and you expect him to be an expert on what to take for the "crippling pain of arthritis?") If you've got arthritis, you're going to take Anacin, Aspirin, Bufferin, or whatever message got through from the advertising.

From time to time, I've asked people (who claim they are not influenced by advertising) why they use certain products. What they say, for the most part, is what is implanted in their heads by the commercials. For example: "It's approved by the American Dental Association," (Crest). "It's got a better ride," (Mercury). "It makes my teeth whiter," (Ultra-brite, Close-Up). "It's all natural," (Herbal Essence).

The point is that people who use products play back the message. The fact is that advertising is ubiquitous. You can't get away from it. It's all around us in newspapers, car cards, matchbook covers, radio, TV, magazines, point-of-sale, packaging, even to where a product is placed in the store. For people to claim they're not influenced in the slightest by advertising is both silly and untrue. (I'm willing to allow rare exceptions, i.e. hermits, flagpole sitters and Sherpa guides.) I'm not arguing it's the most terrific thing in the world; I'm simply stating what is real and what is not real.

What does my psychiatrist friend say about it? "Relax and enjoy it and do as I do — subscribe to *Consumer Reports.*"

45   IDOLS OF THE MARKETPLACE*
John J. Kavanaugh, S. J.

The essay that follows deals with the values found in advertising and suggests that many of these values are destructive ones. A value is a belief a person has about what is good and bad, important or unimportant. It can be argued that our values ultimately shape our behavior so whoever or whatever influences our value system bears a heavy responsibility. I would like to use this concern with values as a point of departure for considering how advertisements work. What follows is a list of questions we might ask ourselves when analyzing print advertisements and commercials.

1. *What are the values championed in the advertisement?* If there are people in the advertisement, what are their values? What values are the creators of the advertisement supporting?

2. *What themes are found in the advertisement?* Let us make a distinction between plot (which is what is happening) and theme (which is what the advertisement is about). Thus two characters may be drinking soda (plot) but the advertisement is about love or passion or jealousy (theme).

---

* John J. Kavanaugh, S. J., "Idols of the Marketplace," from *Media and Values* (Fall, 1986, No. 37). Reprinted with permission.

3. *Where is the action taking place and what significance does this locale have?* How does the background influence and give meaning to the action in the advertisement? In aesthetics we sometimes talk about the figure-ground relationship. How does the background give meaning to the figures?

4. *If there are people in the advertisement, what are they like?* What kind of facial expressions do we find? What about their ages? What can we make of their hair color, hair styles, poses, body language, dress, implied social class? What kind of relationship are we supposed to assume the characters have with one another?

5. *How are images and symbols used in the advertisement?* (For our purposes, an "image" is a mental picture we hold of something and a "symbol" is something that stands for something else, an object that has cultural significance and that has conscious and unconscious meaning to people.)

6. *What persuasive linguistic devices do we find in the text of the advertisement (or dialogue, if we are dealing with commercials)?* Do we find pleading, emotional appeals, scare tactics, use of logic or pseudo-logic or humor? How do the copywriters "define" things like love, happiness, pleasure, duty, or responsibility for us?

7. *What about the use of white (or blank) space, the kinds of type used and the general ambience of the advertisement?* How do these phenomena generate impressions and moods and shape our attitudes?

> *"She said that the only thing she really wanted for Christmas was a pair of Sasson jeans."*
>
> — a blue-collar worker, speaking of his nine-year-old daughter

> *"The human person cannot be relinquished. We cannot relinquish the place in the visible world that belongs to us. We cannot become slaves of things, slaves of economic systems, slaves of production, slaves of our own products. A civilization purely materialistic in outline condemns the human person to such slavery."*
>
> — Pope John Paul II, *Redemptor Hominus*

If we ask ourselves what values we would like to see illuminating the lives of our children, students, parishioners and co-religionists, I think that designer jeans would fall pretty far down the list.

We might speak of human dignity, compassion, a well-grounded individual identity and an ability to relate to others as people and not as things.

Our young friend has reversed this standard. Instead of basing her identity on her potential and qualities as a person, her value in her own eyes rests upon a purchased object. What is forming the life of this young woman? What is most profoundly educating her? Have the social system, the production system and the media system conspired to lead her into a condition of servitude and inhibit the various dimensions of her human personhood?

The answer is clear. Our social myths, our economic gospels and our revelation system of television, advertising, and printed matter are a formation system, educating us towards certain values, attitudes and modes of behavior.

In the most general sense, values always are a function of the culture that forms them, since culture explains all the expressions of who we are.

CULTURAL GROUND

Psycho-socially, culture is a tilling, an elaboration of the human. Like agriculture, culture yields the human product that in turn feeds and sustains us. The culture, in this sense, is our food — our social, psychological and corporate sustenance and nutriment. It provides the very sustenance of our self-understanding, our purpose, our meaning and our fulfillments.

Herein lies culture's danger. It can form us in its own image and likeness rather than in the image and likeness of personhood from which culture has its derivation.

As a child of media-centered late twenty century capitalist culture, this woman-child with her Sasson jeans is operating out of an already fashioned culturally determined belief and behavior system that has implications for every area of her life.

The things she buys determine her identity. The formation of her social identity is based upon commercial imagery and acceptance. Her relationship to her parents is fixated at this level. Sullenness and manipulation characterize her affect. Sensibilities for right order, simplicity, compassion are already deadened. A coalition of pressures from commercialism, advertising and social programming dominates her consciousness. She is manipulated, educated and propagandized. Much of that manipulation is attributable to media.

Before she had ever gotten to primary school — if she is an average child in the United States — she had spent as much time in front of a television set as she would spend in classroom lectures throughout four years of college. Her home life is dominated by television.

The preponderance of programming and advertising in the U.S. delivers a continual message to the viewer: human beings in relationship to each other (in soap operas, series, talk shows, game shows) are trivialized and alienated. People are most likely to be unfulfilled, unfaithful, unhappy, frustrated, foolish. The only times that persons are presented as uniformly happy and ecstatically fulfilled are in commercials: purchasing, collecting or consuming products that resolve problems, deliver self-assurance, win friends.

And television and magazine content is interlaced by the financial fabric of advertising and its covert ideology of happiness through commodities. A commodity-like identity is the end result of the cultural education system in North America.

If we are taught to relate to persons as if they were expendable objects and to relate to things as if they were substitute persons, we are led into the distressing inversion that the pope alludes to when he speaks of becoming slaves to products or slaves to production systems.

OBJECTIFIED VALUES

Value formation is achieved by the very names we give to products. Merit is a cigarette. True goes up in smoke. We eat Life in a box. Joy and Happiness are perfumes. Love, Caring and Hope are cosmetics. New Freedom is a sanitary napkin. Spirit is an automobile. It is precisely the value that is commodified and sold.

As Joan Evans of the Evans Marketing Group in New York has said: "Any industry that sells hope is going to continue to grow. And that's what we're selling." Or as another advertiser said in *Advertising Age*, "Calvin Klein jeans are not blue jeans, they are a sex symbol. Miller isn't a beer. It's blue collar macho...Polo doesn't sell clothing. Polo sells fashion status." The marketeers realize a fact we often repress: it is precisely value that is bought and sold, that has a price, that is quantifiable, that is reduced relative to the status of trinkets.

The valorization of objects is enhanced by the personalization of products that appears in so much advertising. Products are not "Just Born" — they have mothers and fathers. Affection is continually poured out over bottles of mouthwash, toilet paper, diapers, dogs, Mustangs, and paint cans. "This much squeezable softness deserves a hug," the woman says to the toilet paper with a baby's face on the package. Your brandy or your blue jeans are called your "friends."

The language of family relationship is subsumed into corporate identity. "Think of her as your mother." (American Airlines). "World's Greatest Dad." (Seagram's Crown Royal). "We don't love you and leave you." (Xerox). "More dependable than a man." (Payroll Savings Plan). Fidelity and commitment are words describing our relationship to washers and dryers and car stereos.

While this personalization of products is taking place, the actual image of family life in advertising, young women's magazines, rock music and best sellers is severely fragmented. Soap operas, articles in *Cosmopolitan*, bubble gum and pre-teen music portray men and women as being unfaithful to each other. Sexuality is rarely related to covenant or committed intimacy or family. Married people are rarely portrayed as being fulfilled or happy. As an ad for furniture in the New York Times had it, "If your husband doesn't like it, leave him."

BUYING OURSELVES

For over two years now, the most significant advertising phrase for Saks Fifth Avenue has been "We Are All the Things You Are."

Wouldn't they love us to believe it? If everything we are is found at a department store, if we have to purchase our identity, then we are in a condition of servitude, the slaves of products.

The ultimate moral imperative is to consume as a matter of identity. Our very meaning is wrapped up in the economics of production and consumption of more products. Products are portrayed as the condition of happiness: "Nikon: what would life be without it." "Money buys everything." (Polaroid). The media and the economic system coalesce into a book of religious revelation. "Because she believes in us, she'll believe in you. Her Bible is your Bonanza," *Seventeen* magazine boasts to the corporate readership of *Advertising Age*.

Buying is theologized in products called "Spirit," "Jesus Jeans," in diamonds that assure possession of the supernatural, in perfection that can be bought with Beefeaters, in Calvin Klein, whom women are said to "believe in."

The theological virtues have become commodified. Buicks are "something to believe in." "Hope (cosmetics) is all you Need." "Trust Woolite." Love is a diaper, a bottle of Amaretto, a carpet shampoo.

Thus the media-culture-economy formation is complete. We have not only a philosophy of human identity and human relationship collapsed into the world of buying and selling, we have a full blown theological system. The result is cultural ideology as idolatry.

Cultural information system is religious formation system. We form our young in the image and likeness of the products and production systems we have created by our own hands.

Their idols are silver and gold, the work of human hands.
They have mouths but do not speak; eyes, but do not see;
They have ears but do not hear, noses but do not smell;
They have hands but do not feel; feet, but do not walk;
And not a sound comes from their throat.
Those who make them become like them;
So do all who trust in them.

As Psalm 115 suggests, we become like the products we worship. Since our identity and fulfillment is wrapped up in the possessing and consuming of our commodities, we "style" ourselves after products, and where we're not good enough, we are replaced or remodeled. The natural body is to be rejected in favor of the fabricated one.

Everything about our natural bodies is wrong: we're too fat, too thin, we have split ends, pimples, bad breath, body odor, our breasts or hips are too large or too small, we're not manly enough so we need a Brut's perfume or a diet macho beer. "Want a Better Body?" the ad for Formfit says, "Let us rearrange it for you."

CONSUMPTION AS FUEL

In these references to advertisements I am attempting to suggest that there is an economics to issues of identity, relationship, family, commitment, human sexuality, human anxiety, the devaluation of chastity, the rejection of one's natural body. There is also a latent formation system in a culture economically based upon the continual expansion of products, consumer goods and productivity.

This formation system, whether deliberately constructed or not, has a tendency to educate human persons into a mode of thinking, believing and acting that serves the imperatives of the economic system itself.

Perhaps this may be suggested by a set of questions: In an economic system founded upon continually expanding consumption, in a society that already has a surfeit of goods, in a culture whose people are already overconsuming, what kind of person will best fit, what kind of formation will be most appropriate?

How can people be convinced that they must produce and possess more? Is it better to have people with stable and happy lives or unstable and dissatisfied lives? Is it better for them to have a sound personal identity and fulfilling relationships, or to experience a personal and relational emptiness that must be filled in some way?

What kind of person would be considered an economic liability? One who is at home with himself or herself? One who has a sense of justice and compassion? One who is capable of delayed gratification for the sake of longer-range values?

Awareness of the effects of these messages on ourselves and our families is the first step in counteracting them, with efforts to educate a wider public and associated discussions a useful corollary.

Beyond that, however, we must consciously seek to help those we work with uncover cultural ideology and instill methods of solitude, self-understanding, and experiencing of the interior life. A commitment to relationships, the reversal of the culturally taught insensitivity to human suffering and contact with those the culture rejects as worthless, can help counter our built-in biases.

Only direct experience and self-discovery can help us reach beyond the limited script that our objectified values system writes for us. With this transcendence, we will better relate to each other as we learn to savor and appreciate — not merely collect and consume — the goods of the earth.

46

THE PRESENTATION OF GENDER IN ADVERTISING*

ANTHONY SYNNOTT

This essay on gender in advertising has a number of features worth considering. First, it is an excellent example of a content analysis, a research methodology often used by people who work with the mass media. Synnott explains what he does clearly and thus provides a useful introduction to this methodology. Readers of this essay should be able to make their own content analyses of magazine advertisements...and other print media. (It is possible to make content analyses of electronic media, but it is much more difficult.)

In addition, Synnott's findings are quite interesting. He discovers that there is a considerable difference between the way men and women are portrayed in advertisements found in *The New York Times* (Sunday) *Magazine* — a journal read by an extremely influential group of readers (and, one would imagine, a number of feminists).

Synnott is careful to qualify his generalizations. He recognizes, for example, that there is some question about whether or not advertising "reflects" society; there is little doubt, however, that advertising "creates" a reality of its own — the "reality" shown in a given advertisement, and in advertising in general.

The question, then, is what is the relationship that exists between our mass-mediated "reality" and reality itself (assuming we can know reality, a matter about which there is some debate). Many media theorists believe that readers and viewers "internalize" many of the values they see portrayed in the media and "identify" with those they see. That is, without being conscious of what is happening, and much of this occurs at a level below awareness, they accept the values of the heroes and heroines they read about or watch and wish to be like them. This often involves approximating their life-styles, and the products that they are shown using, since it is impossible to do much more than that, generally speaking.

What is most dangerous, however, is that we get a sense of what life is like and what roles we should play from this mass-mediated world. In the case of the advertisements analyzed in *The New York Times Magazine* section, the results are not encouraging, for the advertisements presented a highly distorted picture of everything from what a woman's body should be like to the role of old people in society. Synnott also asks who is responsible for allowing these advertisements (and by implication, all the distortions found in the media) to continue. His answer is that we get the ads that we don't protest about.

* From the *International Journal of Visual Sociology*, Vol. 1, Summer 1983. Reprinted by permission of the publisher, Edition Herodot, Rader Verlag Kongressstr. 5, D-5100, Aachen, W. Germany

Advertisements may or may not reflect reality; but they do *create* a reality. And it is this reality of gender roles, as presented in *The New York Times Magazine* that we discuss here. Feminists have asserted for 20 years, and still assert, that many advertisements are insulting and degrading to women, present false images of reality, are sexist, misrepresent women and are part of the problem, not part of the solution (Friedan, 1963; Greer, 1971; Henry, 1963).

These views, once no doubt minority opinions have become widely accepted, and in recent years considerable attention has been focused on sex stereotyping, especially of women, in the media. A recent report cites over 250 publications relating to this topic (Courtney and Whipple, 1980). Most of this attention has been focused on television (Canadian Radio-Television and Telecommunication Commission, 1982; Canadian Advertising and Advisory Board, 1977; Courtney and Whipple, 1978; National Advertising Review Board, 1975; Ontario Status of Women, 1975; U.S. Commission on Civil Rights, 1979).

However, there has been some research on stereotyping in magazines (Courtney and Lockerety, 1971); but there have been few significant changes over time (Sexton and Haberman, 1974; Venkatesa and Losso, 1975).

Although magazine ads, and TV ads, do not seem to have changed much over the years, public reaction to them has surely changed: hence the surge of publications. The reaction, however, has been not only academic but also political and economic. In 1972 the National Organization for Women (NOW) took the unprecedented step of attempting to take court action against TWA for its "Fly Me" campaign. The Council on The Status of Women offers annual prizes for the most sexist advertisement of the year, and encourages people to boycott the offending product. The prize was won in 1983 by Sanyo, for its advertisement for video-cassette recorders which depicted two female dancers rubbing their thighs with oranges. (*Gazette* June 16, 1983). Such negative publicity against stereotypes is complemented by recent research which indicates that the most effective advertising for many products is realism (Courtney and Whipple 1978, Whipple and Courtney, 1980).

METHOD

Six issues of *The New York Times Magazine* were selected from 1983: January 9 and 23, February 13 and 20, March 20 and 27. A random number system was not used since occasional issues of the magazine are quite untypical (one had a 14 page Ralph Lauren spread; another had a children's clothing special, etc.). Only full page advertisements which prominently displayed living people were used. Thus background or shadowy figures, cartoon characters and drawings, multiple and tiny figures were all omitted; so were insignificant fragments of people, e.g. a foot or a hand, but not heads.

Product associations and the gender-directions of the advertisements are also considered.

There were a total of 183 full-page advertisements in these six issues for 150 products; of these 72 advertisements included pictures of people which met the criteria for analysis. Five of these were duplicates. 32 advertisements portrayed women, 25 presented men, 12 showed couples and three were miscellaneous: a mixed group of children, a mixed group of adults and a mother and her son....

ANALYSIS

The analysis proceeds through various themes; we discuss first youth, beauty and identity; then products and gender, work and activity, body language and expression, and couples.

Women are, without exception, portrayed as young and beautiful; and they usually look wealthy. The men, in contrast are by no means all young; they are not all beautiful; and they do not all look wealthy; one is a cowboy and another a ground mechanic.

The first and most general message of the advertisements is that youth and beauty are essential for women but not for men. The images of themselves and of their sex that men and women see reflected in the pages of *The New York Times Magazine* present different physical realities or options for men and women. Men are still men when they are old and ugly; but women are not still women. Ugly, old women do not exist in *The New York Times Magazine*. The implication is that they do not exist. The identity of most men is therefore affirmed and confirmed, including the old and ugly. The identity of many or most women is denied by such advertising. The image of men in the ads is (relatively) realistic. The image of women is a gross distortion of reality.

These conclusions are probably not perceived immediately and consciously by all readers of the magazine. Nonetheless, the point that seems to be important is that when, and if, the media: T.V., magazines, radio, newspapers, bill-boards etc. reflect the same equation, that *women = young and beautiful*, then in the long-run the not-so-young and the not-so-beautiful must question their identity: their femininity and their worth. All this had been said before, but it still needs to be said that the cumulative impact of such advertising may be a problem.

The New York Times Magazine is only one tiny input into the formulation of this equation. Nonetheless it is this input and its significance which we are considering.

The point should not be over-stated however. Many of the men portrayed in the ads, particularly those in the clothing ads (48% of the male total) are extremely attractive, although tastes will differ. But some are not.

DRESS, BEAUTY AND PRODUCTS

The emphasis on beauty for women has essentially three dimensions. The beauty of the face, which we have already considered; the beauty of the body, and the beauty of the dress. The first is the most important, but the state of dress or undress and body-display are also important. However, the genders are presented quite differently with respect to dress.

Men are portrayed as fully dressed in all 36 advertisements in which the body and dress can be seen. Women, however, are often portrayed in a state of semi-undress or with considerable body-display — in swim suits, bra and panties, or see-through clothing. The female body is displayed, to a greater or lesser degree, in about one-quarter of the ads where the body is visible. Hence the equation is made: *woman = body.*

This body-consciousness and body-display, typified by Maidenform Bra ads, reflects, recreates, or affirms the greater role of the body in social life for women rather than for men. However, whether this is a statement of the obvious or a sexist assertion that "biology is destiny" is a political controversy that cannot be resolved here. Perhaps, as Fisher (1973) has asserted, women are more conscious of, and at home in, their bodies than men are. Nonetheless the question remains: since both men and women wear swim-suits and pants why are not men's bodies displayed in similar style? Suffice it to state here that genders are presented quite differently in the matters of body and dress. The female body is "advertised" far more blatantly than the male.

This conclusion is reinforced when we consider the product-associations of gender. The data is presented in Table 1, and the immediate interpretations of the data indicated that sex roles are portrayed in traditional stereotypes. First, all the beauty product advertisements are portrayed by women: only four it is true, but an equation that *beauty = woman* is made. Secondly, 72 percent of the ads featuring women (excluding those in couples or mixed groups) are for clothes, often body-displaying clothes, compared to only 48 percent of the ads featuring men. Thus women are portrayed as clothes-horses much more frequently than men. Perhaps they are generally

Table I   PRODUCTS AND GENDER

Products	Male		Female		Both	Total
	N	%	N	%	N	N
Dress	12	48	23	72	8	43
Beauty	0	0	4	13	0	4
Other	13	52	5	16	7	25
	25	100	32	100	15	72

more clothes conscious than men, and more beauty conscious. Nonetheless, that 85 percent of the ads featuring women are for clothes and beauty products is quite stereotypical.

There is more to women than clothes and beauty products — but you could not tell that from the ads in *The New York Times Magazine*. The oft-cited visitors from Mars would receive extremely odd impressions of both male and female gender roles and physiques if they perused these ads; but their impressions would be particularly erroneous with respect to women. After all, women do work too.

Other than clothes and make-up, women only advertise cigarettes, Jaguars, Martini and Rossi and Puerto Rico (2). Men, on the other hand, advertise Saab, Hanover Trust, Amstel Beer (2), T.W.A., luxury apartments, Campbell's Soup, cigarettes (5) and IBM computers. Thus although men are featured less often, they are associated with more spheres of life than women are. The message of the magazine is that it is still very much a man's world, with the women as decorative adjuncts. Men are principally associated with a wide range of products; women are almost exclusively associated with physical appearance.

WORK AND ACTIVITY

In this magazine, man's role is to work and to be physically active. Woman's role is not. A woman just has to *be*: to be young and beautiful. There is a clear distinction between men as active, and women as passive; men as doing and women as being. Aristotle would have been proud of *The New York Times*. The data is presented in Table 2.

Most men (60%) are portrayed as working or as physically active in one way or another. They are riding the range (Marlboro), discussing storm-searching or taxes, being proud of their computer or a new model of the architect's plans. One group is having fun on a trampoline, another is off to play cricket (with one beauty wearing a tie and braces!).

Perhaps most interesting of all is that three of the men have names. None of the women do. If a name is a symbol of existence, the logic is clear. Roger

Table 2	ACTIVITY AND GENDER				
		Men		Women	
		N	%	N	%
Active		15	60	3	9
Passive		10	40	29	91
Total		25	100	32	100

Staubach the football great, Jack Mulqueen, the fashion designer, and the Rolls Royce driving owner of luxury Manhattan condominium apartments are all indentified by name. Men seem to be more likely to be "real people" than women are.

Jack Mulqueen's advertisement is particularly curious. The picture features two people, one male and one female. The caption is "I'm Jack Mulqueen." The moral is obvious: the woman does not exist. She has no name.

Most women (91%) are portrayed as neither working nor as physically active. They are doing nothing! Only three advertisements are against this surely insulting portrayal. Two are the same: a hospital worker, who is actually named but almost invisible; the third woman is a scantily clad dancer.

The fact that over 50 percent of adult women in the U.S.A. work in the labor force, and constitute over one-third of the labor force is almost completely ignored. Only two of these 32 female advertisements display working and it is the same person both times. In this respect the advertising stereotype has not changed since the Courtney and Lockerety study of eight magazines in 1970; furthermore, the message conveyed by *The New York Times Magazine* is no different from that conveyed by television, according to the U.S. Commission on Civil Rights (1979).

FACIAL EXPRESSION AND BODY LANGUAGE

Most of the men and the women in the ads have relatively expressionless faces: they look normal, neutral or blank, particularly those advertising clothes or make-up. A significant minority of both sexes look friendly, happy or triumphant and they are smiling. (This is particularly true of the couples: half of them are smiling and happy; the rest may be happy but they are not smiling).

However, a number of the ads are interesting from the point of view of sex-roles. Women seemed to be portrayed, occasionally, in particularly bizarre poses with very odd expressions. There is one lady in red leather with wild eyes and an aggressive pose who looks like she walked through a plate glass window; one is upside down; and a third is in red with red boxing gloves in a most odd pose, with a strange expression and in a vacuum. Yet another is poking a silver branch at an empty bird cage, facing the other way and standing on tip-toe (2). Very surrealistic. A fifth is in white in the dark with shades on, standing on one leg and flying a kite from a ball of wool through a window suspended in mid-air! Not to mention the two Maidenform ads and a cheesecake, glossy pink bra and panties ad.

Compared to these ladies the men seem like regular guys. Only one man is looking at all tough, but his clothes are not.

Thus over a quarter (28%) of the female ads display women as somehow not normal: extremely aggressive, crazy, exposing themselves in public or, in a word, upside-down.

It is a little difficult to interpret this. A charitable interpretation might suggest that female gender-directed ads are successful if they "sell" individuality and occasionally unusual, abnormal behavior; another interpretation might be that the ads merely recognize that women have greater freedom of emotional expression than men in this society. A less charitable view would be that this pattern of depicting women as abnormal in a *negative* way (*extreme* aggression, public semi-flashing etc.) is simply oppressive. Whichever interpretation is accepted, or some other, I hope my descriptions have conveyed the bizarre nature of some of the female ads; nonetheless, the pictures themselves are the best guides.

COUPLES

12 ads portray couples and most seem to be relatively egalitarian in the roles portrayed, in contrast to the single-gender ads. However, some of the ads are difficult to classify. For instance, in one ad a man leans back into a woman, in another the woman leans back into the man; in a third the woman leans away from a man who is leaning towards her, but in a fourth, the woman leans towards the man. Whatever there may be of dominance or subordination, affiliation or independence, seems evenly balanced.

However, three advertisements smack faintly of male dominance. In an ad for More cigarettes, a man offers a light to a lady who is in what Goffman describes as an affiliative pose: unevenly balanced, head canted, hip-slung and smiling with the man saying "It's More You. It's long. It's slim. It's elegant." In another a smiling woman squats beside a reclining man and feeds him a croissant. In a third, the man leads the woman by the hand. Never does a woman lead a man; she merely feeds him.

CONCLUSIONS

The most important conclusion from this study is that genders are presented not only quite differently by *The New York Times Magazine* ads, but also, especially for women, stereotypically. The more specific conclusions are as follows:

1. The women portrayed are, without a single exception, young and attractive and sometimes extremely beautiful. The men, however, range widely both in physical attractiveness and in age. The significance of this has been discussed earlier.

2. All the men in the 36 ads which feature men are fully dressed. However,

about one-quarter of the ads featuring women portray them in varying degrees of undress. Women are thus portrayed as body objects and, to a degree, as sex objects: provocative and erotic.

3. 72 percent of the ads featuring women only advertise dress; and another 13 percent advertise beauty products. Thus women are presented 85 percent oriented towards dress and beauty.

4. Beauty is presented as a woman's domain. 100 percent of the ads for beauty products depict only females. Dress is also presented as predominantly a woman's domain since 53 percent of the ads portray only women while a mere 30 percent depict only men. (The rest depict both.)

5. Although the magazine depicts 28 percent more ads featuring women than men, men are associated with more than three times the number of products. The message is that it is a man's world.

6. 60 percent of the ads featuring men depict them as workers or as physically active or as both. Only 9 percent of the ads depict women as such. Thus 91 percent of the ads portray women as doing nothing: as passive but beautiful.

7. Men are far more likely to be named. 12 percent of men are named compared to, effectively, none of the women.

8. Women are much more likely to be portrayed in bizarre positions or with strange expressions on their faces. They are often portrayed as abnormal.

9. Couples are more likely to be portrayed in less stereotypical ways; but nonetheless there is evidence of male dominance or female body exposure in 42 percent of these ads.

However, some of the significant conclusions do not relate to the presentation of gender, but to the presentation of age and race. The middle-aged and old are almost totally excluded from *The New York Times Magazine*. Only seven people in six ads look as though they are over 40 and all are male.

Even more significant is the absence of blacks. Of roughly 100 individuals portrayed in 72 ads, only two blacks and one Asian are shown — and all three are children. Yet blacks constitute about 15 percent of the total population of the United States and an even larger proportion of New York. This underrepresentation or exclusion might be considered disgraceful. Blacks and other minorities do not exist for this magazine. They are invisible. The title of Ralph Ellison's novel, *Invisible Man*, seems to be as valid now as when it was first published in 1947.

To label the structure of the *New York Times Magazine* as both sexist and racist might be dramatic and convenient, but it would be facile. The *Times* is one of the most prestigious and liberal newspapers in the world. Indeed, ironically, *The Times Magazine* itself covered Friedan's assertions that T.V. commercials insult women, back in 1972 (Hennessee and Nicholson, 1972). Yet in all these ads there are probably not two that most people would find offensive or insulting — but the pattern of ads is surely a different matter.

Labelling is easy. But perhaps the responsibility for change lies not only with the advertising editors of the Magazine and with the companies that advertise, but also and perhaps primarily with ourselves, who seem to respond to these patterns. It may not be true that the public gets the advertisements it likes; but it may be true that it gets the ads that work, and that it gets the ads that it does not protest about.

BIBLIOGRAPHY

Canadian Advertising Advisory Board, *Women and Advertising: Today's Message — Yesterday's Images?* Toronto, 1977.

Canadian Radio-Television and Telecommunication Commission, *Images of Women*, Ottawa: 1982. Cat. No. BC 92–261982.

Courtney, Alice E. and Sarah Wernick Lockeretz, "A Woman's Place: An Analysis of the Roles of Portrayed by Women in Magazine Advertisements," *Journal of Marketing Research*, Vol. VIII. Feb. 1971: 92–5.

Courtney, Alice E. and Thomas W. Whipple, *Sex Stereotyping in Advertising: An Annotated Bibliography*. Cambridge: Market Science Institute, 1980.

Courtney, Alice E. and Thomas W. Whipple, *Canadian Perspectives on Sex Stereotyping in Advertizing*. Ottawa: Advisory Council on the Status of Women, 1978.

Ellison, Ralph, *Invisible Man*, New York: Random House, 1947.

Fisher, Seymour, *Body Consciousness*, Englewood Cliffs, N.J.: Prentice-Hall, 1973.

Friedan, Betty, *The Feminine Mystique*, New York: Dell, 1963.

Gazette, June 16, 1983.

Goffman, Erving, *Gender Advertisements*, London: Macmillan, 1979.

Henry, Jules, *Culture against Man*, New York: Vintage, 1963.

National Advertising Review Board, *Advertising and Women*, New York, 1975.

Ontario Status of Women, *About Face. Towards a Positive Image of Women in Advertising*. Toronto, 1975.

Sexton, Donald E. and Phyllis Haberman, "Women in Magazine Advertisements," *Journal of Advertising Research*, Vol. 14 no. 4, Aug. 1974: 41–46.

U.S. Commission on Civil Rights, *Window Dressing on the Set: An Update*. Washington: 1929. CRI: 2 W72.

Venkatesan, M. and Losco, Jean, "Women in Magazine Ads: 1959–71," *Journal of Advertising Research*, Vol. 15 no. 5, Oct. 1975: 49–54.

Whipple, Thomas W. and Alice E. Courtney, "How to Portray Women in TV Commercials," *Journal of Advertising Research*, Vol. 20 no. 2, April 1980: 53–59.

47   THE POWER OF PACKAGING*
EDWIN E. EWRY

We seldom think about it, but a very high percentage of everything we buy comes in packages. Consider a typical supermarket; it has something like 17,000 products on the shelves, competing for our attention. In many cases, at the point of purchase, packaging makes a difference. That's why manufacturers spend a great deal of money on packaging in an attempt to persuade a shopper to try their product rather than someone else's.

Packaging is no longer just a sophisticated art form; it has been elevated to a science. Decisions about packaging design are often the results of research. There are devices that track (and record) how people look at objects — products, signs, shelf environments. These techniques follow the involuntary movement of the retina as it scans what the eye is observing. In addition, researchers conduct panel discussions to determine what consumers feel about various package designs.

There is a folk saying that goes, "There is no accounting for human taste." While designers cannot ensure that every package will appeal to every consumer, their expertise along with the use of research help create packaging that will grab the attention of shoppers in the competitive retail environment.

The art of packaging involves translating these research findings into the most effective and provocative package. To be successful, package designers along with marketers, must understand the consumer — the feelings elicited by certain colors, the expectations generated by certain product categories and the lure of various packages, their structures and graphics.

We may define packaging, which remains the same over a long period of time, to be an example of "permanent media" while advertising is a medium that can change frequently. Both complement each other in achieving an overall marketing plan.

Since packaging can generate lasting impressions of a product through color, logos, photographs, illustrations and symbols, it serves as an efficient strategic marketing tool, molding a consumer's perception of that product. On the other hand, advertising provides tactical support for the development of product identity.

This essay is written by Edwin E. Ewry, an executive of S&O Consultants, a leading San Francisco-based marketing and design firm that specializes in packaging and corporate and retail identity. This account affords you a first-hand, inside look at the fascinating world of packaging.

SUPERMARKETS — THE BATTLEGROUND

One brand of chunky, low-salt, sugar-free cereal may be more nutritious than another brand, but does it stand a chance on the supermarket shelf, where the choices are endless? A typical supermarket can house as many as 17,000 products with new ones coming on board weekly. In fact, 1986 welcomed more than 8,000 new products.

New stores are contributing some additional shelf space, but their growth is far slower than the dramatic increase in products filling the shelves every year. This has helped make the supermarket one of the most competitive environments in the world.

Unlike advertising that broadcasts different commercials one at a time on radio or television, packages vie for attention simultaneously, making the supermarket shelf a battleground for consumer attention and dollars.

Advertising can be considered a transitory and ever-changing form of communication, but packaging is more permanent. Along with brand names and logos, it identifies a product and remains the same over a long period of time.

To successfully compete in the supermarket environment, markets must maximize the use of all of the resources at their disposal. Packaging is one of those marketing tools that can help the manufacturer regain some control over the retail environment. In addition, as a low-cost investment that keeps working, packaging can be highly effective. For some marketers, whose product volume cannot support a large advertising or promotional budget, well-designed packaging can compensate for that disadvantage.

In creating packaging, we combine marketing, design, and research disciplines to more effectively position companies and their products and services in today's competitive marketplace. Besides new product design and packaging, we use our expertise in the areas of corporate and retail identity, brand and corporate name development and facility design.

While well-designed packaging cannot assure that consumers will pick an item off the shelf, it can certainly maximize the possibility. Since over 60 percent of all supermarket purchases are not planned in advance, impulsive shoppers can be swayed by those products that immediately gain their attention.

Some consumers, however, have already decided what they want to buy; advertising and sales promotion have helped shape that predisposition. But once these shoppers are inside a store and are assaulted by a tremendous amount of information, they may be strongly influenced by what they see — especially when you consider that they see an average of eight products every second.

In addition, if packages can help consumers assimilate information quickly by clearly spelling out their brands' unique selling points ("low-fat," "caffeine-free"), choices become even easier.

Having emphasized the importance of packaging as a strategic marketing tool, we will examine some packaging techniques used by marketers in various categories. The power of packaging will soon be evident as we explore how it is capable of developing a presence for a product on the shelf.

ENTICING THE INDECISIVE

Since impulse categories like snacks, ice cream and cookies generate a high degree of excitement and involvement, shoppers tend to walk away with more items than they originally intended. The crucial moment is at the point-of-purchase. This presents a real challenge to marketers who must ensure that their products stand out on the shelf.

Packaging for impulse categories often incorporates devices that create high appetite appeal to entice consumers. Cookies generally use clear wrappers, which show the appetizing product but risk exposing broken ones, or covered bags, whose visuals of chunky chocolate chips or flaky coconut convey the appeal of the product. A mouthwatering photo or illustration can turn an indecisive shopper into a hungry snacker.

Snack foods take advantage of other packaging techniques that create appetite appeal — ingredient or flavor call-outs such as "salt-free" or "Jalapeno pepper" or foil wrapping — especially to distinguish specialty snacks from basic ones, like a standard bag of potato chips. Colorful and playful graphics also contribute to appetite appeal.

The frozen entree section, one of the fastest growing food categories, also relies on appetite appeal to attract consumers. In this leading-edge category, where conventions have not yet been established, marketers have an opportunity to be innovative. The bland TV dinner pictured on the cartons of yesteryear has been replaced by sophisticated packaging with upscale graphics and high-quality food photography. The frozen dinner is no longer perceived as just a convenience food; consumers are unwilling to trade off ease-of-preparation for quality. The new packaging reflects this change by transforming frozen entrees into home-cooked or restaurant meal substitutes.

BILLBOARDING LEAVES THE HIGHWAY

An in-store billboard — rows and rows of packaged goods with multiple facings whose large, clear product identification is achieved through color, graphics, and brand names — is another effective packaging method which helps marketers establish dominance in a supermarket category.

Billboarding is a great way to display a product in the store. It is no accident that four six-packs of red and white Miller beer all showcase the

Packaging for Green Giant foods. Courtesy of S&O Consultants

brand name in large letters that leap out at the consumer, or that a detergent carves out a large block in the section with its bright colors. The technique is just one of the ways to increase product visibility, an important component of packaging.

Contrast detergents to the small bottles of medicine on the shelf. Packages of aspirin and pain relievers demand that the consumer get quite close to the product. In this case, visibility is not as important; consumers want to study analgesic labels for ingredients and their capabilities and feel confidence in the safety of the product. On the other hand, detergents shout out their message, "extra-duty cleansing power."

Visibility is so key to a package's effectiveness that smart marketers can use packaging to improve shelf impact, if only by 5 or 10 percent, to gain an edge over the competition. Modifications in colors and logos can be as effective as dramatic changes in an entire graphic identity.

Through the use of color, we created a billboard effect for the Green Giant line of frozen vegetables. By designing a "sea of green," we developed a strong section look for Green Giant in the frozen food case. Green has become proprietary for the Green Giant vegetable line whose previous packaging was dominated by white. Later, I will discuss this particular packaging project more in-depth to illustrate the planning, creativity, and research that contributed to its success.

USING THE TRIED-AND-TRUE

Many marketers rely on tried-and-true packaging conventions, especially in established categories. For instance, using certain colors can differentiate flavors, identify entire product categories or create a proprietary identity for a product. As I mentioned before, color can also create appetite appeal and be instrumental in carving out an entire section for a package.

In the beverage category, green often indicates lemon-lime while red is for cherry. And of course, color — fluorescent, day-glo colors conveying cleansing power — have always dominated the detergent category. You can spot these colorful packages from the end of the aisle. Pine cleaners are generally green, bleaches white, and fabric softeners, pastel.

Being aware of color equities for certain categories and specific products can prove successful for marketers. When we were asked to redesign the packaging for Old El Paso food products, we retained the equity of the predominant yellow, along with red, which is strongly associated with the spicy cuisines of Mexico.

Colgate developed a niche in the toothpaste category by selecting red, an unusual color in the predominantly white section. Red has definitely become proprietary for the product. And Campbell's has gained so much equity with its red and white cans that there has been no reason to change its basic packaging over the years.

Structural conventions also guide many marketers. Salt in a cylindrical package and bread in a bag meet consumer expectations. When did you last see cleanser in a glass container, or bread in a box? While some marketers have been successful and set new trends with wine in cartons, juice in aseptic boxes, and coffee in streamlined brick packs, those who dare to break out of the mold run the risk of confusing consumers.

IMPRESSING FOR IMPACT

Finally, marketers must consider each and every presentation mode for a product at retail — a single unit on the shelf or a mass display — in determining how a package is designed. Each mode creates a different perceptual context for the consumer. For example, successful beer marketers utilize design concepts that can effectively display the product as a single can perceived at a close distance, in six-packs and in multiple case stackings attracting attention down the aisle.

In some cases, however, a package that works well in developing a section look may be unmemorable when standing alone, or a striking single unit may not make a strong mass impression.

We designed the packaging for Kraft's processed and natural lines of cheese, which creates an effective mass display in the cheese section. It consistently uses the Kraft brand name and hexagon logo, along with a uniform nomenclature system, color-coding for flavors, and a major blue banding system that unify each line. The result is unmistakably Kraft — and packages that can be identified immediately by consumers.

Keeping some of these techniques in mind, I am going to explore two packaging solutions developed by my company.

SEA OF GREEN

Pillsbury's Green Giant line of frozen vegetables suffered from a lack of presence in the section. Stouffer's concentrated red packaging dominated the category, making it necessary for Green Giant to strengthen its identity by visually organizing and unifying the product line and creating impact in the freezer case.

Our research sister company conducted focus group sessions in San Francisco, New York and Chicago to determine consumer reactions to packaging in the frozen vegetable category and to develop appropriate positioning for Green Giant.

The group discussions concentrated on purchasing patterns, imagery perceptions of Green Giant and competitive brands, Green Giant's current packaging and alternative label designs. The results indicated that the color green would help establish strong brand recognition. In addition, it pointed out the need for clean, uncluttered graphics and product photography to communicate taste appeal.

Besides qualitative focus groups, our research arm has developed a number of standardized research-based products that evaluate packaging. For example, ValiGraphics is a cluster of research methodologies that assess the performance of packaging graphics. It combines the use of the tachistoscope (T-scope), eye-tracking, focus groups, top-of-mind recall and other techniques.

We have also created our Design Visibility Lab (DVL). Its six different instruments objectively measure distinctive dimensions of visual perception, concentrating on the physiological ability of the human eye to see a package under various conditions. The DVL evaluates packaging structures, performance and graphics — size, color and legibility — on the competitive retail shelf.

Armed with the research results on Green Giant, we developed design objectives for the frozen vegetable line — contemporary, uncluttered graphics and photography to convey good taste; consistent use of the Green Giant symbol for strong brand identity; the use of green as a proprietary color; and a unified presentation of product nomenclature.

The prominent use of green on the new package creates a "sea of green" in the freezer case for Green Giant. To visually organize the line of products, the package's left-hand side displays the Green Giant symbol and nomenclature. The right-hand side highlights the product with high-quality photo vignettes of vegetable dishes.

In addition, we created a new shape to hold the formerly freestanding symbol and logotype. It is consistently displayed in the upper left hand corner of the package.

The new packaging system carves out a visually dominant Green Giant section in the freezer case and effectively competes in the market-place. When it was first introduced, sales for the product line increased significantly.

Wonder Egg

The Fazer Wonder Egg presents another interesting case history. It is a specialty candy item — a natural, emptied chicken egg shell filled with high-quality European chocolate — and is a traditional Eastertime treat manufactured and sold in Finland.

Realizing the potential of the American market, which has a high per capita of chocolate consumption, Fazer chose it as a suitable expansion market for its product.

The problem with the egg in the European market was its tissue paper wrapper that did not provide protection from breakage nor a medium for effective graphics. In addition, the paper made it difficult to determine what was inside.

We assumed the responsibility for developing a provocative and utilitarian communications design package for the candy, including point-of-purchase materials, that would combine visibility with protection, communicate a high-quality product and appeal to children, the product users.

The result is a package that accomplishes all of the mentioned objectives. The egg is packaged in a clear plastic thermoformed clamshell that fits into a rectangular box with an oval cut-out. It is suspended in the box window, providing high visibility. The double packaging, common to the cosmetic industry, is unique for candy.

The outer chocolate brown box with hot-stamped gold foil print conveys richness and high quality. Imported European tradition is emphasized to convey a product that may be new to the American market but has a history in the European market. Lavender graphic details emphasize the Eastertime theme.

Although the packaging communicates a premium product, it retains elements appealing to children: a colorful Easter basket; simple, rendered printing for "Wonder Egg"; and information on what the product is and how to use it.

We were also responsible for naming the product "Wonder Egg" — a name that appeals to children, connotes a sense of mystery, and is simple to pronounce.

After an introduction of less than 100,000 into the test market, Wonder Egg proved so successful that sales the following year numbered over one

452

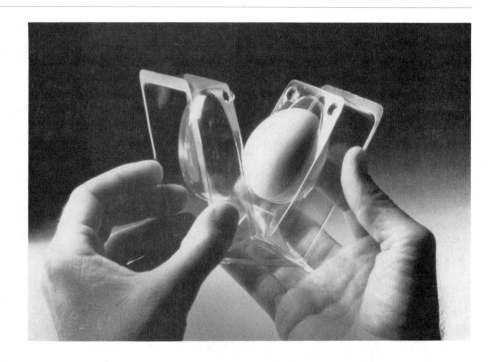

Packaging of Fazer Wonder Egg. Courtesy of S&O Consultants

million. The sales in the United States alone in the second year doubled Fazer's previous worldwide volume for Wonder Egg.

As these and other case histories indicate, packaging serves as a powerful marketing tool, effectively positioning a product on the shelf. It helps consumers assimilate product information more quickly for shopping convenience; creates appetite appeal for products; carves out a section through billboarding; develops a strong brand identity; and establishes dominance in the market category. It is one more resource marketers can use to gain control over the supermarket shelf — one of the most competitive sales environments in the world. Effective packaging can put products on the shelf and can ensure that they end up in the shopping cart.

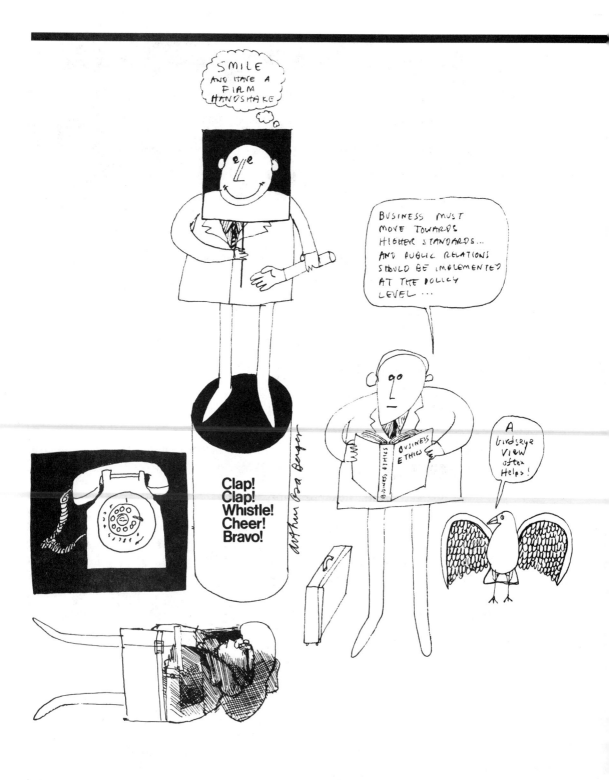

PUBLIC RELATIONS

Public relations has a mixed image; it has the positive, creative aspects to it that we find associated with advertising (without the hucksterism). But it also often seems manipulative and lacking in class — when we think of Hollywood publicity agents, for example. What exactly is public relations? What precisely do people in the field do? Let's consider some of the most important elements of public relations.

First, it is connected with communications. Public relations involves corporations or other entities communicating with "the public" in any one of a variety of different ways. It is unlike advertising in that generally speaking public relations does not involve purchasing airtime for commercials or space in print media for advertisements. (This is not always the case, however, since there is "institutional" advertising, which may be seen as a public relations function.)

What public relations sells, unlike advertising, is an organization's point of view on something, plus its prestige and good name. On any given issue of political or social importance, there are generally a number of different organizations that are trying to get their views known and accepted. It is the public relations experts who have the task of communicating these views.

A second aspect of public relations involves its role in management and corporate policy making. At times public relations experts are called in when an organization faces some kind of a problem or crisis and something has to be done about "damage control." It is much better to have public relations counsel at the policy level to avoid such situations. In this sense, public relations doesn't involve the manipulation of public opinion but, instead, the shaping of institution policy to avoid crises and disasters. The best situation is to have no need for public relations assuming a crisis management role.

Crisis management is the worst-case scenario for corporate public relations executives. Most of their time is spent dealing with the various publics and groups that exist — including, for example, employees, trade organizations, the government, stockholders (in the case of corporations), and the media. Thus, a public relations department of a corporation would be involved in such diverse tasks as publishing employee newspapers or house organs, producing annual reports, and writing promotional materials and news releases for the press.

The influence of this material on the press is the subject of some controversy. It has been estimated that as much as half of the editorial content of some media comes from public relations releases. It is much cheaper for editors to use material written by someone else, of course, and in many small publications a number of the stories come from public relations departments. These stories represent a particular point of view and it is difficult to describe them as news rather than publicity, though they may have news value and human interest appeal. Is it right for editors to use this material as such?

One of the major issues in the field of public relations involves the matter of ethics. The code of professional standards of the Public Relations Society of America says that public relations practitioners should be truthful at all times. But what does this mean? In order to protect their companies, public relations experts have often resorted to telling half-truths and misleading people, to covering things up and to actual lying — which explains why the industry ranks sixth in terms of occupations having high admission rates to mental institutions.

There is the matter of the general ethical values of *some* public relations consultants. In a sense they are "hired guns," willing to put their expertise to use for anyone who can pay — without concern for anything but their fees. This sensibility has caused problems for the industry and tarnished its image and credibility, even though most practitioners of public relations are ethical and responsible. Ironically, public relations itself has an "image" problem.

Public relations is a large and complex industry; it encompasses everything from press agentry to lobbying, from fund-raising to conducting opinion research, from giving gifts to selling advice. It is a vital tool of many different kinds of institutions and organizations that all struggle to make their voices heard. Often it is important for the public welfare that these voices are heard.

At its best, it is a responsible instrument that shapes the policies of organizations in constructive ways; at its worst, it is a tool used to manipulate public opinion for people or organizations with severe image problems...many of whom deserve the images they have.

48 MOVING TOWARD HIGHER STANDARDS FOR AMERICAN BUSINESS *

JOHN A. KOTEN

Arthur W. Page was the first corporate vice president for public relations in America. He was hired by AT&T in 1927 and built the largest and one of the best public relations organizations in the country. Page formulated six principles of corporate behavior that, our author suggests, have stood the test of time and that all public relations practitioners should keep in mind.

These six principles are:

1. Be attentive to the public.
2. Be honest.
3. Have the company do, not tell.
4. Manage for tomorrow.
5. Help the company recognize that the public controls the corporate fate.
6. Interject the best of personal character into the corporate character.

Page did not see public relations as a matter of manipulating public opinion by using various ploys and gimmicks. Corporations got good press and public esteem by doing good things (and letting people know about what they did).

The author of this article, John Koten, also has some ideas about what kind of education people should have to best prepare them for work in public relations. He argues that people should have a broad liberal arts education, and know something about politics, economics, literature, and history. The list might be extended, I would add, to areas such as the arts, psychology, and philosophy.

This is because people who work in public relations should not be seen as mere technicians, who know how to write news releases or video scripts. Public relations, from Page's perspective, is something much more elevated than this — it involves policy making, ethics, and is really a management function.

The various schools and departments of public relations are turning out fifteen candidates for every job in public relations, so the competition is intense. Obviously, most of the people who graduate with public relations degrees cannot find jobs in the field. If these people have not been educated broadly but narrowly "trained" instead, they will be doubly deprived — not suited for work in public relations (as Koten sees things) or many other jobs, and, it might be argued, not suited for life.

* Reprinted with permission of *The Public Relations Review*, Fall 1986.

Arthur W. Page was hired by AT&T in 1927 as America's first corporate vice president of public relations. Management had come to realize that since it conducted a public business, the public should be told what it was doing.

Page immediately set about to see that both the public and employees knew not only what was happening in the business, but what its policies were as well. This doesn't sound terribly revolutionary today, but in the '20s it was new. In the process of informing his constituents, Page built the largest corporate public relations organization in the country, one that many also considered to be the finest.

Page also introduced a new idea when it came to setting goals for business. He considered a statement made to the public on behalf of the company a commitment, one the company absolutely had to meet if it was to operate with integrity and credibility. Said another way, the philosophy he advocated was, "Be sure our deeds match our words" — or vice versa.

Such a commitment could be made by a corporation, he reasoned, in a speech, news release, advertisement or other such public manner. The important thing was to make sure employees also were aware of what those utterances were.

It has been almost sixty years since Page set that standard for the public relations profession; a standard which, in effect, required higher standards for all businesses. In the years since, public relations professionals have been sensitive to their need to match deeds and words, but often the "doing" and "telling" sides of business operate independently. The very words "public relations" have come to be more narrowly defined. Too frequently, they mean publicity and razzle-dazzle, meanings inconsistent with the inherent, strategic role today's corporate communicators *can* and *should* play in shaping corporate behavior.

In an age where the reputation of American business suffers from alleged abuses in the defense industry, record numbers of airline crashes, and environmental disasters like Bhopal; in an age when America's corporate competitiveness is challenged in world markets; in *this* age, the corporate communicator can play a significant role in shaping and restoring American business to a pre-eminent role in our world-wide society.

Page's notion of "doing as well as telling," and five other professional standards advanced by him, are as worthy of business attention today as they were in Page's day. It falls to the communications professional — one who understands how opinion is shaped and how to shape it — to plant Page's six standards of behavior in the corporate realm, and to nourish them on behalf of the profession and American business.

THE PAGE STANDARDS

Page's six standards for public relations management and corporate management are:

Cover of annual report. Reprinted by permission of Wells Fargo & Company. Cover design by Image Arts of San Francisco.

1. Be attentive to the public. As two-way communicators, communications professionals must be sensitive to what the public wants and needs, and tell their companies so they can respond. At the same time, they must communicate the company's character to the public, in order to gain the freedom the company needs to serve effectively.

   The payoff of this idea can be illustrated by a story about Illinois Bell.

   Illinois Bell was having some service problems in the mid-1960s in Chicago. There was dissension within the company about how these problems should be handled.

   The public relations vice president, Hale Nelson, believed in being responsive to the public interest. Concerned about deteriorating public opinion and its ultimate effect on the prices the company charged, Nelson took the bull by the horns and launched a series of newspaper ads announcing, "If *you've* got a problem with your phone service, *we've* got a problem — and we'll fix it in 24 hours."

   The initial reaction in retrospect was not surprising — the public was pleased, but the operations people were outraged. They didn't want to be committed to handling *every* service problem within 24 hours during periods when work forces were thin and problems frequent.

   By boldly stating the performance standard publicly — in effect holding an entire company hostage to what the public wanted — public relations took the initiative.

   Today, a 24-hour response to an out-of-service call is standard operating procedure at Illinois Bell; in fact, 95 percent of our customers have their lines repaired well before those 24 hours pass. Both the public and the company are well served by this policy.

2. Be honest. Corporate communicators — and corporations — can't afford to waffle with the facts. Professional communicators subscribe to the notion that a well-informed public is a supportive one. The truth applies not only in financial communications, but in employee communications, in press releases, in advertising, in dealings with community groups — without exception, in all communications activities.

   If they make a mistake, professional communicators admit it. Such candor is sure to win friends and gain respect. The on-going saga of Coca-Cola — "genuine," "new," "classic," or whatever it's called — is a case in point.

   By adjusting to the public's preference, and admitting it had made a mistake and then doing something about it, Coca-Cola silenced Pepsi's premature trumpeting of victory — and wound up gaining more shelf space than before, a key factor in increasing volume in the soft drink industry. The war is not over, but for the moment public sentiment, however grudging, is on the side of Coke.

3. Ensure that the company does, instead of simply tells. Page was fond of pointing out that the public's perception of an organization is based 90 percent on what the organization does, and 10 percent on what it says.

Johnson & Johnson's handling of the Tylenol poisonings, in 1982 and again in 1986, provides a good example in support of his point.

In the 1982 poisonings, Johnson & Johnson recalled their product even as the media announced the company was blameless. Six weeks later, they reintroduced Tylenol — this time in triple safety-sealed, tamper-resistant packaging.

Largely because Johnson & Johnson *demonstrated* a sense of responsibility to its customers, Tylenol recaptured 70 percent of its market just 20 weeks after the initial tragedy. Public relations teams played a key role in the comeback, from interviews and press conferences to market research and strategic planning.

This year, Johnson & Johnson again *demonstrated* its sense of customer responsibility after a poisoning death in New York state. This time, the company permanently stopped production of its over-the-counter capsule medications because, according to Chairman James E. Burke, "We feel the company can no longer guarantee the safety of these capsules."

The company even offered to replace its capsules for "caplets" at no charge — a marketing activity that reinforces the company's stated concerns for earning customer trust. Johnson & Johnson did some real "doing" in support of telling their message, and the results speak for themselves.

4. Manage for tomorrow. One way of looking to the future is being demonstrated by several of the nation's leading computer manufacturers. AT&T is donating $32 million worth of computers to forty-six college campuses. IBM and Apple similarly have given terminals and software to educational institutions. Brown University in Rhode Island built a $1.5 million computer science laboratory based on contributions from companies such as IBM, Xerox and Gould.

The benefits from this example of managing for tomorrow are shared by everyone involved. Students gain the skills they need to be successful in the information age. Companies gain computer-literate employees for tomorrow, and have a "hands-on" testbed for their products today. Most of all, such long-range planning creates a user-friendly customer base — people who will insist on having the product because they learned skills on it, or because they are familiar with its benefits.

Companies and managers who expect to be around a long time will have a different perspective from those which operate day to day. They are also the ones most likely to be here as well.

Another way to assure the future is to anticipate public reaction and eliminate practices and procedures that create difficulties — not only in the corporate communications organization, but companywide. What are the contact employees saying to customers? Have company procedures been looked at from the customer's or the public's perspective?

In addition to eliminating practices that might cause potential problems, the corporate communicator should also be satisfied that there is an adequate, carefully thought-out information plan in place in case disaster strikes. Consider how much better off NASA would be today if an adequate plan had been followed when the Challenger accident took place.

5. Help the company recognize that the public controls the corporate fate. This means manage the communicator's job as if the whole company depends on it, because it does.

Chrysler Corp. recognized this point when it requested a government-guaranteed loan, and leaned heavily on its communicators to moderate public opinion, which was overwhelmingly against government bailouts.

The company's government relations team played an obvious role. Other public relations professionals, from media relations to research, faced the tremendous challenge of maintaining the public's confidence, in this case, among customers, investors, suppliers and dealers.

When the federal government finally did approve loan guarantees of $1.2 billion, it made them conditional upon obtaining an equal amount of non-guaranteed loans from "the Chrysler family." You can imagine the public relations job necessary to pull off the price rollbacks and deferred payments to suppliers — not to mention union and employee acceptance of wage and benefit cuts. It was no accident that Lee Iacocca became a familiar figure on television screens and national magazine covers. With the help of his communications staff, who understood its value and importance, he won public support for his company.

Communications professionals also recognize that there are times when silence on an issue is equally useful to gain a long-term strategic advantage. Unfortunately, too often silence is a result of not knowing what to do, covering up or just plain failing to seize the moment.

One example, albeit extreme, of successfully using silence occurred during World War II on Ponte Vedra beach in eastern Florida. On June 17, 1942, the Germans landed a small contingent of soldiers on that American soil. They had been brought to our shores by submarine and were part of a two-point invasion (the other was near Amagansett on Long Island) whose mission was to sabotage key American industries and facilities.

Upon landing, the invaders buried a cache of munitions on the sandy beach. A few days later, the munitions were discovered by alert Coast Guardsmen.

Rather than acknowledge this incident publicly, the government wisely chose to maintain silence, not only to confuse the German high command but also to minimize any panic or confusion among Americans who already were nervous and uneasy about being in the war. It wasn't until years later that the "mission" was declassified and the public became aware of what happened. In this instance, public opinion was controlled in a way that kept public focus on the main issue, rather than allowing it to be diverted by a smaller issue.

Corporate communications in *every* case is a *management* function. No corporate strategy should be implemented without first considering the impact of that strategy on external and internal publics. The corporate communications professional is a policy-maker, *not* a publicist or solely the writer of annual reports.

6. Interject the best of personal character into the corporate character. That means being knowledgeable, patient and good-humored.

It's important communicators know and understand their business. To be effective, they should be as knowledgeable as anyone about what's happening inside and outside their company.

Corporate communicators shouldn't be regarded only as crisis-handlers, but also as crisis-preventors. For example, communicators should insist long before a potential tragedy occurs that every employee knows safe working conditions and practices are the cheapest form of insurance a company can have. (One only needs to mention the words "Union Carbide" to understand the full implications of the pro-active role a corporate communicator *should* play.)

If communicators lay the right groundwork with consistent, calm, and reasoned attention to information and contacts, corporations won't think of public relations only when the corporate ship hits turbulent waters. Instead, they'll look to communicators as leaders of the way through the rough waters *and* the calm seas, a source — prepared and able — not only to defuse crises, but to lead the company to new markets and to greater customer acceptance of products and services. The communicator's image should be one of being a pathfinder — a person who seeks the outer perimeters. It's a tall order, but a doable one.

THE POWER OF CORPORATE COMMUNICATIONS

No group in a corporation is better suited to the task of raising business standards than the communications group. Corporate communicators have the means and contacts — the power — to drive corporate behavior in response to public needs and to assure that its behavior is recognized in appropriate ways. The result of such effort is reputation in its broadest sense — achieved not by accident, but by design.

No other group can articulate the practices and policies of the company as well. As a result, corporate communicators help the policy-makers explain the company so the number of people who understand and support corporate objectives is maximized. Most importantly, they should be — and in most cases are — at the table when policy is being formulated. *That* is key to making sure corporate deeds match corporate pronouncements and vice versa.

Knowing corporate communicators help formulate policy is not enough.

There is more, much more, to do on behalf of raising standards for the profession and the corporations they serve.

By using their early-warning systems, corporate communicators can identify factors which positively (or negatively) affect their company's reputation or operations. Reaching into their information banks, they can recommend programs which enhance or support desirable trends — or reverse undesirable ones.

Conversely, they can alter public behavior and public perceptions — and they demonstrate this ability every day. Through a wide variety of means, over time communicators can alter the reputation of their companies. They can cause the public, customers, and employees to act and react.

The extent to which corporate communicators can change public behavior contributes directly to a company's growth. The extent to which communicators can improve employee morale and attitudes increases productivity — thereby keeping reasonable its costs of doing business. Both activities flow right to the bottom line: the ultimate — but not only — measure of corporate performance.

FIRST STEPS TO HIGHER STANDARDS

Corporate communicators can begin by demanding higher standards within their own organizations and departments — by insisting on factual, rather than superficial reporting. They should have a low tolerance for careless, inaccurate communications of any type.

They can insist that hyperbole be translated into common sense. There is no reason why the information coming from a corporate communications department shouldn't be accurate as a financial statement — and as valued. At the same time, because wordsmithing is among our talents, communicators can use our craft to *excite*, to *motivate*, to *dramatize* their companies and their activities in a way no financial statement can do — unless it's colored in red ink.

These are first steps on the road to higher professional standards. They carry the essence of what Page said when he laid the groundwork for the in-house corporate public relations organization.

Page believed that a corporation's performance is an expression of its character — both corporate and individual. His view of corporate character is not unlike the view of the nascent America held by the leaders who founded this country. These leaders recognized that public opinion would not support the British rulers; they in turn relied on writers like Tom Paine, who helped arouse public opinion to such an extent that ultimately a new government was formed.

Another "writer," Thomas Jefferson, synthesized the attitudes of the Colonists and produced a document, the Declaration of Independence, that clearly stated their goals and aspirations. In fact, the Declaration of

Independence contains one of the earliest references to public opinion. The opening paragraph states that "...a decent Respect for the Opinions of Mankind requires that they should declare the causes which impel them to the Separation."

The parallels are obvious between the idea that a nation must be responsive to its public, and Page's notions that a corporation must operate in the public interest. Page believed that a company must manage for the long run — must make customer satisfaction its primary goal. Such a goal, he believed, would lead to investor *and* employee satisfaction.

FOR THE FUTURE

Much of the future of our profession and of American business depends on the preparation of those who follow to carry on the Page tradition.

Education in the broadest sense is the key. Unfortunately, many educational institutions don't fully address the needs of this segment of the profession. They tend to define corporate communications — public relations — too narrowly.

Judging by the "product" corporations see as applicants, many schools concentrate exclusively on the mechanics of the craft: how to write a news release, a video script, a public service announcement; how to conduct a survey; how to talk to the media.

There's nothing wrong with teaching the mechanics — it would be wonderful if more people truly had these skills. The problem is that corporate communications is more — much more — than getting publicity, arranging stunts and putting out the company magazine. To be successful, to reach the highest management positions, communicators must have more than the basic skills. They need a good, general foundation in economics, politics, literature, history.

They need to understand the total environment in which decisions are made. They need skills that will help them identify *what* their corporations have to say. They need skills that will make them contributors to the shaping of that message, not just repeaters of the corporate line.

In other words, knowing how to type does not make a person a novelist. Knowing how to use a calculator does not make someone an investment analyst. Communicators who have the basic communications skills, but don't have a message or a vision, will never assume their rightful place in the corporate world. They will not be in a position to make the contributions to their corporations that more well-rounded persons from other disciplines will make.

Finding the right kind of people to assume such responsibilities has never been easy, but now, as the demands of business continue to grow, it is increasingly difficult. The requirements for entering our field are not as tough as those for other disciplines. Unfortunately, our educational institutions turn off many good candidates by perpetuating the myth that public relations is a field for people who get along well with others.

Each year our schools turn out "qualified" public relations graduates at a rate of about fifteen graduates for every job opening. Such a surplus leads to frustrated graduates, depressed salaries, the best people seeking other vocations. The entire career chain is affected by many schools' self-serving interest in capitalizing on a market that many young people think would be "fun" to be a part of. No wonder that CEOs too frequently turn to "outsiders" to help guide or run corporate communications.

Professionals in the field know it as one that is demanding. It takes people who understand the art of negotiating, how people think, and why they reach the conclusions they do. It takes hard work and long hours. It takes the very best of college graduates to meet today's communications needs.

It's up to today's communicators to change the perception of "public relations." One way they can succeed is by bringing higher standards to reality in their own corporations and by refusing to settle for anything less. Today's communicators must be the shapers of ideals, the keepers of the dream.

The improvement and perpetuation of the profession is self-serving, but why apologize? If done correctly, it will serve our companies, our nation, and all of society. The willingness of our profession to bring new standards of ethics and ethical behavior to the business world can enhance the reputation of all business, because the deeds will match the words.

49 ROOTS OF MODERN PUBLIC RELATIONS: THE BERNAYS DOCTRINE*

MARVIN N. OLASKY

Edward Bernays, one of the founding fathers of public relations, wrote a book in 1928 called *Propaganda*. In it he suggested that the function of public relations is to persuade people, to manipulate them, for their own benefit. A small group of people, then, shaped public opinion by means of what Bernays called "propaganda." Furthermore, this small group of people, an "invisible government," had responsibility for defending democracy.

* Marvin N. Olasky, "Roots of Modern Public Relations: The Bernays Doctrine," from *Public Relations Quarterly*, Winter, 1984, reprinted with permission.

Does this sound radical? Does this sound anti-democratic? (After all, isn't America ruled by "the people"?) Does this sound illogical? Let me put Bernays' ideas in perspective by quoting from an important textbook on American politics, Dye and Zeigler's *The Irony of Democracy*:

> Elites, not masses, govern America. In an industrial, scientific, and nuclear age, life in a democracy, just as in a totalitarian society, is shaped by a handful of men. In spite of differences in their approach to the study of power in America, scholars — political scientists and sociologists alike — agree that "the key political, economic, and social decisions are made by 'tiny minorities.'"

> An elite is the few who have power; the masses are the many who do not. Power is deciding who gets what, when, and how; it is participation in the decisions that allocate values for a society. Elites are the few who participate in the decisions that shape our lives; the masses are the many whose lives are shaped by institutions, events, and leaders of which they have little direct control…Elites are not necessarily conspiracies to oppress or exploit the masses. On the contrary, elites may be very "public regarding" and deeply concerned with the welfare of the masses.

The irony of democracy is that elites must govern if democracy (government "by the people") is to survive, our authors argue.

This is because the masses in America are "apathetic and ill-informed about politics and public policy, and they have a surprisingly weak commitment to democratic values — individual dignity, equality of opportunity, the right to dissent, freedom of speech and press, religious toleration, due process of law." Fortunately, Dye and Zeigler tell us, the masses don't lead but follow. Who do they follow? Democratically minded elites. How do these elites maintain control? By what Bernays called "propaganda."

BIBLIOGRAPHY

Edward Bernays, *Propaganda*. New York: H. Liveright, 1928.

Thomas R. Dye & L. Harmon Zeigler, *The Irony of Democracy*: An Uncommon Introduction to American Politics. 3rd Edition. North Scituate, MA: Duxbury Press, 1975.

Edward Bernays, 1928: "Intelligent men must realize that propaganda is the modern instrument by which they can fight for productive ends and help to bring order out of chaos."

Virtually every public relations practitioner, when asked to name the founder of modern public relations, will say: Ivy Lee. Textbooks love to quote the "Declaration of Principles" Lee sent to newspaper editors in 1906 when he was beginning his practice. "All our work is done in the open," Lee wrote, stressing his plan to "frankly and openly...supply to the press and public of the United States prompt and accurate information...." But how much does a goody two-shoes statement of that sort reflect the reality of public relations work then or now? In practice, Ivy Lee felt compelled to publicize distortions in a way which led Carl Sandburg to call him a "paid liar." In practice, many current practitioners do not want to lie, but they do not do all of their work "in the open," they *do* attempt to persuade rather than merely inform, and they *do* believe that only a fool speaks frankly about matters which could injure a client.

It is time to recognize more fully the work of another public relations founding father whose early statements are much closer to current reality. The writings of Edward Bernays, who created the expression "public relations counsel" during the 1920s, are worth a second look by practitioners who want to *understand* as well as act. It was Bernays, the nephew of Sigmund Freud, who integrated what had been the publicists' trade with the major intellectual trends of the late nineteenth and early twentieth centuries, particularly Freudianism and Darwinism. It was Bernays during the 1920s who gave public relations practitioners not just a job and a paycheck, but a purpose, that of "manipulating public opinion" (Bernays' expression, used positively) in order to counter "the whimsical forces of life and chance."

FACING FACTS FRANKLY

Many contemporary public relations practitioners do not like to think of themselves as engaged in "manipulation" or, even worse, "propaganda." Many euphemistic words are thrown around in an attempt to avoid such stigmatizing self-identification. But Bernays faced facts frankly in 1928 when he wrote a book on public relations and proudly titled it *Propaganda*. He realized that the pursuit of propaganda is the logical step once belief in a God sovereign over human activities is no longer present. "How can you blame the intelligent business man who has millions invested in his industry, and thousands depend on it for jobs," Bernays asked *Atlantic* magazine readers in 1932, "if he attempts by intelligent propaganda to give these shifting tides of taste a direction which he can follow without loss; to control by means of propaganda what otherwise would be controlled disastrously by chance?"

Bernays not only went beyond Ivy Lee in developing the rationale for a public relations style which prized manipulation, but also developed a new methodology. A sound practitioner, Bernays wrote, "takes account not merely of the individual, nor even of the mass mind alone, but also and especially of the anatomy of society, with its interlocking group formations and loyalties." The individual is "a cell organized into the social unit. Touch a nerve at a sensitive spot and you get an automatic response from certain specific members of the organism."

The mechanistic nature of this procedure was, for Bernays, no exaggeration. Whether or not he and others could manipulate so precisely was and is open to question, but Bernays claimed that he could "effect some change in public opinion with a fair degree of accuracy by operating a certain mechanism, just as the motorist can regulate the speed of his car by manipulating the flow of gasoline." The way to that goal was through working on the leaders, and through them their followers: "If you can influence the leaders, either with or without their conscious cooperation, you automatically influence the group which they sway."

What Bernays proposed in *Propaganda*, and proudly argued in an *American Journal of Sociology* article entitled "Manipulating Public Opinion," was nothing less than a new way of looking at public relations; while Lee talked about providing "public information," Bernays' goal was to make a hero of "the special pleader who seeks to create public acceptance for a particular idea or commodity." Public relations, for Bernays, no longer needed to be defended as what sinful men do in a sinful society. Public relations would now be proclaimed as the service which saviors of that sinful society would take upon themselves to perform. It was hard work to be continuously "regimenting the public mind every bit as much as an army regiments the bodies of its soldiers," but someone had to do it.

THE BEHIND-THE-SCENES SPECIALIST

Who? Bernays' vision of the future of public relations was most attractive to practitioners trying to rise above publicist status. Certainly, Bernays wrote, "There are invisible rulers who control the destinies of millions." But those were not the political leaders or big businessmen of common paranoia. No, Bernays insisted that, "It is not generally realized to what extent the words and actions of our most influential public men are dictated by shrewd persons operating behind the scenes." The behind-the-scenes operators were necessary to the operation of a society, and there would not be that many of them: "The invisible government tends to be concentrated in the hands of the few because of the expense of manipulating the social machinery which controls the opinions and habits of the masses...." As to the job description and title of the behind-the-scenes operators, Bernays was precise: "There is an increasing tendency to concentrate the functions of propaganda in the hands of the propaganda specialist. This specialist is more and more assuming a distinct place and function in our national life. [He] has come to be known by the name of 'public relations counsel.'"

Bernays began *Propaganda*, the most important of his many books, with the assertion that, "The conscious and intelligent manipulation of the organized habits and opinions of the masses is an important element in democratic society. Those who manipulate this unseen mechanism of society constitute an invisible government which is the true ruling power of our country." That was an awesome opening note. Since a democratic society is normally considered to be one in which "the people" in general do rule, and an authoritarian society is often considered one in which a small group of people rule, Bernays was trying to square the circle by arguing, in effect, that we must kill democracy to save it.

Others during the 1920s argued similarly but were not audacious enough to consider such a degree of social control "democratic." Bernays, though, considered behind-the-scenes manipulation the type of "democracy" that was still practical: "We are governed, our minds are molded, our tastes formed, our ideas suggested, largely by men we have never heard of. This is a logical result of the way in which our democratic society is organized. Vast numbers of human beings must cooperate in this manner if they are to live together as a smoothly functioning society."

Bernays did not stop there; he contended repeatedly that such a behind-the-scenes system is the *only* one possible in a large-scale society which chooses to avoid outright authoritarian control: "Whatever attitude one chooses to take toward this condition, it remains a fact that in almost every act of our daily lives, whether in the sphere of politics or business, in our social conduct or our ethical thinking, we are dominated by the relatively small number of persons — a trifling fraction of our hundred and twenty million — who understand the mental processes and social patterns of the masses. It is they who pull the wires which control the public mind...."

50 THE NEW ROCHELLE STORY*

BARRY JACOBS

It is hard to understand how images get attached to cities. Perhaps a comedian starts making jokes about a city and others pick upon it? If Johnny Carson starts "taking off" on a city, before millions and millions of people, and makes it the butt of his jokes, that city will have image problems.

However it happens, cities get certain images in the public mind and these images tend to persist. Cleveland, Ohio, for example, has a terrible image

---

* Reprinted with permission from the August 1985 issue of the *Public Relations Journal*. Copyright © 1985 by the *Public Relations Journal*.

because countless comedians have made fun of it as a boring place. On the other hand, San Francisco has a very positive image — one that some writers argue it no longer deserves. It is living on its history, they suggest, and has been eclipsed by Los Angeles as a center for business, arts, culture, sports, and just about everything else. ("And smog," argue the defenders of San Francisco, who describe Los Angeles as an automobile ridden wasteland, and point to the spectacular physical beauty of San Francisco.)

Cities, then, have images and reputations that are very important for them. Sometimes a good image turns bad. When that happens, cities find themselves facing many problems. Businesses don't want to locate or stay in such cities, new employees don't want to live in them, and a vicious cycle starts that can end up devastating a city.

The article that follows is a case study of New Rochelle, a city that changed its image and revived itself. (At one time more than seventy-five downtown stores were vacant, a large department store had moved out, and the city's shopping mall was close to going out of business.) It did this by changing itself and by employing a forward-looking public relations firm to guide it. The firm realized that it was necessary for the people in New Rochelle to feel good about the city before others could be persuaded to change their image of New Rochelle. They undertook a number of projects that did this — including a Festival of Nations, which played up the ethnic diversity of the people who lived there. They also published a book that showed how beautiful the area was. And they changed the look of press releases and publications generated by the city. They did many other things, also.

As the image of the city changed, businesses started returning, which, in turn, bolstered community pride and led to new projects. As the result of all this, property values rose, and the downtown area started picking up. New Rochelle had changed itself and had turned its image around. And that made a great deal of difference.

Norman Rockwell's paintings conjure up an innocent rural America — old-timers playing checkers, kids getting haircuts, families going to church. But Rockwell's model wasn't in Iowa, or anywhere else in the middle of the country, it was a mere 30 minutes from midtown New York City. In depicting its citizens and capturing their wholesome sensibilities, Rockwell made New Rochelle, New York — a bucolic suburb on Long Island Sound — America's hometown.

But the image of the place, enshrined on hundreds of *Saturday Evening Post* covers, has long since been tarnished. As with many other small cities, the advent of social problems in the fifties and sixties saw the archetypal wooden Indian in front of city hall replaced by unemployment lines. With inflation and decay, the general stores went vacant. Hometown, in New Rochelle and elsewhere, became rundown and dirty, and not so homey any more.

In the seventies, New Rochelle's leaders attempted to revive their city and hired Ruder, Finn & Rotman to help with the task. While the leaders brought in new money and new businesses, the public relations firm brought new vigor to the Rockwellian vision of a charming place to live and work. The efforts were successful: New Rochelle today is a model for pairing economic development with public relations in order to make America's hometowns whole again, and city leaders from Massachusetts to Japan have looked for lessons in the city's experience.

While the reasons for its deterioration are similar to those plaguing many other American cities, New Rochelle's long, narrow geographic shape added special problems. Since the twenties, the town that Rockwell loved (situated in the southern part of Westchester County) developed as a city-suburb, but its city and suburban natures had never meshed well: northern New Rochelle, with its exquisite houses and rolling lawns, became the home for well-off Manhattan commuters; the southern segment contained a small downtown of shops, businesses, a couple of department stores, and a less affluent residential section.

After World War II, the great movement to the suburbs that swept people out of the cities carried them past New Rochelle to regions farther north in the county, where homes were newer, larger, and less expensive. As the population grew in these areas, modern shopping malls opened, drawing business away from downtown New Rochelle's stores. Soon some of the northern New Rochellers began moving out, following the population trend. As a result, between the 1960s and 1980s, New Rochelle's population declined from 80,000 to 70,000.

Even as these changes were going on, many of New Rochelle's suburban residents still held an image of their city as the perfect bedroom community — a quiet place to hang one's hat after a hard day at the office — and paid little attention to what was happening downtown. But by the early seventies, even the most insular suburbanites were feeling their city's decline in both their pocketbooks and their egos.

"Taxes were going up and the streets were in disrepair," says Sidney Mudd, former president of Joyce Beverages, a New Rochelle firm, and a leader of the New Rochelle Development Council. "Finally people began to say, 'Why doesn't somebody do something about New Rochelle?'"

They'd waited nearly too long. Over seventy-five downtown stores were vacant; Bloomingdales, the well-known department store, had moved out; and the shopping mall was teetering on a financial brink. Worse was the effect on community morale. People from other Westchester communities, particularly those who had left urban areas in what has been called "white flight," perceived New Rochelle as heavily black (it is 17 percent black) and referred to it in negative terms, saying it was on its way to becoming a Bronx-type slum. New Rochelle's self-image was shaky; it figured the city's good days were through.

It was the business community that rallied to fight the city's demise. About fifteen of the most powerful leaders formed the New Rochelle Development Council in 1975 to help spur growth and halt the decay. Says

Lewis Fechter, the urban planner who's served since then as the Council's executive director, "New Rochelle's initial success in the thirties, forties, and fifties was somewhat responsible for its later problems. The community seemed to believe that change would upset the apple cart." But Fechter and the Council were determined to force through change for the city's own good, and they prodded the local government into undertaking some redevelopment projects. They also began reaching out to corporations around the country (through their own business contacts) to try to interest them in moving their plants, stores, and offices to New Rochelle.

But New Rochelle's leaders realized that, even with the growing list of economic improvements, negative perceptions about the community would still hold back its rebirth. In 1977, therefore, a local councilwoman contacted one of her neighbors, David Finn, a principal of Ruder, Finn & Rotman, who's lived in and commuted from New Rochelle for over thirty years. Finn, whose firm had done public relations work for other cities' urban-development plans across the country, as well as in other nations, had been only vaguely aware of New Rochelle's own struggles at revitalization. He soon began attending meetings of the Development Council and local government on an informal basis, in order to come up with ideas for improving the city's identity.

Finn brought to these meetings a sense of the importance of public relations to a community's redevelopment that went far beyond merely publicizing some isolated improvements. In the words of Amy Binder, managing director of urban communications at Ruder, Finn & Rotman and a longtime resident of New Rochelle, "You can't think about attracting businesses to your city until you get its residents feeling good."

It is this philosophy that's at the heart of one of the first projects Finn undertook for New Rochelle — a survey of fifty community leaders on their attitudes about their city. "We believe," the introduction to the 1977 survey report says, "that only New Rochelle's people have the power to renew the city's reputation."

The survey report — the keystone of the firm's subsequent public relations efforts in the community — confirmed that many residents held negative opinions of New Rochelle. But it also made several suggestions for drawing on those same people's concern for their community in order to rebuild it. Central among these was the idea of setting up volunteer citizen task forces on improving various aspects of the city's life. Just as David Finn had lived in New Rochelle most of his adult life but was only now directing his energies toward helping his city, many other well-known people — including opera singer Robert Merrill and actress Ruby Dee — were called upon to serve on committees on New Rochelle's cultural programs, festivals, publications, ethnic issues, and more. They brought talent and prestige to the effort that convinced people both inside and outside the city that New Rochelle was determined to renew itself.

From the ethnic-issues task force came the idea for setting up a Festival of Nations — a yearly outdoor food, crafts, and culture fair. While other

Westchester communities often disparaged New Rochelle for its "mixed" population, the festival was a means of showing off the city's ethnic diversity and making it a community strength. Every year since 1979, over 20 ethnic groups have set up booths, and between 20,000 and 40,000 visitors partake of the exotic fare. It's been an important way of involving large segments of the community in appreciating its own inherent vitality.

From the publications task force came the idea for a book to remind New Rochelle's residents that, though the city had slipped somewhat, they still lived in a lushly beautiful and historic community that also offered good schools, businesses, and homes. The resulting handsome volume of expensively reproduced photographs by David Finn, with a preface by Robert Merrill, shows off a still-quaint waterfront, expansive green parks, 18th-century historic sites, offices, schools, churches, and synagogues.

While all the task forces have since dissolved or been absorbed into groups like the Arts Council or the Third Sector Initiative, they served their initial purpose well. As the city's leaders worked quietly to bring businesses and jobs back, the volunteer committees got the cream of New Rochelle's commuting talent involved in producing the sort of high-visibility projects that announced to the rest of the residents that changes — good changes — were brewing for their city.

The appearance of the publications being produced by city hall before Ruder, Finn & Rotman formally contracted with the city in 1979 were of poor visual quality. The firm introduced better-designed press releases and information brochures. At the same time, it sent business leaders and the New York metropolitan-area press a sleek package called "New Rochelle in the News," which included reprints of the articles on the city that had appeared within the previous six-month period.

The survey report also called for more support in the local city newspaper for the revitalization effort. Ruder, Finn & Rotman developed, with the *New Rochelle Standard-Star*, a six-part series entitled "Why New Rochelle?" Like the photography book, it listed the city's many strengths and helped to bolster community pride and counteract outsiders' derision.

Since the initial survey, Ruder, Finn & Rotman has continued to come up with ideas for involving residents in the city's improvement. New Rochelle has always been the home of a great number of not-for-profit organizations — nearly 500, in fact. So in 1979, the firm helped organize a meeting of many of them to talk about how they felt about New Rochelle. Out of the meeting was formed an organization called the Third Sector Initiative, coordinated by Ruder, Finn & Rotman and sponsored by the two colleges in the area — Iona College and the College of New Rochelle — as well as the New Rochelle Hospital Medical Center.

Out of the Third Sector Initiative grew College As Citizen, a sort of neighborhood think-tank on how to improve the city. The "College" has monthly meetings attended by members of the city council, business leaders, faculty at the two colleges, and Ruder, Finn & Rotman — as coordinator — to come up with topics of local concern for in-depth urban-policy study. The studies are then undertaken by faculty members whose time is donated by the two colleges. While the city government is in no way bound by the recommendations of these studies, it takes them very seriously, and College as Citizen is credited in most press releases and conversations as the information source.

Over the years, as Ruder, Finn & Rotman has generated ideas for many of these community projects and then coordinated their activities, it has stretched the meaning of public relations in New Rochelle beyond mere publicity. But that doesn't mean it's neglected the value of good press. As each new project took hold, the local and national media became more and more interested in the doings in New Rochelle. Several dozen *New York Times* pieces, as well as those from many other publications, have helped to turn the city's image around. Today, Ruder, Finn & Rotman has a full-time staffperson in New Rochelle working with the local government, the Development Council, College As Citizen, and a wide array of groups through the Third Sector Initiative, to generate more ideas and more publicity.

The results of the New Rochelle redevelopment effort as a whole have been quite spectacular. "Property values in New Rochelle over the last 10 years are the second or third most highly appreciated in lower Westchester County," says Francis Eisner of Oshlape Eisner Real Estate. Thirty corporations have relocated to the city in the last decade, and over a million square feet of new office space has been built. The downtown shopping area still has a few vacancies, but community leaders hope that, with several new projects coming on-line in the next decade (including an office/residential development near the railroad station and a huge luxury-housing development on an island just off the New Rochelle waterfront), the city will be bursting with economic health.

The community, with the help of the public relations effort, seems to have regained its psychological health. No longer do residents put the city down. And those from other Westchester communities now think of New Rochelle as an active, growing city.

Norman Rockwell was a great public relations man for the community, but in a sense he painted New Rochelle into a corner. To throw off the yoke of small-town quaintness and take an active part in modernizing their home-town, Ruder, Finn & Rotman has helped to put the paintbrush in New Rochelle residents' hands and allowed them to feel good about themselves.

BUSINESS AND REGULATION

When we buy a record or go to the movies or watch a television program we think, primarily, about the pleasure we expect to get from our purchase or expenditure of time. We want to be entertained, we want to have some kind of an emotional experience that will be of value to us. Our focus is on some work that has caught our attention — either as the result of advertisements or reviews or comments from our friends (and often a mixture of all three).

The work of art is like the tip of the iceberg. We seldom think about all the people involved in bringing that work into existence — the writers, the directors, the performers, the lighting experts, the sound experts, the editors and all of the others involved. You get a sense of how complicated it is to make a film or television program when you see the list of credits rolling by at the end of the show. It isn't unusual for an hour action-adventure television program to cost more than a million dollars and for a film to cost $10 million.

We are dealing with huge industries that take in billions of dollars in revenues …whose impact upon American culture and society (many scholars and researchers suggest) is profound. And that is where the government comes in, since its mission is to promote the general welfare.

In the case of television and radio, the influence of the government is direct. There are limits on the amount of space available on the radio and television spectrums, which means that the government allocates space to stations that promise to generate programming in the public's interest. After all, if the public owns the airwaves, we should expect that stations would use these airwaves in the public's interest.

Since the media are held to be of central importance in modern societies, they are, quite naturally, the focus of a great deal of attention by scholars and legis-lators. Statistics suggest that there is growing concentration of ownership in the media. What effect is this having? How is this concentration impacting on our social and political institutions?

Think, for example, of the role television commercials now play in elections. Politicians spend hundreds of millions of dollars for these commercials. Does this mean that politics will soon be a field only for the wealthy and telegenic? Should government do something about this? If so, what?

Consider, also, the radio business. It is extremely competitive and has been likened to war, as stations battle other stations for a share of the audience. This share, and the nature of the audience, determines what the stations can charge for advertisements. How does this influence programming? Is this the right way to obtain the best programming? What is the best programming? What should radio do...or is it as good as it can be the way it is?

One of the most important and difficult issues involving the media is the matter of censorship. What should be done about violence on television? An even more difficult subject is sexuality and the media. What should be done about sexually explicit material in the media — and particularly in films and on television? Where do you draw the line between using sexually explicit material for "legitimate" purposes and pornography? Some people feel that this sexually explicit material is degrading and disgusting and should be censored.

Others argue that this material has no harmful effect on people, and that, studies show, it actually is helpful for that element of the public that seeks it out. Besides, as the defenders of sexually explicit material point out, the First Amendment protects freedom of expression and it is more important to protect this right than it is to censor pornographic material. Moreover, nobody has been able to define pornography to the satisfaction of everyone, so one person's "art" is another person's "pornography," and vice versa.

You can see, then, that because the media play such a central role in modern American society, and have the attention of so many people, they are the subject of a great deal of interest. There are not two separate domains — business and government — that exist independent of one another. Business and government are always mixed up in each other's affairs, for legitimate reasons. And this has been so throughout our history. Business and government are like two sides of a piece of paper.

The relation is particularly signficant since radio and television use the public airwaves and must be regulated. This is obvious. What role the government should play in other areas is another matter. We do not want to have the government control our media and press and turn them into instruments of propaganda. And we do not want a few private interests to dominate the media and use them for their own purposes (which might involve elections and other such sensitive areas). How do we prevent concentration of the media? What is the proper role of government relative to the media? These are questions with which we will always have to wrestle.

51   CONCENTRATION OF CONTROL OF THE MEDIA*

BEN BAGDIKIAN

The question of concentration of the media is an important one…and a complicated one. Bagdikian offers data that show that there is growing concentration in ownership of the media and suggests that this has grave implications for the spread of diverse opinions. After all, as the saying goes, "He who pays the piper calls the tune."

In an article recently published in *The Journal of Communication* entitled "The U.S. Media: Supermarket or AssemblyLine" he provides some information supporting his argument. Let me cite a few of the points he makes, which serve as a kind of updating of the article you will be reading and that will give you a few new ideas to consider.

He estimates that as of 1984, some forty-four corporations controlled "half or more of all media output." In 1982, the figure had been fifty corporations, so concentration is getting stronger. As a result of deregulation, he estimates that a half-dozen corporations (including the three networks) will end up controlling "most of the programming and access to the national network." The three networks now provide "most of the content for the 1,000 local commercial stations," and the content of most broadcasting is similar, regardless of which network one is dealing with.

In the magazine industry, "fewer than twenty corporations have most of the business" and though there are 2500 book publishers, "eleven have most of the annual sales of two billion books." Though there are 8000 commercial stations, only a dozen formats are found on these stations, so ultimately there is very little diversity in radio programming.

The result of all this, Bagdikian argues, is that the corporations that own and control the media have the power to affect in profound ways (if not "shape") our attitudes. There is a narrowing of the political and social content of the media — a narrowing that is often not the result of conscious decision making by those who run the media corporations but is, instead, based on their interests and beliefs about what should be covered. At times, however, the owners of the media corporations do affect media content directly, which has political significance and, it can be argued, consequences.

If democracy is based on the free expression of competing opinions, we must wonder what impact this increased concentration of media ownership is having on our political system. And we must consider how we might best deal with this problem.

---

* Ben Bagdikian, Statement to The Federal Trade Commission, Dec. 14, 15, 1978.

Let me give my background briefly as some explanation of the source of my information and opinions. For nineteen years I worked for daily newspapers as a reporter, foreign correspondent, Washington correspondent and an editor. I have been a magazine editor and have written for most national magazines of general circulation. Throughout this period I have done media research and criticism. I was a Guggenheim Fellow researching ownership patterns of the press. For two and a half years I did research at Rand (Corporation, a private "Think Tank") on the impact of modern technology on the future of American informational media and for the last three years on factors that lead to success or failure for newspapers. For the last two years I have been on the faculty of the Graduate School of Journalism at the University of California at Berkeley.

This symposium is looking at the phenomenon of increasing control of information organizations in the United States by a relatively small number of national and transnational corporations. I understand that some important executives in publishing have expressed concern that people outside the corporate end of their business — that is, journalists, researchers, academics, civic activists and others — will approach the problem with a prejudice against their motives. Let me confirm their worst fears by beginning with a quotation on that subject. I quote:

> "I rather think that the influence of the American press...is declining. This, I believe, is because so many newspapers are owned or influenced by reactionary interests and predatory corporations, and are used selfishly to promote the welfare of these reactionary interests, rather than the welfare of the public."
> End of quote.

I would not express my own concern in that language and there are portions of that quotation that seem to me to be exaggerated. But I should point out that the quotation is not from a journalist or academic but from one of the trade's pioneers in chains and conglomerates, the original William Randolph Hearst. He uttered those words in 1924, at which time he was among the first to show the power of owning newspapers, magazines, movie companies and other assorted properties that affect the public mind.

Today we are looking at a phenomenon that might have surprised even Mr. Hearst. In 1924 he and other chain operators controlled 31 corporations that owned 153 papers, or 8 percent of all dailies. Today there are 167 chains that control 1,082 papers, or 61 percent of all papers. It took the first 60 years of this century for chains to control 27 percent of all our papers. It has taken only the last 16 years for chains to reach control of 61 percent of all papers and 75 percent of all daily circulation.

Newspapers are only one medium that influences our culture and our politics. The phenomenon of fewer and fewer people controlling more and more of our public intelligence affects every mass medium in our country. The concentration of control of our newspapers, magazines, broadcasting, books, and movies has reached alarming levels. Fewer than 100 corporate executives have ultimate control of the majority of each medium in the United States. According to the Census of Manufacturers twenty corporations, each with a chief executive officer, control 52 percent of all daily newspaper sales. Twenty corporations control 50 percent of all periodical sales. Twenty corporations control 52 percent of all book sales. Twenty corporations control 76 percent of all record and tape sales. If one counts the three networks and the ten corporations whose sponsorship dominates prime time, thirteen corporations control two-thirds of the audience in television and radio. Seven corporations control 75 percent of movie distribution. These 100 men and women constitute a private Ministry of Information and Culture for the United States.

In fact, there are fewer than 100 corporations because some of them are among the top twenty controllers of more than one medium. For example, 27 percent of all television stations are controlled by newspaper companies. A magazine company, Time, Incorporated, owns magazines, seventeen weekly newspapers, five book publishing houses, a film company, and has interests in cable, and records. RCA owns the National Broadcasting Company, a record company, and the book publishing houses of Random House, Ballantine Books, Alfred Knopf, Pantheon, Vintage and Modern Library. The biggest newspaper conglomerate, Times-Mirror, owns the *Los Angeles Times*, the *Dallas Times-Herald, Long Island Newsday* and other papers, four magazines, TV stations, cable systems, 50 percent of a news service and New American Library. CBS is one of three companies with two-thirds of the prime-time audience, owns twenty magazines, three record companies, and the book publishing houses of Holt, Rinehart and Winston, Popular Library, and W.B. Saunders Co.

This really means that when it comes to the mass media that create a major ingredient of our social and political environment, the men and women who control most of it would fit in this room. If that were the case of a government bureaucracy there would be justified alarm among the public and especially among the enterpreneurs who now control our media environment. And I would share their alarm for two reasons: government has police powers to enforce self-serving propagandistic use of our mass media. And even under the best of conditions it is not safe to repose in a small group of human beings, governmental or not, such closely controlled power over the ideas, information, and values that are propagated by our mass media. The small number of private corporations that are increasingly gaining control over our mass media do not have governmental powers. But they are too small a group of fallible human beings to have such unified control. Even if they should be philosopher-saints in their wisdom, this country was founded on the theory that no small group, even philosopher-saints, should have so much power over public information and discourse.

This pattern of control is compounded by two new developments in media ownership. One is the inclusion of journalism and other media companies in large conglomerate corporations that are also in other industries, industries that regularly are reported — or not reported — by the same corporations' media properties. A company like ITT, deeply involved with foreign governments and domestic policy, that also controls publishing companies is in a position of direct conflict of interest that we would not condone with government officials or agencies. We know that for many years William Randolph Hearst used his newspapers, magazines, wire services and movie production companies to urge the United States to declare war on Mexico, not out of a pure instinct for news but because he feared expropriation of his mining properties in Mexico. Today there is greater potential than ever for using journalism as a by-product by large conglomerates who have an explicit desire to influence public opinion and government policy in their favor.

The other new development is a pattern of several traditionally competing media coming under ownership by the same parent corporation. It has always been assumed that a newspaper article might be expanded to a magazine article which could become the basis for a hardcover book which, in turn, could be a paperback, and then, perhaps, a TV series and finally, a movie. At each step of change an author and other enterprises could compete for entry into this array of channels for reaching the public mind and pocketbook. But today several of our media giants own these arrays, not only closing off entry points for competition in different media, but influencing the choice of entry at the start on the basis of how a later treatment by the same company will profit.

Book publishing, for example, used to be satisfied by a conventional profit in the sale of hardcover books. But now that most book sales are controlled by twenty companies, many of which also own other media, increasingly hardcover books, those basic repositories of information and reflection, are selected not because the public will buy them for themselves, at a profit for the book company, but because they will do well in the same company's magazines, in its mass paperback sales or in its television and movie treatment. Not only does this constrict the basis on which book manuscripts are selected, but it has begun to destroy the special quality of presentation that is unique to each medium and that represents a necessary richness of subject matter and approach. We now see book manuscripts assigned and selected so that a television movie can be made from which a mass paperback based on the television movie can be sold, all by a company that had this media incest orchestrated by its marketing computers.

The question inevitably arises whether the media really have any influence. The answer is not always simple. During the administration of Franklin Delano Roosevelt, the majority of newspapers, then the major medium, were hostile to the New Deal in their news columns and in their editorials. But they were dealing with a population whose desperation at finding food and shelter was more persuasive than the slanted news and angry editorials against Roosevelt's programs. But we do not always deal with desperate overwhelming, personal problems. Instead, between crises we accumulate unspectacular information and ideas that shape our values and those values in turn influence how we meet crises when they arise. In this everyday, unspectacular laying down of the national consciousness I think the evidence is clear that our media do have a subtle but profound effect.

In explicit things like the impact of television on violent behavior, the report of the U.S. Surgeon General, when read in the original, shows beyond doubt that the persistent portrayal of violence on television affects every American's attitude toward violence, regardless of social class.

Perception of our whole society, and of particular groups in our society is learned mostly from our mass media. We are increasingly a society of polarized, homogeneous communities — tending to separate by race, by economics and by social class. We no longer live in small communities where there is personal contact across class lines. We are seeing the disappearance of the community, all-class school. Millions of Americans are growing up without personal knowledge of other Americans who are of a different skin color, or ethnic background, or economic class — except for what they see, read and hear in the mass media.

Media operators, when confronted with this, tend to disclaim all influence on human behavior. When they do so, they fly in the face of the overwhelming weight of evidence of the most careful studies and of common experience. They are also ignoring their own appeals to advertisers. When media operators compete for their share of the $27 billion annual advertising expenditures, they insist to the advertisers that their medium can influence human behavior. If our media cannot influence human behavior then they are selling false goods to the commercial entrepreneurs, the politicians, and the special interest groups who buy space and time to advertise their wares and to influence public opinion.

It would mean that some of our most powerful corporations — IBM, Xerox, Proctor & Gamble, General Motors, General Mills, Mobil Oil — are fools because they spend billions of dollars every year advertising to sell their goods and to influence public opinion. They would be fools if they continued to spend this money without some evidence that it does in fact change the way people think and behave. I do not believe that they are fools and I don't think that media operators treat them as fools.

I see no alternative but to assume that our media have a profound effect on our national culture and values and that we should be concerned about control of our media.

My concern over the nature of control over the media is not so much my disagreement with the personal values and politics of many media owners. I do not want homogeneous newspapers, broadcasts, magazines, and movies, even if all of them were compatible with my personal beliefs. History forces us to be concerned. History tells us that the only safe source of information is pluralistic. History also tells us that potential power must be regarded as real power. Government laws that permit severe regulation do not make the media operators less worried simply because the government says it doesn't really intend to use these powers. I don't believe government when it says that and media operators are wise not to believe it. Licenses to exercise power will be used. But neither can I look with equanimity when the small number of people who control our media say they are benevolent, and that they do not really intend to use their ultimate power of control over information. We are being careless with history unless we assume that whoever has power sooner or later will use it to the fullest.

Media operators sometimes argue that the public would not stand for their using their power to control news. I suggest that the public knows what it will stand for and not stand for only when it knows that it has a choice. For important portions of our social and political life, what the media do not tell us, we do not know. If a local newspaper is ordered by its owner to tell only negative stories about a disliked politician — and occasionally that happens — then the people in that community may never know anything positive about that politician. If television tells 90 million Americans every night that anger, aggression, and shooting are the prime-time norm for human relations, millions of children will grow up with a diminished sense of compassion, tenderness and empathy, and with a greater tolerance for aggression and violence.

In many ways, the American media pattern is superior to that in most developed countries. We have more newspapers than most countries. We have more radio and television stations. We make more movies and publish more magazines. Government does not have a monopoly on all mass communications, as it does in many societies, and it does not have a monopoly or near-monopoly on broadcasting as it does in many democratic countries. Instead we have more than 1,700 daily newspapers, none of them under government control. We have 8,600 radio and 700 commercial television stations, all regulated by government but privately owned, and 10,000 periodicals, and so forth. But the units of these that reach the largest audiences are increasingly coming under the control of a small number of corporations.

When we remember that twenty corporations control access to most of the American audience in each of these media, the very large number of units becomes ominous rather than reassuring. It means that today more than half of this enormous machinery for affecting the public mind, despite its size and power, is controlled by fewer than 100 corporations.

There is a peculiarity of American political organization that makes media concentration and monopoly particularly dangerous. This peculiarity further diminishes the advantage we enjoy in a large number of communication outlets.

To a greater extent than any other developed country, the United States is organized at a local level. We vest in cities, towns and countries important governmental functions that in other societies are governed at a national level. Our education, policing, land use, and other vital functions are decided by each community through its local political machinery. This is why we have local papers rather than national ones and this is why our basic Communications Act called for local broadcast stations, not national ones, on the basis that each community has peculiar needs no national medium can fill.

The developing patterns in daily newspapers illustrate what I mean.

In most developed countries there are a number of papers published in the principal city and distributed in every part of the country the same day. All the serious national and international news is in these papers. Local papers are of relatively small importance because the central functions that affect people's lives are exercised at the national level and presumably will be reported by the national papers. The large number of national papers in these other countries means there is commercial competition. But, more important, it means that there can be differences in basic political or social content, from which people may make a choice, each paper concentrating on a slightly different point of view and reporting a different spectrum of information. If a radical paper buries a story embarrassing to its adherents, a conservative rival will happily report it and the information will enter the public arena.

In this country we have only one truly national paper, *The Wall Street Journal*, transmitted overnight by satellite to printing plants all over the country and delivered by newsstand or mail the same day in every part of the country. But it is a specialized financial paper. We have a few papers of unusual influence, like *The New York Times*, *The Los Angeles Times*, and *The Washington Post*, but they are not available in every part of the country the same day of publication. There are a number of subsidiary reasons for the lack of a national press in this country but the major reason is that no national newspaper can tell the people of a particular city or region what they need to know in order to govern themselves. *The New York Times* is of little help to Des Moines when Des Moines elects members of its school board.

This pattern of localism, and the degree to which the health of urban society depends on it, makes disturbing two contemporary developments in the press. First, is the now almost-standard pattern of local monopoly for daily papers throughout the country. And second, the consolidation of these monopolies into dominating metropolitan publications that preempt the economic base for new papers in each community but do not provide each community with the news it needs.

Monopoly is an established fact in American daily newspapers. There are 1,760 daily papers in the country in about 1,600 communities, and in ninety-seven and one half percent of these communities there is only one local newspaper company. Those of you who live in the 34 cities of the country that still have newspapers in face-to-face competition should realize that you are in a two and one half percent minority.

The other disturbing development is that most of our cities do not have daily papers. We have 7,000 urban places in the country but only 1,760 newspapers, leaving about 75 percent of our urban communities without their own paper. It was not always this way. In 1890 there were 1,348 urban places and 1,600 daily papers, an excess of 19 percent of papers over urban communities. The 75 percent of our urban communities without their own paper often have access to a metropolitan or other paper from another community. And many papers would insist that they try to cover all of the cities where they sell papers. But the fact is that they do not and cannot. It is not unusual for a metropolitan paper to have significant distribution over 40 counties. *The Atlanta Constitution and Journal*, for example, circulates significantly in 55 counties, only 16 of which have their own daily paper. The average county in the United States has 26 local governments, 22 of them with taxing power. A paper that covers 40 counties, in order to do minimal civic reporting, would have to cover over 1,000 governmental bodies. This is just a start of adequate community reporting and no paper comes even close.

These developments put a different light, I think, on the development of chains, conglomerates and other extreme concentrations of control over our mass media. It means that in many media, particularly newspapers and in the uniformity of network programming, large numbers do not mean competition but the opposite.

The most clear example of what I mean is in the case of daily newspapers. There are in the United States 1,759 daily newspapers of general circulation, a figure that has remained almost constant for a generation. These daily papers are owned by 834 companies. If the ownership were distributed evenly this would mean about two papers per company. But of course ownership is not distributed evenly because 167 of these companies, the chains or groups, that own more than one paper in more than one community, own 62 percent of all daily papers. If ownership of chain papers were distributed evenly among chains it would mean between 5 and 6 papers per chain. But that is not the case. The 25 largest chains own 31 percent of all dailies and a majority of all chain papers. But chain-owned papers are bigger than the average American daily, so in terms of circulation, the 25 largest newspaper corporations control 52 percent, or a majority, of all papers sold daily in the United States.

But as we look at the accumulation of media power by the largest companies we see an even tighter concentration. The ten biggest chains control 36 percent of all circulation and 20 percent of all newspaper companies.

Put another way this shows that one percent of all newspaper companies control 36 percent of all papers sold daily and own 20 percent of all newspaper companies.

At the start of 1977 there were 1,759 dailies in the country, and 677 remained independently owned. About 250 of these 677 have less than 5,000 circulation and therefore have too small a cash flow to interest a chain. The larger chains are bidding furiously for the remaining 400 and predictably most will be absorbed. In fact 100 of the remaining 400 were bought by chains in the last twenty months.

The rate at which the big chains are swallowing small chains and accumulating control of our daily printed news is seen in just the last ten years. Ten years ago the ten biggest chains controlled 11 percent of all daily newspaper companies. Today the ten biggest chains control 20 percent of all daily papers. So not only is the independently owned daily paper predictably going to disappear, but control of all papers is rapidly accumulating disproportionately among the biggest corporations in the news business.

Concentrated control of news is different from control of other commodities. The principal difference, of course, is that this is not control of automobiles, detergents and breakfast cereals but control of public information. But this control of public information becomes even more critical when we look at the pattern of local monopoly in daily newspapers.

We have already noted that of the cities that have their own daily paper, 97.5 percent have a local monopoly. This, too, has progressed with frightening speed. From the turn of the century we have gone from almost two-thirds of newspaper cities with competing papers to 2.5 percent. And I believe that it is only a matter of time before competing daily papers in the same city will be a peculiarity of a handful of cities either of great size or where publishers compete with each other for reasons other than economic profit.

This means a great deal when we look at what it means to have most of our news controlled, as it is today, by a few national and transnational corporations. Concentration of control in the marketplace is not limited to newspapers and other media companies. It is true of a large segment of our economy. There is similar and frequently even greater concentration in other industries, and with even a greater rate of accumulation of control from an earlier period of hundreds of individual entrepreneurs. In the automobile industry, for example, two generations ago there were more than 200 individual companies making automobiles in the United States and today there are only four.

But because almost all of our papers are local monopolies and because chains particularly try to stay away from competing papers we have a different situation in the newspaper industry.

In the automobile industry, the remaining giant corporations compete with each other and with foreign companies, all of which acts as a restraint against over-pricing and reduction of quality. General Motors, Ford, Chrysler and American Motors compete with each other and they all compete with Volkswagen, Toyota and so forth.

That is not true in the newspaper business. Of the 1,082 papers owned by chains, half of 1 percent, or fifty, have local printed competition. Of these fifty papers, only seven, or seven-tenths of one percent have face-to-face competition, or competition in the same time of day. Of the fifty chain papers that have any competition at all, whether dividing the market in AM and PM segments between them or in face-to-face competition, sixteen are in agency agreements permitted by the special exemption from antitrust laws. This means that among the fifty chain papers that have any kind of local printed competition, sixteen, or one-third of them can legally fix prices and share profits.

The result is that 97 percent of all chain papers have no economic competition in their cities. If you eliminate the ones with agreements to fix prices and share profits, you still have 95 percent of all chain papers with no local competition. It seems to me that this places a different light on the growing control of news by a few corporations. It means that each of these noncompeting corporations has a network of monopoly operations. So the daily newspaper industry is not comparable to other concentrated industries where at least the giants compete with each other. It is more like the telephone or other utility companies that have sanctioned monopolies. In the ultimate test, a real choice available to the consumer, the consumer loses, 95-to-5.

52   RICH MAN, POOR MAN*
BEN STEIN

This essay is about the crazy world of Hollywood. It deals, specifically, with the envy and greed that pervade the television and film industry. In this bizarre world, writers who may be making hundreds of thousands of dollars a year are full of anger and rage. They feel they are being cruelly exploited by producers who make millions of dollars a year (and don't want to share very much of this money with the writers). The writers feel, with some degree of justification, Stein suggests, that they are the crucial element in determing the success of a television series or film, but that they are not given a fair share of the revenues their work generates.

To understand why the writers feel the way they do, it is useful to keep a few things in mind. First, the writers are experiencing what sociologists call "relative deprivation." This concept explains that people's feelings about whether they are successful or have enough of the good things in life are not based on absolutes, such as "I'm making $350,000 a year." Instead they are affected by a sense of what they have *relative* to what they think they should have or what others have.

This is because success, in American society, is always relative; there is no absolute definition of success. It constantly eludes us and no matter what we achieve, we are generally unsatisfied and want more. (This is not true, many sociologists argue, in all societies; in some countries success is more "absolute" and people are not plagued as much by feelings that they must always surpass their earnings or whatever every year.) Relative deprivation may have its psychological costs but it also generates a great deal of energy and activism.

But more important, for our concerns, is the fact that much of what goes on in Hollywood is irrational and based on chance, on luck, or connections. As Stein writes, "The punk with family connections to an investment bank in New York becomes a powerful producer while the lifelong toiler in the vineyards drives a rented Pinto. The kid who takes the producer's homely daughter to the prom gets

* Permission to use the following copyrighted material is gratefully acknowledged: "Rich Man, Poor Man," by Ben Stein first appeared in *New West/California*, July 1981, pp. 101–102.

to be a coproducer right out of college while the gagman with ten years' experience gets unemployment." It is the illogicality (and the power of money and privilege) that also bothers the writers. In many respects, Hollywood, "the dream factory," is a repudiation of the American Dream — which tells us that success is the reward of those who work hard and thus deserve it.

Hollywood runs on envy. The other fellow's luck, the house in Malibu for just one half hour pilot for a show that ran for six years, the half ownership of an office building in Century City for just a polish on a $100 million-grossing picture — these are the hormones that course through the town's bloodstream, motivating, stimulating, and sometimes crippling the creative energies of a multitude of hungry people. Envy can drive the producer, the writer, the director, the actor to superhuman feats of production, greed, and even art. But envy can also bring Hollywood to the brink of suicide.

This takes us to strike-torn Hollywood circa summer 1981. The writers' strike drags on and on. (Although as this goes to press, a major break in the writers' strike appears to be imminent.) We have already had an actors' strike and a musicians' strike. The directors may go out. Supposedly these strikes are about who is to get what out of the radical restructuring of the television business that is underway. But even the new frontier of TV does not explain the level of bitterness and emotion in Hollywood today. Put simply, Hollywood is not approaching economic issues sensibly.

On any rational basis, this is absolutely the worst time for strikes to take place. The television network business is in terrible shape. Average viewership has fallen off so much in the last two years that the ratings of this year's ratings winner, CBS, would have garnered only third place in 1979. In towns where there is large-scale cable available, network viewership is falling by 3 percent to 4 percent a year, according to a top TV producer. This means less money for the production houses and less money all the way down the line. The movie business is in even worse shape. Adjusted for inflation, box office receipts are running at the lowest rate in ten years. Several medium-size production companies have cut back drastically on features. Even the majors are cutting the number of their features.

It is not sensible for Hollywood to tear itself apart in hard times. But it is the inevitable fruit of bringing together a great many envious people in a situation that encourages the growth of envy the way a tropical jungle encourages giant orchids. First of all, envy is in the Hollywood type from day one. Writers, directors, actors, musicians, all the above-the-line creative people, think of themselves as artists. People do not become artists because they are secure in their minds. They become artists to compete, to show that they can do something better, more originally, more profitably than someone else. They hate it when that someone else looks as if he is doing better than they. If Beethoven could be envious of Rossini (as he was), a staff writer of *Too Close for Comfort* could envy the story editor of *Happy Days*, and both of them could be extremely envious of the producer.

Additionally, the Hollywood MO guarantees jealousy and resentment. This is a company town, as a famous writer once said. But it is a totally atomized, junglelike company town without rules or logic. There is no social contract here that says you must start out at the bottom and work your way to the top, all the while giving obeisance to those above you. There is no gradual accretion of wealth and power due to years of seniority that merit veneration. Things happen randomly, crazily, without logical explanation.

If an instructor in economics at Cal State Northridge sees that Paul Samuelson has won the Nobel Prize in economics, his envy will be tempered with a realistic understanding that Samuelson is a hardworking genius with many years of work in his field. If a director who has put in fifteen years of hard work on the set sees the big picture go to the star's hairdresser, his envy will know no bounds. The punk with family connections to an investment bank in New York becomes a powerful producer while the lifelong toiler in the vineyard drives a rented Pinto. The kid who takes the producer's homely daughter to the prom gets to be a coproducer right out of college while the gag man with ten years' experience gets unemployment. This cruelly illogical distribution of Hollywood's goodies makes people envious.

In this fertile soil envy grows especially lush when one Hollywood type sees another Hollywood type suddenly become as rich as a Rockefeller while the former is only upper middle class. The envy is particularly powerful if the poorer man can be persuaded — perhaps rightly — that the richer man would never have done it except by victimizing the poorer. This rule applies even when the poorer man makes $20,000 a week.

This is how it works. At the Writers' Guild of America (WGA) meeting just before the strike vote, one writer after another stood up to denounce the insulting refusal of the producers to accede to our modest demands. I recognized some of those people at the Hollywood Palladium. A few years before, they were eating hot dogs at Pink's, getting by on an occasional magazine gig. Now they are getting $250,000 a screenplay, plus a parking place at Fox right next to Michael Shamberg's. I saw grown men who could not meet their house payments a few years ago, who now make $5,000 a week writing sit-coms. They stood up at the meetings and railed against the screwing over they got from the producers. Men and women who were worried about memberships at the Mulholland Tennis Club five years ago now make more than a corporate officer at AT&T. Yet they will strike rather than accept an increase in minimums of only 35.3 percent over three years, even though they are already far above the minimums themselves.

This is not economic, profit-maximizing man at work. But it is envious man at work. "Yes," says the writer, "I make $10,000 per show. Yes, if I stay on this show for two years the residuals will allow my children to live as squires in Ireland. Yes, if I stay at work on this sit-com for five years, I can retire with more money than I ever dreamed I would earn in my entire lifetime. But that's nothing! If this show lasts for five years, the producer will make millions. Norman Lear may make $50 million personally. Or if this show lasts for six years, Grant Tinker may take $40 million out of it. For himself. Personally. Larry Gelbart may make tens of millions out of *M*A*S*H*. Garry Marshall may become as rich as an oil sheikh from *Happy Days*, even after Paramount's cut."

The writers (and directors) know perfectly well that if a television series runs long enough to yield about 100 episodes (usually about five years), it can go into syndication. That means it is sold, market by market, for showing by independent television stations at all different times of the day. Very few shows that start out as pilots make it to syndication, perhaps 1 percent. But when a show does make it that far, Katie, bar the door. Entertainment industry experts say that *All in the Family* yields $25 million a year from syndication with no end in sight. *One Day at a Time* pays about $18 million a year. The *Mary Tyler Moore Show* is said to pay off about $15 million a year. *Happy Days* may be worth $15 million a year, minimum. *M*A*S*H*, some say, will eventually produce the most of all. And there are many more. For the producers, it is like striking oil — a great deal of oil.

Of course, they have to share some of it with the distributors. They also pay residuals to writers, directors, and actors. But there is plenty left over to make a few producers staggeringly rich. It makes a lot of writers crazy. Some directors, too. After all, there would be no show without writers, no show without directors.

So they fight back. When the time comes for contract negotiations, they know exactly what to do. Ask for a percentage of the gross from pay television. It may be a fair demand, but it will make the producers insane. Ask for a quota for minority group writers. Ask for a guarantee of drastically higher minimums for TV and movies. Ask for — no, demand — that a certain number of shows be written freelance. If the bastards turn us down, hit the bricks. See how they like that!

But, as Jordan Baker said in *The Great Gatsby*, "It takes two to make an accident." The producers are just as angry at and envious of the writers and directors. To the producers, the writer is a hack, the director a necessary maniac evil. Ask a powerful TV producer if the writers should get a percentage of the gross from pay TV. "Look," he says, "should the cobbler who makes Gucci shoes get a percentage of Gucci's gross? The man who designed the shoe, maybe. Mr. Gucci, definitely. But the cobbler gets his salary, and that's it."

Another producer summed it up even more beautifully. "If I am an architect and a builder and I build a house, I get the profit when it's sold. The maid who cleans up the house doesn't get a percentage. That's the way the world works."

To the producers, the writers and directors are already wildly overpaid. They glide along the show biz pond taking no risks, mostly turning out hack work, yet they get paid whether there is a profit or a loss. "Where are the writers and the directors when we take a loss on a series that didn't work out? Are they making up the loss when we go into deficit financing? We take the risk, and we get the profits. That's the way it always works."

There is also a noneconomic ground for envy by the producers. The writer or director is, at least to the outside world, an artiste! He does not have to manipulate spread sheets. He gets into the Arts and Leisure section of *The New York Times*. He gives lectures at Princeton. He gets asked for his autograph. The producer does not get any of these goodies. He labors in obscurity, even if it is wealthy obscurity. The producer does not like to see, in *People* magazine, some creep with an Underwood whom he could buy or sell with a few thousand dollars.

When the writers or directors demand more this, more that, a percentage of the gross, for God's sake, the producers are in no mood to be reasonable. If they want to walk out, screw 'em. "Let them walk out and get their houses foreclosed, and then they'll learn," a producer told me.

Of course, pay TV, minimums, freelance assignments, quotas are all serious issues. A Hollywood writer, God knows, has plenty of legitimate grievances against the producers. But in a sensible atmosphere, where there is a realization of how tough times are, where mutual interests lie, everything could be settled without ugly confrontation.

But envy and resentment overwhelm good sense. Envy, the unified field of Hollywood forces, pulls the town in upon itself like a ghastly black hole in space. This may be the price we pay for being a community of competitive, artistic, highly motivated people. But I think that is what the doctor says about heart attacks. And we do not need them, either.

53   THE BIG CHILL ON ROCK RADIO*

KEVIN BERGER

The essay that follows is a case study of the rock music industry in San Francisco. It is a revealing portrait of the radio business and of the struggle that stations wage to attract audiences. To give you a perspective on the significance of the music the various stations play, let me offer a quotation from a scholar about the

---

* Kevin Berger, "Rock Radio In the Bay Area: Forward into the Past" is reprinted with permission of *The Bay Guardian* and the author. Aug. 7, 1985.

significance of rock music for young people. The author, Allan Bloom, is a professor who teaches at The University of Chicago. He writes:

> Rock music caused a great evolution in the relations between parents and children. Its success was the result of an amazing cooperation among lust, art, and commercial shrewdness. Without parents realizing it, their children were liberated from them. The children had money to spend. The record companies recognized as much and sold them music appealing to their secret desires. Never before was a form of art (however questionable) directed to so young an audience.
>
> This art gave children's feelings public respectability. The education of children had escaped their parents, no matter how hard they tried to prevent it. The most powerful formative influence on children between 12 and 18 is not the school, not the church, not the home, but rock music and all that goes with it. It is not an elevating but a leveling influence. The children have as their heroes banal, drug-and sex-ridden guttersnipes who foment rebellion not only against parents but against all noble sentiments. This is the emotional nourishment they ingest in these precious years. It is the real junk food.
>
> One thing I have no difficulty teaching students today is the passage in "The Republic" where Socrates explains that control over music is control over character and that the rhythm and the melody are more powerful than the words. They do not especially like Socrates' views on music, but they understand perfectly what he is about and the importance of the issue.
>
> *Wall Street Journal.* May 2, 1983

It is worth keeping Bloom's ideas in mind when you read about the radio music industry in San Francisco and when you think about your development. We might also ask how Bloom would explain the fact that numerous surveys of college students indicate large numbers of them are primarily interested in obtaining good jobs and making a lot of money.

7:15 A.M.: Monday morning. Your clock radio clicks on, and you drag yourself out of bed to face another week. The radio is tuned, as it has been for years, to a local rock station. As the music fills the bedroom and, slowly, your awareness, you all of a sudden shake your head, overcome by an overpowering sense of *deja vu.* Can it be true? Is it really 1976 again?

No, it's 1985. It's just that what's new in rock radio is old music, and the strains of the tunes we grew up to can be heard from car stereo to beach box throughout the Bay Area. You may search for the songs on the cutting edge of new music in vain on the commercial bands: though the proliferation of old songs by the Rolling Stones and Pink Floyd on Bay Area air waves may cause new music lovers to cringe, it brings smiles to the corporate owners of the stations. According to their market research, nostalgia sells.

LOCAL PRODUCT

Album-oriented rock (AOR) radio was a product of the late 1960s and the rock revolution that era spawned. No station was more influential in establishing its format (or lack thereof) than KSAN of the late '60s and early '70s. The brainchild of San Francisco radio legend Tom Donahue, it broke with traditional rock radio in concentrating on the album rather than the single, the artist rather than the package. Long songs not to be found on 45s — a hallmark of sixties rock — received extensive airplay on AOR stations. A new venue for "hit" songs was found and bands without Top 40 singles became stars in their own right, selling out large concert halls and influencing rock music in general. AOR stations became a force for the music business to contend with.

The rock classics that once gave KSAN-style AOR radio its musical integrity are now being recycled to restore AOR radio to financial integrity. Since 1981, AOR stations, once the hottest advertising vehicle around for reaching young adults, have been losing the battle for the radio advertising dollar to CHR (contemporary hit radio), AC (adult contemporary), and country stations.

THE RATING GAME

The national Arbitron ratings, radio's equivalent of the TV Nielsens, tell the tale. In the 1984 overall ratings, called "12 plus" in the business (listeners 12 years and older), contemporary hit stations (like San Francisco's KMEL) turned in an overall rating of 16.9, while adult contemporary stations such as (KYUU) turned in a showing of 13.6. Third on the list were country stations (like KSAN in its most recent incarnation) at 11.8. The AOR stations brought up the rear last year, turning in a dismal 10.8 showing.

The numbers are far from arbitrary. The Arbitron rating for AOR stations means that between 6 am and midnight on an average day last year, 10.8% of the country's listeners with their radios turned on were tuned in to AOR stations — and that was an *increase* from 1983.

These numbers *mean* something. As Ron Fell, publisher of *The Gavin Report*, a radio industry tip-sheet sold to stations nationwide, points out, "The ratings are the only report cards for the national advertisers. And no station can hope to survive without the Cokes and General Motors."

Since 1980, no AOR newcomer has survived in the Bay Area without national advertisers. A floundering KMEL, "the Camel," switched from AOR to CHR in 1984, and "The Quake," KQAK, went under this past spring.

Tom Yates, co-program director of KKCY, the station that replaced The Quake, believes KQAK failed because of their strictly new-wave format.

"That kind of narrow casting always creates a promotion problem for the salespeople," he says. "If a station's format is not attractive enough to the consumers, then the advertisers don't come, and the money doesn't come. That's what killed The Quake."

AOR'S FALL

Burt Baumgartner, a promotion manager at Columbia Records and a former musical director at KSJO, an AOR station in San Jose, characterized AOR's rise and fall.

"AOR exceeded everyone's expectations in the seventies. Long songs like 'Stairway to Heaven' by Led Zeppelin and 'Freebird' by Lynyrd Skynyrd literally made AOR a success. The 18- and 19-year-olds, who were most of the population, listened to AOR stations all day to hear 'Stairway to Heaven' again. And, of course, the advertisers loved that.

"But AOR never changed, and by 1980 people were sick to death of *Frampton Comes Alive*. Then along came disco, and we couldn't play records by Marvin Gaye or The Supremes. Most AOR listeners hated disco, and anytime we'd play something by a black artist, someone would call me at KSJO and say, "Get that disco shit off the air!" Since then, according to Baumgartner, AOR has been stuck in a rut of playing the least offensive material.

The suburban boom of the Seventies also had a significant impact on AOR. As the decade progressed, Arbitron's sample audiences, on whom the ratings are based, grew proportionately dependant on the populations outside of the urban areas. Bonnie Simmons, a deejay and program director at KSAN during its heyday, and now a deejay at KFOG, recalls the change.

"When the ratings book began to be weighed heavily toward the South Bay and East Bay suburbs, it was no longer possible for us at KSAN to survive off the ratings of San Francisco and Berkeley, where we were the most popular," she says. "It gets tough for program directors when you have to take into account several different audiences, and so you are naturally inclined to take fewer chances."

With AOR mired in a slump, along came Lee Abrams, a programming consultant to more than seventy stations, to turn the tide. By 1980, Abrams had made his reputation by convincing stations to play songs like "Stairway to Heaven." Acknowledging that such a strategy had run its course, Abrams told *Variety* that AOR's survival depended on "getting rid of the old 1976–1980 corporate sounding bands, like Led Zeppelin. AOR is going to sound totally different, and we're on our way."

OLDER EARS

Abrams's reputation as a consultant landed him in October of 1982 at San Francisco's KFOG. Formerly an easy listening station, KFOG made the switch to a hard rock format in September of 1982. Abrams was brought in to establish a format for the station. It was his plan to leave the hard rock to crosstown rival, KMEL, and give KFOG a healthy does of softer rock songs by bands like Traffic, spiced with accessible new wave tunes by groups like Men At Work.

John Rivers is KFOG's current program director, the one who, in conjunction with Abrams, or with one of his assistants, decides what goes on the air. Before he came to the Bay Area and KFOG, he worked as program director at stations in Buffalo and Memphis that were both Abrams's clients. Rivers recalls that "no other station in the country would try" the new Abrams format until the executive at General Electric, which then owned KFOG (it was bought by the Susquehanna Corporation, a maker of housing materials, in January of 1984) agreed "to give it a shot." Along with Dave Logan, KFOG's program director at the time, Abrams put the experiment to work.

The new format KFOG was putting out over the Bay Area airwaves was, for the first time, aimed primarily at older listeners, Bay Area residents between the ages of 25 and 34.

"During the seventies, 18–34 was the target that everyone wanted," says Rivers. "But a lot of research was done and the results were that stations were really targeting either older businessmen or 16- to 22-year-olds. The upper end of the 18- to 34-year-old block was being told that you have to take the Motley Crues and the AC/DCs along with the rock classics that you grew up with," he says.

Abrams and Logan, though, knew that the "upper end" was through with the Motley Crues, and so they built a format that relied 75 percent of the time on friendly classics by The Beatles, The Byrds, or one-hit wonders like Thunderclap Newman. The format was bolstered by popular seventies "classical-rock" bands like Yes.

How did Abrams and Logan decide that a 1982 audience would accept such a format?

Said Rivers, "We'd go out and do research and talk to listeners. 'Okay, you were 20 in 1970,' we'd say, 'What do you remember about that?' And they would give you glowing responses about the marches, and being involved in this and that. 'What do you do now? Who did you vote for?' And they'd respond, 'I'm a stockbroker, and I voted for Reagan.' They're very conservative and yet to some degree consider themselves liberal. And they think of their music very similarly. These are the people who were important in creating our format."

But KFOG was determined to avoid the label of an "oldies station." As Rivers said, "All-solid-gold stations aren't making it anymore. They simply aren't." The numbers back him up. KYA, San Francisco's "solid gold" station, rated a 1.0 in the most recent Bay Area findings, lowest of all rock stations. In the 18–49 age group it averaged 16,200 listeners daily, compared to KFOG's 22,000.

QUALITY ROCK

What does the playlist look like that makes up the new AOR sound? Along with hundreds of non-current songs, a recent KFOG weekly playlist included twenty-nine new songs. Speaking of them, Rivers explains, "We choose quality rock, music that will hold up through time. Songs that you will remember in six months." As examples of recent "quality" rock, Rivers cited songs by Corey Hart, Paul Young, and 'til Tuesday.

For the first year and a half, KFOG "took some hard knocks in the ratings," said Rivers. But the tide began to turn in 1984, as the station gained greater audience acceptance and began to climb in the ratings. It has continued its ascent, scoring a 2.7 most recently, putting it in third place behind the local AC station, KYUU (3.8), and the BU (black/urban) station, KSOL (4.4).

KSOL's 4.4 is indicative of the fragmented market in the Bay Area. No single Bay Area FM station can claim a commanding market position and a wide loyal audience that looks anything like L. A.'s CHR station KIIS (9.0). According to Fell, that is because there is no local program director who has the "right combination of courage and market practicality." Fell also believes there are no local deejays "worth rallying behind."

In the Bay Area at least, an FM station's value as an advertising vehicle is not necessarily reflected in its overall 12-plus Arbitron rating. "Advertisers are more concerned with the ratings in the 18- to 34-year-old bracket, or the 25- to 49-year-old demo," says Bernie Wagner, the operations manager and media consultant at KSOL. "The 18–34 demo is the big one, though, the one that all the sales and advertising agencies are after these days." Advertisers scrutinize ratings data closely in searching for the right station and time slot for their particular product.

These days, though, the Arbitron ratings are often not enough. Ken Costa, head of research at the Radio Advertising Bureau in New York, a sales and marketing organization that assists stations and advertisers, reports that "most advertisers now rely heavily on sophisticated lifestyle studies, as well as ratings, to determine the spending power of age groups in certain areas."

IDEAL TARGET

One marketing and advertising coordinator at Warner/Elektra/Atlantic Records, who spoke only on condition he not be named, told the *Bay Guardian* influential advertising agencies have extracted from such studies the ideal target. Not surprisingly, local station owners eager for agency dollars have embraced the same audience target.

"Let me put it this way," he said. "The ad agencies are dictating an affluent, 25- to 49-year-old woman, so that is what everybody in radio is targeting for now. That is where most of the ad money is spent. The agencies are controlling the programming. That is the bottom line of what's happening here. The program director answers to the general manager, the general manager answers to the owner, and that is what constitutes the conservative mood in radio."

The attractiveness of that 25- to 49-year-old listener to potential advertisers launched KKCY into the Bay Area AOR market two months ago. Plus, the music market for that group of listeners was wide open, according to co-program director, Yates.

"Through logical research, as opposed to research that leads to programming by negativity and exclusion, we have been able to identify that no rock-related station — KSOL, KBLX, KYUU, KFOG — is serving that target." For the second time, Yates is joined as program director by Kate Hayes. The first time around, in 1980, they shared that task at the legendary KSAN's thirteenth and final year as an AOR station. Both have long histories in AOR. Hayes reports further on the potential KKCY listener as profiled by "logical research."

"They buy Volvos, Audis and Peugeots. They always buy above the midline. They buy top-end stereo gear, not just those 'Suburban boxes.' But they only take those to the beach. And they buy clothes for their children, because they have a lot of kids."

Yates notes one important finding about some of those 28- to 46-year-old listeners: their musical tastes have grown more eclectic. Many of them are listeners "who don't just like rock." Hayes adds, "Windham Hill made $20 million last year selling to that demo. It seems kind of silly to ignore them." To nail down this older, less rock-oriented audience, KKCY has been playing, along with the soft jazz of Windham Hill, songs as diverse as "I Got a Right to Sing the Blues" by Billie Holliday and Chris Isaak's "Dancin'."

KKCY's deejays benefit from technology undreamed-of by their predecessors of as little as a decade ago. They can choose for airplay any of 5,000 songs — approximately five times as many as any other AOR station — available through a computer terminal in the studio. But in the face of the rigid audience-targeted format, the technology can do nothing to get on the air new songs and new bands. KKCY's weekly playlist is derived from a format that requires a specific mix of songs from specific years. That format allows deejays to choose from only forty current songs.

That format appears to be working. Fully 85 percent of the 363 listeners who wrote the station in its first month of operation were between the ages of 25 and 44.

"THE ROCKER"

This same trend of targeting toward the "upper end" of the 18–34 age group can be discerned in some recent changes made at KRQR ("The Rocker"). According to program director Chris Miller, that station's listeners have in recent years been "18- to 24-year-olds and predominantly male." In terms of musical tastes, this age group has traditionally supported, both in concert and at the record stores, heavy metal music.

Yet this past spring, KRQR decided to cut almost all heavy metal from its playlist. An ad campaign followed, promoting "KRQR, the Ecstasy Without the Agony," a reference to the jettison of metal music. The change came on the heels of the recent Arbitron ratings, in which KRQR fell from 2.7 to 2.1 in the ratings. At an estimated average loss of $1 million in annual revenues per one point drop, this translated into a potential loss of $500,000 for The Rocker — and into more Beatles and less Twisted Sister on the air. Why did the station put older music into the format? Notes Miller, "Several firms have done surveys — and pretty fascinating ones — that say that the music you liked when you were 16 is the music that you will like for the rest of your life."

Does that mean KRQR is now playing older music to satisfy an older audience? Miller hedged. "The music is adjusted by the market indicators, yes."

BUSINESS SENSE

KFOG's number one rating among Bay Area AORs in the 18–34 and 25–49 age groups shows that a musical format based primarily on "rock classics" makes good business sense. KKCY's concentration on old material to hit the desired 25- to 44-year-olds may also make good business sense, just as KRQR's abandonment of heavy metal may push it upward in the ratings. To some record and radio insiders, though, the trend in programming toward an older audience comes with a high cost attached: it may be eliminating any possibility for new musical trends to gain airplay.

Paul Rappaport, the vice president of promotion of CBS records, is unquestionably a member of that older, upscale audience the AOR stations are coveting. But unlike that target audience the programmers and consultants believe in, Rappaport is sick of the same old song.

In a recent issue of *Album Network*, there is a photograph of him standing in front of the Whisky-A-Go-Go in Los Angeles in 1970. He has a beard, long hair and is leaning against a guitar. Beneath the photo, he has written a message to radio program directors.

"I don't look like this any more," he writes. "Like most Americans of my generation, I strive to look and feel young, and want to stay 'with it,' rather than sit around reminiscing."

"If you purport to be looking for upper demos, 25–34, you want a good mixture of currents with some oldies thrown in, and not the oldies format. ...And guess what? I didn't need a focus group to figure this out. New artists are being overlooked."

Rappaport is representative of a group the statistics and the formats don't allow for: older rock fans who *are* interested in hearing new music and new artists. But without exposure on the commercial rock stations, it isn't likely the new music will make it to the fans' ears.

Baumgartner of Columbia Records agrees there's a pall hanging over Bay Area AOR.

"I think the public is very open to hearing new music," he adds. "There is a lot of good stuff out there: If it's played, people will get excited. And that's the only thing that can make radio exciting again."

Miller, KRQR's program director, disagrees. "It's very hard to convince people to try something new. They are very conservative. Stations in the past have played new releases for an hour, and all of them have been monumentally unsuccessful."

Fell, publisher of *The Gavin Report*, cites as proof that listeners are conservative the recent demise of KQAK, the "Rock of the eighties" station that KKCY replaced. "People who want radio stations to be museums, to offer and preserve the best art of the day at great operating losses, don't realize that reaching the most profitable demo — the 30-year-olds, the Yuppies — is the bottom line of doing a good business. The Quake felt they had an obligation to play the best, new, cutting-edge music of the day. And they did a heck of a job of it. But they couldn't stay in business. The Yuppies don't want to identify with that kind of music."

NEW MUSIC

KUSF, a small 3000-watt nonprofit station funded by the University of San Francisco, is cited by many in the business as the station playing the best new music in town. Between 11AM and 6PM on weekdays, KUSF jocks regularly aired records by Robyn Hitchcock, Game Theory, Windbreakers, Graham Parker, and Danny and Dusty. On Sunday evenings, the man at the mike is Howie Klein. Klein, who has worked as a commercial deejay and music journalist in the Bay Area for many years, and is the president of 415 Records (a venue for such local new wave bands as Romeo Void and Translator that is distributed by Columbia Records), says, "It is only through the young audience that good things take off in schools, and then spread to the general audience."

The station does have something of an image problem. Harry Levy, KUSF's soft-spoken, intelligent young program director, acknowledges, "I know that people think we are all punks down here who play nothing but hardcore punk all the time, but that is not true at all."

CLASH AND COODER

Levy has installed a playlist of 60 new songs, six of which must be played an hour. That playlist largely reflects the record sales of local and national independent labels. The volunteer deejays must also play one or two "new wave standards" — "London Calling" by the Clash, for example — each hour. Once these requirements are satisfied, the deejays are free to play what they like, which is usually new and often unconventional rock. Levy says, though, he wants the deejays to understand that songs by Ry Cooder and Rickie Lee Jones can be added to the harder-edged songs. What counts, he insists, is a genuine feel for the music.

KUSF's amateurism and dedication to new music is reminiscent of the old KSAN. "I always thought that there would be another KSAN, that another station would come along and take chances on new artists and songs," says Levy. "But radio in San Francisco has gotten progressively worse. Our rock stations now are programmed for the lowest possible intelligence. It's really too bad that listeners aren't being challenged more."

Not only are we not being challenged by new songs, we're being sedated by too many old ones. Rock hasn't died. It's as vital and dangerous and wonderful as ever. Listen to KUSF. Take a midnight chance at a local club on an unknown band. When you get home, you can always tune your clock radio back to one of the commercial stations, where it's yesterday once more.

54   STATEMENT (TO HOUSE SUBCOMMITTEE)*

Stanley Fleishman

The material that follows is testimony given by Stanley Fleishman, a prominent lawyer and then general counsel of the Adult Film Association of America, at hearings held by the Subcommittee on Communications of the Committee on Interstate and Foreign Commerce of the U.S. House of Representatives. I have also included some questions raised by Congressman Lionel Van Deerlin, who was chairman of the subcommittee.

Mr. Fleishman included, for the record, a long statement with some interesting material on the matter of censorship. Some of this material (based on the findings of a governmental commission) follows and is worth considering when we think about censorship:

1. Extensive empirical investigation provides no evidence that exposure to or use of explicit sexual materials play a significant role in the causation of social or individual harms such as crime, delinquency, sexual or non-sexual deviancy or severe emotional disturbances. This empirical evidence supports the opinion of a substantial majority of persons professionally engaged in the treatment of deviancy, delinquency, and antisocial behavior, that exposure to sexually explicit materials has no harmful causal role in these areas.

2. Studies show that a number of factors, such as disorganized family relationships and unfavorable peer influences, are intimately related to harmful sexual behavior or adverse character development. Exposure to sexually explicit materials, however, cannot be counted as among those determinative factors. Exposure to such materials appears to be a usual and harmless part of growing up in our society and a frequent and non-damaging occurrence among adults.

3. Exposure to sexually explicit materials has positive aspects. Such materials are sought as a source of entertainment and information by substantial numbers of American adults. These materials also appear to serve to increase and facilitate constructive communication about sexual matters. The most frequent purchaser of explicit sexual materials is a college-educated, married adult, in his thirties or forties, who is of above average socio-economic status.

These three quotations, taken from a very long document, offer a number of insights that we can use when we think about sexually explicit films and videos

---

* Testimony given to the Subcommittee on Communications of the Committee on Interstate and Foreign Commerce, House of Representatives, 94th Congress, 2nd Session on The Issue of Televised Violence and Obscenity. July 9, August 17 and 18, 1976. Serial No. 94–140.

(and all other kinds of media). A government commission that investigated pornography concluded that it is not harmful. Pornography resists definition and exists, it seems, in the eye of the beholder.

Mr. FLEISHMAN. Mr. Chairman, I am sure that I was not invited to speak here as a counsel for the Adult Film Association of America, but more likely because of my very extensive experience in the Supreme Court. I argued more than a dozen cases in the U.S. Supreme Court on the subject of censorship.

I was also one of the attorneys for the Smothers Brothers in their first fight on this entire subject. They were the advance guard; they were the ones who got blown up first in this censorship debate.

As I see it, and I disagree with Mr. Cowan, who preceded me, on many subjects, and I agree with him on some — as I see it, that notwithstanding the first amendment, and notwithstanding section 326, the Federal Communications Commission might truly be named the Federal Censorship Commission. They engage in censorship, both in terms of so-called affirmative action, of the kind that Mr. Cowan was talking about. They engage in direct negative censorship.

For example, the *Sonderling* case, where the station was punished for a talk show, and those were the fem forums that were very popular for a while, and the FCC said that was inappropriate and a penalty was involved.

For the pending *Pacifica Foundation* case, where the album by George Carlin, a very fine album, was found to be the basis of a penalty against the Pacifica because, presumably, the record was indecent. The issue that was being raised in the record, which is very interesting and very relevant to what we are talking about here, is the use of words and our whole concept of what is good, what is bad.

Mr. Carlin, in the album, was saying it is OK, for example, to yell on television, or at a baseball game, kill the umpire, but if, God forbid, he said, "F —— the umpire," then the whole world was going to come apart. The burden of his record was, "Why is that?" Why is it that, from the FCC point of view, from everybody's point of view, really, it is OK to say "kill," but not "f ——"?

I think that, somehow, if we are able to resolve that question, many of the problems that we are dealing with here would, perhaps, fall into place a little bit better.

For example, the FCC has proposed legislation directed at so-called obscenity, more broadly defined than the Supreme Court has defined it, and indecency which has never before been thought to be the proper subject of legal suppression.

But, again, the FCC has not spoken in terms of violence, I mean. We have the notion of giving the FCC more power over an area of life which, as you have heard here and I agree completely, is one that is neglected, really, in the broadcast media, and, instead, we are being encouraged to have more violence.

My position, generally, with regard to the broadcast media, and I have thought about it a great deal, is, ultimately, that the broadcaster must have exactly the same right — no more, no less — than a newspaper.

I know the arguments in terms of the broadcaster has a license, but, that, in a way, only presents the problem in terms of how censorship is worked by Government.

I know the problems of monopoly, and I think the answer there has to be in terms of using the monopoly law.

For example, in my lifetime, we had a monopoly in motion pictures. Ultimately, there was an antitrust case resulting in the *Paramount Pictures* case. Prior to that time, what you had was integration. You had the major producers of film also distributing the film and exhibiting the film, and you had that kind of tight monopoly control so that you had limited kinds of film.

Ultimately, as a result of the *Paramount* case, where there was a breakup where production, distribution, and exhibition were not in tight hands, we had the diversity that Mr. Cowan was talking about — in the screen we got diversity — and we were able to open up the screen to an enormous area of human events that heretofore — or theretofore, had been suppressed, including, I might add, a lot on screen that is distasteful, that has excessive violence, that has excessive sex, that has excessive nonsense in it. There is no question about that.

I saw, last night, "The Taxi Driver." Well, 10 minutes of it I didn't see. I could not, for myself, stand the violence on it. That is my taste. I closed my eyes. I suppose if it were on television, I would have gone to another station.

I think that as we approach it, and really the questions that have come out, as I have been sitting here, is: Do we really believe in the first amendment, or do we want to change it? Do we want to say that television is so powerful a medium of expression that we should censor? If we want to do it, we ought to talk in those terms. Then, we can have a good debate.

Should we have censorship? Why should we have censorship? Should we amend the constitution to exempt from the protection of the first amendment the broadcast media?

It is not good — it is not healthy to have euphemisms. It is not good to say:

We are not engaging in censorship. This is self-regulation. We are not engaging in censorship. This is just for the public interest.

The public interest, as I see it, is found in the first amendment. The public interest is best served when Government keeps its hands off content. That is not to say that we have good content with Government out of the picture. That is not what I mean at all. I agree with much of what the speakers before had said in terms of the poor quality of television, in some particulars, the fact that we really have forced feeding by the broadcasters; but, it is not any different, really, if you think about it, than what we get from the Los Angeles Times. It is the paper in town, and we get what the Los Angeles Times gives us, good, bad, indifferent.

That is, as I see it, what the first amendment is really all about.

Now, we hear a lot about of, "Well, surely, we have to protect the minors, don't we?" I mean, "What are we going to do about the poor kids?"

First of all, I am reminded by a statement that Justice Douglas made, dissenting in a case back in 1966, *Ginsberg* v. *New York*. He said, "The juvenile delinquents I have known are mostly over 50 years of age."

As I read the newspapers and some of the shenanigans of some of your cohorts, Mr. Chairman, I must say that, Justice Douglas knew whereof he spoke.

We have in the Supreme Court a case, which, it seems to me, ought to be kept in very sharp focus, and that is, *Bucker* v. *Michigan*.

The principle there announced was that it would, in a democratic society, be entirely inappropriate to have the level of programming — this case, it was a book involved — the level of communication set by what is, quote, "appropriate for the minor." That would reduce all of us, of course, to being minors.

While we are talking about appropriateness and what is the public interest, I saw a very interesting story in the Los Angeles Times which, unhappily, I did not bring with me, but it was a report from the United Methodist Board of some kind where they came to the conclusion that under the family hour, the women — the position of women, the attitude of society towards women was grossly distorted, much more so than it was on general television.

So, one might say, "Well, the family hour may be OK for kids, but poor for women," or wherever else you want to move in this direction.

I have set forth, Mr. Chairman, at great length, findings from a report which has been much maligned, much neglected, and ought to receive much attention today. That was a report by the Commission on Obscenity and Pornography. It took 2 years for that Commission to bring in its report. A great deal of my money and your money was spent in connection with the work done by that Commission.

Unfortunately, when it was presented to the President, President Nixon said that that was immoral and he knew what morality was, and he was rejecting that Commission report, because it was immoral. I have to say, regretfully, that the Congress, including your House and the Senate, without reading the report, put it on the shelf, and it has been put away.

I have prepared a statement, I have some of its findings, at great length. I think that it would be helpful if the Congress were to take a look at it because there is a great deal of wisdom to be found in the entire report.

I would like to read just a brief statement from one of the Commissioners, a Reverend Jones, who was one of the Commissioners on the

Obscenity Commission. He was concurring in the general conclusions of the Commission, but, he had a separate statement, and this is part of it, which seems to have a great meaning for this committee.

> I have long been concerned that the burden of blame and the therapy of reeducation be focused on the true sources of the sexual crimes and maladjustments which plague our country and its citizens. If certain kinds of books or films had been proven the cause, then, I was quite willing to join in the crusade against them: however, it has been very adequately shown, through our research, that the roots of such behavior lie in the home and in the early years of familial and sibling relationships.
>
> It is good, I believe, to stop chasing what may have been our unconscious scapegoats in the media and to concentrate the energies, instead, upon the kind of re-education of the family, which will make for health and sanity.

Mr. Chairman, you mentioned the fact that one of the suggestions made by Mr. Cowan, with regard to locks on televisions, would be okay for those parents who were concerned, but what about the parents who are not concerned with their children?

Mr. VAN DEERLIN. What about the children of the parents who are not concerned?

Mr. FLEISHMAN. Yes; that is an enormous problem. It is an enormous problem, but I don't see how Government can take the place of the parent. The best we can do is to get parents to assume responsibilities because, if we are saying, "Well, we have to think about the parent who doesn't take care of his kid," you have to get rid of matches, I guess, because the kid is going to take a match and burn the house up, if nobody is watching him. There is no end to it. I mean, Government cannot take the place of parents, as I see it.

I have set forth, Mr. Chairman, as exhibit C to my statement, an opinion by Judge Bazelon which seems to me to be of great relevance to this hearing. It shows, in enormous detail, how the FCC engages in censorship, by, as he calls it, the raised eyebrow. Censorship by fear; not unlike, at all, the situation that preceded the family hour.

I think that the opinion of Judge Bazelon would be very helpful for the committee in seeing that the kind of war that the FCC, or Chairman Wiley, engaged in as a weapon to whip everybody into line is not new. This was exactly what was done back when the FCC finally took a stand against the fem talk shows that I spoke about earlier, the *Sonderling* case.

But, the truth of the matter is that since the FCC has the power of life and death over a station, the right to revoke a license, the right to kill, really, the station, its power is enormous and its censorial aspects are plain.

Now, having come to the conclusion that there is no room at all for Government, in terms of content, and that includes both affirmative and negative — there is no more room for Government to say that a station has to have something good for kids, something good for seniors, something good for this, that or the other ethnic group, any more than Government can say, "We are a newspaper." They have to have that. I think that in each instance, Government is precluded by the first amendment from doing so.

Mr. VAN DEERLIN. On what basis, then, does the Commission grant a license and renew a license?

Mr. FLEISHMAN. In my judgment, what it should be — I mean, right now, it is in terms of the public interest and convenience. The public interest, as we know, is a concept that is variable and —

Mr. VAN DEERLIN. In the minds of seven commissioners.

Mr. FLEISHMAN. Exactly, yes; and not in all seven of them. Sometimes it is four against three.

It seems to me that there ought to be the granting of a license on a relatively random basis. That there should not be any inquiry into the content. It is true that there are limited numbers of channels available, but they are not as limited as they once were, and there are more that could be made available, if the FCC wanted to do so.

I would say that the channels should be opened up. They should be made available on a random basis, without regard to content, that a licensee should not have a license in perpetuity. Theoretically, it is not in perpetuity, now, anyhow. It is renewable every 5 years, but, for practical purposes, it is in perpetuity.

I think that a license should be for a single one 5-year term, and then out. Let somebody else get it. You are going to get diversity in that way.

What you have is: You have such a vested interest. A license, after a while, is worth so many millions of dollars that there is no way in the world that the licensee is going to take a chance, in terms of trying to be a little more creative, a little more exploring.

But, if you had a single term of 5 years, and then somebody else comes in and does the best he can, I think that would be very helpful.

I think, as I indicated before, the use of the antitrust laws would be of extreme assistance here. I think that we have a monopoly situation. The networks, now, do have monopolistic control. I think if they didn't have stations, that would be a good beginning. I think that limitations could be imposed in terms of not having a particular radio station or television station bound, hand and foot, to CBS, or one of the other networks, if there was more fluidity, in terms of giving them options to choose what they want.

I think that what Mr. Cowan said in terms of that there ought to be programs for children is right. I think one way that it might be explored is through public broadcasting. We have public broadcasting now. What we ought to say is, "Use it in a creative way to get on the air what we want, and then have open and free competition with the broadcasters." I think that, with public broadcasting, with a broad-based Board of Directors, so that it is, hopefully, not weighted in any one particular direction too much, at least, that we would have the opportunity for having the kind of ballet, children's programs, senior programs, and all the rest that we do think of as valuable, and is valuable, that ought to be there, without having Government come in on private persons and doing what 326 said, that FCC should not do, because, notwithstanding the first amendment, notwithstanding 326, the FCC is very aggressively, very actively, presently engaged in censorship.

Thank you, Mr. Chairman.

55 THE STRANGE POLITICS OF "FAIRNESS"*

DAVID BOLLIER

The heart of the Fairness Doctrine is the notion that in democratic societies, it is necessary to ensure that all voices are heard on important social and political issues and that the media devote a decent amount of time to these issues. Few could argue with these goals; the problem is how do we implement them? How do we serve the public interest best? How do we make certain that the voices of minorities are heard and that all sides of controversies are presented?

In the past, the Fairness Doctrine of the Federal Communications Commission has required broadcasting stations, which use the public airwaves, to be fair and ensure that both sides of controversies (or, in some cases, all sides) are heard. Many radio and television stations have long felt that the Fairness Doctrine actually has inhibited them and prevented the free airing of controversial views since, in some cases, the stations avoided dealing with such topics to prevent "crazies" from having air time.

The print media, which do not use the airwaves (a scarce and valuable commodity), are not covered by such a doctrine and the electronic media now argue that they shouldn't be either, since cable and other new technologies now have opened up access. The other side of this coin is that access without audiences doesn't mean very much.

We find ourselves facing a dilemma. Those who wish to repeal the Fairness Doctrine argue that doing so will enhance our First Amendment Rights and those who oppose the repeal say that just the opposite will happen and the electronic media will become partisan. The public will be left unprotected from broadcasters who use their stations for political purposes. This situation is particularly important because so many people in America get most of their news from television. We might consider the ideas found in the *Red Lion* case here:

It is the right of the viewers and listeners, not the right of the broadcasters, which is paramount…It is the purpose of the First Amendment to preserve an uninhibited marketplace of ideas in which truth will ultimately prevail, rather than to countenance monopolization of that market, whether it be by the Government itself or a private licensee.

That's the goal. How we reach it is another matter.

Deep in the legal jungles of Washington, D.C., a guerrilla war of liberation is smouldering. The rebels, who invoke the spirit of the American Revolution and liken their oppressor to King George, are broadcasters and their lawyers. Previous skirmishes in Congress and the courts have left them frustrated and angry, but now they're readying themselves for what many believe will be their triumphant assault.

The citadel under siege is the Fairness Doctrine, the rules administered by the Federal Communications Commission that impose two basic obligations on broadcasters: (1) to devote a reasonable amount of their broadcast time to controversial issues of public importance and (2) to air contrasting views on those issues.

For years, most television and radio stations observed an uneasy truce with the Fairness Doctrine, providing air-time — often grudgingly — to the handful of critics, mostly citizens groups, who had legitimate complaints about broadcast fairness. But in recent months, emboldened by the deregulatory climate at the FCC, broadcasters have intensified their criticism of the doctrine. They now nourish hopes of defeating it in either of two legal challenges that may go to trial this fall.

Most of the rebels' complaints are familiar. Broadcasters claim that the Fairness Doctrine "chills" their First Amendment right of free speech by forcing them to air others' views. They say that the rules are a costly, time-consuming hassle. And now a powerful new argument has emerged: that the Fairness Doctrine is obsolete because cable television and other new media are providing a diversity of voices.

Ford Rowan, former NBC newsman and author of a 1984 book on the Fairness Doctrine, rhetorically wonders "what Madison, Jefferson, Franklin, or other co-conspirators against King George would have done. Would they have been willing to run the risk that a free electronic press might abuse its power?" (Rowan himself would take the risk.)

What makes the broadcasters' crusade so significant is that it would undercut the "public trustee" foundation of commercial broadcasting. In passing the Communications Act of 1934, Congress directed broadcasters to serve "the public interest, convenience, and necessity." The most meaningful embodiment of that standard, apart from the licence renewal process, is the Fairness Doctrine.

While critics of the doctrine would like to throw out the public interest standard entirely, such an open challenge would face a strategic disadvantage: Congress simply is not prepared to jettison this fundamental premise of our broadcasting system. So broadcasters are instead seeking a radical redefinition of the standard's *meaning* by eliminating the Fairness Doctrine.

This prospect has profound implications for a constellation of other important FCC "content regulations," which govern issue advertising and response time for personal attacks (see box). If the Fairness Doctrine is declared unconstitutional these regulations are also "doomed," according to Robert Gurss, attorney for the Media Access Project, a public interest law firm defending the doctrine. While these apocalyptic consequences are hardly imminent, many broadcasters are eager to take whatever steps possible toward transforming the publicly granted privilege of broadcasting into a corporate asset. Will the rebels succeed?

At first glance the struggle over the Fairness Doctrine seems to take place in a twilight zone in which traditional political alignments go topsy-turvy. Naderites join hands with Phyllis Schlafly because they both favor greater citizen access to the broadcast media. Staunch civil libertarians such as Floyd Abrams and Nat Hentoff make common cause with the broadcasting industry because they believe any FCC scrutiny of broadcast journalists' decision-making violates the First Amendment (while the American Civil Liberties Union dissents from this view). And a handful of corporations such as Mobil Oil and General Motors agree with public interest groups that the Fairness Doctrine should stay.

Now that the FCC itself has blasted the rule that it's supposed to enforce, Fairness politics have become even more bewildering. Such bizarre political alignments inspired Federal Appeals Court Judge J. Skelly Wright's famous observation that when it comes to matters of broadcast fairness, it's difficult "to tell the good guys from the bad guys." Who are we to believe when both sides claim the high ground by giving such similar names to their advocacy groups: the Center for Free Speech and the Freedom of Expression Foundation? (The former defends the Fairness Doctrine, the latter attacks it.)

Despite such confusion and the unusual alliances, however, where you stand on the issue generally depends on where you sit — in the control room, or in the broadcast audience at home. Media professionals generally oppose the Fairness Doctrine; they say it infringes on their free speech. (Group W is the only major broadcast firm that actively supports the doctrine.) Citizens who have a specific message or political cause — consumers, labor unions, religious organizations — generally support it; they say it enhances their free speech. When this conflict arises locally, it's usually resolved through informal negotiations that result in free air-time for the aggrieved party. Now the conflict is flaring into a full-scale constitutional challenge to the Fairness Doctrine.

In 1982, a Syracuse, New York, television station, WTVH, sold 182 minutes of its air-time to utilities promoting nuclear power. In the eyes of the Syracuse Peace Council, a citizens group, the station failed to provide a "reasonable" counterbalance, as required by the Fairness Doctrine. The group filed a complaint with the FCC. "Even the total amount of news programming (on nuclear-related issues, not necessarily nuclear power) didn't equal the amount of advertising time bought by the utilities group," says Liam Mahoney, a peace council activist.

The FCC agreed with the antinuclear group in 1984, ordering WTVH to correct its unbalanced coverage. (See *Channels*, January/February 1985.) But the station refuses to comply with the FCC order and is now mounting a direct constitutional challenge to the Fairness Doctrine — the first such test case since 1969. "When the government ends up controlling the press," warns John DeRoache, general manager of WTVH, "we could end up in the same situation as *Pravda* in Russia. The Fairness Doctrine is an absolute threat to every broadcaster."

Using more temperate language, network journalists such as Eric Sevareid, Bill Monroe, and Dan Rather agree. Rather told the FCC: "Once a newsperson has to stop and consider what the government agency will think of something he or she wants to put on the air, an invaluable element of freedom has been lost."

Activists say that loss is greatly exaggerated; they say the free-speech rights of broadcasters and monied issue advertisers are already adequately protected by their easy access to the airwaves. Those who suffer are the majority of people, who have neither transmitters of their own nor money to buy air-time. "The Fairness Doctrine is the only reason that citizens can have First Amendment rights in the broadcast medium," says media activist Joseph Waz.

Defenders of the Fairness Doctrine also point out that its "chilling effect" has been minimal. Since only one broadcast station has *ever* had its FCC license revoked for violation of the rule — the Rev. Carl McIntyre's WXUR radio station in Media, Pennsylvania, in 1972 — the industry's protestations of creeping Big Brotherism sound overwrought. Of some 6,787 Fairness Doctrine complaints and inquiries to the FCC in 1984 (about 10 percent in letters, the rest in phone calls), only six resulted in official FCC inquiries to stations. Only one case in 1984 resulted in an FCC finding that a station — WTVH Syracuse — had acted "unreasonably." It was the first such slap on a broadcaster's wrist in five years. Is that so burdensome?

Yes, says chairman Mark Fowler's FCC, quoting Judge David Bazelon of the U.S. Court of Appeals: "...even a governmental 'raised eyebrow' can send otherwise intrepid entrepreneurs running for the cover of conformity." In thousands of instances, says the FCC, the mere threat that citizens groups might lodge an official complaint "creates a climate of timidity and fear" and runs up legal fees.

Some broadcasters say they'd rather avoid controversy altogether, by refusing to run advocacy advertisements, than risk contravening the Fairness Doctrine. In comments to the FCC, the National Association of Broadcasters cites forty-five instances in which the doctrine has thus inhibited editorial freedom. The NAB claims the Fairness Doctrine has

squelched a radio series on the B'nai B'rith in Pennsylvania, advertising for
ballot propositions in Charlotte, North Carolina, and a radio show on religious cults in Southern California. Critics charge that many of the instances
cited are years old and scantily documented. The real "chilling effect," they
reply, is broadcasters' resistance to surrendering valuable air-time for controversies that don't pay their way.

As an imperfect means of balancing the First Amendment rights of
broadcasters against those of the public, the Fairness Doctrine seems to
apply a double standard. Why should broadcasters be denied the same freedom of expression print enjoys? The Supreme Court gave its first definitive
answer to that question in 1969, in effect, by posing another question:
Whose First Amendment is it, anyway? The landmark *Red Lion Broadcasting* v. *FCC* decision concluded that "it is the rights of viewers and
listeners, not the right of the broadcasters, which is paramount." The court
upheld the doctrine.

The FCC has the power to safeguard these rights, in the court's view,
because broadcast frequencies are inherently scarce and selectively granted
to trustees acting in the public's interest. "There is no sanctuary in the First
Amendment to unlimited private censorship operating in a medium not
open to all," the court said. Thus, broadcasters are free to have their say, but
as public trustees they must avoid "private censorship" of others.

This unequivocal language quelled critics of the Fairness Doctrine for
most of the 1970s. But with Ronald Reagan's election and his appointment
of Fowler as FCC chairman in 1981, the political climate quickly changed.
Fowler and many broadcasters began asserting that the proliferation of new
media undermines the Fairness Doctrine's "scarcity rationale."

The first stop in the crusade to repeal the doctrine was the Senate, where
Senator Bob Packwood (R-Oregon) held hearings in early 1984 on a "Freedom of Expression" bill. The legislation would have eliminated all content
regulation of broadcast media, including the Fairness Doctrine and Equal
Time Rule (which applies to political candidates). But the bill was defeated
11 to 6 in the Senate Commerce Committee even though it had been greatly
weakened by amendment and even though Packwood then held sway as
committee chairman. In the House, the repeal campaign ran up against
Representative Tim Wirth (D-Colorado), chairman of the House telecommunications subcommittee, who adamantly opposes any repeal or modification of the Fairness Doctrine.

Broadcasters then tried to convince the FCC to rescind the doctrine. But
this tactic ran aground on an unresolved legal question: Is the Fairness
Doctrine a statutory creation that only Congress can repeal, or an
administrative rule the FCC can erase?

It was first enunciated as an FCC rule in 1949, but ten years later
Congress mentioned the doctrine, in passing, as part of its 1959 amend-
ments to the Communications Act. Now broadcasters are claiming that
Congress did not *mandate* the Fairness Doctrine in 1959 but only
recognized it as a rule. If so, the FCC would have the authority to rescind

the doctrine, as it would doubltless like to do. Yet the commission last year refrained from claiming that authority. Henry Geller, director of the Washington Center for Public Policy Research, explains with a chuckle: "The FCC was scared stiff that if it made a statutory determination, twenty minutes later Congress would pass legislation telling the FCC to drop dead." Instead, the commission merely issued a report last August urging Congress to repeal the doctrine.

Stymied in Congress and half-disappointed by the FCC, broadcasters are seeking relief in the federal courts. They glimpsed an encouraging sign in two footnotes buried in a July 1984 Supreme Court decision that struck down a law against editorializing by public broadcasting stations. In *FCC* v. *League of Women Voters of California*, the court said it might reconsider its *Red Lion* decision if there were "some signal from Congress or the FCC" that new communications technologies have invalidated the "scarcity rationale" for the Fairness Doctrine, or if the commission determined that the doctrine chills free speech. The FCC virtually sent up signal flares to make both points in its August report.

It may be impossible to read the Supreme Court's mind in two of its footnotes, as Henry Geller contends, but many broadcasters regard the footnotes as the court's invitation to bring a test case on the Fairness Doctrine, and are charging ahead with two separate constitutional challenges, filed in the U.S. Court of Appeals.

The first case, brought last October by WTVH's owner, the Iowa-based Meredith Corporation, could be argued as soon as next fall. The suit represents "the most serious challenge to the Fairness Doctrine since *Red Lion*," according to opposing attorney Gurss of the Media Access Project. But the case also has its weaknesses. For example, Gurss says, "WTVH may have a hard time showing that it suffered an injury" since, in response to a later request by the antinuclear group, it voluntarily gave the group air-time.

The second case against the Fairness Doctrine was filed in the same month by the 2,200-member Radio-Television News Directors Association (RTNDA). Rallying behind the suit are the National Association of Broadcasters, Gannett, Post-Newsweek Stations, and other major broadcasters. CBS is providing most of the legal resources.

"Broadcasters agreed that this is the way to go," says Ernie Schultz, executive vice president of RTNDA. "After examining the merits of the WTVH case, we decided that is was not as good a vehicle for challenging the Fairness Doctrine." Blaming the FCC for a failure of nerve, the RTNDA seeks to force the commission to decide whether it has authority to rescind the doctrine. At the same time, the suit asks the court to find the Fairness Doctrine unconstitutional.

Defenders of the doctrine claim the RTNDA case doesn't belong in court and are seeking to have it dismissed. One reason it should be, in Geller's view, is that the court should not review the constitutionality of the Fairness Doctrine before the FCC explores alternative rules, less "chilling" to broadcasters' rights, that would achieve the Fairness Doctrine's goals.

COMPANION RULES ON BROADCAST FAIRNESS

Several regulatory companions to the Fairness Doctrine developed out of FCC and court decisions over the years. Each *has complex exceptions, qualifications, and ambiguities. Two of the most important:*

PERSONAL ATTACK RULE

When a TV or radio station airs an attack on the honesty, integrity, character, or any similar trait of a person or group, the station must notify the subject within seven days, provide a tape or transcript of the attack, and offer a reasonable opportunity for rebuttal, even if there is no paid sponsor for it. This rule does not apply to attacks made on news shows or by political candidates.

THE CULLMAN DOCTRINE

If a broadcaster airs a paid advertisement that deals with a controversial issue of public importance, it must also air opposing views, even if there is no paid sponsor for those views. This rule is frequently invoked during campaign seasons, when business lobbies buy air-time to promote certain ballot initiatives or referendums.

Several other FCC rules deal with broadcast fairness during election campaigns:

EQUAL TIME RULE (more formally known as the Equal Opportunities Rule)

If a broadcaster sells or gives air-time to one candidate for public office, it must offer equal access to all candidates for the office. ("Equal" applies to both the amount of air-time and the audience size.) Again, the broadcaster cannot edit or censor the candidate's presentation. News shows are exempt.

REASONABLE ACCESS PROVISION

The result of a 1972 election law, this rule guarantees that candidates for federal office have reasonable access to buy unedited air-time during campaigns. The rule prevents a station from freezing out candidates it may dislike.

THE ZAPPLE DOCTRINE

An offshoot of the Equal Opportunities Rule, the Zapple Doctrine says that stations giving or selling air-time to the *supporters* of one candidate must provide an equal opportunity to supporters of opposing candidates.

POLITICAL EDITORIALIZING RULE

If a station endorses a candidate for public office in an editorial, the station must notify other legally qualified candidates for that office within 24 hours and offer them an opportunity to reply. If the station airs its editorial within 72 hours before an election, it must give candidates advance notice so that they can respond.

But if the court gets past such questions and considers the merits of the RTNDA or WTVH cases, the pivotal issue may turn out to be whether the growth of new communications technologies renders the Fairness Doctrine obsolete by ending the scarcity of frequencies. Opponents say there's no need for a doctrine to assure a diversity of voices in broadcasting because there are now so many media outlets.

Defending the doctrine, Gurss looks at "scarcity" another way, arguing that there will be a scarcity of media outlets as long as there are more applicants for broadcast licenses than there are frequencies to be licensed. Those who get the licenses shouldn't be the only ones able to speak on the air.

The two definitions of scarcity are as far apart as the basic assumptions of the defenders and opponents of the Fairness Doctrine. Running a public franchise is different from running a private company. Serving the democratic process is not always as profitable as serving advertisers. The Fairness Doctrine forces the basic question: Which notion of broadcasting shall prevail?

It is not an all-or-nothing proposition, of course, because the Fairness Doctrine in practice exacts only marginal concessions from most broadcasters. They retain their First Amendment rights to have their own say on the air, while allowing others to stand on the same soapbox. They are not

LEGAL LANDMARKS IN THE HISTORY OF THE FAIRNESS DOCTRINE

1929: Broadcasters are first required to air contrasting views on public issues in *Great Lakes Broadcasting Inc.*, a ruling by the Federal Radio Commission.

1934: Congress passes the Communications Act, which creates the FCC and mandates that Broadcasters serve the public interest.

1941: The FCC rules in *Mayflower Broadcasting Inc.* that the public interest requires an outright ban on editorializing by broadcasters. "The broadcaster cannot be an advocate," the commission says.

1949: The FCC loosens its Mayflower decision, articulating the Fairness Doctrine as it is known today. While stations may editorialize freely, they are obligated to present "different attitudes and viewpoints concerning those vital and often controversial [community] issues."

1969: For the first time, in *Red Lion Broadcasting* v. *FCC*, the Supreme Court explicitly rules that the Fairness Doctrine is constitutional. Broadcasting's characteristics justify rules not applied to other media.

1973: In *CBS* v. *Democratic National Committee*, the court allows broadcasters to reject all opinion advertisements that individuals or groups may wish to air. There is no private right to purchase air-time. (In *CBS* v. *FCC*, eight years later, however, the court gives candidates for public office privileged access to the air during campaign season.)

1975: For the first and only time, the court forces a station (WHAR, Clarksburg, West Virginia) to cover a "controversial issue of public importance" (strip mining).

censored, and have great leeway in choosing how and when they will balance their coverage. Public obligations and private enterprises can coexist. Surely the Fairness Doctrine represents a small sacrifice in light of licensees' lucrative returns.

The two conceptions of broadcasting that may meet in court this fall bring to mind an old political metaphor: two teams locked in competition, one team thinking it's playing football, the other rugby. Which one is playing by the right rules? As long as a public resource, the airwaves, is devoted above all else to private profit-making, the clashes over broadcast fairness will persist. In the meantime, the Fairness Doctrine provides useful time-outs for getting the two teams together and reminding the visiting team who it is, after all, who owns the field.

56 BROADCAST REGULATION: AN ANALYTIC VIEW*

E. G. KRASNOW, L. D. LONGLEY, AND H. A. TERRY

Broadcast regulation, Krasnow, Longley, and Terry tell us, is generally shaped as a result of interaction among six "primary determiners": the FCC, the courts, the White House, various citizen groups, the industry, and Congress. We often become so involved with one or another of these entities that we lose sight of the big picture.

The material that follows is a chapter from their book, *The Politics of Broadcast Regulation*, which remedies this situation by giving us a "systemic view" of broadcast regulation — a perspective that shows us how the six groups interact in the shaping of broadcast policy. There are three major actors in this scenario: the FCC, the broadcasting industry, and Congress; the other entities play secondary roles, generally speaking. The matter of broadcast regulation is complicated by competition within the broadcast industry. What benefits one group usually harms a different one, so there is a constant tug of war between industry groups.

Krasnow et al. offers some generalizations about policy making:

1. Participants seek conflicting goals from the process.
2. No one group has enough power to dominate the policy-making process.
3. Participants have unequal strengths in the struggle for control and influence.
4. Component subgroups of participant groups often disagree on policy options.
5. Changes are made by small steps.

* From *The Politics of Broadcast Regulation*, 3rd ed., by Erwin Krasnow et al. Copyright © 1982 St. Martin's Press, Inc., and used with the publisher's permission.

6. Legal and ideological symbols play a significant role in the process.
7. The process is usually characterized by mutual accommodation among participants.

These generalizations provide a framework for understanding policy making as it relates to the broadcast industry and explains why the different competing groups pursue relatively moderate goals. The system is designed to prevent any one group from gaining too much, though one might argue that this system makes it difficult to get anything done at all. In some cases, the authors write, when an issue is seen as crucial by some group, accommodation often breaks down.

Broadcast regulation, we have seen, is shaped by six primary determiners — the FCC, the industry, citizen groups, the courts, the White House, and Congress. In addition there are miscellaneous participants — the Federal Trade Commission or the Commission on Civil Rights, for example — sometimes involved in specific broadcast-related issues but whose participation in the regulatory process, while important, is less constant. We have also seen that the six primary determiners rarely can accomplish much by unilateral action. The president, for example, names members of the FCC but checks out potential appointees in advance with significant interest groups (the industry and, infrequently, citizen groups). In the end, the Senate must formally approve nominations. The determiners, in other words, interact with each other in a complex fashion. Often those interactions are as important as, or more important than, what the determiners do on their own. Any attempt to understand what goes on in broadcast regulation must explain regulation as the outcome of complex interaction patterns within a dynamic system — what we will term the "broadcast policy-making system."

It is remarkable that so little effort has been devoted to the systematic understanding of broad-scale regulatory systems such as those affecting broadcasting. That is not to say that people have not attempted to understand broadcasting regulation. It is to point out that they have tended to shy away from attempts to explain it in analytic systems terms. There is a significant research literature surrounding each of the determiner groups we have identified. That literature is often interdisciplinary because political scientists, economists, historians, sociologists, and even psychologists have something to say about each of these groups. On occasion, the perspectives of one field are used to criticize or enlighten research that approaches the subject from another perspective. We have a body of literature about judicial behavior, relevant to an understanding of the role of the courts in broadcast regulation,[1] and interest group behavior, relevant to understanding both the industry and citizen groups.[2] Presidential[3] and congressional[4] decision making has occupied the attention of scholars for decades. Many persons have delved deeply into theories of regulatory agency behavior, with at least some of that attention being devoted to the FCC.[5] Rarely do these scholars make the error of assuming that one group exists in a vacuum; there is always some recognition that other groups influence the behavior of the participant being most directly studied. Often, however, that single group of greatest interest becomes the focus of attention.

The problem with such an approach is that it does not conform to reality. The moment one has understood and perhaps even predicted an administrative agency's act, for example, one finds that that action can be undone by the judiciary. It is possible to reach a finely detailed understanding of how and why Congress produced a particular law, but unless it is also understood that the consequences of that law will be profoundly influenced by how an administrative agency implements it or how courts interpret it or how affected industries behave under it, the perspective will be too narrow to result in real understanding of policy making.

It would be marvelous if there were an agreed upon general theory of the politics of regulation that incorporated the behavior of all the significant determiner groups.[6] Unfortunately, as yet no such accepted theory exists. Theories are easier to develop and test for simple laboratory-like phenomena than for more complex events and systems. Scholars have not yet even achieved consensus about which of several competing theories of regulatory agency behavior should be used for the analysis of an organization such as the FCC.[7]

This lack of agreement on a general theory, however, does not mean that the attempt to gain at least some systematic understanding of the broadcast regulatory process is futile. It simply means that the objective is not quite what it would be if there were a unified theory. With such a theory, at its most refined state, the objective would be to predict the behavior of the entire system. Lacking such a general theory, present goals must be more modest. We shall propose here a generalized model and develop some statements about its behavior. The model will help explain things and perhaps even allow some "retrodiction": it assists in understanding what has gone on even if it is not, like many models, developed to a stage where it permits prediction. In part two of this book, we will present five case studies of the broadcast regulatory system in action. The model and generalizations proposed here can then be seen in action.

A SYSTEMS APPROACH TO BROADCAST REGULATION

The politics of broadcast regulation can be seen in terms of an analytical framework or model we term the "broadcast policy-making system." Such a framework can be used both to understand the regulatory process and to suggest to scholars a conceptual orientation for work in this area.

As is the case with any model, the one we are suggesting is a simplification of reality. Yet to simplify is to streamline, to strip off surface complexities in order to show the essential elements of a system. Because virtually any economic or political process may be analyzed graphically in terms of such a systems approach, it also affords a uniform way to evaluate and compare a variety of situations or processes. A model directs attention to, and focuses on, key relationships and activities. By doing this, it helps define order in a real political world with many subtleties. An analytic system of this type is, in the words of political scientist Robert A. Dahl, "an aspect of things in some degree abstracted from reality for purposes of analysis."[8] Its primary test is not whether it is elegant or neat but whether it fosters an understanding of the political process or processes being studied.

Figure 1 represents the broadcast policy-making system. The six recurring participants in the regulatory process are the authoritative decision-making agencies at the heart of the model. The figure also charts various channels of influence among these six participants. It is significant that there is no one pathway through the core of the broadcast policy-making

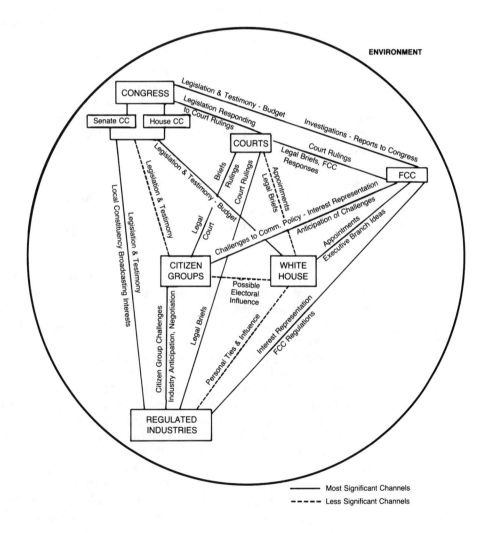

system, and any one of the various routes necessarily involves many participants. The key to understanding the politics of broadcast regulation lies in simultaneously analyzing the individual participants and their interactions. As Gary Wamsley and Mayer Zaid point out, "Policy is as much or more a product of factors within the interstices of the system's 'black box'...as it is of pressures or inputs from outside."[9] Although outside pressure, or "inputs," and the internal politics of each of the decision-making bodies can raise issues and define alternatives, it is the political relationships of, and interactions among, the six key determiners that are truly crucial to broadcast regulation.

Three of the principals (the White House, the courts, and citizen groups) usually play a less immediate, sustained, and direct role than the other three (the FCC, Congress, and the regulated industries). Thus, the primary channels of influence, information, and contact are traced among these three most significant determiners as the outer triangle in figure 1.

The system produces policy dynamically. Policy decisions — which might be called "outputs" — emerge from the interaction of some or all of the participants. Although the need for policy decisions may sometimes be stimulated by parties outside the system — for example, by an action of the Federal Trade Commission — in most instances, the functioning of the system itself generates the need for still more policy decisions. In other words, although some policy decisions may have long lives, many remain accepted and unchanged only briefly: one day's policy outputs in this system commonly become the inputs for the next day's policy making.

The policy outputs of this system are varied. They include "public" policies such as FCC rules and regulations, final court actions, laws enacted by Congress, and executive orders. An example of legislation would be the statutory requirement that all television sets sold after a certain date have UHF as well as VHF receiving capacity; an example of an agency decision would be the FCC's desire that incumbent broadcast station licensees should have preferred status, in renewal proceedings, over challengers for their licenses. Outputs may even take the form of decisions not to do something, exemplified by recent trends in "deregulation" such as the FCC decision not to supervise the number of commercials radio stations carry, or its decision not to concern itself with the entertainment programming format those stations use. In our model, policy outputs may even include many of the actions of the regulated industries, whose implementation of or operation under FCC rules and regulations or the Communications Act of 1934 is, in many cases, authoritative because it is unchallenged.

In most instances, such policy outputs (or authoritative decisions) bestow rewards or impose penalties on other affected interests. Reactions of those interests — or, occasionally, outside interests — stimulate the system to generate further policy output. They become, in effect, input back into the system. Some inputs are specific, such as a demand by a citizen group that a broadcast station not be permitted to change its format. Other inputs are exceedingly general, such as the mood that can be cast over an independent regulatory commission by a president or by the current public image of the agency. It is important to realize, too, that the system does more than merely respond to demands; it also molds political demands and policy preferences.

The system, of course, does not function in a vacuum. It operates in the context of an environment consisting of many factors, including the historical development of broadcast regulation, the basic technical and economic characteristics of broadcasting, and broad legal prescriptions. The environment outside the system also encompasses other factors, such as public attitudes toward broadcasting and government regulation and the actions of related systems — the Federal Trade Commission, for example — which may at times inspire and influence the broadcast policy-making system. It even includes actions and groups beyond the United States, for the spectrum is an international resource and U.S. broadcast networks and programs have a worldwide effect. In recent years, for example, U.S. policies toward spectrum allocation for radio and toward the location and function of communications satellites have had to be reconciled with the desires of our international neighbors. The United Nations Educational, Scientific and Cultural Organization (UNESCO) has debated policies toward a "new world information order" that, although perceived by third world nations to be important to their development, are seen by Western nations as antithetical to notions of press freedom. The major demands and supports — outputs and inputs — that determine what the system does, however, generally originate from within.

Policy outputs — the immediate short-range policy decisions — should be distinguished from policy outcomes — the longer-range consequences of such decisions. As David Easton puts it:

> An output is the stone tossed into the pond and its first splash; the outcomes are the ever widening and vanishing pattern of concentric ripples. The actual decisions and implementing actions are the outputs; the consequences traceable to them, however long the discernible claim of causation, are the outcomes.[10]

From the perspective of the participant groups, there are often clear "winners" and "losers" only when it comes to momentary outputs. It is harder to determine a winner or loser in looking at long-range outcomes. The "success" of an individual output ought to be measured by means other than the degree to which it meets immediate needs — either social ones or those of the participant groups. Success also includes the effect of the outputs on patterns of present and future inputs, and, of course, its relationship to outcomes.

When a policy output — or a long-range outcome — fails to meet the expectations of affected parties or is seen as an inappropriate or inadequate solution to the problems that gave rise to those expectations, that output is likely to be overturned by subsequent actions as frustrated demands arise anew. Indeed, if the system is perceived as being unresponsive to the expectations of key participants over a substantial period of time, then even its most basic features may prove vulnerable. So far, however, the broadcast policy-making system has, as a system, proved very durable.

SOME GENERALIZATIONS ABOUT POLICY MAKING

One important feature of the broadcast policy-making system is that it is highly turbulent. Largely because communications is influenced by rapidly changing technology, few specific policy decisions are stable and long-lasting. The system is always responding to new or changed conditions, with consequent incessant interaction among its participants. The operation of the policy-making system in specific instances is inherently unique; each policy-making problem is likely to differ in important respects from all others. However, certain recurring patterns about the politics of broadcast regulation can be identified:[11]

1. *Participants seek conflicting goals from the process.* Pluralism and dispersion of power in policy making do not by themselves suggest that the process is inevitably a struggle for control or influence. Conceivably the participants in such a process could share certain perspectives concerning what is to be done. Such is rarely the case, however, in the broadcast policy-making process; the gains of one set of participants are usually made at the cost of the interests of another. The policy demands of different groups often conflict; they must usually compete for scarce rewards.

2. *Participants have limited resources insufficient to continually dominate the policy-making process.* In a pluralistic complex such as that outlined in figure 1, policy-making power tends to be divided. Although the FCC frequently initiates policy proposals, it lacks the ability to implement most of them single-handedly. To prevail, it must win significant support from other participants. Similarly, none of the other five participants has hierarchical control over the policy making process, which is simply to say that nobody dominates the process consistently. In such a system policy making results from the agreement — or at least the acquiescence — of multiple participants, not from the domination of one. Coalitions of diverse participants work together and reward those belonging to them.

3. *Participants have unequal strengths in the struggle for control or influence.* Inequality among participants can arise because one party is inherently stronger, cares more, or develops its potential more effectively. In the 1970s, for example, citizen groups had considerably less strength than the Federal Communications Commission and the broadcast industry in their ability to influence policy concerning radio station format changes. Even when one federal court agreed with the views of a citizen group, another federal court — supported by the FCC and by broadcasters — prevailed. Favorable public opinion, legal symbols,

congressional allies, and the like are all potential sources of strength that participants have access to in differing degrees and that they may use with varying success on different issues.

4. *The component subgroups of participant groups do not automatically agree on policy options.* Each of the six groups we have identified consists of many subgroups: citizen groups range from liberal to conservative; the FCC is organized into bureaus representing interests that may conflict, such as cable television and broadcasting; there is not one single court but, instead, a hierarchy of courts, and it is common for a superior court to overturn the actions of an inferior court; radio broadcasters may sometimes view issues differently than television broadcasters. Thus, while it is useful to refer to the six principal participants as if each was one, it is important to recognize that each group may be unable — or find it very difficult — to agree on a common objective or course of action.

5. *The process tends toward policy progression by small or incremental steps rather than massive change.* One means of minimizing opposition to a policy initiative is to show its close relationship to existing and generally accepted policy. Frequently, earlier actions are cited to prove that the desired change is not unprecedented but only a logical continuation of past concerns and policies. One of the beauties of administrative law is that precedents usually can be found for almost any initiative. Although agencies are not as bound by precedent as are courts, they still hesitate to turn their backs on the past when it is pointed out to them. Such slow and gradual shifts in policy are not only strategic but probably inevitable, given the multiplicity of participants with conflicting goals, unequal strengths, and limited resources. Incrementalism tends to be at least a safe, if not necessarily the safest, course of action. As a result, however, the system is rarely bold or innovative and has a hard time responding to environmental pressures for massive change. The five case studies that follow show that the political resources necessary to accomplish significant policy innovations are greater than those necessary to achieve more incremental change or to preserve the status quo.

6. *Legal and ideological symbols play a significant role in the process.* Throughout the evolution of policy a recurring theme of participants is the legal and ideological symbolism they may attach to a discussion of alternatives. In many instances policies are seen as threatening or protecting the "rights" of broadcasters or the "rights" of listeners and viewers, without refined and, most importantly, commonly agreed upon specification of the meaning of those concepts. Broadcast policy-making discussions can also become embroiled in arguments over stock, symbolic rhetoric such as "localism," the "public interest," "access to broadcasting," or "free broadcasting." The terms become symbols cherished by participants in and of themselves without careful thought, or they are not commonly understood, so that ideological rhetoric sometimes supersedes real issues and actions in importance.

7. *The process is usually characterized by mutual accommodation among participants.* Customarily, participants in broadcast policy making do not attempt to destroy one or more of their opponents. Rather, the process is characterized by consensual, majority-seeking activities. Mutual adjustment among participants may occur in a variety of ways, including negotiation, the creation and discharge of obligations, direct manipulation of the immediate circumstances in which events are occurring, the use of third parties or political brokers capable of developing consensual solutions, or partial deferral to others in order to effect a compromise. To some participants, on some issues, however, accommodation is difficult if not impossible, and on these issues policy debate is intense and the perceived stakes the greatest.

The five case studies that follow (Ed. note: see original publication, *The Politics of Broadcast Regulation* for case studies) provide an opportunity to examine the politics of broadcast regulation in actual instances of struggle over policy alternatives. We will see the six key participants in the regulatory process using their varying (sometimes insufficient) financial, political, and social resources to attempt to obtain their desires in the face of probable or actual opposition from other participants. We will also see that, if they wish to be even incrementally successful, the participants must be relatively moderate in their goals, must respect legal and ideological symbols, must organize their resources (and the resources of their supporters) carefully, and must exhibit a willingness to adjust their positions in light not only of the positions of others and the resources available to them, but also the presence of potential or very real opponents. The politics of broadcast regulation is not dominated by a single group or interest; rather, the politics of broadcasting consists of complex interactions among multiple determiners of regulatory policy.

NOTES

1. See, for example, Henry J. Abraham, *The Judicial Process*, 4th ed. (New York: Oxford University Press, 1980); Joel B. Grossman and Richard S. Wells, *Constitutional Law and Judicial Policy Making*, 2nd ed. (New York: Wiley, 1980); Glendon Schubert, *Judicial Behavior: A Reader in Theory and Research* (Chicago: Rand McNally, 1964); Sheldon Goldman and Austin Sarat, eds., *American Court Systems: Readings in Judicial Process and Behavior* (San Francisco: W. H. Freeman, 1978); and especially Louis Jaffe, *Judicial Control of Administrative Action* (Boston: Little, Brown, 1965).
2. See, for example, David B. Truman, *The Governmental Process: Political Interests and Public Opinion*, 2nd ed. (New York: Knopf, 1971); Norman J. Ornstein and Shirley Elder, *Interest Groups, Lobbying and Policymaking* (Washington, D.C.: Congressional Quarterly Press, 1978); Congressional Quarterly, *The Washington Lobby*, 3rd ed. (Washington, D.C.: Congressional Quarterly

Press, 1979); and especially Jeffrey M. Berry, *Lobbying for the People* (Princeton, N.J.: Princeton University Press, 1977); Andrew S. McFarland, *Public Interest Lobbies* (Washington D.C.: American Enterprise Institute for Public Policy Research, 1976); and Timothy B. Clark, "After a Decade of Doing Battle, Political Interest Groups Show Their Age," *The National Journal*, July 12, 1980, pp. 1136–1141.

3. See, for example, Richard M. Pious, *The American Presidency* (New York: Basic Books, 1979), especially chapter seven; Richard E. Neustadt, *Presidential Power: The Politics of Leadership from FDR to Carter* (New York: Wiley, 1980); Thomas A. Timberg, *The Federal Executive: The President and the Bureaucracy* (New York: Irvington, 1978); and Richard P. Nathan, *The Plot That Failed: Nixon and the Administrative Presidency* (New York: Wiley, 1975).

4. See, for example, Lawrence C. Dodd and Bruce I. Oppenheimer, *Congress Reconsidered*, 2nd ed. (Washinton, D.C.: Congressional Quarterly Press, 1981); Congressional Quarterly, *Inside Congress*, 2nd ed. (Washington, D.C.: Congressional Quarterly Press, 1979); and especially John W. Kingdon, *Congressmen's Voting Decisions*, 2nd ed. (New York: Harper & Row, 1981); Aage R. Clausen, *How Congressmen Decide: A Policy Focus* (New York: St. Martin's Press, 1973); Randall B. Ripley and Grace A. Franklin, *Congress, the Bureaucracy and Public Policy*, rev. ed. (Homewood, Ill.: Dorsey Press, 1980); and Lawrence C. Dodd and Richard L. Schott, *Congress and the Administrative State* (NY: Wiley, 1979).

5. See, for example, Marver Bernstein, *Regulating Business by Independent Commission* (Princeton, N.J.: Princeton University Press, 1955); Sam Peltzman, "Toward a More General Theory of Regulation," *Journal of Law and Economics*, 19 (August 1976), 211–240; Michael Porter and Jeffrey Sagansky, "Information, Politics, and Economic Analysis: The Regulatory Decision Process in the Air Freight Case," *Public Policy*, 2 (Spring 1976), 263–307; Richard A. Posner, "Taxation by Regulation," *Bell Journal of Economics and Management Science*, 2 (Spring 1971), 22–50; and George J. Stigler, *The Citizen and the State: Essays on Regulation* (Chicago: University of Chicago Press, 1975). See also various additional works on regulation cited in the annotated bibliography of this book.

6. For an example of what such a theory might have to include, see James Q. Wilson, "The Politics of Regulation," in *The Politics of Regulation*, ed. James Q. Wilson (New York: Basic Books, 1980), pp. 357–394.

7. Compare, for example, Wilson's work, ibid., with Bruce M. Owen and Ronald Braeutigam, *The Regulation Game* (Cambridge, Mass.: Ballinger, 1978), pp. 1–36. An excellent review of several theoretical ways of looking at the FCC is found in G. Gail Crotts and Lawrence M. Mead, "The FCC as an Institution," in *Telecommunications: An Interdisciplinary Survey*, ed. Leonard Lewin (Dedham, Mass.: Artech House, 1979), pp. 39–119. See also Glen O. Robinson, "The Federal Communications Commission: An Essay on Regulatory Watchdogs," *Virginia Law Review*, 64 (March 1978), 169.

8. Robert A. Dahl, *Modern Political Analysis*, 2nd ed. (Englewood Cliffs, N.J.: Prentice-Hall, 1970), p. 9.

9. Gary Wamsley and Mayer Zaid, *The Political Economy of Public Organizations* (Lexington, Mass.: Heath, 1973), p. 89.

10. David Easton, *A Systems Analysis of Political Life* (NY: Wiley, 1965), p. 352.

11. The generalizations that follow were suggested in part by Charles E. Lindblom, *The Policy-Making Process* (Englewood Cliffs, N.J.: Prentice-Hall, 1968).

NEW
TECHNOLOGY

We are now living in the middle of what one researcher, Fred Williams, has called a "communications revolution." There are so many changes taking place in the field of telecommunications and related industries, that it is very difficult to determine what the ultimate impact of these changes will be.

Rather than focusing upon the future, and theories of what might happen, it is useful to examine what impact the new technologies are having now. For example, consider how people are using remote control tuning devices with their television sets. A phenomenon has developed called "flipping" in which viewers jump from channel to channel continually, since this can be done by simply pressing a button on a remote control tuner.

J. Walter Thompson, a large advertising agency, made a study of this phenomenon and discovered that approximately one third of all television watchers were "flipping" (and that more than half of viewers between the ages of eighteen and twenty-four were). Advertisers are worried because viewers often flip at the first sign of a commercial, a process called "zapping." Another phenomenon, called "zipping," involves fast forwarding through commercials in movies and other programs when people play them back on Video Cassette Recorders (VCRs).

The flipping phenomenon suggests that many people no longer watch programs but, instead, watch television...and jump around from program to program continually. By flipping, zipping, and zapping, people avoid or miss many commercials, which creates enormous problems for television networks and stations, who sell time on the basis of audiences they claim to "deliver" to advertisers.

As a result of flipping, commercials are often much shorter (fifteen seconds is becoming standard) and programs have become faster-paced. After all, if viewers become bored, all it takes is a press of a button and they are watching something else.

The remote control device is relatively simple one, yet is has had a profound impact on the television industry. The VCR is probably the most revolutionary of all the new technological devices. It frees viewers from the control of stations and networks and allows them to "schedule," as it were, their own television viewing.

Until VCRs were developed, viewers could only watch programs that were broadcast or cablecast to them. You had to select from what was available when it was available and if you didn't like anything, you had no alternatives (other than not watching television, that is). With the development of VCRs, however, viewers are king and can tape programs and view them when they want to watch them. (This process is known as "time shifting.") And they can rent films and other kinds of programs to watch at their convenience for nominal fees.

As a result of economies made possible by mass production, VCRs now cost less than $300; it is estimated that by 1990 approximately 50 percent of American households will have them. The impact of VCRs on network television broadcasting keeps growing and some researchers believe that the VCR will lead to a restructuring of television broadcasting.

In many middle-Eastern countries, families have several VCRs. Some of these countries restrict the kinds of programs they allow on television, but the people get around these restrictions by importing (often smuggling in) films and other materials they wish to view. So the VCR has pretty much destroyed the power of governments to censor television and films.

The remote control device and the VCR are aspects of new technology that we are all familiar with. There are, in addition, many other phenomena to consider, such as the development of cable television, of satellites (and direct broadcasting from satellites to home receiving dishes), of teletext and videotex "electronic publishing" information services, of computers, of videodiscs, videogames, compact discs, digital audio recorders (DARs), and fiber optics. And these phenomena are just the beginning.

The same applies to other areas. Things move so quickly that books on new technology tend to be obsolete by the time they are published. If it takes a year to write a book and approximately a year to publish the book (which tends to be the case), you have material that is two years old when it is published.

There are also human factors that must be considered. For example, it may be possible for many people to work at home in this "wired" nation, but studies have found that people, as a rule, don't like to stay at home; they prefer to go into the office, be with people, and have lunch with their friends. We are, after all, social animals. There is often a gap between what we can do and what we want to do (or feel we should do). The new technologies are "privatizing" our lives in many respects. Whether this is progress remains to be seen.

57   THE NEW TECHNOLOGIES*

LYNNE SCHAFER GROSS AND R. DEAN MILLS

In recent years we have seen an incredible number of new devices that play an increasingly significant role in the making and distributing of our mass media. I am talking about such things as computers, satellites, videocassette recorders (VCRs), fiber optics, cable systems, digital audio recorders, compact disks, Videodroids (for editing film via video), and laser disks, to name some of the most important. The essay that follows deals with many of these new technologies and will provide you with a broad overview of the most important of them and the role they may be playing in the future.

These devices have had a revolutionary impact on the media and on society; we now live in an information society in which more than half of our Gross National Product is generated by the creation and distribution of information — as contrasted with the production of goods. The new media technologies also have implications for our social order and our political systems.

Technology always poses a problem to people: who will be boss? There are people, "technological determinists," who believe that all technologies have imperatives built into them and that, ultimately, technology is the basic shaping force in societies. Our new world, they believe, will be technologically determined. Technology will take command, so to speak.

Other thinkers dispute this. They argue that people create technologies and have the power and the responsibility to use them in humane ways. From this perspective, the new technologies are tools used by people for particular purposes and do not, like Frankenstein's monster, take on a life of their own once they have been created. We ought to keep this "debate" in mind when we think about the new technologies and their impact.

As far as the mass media, in particular, are concerned, there is another matter that deserves consideration. Let's take the case of television. We may develop cable systems, shoot endless numbers of satellites in the air, spread fiber-optics systems far and wide, invent new cameras, and develop new and advanced audio and video editing systems, but what impact does all this have on the programs we make? In the 45 years since television was created, we do not seem to have been particularly creative in developing new kinds of programs. So it seems likely that our new technologies will end up being transmission agents for the same old films and television shows. We will end up spreading the cultural "wasteland" further, faster, and cheaper. But is this progress?

---

* Lynne Schafer Gross and R. Dean Mills, "The New Technologies." This article was written especially for this volume. Copyright © 1987, Lynne Schafer Gross and R. Dean Mills.

The record for mass communication prognostication is almost unblemished. Seldom has anybody gotten it right:

Why didn't somebody guess that Johannes Gutenberg's jerry-rebuilt wine press and movable type would redraw the face of Europe?[1]

Why did the telephone, which some early forecasters saw as a medium for bringing concerts and news into the living room, end up being an individual, rather than a mass, medium?[2]

How was it that radio, which its inventors originally perceived to be simply a wireless telephone, turned out to be the mass entertainment and news medium that the telephone was supposed to be?[3]

How could the experts have been so wrong in the 1940s, when they predicted that facsimile machines would replace the daily newspaper?[4] (And again in the 1970s, when a new group of experts pronounced that the newspaper had met its match, this time in videotex?)

And why don't we all have video telephones? They have been technologically feasible since the turn of the century. And innumerable business executives from a number of countries have predicted that, any year now, they would be in every household.[5]

In this essay, we try to explain why predictions about new communications technologies are so tricky. We illustrate with examples of unexpected successes and unexpected duds. Along the way, we try to sort out what factors determine success or failure for a new technology. And, finally, ignoring the clear lessons of our narrative and our better instincts, we will make some predictions of our own.

We narrow our focus in this chapter by dealing primarily only with those technologies that (1) promise a new system of delivery of entertainment or information and that (2) are aimed at a mass audience. We do not discuss such technological refinements as high definition or 3-D television, compact audio disk players and digital audio tapes, which represent changes in format rather than in delivery. Nor do we talk here about the computer, which is discussed elsewhere in this book.

We must also note, for the record, that most of the "new" aren't actually all that new. In fact, some of them have been around since the 1940s, and even the newest are over five years old. However, they are often grouped as new technologies because they threatened (or seemed to threaten) older, more established media — broadcast television, film, newspapers, and magazines.[6]

Although prognosticators have erred constantly, they have not erred consistently. Sometimes, when genuinely innovative technologies were on the brink of transforming the social, economic and political landscape, observers ignored them or grossly misunderstood them. In other cases, technologies described with much ballyhoo as revolutionary turned out to be marketing flops. In some cases, the same technology was underestimated at one point, overestimated at another.

The first kind of error, underestimation, seems to be rooted deep in the human psyche. The human mind finds it difficult, if not quite impossible, to imagine something truly different from anything it has encountered. So when a new technology comes along, the mind either fails to see it or attempts to hang it on the metaphorical peg of an existing technology. The telephone was seen as an extension of the concert hall, or as merely a talking telegraph. The radio was seen as simply a wireless telephone, of interest only to ship captains. Television was seen as simply radio with pictures, or as a movie theater that happened to be in the living room — rather than as a medium that would, as it turned out, restructure American family life. Similarly, two newer technologies, video cassette recorders and cable television, were at first perceived as merely interesting adjuncts of existing technologies.

The video cassette recorder, when it first emerged as a consumer product in 1975, seemed to be simply an extension of an existing technology, television. And in some ways it seemed analogous to another old technology, sound recording. It was natural for everyone to perceive the VCR as simply a recorder of television programs — a device to record the occasional program that the viewer would want to see several times.

Instead, of course, the VCR turned out to be one of those media sleepers — a new technology that unexpectedly rearranges people's daily routines. In fact, after only a dozen years on the consumer market, VCRs have changed not only television viewing habits but a whole range of social and media behaviors.

As with any new technology that finds a secure market niche, VCRs are also shaking up the old technologies. They may provide the death blow to neighborhood movie theaters, already on the ropes at the hands of television and cable television. With their voracious appetite for new material, they may help change the way movies are sold and produced. And by giving consumers more direct control over their viewing habits, VCRs may force the once unchallengeable television networks into changing their way of doing business.

No one could have predicted such far-reaching effects for the rich person's toy that Sony first sold in 1975. People could use the Betamax ($2,300 for both recorder and the special Sony set that was part of the package) only to record programs while they were watching them. They were toys for the true videophile, people who built up archives of programs to see over and over.

After JVC introduced its VHS (video home system) format a year later, competition led to cheaper units and enhanced features. The one-hour cassettes of the first Betamax were replaced by two-hour cassettes, giving owners enough tape to accommodate feature films — the first indication of the dominant role that VCRs were about to carve out for themselves. Timers gave viewers the power to time-shift — record programs for viewing at a later time. Or they could even go to the grocery store — or to classes — without worrying about missing their favorite soaps. The VCR would tape programs for them while they were out. Pause buttons enabled them to eliminate commercials while they recorded. Fast forward let them zap commercials during playback. They could even record one program while viewing another, finally giving the viewer victory in that age-old battle with network programmers who scheduled two good programs for the same hour.

Today, the VCR remains a device for time-shifting (what VCR owner watches the David Letterman show during its real-time, early-morning broadcast hours?). That alone disturbs the networks, whose executives fret about the effects time-shifters and commercial-zappers will have on advertising revenues. But the VCR has also given rise to a whole new way of distributing and viewing prerecorded movies. In fact, the most important impact of VCRs may be the one that has little to do with television directly: The family living room is replacing the neighborhood movie theater. VCRs appear already to have stolen away from theaters one of the last major contingents of older customers — X-rated movie fans. For many video stores, adult movies constitute a large fraction of the business.

And now there's at least some evidence that theater owners' last hope, the teen-age and young adult audience, may also be deserting to the new technology. Teenagers, who according to conventional wisdom would stick to movie theaters because it was a way of getting out of the home, are finding VCRs attractive for the same reasons adults have. Your VCR shows the movies you want (What tonight? A classic? A foreign film? Musical comedy? Pee Wee Herman?) when you want them (Before dinner, with drinks? After dinner? In bed? No problem.). And you don't have to worry about parking places and muggers. Or endure sticky floors, the smell of stale popcorn, or the tall guy who always sits in front of you and the mouthy people who always sit behind you.

Dr. Joyce Brothers, the television psychologist, says the VCR has an even stronger appeal to some teenagers. "It's harder to get your girl from a movie theater into bed than simply to move into the next room or lie down in front of the TV."[7]

Success story that they are, even VCRs had a thicket full of legal and marketing problems to work their way through — demonstrating the difficulties that any new technology faces in carving out a niche for itself in a tough market. In 1976, Universal Studios and Walt Disney Productions brought suit against Sony in an attempt to prohibit the manufacture of the Betamax and even the use of units already sold, claiming that the machines violated copyright laws because they could copy material off the air. In 1984, however, the U.S. Supreme Court decided in favor of Sony, and the 13 million-plus people who had VCRs did not have to throw them in the trash.

Ironically, after Sony won that battle it lost a crucial marketing war, one consumers had watched nervously from the sidelines as they tried to decide which kind of VCR to buy. Although Sony had the first recorder and superior technology (the Betamax, most experts agreed, offered clearer pictures), it lost out to the VHS standard and stopped manufacturing the Betamax in 1986. Greed may have led to its downfall, because Sony was stingy about licensing its machine to other companies. While Sony touted the Betamax, a whole raft of firms were publicizing and advertising the VHS format.

VHS itself is far from secure over the long haul. Sony has now introduced 8-millimeter VCRs. The system, with its smaller cassettes, offers the advantage of more compact VCR cameras for home "movies."

But in whatever format, the VCR clearly has a secure niche in the media mix. As of 1986, they were poised to take over second place, after broadcast, as the most popular delivery system for television. VCRs were in 38 percent of American homes and cable television in 40.[8]

Cable television itself has confounded prognosticators over a forty-year period. It entered the marketplace virtually unnoticed, and within a few decades was in 40 percent of American homes. Clearly, the experts underestimated it. But that was in its infancy and boisterous adolescence. As it matured as a technology, experts and laypersons began to *overestimate* its possibilities. Some predicted cable would kill network television. Some futurists saw in it nothing less than a new kind of democracy, in which voters could instantly voice their opinions on governmental policy through interactive video systems. The reality, as we now know, fell somewhere in between.

Cable television developed in the late 1940s as, literally, an extension of the television antenna. That perception is enshrined in its original name, CATV — community antenna television. Beginning in the late 1940s, in areas where television reception was nonexistent or weak, neighbors strung cable to their homes from a master antenna strategically placed, usually atop the highest hill, to pick up good signals.

Cable was strictly a small business that struggled for many years as a political underdog of television delivery. The FCC and Congress, pressured by broadcast interests, set up restrictions governing how many stations cable systems could import from distant places, which local stations it had to carry, what programs it was not allowed to show if they were shown on local television, and how much it had to pay in copyright fees. Local governments became involved by issuing franchises.

The ma and pa companies that owned the cable systems during the forties to early seventies eked out a living, but the medium was certainly not glamorous.

Certainly the programming was not flashy. For the most part it was merely retransmission of signals picked off from broadcast stations. Any programs originated by the cable systems themselves were usually primitive: a stationary camera focused on a thermometer and barometer, for example, so viewers could check the weather on their home screens. At one point, in 1969, the FCC mandated that all cable systems with 3,500 or more subscribers had to originate local programming. But the rule was never enforced, mainly because many of the cable companies said they couldn't afford local programming.

In the late 1970s, all that changed. A young company, Home Box Office, started using satellites to send movies and special events to cable systems owned by its parent, Time, Inc. HBO quickly found other cable companies also wanted the service, and subscribers proved eager to pay the extra $8 or so a month to get late-run movies in their living rooms. In the meantime, other cable companies were experimenting with interactive cable.

Suddenly, cable was hot. Cities that had never considered having cable, since they were already well-served by strong broadcast signals, suddenly had upwards of fifteen companies vying for franchises. Promises filled the sky — and city council chambers. Companies promised local programming facilities for seniors, blacks, policemen, city council meetings, and even lost dogs. They promised "Gee whiz" interactive services that would perk the coffee, help the kids with homework, do the shopping, protect the home and teach the handicapped.

One highly publicized system, QUBE, initiated in Columbus, Ohio, in 1977 by Warner-Amex did, indeed, offer interactive services. Qube polled people on their thoughts about local and national issues, and designed interactive games. The biggest hit was every Monday-morning quarter-back's fantasy — a service that allowed viewers to call plays during foot-ball games, as they were being played. Viewers could see what percentage of their fellow fans agreed with them instead of the coach.

But promising all these services and actually initiating and paying for them were two different things. Many of the satellite cable networks failed, and the lost dogs (not to mention most of the local human beings) never got their channel or their TV studio. Even QUBE closed its wires in 1984. Cable TV entered, in the euphemistic phraseology of the trade, "a period of consolidation and retrenchment" in the 1980s.[9] But it is still a viable medium.

Video cassette recorders were an unqualified success. Cable was a qualified success. Among recent technologies, they are the rarities, tech-nologies whose potential was underestimated. The more common error recently has been in the opposite direction. We have overestimated the importance, indeed, the survival, of many new technologies. The bad guesses seem to have resulted from three phenomena: (1) the willingness, even eagerness, of corporate executives and consumers alike to believe the hype that accompanied the market introduction of the technologies, (2) the failure to distinguish between genuine technological breakthroughs and gimmicks that were simply variations, usually costly variations, on existing technologies, and (3) the failure to understand the extent of the regulatory and economic problems any new technology faces.

Platoons of public relations and advertising people work hard to make small technological changes sound like revolutionary ones. Consider the breathless language of an advertisement for TeleFirst, an ABC service that offered to broadcast movies for automatic recording by VCRs in the late-evening and early-morning hours: "Ready to introduce you to a whole new concept in home entertainment." TeleFirst did not survive its six-month test period in 1984. Or this advertisement for the United States Satellite

Broadcasting Company, which portrayed the satellite operation as nothing less than a fourth network: "USSB will compete with the other three networks for the very best programming in first-run entertainment, news and sports — from Hollywood to every major production center on the globe."[10] USSB, too, lasted only six months.

And, let's face it. Many of us Americans want to believe the hype. Since the nineteenth century, Americans have placed child-like faith in the power of technology to solve, or at least ameliorate, the dreary problems of living. We do like our electronic toys, many of us, and we're quite ready to believe they will make revolutionary changes in our lives. We believe, that is, until the next revolutionary toy comes along.

When we make this second kind of mistake — whether the we in question is consumers at the local electronic emporium or the media executives who pour millions of dollars into a doomed technology — we do so by ignoring the obvious: Genuine breakthroughs in mass communication come when a new technology delivers information or entertainment, or both, better than an existing technology.

The telegraph was a genuinely new way of delivering the written word at fantastic speeds compared to the postal service. The telephone was a genuinely new way for people to talk with one another over increasingly longer distances. The radio brought both information and entertainment from around the world directly and instantly to the living room, the first time anything like that had ever happened. Television added to that moving visual information. And so on.

Compared to those abrupt changes in the way information and entertainment could be delivered, or even the more modest changes in delivery offered by VCRs and cable television, most of the so-called "new technologies" are (or were) pretty tame stuff. Their introduction follows a predictable pattern. The technology that makes a new consumer product possible is introduced. A company publicizes the idea, using its full panoply of public relations and advertising hype. Revolutionary social and economic benefits are foreseen. The service is tried on an experimental basis. And it flops.

Direct broadcast satellite (DBS) is an example of a very elaborate technology that during the early 1980s received enormous hype and then fell flat on its face. Here was a device that, from 22,300 miles up in space, could transmit signals to two-and-a-half-foot dishes on people's rooftops. Companies entering the field had to plan on at least $700 million to launch the service. Nevertheless, when the FCC invited companies to apply to operate DBS services, thirteen did.

The impetus had come from one company, Satellite Television Corporation (STC), which in 1979 told the FCC it wanted to develop a programming service that would go directly to homes. The idea was opposed by the traditional networks because the establishment of DBS would mean people could receive programming directly, without the intermediaries of broadcast stations. However, the FCC sided with STC and, in 1980, invited applications. The applicants included the three broadcast networks, who had decided to join them in case they couldn't beat them.

Of the thirteen ideas submitted, the FCC approved eight in 1982 and expected that the services would be operational in 1985. Most of the proposed services planned to program movies, sports, and other entertainment. The FCC mandated that "due diligence" reports be given in 1984 to make sure that the companies were progressing toward DBS service and not sitting on the frequencies for future use.

With great fanfare, market surveyors proclaimed that 23 percent of consumers would be likely to buy the rooftop dishes and another 20 to 35 percent would be somewhat likely.[11] The whole idea looked so promising that one other company, United States Satellite Broadcasting Company, essentially snuck into the arena.

In 1982 it petitioned the FCC to begin a vaguely described DBS service, which the FCC approved. It then purchased time on a Canadian satellite that could beam signals to four-foot receiving dishes. United set up five channels of service and offered them in the Midwest for $40 per month and a one-time installation cost of $300. After six months of operation, United folded its tent, having attracted only about a thousand customers.

Meanwhile, several of the original DBS applicants flunked their "due diligence" tests and others didn't even bother to fill out the forms. Then, in a very surprising move, Satellite Television Corporation, the company that had pioneered the DBS concept, announced it was pulling out of the business after having spent five years and $140 million gearing up for it. This left the DBS in turmoil, where it remains.

Dreams that DBS would challenge the major television networks are clearly dead. Today the technology is used largely by individual hard-core television fans who buy the large ten-foot dishes to pick off signals directly from satellites. But HBO, ESPN, the Disney Channel and others have begun to scramble the signals, making even that use less attractive.

Teletext and videotex are two other technologies that drew enormous interest from prognosticators, who predicted great things particularly from the interactive capabilities of videotex. And the corporate managers of major media corporations like Times-Mirror and Knight-Ridder thought enough of the idea to invest millions of dollars in experimental videotex systems. But the consumer remained unimpressed, stubbornly preferring the mundane, but still user-friendly technologies of newspapers and yellow pages.

Both text services show words and graphics on a TV screen, but the method of delivery is different. Teletext is transmitted on part of the traditional television signals and can be picked up by ordinary television sets equipped with special decoders. Users can select what they want from a limited number of "pages," usually about 200.

Videotex is a genuinely interactive system transmitted through cable TV or telephone wires. In addition to selecting from a wide range of constantly updated information, videotex users can send messages back to the cable company source. Teletext users could, for example, find out what plays were being offered by local theaters. Videotex users can actually purchase tickets through the system.

Of course, someone always has to pay for a new technology. In some foreign countries, particularly France, where text services became popular, national governments underwrote the cost. In the United States, the consumer had to pay, either through a fixed monthly rate or through fees paid for the time they spent "on line."

In the early 1980s several American experiments were begun in both teletext and videotex, a number of them by companies who owned newspapers and were hedging their bets in case text services replaced newspapers. In fact for a while newspaper owners were so intent on getting into the field that they worked actively to bar AT&T from electronic publishing. In a famous 1982 agreement, AT&T gave up its local telephone companies but was allowed to engage in other communications activities, including text services. But, at newspapers' insistence, the agreement was modified to prohibit AT&T's entry into the text services until 1990.

In 1982 predictions were being made that both teletext and videotex would become widely available in the not-too-distant future,[12] so the newspaper publishers were glad to have AT&T out of the way for several years. It was a pyrrhic victory. Knight-Ridder, Times-Mirror, Group W, Time, CBS, and NBC tried text services. Although some consumers were generally impressed, they weren't willing to spend the money to keep them in their homes, and the services almost all folded.

Video discs are another new technology that failed as a mass medium, at least the first time around, and now are looking for a more modest role in life. Development of video discs first began in earnest in the 1960s, but for many years they were plagued by those twin curses of most new technologies, over-promotion and under-development. Announcement after announcement said the video disc would be on the market "next year," but many next years came and went, and still no disc.

As with video cassette recorders, there actually were two different disc systems. The less advanced was the capacitance disc developed by RCA. It had a diamond stylus that moved over grooves similar to those of a phonograph record.

The second system, the laser disc, had a very muddled parentage that included marriages, divorces, and partial custody by a large number of companies, including MCA, Philips, Magnavox, IBM, and Pioneer. The laser disc used a laser beam that read information embedded in a plastic disc, a technology that guaranteed the disc would never wear out and that any frame could be quickly accessed and viewed in freeze-frame almost indefinitely. Unlike VCRs, both were playback-only systems; they could not record programs off the air.

The laser disc, then owned by MCA-Philips and called DiscoVision, was the first on the market. The first models of the machine itself sold out shortly after its 1978 introduction, but the discs were so technically flawed that their sale and manufacture had to be discontinued.

In 1981, RCA introduced its capacitance disc player, called Selectavision, and predicted it would sell 200,000 in the first year. And at first they sold fast: 26,000 players and 200,000 discs the first week. But the pace quickly dropped and RCA fell far short of its 200,000 goal in the first year. In fact, after three years only 500,000 machines had been sold and RCA abandoned Selectavision.[13] The company blamed videocassette recorders, which could record as well as play back. When RCA threw in the towel, in 1984, the laser disc, now owned by Pioneer, was still suffering from technical glitches, and video discs seemed dead.

However, Pioneer managed to solve the manufacturing problems and began marketing the disc players to education and industry. In these markets the technology has been tied to computers, and its vast storage capability and its ability to freeze pictures and access them quickly seem to be genuine assets. So the future of the disc is unsure, at best, but it may have a reincarnation.

With some new technologies, the infatuation and marketing hype is matched by consumer enthusiasm, leading to fantasies of even greater success. Then the bottom falls out. A case in point is subscription television (STV), which was very successful in the late 1970s and is now virtually dead.

Subscription TV is actually one of the oldest of the "new" technologies, having been tested in the early 1950s. Some of the subscription TV systems delivered the program, usually a late-run movie, to the home TV set through wires. Others sent the programming over the air but scrambled it so that home viewers needed to use a special "black box" in order to receive the signal.

Most of the early experiments were low-key and failed primarily because of equipment malfunctions. But in 1957 a high-profile motion picture exhibitor, Henry Griffing, set up an operation in Oklahoma that was supposed to deliver first-run movies by wire. Griffing was strong in sizzle (publicity) and weak in steak (money and programming), and his project bombed.

But it enjoyed so much publicity that broadcasters and motion picture exhibitors got scared enough of subscription TV to lobby against it. The broadcasters were afraid STV would outbid them for movies. Motion picture exhibitors were afraid people would stay home to watch movies rather than going to theaters — anticipating the problem they would eventually face from a different technology, the VCR.

What followed was a shaky decade for STV, during which the FCC allowed it to operate but saddled it with so many pro-broadcasting restrictions that it was stifled. For example, no more than one STV operation was allowed in any one community, and STV systems were prevented from "siphoning" — outbidding broadcasters for programming. At one point STV was even outlawed in California, through a referendum passed by voters, who were influenced by a very strong anti-STV campaign launched by motion picture exhibitors.

Ironically, what changed life for STV was the success of cable TV; but salvation came too late to be longlasting. And the savior, it turned out, would soon become the executioner. Home Box Office succeeded in having the FCC lift some of the restrictions that inhibited STV, including the anti-siphoning and one-to-a-community policies. Starting about 1977, STV experienced a huge boom and UHF stations all over the country began offering scrambled movie services for a fee of about $19.00 a month.

For several years the bloom was on the rose. Predictions were made that STV was on "the threshold of an era of expansion comparable to that of television itself in the 1950s.[14] Since the STV operations were garnering profits at 20 to 25 percent of revenues (in contrast to conventional television, which was less than 18%), these predictions seemed justified. Oak Media, the largest STV company, at one point had 600,000 subscribers in five cities around the country.

Then in the mid 1980s the bottom fell out, because STV could not hold its own against the rapidly expanding cable systems, which enticed subscribers not with just one but several pay-TV services on top of an array of free channels. Subscribers defected in droves, and seven systems shut down in 1983. Even Oak Media, the biggest, closed down or sold out all its systems by 1985. By 1987 only one subscription TV service, SelecTV in Los Angeles, was still on the air, and it was hanging on primarily because it had a satellite feed to other media.

Sometimes the hype for a particular medium is so great that the medium appears to be a failure when, in fact, it is a moderate success. Low-power television (LPTV) is a good example. It was touted as a truly democratic medium — one that, because of the low cost of the technology ($50,000 to start up, compared to about $2 million for conventional stations), would allow the ordinary American, or at least groups of ordinary Americans, to own a TV station. In 1980, then FCC Chairman Charles Ferris said LPTV "offers the same intriguing possibilities as the advent of commercial television broadcasting in the late 1940s."[15]

Although it has not achieved success at all comparable to commercial television, some LPTV stations are moderate successes. First authorized by the FCC in 1980, these stations, as their name implies, have very limited power — ten watts for VHF and one thousand watts for UHF. This means they can cover only a radius of twelve to fifteen miles. They are sandwiched in between regularly operating stations. For example, if a city has a channel 4 and a channel 6, a low-power station could operate on channel 5 provided it did not interfere with either of the other full power stations.

The FCC drew up plans for these stations with the purpose in mind of allowing groups not usually involved with TV ownership to have a TV voice in the local community. In particular, it hoped women and minorities would apply. Some did, but a great number of applications were from large companies such as Sears, Federal Express, and even ABC and NBC.

The FCC received over 5,000 applications before April of 1981 when it decided to impose a freeze on new applications so it could sort out those already submitted. This huge number of applications seemed evidence that many groups and individuals felt there was a bright, profitable future in LPTV.

When the FCC began approving applications late in 1981 — first to rural areas and then to cities — it held to its original purpose, however, and made most of the awards to people who were not part of the broadcasting establishment. All has not been rosy for these novices, and many have not activated their stations or have sold their licenses to other groups. Others have found they could not afford to undertake local programming and instead went to the same well as everyone else — services that provide movies. Others, however, have been able to sell advertising and make modest profits with programs that deal with hunting season, high school band concerts, Yugoslav-American customs, and farm reports.

These biographies of new technologies — obituaries, in several cases — are daunting for the corporate executives who must bet their best guesses with their stockholders' money, and also for those of us who are addicted to technology and want to see the good ideas survive.

Is there a pattern that will help executive and armchair fan alike predict which new technologies will make it? We think so. If it is to succeed, a new delivery system for mass communication must: (1) offer information or entertainment that the consumer wants; (2) offer it in a more attractive, efficient, or helpful way than existing technologies; (3) offer it at a competitive price; (4) fare well in the competitive and economic battles that any new technology faces in today's crowded market; and (5) have a good sense of timing. A successful new technology, in other words, is one that finds the right market niche at the right time.

Consider the case of videotex, the service that Knight-Ridder introduced in Miami (as Viewtron) and Times-Mirror tried in Southern California (Gateway). Videotex fascinated those of us who like new gadgets. And its interactive nature seemed to offer a better way of getting individualized information. But in fact, it turned out to be simply a more cumbersome and more expensive way of delivering information that people could already get in newspapers, magazines, books, and the yellow pages. And those ancient print media were by comparison very user-friendly. Try taking videotex to the breakfast table with you. Or onto the bus. Or to the bathroom.

Direct broadcast satellites failed to some degree in all areas. The programming was the same old movies (or new movies) that everyone else was showing, and it tried to make the scene after cable TV and backyard dishes (both technologies offering a vastly wider program selection) were already established. Most of all, it was just too expensive — for both developers and consumers.

Subscription television for a time met most of the criteria we have listed. It provided subscribers late-run movies, at an affordable price, in the comfort of their own living rooms. But it got a late start because of regulatory problems (themselves caused, of course, in large part by broadcast and movie interests quite conscious of the STV threat). And by the time those problems were solved, two other new technologies, cable television and videocassette recorders, offered the same services in even more attractive packages. With cable, viewers could buy excellent reception of dozens of channels in addition to pay movies. And VCRs offered consumers personal choice and convenience of a kind STV could never match.

The jury is still out on low-power TV. It does meet some of our criteria. Properly executed, LPTV would offer viewers something they do not now get: locally based news and entertainment. And it is conceivable that local television stations could even survive economically, if they are able to attract some of the local advertising dollars that now go into radio. But the question is, will LPTV be able to survive the competition with existing broadcast and cable services? Here, the evidence is not encouraging. Given a choice, television viewers almost always go for the slickest programming. That is one reason American movies are as popular in Nairobi as they are in Nantucket. It is the reason few viewers bothered to tune in to the amateurish productions that filled local access cable channels, and the reason that made it easy for cable owners to kill them off.

Cable, of course, was not dependent upon its local programming. In fact, one of the main reasons cable has survived is that it has something for everyone at a fairly economical price. Among its myriad channels, there is bound to be some sort of programming to appeal to everyone in the family. It succeeded in being a service whose time had come mainly because it hung around for so long. And this longevity led to enough clout to receive some favorable regulation. Although it is not an unqualified success, cable has had enough perseverance — and, on occasion, luck — to meet some of our criteria some of the time.

The one unqualified success story, VCRs, found a toehold in the market, recording programs off the air, very early. Then it quickly seized a much bigger niche, playing back prerecorded movies. It delivered programming consumers have always loved, movies, in an almost irresistibly attractive way, straight to the living room, anytime they wanted it. Its timing was impeccable. STV and cable TV had fought the battle of being allowed to compete with networks by showing movies. They had many scars to show, but the networks, too, were somewhat worn down and had lost some of the battles. Favorable legal decisions helped. But even VCRs remain in some ways vulnerable in the volatile mass media market.

That brings us to our first prediction: We have seen the last of truly revolutionary changes in the delivery of radio and television programming.

We now have the technological capability to deliver sound and moving pictures from any part of the earth to any other part of the earth. Indeed, we can even deliver them from space. To some extent, any improvements at this point, in the technological sense, have to be refinements or clever combinations of existing technologies. It is something like transportation. After you know how to transport goods and human bodies at high speeds by land, sea, and air, there's not much change you can make that's revolutionary — unless you can figure out how to beam bodies instantaneously through space, à la *Star Trek*.

We do not want to carry this too far, of course. Clearly technology in mass communication will continue to develop. Some new technologies (and creative combinations of the old ones) will make lots of money for the people who develop them. Some technological innovations may even make life more pleasurable, perhaps even more efficient for the consumers who buy them.[16] But at this mature stage in the development of communications technology, the changes in people's lives wrought by the new technologies are likely to be evolutionary. And we should be wary of any claims about revolutionary developments in the field.

Prediction two: Eventually there will be a better cassette technology than VHS that will probably be tied to high-definition TV. There will be a gradual turnover to it similar to what happened with color TV. By then —

Prediction three: The neighborhood movie theater will finally die, not to be resurrected. Only very specialized theaters — foreign language in some ethnic neighborhoods, classic and foreign film theaters in a few big cities — will survive.

Prediction four: STV is dead, and its cousin, pay-per-view, will die too unless there is a way people can access what movie they want when they want it. Only if STV can work out a way to give consumers the anytime, any place advantage offered by cassettes will it have a chance to survive — by saving consumers a trip to the local video store.

Prediction five: More cable TV services will fold until there are only about twenty channels offered for a more modest fee than at present. Cable penetration will then go up.

Prediction six: Low-power TV will survive if there are no alternatives for very local programming. If regular TV stations or cable do a good job in this area, the LPTV novelty will wear off, and advertisers and owners won't keep up the concept.

Prediction seven: Videotex will make a comeback, offering an efficient and attractive way of delivering telephone numbers, recipes, banking services, and information about goods and services. This will happen once the federal prohibition on AT&T's entry into the interactive market expires in 1990. Ma Bell will make it work because it already has in place access to almost every home in the United States, through the telephone system. And Ma Bell also has the capital to see this revived videotex through the expensive early years.

Prediction eight: DBS will never get off the ground unless it will be to broadcast network programs in high-definition TV while stations are broadcasting the same material on the old system. This would make possible the gradual transition to HDTV.

Prediction nine: Discs will eventually come back to the consumer market, perhaps by offering cheap, high-definition video and audio, at first for the youth market. People will get used to the format in the workplace, where they will be used for information retrieval, and they will co-exist as audio cassettes and compact discs do now.

Prediction ten: At least one of these predictions, and quite possibly all of them, will be proved wrong, and in an embarrassingly short time.

NOTES

1. For a fascinating account of the changes that printing made in European politics, culture, and social life, see Elizabeth Eisenstein, *The Printing Press as an Agent of Change: Communications and Cultural Transformations in early Modern Europe* (Cambridge, England: Cambridge University Press, 1979).

2. Detailed in William Beck Banning, *Commercial Broadcasting Pioneer: The WEAF Experiment, 1922–1926* (Cambridge: Harvard University Press, 1946). "The Wondrous Telephone," a popular song from 1877, depicts the telephone as, in effect, the radio: "You stay at home and listen/To the lecture in the hall/Or hear the strains of music/From a fashionable ball."

3. One of the best accounts is in Erik Barnouw, *A Tower in Babel* (New York: Oxford University Press, 1966). In fact, the whole Barnouw trilogy (*The Golden Web* and *The Image Empire* as well as *A Tower in Babel*) is well worth reading.

4. Edwin Emery, Phillip H. Ault, and Warren K. Agee, *Introduction to Mass Communications* (New York: Dodd, Mead, and Company, 1963), p. 63.

5. An account of the great, unsatisfied expectations surrounding the video telephone can be found in Brian Winston, *Misunderstanding Media* (Cambridge: Harvard University Press, 1986).

6. Four books that detail the new technologies are: Lynne Schafer Gross, *The New Television Technologies* (Dubuque, Iowa: Wm. C. Brown Company Publishers, 1986), Loy A. Singleton, *Telecommunications in the Information Age* (Cambridge, Massachusetts: Ballinger Publishing Company, 1987), George E. Whitehouse *Understanding the New Technologies of the Mass Media* (Englewood Cliffs, N.J.: Prentice-Hall, 1986), and Frederick Williams, *Technology and Communication Behavior* (Belmont, California: Wadsworth Publishing Company, 1987).

7. Joseph Vitale, "Video Rites of the New Saturday Night," *Channels*, January, 1987, pp. 62–64.

8. "Tape Measure," *Broadcasting*, December 29, 1986, p. 8.

9. "Cable's Lost Promise," *Newsweek*, October 15, 1984, pp. 103–105.

10. The advertisements appeared in a number of trade journals in late 1983 and early 1984.

11. "Public Has an Appetite for DBS," *Variety*, April 27, 1983, p. 1.

12. Joseph Roizen, "Teletext — A Service That's Coming of Age," *E/ITV*, September, 1982, p. 42.

13. "RCA Gives Up on Videodisc System," *Los Angeles Times*, April 5, 1984, pt. IV, p. 1.

14. "STV: Scratching Out Its Place in the New-Video Universe," *Broadcasting*, April 7, 1980, p. 46.

15. U.S. Federal Register, October 17, 1980, p. 69191.

16. In the 1980s, the telephone is finally threatening to become a mass medium of sorts. SurfLine, a 976 service number, gives residents of Southern California up-to-the-hour information on where the best waves are. In 1986, Surfline received a million calls, each of which cost the caller 95 cents. SurfLine is only one of a number of pay-per-dial numbers offering news, information, and entertainment since Pacific Bell introduced the lines in late 1983. In 1986, the 976 lines handled 31 million calls, the bulk of them undoubtedly variants on the Dial-a-Porn theme.

58   THE DIGITAL COMPUTER AS A CREATIVE MEDIUM*

A. Michael Noll

There is a widespread conception that computers are "dumb" devices. They can do all kinds of incredible computational work and be used, with the right software, for all kinds of tasks (such as word processing or making spreadsheets). But, as we keep hearing, they only do what they are told. So if you ask a computer a stupid question, so to speak, you'll get a stupid answer. It is this thinking that is behind the famous statement "garbage in, garbage out" (GIGO).

Computers, then, may be great facilitators, but they certainly have little to do with the creative process, as we generally understand it. It is humans who are creative, who can develop their powers of imagination and generate new ideas, works of art, and new products — generally by combining old ideas and facts in different ways. Creativity is a mystery; we don't really know why some people are so remarkably generative and others don't seem to be creative or imaginative at all.

Creativity is often connected with the ability to break out of old patterns, to escape from conventional ways of seeing things or doing things. And these attributes are, in turn, connected to such things as having a sense of humor or being something of an iconoclast. The important thing is to be able to "break form" and have the courage and confidence to try something original.

The essay that follows, one of the earliest on the subject of computers and creativity, puts many of our notions about computers to the test and contains some interesting surprises. It compares a work of art done by a famous painter and another, similar work, generated by a computer and shows that a large number of people who were asked about the two works were, one might say, "captives" of their prejudices and erroneous ideas about computers.

One area involving creativity not discussed in the essay, but related to the topic, involves computers and writing. The computer has revolutionized writing because word processing programs enable writers to generate first drafts very quickly and then revise these drafts as many times as they wish. It is the ability to revise and edit drafts that is crucial to good writing; very few writers are able to write good first drafts. Thus, the computer has been an incredible aid to writers, many of whom don't have the slightest idea of how a computer works or how to program one. Computers, then, greatly facilitate the creative process and since writing involves, in large measure, writers finding out what they think about things (by writing about them), computers are intimately connected with creativity.

* © 1976 IEEE. Reprinted with permission, from *IEEE Spectrum*, Vol. 4, No. 10, pp. 89–95, October 1967.

The notion of creating art works through the medium of machines may seem a little strange. Most people who have heard about the experimental use of digital computers in creative endeavors have probably shrugged them off as being of no consequence. On the one hand, creativity has universally been regarded as the personal and somewhat mysterious domain of man; and, on the one hand, as every engineer knows, the computer can only do what it has been programmed to do — which hardly anyone would be generous enough to call creative.

Nonetheless, artists have usually been responsive to experimenting with and even adopting certain concepts and devices resulting from new scientific and technological developments. Computers are no exception. Composers, film animators, and graphic artists have become interested in the application of computers in their creative endeavors. Moreover, recent artistic experiments with computers have produced results that should make us re-examine our preconceptions about creativity and machines. Some of the experiments, described in this article, suggest, in fact, that a tight interaction between artist and computer constitutes a totally new, active, and exciting artistic medium.

HOW DOES AN ARTIST WORK?

There is an anecdote attributed to Henri Matisse about how to approach the creative act of painting. You take a blank white canvas, the French artist said, and after gazing at it for a while, you paint on it a bright red disk. Thereafter, you do nothing further until something occurs to you that will be just as exciting as the original red disk. You proceed in this way, always sustaining, through each new gambit with the paint and brush, the initial high visual excitement of the red disk.

The anecdote is a somewhat simplified version of Matisse's idea, but even if we take it lightly, it can do a number of things for us. For one thing, it dispels some of the sense of mystery that hovers over the procedures of the creative person. It tells us something concrete and easily visualized about the creative process while emphasizing the role of the unexpected ideas for which the artist lies in wait and for which he sets a formal "trap" in his medium.

Even a relatively "passive" medium — paint, brushes, canvas — will suggest new ideas to the artist as he becomes engaged. The resistance of the canvas or its elastic give to the paint-loaded brush, the visual shock of real color and line, the smell of the paint, will all work on the artist's sensibilities. The running of the paint, or seemingly "random" strokes of the brush, may be accepted by him as corporate elements of the finished work. So it is that an artist explores, discovers, and masters the possibilities of the medium. His art work is a form of play, but it is serious play.

Most of all, the Matisse anecdote suggests that the artistic process involves some form of "program," one certainly more complex than the anecdote admits, but a definite program of step-by-step action. Without doing too much violence to our sense of what is appropriate, we might compare it to a computational hill-climbing technique in which the artist is trying to optimize or stabilize at a high level the parameter "excitement."

Once we have swallowed this metaphor, it becomes less improbable to imagine that computers might be used, in varying depths of engagement, as active partners in the artistic process. But computers are a *new* medium. They do not have the characteristics of paints, brushes, and canvas. Nor are the "statements" that grow out of the artist's engagement with them likely to be similar to the statements of, for example, oil paintings. An interesting question to explore, then, is how computers might be used as a creative medium. What kinds of artistic potentials can be evolved through the use of computers, which themselves are continually being evolved to possess more sophisticated and intelligent characteristics?

THE CHARACTER OF THE COMPUTER MEDIUM

In the present state of computer usage, artists are certainly having their problems in understanding engineering descriptions and in learning how to program computers in order to explore what might be done with them. However, they *are* learning, and they have already used digital computers and associated equipment to produce musical sounds and artistic visual images.[1-4]

The visual images are generated by an automatic plotter under the control of the digital computer. The plotter consists of a cathode-ray tube and a camera for photographing the images "drawn" on the tube face by deflections of the electron beam. The digital computer produces the instructions for operating the automatic plotter so that the picture-drawing capability is under program control. Musical sounds are produced by the computer by means of a digital sampled version of the sounds that must then be converted to analog form by a conventional digital-to-analog converter.

For both of these artistic applications, a challenging problem is the composition of special-purpose programming languages and subroutines so that the artist can communicate with the computer by using terminology reasonably similar to his particular art. For example, a special music compiler has been written so that the composer can specify complex algorithms for producing a single sound and then pyramid these basic sounds into a whole composition. A similar philosophy has been used in a special language developed for computer animation called Beflix.[5] Both applications share the drawback that the artist must wait a number of hours between the actual running of the computer program and the final generation of pictorial output or musical sounds when he can see or hear the results.

Since the scientific community currently is the biggest user of computers, most descriptions and ideas about the artistic possibilities for computers have been understandably written by scientists and engineers. This situation will undoubtedly change as computers become more accessible to artists who obviously are more qualified to explore and evolve the artistic potentials of the computer medium. Unfortunately, scientists and engineers are usually all too familiar with the inner working of computers, and this knowledge has a tendency to produce very conservative ideas about the possibilities for computers in the arts. Most certainly the computer is an electronic device capable of performing only those operations that it has been explicitly instructed to perform. And this usually leads to the portrayal of the computer as a powerful tool but one incapable of any true creativity. However, if creativity is restricted to mean the production of the unconventional or the unpredicted, then the computer should instead be portrayed as a creative medium — an active and creative collaborator with the artist.

COMPUTERS AND CREATIVITY

Digital computers are constructed from a myriad of electronic components whose purpose is to switch minute electric currents nearly instantaneously. The innermost workings of the computer are controlled by a set of instructions called a program. Although computers must be explicitly instructed to perform each operation, higher-level programming languages enable pyramiding of programming statements that are later expanded into the basic computer instructions by special compiler programs. These programming languages are usually designed so that the human user can write his computer program using words and symbols similar to those of his own particular field. All of this leads to the portrayal of the computer as a tool capable of performing tasks exactly as programmed.

However, the computer is such an extremely powerful tool that artistic effects can sometimes be easily accomplished that would be virtually impossible by conventional artistic techniques. For example, by calculating and drawing on the automatic plotter the perspective projections from two slightly different directions of some three-dimensional object, the computer can generate three-dimensional movies of novel shapes and forms. Such three-dimensional animation, or kinetic sculpture, is far too tedious to perform by any other method. The computer's ability to handle small details has made possible intriguing dissolves and stretches, such as those executed by Stan Vanderbeek, without the tedium of conventional hand animation. Mathematical equations with certain specified variables under the control of the artist have also been used by John Whitney to achieve completely new animation effects. Much of "op art" uses repetitive patterns that usually can be expressed very simply in mathematical terms.

Computers most certainly are only machines, but they are capable of performing millions of operations in a fraction of a second and with incredible accuracy. They can be programmed to weigh carefully, according to specified criteria, the results of different alternatives and act accordingly; thus, in a rudimentary sense, computers can appear to show intelligence.[6] They might assess the results of past actions and modify their programmed algorithms to improve previous results; computers potentially could be programmed to learn. And series of numbers can be calculated by the computer that are so complicatedly related that they appear to us as random.

Of course, everything the machine does must be programmed, but because of the computer's great speed, freedom from error, and vast abilities for assessment and subsequent modification of programs, it appears to us to act unpredictably and to produce the unexpected. In this sense, the computer actively takes over some of the artist's creative search. It suggests to him syntheses that he may or may not accept. It possesses at least some of the external attributes of creativity.

THE MONDRIAN EXPERIMENT

How reasonable is it to attribute even these rudimentary qualities of creativity to an inanimate machine? Is creativity something that should only be associated with the products of humans? Not long ago, in 1950, A. M. Turing expressed the belief that at the end of the century "one will be able to speak of machines thinking without expecting to be contradicted."[7] Turing proposed the now well-known experiment consisting of an interrogator, a man, and a machine, in which the interrogator had to identify the man by asking the man and the machine to answer questions or to perform simple tasks.

A crude approximation to Turing's experiment was performed using Piet Mondrian's "Composition With Lines" (1917) and a computer-generated picture composed of pseudorandom elements but similar in overall composition to the Mondrian painting.[8] Although Mondrian apparently placed the vertical and horizontal bars in his painting in a careful and orderly manner, the bars in the computer-generated picture were placed according to a pseudorandom number generator with statistics chosen to approximate the bar density, lengths, and widths in the Mondrian painting. Xerographic copies of the two pictures were presented, side by side, to 100 subjects with educations ranging from high school to post-doctoral; the subjects represented a reasonably good sampling of the population at a large scientific research laboratory. They were asked which picture they preferred and also which picture of the pair they thought was produced by Mondrian. Fifty-nine percent of the subjects preferred the computer-generated picture;

The picture on the left, "Composition With Lines" (© Rykmuseum-Kröller-Müller), is a reproduction of a work by the Dutch painter Piet Mondrian. The picture on the right was generated by a digital computer using pseudorandom numbers with statistics approximating the Mondrian painting (© A. Michael Noll 1965). When xerographic reproductions of both pictures were shown to 100 subjects, the computer-generated picture was preferred by 59 of them. Only 28 subjects identified the Mondrian painting. Apparently, many of the observers associated randomness with human creativity and were therefore led astray in making the picture identifications.

only 28 percent were able to identify correctly the picture produced by Mondrian.

In general, these people seemed to associate the randomness of the computer-generated picture with human creativity whereas the orderly bar placement of the Mondrian painting seemed to them machinelike. This finding does not, of course, detract from Mondrian's artistic abilities. His painting was, after all, the inspiration for the algorithms used to produce the computer-generated picture, and since computers were nonexistent fifty years ago, Mondrian could not have had a computer at his disposal. Furthermore, we must admit that the reduction in size of the original painting and its xerographic reproduction degrades its unique aesthetic qualities. Nevertheless, the results of the experiment in light of Turing's proposed experiment do raise questions on the meaning of creativity and the role of randomness in artistic creation. In a sense, the computer with its program could be considered creative, although it can be argued that human creativity was involved in the original program with the computer performing only as an obedient tool.

These questions should perhaps be examined more deeply by more ambitious psychological experiments using computer-generated pictures as stimuli.

TOWARD REAL-TIME INTERACTION

Although the experiments described show that the computer has creative potentialities beyond those of just a simple tool, the computer medium is still restrictive in that there is a rather long time delay between the running of the computer program and the production of the final graphical or acoustic output. However, recent technological developments have greatly reduced this time delay through special interactive hardware facilities and programming languages. This tightening of the man-machine feedback loop is particularly important for the artist who needs a nearly instantaneous response.

For example, in the field of music an electronic graphic console has been used to specify pictorially sequences of sounds that were then synthesized by the computer.[9] Functions for amplitude, frequency, and duration of a sequence of notes were drawn on the face of a cathode-ray tube with a light pen. If desired, the computer combined specified functions according to transparently simple algorithms. Thus, the fine details of the composition were calculated by the computer and the overall structure was precisely specified by the graphical score. The feedback loop was completed by the computer-generated sounds heard almost immediately by the composer, who could then make any desired changes in the score.

A similar man-machine interactive system has been proposed for choreography.[10] In this system, the choreographer would be shown a computer-generated three-dimensional display of complicated stick figures moving about on a stage. The choreographer interacts with the computer by indicating the spatial trajectories and movements of the figures. Random and mathematical algorithms might be introduced by the computer to fill in certain fine details, or even to give the choreographer new ideas to evaluate and explore.

A NEW ACTIVE MEDIUM

The beginnings of a new creative partnership and collaboration between the artist and the computer clearly emerge from these most recent efforts and proposals. Their common denominator is the close man-machine interaction using the computer to generate either musical sounds or visual displays. The computer acquires a creative role by introducing randomness or by using mathematical algorithms to control certain aspects of the artistic creation. The overall control and direction of the creative process is very definitely the artist's task. Thus, the computer is used as a medium by the artist, but the great technical powers and creative potentialities of the computer result in a totally new kind of creative medium. This is an *active* medium with which the artist can interact on a new level, freed from many of the physical limitations of all other previous media. The artistic potentialities of such a creative medium as a collaborator with an artist are truly exciting and challenging.

INTERACTIVE AESTHETIC EXPERIENCES

In the previous examples the artist sat at the console of the computer and indicated his desires to the computer by manually using push buttons or by drawing patterns on an electronic visual display. These are probably efficient ways of communicating certain types of instructions to the computer; however, the communication of the actual subconscious emotional state of the artist could lead to a new aesthetic experience. Although this might seem somewhat exotic and conjectural, the artist's emotional state might conceivably be determined by computer processing of physical and electrical signals from the artist (for example, pulse rate and electrical activity of the brain). Then, by changing the artist's environment through such external stimuli as sound, color, and visual patterns, the computer would seek to optimize the aesthetic effect of all these stimuli upon the artist according to some specified criterion.

This interactive feedback situation with controlled environment would be completely dynamic. The emotional reaction of the artist would continually change, and the computer would react accordingly either to stabilize the artist's emotional state or to steer it through some preprogrammed course. Here then is a completely new aesthetic experience utilizing man-machine communication on the highest (or lowest, if you will) subconscious levels and computer processing and optimization of emotional responses. Only a digital computer could perform all the information processing and generate the sights and sounds of the controlled environment required for such a scheme. One is strongly tempted to describe these ideas as a consciousness-expanding experience in association with a psychedelic computer!

Although such an artistic feedback scheme is still far in the future, current technological and psychological investigations would seem to aim in such a direction. For example, three-dimensional computer-generated color displays that seem to surround the individual are certainly already within the state of the art. Electroencephalograms are being scrutinized and studied in great detail, using advanced signal analysis techniques; it is not inconceivable that some day their relation to emotional state might be determined.

ARTISTIC CONSEQUENCES

Predictions of the future are risky in that they may be really nothing more than what the person predicting would like to see occur. Although the particulars should be viewed skeptically, they actually might be unimportant; if the art of the future follows the directions outlined here, then some general conclusions and statements can be made that should be independent of the actual particulars.

The aesthetic experience will be highly individualistic, involving only the individual artist and his interactions with the computer. This type of participation in the creative and aesthetic experience can be experienced by artist and nonartist alike. Because of the great technical and creative power of the computer, both the artist and nonartist are freed from the necessity of strong technical competence in the use of different media. The artist's "ideas" and not his technical ability in manipulating media could be the important factor in determining artistic merit. Conceivably, a form of "citizen-artist" could emerge, as envisioned by Allon Schoener.[11] The interactive aesthetic experience with computers might fill a substantial portion of that great leisure time predicted for the man of the future.

The artist's role as master creator will remain, however, because even though the physical limitations of the medium will be different from traditional media, his training, devotion, and visualization will give him a higher degree of control of the artistic experience. As an example, the artist's particular interactions with the computer might be recorded and played back by the public on their own computers. Specified amounts of interaction and modification might be introduced by the individual, but the overall course of the interactive experience would still follow the artist's model. In this way, and for the first time, the artist would be able to specify and control with certainty the emotional state of each individual participant. Only those aspects deliberately specified by the artist might be left to chance or to the whims of the participant. All this would be possible because the computer could monitor the participant's emotional state and change it according to the artist's specifications. The artist's interaction with the computer would be of a new order because the physical restrictions of the older media would be eliminated.

This is not to say that the traditional artistic media will be swept away; but they will undoubtedly be influenced by this new active medium. The introduction of photography — the new medium of the last century — helped to drive painting away from representation, but it did not drive out painting. What the new creative computer medium will do to all of the art forms — painting, writing, dance, music, movies — should be exciting to observe. We might even be tempted to say that the current developments and devices in the field of man-machine communication, which were primarily intended to give insight into scientific problems, might in the end prove to be far more fruitful, or at least equally fruitful, in the arts.

REFERENCES

1. Mathews, M. V., "The digital computer as a musical instrument," *Sci.*, vol. 142, no. 3592, pp. 553–557, No. 1, 1963.
2. Rockman, A., and Mezei, L., "The electronic computer as an artist," *Canadian Art*, vol. XXI, pp. 365–367, Nov./Dec. 1964.
3. Noll, A. M., "Computers and the visual arts," *Design Quarterly*, no. 66/67, pp. 65–71, 1967.
4. Zajac, E. E., "Computer animation: a new scientific and educational tool," *J. Soc. Motion Picture and Television Eng.*, vol. 74, pp. 1006–1008, Nov. 1965.
5. Knowlton, K. C., "A computer technique for producing animated movies," *Am. Fed. Infor. Proc. Soc. (AFIPS) Conf. Proc.*, vol. 25, pp. 67–87, 1964.
6. Minsky, M. L., "Artificial Intelligence," *Sci. Am.*, vol. 215, pp. 246–260, Sept. 1966.
7. Turing, A. M., "Computing machinery and intelligence,' *Mind. A quarterly review of psychology and philosophy*, vol. 59, N.S., pp. 433–460, Oct. 1950.
8. Noll, A. M., "Human or machine: a subjective comparison of Piet Mondrian's 'Composition with Lines' (1917) and a computergenerated picture," *The Psychological Rec.*, vol. 16, pp. 1–10, Jan. 1966.
9. Mathews, M. V., "A graphical language for composing and playing sounds and music," presented at the 31st Conv. of the Audio Engineering Society, Oct. 1966 (preprint no. 477).
10. Noll, A. M., "Choreography and computers," *Dance Magazine*, vol. XXXXI, pp. 43–45, Jan. 1967.
11. Schoener, Allon, "2066 and all that," *Art in America*, vol. 54, pp. 40–43, Mar.–Apr. 1966.

59   IN COMPUTERLAND WITH *TRON* *

RICHARD SCHICKEL, *TIME* MAGAZINE

TRON wasn't the blockbuster hit movie that the Disney organization thought it would be, but it was a technical marvel as well as being a pretty unusual adventure story. What is most remarkable about the film is that more than half of it (53 minutes out of a total of 93 minutes) was done via computer animation. And many of the backgrounds also used computer animation. It is a fantastic film, in every sense of the word, and it may be that the fantasy somehow gets in the way of the story so that people don't get emotionally involved. Thus *TRON* emerged, one might argue, as a wonderful experiment that was a technical success (though the

---

patient or filmgoer "died" — in the sense of staying away from the box office).

To understand the significance of this movie, Richard Schickel, who wrote this article, ties it to the whole matter of movie going in America and to the fortunes of the Disney organization. Statistics show that young people are the main moviegoers; people over 35 tend to stay away, though they can be lured to the movie house for certain films. And the Disney organization had not been terribly successful with its live action features for a number of years.

Since young people make up 50 percent of the ticket buyers, it is logical to make films that will appeal to them. And *TRON*, it was hoped, might find an audience that would love its remarkable special effects. *TRON* was, in a sense, an attempt by the Disney people to move into the twentieth century and produce films in the same class as *Star Wars* or *E.T.*

The Disney studios had got in a rut for two reasons, Schickel says: they paid very little (and thus did not attract top talent) and they give directors very little freedom. As a result, Disney had not had a "megahit" since *Mary Poppins*, in 1964 and the people who ran the organization were upset about being "hitless wonders." It is against that background that we must understand *TRON*.

Regardless of its financial fate, Schickel argues, *TRON* was an important film — as a sign of the Disney studios' new progressiveness and as a technological marvel that showed what computer animation could do for the movie industry. *TRON* gave audiences, Schickel felt, "their first long look at some part of what their moviegoing future will hold." Since 1982 films have made more use of computer animations and computer generated special effects, but we have not had a film the likes of *TRON*.

"It seems very pretty," she said when she had finished it, "but it's rather *hard to understand."*

— Alice in *Through the Looking-Glass*

Sympathies, Alice. As you once remarked, it is never easy to live in someone else's dream. But even our dreams have grown more complicated, and more menacing, than they were in your day. Stepping sweetly through a mirror or sliding slowly down a rabbit hole at a speed that permits you to grab a marmalade jar off a shelf as you pass by has become...well...child's play by modern standards.

Consider, for example, the frabjous fate of a fractious computer programmer named Flynn, who is the protagonist of a new movie called *TRON*, which has hopes of joining the parade of hit movies that has made this — so far — the biggest summer the box office has ever known. It is no white bunny with a watch tucked into his waistcoat that leads Flynn into a nether world. He is transported there — zap! tingle! sizzle! — via laser beam. As for his looking glass, it is the display screen of a computer terminal. When he passes through it, he is inside the glowing grids of a vast computer system.

And the Jabberwocks that come burbling through these tulgey woods, they are electronic programs Flynn created to amuse adolescent addicts of video games.

Taking on the human forms of their "users" in the real world, a few creatures, like the heroic Tron and a mild-mannered bundle of circuits named Ram, become Flynn's allies in the fight to restore humane values to the electronic underworld. But most are like Sark, the servant of the tyrannical MCP (Master Control Program), a onetime chess programmer who has evilly usurped the knowledge and power of thousands of other programs. Now he boasts that he is 2,415 times as smart as the average human and able to run the world, according to his calculations, 900 to 1,200 times as efficiently as mere mortals.

Luckily for fans of fast action, MCP is a computer with a sense of (grim) humor. This god of the machine sentences enemies to his system's "game grid," where they must function as gladiators in deadly video wars. Sometimes they race on "light cycles" that move with the speed of light. Other times they face off in the "ring game," a form of jai alai, with deresolution (disconnection from the power source) as the price of failure. Deadly "grid bugs" stalk the unwary in this world where "logic probes" and "recognizers" are the weapons of oppression, and the only way out leads through the "input-output tower." In short, writer-director Steven Lisberger, 31, has given witty and dramatic visual forms to computer technology's well-known phrases, investing them with a new symbolic life.

Obviously, the creators of *TRON* aspire to something more than the innocent delights of a Lewis Carroll. They share with the creators of contemporary science fiction a desire to provide moral entertainment for their audience. But just as the highest pleasure offered by Alice lies not in story, character or preachment, but in the brilliant play of language, so, too, the highest pleasure of *TRON* lies in the often astounding play of the film maker's language: imagery, One can say of it, as one can say of few films, that it offers sights that no eye, no camera, has ever before beheld. For to create the inner world of a computer, Lisberger called upon computers to do the work.

Some 53 minutes of his film consist of animation done purely by electronic means, without resort to pen, pencil or brush. Many of the backgrounds for the picture's fantasy sequences, which constitute well over half the film's 96-min. running time, were also generated by computers, which meant that the actors (led by Jeff Bridges as Flynn, Bruce Boxleitner as Tron, Cindy Morgan as Lora, the scientist they both love, and David Warner as Sark) had to perform their most complicated actions on a bare stage with only a neutral backdrop behind them. These sequences were shot in black and white. Color was then added to the electronic "veins" of the actors' costumes, frame by frame through backlight animation.

Though computer animation has been used frequently in television (Bufferin commercials, the opening titles on NBC's *Nightly News*), *TRON* represents an unprecedented orchestration of this relatively new technology.

It thus stands in relationship to what has gone before as *Snow White and the Seven Dwarfs* did to conventional animation when it was released in 1937 and as *2001: A Space Odyssey* did to optical-effects pictures when it was released in 1968.

Four computer animation firms served as subcontractors to the film, and all their machines work in somewhat different ways. In essence, though, each relies on the basic geometric elements out of which our physical universe is composed. Artists' renderings are reduced to blueprints that guide the computer animator at his console. Says Larry Elin, head of the production team at MAGI, of Elmsford, N.Y.: "It's like having a box full of little wooden shapes that you can plunk together to make more complex shapes, with the added attraction that you can also subtract a shape or part of a shape. It's kind of like sculpting." Except, of course, that the sculptor sits at a computer keyboard and never physically touches the object he is creating.

There are other elements at his fingertips as well. The computer's memory bank includes algorithms that tell it how to shade the object and how to change perspectives as it is moved around relative to whatever light source the director or designer has imagined for the shot. And, of course, computer programming offers a choice of "camera angles" no cinematographer could ever obtain in the real world. As Richard Taylor, one of *TRON*'s effects supervisors, explains: "You can do things with computer simulation that are to the mind impossible. There are no physical limitations to the objects. They can pass through each other, for instance. They can metamorphize from one thing into another. You can see something happen that you know is impossible, but if it's done perfectly, as the computer can do it, it looks as though it is real." Herein lies *TRON*'s true glory; it literally expands our capacity to see.

Whatever the immediate commercial and critical fate of the movie when it opens July 9, it is safe to say that it will remain a historical bench mark. Lisberger's claim is no empty boast: "This picture has nothing to be judged against."

Not that *TRON's* commercial fate is unimportant; no picture whose costs are $21 million (and still rising as the rush to completion speeds up) escapes bottom-line anxiety. This summer that fate is harder than ever to predict. June has been the biggest single month at the box office since people started counting. The rush started on Memorial Day weekend, when *Rocky III* took in $12.4 million in three days, the industry's second biggest opening weekend (after *Superman II*). A week later *Star Trek II* did $14 million in three days. Then Steven Spielberg's *E.T.* landed and in two weeks amassed $44 million to $45 million, another record. This hot streak has optimists saying that the market can now expand beyond its traditional average of about 1 billion admissions annually. Pessimists are saying that the June releases may have "borrowed" attendance from July and August, when they expect things to level off again. If the former are right, then *TRON* will benefit from a new movie consciousness in the country. If the latter are right, then its market may already have been skimmed, especially since it will miss the July 4 weekend, traditionally one of the year's two biggest play dates (the other being New Year's).

These speculations are of more than usual concern to the film's producer, for *TRON* represents the most significant effort yet by one of the most public of U.S. public companies, Walt Disney Productions, to regain its former pre-eminence as a film producer. In the years since its founder's death in 1966, the company has grown rich (gross revenues went over $1 billion for the first time in 1981) by following his basic plans for expansion and diversification through its theme parks and merchandising. During that time, though, the area that the company describes in its latest annual report as its "creative heart" has steadily withered. Where once motion picture production accounted for more than 50 percent of Disney's revenue, it now represents only about 10 percent.

The reasons lie as much with American sociology as with Disney management. Though the studio's animated films have continued to do well (last year's *The Fox and the Hound* returned more than $18 million to Disney from its domestic release), the studio has not had a megahit since *Mary Poppins* in 1964. Most of its recent live-action features have drifted off into an irrelevance that borders on joke status — *The Cat from Outer Space, Unidentified Flying Oddball, Herbie Goes Bananas.* These were tired imitations of the kind of guileless comedies the studio had done well with in the fifties and early sixties when there was still something identifiable as a family audience, in which Mom, Pop, and their 2.5 children betook themselves to the movies as a group.

Nowadays that audience is fragmented; the oldsters mostly stay home and the youngsters (who make up some 50 percent of the ticket buyers) are looking for something more powerfully imagined than Disney could provide. *Star Wars, Close Encounters, Raiders of the Lost Ark, E.T.* — they all might have been made at Disney, but they weren't, even though their creators, George Lucas and Steven Spielberg, acknowledge a spiritual indebtedness to Disney movies, the formative experiences of their child-hood.

The problems in recruiting people of their caliber to Disney were simple: money and freedom. Or lack of same. The studio had traditionally developed all its projects in-house, using staffers who did not dare ask for profit participation or very large salaries. Animator Donald Bluth, who led a group of apostates out of Disney in 1979 (and whose first feature, *The Secret of NIMH*, opens across the country, ironically, the same day as *TRON* does), maintains that in recent years the studio's training program for new animators was inadequate. They were skimping on production values even in the animation department, the heart of the heart: "Things that make the experience real, like contact shadows under characters, sparkles on the water," were reduced, breaking the magic. He also thinks the studio's top executives are overly preoccupied with matters like EPCOT, the futuristic entertainment that opens Oct. 1 adjacent to Florida's Disney World, and the new Tokyo Disneyland that opens next spring.

As for creativity, there is no question that Disney's corporate inheritors have been highly conservative — "the Lawrence Welks of the business," as one *TRON* contractor puts it. Eventually, they lost their ability not only to lead their special market but even to follow it intelligently. There were pictures like *Fame* (with its raw language) and *Blue Lagoon* (with its nudity) that some at Disney cast envious eyes upon, but that Company President Ron Miller (who is also Disney's son-in-law) felt he dare not attempt. "The people...who have supported Disney for years wouldn't stand for it."

Yet Disney is a proud company, with a strong sense of its own traditions. Whatever movies may contribute to the balance sheet, they continue to be of huge importance to the corporate image. It is galling to have been for almost two decades the hitless wonder of Hollywood.

"Someone somewhere is going to be offended by anything you do. And when you try to make something that doesn't offend somebody, you also make a picture that doesn't interest anybody. Whenever a founding figure disappears, there is a period of people finding their way and whether it's taken too long or not long enough I can't say. But it was about two years ago that the company made the decision that it was going to have to broaden the types of pictures that it made." The speaker is Thomas Wilhite, 29, trim, prematurely gray and punctilious of manner in a way that is foreign to Hollywood *Wunderkinder*. Wilhite came to Disney as director of public relations in 1979, and last year was appointed by Miller to be operating head of motion picture and TV production. Charged with attracting new people and ideas to the studio, he has the authority to offer inducements like profit sharing and a large measure of creative freedom to the likes of Lisberger. *TRON* is the first important product of his regime, and he jokes that if it flops he may be back in publicity, or perhaps his native Iowa, before the summer ends.

The decision to go with the dream Lisberger has nurtured since 1976, when he first tried his hand at the video game Pong, was courageous. There was the matter of cost, and of employing a technology that had never been used on a large scale; there was the young director's comparative inexperience (he had made only one long animated film, for television); and there was the subject matter itself. Wilhite admits that when the commitment to film *TRON* was made, "we were not so foresighted as to see that in two years video games and computers would be so massive a business." What they could see in Lisberger's presentation was "a new mythology" that was both original and attractive.

In the beginning there was a certain amount of tension — more social and stylistic than professional — as Lisberger's production team invaded what one of them termed "the Mickey Mausoleum," and another labeled "the land of brogans and bow ties." The Tronies tended toward leather jackets, rock music and a certain amount of swearing in the corridors — very un-Disney. On the other hand, one after another among them speaks of what Disney meant to them when they were growing up. Richard Taylor says, "We all felt we'd like to pay Disney back for that magic." "There are a lot of ghosts around that lot," adds Lisberger. "At night in the parking lot we would expect to see Thumper coming along to help us out." There was also a growing sense that with *TRON*, for the first time in years, the studio was embarked upon a project that might make a difference in the way it was regarded both in the industry and in the world at large and, just possibly, in the history of movie technology.

Lisberger believes that the computer-video games generation will see in it new "possibilities in visualization," and surely they will flock to the film. About the older crowd he is less certain. Besides proposing that the film be rated "Child Guidance Recommended," meaning that "if you are over 17 you should take a kid with you," he hopes it will make a beginning at showing computerphobes "why so many people are so excited about computers and video games."

Some viewers may be distracted from the film's visionary qualities by certain defects of a more traditional sort — lack of subtle character definition, a certain jumpiness in the story line, the occasional failure to explain how actions and consequences link up. One promising computer character, the "bit," floats into a sequence looking like a potential Cheshire cat (or even an Artoo Detoo) and then disappears, never to be seen again. Lisberger says he was a victim of technical problems that a tight schedule did not give him time to solve. This sort of omission may limit the film's grosses and prevent it from reaching the commercial levels of a *Star Wars* or an *E.T.*

Still, it is hard to see how a film so original in conception and execution (and so firmly tied to the electronic preoccupations of its adolescent target audience) can fail. Indeed, it has already succeeded in two of its most important missions. It has opened up to the movies not only a new range of technology but a whole new way of seeing. "In a few years," predicts Associate Producer Harrison Ellenshaw, "we'll all look back at *TRON* and have a giggle and say, 'Look at how primitive it is, look how far we've come.'" Says Robert Abel, founder of a firm that produced some of the film's computer images: "*TRON* is truly the tip of that iceberg everybody talks about. It is the first visible effort. Beneath it lies a whole field ready to explode."

At least as important, the film has proved that the Disney studio has the potential to scramble back to the top. "It is counterproductive to pretend that another Walt Disney is going to show up one day in this company," admits Wilhite. "Walt Disneys do not work for other people. They work for themselves ultimately. But in lieu of Disney, who was a visionary, running the film area, we should become a home for visionaries, people who really have something they want to say." Lisberger, like so many of his young colleagues, sees this as the closing of a circle. "I really think it was the imagination of the early Disney films that started me a long time ago. They turned me on so much I've been trying to do something similar ever since." To put the matter simply, Lisberger's computer gamesmanship has put Disney firmly and excitingly back in the movie game. And given audiences their first long look at some part of what their moviegoing future will hold.

60 THE PROMISES AND PERILS OF VIDEOTEX*

Paul Hurly

Videotex, our author tells us, "is a generic name for systems that provide easy-to-use low-cost, computer-based services via communication facilities." There are a number of different types of videotex such as Viewdata, Teletext, and Open-Channel Teletext. All of these are explained in the essay.

The title of the essay, "The Promises and Perils of Videotex" suggests that this new technology poses a number of problems for us — in the areas of use and regulation. For example, it has been argued that the new technologies are leading to a major split in American society between those who have access to them and those who do not. (In an information society, access to information has been, to a great degree, tied to class level.) How do we make certain that large numbers of people will have access to videotex? How do we ensure that people will be able to afford it? And what role should the government play?

The premise, behind the discussion, is that videotex is a viable phenomenon. That premise, however, is questionable. In an essay "Videotex: Anatomy of a Failure," Michael Noll argues that videotex has been a failure in England and many other countries and has very little chance of being a success in America.

Why? Because the average person has no use for videotex. We don't need access to gigantic databases and don't seem to want to spend money to use them. Noll cites some interesting statistics. In Britain, where $50 million was invested in developing a viewdata system called Prestel, only 42,000 terminals were in use as of 1984 (of which 40 percent were in homes). The British Post Office had forecast one million users by 1981. The British have, Noll suggests, "a product in search of a market." (On the other hand, teletext has been a success there…perhaps because it is much simpler and free.)

Hurly, on the other hand, is much more positive about the future of videotex. For example, the United States and Canada have agreed on a viewdata standard and technological developments are making accessing the databases less expensive. Some analysts fear that videotex will become so popular that it will divide our society into small subgroups that have little in common with one another. Hurly believes that the government must take an active role and regulate videotex to make certain it serves the general public and not just the interests of certain elites. Whether videotex will be a success in America remains to be seen.

---

* Reprinted with permission from *The Futurist*, published by the World Future Society, 4916 St. Elmo Avenue, Bethesda, Md. 20184.

REFERENCE

Noll, Michael (1985). Videotex: Anatomy of a failure. *Information and Management.*

The role of videotex as a communications tool is growing rapidly throughout North America and Europe. Videotex systems and services are gradually introducing significant changes to our social, political, and economic milieu. Some of these changes are the inevitable result of technology. A few may be the harbingers of emerging perils.

Videotex is in widespread use throughout the world — in Venezuela, Japan, Finland, Australia, the Soviet Union, Belgium, and Switzerland, just to name a few countries. Videotex applications can be classified in five general categories: retrieval (news, sports, weather, travel schedules, stock market reports), computing (computer-assisted instruction, management information services, income-tax aids), transactional (teleshopping, tele-banking), messaging, and downline loading (transmitting telesoftware programs to intelligent terminals).

Society has reached an important decision point. Should we allow a technology like videotex to transform society seemingly at will, or should we direct the change process triggered in part by videotex toward goals consistent with our present values?

Videotex is a generic term for systems that provide easy-to-use, low-cost, computer-based services via communication facilities. There are several basic types:

Viewdata is fully-interactive videotex. The user's requests for services or information are actually sent to, received by, and acted upon by the system computer. In North America, the terms "videotex" and "videotext" have become synonymous with viewdata.

Teletext is pseudo-interactive or broadcast videotex. While the user can select the information or service to be received, only a one-way communication link is involved.

A final variation of videotex is *open-channel teletext*. One version of open-channel teletext, called closed captioning, has become an important communication aid for the deaf. Other applications include cable television information channels, open captioning, and airline arrival/departure displays.

Videotex services may be transmitted to the receiver's terminal by coaxial cable, fiber-optic cable, telephone line, radio, conventional satellite or Direct Broadcast Satellite TV, or microwave. Both viewdata and teletext may be transmitted by narrow- or broadband video frequencies. Narrowband employs part of the unused portion of a video signal, while broadband makes use of the entire video channel and thus can transmit more data.

Videotex in higher education: San Francisco State University operates a community videotex service available free to all 110,000 cable subscribers in the city. It is a unique system that allows the user to use a TouchTone telephone to access its student-produced database. No special equipment is required at home. Photos courtesy of Audio-Visual ITV Center, San Francisco State University

Videotex data can be displayed on a wide range of devices, including TV sets, microcomputers, or other terminals with a cathode ray tube, and thermal or impact printers.

ISSUES, PROMISES, AND PERILS

As the importance of videotex as a communications technology grows, a number of issues arise concerning its use and regulation. Among the issues to be faced are:

Regulation

Critics argue that government administration of telecommunications is essential to ensure equitable access. Some, believing that the planning of systems like videotex should no longer be monopolized by so-called experts, call for participatory strategies. These advocates point to the deteriorating state of commercial television in the United States and the lead that European public telecommunications authorities have in videotex and fiber optics to demonstrate the weaknesses of present U.S. regulatory methods.

Rate setting

High videotex costs established by market demand may exclude access to videotex by lower socio-economic groups. Government-approved tariffs could help lower access charges and thus promote greater dissemination, but could also increase the financial risk of investing in videotex, possibly reducing the present level of participation by private enterprise.

Billing

Techniques sensitive to individual user practices require more expensive viewdata systems. Centralized billing systems can provide savings to users and service providers, but the amount of detail collected can expose users to a possible breach of privacy.

System ownership

The involvement of major broadcasters such as CBS in teletext tests and of newspaper and book publishers such as Knight-Ridder and Reader's Digest in viewdata systems raises serious concerns regarding the increasing concentration of the private ownership of information distribution systems in North America. Is this growing monopoly, and the power it confers, in the best interest of the general public?

System compatibility

If the ultimate promise of videotex is a global communications village, a single international videotex specification will be required. Network interconnection can be promoted most effectively through system compatibility.

The peril is that, with so much money already invested by industry and users in videotex equipment that complies with other standards, there will be little incentive to move beyond the current situation. If a user's equipment has access to only one system, the result would be like needing two telephones, one for local calls and the other for long distance.

Transborder data flow

TBDF is the movement of data or information by electronic means across national boundaries. There are four basic benefits. First, TBDF will promote the global village concept. Second, it will give the largest number of people access to information. Third, it will allow information to be processed where the costs are lowest. And fourth, it will reduce the cost of retrieving and storing information.

Major concerns regarding TBDF have been raised by various nations and groups. One peril is that the free movement of information could undermine national sovereignty and cultural identity. An economic peril is that the outflow of funds to purchase information from foreign data bases could result in job loss and weakened economies in some countries. A third peril is the potential for invasion of privacy due to jurisdictional ambiguities, the vulnerability of communication transmissions, and the lack of strong national legislation regarding data theft.

Employment

While new jobs are being created and old jobs made more interesting by the adoption of videotex, the gradual introduction of videotex into the integrated office will facilitate the elimination of many white-collar, middle-management jobs. Furthermore, videotex will not transform boring tasks into stimulating jobs, and it has introduced some of its own dull tasks.

For example, copying line drawings or photographs with an optical digitizer or copying typing (word processing) for a videotex program are not more fulfilling activities because they are done electronically rather than electrically. Or suggesting that cab drivers follow routes prescribed by a map projected electronically by videotex in the taxicab may be more efficient but takes all sense of individual decision-making out of the task.

Editor's Note: The concept of the global village comes from Marshall McLuhan.

Privacy and security

While important judicial and technical strides regarding privacy have been made in Europe, neither the United States nor Canada has effective measures in place to ensure personal data privacy and to prosecute violators. The U.S. military has begun to harden data communication facilities, but successful attacks on data bases by radical groups in Europe have graphically demonstrated their vulnerability. The massive compilation and correlation of personal information now possible using modern computers make it extremely difficult to enforce any reasonable form of privacy and confidentiality controls on videotex systems.

Participatory democracy

Although videotex polling mechanisms have been hailed by political scientists as a vehicle for implementing participatory democracy, the peril is that society will adopt rule by electronic plebiscite. There must be requirements that the participants be well informed, be able to comprehend issues, be able to distinguish parochial from national interests, and empathize with opposing viewpoints for participatory democracy via videotex — or any other medium — to be successful.

For example, commentator and columnist Andy Rooney criticized television ads prior to this year's U.S. elections that encouraged all Americans to get out and vote. "I don't want some ignorant person canceling out my vote," Rooney proclaimed. He pleaded for voters who couldn't name their local candidates or tell a Republican from a Democrat to stay home.

The need for proper controls was illustrated by an experiment in Columbus, Ohio, on video polling, using the Warner-Amex Communications system called QUBE. One couple reported coming home to discover that their pre-school son had turned on the television and had participated in a QUBE poll intended for adult viewers.

Cultural dissemination and diversity

Videotex promises to become an electronic library, publishing vehicle, archive, and gallery. Open access will put the best of what is known at everyone's fingertips. The peril is that, with the rapid rise of "information overload," it will be difficult to locate the best.

Communications critic Gary Gumpert has referred to the advent of mini-communication or "mini-com." Unlike mass communication, mini-com, utilizing such technologies as videotex, can deliver nonstandard information or entertainment to specific, selected audiences.

Some critics of mini-com fear that the lack of the single unifying symbols that the mass media have in the past projected will cause national identity to be fragmented and unfocused. Others argue that the existence of large, centralized videotex data bases further removes from small communities, subgroups, and individuals the power to shape what is communicated and concentrates power in the hands of an elite.

VIDEOTEX SYSTEMS IN EUROPE AND THE UNITED STATES

Public videotex systems have been available in most Western European nations since 1981. The United Kingdom also has a large number of private videotex systems. These generally fall in one of two categories: intracompany communication systems, or services provided by a company to selected clients, such as stock brokerage firms providing online videotex market forecasts and analysis, and stock ticker and stock marketing services.

British Telecom's Prestel videotex format, along with the Antiope-DIDON and Antiope-Teletel formats coordinated by Intelematique of France, provided the world's first public videotex systems featuring both visual displays as well as words and numbers. Prestel has introduced such capabilities as the digital reproduction of photographic images, to be used by such services as real estate companies to picture their listings.

West Germany used the Prestel videotex protocol to create a domestic system called Bildschirmtext. This system allows users to gain access to a wide variety of data bases, from airline schedules to mail order company catalogs.

France has promoted the public acceptance and use of Teletel by distributing more than 250,000 Minitel viewdata terminals free of charge. The videotex system is testing the use of a "smart card" for teleshopping and other transactional services.

A common European videotex format called CEPT was adopted in 1983. This will open the way for a fully integrated viewdata network that will permit system users to gain access to data bases anywhere on the continent, in much the same manner as a telephone user can place a long-distance phone call to any nation in the world.

The United States and Canada approved a common viewdata standard in 1984 called the North American Presentation Level Protocol Syntax (NAPLPS). While direct viewdata network interconnection between Europe and North America is still some way off, NAPLPS will gradually help the growth of the North American viewdata market. This is likely to occur for two reasons:

First, the common NAPLPS standard will increase the market for one type of equipment, thus slowly decreasing the cost of terminals and system hardware. Second, a common standard will help to promote greater access between systems and data bases.

While national boundaries in Western Europe have served as an impediment to a continental viewdata network, competition between corporate-owned systems in the United States has been a far greater barrier to the development of a national viewdata network.

A number of major equipment manufacturers, including IBM, Commodore, Wang, and DEC, now manufacture NAPLPS software decoders for microcomputers. This, coupled with the declining cost of modems, will open up an enormous potential pool of terminals in offices and homes to viewdata systems in the United States.

Social-class divisions

While videotex has the capability of making information universally available to all, some predict that the gap between socio-economic classes will be heightened by the availability or lack of availability of information technologies. If this occurs, the haves and have-nots will be divided by access to videotex and computers as well as by economic wealth.

Information handling

Viewdata services, due to their interactive dimension, make it easier to locate specific information. Videotex services are providing customized information presentation and synthesis for users.

Yet research by Nobel laureate Herbert Simon has shown the fallacy in the argument that making more information available improves decision-making. Limitations in human memory and reasoning limit the number of facts that can be weighed when solving a problem.

The utility of information is judged by its accuracy, timeliness, and applicability. When data bases are not updated consistently or strict editorial controls enforced, these measures of videotex's effectiveness can be compromised.

There are other perils. The intermingling of sponsored pages with content pages and the lack of clearly defined editorial standards may blur the distinction between fact and opinion on videotex. People may forget that videotex data can be just as subjective as other sources.

For example, a Canadian citizen was recently charged with knowingly publishing false information that harmed or was likely to harm social or racial tolerance. In addition to allegedly publishing this information in pamphlet form, he had created an electronic "bulletin board" in the United States that Canadians could gain access to via computer.

The control of information is a growing public concern, but censorship by omission is hard to detect. Detection of censorship will become increasingly arduous with the information explosion.

Interpersonal communication

Videotex communication may be effective for such tasks as problem-solving, discussion of ideas, and policy decision-making. However, the lack of verbal communication is a major problem. People form less accurate perceptions of others via media.

Electronic bulletin boards, telegaming that involves networks of simultaneous players, and computer conferencing have created new subgroups and communities across North America. Videotex has fostered new forms of socialization and expanded some people's sense of community. But the absence of immediacy and other interpersonal communication factors, along with the lack of tactile experience, is identified by critics of videotex as a serious weakness. Some fear a consequence of the electronic cottage will be electronic seclusion.

Teleservices

Videotex will change the television set from a passive to an interactive device. Teleservices like travel reservations and ticket ordering, teleshopping, and telebanking will improve the convenience of services for consumers; will help manufacturers, wholesalers, and retailers to pare costs; and will allow businesses to receive immediate payment through electronic funds transfer.

On the other hand, the proliferation of TV-based services may reduce public participation in live events and travel for business or pleasure. The definition of a "vidiot" might be the person who prefers videotex to human or social interaction.

As computer-communication improvements reduce travel, the travel and hospitality industries could be adversely affected. Teleshopping could seriously reduce the consumer's range or choice of services, limiting, for example, the method of payment. And some businesses could become unviable due to competition from videotex marketing and retailing activities.

STRATEGY CHOICES

As the implementation of videotex evolves and the technology is refined, its impact on society is likely to broaden. Gradually, videotex is finding niches or roles it can play as business and institutions identify the unique attributes of the technology and methods by which videotex may complement existing media. Society is faced with two fundamental choices in determining the course videotex will take.

One strategy is basically hands off — laissez faire. Market and social forces would render judgment and shape the direction of videotex. This is the strategy in place today, and some of its effects are already visible. For example, critics of current videotex operations point to the blue-ribbon price tag — and the fact that no one really asked for it in the first place — as reasons that consumers are wary. And telecommunications officials have admitted that they are marketing videotex chiefly for additional revenues needed to offset slow growth in telephone service.

Alternatively, governments could recognize the concerns being expressed by various groups and begin to regulate the videotex industry more closely, accepting that videotex is becoming an essential service required for the benefit of all, not just for those who can now afford it or visualize an application.

The advent of each new communication or travel technology has required a certain measure of regulation. The establishment of uniform railway line widths, an efficient interstate freeway system, highway and air travel safety rules, and reasonably equitable rural-urban telephone rates have ultimately assisted each innovation. Acceptance of each system increased as public confidence and access were facilitated.

Even in the present deregulatory climate in North America, a strong case can be argued for the regulation of videotex services. Some measure of government assurance that videotex will benefit the majority of society and that personal privacy will not be infringed upon would benefit both the videotex industry and the citizen.

61   HOW I BECAME A VIDEO ARTIST*

LYNN HERSHMAN

If you look in the arts pages of newspapers you now find articles about a new kind of artist working in a "new" medium — video. What is video art and how does it differ from television? What are video artists trying to do? Is video really an art form or are video artists putting us all on?

In an essay entitled "Notes on Video as an Artistic Medium," which appeared in *The New Television: A Public/Private Art*, Wulf Herzogenroth offers some suggestions about what video art is. I will summarize his argument and offer some quotations of interest.

Video is different from other art forms such as painting, photography, film, and theatre in that it allows: "(1) Instant control of the picture, (2) numerous electronic possibilities, and (3) picture playback on monitors." The instantaneous aspect of video, he suggests, allows us to draw reality directly into the artistic process, and this can be exploited in "live, closed-circuit environments." The instant control of recording on monitors opens up all kinds of possibilities to artists…especially since these images can be manipulated in a wide variety of ways (as a look at MTV, for instance, shows). Also, video artists can use monitors in creative ways — in groups, in different rooms, etc. for various reasons.

Herzogenroth suggests that there are three essentials involved in what he calls "the specifically artistic use of video." These are:

---

* Lynn Hershman. "How I Became a Video Artist." This article was written especially for this volume. Copyright © 1987. Lynn Hershman.

1. "Video as mirror:" video as an instrument of recognition, of perception of one's own limitations, reversal of left and right, mirroring and illustration of the reflections of one's own ego, confrontation with oneself.

2. Video as documentary medium: photos (real or invented) and *objets trouvés* are combined by artists into works that evoke a quality of the subject or owner and thereby become topographies of people, events or memories.

3. Video as electronic medium: the electronic image makes possible completely new forms and synthetic colors, picture mixing, alteration and feedback between the picture transmitted and the camera.

When you watch a work of video art you generally see it on a television screen. But there's a world of difference between experimental videos and what the mass medium of television generally broadcasts.

REFERENCE

Herzogenroth, Wulf (1978). *The new television: A public/private art.* M.I.T. Press.

When I begin to consider why I use the medium of video, I have to consider the origins of my aesthetic implants and the influence of the politics of the sixties. I was a student at the University of California, Berkeley during the Free Speech Movement, where theatre and performance fused daily into life. Venues for spirited individual empowerment were invented and performed. Art that was created as a result of those years moved out of traditional museum and gallery situations and into normal experience. Art forms, like life styles became alternative. As early as 1968, I was using rented hotel rooms as specific sites for environments. The pedestal that retained sculpture as a precious object dissolved as art merged with context and became a direct part of the space in which it was seen. Audiences moved from a rather elite group of art patrons to a broad public that participated in the work itself.

From 1968 to 1981, I made work that took place in such direct sites as a project home in Australia, department store windows in New York, casinos in Las Vegas, and even the walls of San Quentin Prison. I was the Project Director of Christo's Running Fence, a work that took place in the landscape of 24½ miles in Marin and Sonoma counties. In the early 1970s I founded a museum, an alternative museum for works of this nature, titled the Floating Museum. All of these works were dedicated to the idea of bringing art directly into public arenas, and to involve individuals in all aspects of society. Essentially, they were aesthetic reflections of a dialogue that began in the 1960s.

In order to advertise these site specific works, I made videotaped commercials intended for broadcast. To me they were electronic Haiku that in less than a minute could impart not only the essence of the event, but were, in themselves, art. The installations themselves were always temporal. Designed to last for a fixed amount of time, usually no more than a few weeks, then they would dissolve into memory. The only thing left was documentation. There was an attitude that once an art work was made, even if it existed a few seconds, it would interfere with time and history and therefore exist forever. Art made during the 1970s was labeled *Conceptual*. It dealt with idea more than the object. With experience more than relic. It was the product of an idealistic anti-materialistic generation whose very ephemeral nature rendered much of its force invisible.

What remained of these large scaled events were always the videotapes. They not only proved that the works happened, but had an impact of reaching broad audiences in themselves. In most cases, more people saw the "videotape commercials" than the work. It occurred to me that the electronic community access could potentially be more important than either a gallery or a street, and could more easily and effectively address the philosophical underpinnings of my work.

Because my video commercials were seen by some museum administrators, I was in 1980 given a small grant (about $500) to go into a broadcast studio and have full access to facilities to create a videotape. The work I made (titled TESTPATTERNS) portrayed television as a personified actor who traced his origins to Kennedy's assassination; he was chromakeyed into cannibalized elements of news. This piece showed me the potentials of the medium. I remember being intensely excited about the fluid and plastic possibilities of this form, the painterly qualities of electronic color and effect, and the sculptural qualities of time, all the while having the inbred context of a communication vehicle. The effect of this experience was not only psychic, but physical. To this day I feel intensely energized from being around videotapes or editing equipment, perhaps in the same way some journalists feel about type and printers ink. And it was clear from this initial project that all of my future efforts would be geared toward using the media of videotape to find my voice in art.

In a way, video became an alternative space, just like the earlier environments. Video art was heavily dominated by women. I believe they fell into this field because it was the only access opened at that time. Remember, until the mid-1980s there were virtually no women film directors. But the possibilities in television and video were still open, as was the entire developing language of the medium. What interested me was using the range of possible images as liquid drawings, to use effects as sculpture, and all the while, use both as an imploding tactic for narratives about the very act of watching television. Kind of like using a system against itself. Of going further into the cultural boundaries it presented and amplifying on that as an element of content. The works that most clearly emphasize this are *Rebecca at 28, Confessions of a Chameleon*, and *Lorna*.

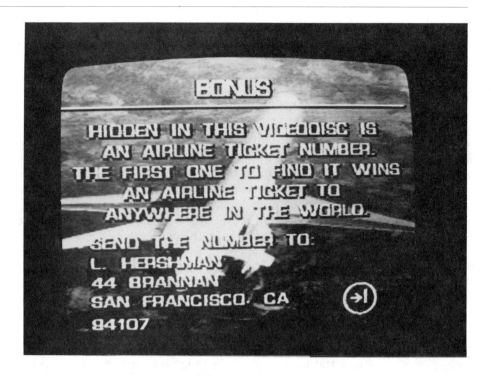

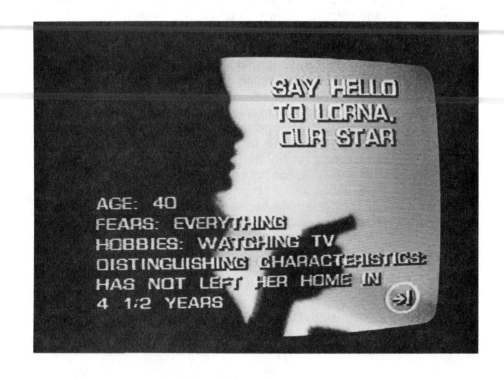

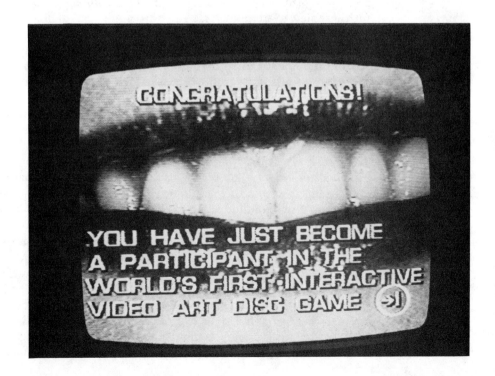

Rebecca is a study of an alcoholic woman who uses the process of the documentary as a vehicle for behavioral change. She breaks from interviews and directly addresses the camera, talking about how the making of the tape made her see herself differently.

Confessions was done completely with a "talking head" of a woman of 43 talking about the difficulties of her divorce, sexual fantasies, and fears. As she speaks she becomes three distinct characters. The video effects echo her dialogue, adapting the form to content. This work goes beyond what is considered "polite" for television, and is designed to make audiences uncomfortable because it trespasses into the utterly unbearable horror of truth. Yet, because of its format, all that the main character says is considered fiction.

Lorna was designed into an interactive laser disk that directly speaks to its audiences, and in fact, depends on their participation and decisions in order to function. Technological changes in media have inspired a change in the traditional way art is seen. Interactive technology generally involve systems that need user/participants in order to function. Rather than offering pre-sequenced narrative information to a passive viewer, interactive media insists upon an active choice by observers. Both function together as a unit, as a cyborg. Interactive technology thus represents the antithesis of communication and art as we have known it. For the radical changes in the terms of communication are reflected in art. Traditionally art was structured like other realms of life — hierarchically. The art world functioned on the presumption that viewing art is passive, while only making art is active. But these new systems reverse this into a new paradigm.

My experience with interactive media happened purely by chance. A friend showed me an article about interactive laser disks and I was presumptuous enough to assume that the capabilities were easily understood, but it took me over three years to produce a disk, because I had first to deconstruct my own presumptions of traditional story telling — a one way process from story teller to listener; bringing the listener into the story as an active participant forced the development of a non-linear format that seemed alien to the narrative form.

My disk was called *Lorna* and was composed from short, fragmented sequences of action, each telling part of a story. But only part. These parts were arranged so that they could be called up by a viewer who could direct the action and heroine at will. The viewer/user could thus not only participate with the heroine, but identify with limits imposed by the medium. Further, they could through their own strategies, design outcomes to overcome the imposed limitations of the medium.

Lorna tells the story of a woman captured by the fears media transmit to her via magazines and television. Her dilemma is that as she stays home out of fear of the world, she watches more television, which paradoxically increases her agoraphobia, or fear of public places. By unravelling the form of the media, like Penelope's nightly unwavings in The Odyssey, she comes to understand them and ultimately is freed from them. Instead of living by remote control, or even remotely living, a player of *Lorna* is forced into serious action. The traditional narrative is replaced by random adventure. Works of Stephane Mallarme as well as John Cage and Marcel Duchamp used similar ideas in their chance operation works. Multiple levels of appearance develop, all of which explore an inverse labyrinth that lead into the inward depths of the individual user. Sequences of Lorna's life are pressed into the disk like amorphous vignettes that wait like recombinant molecules to be vitally decomposed. Each disk has 54,000 still frames capable on each side. There is a capacity for two sound tracks working separately or together. Images can be seen backwards, forwards, or at increased and decreased speeds. Situations can be seen from several points of view, like an electronic Cubism that presents numerous perspectives with no vanishing lines. People who played *Lorna* formed a bond with her and made a clear metaphoric association and identification with her. By scrutinizing Lorna's situation, viewers saw their own lives and the implications of media, and could thus manipulate options in Lorna's life that transferred to theirs. People who played the disk mentioned that the experience changed the way they saw things after the installations.

Players became empowered by the ability to change what they saw on the screen, and could create alternative versions of reality, each determined by choice. Their own choice. Information as taken away from an invisible omniscient and placed directly in their own hands. If Lorna, in its very primitive state can have this effect, than the potential for this expanded experience would be to aid individuals in understanding and questioning their environments, in creating options in their life through conscious choice, and by doing so affect the quality of life throughout human society. The implications of this reversal to the relationship between the individual and technological systems is truly immense. Changing these relationships creates the potential for the bath of media transmitted information that today surrounds and alienates individuals to be replaced by media structured in favor of viewer input.

I am interested in continuing to work with the boundaries of the electronic art media experience. Perhaps Compact Disk Interatives, perhaps broadly distributed feature videotapes that push ineffably into the borders of our culture.

INTERACTIVE MEDIA AND HUMAN RESPONSE

"TOUCHING IS THE TRUE REVOLUTION"

Nikki Giovanni

A while ago, Jack Burnham, an artist and critic, was pondering Marcel Duchamp's break through the picture plane and Luciano Fontano's direct penetration of the canvas when he observed that: "Art is moving towards coitus, towards sex, which is what we wanted all along."[1] One might more accurately suggest that what we have really wanted all along was a connection, a means by which to actively respond and communicate: a dialogue with our environment and our community. Traditionally, there has been a presumption that viewing art is passive, and only the making of it is active. New media insists upon participation of viewers. It is meaningless without it. Computers and interactive video and disks, also scan systems, and satellites have consummated a Techno/Faustian marriage that has bred Cyborgian progeny. The umbilical cord is electric. This new generation of users and user friendly technology represents the antithesis of communication as it has been known. The relationship between individuals and interactive media systems reverses expectations as viewers activate, change and determine the information/reality on their screen. The idea of choice, will and chance are refined into compositional process. In an obvious metaphor, screens can be touched and programmed to respond to body heat. Rather than being remotely controlled by media environments, the controls quite literally are now in the hands of users, as is the key to a new era of individual freedom and empowerment. Clearly, the reformulation of a fundamental dialogue has begun.

In television/past, watching was an addictive event that negated individual power in the following ways:

1. Programs/past both venerate and impersonate ordinary (wo)man, so viewers see simulated reflections of themselves while simultaneously being messaged into passive dependency. Imitations are more perfect than the original. The refined stereotype lacks the flaws, vulnerability and culpability of its prime source, leaving the prime source (ordinary (wo)man) feeling that much more removed and inadequate. Viewers watch these images of an archetypal super-self, but are incapable of directing the action that has captured their fantasies.
2. Television literally puts its viewers into an altered state. The 60 decible hum emitted from the set causes the brain to relax into an alpha mode, which is a passive and non-responsive behavior.
3. Like most abusive substances, television costs: time, money, energy and passion.

Because direct response is discouraged and repressed, the television audience harbors subliminal feelings of impotency that all too often surface as undirected nihilistic rage.

Screens have layered cultural perceptions of reality. Like levels of skin, they separate, cushion, and protect viewers from the unbearable horror of

"Interactive Media and Human Response" is adapted from *High Performance*, No. 37, Spring 1987.

truth. Successive screens distance viewers from content and codify illusion. Truth and fiction blur. Action becomes icon and logo. In turn, they rely on movement and plasticity of time — *iconoplastics* and *logo-motion*.

Like sex, interactive media is not new. Some versions of interactive television existed in the 1920s. In the 1950s a children's program titled "Winky Dink and You" was introduced to commercial television. This program created simple interaction through the use of a plastic sheet that directly attached to the TV. WINKY DINK could encounter serial dilemmas and ask children to draw solutions to his problem with their crayons, right on the screen. Edward R. Murrow used a primitive idea of inter active viewing in "Person to Person." In the 1970's, the National Science Foundation supported three projects that utilized one way audio and video in homes and employed simple transmission back to the studio. Among these was the Warner AMEX QUBE system in Columbus, Ohio. The format was multiple choice responses to options and questions posed within the programs that the community watched. This innovative model and that of Berkes Community Television in Reading, Pennsylvania, borrowed from the social experience of church and town meetings and were significant in shaping participant's behavior through direct communication.[2]

Interactive video, disks, satellite links and computers open, like Pandora's box, a new range of possibilities. Its appeal as an art form is inevitable. Artists like Douglas Davis anticipated the idea of direct touch and inter communication in early pieces like the Austrian tapes of 1974, in which he reached out to touch the anonymous omnipresent audience, and invited them to touch back.

New media, particularly those using "virtual space" employ multiple perspectives to form an electronic cubism that is capable of shaping time. Random access bears a striking relationship to the ideas of chance developed by Marcel Duchamp. It is therefore not suprising that John Cage has embraced this new technology in a work released in January 1987 "THE FIRST MEETING OF THE SATIE SOCIETY."

This work is programmed by a data base that includes such disparate text sources as Henry Thoreau, Marcel Duchamp, James Joyce and Marshall McCluhan. Participants use chance to rearrange passages they integrate into new poetic mesostic texts. A computer program titled MESOLIST was made at Cage's request by Jim Rosenberg in conjunction with IC, a program made by Andrew Culver that simulates the I Ching chance operations.

Kit Galloway and Sherie Rabinowitz have pioneered remarkable media environments that depend upon satellite links to bring together individuals, communities and countries. Their work is intrinsically political and driven by an aesthetic that combines global unity into a revolution of joined responses. Timothy Leary designed MINDMIRROR, a program for the Apple II through Electronic Arts that uses persona and cultural archetypes as a vehicle for personality and behavioral retraining. He says that computers and interactive media systems are the most subversive thing he has done. In *Lorna* the empowering effect was in the gap between touching the remote and changing the reality effect on the screen, the user/consumer/participant was affected via behavior and perception.

Laser technology, computer, and interactive media systems represent a major step toward breaking down barriers between art and audience. As choices for users expand, issues of creativity formerly considered the exclusive domain of fine arts may become concerns for the entire human community. Perhaps like the great nineteenth century poet, Isadora Ducasse predicted, eventually poetry will be made by everyone.

Optimistically the participation of audiences may lead to a rediscovery of personal values and a reordering of life. But it is likely that the technological dimension of the electronic revolution will precede its spiritual emergence. As in each past instance of a change of ethos that was stimulated by a shift in sociotechno relationship, the result invites both the potential for greater freedom as well as the possibility for the invention of still more inhumane horrors, like issues of invasion of privacy or retention of identity. The human community has never been as alienated or lonely as it appears to be now during this communications revolution. New Media is in a constant state of becoming. It is active as opposed to stored. And it is vital precisely because it is not fixed, but permanently in flux. By the time you look back, it has changed, making presumptions obsolete. When a work of art breaks with presumptions, it is subversive and acts as a vehicle for transformation of social beings from what they were to new dimensions of consciousness and human freedom.

Yet there exists the hope that we, as a community of individuals, will retain the ability to move toward an enlightened personal dimension of responsibility. The choice, at least, is ours.

NOTES

1. Video interview with the author.
2. Carey, John and Quarles, Pat. "Interactive Television." In *Transmission* ed. Peter d'Agostino. New York: Tanem Press, 1985, pp. 106–17.

NAME INDEX

SUBJECT INDEX